*The New Handbook
of Psychotherapy
and Counseling with Men*

The New Handbook of Psychotherapy and Counseling with Men

*A Comprehensive Guide
to Settings, Problems, and
Treatment Approaches*

*Revised and Abridged
from the Previous Edition*

Glenn E. Good
Gary R. Brooks
Editors

JOSSEY-BASS
A Wiley Imprint
www.josseybass.com

Published by Jossey-Bass
A Wiley Imprint
989 Market Street, San Francisco, CA 94103-1741 www.josseybass.com

Jossey-Bass books and products are available through most bookstores. To contact Jossey-Bass directly, call our Customer Care Department within the U.S. at 800-956-7739, outside the U.S. at 317-572-3986, or fax 317-572-4002.

Jossey-Bass also publishes its books in a variety of electronic formats. Some content that appears in print may not be available in electronic books.

Figures 15.1 and 15.2 from Kieser, D. J. (1983). The 1982 interpersonal circle: A taxonomy for complementarity in human transactions. *Psychological Review, 90*, 185–214. Copyright © 1983 by the American Psychological Association. Reprinted with permission.

Library of Congress Cataloging-in-Publication Data

The new handbook of psychotherapy and counseling with men : a comprehensive guide to settings, problems, and treatment approaches / Glenn E. Good, Gary R. Brooks, editors.— Rev. and abridged ed.
p. cm.
Includes bibliographical references and indexes.
ISBN 0-7879-7834-5 (alk. paper)
1. Counseling. 2. Psychotherapy. 3. Men—Counseling of. 4. Masculinity.
5. Boys—Counseling of. I. Good, Glenn E., date- II. Brooks, Gary R., date-
BF637.C6N485 2005
158'.3'081—dc22
2004024491

Printed in the United States of America
FIRST EDITION
PB Printing 10 9 8 7 6 5 4 3 2 1

CONTENTS

ACKNOWLEDGMENTS

Sometimes ideas that seemed inspired at the outset turn out to be less creative and Promethean than originally hoped. Sometimes a product after final assemblage bears little resemblance to the one originally envisioned. At other times, however, ideas turn into finished products that emerge as even more gratifying than had ever been imagined. We believe that this book falls into the latter category. It is our immodest belief that the exceptional contributions of thoughtful scholars and therapists have resulted in a handbook that adds substantially to the cause of helping counselors and therapists work more effectively with boys and men.

First, to recognize those who made this book possible, we wish to acknowledge our tremendous debt to Alan Rinzler, our executive editor at Jossey-Bass Publishers. Alan's vision, involvement, and support made this book possible. We would also like to thank Amy Scott and Seth Schwartz, assistant editors, and Jeri Lambert, production coordinator, for their conscientious work in helping complete this project. We also express our gratitude to the chapter contributors; they worked hard to provide chapters that advance the field.

Because this book is built on the pioneering work of others, profound appreciation is offered to men's studies pioneers, such as Drs. Joseph Pleck, James O'Neil, Ronald Levant, Murray Scher, Mark Stevens, Gregg Eichenfield, Michael Kimmel, Harry Brod, Robert Brannon, Tom Skovholt, and James Doyle, whose scholarly contributions provided the foundation for this project. We also express our deep appreciation to the members of the Society for the Psychological Study of Men and Masculinity (SPSMM; Division 51 of the American Psychological Association).

Dr. Good would like to acknowledge the support of his immediate family—his wife, Dr. Laurie Mintz, and their delightful daughters, Jennifer and Allison—for their love, patience, and understanding during this project. He also expresses gratitude to his family of origin, Drs. Jeanne and Robert Good, for their nurturance and encouragement, and to his sister Ellen Wakeman, who tolerated him during their upbringing. He would like to express his gratitude to Drs. Murray Scher, Mark Stevens, and Gregg Eichenfield, with whom he collaborated on a project with similar objectives more than a decade earlier. He expresses his gratitude to his SPSMM colleagues who provide friendship and intellectual clarity. He would also like to express his appreciation of his colleagues and the graduate students in the Department of Educational, School, and Counseling Psychology at the University of Missouri-Columbia, who make each workday a pleasure. Finally, it is Dr. Good's distinct pleasure to acknowledge Gary Brooks's tremendous creativity, dedication, generosity, and everlasting upbeat energy. It is hard to imagine a guy who could get more accomplished while maintaining such enjoyable relational interactions along the way!

Dr. Brooks deeply values the intellectual contributions, friendship, and emotional support of his SPSMM colleagues—those represented in this book, as well as Louise Silverstein, Neil Massoth, Don-David Lusterman, Roberta Nutt, and the late Roy Scrivner. He continues to be buoyed by the love and support of his wife, Patti, and daughters, Ashley and Allison. Finally, Dr. Brooks clearly realizes that he has never made a more astute move than his decision to seek partnership with Glenn Good. Glenn's breadth of knowledge and organizational skills are exceeded only by his warmth, compassion, and delightful relational style.

Last, yet definitely not least, we would like to express our deep appreciation of the men, women, adolescents, children, and families who have the courage to seek psychotherapeutic consultation. You have entrusted us with your secrets, hopes, doubts, and concerns. You have also challenged us to meet you where you were and to understand your experiences and their meaning to you, and allowed us to accompany you on the journey. You were willing to risk trying new ideas, experiences, and behaviors—to risk imagining better lives, relationships, and futures. Finally, you taught us how to serve you effectively and how to improve the services that mental health professionals provide to others. For all of this, we are most appreciative.

GLENN E. GOOD
Columbia, Missouri
GARY R. BROOKS
Temple, Texas

*The New Handbook
of Psychotherapy
and Counseling with Men*

Introduction

Glenn E. Good
Gary R. Brooks

Contemporary boys and men face opportunities to live lives more richly varied and broadly fulfilling than at any previous historical era. Many men have taken advantage of these new possibilities and have begun to reshape critical aspects of their lives. But before discussing these men and these abundant possibilities, we must first take note of men whose lives are in crisis. For these men, the past few decades have been "a time of fallen heroes . . . [when] men have been brought to earth, their strengths put in perspective by their flaws" (Betcher & Pollack, 1993, p. 1). For some, the past few decades ushered in a period they experienced as eroding traditional male values and damaging the image of masculinity itself. During this period, the "dark side of masculinity" has taken center stage (Brooks & Silverstein, 1995).

MEN AT THE CROSSROADS

The media, institutions, businesses, society, and the individuals within it seek to understand the nature of men and masculinity. From the Million Man March to metrosexuals, from Promise Keepers to *Queer Eye for the Straight Guy*, from Marlboro to Viagra, efforts are being made to define, support, change, and market masculinity. Although these phenomena reflect widely disparate underlying philosophies and politics, they share the underlying theme of change and uncertainty among men.

Men as Perpetrators

No theme characterized the last decade of the twentieth century more than that of the constant media attention given to the iniquitous acts of men. From the seemingly inexplicable shooting rampages of Columbine High School and Little Rock, Arkansas, to the hate crimes of Jasper, Texas, to the terrorist attacks of 9/11, males have been the ones to perpetrate violence and hatred.

In part because of the attention focused on the O. J. Simpson trial, domestic violence came out of the shadows and was finally recognized as a major national problem. Social scientists produced data indicating that male violence against women is far more frequent than was commonly understood. Prevalence studies indicated that between 21 and 34 percent of women in the United States are physically assaulted by their intimate adult partners (Goodman, Koss, Fitzgerald, Russo, & Keita, 1993).

1

Another area of increased alarm has been the recognition of the widespread perpetration of sexual harassment of women by men. Again, a public event, the Clarence Thomas hearings, seemed to galvanize public awareness of this issue. Large-scale surveys of working women have suggested that one of every two women is harassed at some point during her academic or working life (Fitzgerald, 1993).

Rape, sexual coercion, and sexual assault have also been recognized as "male" acts that are far more common than previously recognized (Goodman, Koss, Fitzgerald, Russo, & Keita, 1993). Once rape was narrowly defined and considered to be a rare behavior of a very small percentage of deviant men. Recently, however, the focus has broadened to sexual coercion and acquaintance rape as more frequent behaviors among a broad spectrum of men. Research has indicated that between one-third and one-half of males admit to some act of sexual aggression or coercing of women into unwelcome sexual activity (Kaplan, O'Neil, & Owen, 1993; Ward, Chapman, Cohn, & Williams, 1991).

Men as Psychologically Undeveloped

Over the past decade there seems to be increasing attention to male behaviors that might formerly have been dismissed as an inherent aspect of biological manhood. Television and films have been home to frequent comedic parodies of "macho" male behavior. More serious treatises, such as the Hite Report (Hite, 1987), *Refusing to Be a Man* (Stoltenberg, 1989), *The End of Manhood* (Stoltenberg, 1993), *Men Are Not Cost-Effective* (Stephenson, 1991), and *Successful Women, Angry Men* (Campbell, 2000) have echoed a similar message of increasing dissatisfaction with male patterns of conduct.

The sexual conduct of public figures such as Hugh Grant, Mike Tyson, Gary Hart, Robert Packwood, Bill Clinton, Newt Gingrich, Rudy Giuliani, and Koby Bryant has caused some to call for a serious study of normative male sexuality (Good, 1998; Levant & Brooks, 1997). Among the causes of concern have been the ever increasing use of pornography among men (Brooks, 1995; Gaylor, 1985; Kimmel, 1990) and the greater tendency for men to be more prone to engage in nonrelational or casual sexual activity (Levant, 1997; Oliver & Hyde, 1993).

As more and more women have taken their place in work roles outside the home, men have been roundly criticized for failing to shoulder their proper share of work as parents and as domestic laborers. These complaints have regularly been buttressed by research indicating that although men are increasing their involvement, they still typically spend minimal time with their children (Gottfried & Gottfried, 1988; Pleck, 1997; Silverstein, 1996). Other research reflects men's laxity in taking on full responsibility as domestic labor partners (Blain, 1994; Sanchez & Kane, 1996). Hochschild (1989) and Campbell (2000) brought great attention to the extra burden falling on women because of men's resistance to change.

Men have increasingly been criticized for their failures as emotionally expressive and psychologically supportive partners. Popular self-help books have been sold to help women find ways to communicate with their withdrawn and noncommunicative male partners. Communications research has indicated that although men tend to be facile at "report talk," they are grossly deficient in "rapport talk" (Tannen, 1990, 1993). Levant (1997, 2001) argued that "alexithymia" (the inability to recognize and express feelings) is normative among modern men, and Good (1998) recommended that greater emphasis be given to developing males' "emotional competence."

Men as Victims

Amid the depressing litany of complaints against contemporary men and modern manhood, a new perspective has begun to emerge. Epitomized by Faludi's *Stiffed: The Betrayal of the American Man* (1999), this perspective allows for consideration of ways that men have suffered from various cultural shifts and pressures of the past half-century. Similarly, Pollack (1998) and Gurian (1999) provoked considerable reaction to their argument that boys, as well as girls, are harmed by a culture that poorly recognizes their needs and stresses.

Perhaps no single set of facts calls attention to men's situation as much as that of the repeated finding that men die seven to nine years earlier than women (Angier, 1999; Courtenay, 1998; Verbrugge, 1985). The death rate for American men is higher than that for women in every decade of life, and women have an overall life span expectancy that surpasses men in every age group, regardless of race (Klonoff, Landrine, & Scott, 1995).

Closely related to this perspective on men's mortality is a new recognition about men's violence. At a time when men's violence against women is finally receiving an appropriately higher degree of attention, we are also beginning to realize that men also are victims of violence. Men perpetrate the great majority of violent acts and homicides, yet they also constitute more than 85 percent of the victims of homicide (Angier, 1999; Department of Health and Human Services [DHHS], 2000). The situation for African American men is even more problematic (Franklin, 1998); some have referred to African American men as "an endangered species" (Gibbs, 1988).

Although the *Diagnostic and Statistical Manual of Mental Disorders-TR* (American Psychiatric Association, 2000) indicates that women suffer major depression twice as often as men, men have a suicide rate four times greater than women (DHHS, 2000). Men constitute between two-thirds and four-fifths of the population of abusers of alcohol and illicit substances (DHHS, 2000; Diamond, 1987); Grant, Harford, Hasin, Chou, & Pickering, 1992; Isenhart, Chapter Eight of this volume). Further, men make up more than 70 percent of the U.S. homeless population (Marin, 1991).

Lisak (1994; see also Chapter Nine of this volume) has written extensively about the alarmingly high rates of physical abuse of young males. Lisak observes that 10 to 20 percent of boys report childhood physical abuse, but he also notes that the figures are probably gross underestimates because of the tendency for this treatment to be dismissed as "strict discipline."

This thesis on men's distress could go on for many more pages. This matter is thoroughly amplified in several chapters of this volume. The critical point is that contemporary men, regardless of the many advantages and entitlements of a culture that generally treats men quite well, are nevertheless experiencing considerable subjective pain. Men continually struggle to satisfy their fantasized male judges and harshest internalized male critics—the "male chorus" (Pittman, 1990). Men who don't live up to the rigorous standards of the manhood code are clearly experiencing anguish. But it isn't just these men who are hurting. The paradox of modern masculinity is that regardless of a man's accomplishments or successes, he is, in some maddening ways, continually driven toward greater accomplishments—it is never enough. He may be fixated on overtaking the men above him on the various hierarchical ladders of achievement and also horrified at the prospect of being overtaken by other men hell-bent on moving up the same ladder.

The situation of men during the late twentieth century was well captured by observers of traditional men's pursuit of personal power and happiness. The pursuit of power and control denies men love and sensuality, and leaves only the desire and excitement of conquest and acquisition. Men are generally distant from their children and partners, and their working lives are dominated by competition and mistrust. The higher men go up the ladder of success, the harder it is for them to trust other men and to form real friendships (McLean, 1996). The pleasures of relaxed, anonymous movement through the world, of easy conversation with others, of trust and love as part of a community, are unavailable for them (French, 1991).

THEORIZING ABOUT MEN'S DISTRESS

Before considering how to ameliorate the subjective distress of contemporary men, we must first have some notion about the etiological roots of men's conduct. That is, why do men behave the way they do? This question leads to one of the most complex and perplexing areas in all of men's studies.

Essentialism

Essentialism, the idea that there are basic, inherent, or essential differences between women and men, has become increasingly popular over the past decade. Perhaps the most visible exposition of this view has been the work of John Gray (1992), author of *Men Are from Mars, Women Are from Venus.* For Gray, the matter is straightforward: basic *physiological* differences between women and men cannot help but create similarly basic *psychological* differences that make relationships extremely difficult.

These "essential" differences between women and men have been attributed to a range of causes. Some theorists have invoked biology, citing pronounced sex differences in hormonal makeup (Barash, 1979) or in brain structure and neurochemistry (Kimura, 1992; LeVay, 1993; Moir & Jessel, 1991). Others point to radically different evolutionary heritage and adaptive challenges faced by women and men (Archer, 1996; Buss, 1995, 2000).

These essentialist perspectives are interconnected, of course, because the evolutionary perspective is posited as a primary explanation for the essential biological differences. In terms of the age-old "nature versus nurture" debate, proponents of evolutionary psychology are outspoken in their criticism of nurture exclusivists—those they view as emphasizing social causes of behavior and ignoring evolved biological differences. "The perspective of evolutionary psychology jettisons the outmoded dualistic thinking inherent in much current discourse by getting rid of the false dichotomy between the biological and social" (Buss, 1995, p. 167).

Essentialist theorists have made important contributions to men's studies. Their work serves as a sobering reminder that practitioners must not ignore the "bio" aspect in the modern trend toward biopsychosocial thinking. Because of their high regard for the relative immutability of the inherent differences between women and men, essentialist theorists tend to be relatively conservative in their view of possibilities for change. Instead, they make an important plea for men and women to develop far greater appreciation of each other's inherent differences and learn to create respectful communication. Gray (1992), for example, suggests that "the confusion we are experiencing today is definitely due to the lack of acceptance of our differences." For Gray, the secret to relational harmony is "accepting who we are and embracing how others are different" (p. 35).

David Buss, a leading spokesperson for the evolutionary psychology perspective, offers a range of insights and thoughtful perspectives about how women and men might have come to be the way they are. Unfortunately, however, he provides a far more modest agenda about how things might be changed. Buss is appropriately critical of narrow thinking and argues forcefully for an "interactionist" perspective to social problems. He writes extensively about creating "harmony between the sexes" and has provided much food for contemplation. As yet, however, his recommendations have been focused primarily on improved mutual understanding. He has provided few ideas beyond his suggestion that the key to harmony is "fulfilling each other's evolved desires" (1994, p. 221). That is, men and women need to become proficient at giving each other what they have learned to desire. Further, Buss (2000) noted that teaching men and women about the advantages of "cooperation" and "reciprocity" will help "manage competitive mechanisms" that have evolved over the centuries.

In summary, the various efforts to understand the essential differences between men and women have generated enormous discussion and controversy. Despite this controversy, no serious men's studies scholar can ignore the importance of the research into sex differences in hormones and brain structure, nor the theories of differences in evolutionary adaptation. One simply must know all that one can about the building blocks and raw materials of our behavior. At the same time, this line of study is intrinsically limited, as it can only go so far in offering ideas for change. Those who hope for transcendence beyond traditional male roles need to make special efforts to understand the social construction of masculinity—the ways that the raw materials are shaped and manipulated by sociocultural pressures.

Gender Role Strain Theory

Within psychology another critical perspective has appeared: the gender role strain (GRS) paradigm (Pleck, 1981, 1995). Prior to Pleck, most ideas about women and men were anchored in the gender identity paradigm. According to the gender identity paradigm, there are two distinct and oppositional identities of "masculine" and "feminine," and psychological health depends on incorporation of sufficient characteristics of the proper sex role. In this view, healthy psychological adjustment depends on achieving a secure gender identity. Although androgyny—the incorporation of other-gender characteristics— is thought to be beneficial, it is so only *after* a comfortable sense of gender identity has been accomplished.

The GRS paradigm takes a markedly different view of men's behavior. According to the GRS paradigm, gender roles are not only socially constructed but also highly problematic. Among the assumptions of the GRS paradigm are that (1) gender role norms are often inconsistent and contradictory, (2) a high proportion of gender role norms are violated frequently, (3) social condemnation and stressful psychological consequences commonly follow role violations, and (4) many characteristics and behaviors prescribed by gender role norms are psychologically dysfunctional.

The Interactive Systems Model of Gender Role Strain

The interactive systems model of GRS (Brooks & Silverstein, 1995) has been proposed as a more complex integration of cultural, psychological, and political variables affecting men's behavior. The interactive systems model reflects a synthesis of several theoretical approaches: the GRS paradigm, an ecological perspective on the origins of gender roles, the Bowen family systems theory view of the impact of chronic anxiety on behavior (Bowen, 1978), and the social constructionist analysis of gender-linked power differentials within patriarchal society (Brooks & Silverstein, 1995, p. 307).

The interactive systems model draws from the GRS paradigm in that it incorporates the idea that men's problems and challenges are best conceptualized as a product of role stress and not of problematic gender identity. That is, to be psychologically healthy, men and women do not need to acquire fixed gendered identities that are inherently alien and potentially adversarial. Instead, because men's roles are socially created, they may be altered in response to changing times and social demands.

The model draws from Bowen family systems theory by adopting Bowen's (1978) belief that anxiety results when persons "give up self." In this formulation, we see that men have been resolutely socialized to limit themselves to narrow and stereotyped roles—warriors, providers, and sexual performers, but not nurturers and emotional communicators. This narrow socialization requires that men deny aspects of self, a process that generates overwhelming anxiety. The resultant anxiety perpetuates rigid definitions of acceptable male conduct and further alienation from one's full human potential.

The interactive systems model enriches the psychological perspectives of the GRS paradigm and Bowen theory by embracing the broader sociopolitical perspectives of feminism and the ecological perspective of anthropologist David Gilmore (1990). Feminist theory holds that the behaviors of men and women cannot be fully understood without attention to the considerable power inequities between the groups. Miller (1986) noted that membership in a group holding power over others generates personality characteristics that are associated with the use and abuse of power. Reciprocally, membership in a disempowered group produces personality characteristics that reflect this powerlessness and dependence on the dominant group. In this analysis, women, like members of other subordinate groups, have needed to develop interpersonal empathy and emotional sensitivity. Men, in contrast, have been free to develop a sense of entitlement and to exercise their power.

Gilmore's ecological insights add further complexity to this analysis. He studied a wide array of contemporary cultures and found that almost all societies have a "manhood cult" based on the ideas of competition, risk taking, stoic emotional reserve, and rejection of "feminine" aspects of self. But he also found that a manhood cult was not present in all societies. The presence or absence of this value system was closely tied to certain critical ecological variables. The degree to which a society adopts strict ideas of manhood is closely related to two critical ecological variables: the availability of natural resources and the degree of external threat. In the ecological context of plentiful resources, relative ease in the production of food, and the absence of external threat, role pressures are less intense. Therefore, according to Gilmore's research, rigid standards of manhood are not inevitable, but rather are dependent on ecological context.

In summary, the interactive systems model can be viewed as an effort to explain men's behavior through integration of several other perspectives. First, it incorporates the social constructionist idea that men behave in accordance with the powerful pressures of gender socialization. Further, because the model identifies the role of psychological, cultural, and political variables, it offers much broader potential for intervention and change.

NEW HOPE FOR MEN

Many men are in crisis. Many are resentful of the sweeping cultural changes of the past quarter-century and seek nothing more than a return to seemingly happier days when men were men and women (and gays) knew their place. Most men, however, recognize that the clock will not be turned back, that things will never again be the same. Furthermore, a great many men sense that change may ultimately be in their best interest.

The Men's Movement

Beginning in the late 1960s and early 1970s, a new type of scholarship appeared with a curious agenda—to examine the inner workings and secrets of *men's* lives. Admittedly, most academic scholarship had always talked about the lives of mythical and heroic men. But this new scholarship, providing the basis for what would become men's studies, was about the lives of ordinary men. It was about how the average man struggled to bring meaning to his life. Several men wrote paradigm-shifting books suggesting that men, as well as women, could be hampered by rigid traditional gender role expectations. Brenton

(1966), Fasteau (1975), Farrell (1974), Goldberg (1976), Pleck and Sawyer (1980), and Nichols (1975) provided impressive arguments about the hazards of traditional masculinity in contemporary times.

This new line of men's studies scholarship heralded the appearance of a "men's movement" that has gained considerable momentum and attention over the last thirty years. Similar to the women's movement that preceded it, the men's movement has been fueled by a commitment to countering sociocultural forces constraining people's lives. Unlike the women's movement, however, this men's movement has had no dramatically obvious mandate, no clear theoretical underpinnings, and no central organization. In brief, there is considerable disagreement about what the men's movement actually is or has been.

For example, Shiffman (1987) observed that "the men's movement can be described structurally as consisting of a national profeminist organization, networks of activists engaging issues of violence against women, networks of academics working on issues of masculinity, men's support groups, an annual national conference on men and masculinity, and various local and regional events" (p. 297). In contrast, Williamson (1985) argued that "the North American men's movement cannot be traced along one historical line. There have been a number of differing directions characterized by sporadic growth and instability" (p. 308).

Clatterbaugh (1990) described a number of men's organizations. "Nonfeminist" men joined with Fathers' Rights groups (for example, Men's Equality Now) to protest what they viewed as mistreatment of men in the court system. Other groups of men, impressed with the work of Joseph Campbell and Robert Bly, focused on pursuit of essential masculinity or "the deep masculine spirit" (Bly, 1990; Clatterbaugh, 1990). From a very different direction, the gay liberation movement also provided impetus to the men's movement. Originating with the Mattachine Society in the 1950s on the West Coast and energized by the Stonewall Riots of 1969, the gay liberation movement not only pushed for greater tolerance of gay lifestyles but also became a leading voice against the most oppressive aspects of hegemonic masculinity.

Although vigorously opposed to the philosophies and political perspectives of the men's rights groups (and the subsequent Coalition of Free Men), the National Organization of Men Against Sexism became the group most inclusive of the broader men's movement philosophies. Adopting a strong profeminist position, the group incorporated the antiviolence community, veterans of consciousness-raising groups, mythopoetic men, men's studies scholars, gay liberation activists, and civil rights advocates. In 1975, that organization began an annual Men and Masculinity Conference that has brought men together for almost thirty years.

This recognition of men's studies and men's issues has also reverberated in many professional organizations of the mental health professions. Most notably, the American Psychological Association recognized the Society for the Psychological Study of Men and Masculinity, a group that "promotes study of how gender shapes and constricts men's lives, and is committed to an enhancement of men's capacity to experience their full human potential" (Society for the Psychological Study of Men and Masculinity, 2000) and publishes the professional journal *Psychology of Men and Masculinity.*

The decade of the 1990s witnessed a continuation of men's search for answers to their distress, their loneliness, and their existential or spiritual emptiness. Although the men of the Promise Keepers, the Million Man March, the Fathers' Rights groups, the wilderness retreats, and the profeminist men's organizations have different faces and hold some differing philosophies, they are united in promoting the cause of more fulfilling lives for men.

Psychotherapy for Men

Inevitably, the sweeping cultural changes have reverberated into the mental health community. Research by Good and colleagues (1989) found that men's reluctance to use psychological services was closely tied to their conceptions of masculinity. Although they were once dismissed as hopelessly resistant to any form of help seeking, men are now finding their way, both directly and indirectly, into treatment settings. Some men recognize their distress and make independent decisions to seek therapy help. Many more, however, are urged, coaxed, or mandated into treatment by loved ones, bosses, physicians, or legal authorities (Addis & Mahalik, 2003). In the midst of sweeping cultural changes that force men to shape new masculine roles, the resulting increase in the number of male clients and the diversity of issues they present pose challenges for counselors and therapists. To what extent have we developed new therapies and appropriate services to help men? Are we prepared to meet these new challenges?

As is often the case, the honest answer to these questions is ambiguous—yes *and* no. In some ways, the mental health community is poorly prepared to meet the needs of many men. Many observers (Addis & Mahalik, 2003; Robertson & Fitzgerald, 1992; Scher, 1990; Shay & Maltas, 1998; Silverberg, 1986) have noted that men are highly unlikely to see psychotherapy as a good thing and will seek therapy only when there is no other alternative. Some (for example, Heesacker & Prichard, 1992; Wilcox & Forrest, 1992) have argued that therapy is too reliant on "feminine" modes of intervention and that newer therapies more congruent with "masculine" styles must be developed. Brooks (1998) argued that traditional men hate psychotherapy because of (1) the popular stereotypes of the male client as weak and ineffectual, (2) the conflicts between the demands of the male role and the role of the ideal therapy client, (3) traditional men's sense that there is a collusion among women and members of the therapy community against men, and (4) the failure of the therapy community to recognize men's special needs.

For some time, mental health professionals have recognized that men are reluctant to take on the client role. We have realized that men's help seeking is often tentative and complicated by conflicting motives, making it difficult for counselors to establish therapeutic alliances. But the problem is much larger: many counselors and therapists don't fully understand men's experiences. Many don't see the connection between men's problematic behaviors and their psychic pain. Many don't feel adept at engaging reluctant men in treatment. Many don't understand how to customize traditional therapy modalities to serve men better. Finally, many don't see how to integrate the progress made in a man's therapy work into systemic change that will benefit him and his loved ones.

In spite of these substantial problems, there are many positive trends. There is no doubt that the psychotherapy community is becoming far more sensitive to cultural diversity issues (Comas-Diaz & Griffith, 1988; Sue & Sue, 1990). Within the rubric of cultural diversity, many are now recognizing that gender is a critical cultural variable and a central mediator of experience in clients' lives. Recognition came first to the many ways that gender-blind diagnoses and therapies harmed women. Gender studies scholarship, first applied to women, soon came to be considered in terms of the experiences of both men and women. Gender scholars began to call for psychotherapies that are gender aware (Good, Gilbert, & Scher, 1990), gender sensitive (Philpot, Brooks, Lusterman, & Nutt, 1997), or gender fair (Nutt, 1991). These approaches call for therapists to consider women's and men's gender context when conducting assessments and developing intervention strategies.

We believe it is now critical that men be recognized as a special culture and that diversity training include attention to the area of men and masculinity. Further, we believe that some therapy situations should be considered as a form of cross-cultural counseling, calling for the special considerations of that sensitive situation. It is our conviction that when boys' and men's experiences are better understood, therapeutic bonds will be far easier to establish. Therapists will be far more empathic and compassionate toward men. Men will be far more eager to use psychotherapy. We believe ardently in the need to improve the relationship between men and the therapy community.

A landmark event in this cause was the publication of the *Handbook of Counseling and Psychotherapy for Men* (Scher, Stevens, Good, & Eichenfield, 1987). That pioneering book broke new ground, providing a single reference source that embraced many of the ideas of therapists who were working in widely diverse settings. For its time, that handbook offered the best of the information available about the diversity of therapy approaches for men.

Much has taken place in the seventeen years since publication of that handbook. There has been an exponential increase in research and writing about men's lives and about therapy for men. Innovative new therapies have appeared in a wide variety of mental health disciplines. Clearly, there has been a pressing need for a new handbook that reflects these vital new developments. We believe that this new paperback edition fills that void by capturing recent developments and by offering a vital resource for counselors and therapists desiring to provide effective services to their male clients.

OVERVIEW OF THE BOOK

This edition is divided into six important sections: (1) settings in which boys and men are likely to be seen, (2) problems men are likely to present, (3) developmental issues of boys and men, (4) therapeutic approaches and modalities for working with boys and men, (5) special considerations and skills for therapy with men, and (6) multicultural and diversity-related considerations for therapy with boys and men.

The chapters of Section One consider the counseling and therapy needs of boys and men in terms of the physical setting in which services are provided. Although men may be underrepresented in therapists' private offices, boys and men are abundant in school, medical, business, university, rehabilitation, and veterans' settings. In this section, the authors provide male-friendly interventions that are sensitive to the physical context, special needs, and expectations of participants in these settings.

The chapters of Section Two examine some of the far too common problems that men experience—depression, substance abuse, and psychological trauma. These chapters "contextualize" men's problems and situate these problems within a framework that recognizes the social construction of masculinity. They identify how male socialization processes dispose many boys to become troubled men. The chapters demonstrate how men are continually given mixed messages about violence, sexuality, alcohol, dominance, and emotional sensitivity. Finally, they incorporate the GRS model to show that although men are sometimes victimizers they are also victimized.

The chapters of Section Three explore the normative challenges and developmental opportunities of the male life cycle. They examine the issues of boyhood, the development of men's careers, and the challenges associated with midlife. Virtually all men struggle with negotiating the limitations and restrictions associated with narrow constructions of proper masculine behavior. Most boys and men share (or will share) certain common experiences and challenges—the taunting, bullying, and shaming of boy culture and the insidious existential dilemmas of midlife. Most men struggle to make emotional connections with others, despite harsh pressures to maintain a rugged and stoic external facade. Work and career add additional complexity to men's lives, sometimes becoming so central that all else suffers. Most men wrestle with the impossible conflict between career fixation and a broader definition of self. These chapters add a crucial perspective by broadening the focus from the serious problems experienced by some men to the difficulties encountered by almost *all* men.

The chapters of Section Four seek to directly address the formerly prevalent "gender-blind" nature of major therapy theories and interventions. Consistent with the welcome trend to customize therapy to the cultural values and needs of clients, these chapters make it abundantly clear that therapists can no longer accept the uniformity myth that one therapy "size" fits all. These chapters provide explicit suggestions about how to apply current models of psychotherapy to the specific issues of boys and men.

The chapters of Section Five examine therapists as "gendered" beings, in that therapists and their clients both bring gender-based assumptions and values into their therapeutic relationships. In this section, the authors illustrate that therapists' gender awareness and self-knowledge make a critical difference in their therapeutic relationships and to the subsequent outcomes of their encounters with boys and men.

The chapters of Section Six are especially important because they challenge the myth of homogeneity in men's lives. Men's studies scholars have come to realize that there are many masculinity ideologies that depend in part on men's ethnicity, acculturation, social class, sexual orientation, physical abilities, and geographical region. For example, it is absurd to speak of male dominance, privilege, power, and entitlement when considering gay or African American men as one would speak of it when considering white, upper-class, heterosexual men. Marginalized men likely experience masculinity differently than do men with greater access to the historical "perks" of manhood. The diversity perspective does not negate the importance of understanding the vast commonalties among all men. Rather, it simply highlights the need for therapists to consider simultaneously all critical areas of cultural influence in their clients' lives. To the extent that therapists are familiar with the most salient values and meanings in their clients' lives, they will have that many more avenues of entry into their clients' worlds and will have far greater capacity for therapeutic empathy.

OUR HOPES

Our years of study of men and masculinity have consistently provided us with some of the most gratifying experiences of our professional lives. It has allowed us to develop many meaningful relationships and has greatly enhanced our personal lives. As excited as we have been by this dynamic field of scholarship, we also realize that this area is one of considerable sensitivity and strongly held beliefs. It seems unfortunate to us that this area of study has sometimes generated unnecessarily harsh acrimony and polarization. We believe that this book surmounts the primary sources of tension and sensitivity, because it views women's and men's interests as reciprocal, considers men as inherently well intentioned, and holds great optimism for men's capacity to accommodate to the needs of a rapidly changing culture.

The GRS paradigm that undergirds the therapeutic interventions of this book recognizes that women *and* men are harmed by narrow, restrictive gender roles and unforgiving processes of gender socialization. Counselors and therapists can help women and men recognize that they are jointly invested in challenging restrictive processes and creating greater role opportunities for women and men. Rigid gender socialization into narrow roles is *not* in the best interests of men or women. To function successfully in a complex and changing culture, women and men must have full access to the widest range of social, emotional, and psychological skills. Counseling and psychotherapy can provide pivotal impetus and guidance for achieving those skills. Therapists and counselors can help women and men approach each other with compassion and respect and can empower them to develop their inherent capacities to be fully functioning human beings.

References

Addis, M. E., & Mahalik, J. R. (2003). Men, masculinity, and the contexts of help-seeking. *American Psychologist, 58*, 5–14.

American Psychiatric Association. (2000). *Diagnostic and statistical manual of mental disorders* (4th ed., Text Revised). Washington, DC: Author.

Angier, N. (1999, February 17). Why men don't last: Self-destruction as a way of life. *The New York Times*, p. G8.

Archer, J. (1996). Sex differences in social behavior: Are the social role and evolutionary explanations compatible? *American Psychologist, 51*, 909–917.

Barash, D. (1979). *The whisperings within*. New York: Penguin Books.

Betcher, R. W., & Pollack, W. S. (1993). *In a time of fallen heroes: The re-creation of masculinity*. New York: Atheneum.

Blain, J. (1994). Discourses of agency and domestic labor: Family discourse and gendered practice in dual-career families. *Journal of Family Issues, 15*, 515–549.

Bly, R. (1990). *Iron John: A book about men*. New York: Vintage Books.

Bowen, M. (1978). *Family therapy in clinical practice*. Northvale, NJ: Aronson.

Brenton, M. (1966). *The American male*. New York: Coward-McCann.

Brooks, G. R. (1995). *The centerfold syndrome: How men can overcome objectification and achieve intimacy with women*. San Francisco: Jossey-Bass.

Brooks, G. R. (1998). *A new psychotherapy for traditional men*. San Francisco: Jossey-Bass.

Brooks, G. R., & Silverstein, L. B. (1995). Understanding the dark side of masculinity: An integrative systems model. In R. F. Levant & W. S. Pollack (Eds.), *A new psychology of men* (pp. 280–333). New York: Basic Books.

Buss, D. M. (1994). *The evolution of desire: Strategies of human mating*. New York: Basic Books.

Buss, D. M. (1995). Psychological sex differences: Origins through sexual selection. *American Psychologist, 50*, 164–168.

Buss, D. M. (2000). The evolution of happiness. *American Psychologist, 55*, 15–23.

Campbell, B. M. (2000). *Successful women, angry men*. Berkeley, CA: Berkeley Books.

Clatterbaugh, K. (1990). *Contemporary perspectives on masculinity: Men, women, and politics in modern society*. Boulder, CO: Westview Press.

Comas-Diaz, L., & Griffith, E. H. (1988). *Clinical guidelines in cross-cultural mental health*. New York: Wiley.

Courtenay, W. H. (1998). Better to die than cry? A longitudinal and constructionist study of masculinity and health risk behavior of young American men. (Doctoral dissertation, University of California at Berkeley). *Dissertation Abstracts International, 59*(08A), (Publication No. 9902042).

Department of Health and Human Services. (2000). *Healthy people 2010. Understanding and improving health*. Washington, DC: U.S. Government Printing Office.

Diamond, J. (1987). Counseling male substance abusers. In M. Scher, M. Stevens, G. Good, & G. Eichenfield (Eds.), *Handbook of counseling and psychotherapy with men* (pp. 332–342). Thousand Oaks, CA: Sage.

Faludi, S. (1999). *Stiffed: The betrayal of the American man*. New York: Morrow.

Farrell, W. T. (1974). *The liberated man*. New York: Bantam.

Fasteau, M. F. (1975). *The male machine*. New York: Dell.

Fitzgerald, L. (1993). Sexual harassment: Violence against women in the workplace. *American Psychologist, 48*, 1070–1076.

Franklin, A. J. (1998). Treating anger in African American men. In W. S. Pollack & R. F. Levant (Eds.), *New psychotherapy for men* (pp. 239–258). New York: Wiley.

French, M. (1991). *Beyond power: On women, men and morals.* London: Cardinal.

Gaylor, L. (1985, July/August). Pornography: A humanist issue. *Humanist,* pp. 34–40.

Gibbs, J. T. (1988). *Young, black, and male in America: An endangered species.* Dover, MA: Auburn House.

Gilmore, D. D. (1990). *Manhood in the making: Cultural concepts of masculinity.* New Haven, CT: Yale University Press.

Goldberg, H. (1976). *The hazards of being male.* New York: New American Library.

Good, G. E. (1998). Missing and underrepresented aspects of men's lives. *SPSMM Bulletin, 3*(2), 1–2.

Good, G. E., Dell, D. M., & Mintz, L. B. (1989). Male role and gender role conflict: Relations to help seeking in men. *Journal of Counseling Psychology, 36,* 295–300.

Good, G. E., Gilbert, L. A., & Scher, M. (1990). Gender aware therapy: A synthesis of feminist therapy and knowledge about gender. *Journal of Counseling and Development, 68,* 376–380.

Goodman, L. A., Koss, M. P., Fitzgerald, L. F., Russo, N. F., & Keita, G. P. (1993). Male violence against women. Current research and future directions. *American Psychologist, 48,* 1054–1058.

Gottfried, A. E., & Gottfried, A. W. (1988). *Maternal employment and children's development.* New York: Plenum Press.

Grant, B. F., Harford, T. C., Hasin, D. S., Chou, P., & Pickering, R. (1992). DSM-III-R and the proposed DSM-IV alcohol use disorders, United States, 1988: A nosological comparison. *Alcoholism: Clinical and Experimental Research, 16,* 215–221.

Gray, J. (1992). *Men are from Mars, women are from Venus.* New York: HarperCollins.

Gurian, M. (1999). *A fine young man: What parents and educators can do to shape adolescent boys into exceptional men.* New York: Tarcher.

Heesacker, M., & Prichard, S. (1992). In a different voice, revisited: Men, women, and emotion. *Journal of Mental Health Counseling, 14,* 274–290.

Hite, S. (1987). *The Hite report on women and love: A cultural revolution in progress.* New York: Knopf.

Hochschild, A. (1989). *The second shift.* New York: Viking.

Kaplan, R. S., O'Neil, J. S., & Owen, S. V. (1993, August). *Misogynous, normative, progressive masculinity and sexual assault: Gender role conflict, hostility toward women and hypermasculinity.* Paper presented at the annual convention of the American Psychological Association, Toronto, Canada.

Kimmel, M. S. (Ed.). (1990). *Men confront pornography.* New York: Crown.

Kimura, D. (1992, September). Sex differences in the brain. *Scientific American,* pp. 119–125.

Klonoff, E., Landrine, H., & Scott, J. (1995). Double jeopardy: Ethnicity and gender in health research. In H. Landrine (Ed.), *Bringing cultural diversity to feminist psychology: Theory, research, and practice* (pp. 335–360). Washington, DC: American Psychological Association.

Koss, M. P. (1993). Rape: Scope, impact, interventions, and public policy responses. *American Psychologist, 48,* 1062–1069.

Levant, R. F. (1997). Nonrelational sexuality in men. In R. F. Levant & G. R. Brooks (Eds.), *Men and sex: New psychological perspectives* (pp. 9–27). New York: Wiley.

Levant, R. F. (2001). Desperately seeking language: Understanding, assessing, and treating normative male alexithymia. In G. R. Brooks and G. E. Good (Eds.), *The new handbook of psychotherapy and counseling with men: A comprehensive guide to settings, problems, and treatment approaches* (pp. 424–443). San Francisco: Jossey-Bass.

Levant, R. F., & Brooks, G. R. (1997). *Men and sex: New psychological perspectives.* New York: Wiley.

LeVay, S. (1993). *The sexual brain.* Cambridge, MA: MIT Press.

Lisak, D. (1994). The psychological consequences of sexual abuse: Content analysis of interviews with male survivors. *Journal of Traumatic Stress, 7,* 525–548.

Marin, P. (1991, July 8). Born to lose: The prejudice against men. *The Nation,* pp. 46–51.

McLean, C. (1996). The politics of men's pain. In C. McLean, M. Carey, & C. White (Eds.), *Men's ways of being* (pp. 11–28). Boulder, CO: Westview Press.

Miller, J. B. (1986). *Toward a new psychology of women* (2nd ed.). Boston: Beacon Press.

Moir, A., & Jessel, D. (1991). *Brain sex: The real difference between women and men.* New York: Carol Publishing Group.

Nichols, J. (1975). *Men's liberation: A new definition of masculinity.* New York: Penguin Books.

Nutt, R. (1991). Ethical principles for gender-fair family therapy. *Family Psychologist, 7,* 32–33.

Oliver, M. B., & Hyde, J. S. (1993). Gender differences in sexuality: A meta-analysis. *Psychological Bulletin, 114,* 29–51.

Philpot, C., Brooks, G. R., Lusterman, D. D., & Nutt, R. L. (Eds.). (1997). *Bridging separate gender worlds.* Washington, DC: American Psychological Association.

Pittman, F. (1990). The masculine mystique. *Family Therapy Networker, 14*(3), 40–52.

Pleck, J. H. (1981). *The myth of masculinity.* Cambridge, MA: MIT Press.

Pleck, J. H. (1995). The gender role strain paradigm: An update. In R. F. Levant & W. S. Pollack (Eds.), *A new psychology of men* (pp. 11–32). New York: Basic Books.

Pleck, J. H. (1997). Paternal involvement: Levels, sources, and consequences. In M. E. Lamb (Ed.), *The role of the father in child development* (3rd ed., pp. 66–103). New York: Wiley.

Pleck, J. H., & Sawyer, J. (1980). *Men and masculinity.* Upper Saddle River, NJ: Prentice Hall.

Pollack, W. S. (1998). *Real boys: Rescuing our sons from the myths of boyhood.* New York: Basic Books.

Robertson, J. M., & Fitzgerald, L. F. (1992). Overcoming the masculine mystique: Preferences for alternative forms of therapy among men who avoid counseling. *Journal of Counseling Psychology, 39,* 240–246.

Sanchez, L., & Kane, E. W. (1996). Women's and men's constructions of perceptions of housework fairness. *Journal of Family Issues, 17,* 385–387.

Scher, M. (1990). Effect of gender-role incongruities on men's experience as clients in psychotherapy. *Psychotherapy, 27,* 322–326.

Scher, M., Stevens, M., Good, G., & Eichenfield, G. (Eds.). (1987). *Handbook of counseling and psychotherapy with men.* Thousand Oaks, CA: Sage.

Shay, J. J., & Maltas, C. P. (1998). Reluctant men in couple therapy: Corralling the Marlboro man. In W. S. Pollack & R. F. Levant (Eds.), *New psychotherapy for men* (pp. 97–126). New York: Wiley.

Shiffman, M. (1987). The men's movement: An empirical investigation. In M. S. Kimmel (Ed.), *Changing men: New directions in research on men and masculinity* (pp. 295–314). Thousand Oaks, CA: Sage.

Silverberg, R. (1986). *Psychotherapy for men: Transcending the masculine mystique.* Springfield, IL: Thomas.

Silverstein, L. B. (1996). Fathering is a feminist issue. *Psychology of Women Quarterly, 20,* 3–37.

Society for the Psychological Study of Men and Masculinity. (2000). SPSMM mission statement. *SPSMM Bulletin, 5*(3), 26.

Stephenson, J. (1991). *Men are not cost-effective.* Napa, CA: Deimer, Smith.

Stoltenberg, J. (1989). *Refusing to be a man: Essays on sex and justice.* New York: Meridian.

Stoltenberg, J. (1993). *The end of manhood.* New York: Penguin Books.

Sue, D. W., & Sue, D. (1990). *Counseling the culturally different: Theory and practice.* New York: Wiley.

Tannen, D. (1990). *You just don't understand: Women and men in conversation.* New York: Morrow.

Tannen, D. (1993). *Gender and conversational interaction.* New York: Oxford University Press.

Verbrugge, L. M. (1985). Gender and health: An update on hypothesis and evidence. *Journal of Health and Social Behavior, 26,* 156–182.

Ward, S. K., Chapman, K., Cohn, E., & Williams, K. (1991). Acquaintance rape and the college social scene. *Family Relations, 40,* 65–71.

Wilcox, D. W., & Forrest, L. (1992). The problems of men and counseling: Gender bias or gender truth. *Journal of Mental Health Counseling, 14,* 291–304.

Williamson, T. (1985). A history of the men's movement. In F. Baumli (Ed.), *Men freeing men: Exploding the myth of the traditional male* (pp. 308–324). Jersey City, NJ: New Atlantis Press.

SECTION ONE

TREATMENT IN CONTEXT

CHAPTER ONE

A Male-Friendly Therapeutic Process with School-Age Boys

Mark S. Kiselica

Outpatient psychotherapists, school counselors, school psychologists, and school social workers typically require their clients to visit their offices for formal counseling sessions, during which clients are expected to be introspective and to verbalize intimate thoughts and feelings. Although many clients are comfortable with and helped by this approach to counseling and psychotherapy, it is incompatible with the relational styles of many boys and with their conceptions about the helping process. For example, males with a traditional gender role orientation tend to prefer group activities (Andronico, 1996; Jolliff, 1994) that are competitive (Griffin-Pierson, 1990) and involve sports or the manipulation and organization of data and objects (Kiselica, 1995). Furthermore, traditional teenage boys experiencing adjustment difficulties tend to respect and trust professionals who are willing to leave their offices, participate in youth recreational activities, and help their clients to address the clients' practical concerns (Hendricks, 1988; Kiselica, 1995; Kiselica, Stroud, Stroud, & Rotzien, 1992; Sander & Rosen, 1987). Consequently, traditional young men are likely to feel ill at ease with counseling and psychotherapy as it is customarily practiced (Kiselica, 1992, 1995; Kiselica & Horne, 1999) and may be reluctant to work with practitioners who either condemn or do not understand traditional male relational styles and expectations about the helping process (Hendricks, 1988; Kiselica, 1992, 1995; Kiselica & Horne, 1999; Sander & Rosen, 1987).

To correct for this mismatch between the parameters of conventional counseling and psychotherapy and the relational styles and expectations of traditional adolescent males, practitioners must make adjustments in the process of counseling and psychotherapy with traditional young men. The purpose of this chapter is to recommend that such adjustments adhere to a male-friendly therapeutic process with traditional school-age boys. A male-friendly process is one in which the counselor employs a wide variety of strategies and activities that are likely to appeal to traditional male youth and facilitate the establishment and maintenance of rapport with this population.

I begin this chapter with a description of the traditional male relational style. I argue that there is a mismatch between the characteristics of the conventional counseling environment

This chapter is a revised version of "A Male-Friendly Therapeutic Process with Adolescent Boys," which was presented at the Annual Convention of the American Psychological Association, Boston, Massachusetts, August, 1999.

and the relational styles of traditional school-age boys, and I present a proposal for transforming the therapeutic process with boys through the application of a male-friendly approach to counseling and psychotherapy. Data from empirical research evaluating the efficacy of counseling with teen fathers are used as the foundation for recommending the following: questioning the rigid use of fifty-minute sessions; using informal activities, alternative time schedules, and alternative settings; employing humor, self-disclosure, and other rapport-building tactics; and helping boys through group counseling. I consider the implications of a male-friendly approach for redefining professional conceptions about boundaries in the client-therapist relationship and transforming the practice of school-based counseling. I conclude the chapter with a discussion of the myths and realities about alexithymia in boys.

As a preliminary note, I recognize that there are many theoretical approaches to working with troubled school-age boys. Many mental health professionals prefer to counsel the entire family in an attempt to change the family system in a way that facilitates the growth and emotional well-being of the identified client. Other practitioners are inclined to work with boys in individual counseling or psychotherapy, while still others artfully juggle family and individual sessions. The recommendations discussed here are offered as suggestions for establishing and maintaining rapport during individual and group therapeutic encounters between clinicians and boys who have a traditional male relational style.

WHAT IS A TRADITIONAL MALE RELATIONAL STYLE?

Boys who exhibit a traditional male relational style tend to be uncomfortable verbalizing their intimate thoughts and feelings in contexts in which there is likely to be disapproval regarding the expression of emotions by males (Fischer et al., 1993; LaFrance & Banaji, 1992; Shields, 1995). For example, many traditional males are wary of acknowledging when they are frightened or sad or of allowing themselves to cry because they believe that others will view such expressions as a sign of weakness (Levant, 1995). Traditional boys also develop friendships and experience closeness to others through instrumental activities, such as participating in sports, going fishing or swimming, hanging out in the streets, working on a project that requires manual labor, or playing on a computer (Clinchy & Zimmerman, 1985; Kiselica, 1992, 1995; Surrey, 1985). Simply put, traditional boys present themselves to the world as "doers" rather than as "feelers" (Kiselica, 1992), even though they experience and are capable of expressing very powerful emotions, such as joy, sorrow, happiness, and anger (see Heesacker et al., 1999).

TRADITIONAL BOYS IN COUNSELING AND PSYCHOTHERAPY

Traditional boys are often ill suited for counseling and psychotherapy as it is commonly practiced. More than twenty years ago, Monroe Bruch (1978) explained in a special issue of *The Counseling Psychologist* on helping men that there is a mismatch between the relational styles of traditional males and that of most helping professionals. Borrowing Holland's (1973) typology, Bruch (1978) suggested that the helping environment is best suited for individuals who would be classified as having a "social" personality type (p. 27). That is, clients who are skilled at and comfortable with the self-disclosure of thoughts and feelings and who are introspective can easily relate to counselors because counselors use the same relational style. Thus, males who have social personality types tend to respond well to counseling activities. However, many males, especially traditional males (and, I might add, many females) are not social types, and their relational styles are not congruent with the social environment of counseling. For example, men who have "conventional" and "realistic" personalities avoid less structured interpersonal and exploratory activities, such as counseling, and prefer activities involving the manipulation and organization of data and objects. Consequently, they are likely to feel ill at ease with counseling as it is customarily practiced (Bruch, 1978).

Because of this mismatch between the relational style of the client and the norms of the counseling setting, the traditional male client tends to feel uncomfortable, has difficulty responding in a manner that the counselor prefers, and is disinclined to continue in counseling. Many counselors erroneously view these behaviors as acts of resistance (Kiselica, 1992, 1995) and as evidence that the client is hypoemotional (Heesacker et al., 1999) and does not want to address his problems rather than viewing the situation as a possible problem of a lack of fit between the client and the counseling environment (Kiselica, 1992, 1995). In a conference address pertaining to this issue (Kiselica, 1992), I argued that this problem is analogous to a clothing manufacturer who has designed a one-size-fits-all glove, in which the glove actually fits a small percentage of customers. The remainder of people whose hands do not fit into the gloves either will have very numb hands on a bitter cold day because the gloves are too small to wear or their hands will feel lost inside the gloves because the gloves are too large. In this situation, is it surprising that the hands of some of the customers become stiff? That other customers dislike the gloves because they are oversized? Would it not behoove the manufacturer to develop different gloves for different people?

Returning from this analogy back to therapeutic considerations, I contend that many boys avoid and drop out of counseling and psychotherapy because they are uneasy with the manner in which helpers typically relate to them (Kiselica, 1992, 1995). If this hypothesis is true, and there is considerable empirical support for this conjecture (see Achatz & MacAllum, 1994; Brown, 1990; Hendricks, 1988; Sander & Rosen, 1987), then it makes sense that helping professionals adapt their relational styles to the personalities of traditional boys to make the helping process more appealing and more effective with this population.

A MALE-FRIENDLY APPROACH TO COUNSELING AND PSYCHOTHERAPY

How can this adaptation be accomplished? How should the helper relate to young men with a traditional relational style? To put it in another way, how can we construct and deliver a male-friendly approach to counseling and psychotherapy with school-age boys?

In my attempt to answer these questions, I will draw extensively from the findings of a variety of studies pertaining to the provision of services to teen fathers. Historically, adolescent fathers have been greatly misunderstood, underserved, and treated in a pejorative manner by social service providers in the United States (Kiselica, 1995, 1999). Consequently, they have been unlikely to participate in teen parenting programs, even though the best available data demonstrate that the majority of teen fathers want help with the challenges of parenthood (Achatz & MacAllum, 1994; Brown, 1990; Hendricks, 1988; Sander & Rosen, 1987). Other data, which are summarized here, indicate that the use of counseling services by teen fathers increases substantially when service providers tailor teen parenting programs to the needs of adolescent fathers and employ nontraditional approaches to counseling (Achatz & MacAllum, 1994; Brown, 1990; Hendricks, 1988; Sander & Rosen, 1987). Because these data are drawn from studies that were conducted in many different rural and urban areas of the United States and with samples of white (non-Hispanic), African American, and Hispanic males, they are likely to have strong external validity for working with other boys. Collectively, these data suggest that effective helping must begin with a reexamination of the time constraints imposed on male clients and the use of formal office settings during counseling and psychotherapy.

A Reexamination of the Fifty-Minute Hour and the Use of Formal Office Settings

Traditional boys tend to develop trusting relationships with their friends over time, by hanging out, doing things together, and gradually letting others into their psychological world. Consequently, they are a bit like fish out of water when they are thrust into formal counseling situations in which they are expected to remain seated and spill their guts for an hour at a time once a week. The so-called fifty-minute hour, which has become the standard time frame for counseling and psychotherapy sessions in the United States, is an artificial and odd concept to many boys and is especially foreign to some ethnic groups, such as Native Americans. For many boys meeting a counselor or psychotherapist for the first time, fifty minutes is too long a period to sit around talking. For others who are in a crisis, a fifty-minute session—particularly fifty minutes once a week—is inadequate for managing a crisis. Some teenage boys perceive mental health practitioners who adhere rigidly to this one-hour-per-week standard as being hypocritical about wanting to be helpful (Kiselica, 1992).

The reliance on formal office settings for the work of counseling and psychotherapy is also problematic for many boys with a traditional relational style. Most practitioners who work with school-age boys do so within the confines of their offices. Yet traditional boys are accustomed to developing intimate relations in less formal settings. Boys who are good buddies with one another get to know each other inside and out through the instrumental activities they share. For example, over the course of any sporting season, boys on the same team get to know each other quite well, including significant information about each other's psyche. Although boys on the same team may not sit down and have face-to-face, heart-to-heart chats, they do share stories and bits and pieces of significant emotional material about their lives with one another while changing in the locker room, horsing around together and hanging out after practice and between games, and traveling to and from practices and games. In a similar fashion, guys who tinker with automobiles or youths who are members of gangs develop close friendships through their shared activities in garages and street hangouts, respectively. Intimate kinships develop in these varied settings. However, traditional males view formal office settings as, well, formal, and not as the kind of place where you let others see what makes you tick inside. Asking a traditional male to step into a formal office setting and open up his psyche is analogous to asking an opera singer to perform an inspired rendition of an aria in a toolshed without the support of an orchestra. The setting is just not conducive to the production of one's best performance.

Alternative Time Schedules and Settings

In light of these considerations, it is time for mental health professionals to reexamine the standard use of the fifty-minute hour and formal office settings with traditional male adolescents. Instead, as Hendricks (1988) has suggested, to the extent possible, the time for meetings with boys should be convenient for them. It is better to be more general rather than rigid and specific regarding the scheduling of appointments and to establish drop-in periods. For example, a practitioner can ask, "Can you come in the morning between the hours of nine and eleven, or is the afternoon better for you between the hours of three and six?" Because some boys, especially those from emotionally disengaged families, are not very good at following through on making and keeping appointments, Brown (1990) advised counselors to be persistent in their efforts to serve young men, even though they may feel frustrated at times. She noted that patience and persistence frequently prove successful in engaging this population in counseling. Furthermore, as I have discussed elsewhere (Kiselica, 1995, 1999), once boys gradually get to know their counselors and experience the benefits of good treatment, they tend to become more committed to counseling and psychotherapy and tolerant of higher expectations by the therapist that the client show up for expected appointments.

Having initial interactions outside the office setting can speed up the process of establishing rapport with traditional boys. The professional can conduct much of the early information gathering in a gym or outside, where the clinician and boy take turns shooting baskets or tossing a football while they talk about each other's favorite teams (Kiselica, 1995, 1999). Or the two might go for a walk, share a snack and a soda, and chat about the young man's interests as they walk side by side (Kiselica, 1995, 1999). Other strategies include conducting sessions in the client's home, at a park, or in a restaurant and talking about each other's lives while playing checkers, working together on a manual project, or fishing or hiking in the woods together.

Without question, school-based practitioners who attempt to employ these nonconventional, rapport-building strategies are likely to be discouraged by school officials who have rigid expectations about how and where counseling should occur. As a solution to this problem, in a later section of this chapter I suggest some of the system-change strategies that can help school officials to accept a transformed practice of school-based counseling with boys.

Humor and Self-Disclosure

Across the many different settings suggested earlier, the counselor should be prepared to inject a little humor and self-disclosure into the conversation. Traditional boys tend to relieve tension by telling jokes, and they typically feel comfortable with people who can loosen things up a bit with a well-timed joke or two. Although traditional boys may find it difficult to disclose very personal matters to others directly, they tend to open up to others who take the lead with self-disclosure. Therefore, it is recommended that the counselor be prepared to share an appropriate amount of personal information about himself or herself with the client. For example, when I have determined that it is safe to do so, I often show boys I counsel photos of my wife and children and tell them about where I was raised and where I live. Telling a little bit about oneself to the client engenders trust and models self-disclosure for the client. In summary, sharing light conversations that are characterized by gradual and mutual self-disclosure and are held outside of the office can pave the way for discussions regarding more substantive matters.

Other Rapport-Building Tactics

Once the practitioner senses that it is OK to broach more personal topics, heavy reliance on open-ended questions such as "How are you feeling?" tends to be ineffective. Instead, it is recommended that the counselor conduct issue-specific discussions (Barth, Claycomb, & Loomis, 1988) centered on how the counselor can help the young man with his most pressing concern (Hendricks, 1988). I emphasize the word *his* because the client may have a different agenda for the counseling session than the clinician does. For example, it is common for adolescent boys to want help with practical matters, such as finding a job, getting a car license, or settling a dispute with a girlfriend, whereas the counselor may intend to discuss the boy's academic difficulties or conflicts between the youth and his teacher or family. Although the counselor cannot ignore the latter issues, which are often the basis for counseling referrals, he or she is advised to proceed carefully and to follow the client's cues regarding his comfort level with any topic. In other words, the counselor should take it slow and follow the boy's lead. After the youth grows more comfortable and trusting, the counselor can be more direct and less tentative and switch the focus of counseling to more emotionally charged issues.

Empathy, availability, and honesty are essential to the development and maintenance of rapport (Brindis, Barth, & Loomis, 1987; Kiselica, 1996). A troubled boy needs to know that he can count on the counselor during times of crisis. Therefore, it is essential early on to assure him of one's availability for as long as it is needed and to empathize with his feelings about his problems. Furthermore, it is a good idea for the counselor to act in a way that demonstrates respect for the lad's autonomy. For example, the counselor is advised to provide his or her business card, which should list the counselor's name, work address and phone number, and the hours during which the counselor can be contacted (Hendricks, 1988).

These measures will help many boys to feel comfortable visiting a counselor in his or her office. In the following section I recommend additional tactics for making office visits a success.

Male-Friendly Strategies During Office Visits

According to Hendricks (1988), there are many things the clinician can do to put a boy at ease once he arrives at the clinician's office:

1. Ask the client for his permission to call him by his first name.
2. Encourage him to relax by offering a soft drink before beginning the session.
3. Have all calls held during the interview. Doing so contributes to his sense of importance.
4. Have magazines displayed with which a teenage boy can identify, especially sports publications.
5. Be knowledgeable about the slang he may use.
6. Be prepared to discuss events going on in the community.
7. Keep interview sessions brief—a maximum of forty-five minutes.

The manner in which one talks to a boy can greatly influence his response. During the early stages of counseling, it is advisable to not ask too many questions because boys often associate such questioning with being in trouble. Once again, the counselor should be prepared to do a lot of listening and to follow the boy's lead about what topics he is ready to discuss. This approach communicates to the youth that the counselor is there to address the youth's own pressing needs (Hendricks, 1988). "Moreover, trust, rapport, and constructive communication are likely to be established more rapidly when the youth and clinician sit side-by-side rather than opposite each other" (Hendricks, 1988, p. 719). This seating arrangement tends to reduce suspicion and self-consciousness (Hendricks, 1988). Kiselica (1999) recommended that a counselor wearing a long-sleeved shirt role up his or her shirtsleeves, thereby conveying to the youth that the counselor is ready to work for and with the youngster. It can also help to toss a miniature football around while the counselor and client talk about disturbing subjects (Kiselica, 1995).

Another critical task during the initial stages of counseling is to explore the boy's view about counseling. Through this process misconceptions about the purpose of counseling can be corrected. In addition, the counselor can prepare the client for some of the work that might lie ahead (Kiselica, 1995).

Working Efficiently: Group Counseling Services for Boys

Practitioners who work in school settings understandably might be concerned about how they can follow the recommendations offered here in light of the many demands that tax their time and energies. For example, on average there is only 1 counselor for every 513 students in U.S. elementary and secondary schools (Barstow, Urbaniak, & Holland, 1999). I have personally supervised school counseling practicum students and interns working in school districts in which the student-to-counselor ratio is nine hundred to one. School counselors employed in these districts will have difficulty finding the time to work individually with troubled boys, especially in the manner that I have suggested here. Yet school counselors and other professional helpers who work in schools have an ethical obligation and face public pressure to address the needs of troubled boys.

These conflicting demands place some school-based helpers in a difficult if not impossible situation. It is highly unlikely that school-based practitioners who are overwhelmed with student-to-counselor ratios of five hundred to one or higher can deliver effective counseling services. Such circumstances call for systematic changes in the schools, which is an issue I address later in this chapter. Until such changes occur, however, school-based helpers must strive to find an efficient way to help troubled boys in the face of such difficult circumstances.

Counseling boys in groups may be a partial solution to this problem. Group counseling approaches are more efficient than individual approaches to counseling because they allow counselors to address the needs of many clients in the same session. In addition to this practical advantage, group counseling makes clinical sense for counseling with boys in school, agency, and private practice settings because, as Jolliff (1994) and Andronico (1996) have observed, boys and men are accustomed to working and playing together in groups. Therefore, group counseling is a powerful treatment modality with males (Andronico, 1996; Jolliff, 1994), and it works particularly well with school-age boys when it is incorporated into holistic programs that include recreational and educational activities (Kiselica, 1996; Kiselica, Rotzien, & Doms, 1994).

Over the course of the past ten years, I and several of my colleagues have designed an approach to group counseling that is designed to appeal to the relational styles of traditional boys (see Kiselica, 1995, 1996, 1999; Kiselica, Rotzien, & Doms, 1994). In brief, our approach involves incorporating informal, rapport-building strategies such as helping boys to establish rapport through participation in recreational activities integrated with group psychoeducational activities that target the particular concerns of the group. For example, we have developed after-school programs for expectant teenage fathers in which the participants introduce themselves and then play basketball for approximately half an hour. Afterward, while having a drink or a snack, the boys watch and react to educational videos that are designed to help them clarify their attitudes about fatherhood and to express their feelings about becoming a parent. Other sessions are focused on teaching the participants important life skills, such as child care and financial and time management skills. This approach to counseling taps the instrumental, group-oriented relational style of traditional boys while capitalizing on the support that is created through the formation of a therapeutic group.

Professionals can apply this model in their work with boys facing a wide range of emotional difficulties. Informal recreational activities can be merged with psychoeducational sessions targeting the stereotypic problems of boys, such as disruptiveness and aggression, as well as other problems, such as shyness, gender identity issues, and incest, problems that hundreds of thousands of boys experience but that are commonly ignored by society (see Kiselica & Horne, 1999).

A REEXAMINATION OF PROFESSIONAL CONSTRAINTS

Undoubtedly, some practitioners will be uncomfortable with the ideas that I have proposed here because they are at odds with traditional conceptions of boundaries in the client-practitioner relationship. As Arnold Lazarus (1990, 1995) has pointed out, most mental health practitioners are trained to maintain a high degree of professional distance from their clients in order to maintain their objectivity about their clients' problems. Furthermore, the ethical standards used in psychology, counseling, psychiatry, and social work discourage practitioners from developing dual relationships with clients—that is, from having a personal and a professional relationship with a client at the same time. Although these conventions of clinical practice certainly have many merits, such as preventing the exploitation of clients, Lazarus and other prominent leaders of the mental health professions, such as Nancy Boyd-Franklin (1989) and Derald Wing Sue (1997), and organizers of highly acclaimed, successful community-based service programs for adolescents, such as Michael Carrera (1992), have questioned the strict interpretations of and adherence to these conventions. For example, Lazarus (1990, 1995) has argued that rigid boundaries between client and therapist sometimes have the effect of shackling the humanity of the therapist and consequently impair the client-therapist relationship. Similarly, Boyd-Franklin (1989) and Sue (1997) have noted that the standard way of conducting psychotherapy creates such a distance between the client and the practitioner that some populations, such as impoverished, inner-city African Americans, consider counseling and psychotherapy to be a strange and foreign endeavor that should be avoided. Carrera (1992) urged that traditional service programs, which impoverished inner-city boys view as lacking heart, be replaced by holistic, highly personal educational programs.

I argue that the same types of problems permeate much of the mental health work going on with traditional boys and that it is time to transform counseling and psychotherapy with boys, a transformation that requires us to reexamine how rigidly we interpret concepts such as client-therapist boundaries and dual relationships. We have to do a better job of creating safe but humane boundaries in counseling and psychotherapy with boys. Although confused and troubled boys can be helped by someone who listens to and analyzes their problems with an objective stance, there is strong empirical evidence that they can be helped even more by practitioners who are also willing to get out of their offices, visit their clients' homes, take boys out to lunch, play with boys in school yards, drive them to job interviews, and work on projects with them (Achatz & MacAllum, 1994; Brown, 1990; Hendricks, 1988; Sander & Rosen, 1987). This is not to say that professionals should take the place or do the work of parents and other family members. On the contrary, it is preferable that the practitioner assist families to engage and help troubled boys with their intrapsychic and extrapsychic concerns. Nevertheless, whether the work is focused on mobilizing the family members to help their sons or on working with boys individually in therapy, I am convinced that the most effective practitioners are those whom boys perceive to be active, involved mentors who make a positive difference in boys' lives by addressing their practical needs and their emotional difficulties in a friendly, loving, and involved manner.

Addressing Constraints Imposed by School Systems

School counselors, school psychologists, and school social workers remain somewhat limited in their attempts to help boys by the constraints imposed by school systems. On the whole, school district policies regulating and defining the work of school-based helpers dictate and reward a conservative, outdated approach to counseling boys. School practitioners cannot help boys if they continue to be overwhelmed by inexcusably high student-to-counselor ratios and if they are forced to practice in a way that comes across as being foreign to U.S. boys. The legions of boys who are struggling with cultural values conflicts, confusion about what it means to be male, sexual identity issues, teenage fatherhood, physical and sexual abuse, aggressive tendencies, learning difficulties, anxiety, depression, hyperactivity and attention difficulties, and substance abuse warrant a radical transformation of the way we conduct counseling and psychotherapy with boys (see Horne & Kiselica, 1999; Kiselica & Horne, 1999). Schools must play an integral part in this transformation, beginning with a reexamination of the demands placed on school-based counselors and the manner in which they are required to provide their professional services.

School counselors, school psychologists, and school social workers can be crucial agents for changing school-based services for boys by participating in several initiatives. First, it is recommended that helpers employed in archaic school systems obtain and read *Developing and Managing Your School Guidance Program,* by Gysbers and Henderson (2000). This resource is necessary reading for any school-based counselor who is frustrated by high student-to-counselor ratios and by responsibilities that have nothing to do with counseling, such as performing the quasi-administrative tasks of monitoring hallways and processing student schedules. Gysbers and Henderson describe a model for how school counselors can work over time with other school personnel, parents, school board members, and students to create support for the hiring of additional school counselors and to update and expand the roles of counselors in schools. Second, school practitioners are urged to read the works of Carrera (1992), Dryfoos (1994), and Tyack (1992), all of whom describe the benefits (for example, reduced vandalism, dropout, delinquency, and teen parenthood rates) of innovative counseling and social services for youth, and to inform key power brokers in their communities about the effectiveness of these innovative approaches to counseling in schools. Lastly, school-based helpers can fortify their arguments for transforming counseling with boys by capitalizing on the growing public discontent regarding the failure of schools to address adequately the social and emotional needs of schoolchildren. Sadly, the gruesome killings and suicides at Columbine High School and similar tragedies at many other schools throughout the United States have awakened the country to the disturbing fact that "too many of our nation's sons are in trouble and troubled in a society that tends to disregard their problems or give them mixed messages about receiving help" (Kiselica & Horne, 1999, p. xvii). In response to this problem, there has been an urgent demand by the public to place more counselors in schools. As evidence of this demand, Congress is currently reviewing new legislative proposals that are designed to fund the hiring of one hundred thousand new school counselors, psychologists, and social workers (Barstow et al., 1999). Mental health professionals must continue to support this type of legislation so that we can ensure that caring and competent counseling professionals help boys to reach their fullest potential.

MYTHS AND REALITIES REGARDING ALEXITHYMIA AND BOYS

As a closing note, any mental health practitioner, whether employed in a school or a nonschool setting, should understand the subject of alexithymia and its alleged occurrence in boys. *Alexithymia* is defined as a very serious emotional disturbance characterized by a constellation of symptoms, including stiffness of posture and an expressionless face, difficulty identifying and describing feelings, a concrete and reality-based cognitive style, an impoverished imagination, and psychosomatic ailments (Krystal, 1982; Sifneos, 1973). According to Krystal (1982), alexithymia is common among people who have suffered from severe trauma and individuals with addictions who are going through drug withdrawal.

Unfortunately, recent writings about alexithymia have created the widespread impression that the disorder is gender specific and limited to males. For example, Pollack (1995, 1999) and Pollack and Chu (1997) have proposed that boys experience a normative developmental trauma of a premature, forced emotional separation from their mothers, which creates low levels of alexithymia, which in turn is the root cause of aggression, suicide, drug abuse, and other difficulties in boys. Although it is true that some boys experience alexithymia, there is no empirical support for the claim that boys are more likely than girls to suffer from alexithymia. On the contrary, the best available data indicate that there are no significant gender differences in the occurrence of alexithymia (Levant, 1999; Mallinckrodt, King, & Coble, 1998). Nevertheless, widespread misconceptions about alexithymia have contributed to stereotypes depicting boys as emotionally mummified creatures (Kiselica, 1997). These stereotypes have the potential to cause practitioners to view male clients as being more psychopathological than they actually are (Heesacker et al., 1999).

As I have argued here and elsewhere (Kiselica, 1997), a more accurate portrayal of boys is to understand that they are not emotionally constricted but that they tend to express their emotions in ways that are different from those used by most females and most counselors. Furthermore, the counseling process strategies described in this chapter are designed to help practitioners to understand the relational styles of traditional boys and how to adapt counseling to match those styles.

What, then, should counselors do with the minority of boys who display the serious condition of alexithymia? Levant (1995) has appropriately argued that males with alexithymia need training in how to access and express a wide range of emotional states, especially vulnerable and caring emotions. Clearly, boys (and girls) with alexithymia can benefit from the type of emotional self-awareness training techniques that Levant and his colleagues have developed (see Levant, 1993, 1995; Levant & Kelly, 1989). Although it is beyond the scope of this chapter to describe these techniques in detail, practitioners interested in an overview of emotional self-awareness procedures are referred to the writings of Levant on the subject (Levant, 1993, 1995; Levant & Kelly, 1989). The male-friendly therapeutic process described in this chapter can help practitioners working with boys with alexithymia to develop a sound foundation of trust on which the construction of emotional self-awareness skills can begin.

If we really intend to help school-age boys, we must understand that their ways of relating tend to be different from the preferred relational style of most mental health professionals. Consequently, we must adjust counseling and psychotherapy to fit the ways that boys approach the world so that boys will feel comfortable with counselors and the work they do. By reexamining our use of the fifty-minute hour, working with boys in informal settings, using humor and self-disclosure, employing male-friendly rapport-building strategies, counseling boys in groups, confronting professional and institutional constraints, and understanding the myths and realities pertaining to alexithymia among boys, we will succeed in helping school-age boys to lead more happy and fulfilling lives.

References

Achatz, M., & MacAllum, C. A. (1994). *Young unwed fathers: Report from the field.* Philadelphia: Public/Private Ventures.

Andronico, M. P. (1996). Introduction. In M. P. Andronico (Ed.), *Men in groups: Insights, interventions, and psychoeducational work* (pp. xvii–xviv). Washington, DC: American Psychological Association.

Barstow, S., Urbaniak, J., & Holland, H. Z. (1999, June). Washington update: "100,000 New Counselors" voted in. *Counseling Today, 1,* 10–11.

Barth, R. P., Claycomb, M., & Loomis, A. (1988). Services to adolescent fathers. *Health and Social Work, 13,* 277–287.

Boyd-Franklin, N. (1989). *Black families in therapy: A multisystems approach.* New York: Guilford Press.

Brindis, C., Barth, R. P., & Loomis, A. B. (1987). Continuous counseling: Case management with teenage parents. *Social Casework: The Journal of Contemporary Social Work, 68,* 164–172.

Brown, S. (1990). *If the shoes fit: Final report and program implementation guide of the Maine Young Fathers Project.* Portland, ME: University of Southern Maine, Human Services Development Institute.

Bruch, M. A. (1978). Holland's typology applied to client-counselor interaction: Implications for counseling with men. *Counseling Psychologist, 7,* 26–32.

Carrera, M. A. (1992). Involving adolescent males in pregnancy and STD prevention programs. *Adolescent Medicine: State of the Art Reviews, 3,* 1–13.

Clinchy, B., & Zimmerman, C. (1985). *Growing up intellectually: Issues for college women* (Work in Progress No. 19). Wellesley, MA: Wellesley College, Stone Center for Developmental Services and Studies.

Dryfoos, J. G. (1994). *Full-service schools: A revolution in health and social services for children, youth, and families.* San Francisco: Jossey-Bass.

Fischer, P. C., Smith, R. J., Leonard, E., Fuqua, D. R., Campbell, J. L., & Masters, M. A. (1993). Sex differences on affective dimensions: Continuing examination. *Journal of Counseling and Development, 71,* 440–443.

Griffin-Pierson, S. (1990). The competitiveness questionnaire: A measure of two components of competitiveness. *Measurement and Evaluation in Counseling and Development, 23,* 108–115.

Gysbers, N. C., & Henderson, P. (2000). *Developing and managing your school guidance program* (3rd ed.). Alexandria, VA: American Counseling Association.

Heesacker, M., Wester, S. R., Vogel, D. L., Wentzel, J. T., Mejia-Millan, C. M., & Goodholm, C. R. (1999). Gender-based emotional stereotyping. *Journal of Counseling Psychology, 46,* 483–495.

Hendricks, L. E. (1988). Outreach with teenage fathers: A preliminary report on three ethnic groups. *Adolescence, 23*(91), 711–720.

Holland, J. L. (1973). *Making vocational choices: A theory of careers.* Englewood Cliffs, NJ: Prentice Hall.

Horne, A., & Kiselica, M. S. (Eds.). (1999). *Handbook of counseling boys and adolescent males: A practitioner's guide.* Thousand Oaks, CA: Sage.

Jolliff, D. (1994). Guest editorial: Group work with men. *Journal for Specialists in Group Work, 19,* 50–51.

Kiselica, M. S. (1992, March). Alternative models of masculinity. In L. H. Glenn (Chair), *Connectedness not dependence: Gender issues and relationship excellence.* Symposium conducted at the annual convention of the American Association for Counseling and Development, Baltimore.

Kiselica, M. S. (1995). *Multicultural counseling with teenage fathers: A practical guide.* Thousand Oaks, CA: Sage.

Kiselica, M. S. (1996). Parenting skills training with teenage fathers. In M. P. Andronico (Ed.), *Men in groups: Insights, interventions, and psychoeducational work* (pp. 283–300). Washington, DC: American Psychological Association.

Kiselica, M. S. (1997). Is emotional constriction in boys and men the product of a normative or an aberrant developmental pathway? In W. S. Pollack (Chair), *Rescuing Ophelia's brothers: What about boys?* Symposium conducted at the annual convention of the American Psychological Association, Chicago.

Kiselica, M. S. (1999). Counseling teen fathers. In A. Horne & M. S. Kiselica (Eds.), *Handbook of counseling boys and adolescent males: A practitioner's guide* (pp. 179–197). Thousand Oaks, CA: Sage.

Kiselica, M. S., & Horne, A. (1999). Preface: For the sake of our nation's sons. In A. Horne & M. S. Kiselica (Eds.), *Handbook of counseling boys and adolescent males: A practitioner's guide* (pp. xv–xx). Thousand Oaks, CA: Sage.

Kiselica, M. S., Rotzien, A., & Doms, J. (1994). Preparing teenage fathers for parenthood: A group psychoeducational approach. *Journal for Specialists in Group Work, 19,* 83–94.

Kiselica, M. S., Stroud, J., Stroud, J., & Rotzien, A. (1992). Counseling the forgotten client: The teen father. *Journal of Mental Health Counseling, 14,* 338–350.

Krystal, H. (1982). Alexithymia and the effectiveness of psychoanalytic treatment. *International Journal of Psychoanalytic Psychotherapy, 9,* 353–378.

LaFrance, M., & Banaji, M. (1992). Toward a reconsideration of the gender-emotion relationship. In M. S. Clark (Ed.), *Review of personality and social psychology* (Vol. 14, pp. 178–201). Newbury Park, CA: Sage.

Lazarus, A. A. (1990). Can psychotherapists transcend the shackles of their training and superstitions? *Journal of Clinical Psychology, 46,* 351–358.

Lazarus, A. A. (1995). Boundaries in the physician-patient relationship. *JAMA, 274,* 1345–1346.

Levant, R. F. (1993, August). *Men and psychotherapy: Assessment and treatment of alexithymia in men.* Paper presented at the annual convention of the American Psychological Association, Toronto.

Levant, R. F. (1995). Toward the reconstruction of masculinity. In R. F. Levant & W. S. Pollack (Eds.), *A new psychology of men* (pp. 229–251). New York: Basic Books.

Levant, R. F. (1999, August). Boys in crisis. In R. F. Levant (Chair), *New work in the psychology of boys.* Symposium conducted at the annual convention of the American Psychological Association, Boston, MA.

Levant, R. F., & Kelly, J. (1989). *Between father and child.* New York: Viking.

Mallinckrodt, B., King, J.L., & Coble, H.M. (1998). Family dysfunction, alexithymia, and client attachment to therapist. *Journal of Counseling Psychology, 45,* 497–504.

Pollack, W. S. (1995). No man is an island: Toward a new psychoanalytic psychology of men. In R. F. Levant & W. S. Pollack (Eds.), *A new psychology of men* (pp. 33–67). New York: Basic Books.

Pollack, W. S. (1999). *Real boys: Rescuing our sons from the myths of boyhood.* New York: Henry Holt.

Pollack, W. S., & Chu, J. (1997, August). Lost boys: Finding boys' voices. In W. S. Pollack (Chair), *Rescuing Ophelia's brothers: What about boys?* Symposium conducted at the annual convention of the American Psychological Association, Chicago.

Sander, J. H., & Rosen, J. L. (1987). Teenage fathers: Working with the neglected partner in adolescent childbearing. *Family Planning Perspectives, 19,* 107–110.

Shields, S. A. (1995). The role of emotion beliefs and values in gender development. In N. Eisenberg (Ed.), *Review of personality and social psychology* (Vol. 15, pp. 212–232). Thousand Oaks, CA: Sage.

Sifneos, P. E. (1973). The prevalence of "alexithymic" characteristics in psychosomatic patients. *Psychother. Pychosom., 22,* 255–262.

Sue, D. W. (1997, November). The psyche of the nation in terms of racial and cultural relations. Address conducted for the Multicultural Lecture Series, The College of New Jersey, Ewing, NJ.

Surrey, J. L. (1985). *Self-in-relation: A theory of women's development* (Work in Progress No. 13). Wellesley, MA: Wellesley College, Stone Center for Developmental Services and Studies.

Tyack, D. (1992). Health and social services in public schools: Historical perspectives. *Future of Children, 2,* 19–31.

CHAPTER TWO

Counseling Men in Medical Settings

The Six-Point HEALTH Plan

Will H. Courtenay

Gender-based medicine and health care are receiving increased attention among health professionals (Courtenay, 2000c; Courtenay & Keeling, 2000a, 2000b; Eisler & Hersen, 2000; Lent & Bishop, 1998). In addition to having different reproductive health needs, women and men have different risks for specific diseases and disabilities (Courtenay, 1999, in press-a). They also differ in their perceptions of health. Research consistently indicates, for example, that men are less likely than women to perceive themselves as being at risk for most health problems, even for problems that men are more likely than women to experience (see Courtenay, 1998b, in press-b). Furthermore, gender-specific interventions are often necessary to achieve positive clinical outcomes. As noted elsewhere (Courtenay, 1998a), a substantial body of research has demonstrated that—based on their readiness to change health-related behaviors—women and men require different interventions and that failure to tailor interventions to these gender-specific needs significantly reduces the chance of behavioral change. Other studies have found that using such approaches as future awareness and imagining symptoms to modify risk behaviors is more effective with men than with women (DePalma, McCall, & English, 1996; Rothspan & Read, 1996).

MEN, MASCULINITY, AND HEALTH

Feminist scholars were among the first to address gender and health, noting, for example, the absence of females as subjects in health research and the use of males as the standard for health. The result, however, is that "gender and health" has now become synonymous with "women's health" (see, for example, Bayne-Smith, 1996). Although health science has frequently used males as study subjects, research typically neglects men's gender. The health risks associated with men's gender are taken for granted and have remained largely unexamined. In fact, several authors have recently argued that medical researchers, psychologists, and other health professionals have all contributed to cultural portrayals of men as healthy and women as the "sicker" gender and thus to the "invisibility" of men's poor health status (Annandale & Clark, 1996; Courtenay, 2000a; Gijsbers van Wijk, Vliet, Kolk, & Everaerd, 1991). Little is understood, for example, about why men in the United States, on average, die nearly seven years younger than women and have higher death rates than women for all fifteen leading causes of death (Courtenay, 2000d).

The explanatory power of biological factors in predicting gender differences in morbidity and mortality is comparatively small (Krantz, Grunberg, & Baum, 1985; Verbrugge, 1989). In working with men, it is therefore particularly relevant to address psychological and social factors. A growing body of research indicates, for example, that masculinity and men's beliefs about manhood are significantly associated with men's health. Men who adopt traditional beliefs about manhood and dominant norms of masculinity have greater health risks than their peers with less traditional beliefs and engage in riskier behaviors, such as smoking; alcohol and drug use; and unhealthy behaviors related to safety, diet, sleep, and sex (see Copenhaver & Eisler, 1996; Courtenay, 1998a; Eisler, 1995). Indeed, many of the attitudes and behaviors that men and boys in the United States are typically encouraged to adopt are the very same attitudes and behaviors that increase their health risks (Courtenay, 2000a, in press-b). Taken together, these findings demonstrate that men's gender—not simply male biological sex—mediates men's health and preventive practices. They also show why it is necessary for medical and mental health professionals to address the influences of men's gender when working with men.

Any contact a health professional has with a man provides an important opportunity. Men represent 65 percent of those who have not visited a physician in two to five years and 70 percent of those who have not visited a physician in more than five years (U.S. Department of Health and Human Services, 1998a). Even among persons with health problems, men are significantly more likely than women to have had no recent physician contacts, regardless of income or ethnicity (U.S. Department of Health and Human Services, 1998b). Therefore, any encounter a health professional has with a man—particularly a young or middle-aged man—may be the only opportunity for assessment and intervention that any health professional will have with that man for a very long time. Furthermore, even one contact with a male patient can have significantly positive effects on both behavioral and clinical outcomes. A meta-analysis demonstrated that it is not the number of contacts or the amount of time spent with patients but rather how the time is spent that produces positive results (Mullen, Mains, & Velez, 1992).

Although many counseling and psychological interventions with men have been recommended in the past two decades (Courtenay, 2000b), few psychosocial techniques have been developed for health professionals who work with men in health care settings (Courtenay, 1998c; Sutkin & Good, 1987). Even more rarely are health interventions designed to address the unique needs of various populations of men, such as gay and bisexual men (Scarce, 1999) and men in prison (Courtenay & Sabo, in press). Despite the fact that on average African American men die eight years younger than European American men (U.S. Department of Health and Human Services, 1996), only recently have the specific psychosocial health needs of African American men been addressed (L. E. Davis, 1999). Given this lack of clinical guidance, it is not surprising that men receive significantly less physician time in medical encounters than women, and that men are provided with fewer and briefer explanations—both simple and technical (see Courtenay, 2000b).

PRACTICE GUIDELINE FOR THE TREATMENT OF MEN

I have developed a clinical practice guideline health professionals who work with men (Courtenay, 1996a). Its recommendations are based on an extensive review of biopsychosocial research related to men's gender and health, located through keyword searches in MEDLINE and PsycLIT. This guideline identifies behavioral and psychosocial factors that affect the onset, progression, and management of men's health problems; reviews evidence demonstrating the effectiveness of various interventions; and outlines specific recommendations for addressing these factors when working with men in clinical practice. I summarize its findings and recommendations in this chapter.

Communication between clinicians and their patients—and the health education provided through this relationship—is emphasized here. Health professionals whose responsibility it is to counsel men in medical settings are in a unique position to assist men. An extensive review of scientific evidence reveals that patients are more likely to be helped to prevent future disease by clinicians who ask, educate, and counsel them about personal health behaviors than by those who perform physical examinations or tests (U.S. Preventive Services Task Force, 1996). Furthermore, patients' feelings and attitudes about their health are influenced both by the information they receive and by the way in which they receive it (Hall, Roter, & Katz, 1988; Horne, Vatmanidis, & Careri, 1994). These findings have led to the recent conclusions that "talking is more important than testing" (Woolf, Jonas, & Lawrence, 1996, p. xxxvii) and that offering prevention advice and communicating effectively with patients is the most important skill for clinicians to acquire in the twenty-first century (Koop, 1996).

The American Medical Association (1991a) has referred to the lack of effective clinician-patient communication as a health hazard for men. Poor communication is associated with inaccurate diagnoses, poor compliance and outcomes, and low knowledge and knowledge retention (H. Davis & Fallowfield, 1991).[1] Conversely, effective patient and clinician communication has been found to be associated with improved compliance and better patient health status as measured physiologically, behaviorally, and subjectively (Cramer, 1991; Cramer & Spilker, 1991; Hall et al., 1988; Kaplan, Greenfield, & Ware, 1989; Meichenbaum & Turk, 1987). Because the learning patterns and conversational styles of women and men in this society differ distinctively and because women and men respond to and accept information differently (Golombok & Fivush, 1994; Tannen, 1990), it is imperative that health professionals incorporate what is currently understood about these gender differences into their interventions with men if these interventions are to be effective.

This chapter consists of six sections. Each section represents one of six types of interventions discussed in the guideline. Together, the section titles form the acronym HEALTH: humanize, educate, assume the worst, locate supports, tailor plan, and highlight strengths.

HUMANIZE

The first step in working with men is to humanize. Humanizing means validating, legitimizing, or normalizing their health problems and concerns. Conveying to patients that their feelings and experiences are understandable or legitimate—and that other people would probably feel the same way—is considered essential to effective communication with patients (Grüninger, 1995). Humanizing is especially important with men. Attending to health matters has historically been socially sanctioned and encouraged among women but not among men (Courtenay, 2000a, 2000e; Oakley, 1994). Consequently, many men associate health matters with womanly matters, and men receive strict social prohibitions against doing anything that women do (Courtenay, 2000e). Because disease,

---

[1]The terms *compliance* and *adherence* are used interchangeably throughout this chapter.

disability, and behavioral responses to illness are antithetical to traditional meanings of manhood (Courtenay, 2000a), men can experience shame when they have health problems. For example, one in five men report embarrassment as a reason for not discussing prostate, colon, or rectal cancers with a physician (American Medical Association, 1991b). Humanizing is especially important with patients who have chronic or permanently disabling or life-threatening conditions, which can seriously undermine men's identity as men (Charmaz, 1995).

Permission to have physical problems or health concerns and to discuss them openly has been referred to as a primary health care need of men (DeHoff & Forrest, 1984). Clinicians can help men learn that asking for help, acknowledging pain, expressing fear, crying, or needing bed rest are normal, human experiences—they are not unmanly. Other authors reviewing research on masculinity have suggested that when male patients have difficulty expressing discouragement, fear, or concern about giving up control during physical or psychological examinations, clinicians should communicate that these experiences are both normal and appropriate (Copenhaver & Eisler, 1996). Humanizing is a form of validation that some practitioners consider to be the most effective approach in beginning consultation with men (Rappaport, 1984). Humanizing may also contribute to the development of trust, which is also considered to be a critical first step in helping men (R. May, 1990). Specific factors that should be humanized include help seeking, illness and vulnerability, pain, and sexuality.

Humanizing Help Seeking

Men are significantly less likely than women to seek health care, except perhaps when their condition is serious (Courtenay, 2000a). There is evidence that this difference is seen because men have less intention to seek help from a variety of sources when they need it (see Ashton & Fuehrer, 1993; Good, Dell, & Mintz, 1989; Rule & Gandy, 1994; Sawyer & Moss, 1993). In fact, it has been suggested that men are least likely to ask for help when they are most in need of it (Rappaport, 1984). Among people who are depressed, for example, men are more likely than women not to seek mental health services, to withdraw from others, and to try to manage their depression on their own (Courtenay, 1998b, 2000a). Men learn these behaviors early in their lives. Parents and other adults not only actively discourage boys from seeking their help but often punish them when they do (Courtenay, 2000e). Seeking help can undermine men's sense of independence, which for some men is essential for self-respect (Tannen, 1990); this requirement for independence is believed to be true as well for African American men (Lee, 1990) and Latino men (Marks, Garcia, & Solis, 1990). Men can experience needing help as demeaning (Charmaz, 1995) and may subsequently develop feelings of inadequacy (Heppner & Gonzales, 1987) and shame (Brooks, 1998). Consequently, men may undergo considerable inconvenience rather than ask for help (DePaulo, 1982).

Health care visits pose a variety of threats to the roles most familiar to men (Sutkin & Good, 1987). They necessarily mean surrendering some autonomy and relinquishing some control. Lying still in bed or on a consulting table is contrary to the action-oriented and problem-solving coping styles that many men adopt. Clinicians' reconceptualization of help seeking as positive behavior can disconfirm men's anticipated response of disdain. Clinicians can offer reinforcement by saying, "I'm glad you phoned me. It's an important first step" or "Contacting me when you did was the best thing you could have done." Reframing men's help seeking as an act of strength, courage, and self-determination may decrease any embarrassment or self-doubt that they may experience in asking for help. Some clinicians consider reframing to be important when beginning work with men (J. A. Allen & Gordon, 1990). Clinicians could say, for example, "I know it can be a real challenge to ask for help, but I'm glad to see that didn't stop you." Clinicians can also assess men's intention of keeping follow-up appointments by saying, "You know, a lot of men have trouble keeping their follow-up appointments. Does that ever happen to you?" When asked nonjudgmentally, such questions help to predict future adherence and determine the need for treatment compliance techniques (Meichenbaum & Turk, 1987).

Humanizing Illness and Vulnerability

Because illness and vulnerability threaten stereotypically masculine notions of competence, vitality, and strength (Charmaz, 1995), men may experience illness and vulnerability as personal flaws or as failures to successfully demonstrate manhood (Courtenay, 2000d). Simply saying, "You know, everybody gets sick sometimes" can bring relief to men and help to establish rapport. Clinicians can also directly label the influence of gender: "Getting sick doesn't mean you're less of a man." When they are ill, men are less likely than women to restrict their activities or stay in bed for both acute and chronic conditions (Courtenay, 2000d). Some men consider staying in bed to rest or recover to be pampering, and by traditional standards men should not pamper their bodies (Courtenay, 2000e). Men may think of themselves as lazy if they miss work after an operation. Clinicians can humanize the need for convalescence and bed rest by saying to men, "Staying in bed and taking care of yourself when you're sick doesn't mean you're a bad employee or not a team player."

Humanizing Pain and Fear

It is also important for clinicians to make human the experience of pain and fear and to give men permission to acknowledge physical discomfort. Research consistently indicates that, compared with women, men report less pain for the same pathology, less severe pain, greater tolerance of pain and higher pain thresholds, and shorter duration of pain (Miaskowski, 1999; Unruh, 1996; Unruh, Ritchie, & Merskey, 1999). Men and society in general often view admitting and displaying fear and pain as unacceptable behaviors for men (Brooks, 1998; Courtenay, 2000a; Sutkin & Good, 1987). Not surprisingly, men are less likely than women to cry (Kraemer & Hastrup, 1986; Lombardo, Cretser, Lombardo, & Mathis, 1983) and they report less fear than women do (Croake, Myers, & Singh, 1987; Liddell, Locker, & Burman, 1991). Men are often uncomfortable in situations that require the expression of tender or painful emotions, because they believe that expressing such emotions is a violation of traditionally masculine behavior (Copenhaver & Eisler, 1996). Men may need to experience literally intolerable pain before they can acknowledge to themselves or to others that they are hurting. Failing to acknowledge or display physical pain can have far-reaching implications for men's health: it can influence the decision to seek help, delay intervention, and undermine diagnosis and treatment planning.

Clinicians should label conditions known to be painful as such: "Kidney stones can be very painful. I don't want you to hesitate for a moment if you think you might need to come back to the emergency room." Clinicians could express surprise when men deny that their kidney stones are painful. It may also be necessary to humanize the need for pain medication. Sutkin and Good (1987) suggest that a "tough guy" will characteristically wait six hours before requesting or taking a pain medication that is effective for four hours. Clinicians can compensate for this behavior by saying, "There are no medals for enduring pain, so I want you to let me know if you experience even the slightest bit of discomfort." For men who are refusing medication, clinicians can say, "It's routine for people to receive pain medication for this procedure. Are you sure you don't want the doctor to write you a prescription?"

Humanizing Sexuality

It is also important to humanize sexuality. Men's sexual performance is a measure of masculinity in this society (Fracher & Kimmel, 1992). Furthermore, masculinity is measured by superhuman standards that require men to be perpetually interested in and ready for sex (Zilbergeld, 1992). These cultural stereotypes, however, are inconsistent with many men's experience. At least one out of four American men is unable to get or maintain an erection for sex (Goldberg, 1993). Erectile dysfunction is also a common side effect of prostate surgery and a variety of medications. Difficulty getting or maintaining an erection can threaten a patient's self-image as a man and undermine a fundamental aspect of his gender identity (Charmaz, 1995). Not surprisingly, at least three out of four men with sexual concerns report not discussing those concerns with their physician and report that they are deterred from doing so by embarrassment (American Medical Association, 1991b; Metz & Seifert, 1990).

Humanizing sexuality gives men permission to discuss their concerns by normalizing sexual problems or fears among men (Fracher & Kimmel, 1992; Kaplan, 1974). Clinicians can say, "Most men have concerns about sex; it's normal. And I hope you're comfortable telling me if you do" or "I'd be surprised if you didn't worry about that; most men do." In fact, one study found that most men with sexual concerns preferred that clinicians initiate the discussion (Metz & Seifert, 1990). Many men can also use help in identifying unrealistic and less-than-human perceptions of manhood that contribute to sexual anxiety and help in learning how more human perceptions of sexuality can reduce stress and sexual dysfunction. Men with erectile dysfunction may benefit from being told that it is a common condition—that almost every man experiences occasional and transient erectile problems at some point in his life (Fracher & Kimmel, 1992; Zilbergeld, 1992). Clinicians can say, "Although the world often expects you to act like a machine, you aren't one. Your body can't really be expected to turn on and off at will. If you relax and don't expect so much out of yourself, you'll be surprised. Your anxiety will diminish and you'll feel a lot more pleasure."

Defining a Healthy Manhood

Although disease and disability are often unpleasant, they also provide men with the opportunity to redefine their lives and their manhood (Charmaz, 1995; D. F. Gordon, 1995). Indeed, many men may need to undergo this "reconstruction" of masculinity if they are to substantially improve their health (Levant & Kopecky, 1995). In a supportive manner, clinicians can challenge their patients' preconceived beliefs about what a man should be or what a man must do and discuss how these beliefs can damage them physically and psychologically (Brooks, 1998; Copenhaver & Eisler, 1996). This strategy is considered a consciousness-raising intervention (Copenhaver & Eisler, 1996), and research indicates that raising consciousness is an effective means of helping people to begin changing unhealthy behavior (Prochaska, Norcross, & DiClemente, 1994). For example, when humanizing help seeking, clinicians can say, "How do you think being a man influences your ability to ask for help?" Clinicians can then help male patients to see how their options are often limited not by their disability or illness but by their beliefs about manhood and other gender-related factors and help them explore more realistically human and healthy self-perceptions. Moderate self-disclosure by clinicians—particularly if the clinicians are men—may make male patients feel safer in exploring these issues. Self-disclosure establishes a basis of similarity and promotes trust; it has also been found to increase treatment adherence and to increase patients' sense of competence and self-efficacy (Copenhaver & Eisler, 1996; R. May, 1990; Meichenbaum & Turk, 1987). Clinicians might say, "I know what you mean, I have a hard time admitting when I'm sick too" or "I often feel like I'm just supposed to handle things on my own."

THE IMPORTANCE OF EDUCATION

The next step is to educate men about their health. As noted, health education interventions are an essential aspect of disease and injury prevention (Council on Scientific Affairs, 1990; U.S. Preventive Services Task Force, 1996; Woolf et al., 1996). According to strong evidence from recent reviews and meta-analyses, besides increasing patient and health practitioner satisfaction (Grüninger, 1995) health education improves compliance (Cramer, 1991; Cramer & Spilker, 1991; Hall et al., 1988; McCann & Blossom, 1990; Meichenbaum & Turk, 1987); reduces risk factors, disease, and death; and promotes healthy behaviors such as exercise, healthy diet, and blood pressure control (R. G. Frank, Bouman, Cain, & Watts, 1992; Grüninger, 1995; Mullen et al., 1992; U.S. Preventive Services Task Force, 1996). Similarly, psychoeducational interventions have been found to have a significantly positive effect on pain, psychological distress, and recovery and to be cost-efficient as well (Byers et al., 1995; Devine, 1992; Horne et al., 1994). Education is also essential if patients are to become active participants in their own health care (Make, 1994).

Educating Men About Their Health

There is strong evidence that men need to be educated about their health. If they are to maintain good health, it is critical that they be familiar with symptoms of life-threatening disease, know how the body should function, and know their family health histories (DeHoff & Forrest, 1984; Goldberg, 1993). Research consistently indicates, however, that men are less knowledgeable than women about health in general and about specific diseases such as heart disease, cancer, and sexually transmitted diseases (Courtenay, 2000e). Men also ask fewer questions than women do when visiting a physician (Wallen, Waitzkin, & Stoeckle, 1979; Waitzkin, 1984, 1985). Asking a question necessarily means admitting that there is something one does not know, which is often difficult for men to acknowledge (Tannen, 1990). Consequently, the American Medical Association has concluded, based on two national surveys, that men are "surprisingly uninformed" about basic health issues and that health professionals have a responsibility to educate men (American Medical Association, 1991a, 1991b).

Too often, however, health professionals fail to provide the health education that could reduce men's risks. Historically, health education generally and cancer education specifically have been directed primarily at women (Oakley, 1994; Reagan, 1997). Men also receive less information from physicians. In fact, no study has ever found that women receive less information from physicians than men do (Roter & Hall, 1997). This failure to educate men can result in a self-fulfilling prophecy and reinforce a damaging irresponsibility toward health matters among men. This need not be the case. Research indicates that health promotion and education can produce positive changes in knowledge, behavior, and health outcomes among men (Baer, 1993; Danielson, Marcy, Plunkett, Wiest, & Greenlick, 1990; Little, Stevens, Severson, & Lichtenstein, 1992); indeed, these changes are sometimes even greater than those found among women (Bjornson et al., 1995; Hornbrook et al., 1994; Oleckno & Blacconiere, 1990). Furthermore, obtaining information from conversation appeals to many men (Tannen, 1990) and can also be reassuring. Hendricks (1999) cites evidence, for example, that learning about diabetes, its associated health-related problems, its treatment, what outcomes can be expected from treatment, and when patients can expect these outcomes reduces fear and anxiety among African American men with the disorder.

Specific educational interventions vary depending on a man's current health, his presenting concern, and his future risks, as well as on the clinician's role and responsibilities. In general, clinicians can begin to educate men by saying, "I don't know about you, but most men know very little about their bodies and their health, and that lack of knowledge actually increases their health risks" or "Most of the things that have the biggest impact on your health are completely within your control." Because they have had relatively little experience with the health care system, many men need basic information such as how to ask for help, whom to contact to schedule a follow-up appointment, whom to phone with questions after discharge, and what kinds of questions to ask their health care providers. When counseling men, clinicians should word advice clearly, simply, and directly (Make, 1994; U.S. Preventive Services Task Force, 1996). Because patients see health professionals as experts, a direct statement such as "I must insist that you do your rehabilitation exercises daily" can have a strong positive effect (U.S. Preventive Services Task Force, 1996). To promote preventive care and behavioral change, it is considered essential to provide alternative behaviors (R. G. Frank et al., 1992). It is not enough simply to educate men about the importance of taking medication as prescribed. Clinicians must also suggest strategies for adhering to the prescribed regimen, such as establishing a dosing schedule and checklist and using a pillbox with daily compartments or an alarm (Cramer, 1991; Meichenbaum & Turk, 1987).

Clinicians should not be afraid to be enthusiastic in their interventions with men. Research indicates that men respond positively to active encouragement to engage in preventive health behavior (Myers et al., 1991). Because many men are less comfortable receiving information than giving it (Tannen, 1990), clinicians can communicate to male patients that the information they are being offered is provided routinely; patients may be less likely to feel that clinicians have singled them out as being ignorant (Rappaport, 1984). Clinicians can say, "We tell all of our patients . . ." or "You may already know this, but let me review it for the sake of good form." Then, clinicians can supplement what they say with written materials. Although written materials alone may not help patients to change their behavior (Grüninger, 1995), they may be more helpful to men than to women (R. May, 1990). It is essential, however, to make sure that patients can read and understand these materials (Meichenbaum & Turk, 1987).

Despite some inconsistent findings regarding the use of fear in motivating people to change unhealthy behaviors, health educators agree that some aspects of fear can be used effectively with some patients (Meichenbaum & Turk, 1987). In one study, fear of developing cancer was among the best predictors of testicular self-examination among young men (Katz, Meyers, & Walls, 1995). It is essential, however, that an intervention using fear also foster men's sense of efficacy in remedying the problem (Meichenbaum & Turk, 1987). Clinicians can offer information that induces a relatively low level of fear, provides positive reinforcement, and focuses on the immediate effects of modifying behavior, such as the reduction in high blood pressure and increased lung capacity that occur when patients stop smoking (Job, 1988): "Your diet is raising your risk of heart disease. But even the minor changes we've discussed will not only reduce this risk but also lower your cholesterol and increase your vitality."

Conveying the Importance of Screening, Self-Examination, and Early Detection

Men need to be taught how to do self-examinations. They also need to be taught the importance of screenings and early detection. Screening tests are essential for preventing disease, detecting preclinical conditions, and identifying a variety of diseases at an early stage when successful treatment is more likely (Courtenay, 2000d; U.S. Preventive Services Task Force, 1996; Woolf et al., 1996). Men, however, are less likely than women to practice self-examination or to attend health screenings (Courtenay, 2000d); African American men may be even less likely than European American men to do so (Pierce, 1999). Self-exams are particularly important for men. Because they seldom visit physicians, self-examination is the only way most men will detect a variety of diseases when they are still curable (Goldberg, 1993). Self-exams relevant to men include those for skin and testicular cancer, hypertension (for men at risk for heart disease or stroke), and sexually transmitted diseases. Health professionals can do much to encourage men to practice self-examination. Expressions of concern and personal instruction by clinicians have been associated with the intention to conduct self-exams (Brubaker & Wickersham, 1990; Neef, Scutchfield, Elder, & Bender, 1991).

Educating patients about their specific health risks is an essential aspect of disease and injury prevention (U.S. Preventive Services Task Force, 1989). It is particularly important to provide this information for men. One recent and extensive review of large studies, national data, and meta-analyses demonstrates that males of all ages are more likely than females to engage in more than thirty behaviors that increase the risk of disease, injury, and death (Courtenay, 2000d). Despite these findings, men receive less advice from physicians about changing risk factors for disease during checkups than women do (C. Friedman, Brownson, Peterson, & Wilkerson, 1994). Only 29 percent of physicians routinely provide age-appropriate instruction on performing self-exams for testicular cancer, compared with 86 percent who provide age-appropriate instruction to women on performing breast self-exams (Misener & Fuller, 1995). Clinicians must assess the need for self-examination skills among all their male patients.

To determine a man's specific risks, a health risk assessment can be useful. One such assessment has been developed specifically for men and includes items addressing both health behaviors and beliefs, including beliefs about manhood (Courtenay, 1996b). Once men's risks are identified, clinicians can provide counseling as indicated. When counseling men about modifying unhealthy behaviors, clinicians may emphasize the personal relevance of change and link it with individual men's circumstances (Meichenbaum & Turk, 1987), such as being healthy for their children. Men should also be invited to discuss what they believe they can do to reduce their health risks or modify their behaviors (J. P. May & Martin, 1993). In general, there is sufficient evidence regarding effective outcomes to strongly recommend counseling patients about avoiding tobacco, exercising regularly, limiting consumption of dietary fat, not driving while impaired by alcohol or other drugs, wearing bicycle helmets, and using condoms (U.S. Preventive Services Task Force, 1996). There is also sufficient evidence to recommend counseling patients about avoiding excess sun exposure; consuming fiber, fruits, and vegetables; using safety belts; reducing alcohol consumption in drinkers who may misuse alcohol; avoiding recreational activities while intoxicated; removing from the home or safely storing firearms in the home to prevent youth violence; and caring for their teeth (U.S. Preventive Services Task Force, 1996). Because most of these factors are significantly more common among men than among women (Courtenay, 2000d), it is particularly important to provide counseling to men.

Ensuring Comprehension

To foster compliance, it is important to make sure that patients understand what they have been told (Meichenbaum & Turk, 1987). Ensuring comprehension is especially important in the case of men, who can have difficulty admitting that they do not understand (Moore, 1990; Tannen, 1990). Simply asking patients to restate the information they have been given or to rehearse a regimen is an effective technique (Meichenbaum & Turk, 1987). If a clinician has explained to a patient how to perform a certain task—how to use a mechanical ventilatory support, for example—he or she should ask the patient to demonstrate the procedure (Kacmarek, 1994). The clinician can further clarify whether the patient has understood the information he was given—and how he will implement that knowledge—by asking, "Given what we discussed about your diet, what changes do you think are realistic for you to make to lower your blood pressure?"

Similarly, it is important for clinicians to recognize that men may have questions that they will not ask. Admitting that there is something they do not know or that they need to learn from someone else may be difficult for men (Rappaport, 1984; Tannen, 1990). Women ask more questions—and more direct questions—than men do when visiting a physician (Kaplan, Gandek, Greenfield, Rogers, & Ware, 1995; Waitzkin, 1984, 1985; Wallen et al., 1979). Consequently, clinicians should actively encourage men to ask questions, by saying, for example, "I'll try to cover everything, but your questions will be very helpful." Regardless of what exactly one says, it is essential to issue a direct invitation; merely informing patients that one is open to questions is not enough (Robinson & Whitfield, 1985). Clinicians can conclude a consultation by saying, "I've explained a lot to you. I'd be surprised if you didn't have some questions" or "You know, people often leave here without talking about the things that they're most concerned about."

ASSUMING THE WORST

One of the most common and enduring cultural stereotypes about men is that they are healthier and more resistant to disease than women are, despite a wealth of evidence to the contrary (Courtenay, 2000e). Men who attempt to conform to these cultural stereotypes increase their health risks. They may try to appear strong and healthy, believe that they are invulnerable to risk, minimize pain and deny feelings that others may perceive as signs of weakness, and report their health inaccurately (Courtenay, 2000a).

Men's Perceived Invulnerability to Risk

Studies consistently indicate that men are less likely than women to perceive themselves as being at risk. This difference holds true for a variety of health problems (see Boehm et al., 1993; Cohn, Macfarlane, Yanez, & Imai, 1995; Cutter, Tiefenbacher, & Solecki, 1992; Flynn, Slovic, & Mertz, 1994; Savage, 1993; Weissfeld, Kirscht, & Brock, 1990), including problems associated with sun exposure (Banks, Silverman, Schwartz, & Tunnessen, 1992; Mermelstein & Riesenberg, 1992); cigarette, alcohol, and other drug use (Spigner, Hawkins, & Loren, 1993); and physically dangerous activities (Zuckerman, 1994). Men's perceived invulnerability can prevent them from practicing preventive care or changing unhealthy behavior, thus actually increasing their health risks (Janz & Becker, 1984; Kreuter & Strecher, 1995; Mermelstein & Riesenberg, 1992; Reno, 1988; Rosenstock, 1990; Taylor, 1986; Weinstein, 1987). Perceived invulnerability has also been linked with poor compliance (H. S. Friedman & DiMatteo, 1989).

Men's Reported Health Needs

The American Medical Association contends that clinicians need to be more active than they are in inquiring about men's symptoms (American Medical Association, 1991a). This inquiry is especially important because the information men provide to clinicians does not always accurately reflect their needs. Research indicates that, except for anger, men express fewer emotions and disclose fewer fears and feelings of vulnerability than do women (Allen-Burge, Storandt, Kinscherf, & Rubin, 1994; Balswick, 1982; Belle, Burr, & Cooney, 1987; Chino & Funabiki, 1984; Grigsby & Weatherley, 1983; Hyde, 1986; Stapley & Haviland, 1989; Tannen, 1990; Williams, 1985). This stoicism is especially true of men who endorse traditional beliefs about masculinity (Copenhaver & Eisler, 1996; Saurer & Eisler, 1990; Thompson, Grisanti, & Pleck, 1985). These factors influence men's clinical consultations. Men provide less emotional and personal information than do women in reporting their health (Corney, 1990; Verbrugge, 1985). Men may deny their physical or emotional distress and conceal their illnesses or disabilities in an effort to preserve their masculinity or in the hope that their doctor will admire their stoicism or courage (Charmaz, 1995; Sutkin & Good, 1987). Men may also deny that they engage in risky behavior. One large study of safety belt use that compared self-reports with actual use found that among drivers who had been observed not wearing safety belts—more than three out of four of whom were men—one-third had reported that they always wore safety belts (Preusser, Williams, & Lund, 1991).

Assessing Men's Health Needs

Taken together, the preceding research suggests that men fail to convey the information clinicians need to provide effective medical care and that clinicians must therefore assume the worst. It is also essential to assume the worst in order to compensate for gender stereotypes, which influence the diagnostic decisions of—among others—mental health clinicians (Adler, Drake, & Teague, 1990; Fernbach, Winstead, & Derlega, 1989; Ford & Widiger, 1989; Potts, Burnam, & Wells, 1991; Waisberg & Page, 1988). One large study found that clinicians were less likely to identify the presence of depression in men than in women and that they failed to diagnose depression in nearly two-thirds of men who were depressed (Potts et al., 1991). Similarly, when patients are matched by symptoms or diagnoses, men are less likely than women to receive prescriptions for antidepressants and other psychotropic drugs (Hohmann, 1989; Taggart, McCammon, Allred, Horner, & May, 1993).

Men's desire to appear strong and healthy, to believe that they are invulnerable to risk, to conceal physical and emotional distress, and to report their behaviors inaccurately are all factors that must be considered when working with men. First, these factors make it difficult to conduct an accurate assessment. Second, as a result of these factors, men's physical and mental conditions are often serious when they finally seek help (Fabrega, Pilkonis, Mezzich, Ahn, & Shea, 1990; Gerber, Thompson, Thisted, & Chodak, 1993; Sawyer & Moss, 1993; Thomas & Kelman, 1990; Verbrugge, 1980, 1982). Assuming the worst compensates for these factors and for the tendency among clinicians to underestimate men's vulnerability.

Getting the Necessary Information

To diagnose men's condition accurately and to plan their treatment, it is essential to elicit information about their symptoms and feeling states. Asking men how they feel is not recommended, however. It has been argued that this question is difficult for men to respond to (Rubin, 1983) and that it often elicits nothing more than a shrug of the shoulders or an unreflective "Fine" (Rappaport, 1984). Instead, clinicians should inquire indirectly: "Tell me, how do you experience that?" or "What is that like for you?" These questions are uncommon and may be less likely to prompt an automatic response. Similarly, when assessing depression in men, it may be helpful to avoid the words *feel* and *depressed* and instead ask, "Do you ever get a little down?" Men may find it easier to admit that they get down than that they feel depressed.

A clinician who suspects that a man may be concealing his symptoms should question him further. If a sixty-year-old African American man who has diabetes and a family history of stroke is not reporting any symptoms, the clinician should ask him if he has experienced any sudden weakness or numbness, any loss of vision or speech, and any dizziness or headaches. Individualized feedback on specific health risks can increase men's accurate perceptions of their own susceptibility to these risks (Kreuter & Strecher, 1995). In response to perceptions of vulnerability that are inconsistent with men's actual risks, a clinician can say, "I know it's important to you to think of yourself as strong and healthy. But that attitude can lead you to take unnecessary risks with your health."

LOCATING SUPPORTS

Men are taught to value independence, autonomy, and self-sufficiency in themselves (Courtenay, 2000e; Majors & Billson, 1992; Marks et al., 1990). Consequently, compared with women, men have significantly fewer and less intimate friendships, fewer lifetime ties, and smaller and less multifaceted social networks, and they receive less support from network members (Courtenay, 2000d). Traditional beliefs about masculinity may make men even less likely to seek help from their friends, partners, and families (Burda & Vaux, 1987; Good et al., 1989; Pleck, 1981).

Exaggerated self-sufficiency and lack of social support contribute to the shortening of men's lives. There is overwhelming evidence that a lack of social support constitutes a major risk factor for mortality, especially for men. Men with the lowest levels of social support are two to three times more likely to die than those with the highest levels of support, even after controlling for health status and other possible confounding factors (Courtenay, 2000d). In contrast, high levels of social support are associated with the maintenance of positive health practices, modification of unhealthy behavior, and compliance with treatment (Courtenay, 2000d). Marriage also plays an important role in men's health; whether single, separated, widowed, or divorced, unmarried men have greater health risks than any other group (Courtenay, 2000d).

Involving Friends and Family

Assessing social support is considered essential to promoting behavioral change and preventive behavior (R. G. Frank et al., 1992). Involving friends and family as sources of support can also be essential to improving clinician-patient relationships and clinical outcomes (Delbanco, 1992). Clinicians should recognize the importance of extended family for African American men specifically and the need to involve family members collaboratively in these patients' care (Pierce, 1999). Because men have fewer social supports than do women and are less likely to use the ones they have, it is essential for clinicians to help men to identify the sources of support that are available to them. Sources of support may include significant others, friends, family members, coworkers, classmates, and groups. Clinicians can ask men, "Who are the people you are most comfortable asking to give you a hand?"

Clinicians should assess—and help patients to assess—whose involvement patients find helpful. Other people's involvement, in and of itself, is not necessarily supportive (Meichenbaum & Turk, 1987). A family member, friend, or health professional who has difficulty seeing vulnerability in men can undermine male patients' motivation to mobilize support. Once men's supports are identified, clinicians can encourage them to reach out to others. Otherwise, they may not. In a postoperative consultation, one man said, "You know, I was going into surgery and no one knew. It seemed like it would have been complaining to tell them." Clinicians can assist men in recognizing that everyone needs help sometimes and remind them that people really like to help and that their friends are probably happy to be asked.

Using Familiar Concepts

In talking with male patients about social support, clinicians should consider using concepts that are easily recognizable and familiar to many men (B. Gordon & Pasick, 1990), such as teamwork, networking, and strategic planning. Clinicians can suggest that men set regular times to meet with friends. It may be difficult for men to contact other men to get together; they may think that doing so puts them in a one-down position (Tannen, 1990). The regular ball game, movie, or dinner out provides men with regular contact and support without having to ask for it or betray their need for it. Clinicians can provide encouragement for any attempts—however small—men make to reach out to others (B. Gordon & Pasick, 1990). Clinicians should also consider referring men to support or educational groups that are available to and appropriate for male patients and should encourage them to participate if a referral is made. It is also important not to overlook or underestimate contacts that men already have with others through activities such as work, church, or sports (B. Gordon & Pasick, 1990; Pasick, 1990).

Clinicians as Sources of Support

Health care providers are also an important source of support for men (Kaplan et al., 1989). For unmarried men in particular, professionals may be one of the few sources of support that are available. Although men may be reluctant at first to look to clinicians for support, research indicates that they will respond positively to efforts at follow-up contact. Telephone follow-up specifically has been found to improve counseling effectiveness and behavioral change (U.S. Preventive Services Task Force, 1996), reduce noncompliance, and improve appointment keeping (Meichenbaum & Turk, 1987).

CUSTOMIZING EACH PLAN

The importance of developing and implementing realistic health maintenance plans with patients has been addressed elsewhere; a well-tailored plan fosters behavioral change and improves treatment adherence (see Grueninger, Goldstein, & Duffy, 1990; Meichenbaum & Turk, 1987; Prochaska et al., 1994). Tailoring a plan is especially important with men, who are much less likely than women to persist in caring for a health problem (Courtenay, 2000d). The type of plan, the extent of the plan, and its specific components depend on each man's individual needs, as well as on the clinician's role and functions. The following discussion identifies aspects of a plan that warrant particular attention when working with men.

Planning a Healthy Future

Essentially, tailoring a plan means developing a health maintenance schedule, like the maintenance schedule for a car; this analogy may prove useful when introducing the concept to male patients. Tailoring the plan means individualizing it to the patient's needs, age, intellectual capacity, attitudes, cultural background, and circumstances; this information is considered essential both in establishing a plan and in fostering adherence (Meichenbaum & Turk, 1987). For the plan to be successful it must be realistic, it must be broken down into attainable steps, and the patient must have the skills necessary to carry it out (Meichenbaum & Turk, 1987; Prochaska et al., 1994; U.S. Preventive

Services Task Force, 1996). Discussing the pros and cons of various treatment possibilities with patients and inviting their suggestions and preferences is useful not only in tailoring a plan but also in fostering compliance (Meichenbaum & Turk, 1987). For example, clinicians may suggest that men choose a day of the month to do self-examinations—a day with personal relevance that they can easily remember, such as a birth date.

Ideally, men's comprehensive health maintenance plans include periodic physicals, screenings, self-examinations, preventive behaviors, self-care techniques, and vitamin and medicine schedules. The plans should include a physical examination every few years for young men and every year for men over fifty (Goldberg, 1993). Physical examinations provide the opportunity for screenings, further assessment, referrals, and the early detection of disease. Screenings should include periodic blood pressure measurement, periodic weight measurement, blood cholesterol screening every five years, periodic sigmoidoscopy, and annual fecal occult blood testing for colorectal cancer for men over fifty; the plan should also include annual flu and pneumonia immunizations for men sixty-five and older (U.S. Preventive Services Task Force, 1996).

Fostering Adherence

It is well-known that patients do not always follow their doctors' advice. Men's beliefs about masculinity may undermine their compliance with the plan. Among men with heart disease, men with traditional beliefs have been found to be less likely to follow their physicians' orders and to make fewer healthy lifestyle changes after hospital discharge than their less traditional peers (Helgeson, 1995). Therefore, in tailoring a plan with a patient it is important to assess his intention of complying with treatment recommendations and to utilize adherence-enhancement techniques as necessary (Meichenbaum & Turk, 1987). Clinicians may ask their male patients to describe specifically how they intend to carry out their plans (U.S. Preventive Services Task Force, 1996). For example, they can assess men's intention to rest during recovery by asking, "What arrangements have you made at work to cover your absence?" The more specific patients are in describing how they intend to carry out their regimen, the more likely they are to be compliant (U.S. Preventive Services Task Force, 1996).

It is important to anticipate nonadherence. Inquiring into patients' history of compliance can be effective in fostering adherence if it is done in a nonjudgmental and nonthreatening manner (Meichenbaum & Turk, 1987; U.S. Preventive Services Task Force, 1996). Several studies have found that clinicians who work with patients to overcome obstacles to adherence increase compliance (McCann & Blossom, 1990). Male patients can be asked, "Do you ever miss your medical appointments?" and "Do you sometimes stop taking your medicine when you start to feel better?" Clinicians can also assess patients' commitment to a proposed plan by asking directly, "Will you stick to this plan?" or "How are you going to carry out this plan?" (Grueninger et al., 1990; Hewson, 1993). Developing a written or verbal contract is also effective in fostering compliance in some patients (Meichenbaum & Turk, 1987).

HIGHLIGHTING STRENGTHS

Men's behavior and coping styles are associated with both positive and negative health outcomes. Being aggressive, competitive, and achievement oriented, for example, increases men's risk of heart disease (see Strube, 1991). But these same characteristics can be turned into a health advantage. Being competitive and achievement oriented may be exactly what makes men more successful than women at quitting smoking, even though more women than men say they want to quit (Courtenay, 2000d). Similarly, although traditional beliefs about manhood can increase men's risks, certain characteristics that are considered traditionally masculine ways of coping are highly adaptive for men (and women). These characteristics include having the ability to act independently, to be assertive, and to be decisive (Cook, 1985; Eisler, 1995; Nezu & Nezu, 1987; Sharpe & Heppner, 1991; Sharpe, Heppner, & Dixon, 1995). Reliance on traditionally masculine characteristics can help to enable men to cope with cancer (D. F. Gordon, 1995) and chronic illness (Charmaz, 1995). Interpreting testicular cancer as a battleground for proving their courage gives some men greater self-confidence (D. F. Gordon, 1995).

Highlighting patients' strengths fosters motivation and compliance (Meichenbaum & Turk, 1987). It also conveys respect for their efforts and achievements, which is an important aspect of effective patient-clinician communication (Grüninger, 1995). Commenting on men's strengths before exploring their feeling states may reduce embarrassment and allow them to express their emotions more freely (Rappaport, 1984). For example, clinicians may say, "It's great that you took control of things the way you did and got yourself in here so quickly. But even when we take decisive action, it doesn't always reduce our fears." Identifying men's strengths may also foster clinicians' sense of empathy and compassion, which some contend are essential factors in helping men to change (Brooks, 1998; Schinke, Cole, Williams, & Botvin, 1999). Highlighting men's strengths can also mean drawing on their cultural strengths. When discussing diet planning with African American men, for example, Hendricks (1999) suggests identifying high-fiber soul foods familiar to these patients and incorporating those foods into the plan.

In the following sections I discuss how to highlight men's strengths by reinforcing specific coping strategies.

Teamwork

The most fundamental way to begin highlighting men's strengths is to encourage them to become active participants in their own health care. The relationship between health professionals and patients is increasingly viewed as a partnership in which health care is the shared work of patients and clinicians (Grüninger, 1995; Make, 1994; Meichenbaum & Turk, 1987; Woolf et al., 1996). Collaborative treatment that encourages patients' active involvement is associated with treatment adherence and improved outcomes (Deber, 1994; McCann & Blossom, 1990; Meichenbaum & Turk, 1987; O'Brien, Petrie, & Raeburn, 1992). Men may tend to perceive health care as something that is done to them, not something that they participate in. The patient-clinician relationship, however, can be the ideal type of interaction for men, provided it is approached as teamwork. Although men are taught to value independence and self-sufficiency, many men have also learned to value the camaraderie and partnership fostered among men through sports, the military, and fraternities (Heppner & Gonzales, 1987). Similarly, men's friendships often focus on working together on tasks or activities (Buhrke & Fuqua, 1987; Miller, 1983).

Asking "Where do you want to start?" (Grüninger, 1995) enlists men's involvement and reinforces their active participation. Clinicians can convey to male patients that they are an integral part of the clinical team and that the success of their treatment depends on their cooperation. Clinicians may ask, "How do you think I can best help you to follow this regimen?" or "What do you think is the best way for you to track your cholesterol levels?" Exploring patients' expectations and prior experiences, answering their questions, inviting their opinions, inquiring into their priorities and preferences, avoiding jargon, and being friendly will all help to make them feel like part of the team (Grüninger, 1995; Meichenbaum & Turk, 1987).

Denial as a Positive Coping Strategy

The negative effects of men's tendency to deny or minimize risk were cited earlier. Denial, however, can also help men to cope with illness—particularly when denial is used not to dismiss that one is ill but to minimize the severity of a problem (Helgeson, 1995). Denial is associated both with noncompliance and with positive consequences, such as resuming work and sex, better medical outcomes, and effective coping after surgery (Helgeson, 1995; Levine et al., 1987). This research suggests that clinicians need to recognize how patients are using denial. Identifying how men use denial as a positive means of coping will also convey respect (Grüninger, 1995). Clinicians can say, for example, "I admire the positive perspective you have on your recovery."

Intellectual Coping

Intellectual, logical, and rational approaches are highly valued coping mechanisms among men (Eisler, 1995; Meth, 1990). Although these coping mechanisms can create problems for men in their interpersonal relationships, they are an asset when men are learning about their health. Because men's conversational styles tend to focus on conveying and exchanging factual information (Moore, 1990; Tannen, 1990), men may be particularly responsive to health education interventions (Helgeson, 1995). Similarly, effective decision making about changing unhealthy behavior requires that individual patients assess the pros and cons of change (Grüninger, 1995; Prochaska et al., 1994). Clinicians should make positive use of men's tendency to weigh their options rationally by discussing with them the costs and benefits of change and emphasizing the intellectual aspects of health care.

Action-Oriented, Problem-Solving, and Goal-Setting Coping

Men engage in more action-oriented, problem-solving, and goal-setting coping than women do (Nezu & Nezu, 1987; Stone & Neale, 1984), including when they are coping with health problems (Fife, Kennedy, & Robinson, 1994; D. F. Gordon, 1995; Helgeson, 1995). Although an action-oriented, problem-solving coping style can hinder men's recovery from illness, it can also help them to recover and reduce their future risk (Charmaz, 1995; D. F. Gordon, 1995; Helgeson, 1995). Clinicians may help patients conceptualize their task as conquering or outsmarting an illness by saying, "I'm impressed by how determined you are to outsmart this disease. And if you keep up that approach, there's a good chance you will!" Men with traditional attitudes about masculinity may be particularly responsive to interventions that emphasize problem-solving skills (Robertson & Fitzgerald, 1992). Teaching problem-solving skills has also been found to be effective in reducing risks among young African American men (Schinke et al., 1999).

A goal-oriented approach to solving problems can be used to men's health advantage. For example, setting dates for achieving specific health goals can contribute to positive outcomes and foster adherence (Little et al., 1992; Meichenbaum & Turk, 1987). Clinicians can reconceptualize patients' goals after surgery as recovery and reframe health goals as targets to shoot for. Clinicians can also capitalize on men's interest in keeping score when monitoring cholesterol or blood pressure by saying, "What are the odds that you can bring your cholesterol down by the next time I see you?"

Healthy Sense of Control

For many men, being in control is an essential part of being a man. As noted earlier, illness can threaten men's sense of being in control. Furthermore, men are more likely than women to believe that they have very little or no control over their future health, a belief that can increase men's risk-taking behaviors (Courtenay, 1998a). To maintain healthy behaviors and modify unhealthy ones, it is essential that patients have a sense of self-efficacy and that they believe that they can respond effectively to reduce a health threat (Grüninger, 1995; Schinke et al., 1999; Taylor, 1990). Patients are also more likely to adhere to treatment when they feel that they have some control over their illnesses (O'Brien et al., 1992). College men who have a personal sense of control over cancer, for example, are significantly more likely to practice monthly testicular self-examination than those who do not (Neef et al., 1991). These findings suggest that clinicians should attempt to foster men's sense of self-efficacy by focusing on the positive aspects of control. Clinicians can suggest to men that they take "personal responsibility" for their well-being and "take charge" of their health, for example.

CONCLUSION

In this chapter I have summarized the findings and recommendations of a clinical practice guideline for working with men. I identified six general strategies, represented by the acronym HEALTH: humanize, educate, assume the worst, locate supports, tailor plan, and highlight strengths. These interventions are critical because men have serious health risks and because these risks are compounded by men's gendered health behaviors and beliefs.

It is important to note that clinicians—particularly male clinicians—need to examine their own health behavior. Like male patients, male clinicians are more likely than their female counterparts to engage in behaviors that increase their health risks (D. G. Allen & Whatley, 1986; Council on Scientific Affairs, 1990; E. Frank & Harvey, 1996; Lewis, Clancy, Leake, & Schwartz, 1991; Norman & Rosvall, 1994), and this gender difference influences their work with male patients. Physicians who themselves practice good health habits are more likely to counsel their patients about healthy behaviors, and those with poor health habits are especially unlikely to do so (Lewis et al., 1991; Wells, Lewis, Leake, & Ware, 1984). Similarly, mental health professionals who have difficulty accepting or expressing their own feelings may have difficulty assisting male patients to express their emotions (Heppner & Gonzales, 1987).

Clinicians should also be aware of their views about what it means to be a man and of how these views influence their work with men. Health professionals may subtly or even unconsciously convey contempt for male patients who do not "act like men" (Heppner & Gonzales, 1987). To assess their beliefs, clinicians should ask themselves, "How do I feel when I see a man who is not in control of his emotions?" "Am I likely just to see a man's hostility and fail to see the pain and sadness underneath?" "Do I simply assume that all male athletes are heterosexual?" "Does my manner make men feel safe?" Clinicians may need to find means of compensating for their own stereotypes and means to validate, respect, and foster the unique ways each man becomes involved in his health care.

References

Adler, D. A., Drake, R. E., & Teague, G. B. (1990). Clinicians' practices in personality assessment: Does gender influence the use of *DSM-III* axis II? *Comprehensive Psychiatry, 31,* (2), 125–133.

Allen, D. G., & Whatley, M. (1986). Nursing and men's health: Some critical considerations. *Nursing Clinics of North America, 21*(1), 3–13.

Allen, J. A., & Gordon, S. (1990). creating a framework for change. In R. L. Meth & R. S. Pasick (Eds.), *Men in therapy: The challenge of change* (pp. 131–151). New York: Guilford Press.

Allen-Burge, R., Storandt, M., Kinscherf, D. A., & Rubin, E. H. (1994). Sex differences in the sensitivity of two self-report depression scales in older depressed inpatients. *Psychology and Aging, 9*(3), 443–445.

American Medical Association. (1991a, October). *Lack of doctor-patient communication hazard in older men* [News release]. Chicago: Author.

American Medical Association. (1991b, October). *Results of 9/91 Gallup survey on older men's health perceptions and behaviors* [News release]. Chicago: Author.

Annandale, E., & Clark, J. (1996). What is gender? Feminist theory and the sociology of human reproduction. *Sociology of Health and Illness, 18*(1), 17–44.

Ashton, W. A., & Fuehrer, A. (1993). Effects of gender and gender role identification of participant and type of social support resource on support seeking. *Sex Roles, 28*(7–8), 461–476.

Baer, J. T. (1993). Improved plasma cholesterol levels in men after nutrition education program at the worksite. *Journal of the American Dietetic Association, 93*(6), 658–663.

Balswick, J. O. (1982). Male inexpressiveness: Psychological and social aspects. In K. Solomon & N. B. Levy (Eds.), *Men in transition: Theory and therapy* (pp. 131–150). New York: Plenum.

Banks, B. A., Silverman, R. A., Schwartz, R. H., & Tunnessen, W. W. (1992). Attitudes of teenagers toward sun exposure and sunscreen use. *Pediatrics, 89*(1), 40–42.

Bayne-Smith, M. (Ed.). (1996). *Race, gender, and health.* Thousand Oaks, CA: Sage.

Belle, D., Burr, R., & Cooney, J. (1987). Boys and girls as social support theorists. *Sex Roles, 17*(11–12), 657–665.

Boehm, S., Selves, E. J., Raleigh, E., Ronis, D., Butler, P. M., & Jacobs, M. (1993). College students' perception of vulnerability/susceptibility and desire for health information. *Patient Education and Counseling, 21,* 77–87.

Brooks, G. R. (1998). *A new psychotherapy for traditional men.* San Francisco: Jossey-Bass.

Brubaker, R. G., & Wickersham, D. (1990). Encouraging the practice of testicular self-examination: An application of the theory of reasoned action. *Health Psychology, 9*(2), 154–163.

Buhrke, R. A., & Fuqua, D. R. (1987). Sex differences in same and cross-sex supportive relationships. *Sex Roles, 17*(5–6), 339–352.

Burda, P. C., & Vaux, A. C. (1987). The social support process in men: Overcoming sex-role obstacles. *Human Relations, 40*(1), 31–44.

Byers, T., Mullis, R., Anderson, J., Dusenbury, L., Gorsky, R., Kimber, C., Krueger, K., Kuester, S., Mokdad, A., Perry, G., & Smith, C. A. (1995). The costs and effects of a nutritional education program following work-site cholesterol screening. *American Journal of Public Health, 85*(5) 650–655.

Bjornson, W., Rand, C., Connett, J. E., Lindgren, P., Nides, M., Pope, F., Buist, A. A., Hoppe-Ryan, C., & O'Hara, P. (1995). Gender differences in smoking cessation after 3 years in the Lung Health Study. *American Journal of Public Health, 85*(2), 223–230.

Charmaz, K. (1995). Identity dilemmas of chronically ill men. In D. Sabo & D. F. Gordon (Eds.), *Men's health and illness: Gender, power, and the body* (pp. 266–291). Thousand Oaks, CA: Sage.

Chino, A. F., & Funabiki, D. (1984). A cross-validation of sex differences in he expression of depression. *Sex Roles, 11,* 175–187.

Cohn, L. D., Macfarlane, S., Yanez, C., & Imai, W. K. (1995). Risk-perception: Differences between adolescents and adults. *Health Psychology, 14*(3), 217–222.

Cook, E. P. (1985). *Psychology androgyny.* New York: Pergamon Press.

Copenhaver, M. M., & Eisler, R. M. (1996). Masculine gender roles stress: A perspective on men's health. In P. M. Kato & T. Mann (Eds.), *Handbook of diversity issues in health psychology* (pp. 219–235).

Corney, R. H. (1990). Sex differences in general practice attendance and help seeking for minor illnesses. *Journal of Psychosomatic Research, 34*(5), 525–534.

Council on Scientific Affairs. (1990). Education for health: A role for physicians and the efficacy of health education efforts. *JAMA, 263*(13), 1816–1819.

Courtenay, W. H. (1996a). *Clinical practice guideline for the treatment of men.* Paper submitted in partial fulfillment of the doctoral degree, University of California, Berkeley.

Courtenay, W. H. (1996b). *Health Mentor: Health Risk Assessment for Men.*™ Berkeley, CA: Author. (Copies available from Men's Health Consulting, 2811 College Avenue, Suite 1, Berkeley, CA 94705-2167.)

Courtenay, W. H. (1998a). Better to die than cry? A longitudinal and constructionist study of masculinity and the health risk behavior of young American men (Doctoral dissertation, University of California at Berkeley). *Dissertation Abstracts International, 59*(08A). (Publication No. AAT 9902042)

Courtenay, W. H. (1998b). College men's health: An overview and a call to action. *Journal of American College Health, 46*(6), 279–290.

Courtenay, W. H. (1998c). Communication strategies for improving men's health: The 6-Point HEALTH Plan. *Wellness Management, 14*(1), 1, 3–4.

Courtenay, W. H. (1999). Youth violence? Let's call it what it is. *Journal of American College Health, 48*(3), 141–142.

Courtenay, W. H. (2000a). Constructions of masculinity and their influence on men's well-being: A theory of gender and health. *Social Science and Medicine, 50*(10), 1385–1401.

Courtenay, W. H. (2000b). Social work, counseling, and psychotherapeutic interventions with men and boys: A bibliography. *Men and Masculinities, 2*(3), 330–352.

Courtenay, W. H. (2000c). Teaming up for the new men's health movement. *Journal of Men's Studies, 8*(3), 387–392.

Courtenay, W. H. (2000d). Behavioral factors associated with disease, injury, and death among men: Evidence and implications for prevention. *Journal of Men's Studies, 9*(1), 81–142.

Courtenay, W. H. (2000e). Engendering health: A social constructionist examination of men's health beliefs and behaviors. *Psychology of Men and Masculinity, 1*(1), 4–15.

Courtenay, W. H., & Keeling, R. P. (2000a). Men, gender, and health: Toward an interdisciplinary approach. *Journal of American College Health, 48*(6), 1–4.

Courtenay, W. H. (Guest Ed.), & Keeling, R. P. (Ed.). (2000b). Men's health: A theme issue. *Journal of American College Health, 48*(6).

Courtenay, W. H., & Sabo, D. (in press). Preventative health strategies for men in prison. In D. Sabo, T. Kupers, & W. London (Eds.), *Confronting prison masculinities: The gendered politics of punishment.* Philadelphia: Temple University Press.

Cramer, J. A. (1991). Overview of methods to measure and enhance patient compliance. In J. A. Cramer & B. Spilker (Eds.), *Patient compliance in medical practice and clinical trials* (pp. 3–10). New York: Raven Press.

Cramer, J. A., & Spilker, B. (Eds.). (1991). *Patient compliance in medical practice and clinical trials.* New York: Raven Press.

Croake, J. W., Myers, K. M., & Singh, A. (1987). Demographic features of adult fears. *International Journal of Social Psychiatry, 33*(4), 285–293.

Cutter, S. L., Tiefenbacher, J., & Solecki, W. D. (1992). En-gendered fears: Femininity and technological risk perception. *Industrial Crisis Quarterly, 6*(1), 5–22.

Danielson, R., Marcy, S., Plunkett, A., Wiest, W., & Greenlick, M. R. (1990). Reproductive health counseling for young men: What does it do? *Family Planning Perspectives, 22*(3), 115–121.

Davis, H., & Fallowfield, L. (1991). Counseling and communication in health care: The current situation. In H. Davis & L. Fallowfield (Eds.), *Counseling and communication in health care* (pp. 3–22). New York: Wiley.

Davis, L. E. (Ed.). (1999). *Working with African American males: A guide to practice.* Thousand Oaks, CA: Sage.

Deber, R. B. (1994). Physicians in health management, 7: The patient-physician partnership: Changing roles and the desire for information. *Canadian Medical Association Journal, 151*(2), 171–176.

DeHoff, J. B., & Forrest, K. A. (1984). Men's health. In J. M. Swanson & K. A. Forrest (Eds.), *Men's reproductive health* (pp. 3–10). New York: Springer.

Delbanco, T. L. (1992). Enriching the doctor-patient relationship by inviting the patient's perspective. *American College of Physicians, 116*(5), 414–418.

DePalma, M. T., McCall, M., & English, G. (1996). Increasing perceptions of disease vulnerability through imagery. *Journal of American College Health, 44*(5), 227–234.

DePaulo, B. (1982). Social-psychological processes in informal help-seeking. In T. Wills (Ed.), *Basic processes in helping relationships* (pp. 255–280). New York: Academic Press.

Devine, E. C. (1992). Effects of psychoeducational care for adult surgical patients: A meta-analysis of 191 studies. *Patient Education and Counseling, 19*(2), 129–142.

Eisler, R. M. (1995). The relationship between masculine gender role stress and men's health risk: The validation of a construct. In R. F. Levant & W. S. Pollack (Eds.), *A new psychology of men* (pp. 207–225). New York: Basic Books.

Eisler, R. M., & Hersen, M. (2000). *Handbook of gender, culture, and health.* Mahwah, NJ: Erlbaum.

Fabrega, H., Pilkonis, P., Mezzich, J., Ahn, C. W., & Shea, S. (1990). Explaining diagnostic complexity in an intake setting. *Comprehensive Psychiatry, 31*(1), 5–14.

Fernbach, B. E., Winstead, B. A., & Derlega, V. J. (1989). Sex differences in diagnosis and treatment recommendations for antisocial personality and somatization disorders. *Journal of Social and Clinical Psychology, 8*(3), 238–255.

Fife, B. L., Kennedy, V. N., & Robinson, L. (1994). Gender and adjustment to cancer: Clinical implications. *Journal of Psychological Oncology, 12*(1), 1–21.

Flynn, J., Slovic, P., & Mertz, C. K. (1994). Gender, race, and perception of environmental health risks. *Risk Analysis, 14*(6), 1101–1108.

Ford, M. R., & Widiger, T. A. (1989). Sex bias in the diagnosis of histrionic and antisocial personality disorders. *Journal of Consulting and Clinical Psychology, 57*(2), 301–305.

Fracher, J., & Kimmel, M. S. (1992). Hard issues and soft spots: Counseling men about sexuality. In M. S. Kimmel & M. A. Messner (Eds.), *Men's lives* (2nd ed., pp. 428–450). New York: Macmillan.

Frank, E., & Harvey, L. K. (1996). Prevention advice rates of women and men physicians. *Archives of Family Medicine, 5*(4), 215–219.

Frank, R. G., Bouman, D. E., Cain, K., & Watts, C. (1992). Primary prevention of catastrophic injury. *American Psychologist, 47*(8), 1045–1049.

Friedman, C., Brownson, R. C., Peterson, D. E., & Wilkerson, J. C. (1994). Physician advice to reduce chronic disease risk factors. *American Journal of Preventive Medicine, 10*(6), 367–371.

Friedman, H. S., & DiMatteo, M. R. (1989). *Health psychology.* Englewood Cliffs, NJ: Prentice Hall.

Gerber, G. S., Thompson, I. M., Thisted, R., & Chodak, G. W. (1993). Disease-specific survival following routine prostate cancer screening by digital rectal examination. *JAMA, 269*(1), 61–64.

Gijsbers van Wijk, C.M.T., Vliet, K. P. van, Kolk, K. P., & Everaerd, W. T. (1991). Symptom sensitivity and sex differences in physical morbidity: A review of health surveys in the United States and the Netherlands. *Women and Health, 17*(1), 91–124.

Goldberg, K. (1993). *How men can live as long as women: Seven steps to a longer and better life.* Fort Worth, TX: Summit Group.

Golombok, S., & Fivush, R. (1994). *Gender development.* Cambridge, MA: Cambridge University Press.

Good, E. G., Dell, D. M., & Mintz, L. B. (1989). Male role and gender role conflict: Relations to help seeking in men. *Journal of Counseling Psychology, 36*(3), 295–300.

Gordon, B., & Pasick, R. S. (1990). Changing the nature of friendships between men. In R. L. Meth & R. S. Pasick (Eds.), *Men in therapy: The challenge of change* (pp. 261–278). New York: Guilford Press.

Gordon, D. F. (1995). Testicular cancer and masculinity. In D. Sabo & D. F. Gordon (Eds.), *Men's health and illness: Gender, power, and the body* (pp. 246–265). Thousand Oaks, CA: Sage.

Grigsby, J. B., & Weatherley, D. (1983). Gender and sex role differences in intimacy of self-disclosure. *Psychological Reports, 53,* 891–897.

Grueninger, U. J., Goldstein, M. G., & Duffy, F. D. (1990). A conceptual framework for interactive patient education in practice and clinic settings. *Journal of Human Hypertension, 4*(Suppl. 1), 21–31.

Grüninger, U. J. (1995). Patient education: An example of one-to-one communication. *Journal of Human Hypertension, 9*(1), 15–25.

Hall, J. A., Roter, D. L., & Katz, N. R. (1988). Meta-analysis of correlates of provider behavior in medical encounters. *Medical Care, 26*(7), 657–675.

Helgeson, V. S. (1995). Masculinity, men's roles, and coronary heart disease. In D. Sabo & D. F. Gordon (Eds.), *Men's health and illness: Gender, power, and the body* (pp. 1–21). Thousand Oaks, CA: Sage.

Hendricks, L. E. (1999). *Working with African American males: A guide to practice*. Thousand Oaks, CA: Sage.

Heppner, P. P., & Gonzales, D. S. (1987). Men counseling men. In M. Scheer, M. Stevens, G. Good, & G. A. Eichenfield (Eds.), *Handbook of counseling and psychotherapy with men* (pp. 30–38). Thousand Oaks, CA: Sage.

Hewson, M. G. (1993). Patient education through teaching for conceptual change. *Journal of General Internal Medicine, 8*(7), 393–398.

Hohmann, A. A. (1989). Gender bias in psychotropic drug prescribing in primary care. *Medical Care, 27*(5), 478–490.

Hornbrook, M. C., Stevens, V. J., Wingfield, D. J., Hollis, J. F., Greenlick, M. R., & Ory, M. G. (1994). Preventing falls among community-dwelling older persons: Results from a randomized trial. *Gerontologist, 34*(1), 16–23.

Horne, D. J., Vatmanidis, P., & Careri, A. (1994). Preparing patients for invasive medical and surgical procedures, 1: Adding behavioral and cognitive interventions. *Behavioral Medicine, 20*(1), 5–13.

Hyde, J. S. (1986). Gender differences in aggression. In J. S. Hyde & M. C. Linn (Eds.), *The psychology of gender* (pp. 51–66). Baltimore: Johns Hopkins University Press.

Janz, N., & Becker, M. (1984). The health belief model: A decade later. *Health Education Quarterly, 11*(1), 1–57.

Job, R. F. (1988). Effective and ineffective use of fear in health promotion campaigns. *American Journal of Public Health, 78,* 163–167.

Kacmarek, R. M. (1994). Make discussion. *Respiratory Care, 39*(5), 579–583.

Kaplan, H. S. (1974). *The new sex therapy: Active treatment of sexual dysfunctions*. New York: Brunner/Mazel.

Kaplan, S. H., Gandek, B., Greenfield, S., Rogers, W., & Ware, J. E. (1995). Patient and visit characteristics related to physicians' participatory decision-making style: Results from the Medical Outcomes Study. *Medical Care, 33*(12), 1176–1187.

Kaplan, S. H., Greenfield, S., & Ware, J. E. (1989). Assessing the effects of physician-patient interactions on the outcomes of chronic disease. *Medical Care, 27*(Suppl.), S110–S127.

Katz, R. C., Meyers, K., & Walls, J. (1995). Cancer awareness and self-examination practices in young men and women. *Journal of Behavioral Medicine, 18*(4), 377–384.

Koop, C. E. (1996). Foreword. In S. H. Woolf, S. Jonas, & R. S. Lawrence (Eds.), *Health promotion and disease prevention in clinical practice* (pp. vii–ix). Baltimore: Williams & Wilkins.

Kraemer, D. L., & Hastrup, J. L. (1986). Crying in natural settings: Global estimates, self monitored frequencies, depression, and sex differences in an undergraduate population. *Behavior Research and Therapy, 24*(3), 371–373.

Krantz, D. S., Grunberg, N. E., & Baum, A. (1985). Health psychology. *Annual Review of Psychology, 36,* 349–383.

Kreuter, M. W., & Strecher, V. J. (1995). Changing inaccurate perceptions of health risk: Results from a randomized trial. *Health Psychology, 14*(1), 56–63.

Lee, C. C. (1990). Black male development: Counseling the "native son." In D. Moore & F. Leafgren (Eds.), *Problem solving strategies and interventions for men in conflict* (pp. 125–137). Alexandria, VA: American Association for Counseling and Development.

Lent, B., & Bishop, J. E. (1998). Sense and sensitivity: Developing a gender issues perspective in medical education. *Journal of Women's Health, 7*(3), 339–342.

Levant, R. F., & Kopecky, G. (1995). *Masculinity reconstructed: Changing the rules of manhood— at work, in relationships, and in family life*. New York: Dutton.

Levine, J., Warrenburg, S., Kerns, R., Schwartz, G., Delaney, R., Fontana, A., Gradman, A., Smith, S., Allen, S., & Cascione, R. (1987). The role of denial in recovery from coronary heart disease. *Psychosomatic Medicine, 49*(2), 109–117.

Lewis, C. E., Clancy, C., Leake, B., & Schwartz, J. S. (1991). The counseling practices of internists. *American College of Physicians, 114*(1), 54–58.

Liddell, A., Locker, D., & Burman, D. (1991). Self-reported fears (FSS-II) of subjects aged 50 years and over. *Behavior Research and Therapy, 29*(2), 105–112.

Little, S. J., Stevens, V. J., Severson, H. H., & Lichtenstein, E. (1992). Effective smokeless tobacco intervention for dental hygiene patients. *Journal of Dental Hygiene, 66*(4), 185–190.

Lombardo, W. K., Cretser, G. A., Lombardo, B., & Mathis, S. L. (1983). Fer cryin' out loud—there is a sex difference. *Sex Roles, 9*(9), 987–995.

Majors, R., & Billson, J. M. (1992). *Cool pose: The dilemmas of black manhood in America.* New York: Simon & Schuster.

Make, B. (1994). Collaborative self-management strategies for patients with respiratory disease. *Respiratory Care, 39*(5), 566–579.

Marks, G., Garcia, M., & Solis, J. M. (1990). Health risk behaviors of Hispanics in the United States: Findings from HHANES, 1982–84. *American Journal of Public Health, 80*(Suppl.), 20–26.

May, J. P., & Martin, K. L. (1993). A role for the primary care physician in counseling young African-American men about homicide prevention. *Journal of General Internal Medicine, 8,* 380–382.

May, R. (1990). finding ourselves: Self-esteem, self-disclosure and self-acceptance. In D. Moore & F. Leafgren (Eds.), *Problem solving strategies and interventions for men in conflict* (pp. 11–21). Alexandria, VA: American Association for Counseling and Development.

McCann, D. P., & Blossom, H. J. (1990). The physician as a patient educator: From theory to practice. *Western Journal of Medicine, 153*(1), 44–49.

Meichenbaum, D., & Turk, D. C. (1987). *Facilitating treatment adherence: A practitioner's guidebook.* New York: Plenum.

Mermelstein, R. J., & Riesenberg, L. A. (1992). Changing knowledge and attitudes about skin cancer risk factors in adolescents. *Health Psychology, 11*(6), 371–376.

Meth, R. L. (1990). The road to masculinity. In R. L. Meth & R. S. Pasick (Eds.), *Men in therapy: The challenge of change* (pp. 3–34). New York: Guilford Press.

Metz, M. E., & Seifert, M. H. (1990). Men's expectations of physicians in sexual health concerns. *Journal of Sexual and Marital Therapy, 16*(2), 79–88.

Miaskowski, C. (1999). The role of sex and gender in pain perception and response to treatment. In R. J. Gatchel & D. C. Turk (Eds.), *Psychological factors in pain: Critical perspectives* (pp. 401–411). New York: Guilford Press.

Miller, S. (1983). *On men and friendship.* Boston: Houghton Mifflin.

Misener, T. R., & Fuller, S. G. (1995). Testicular versus breast and colorectal cancer screen: Early detection practices of primary care physicians. *Cancer Practice, 3*(5), 310–316.

Moore, D. (1990). Helping men become more emotionally expressive: A ten-week program. In D. Moore & F. Leafgren (Eds.), *Problem solving strategies and interventions for men in conflict* (pp. 183–200). Alexandria, VA: American Association for Counseling and Development.

Mullen, P. D., Mains, D. A., & Velez, R. (1992). A meta-analysis of controlled trials of cardiac patient education. *Patient Education and Counseling, 19*(2), 143–162.

Myers, R. E., Ross, E. A., Wolf, T. A., Balshem, A., Jepson, C., & Millner, L. (1991). Behavioral interventions to increase adherence in colorectal cancer screening. *Medical Care, 29*(10), 1039–1050.

Neef, N., Scutchfield, F. D., Elder, J., & Bender, S. J. (1991). Testicular self-examination by young men: An analysis of characteristics associated with practice. *Journal of American College Health, 39*(4), 187–190.

Nezu, A. M., & Nezu, C. M. (1987). Psychological distress, problem solving, and coping reactions: Sex role differences. *Sex Roles, 16*(3–4), 206–214.

Norman, J., & Rosvall, S. B. (1994). Help-seeking behavior among mental health practitioners. *Clinical Social Work Journal, 22*(4), 449–460.

Oakley, A. (1994). Who cares for health? Social relations, gender, and the public health. *Journal of Epidemiology and Community Health, 48*(5), 427–434.

O'Brien, M. K., Petrie, K., & Raeburn, J. (1992). Adherence to medication regimens: Updating a complex medical issue. *Medical Care Review, 49*(4), 435–454.

Oleckno, W. A., & Blacconiere, M. J. (1990). Wellness of college students and differences by gender, race, and class standing. *College Student Journal, 24*(4), 421–429.

Pasick, R. (1990). Raised to work. In R. L. Meth & R. S. Pasick (Eds.), *Men in therapy: The challenge of change* (pp. 35–53). New York: Guilford Press.

Pierce, R. (1999). Prostate cancer in African American men: Thoughts on psychosocial interventions. In L. E. Davis (Ed.), *Working with African American males: A guide to practice* (pp. 75–90). Thousand Oaks, CA: Sage.

Pleck, J. H. (1981). *The myth of masculinity.* Cambridge, MA: MIT Press.

Potts, M. K., Burnam, M. A., & Wells, K. B. (1991). Gender differences in depression detection: A comparison of clinician diagnosis and standardized assessment. *Psychological Assessment, 3*(4), 609–615.

Preusser, D. F., Williams, A. F., & Lund, A. K. (1991). Characteristics of belted and unbelted drivers. *Accident Analysis and Prevention, 23,* 475–482.

Prochaska, J., Norcross, J., & DiClemente, C. (1994). *Changing for good: The revolutionary program that explains the six stages of change and teaches you how to free yourself from bad habits.* New York: Morrow.

Rappaport, B. M. (1984). Family planning: Helping men ask for help. In J. M. Swanson & K. A. Forrest (Eds.), *Men's reproductive health* (pp. 245–259). New York: Springer.

Reagan, L. J. (1997). Engendering the dread disease: Women, men, and cancer. *American Journal of Public Health, 87*(11), 1779–1787.

Reno, D. R. (1988). Men's knowledge and health beliefs about testicular cancer and testicular self-exam. *Cancer Nursing, 11*(2), 112–117.

Robertson, J. M., & Fitzgerald, L. F. (1992). Overcoming the masculine mystique: Preferences for alternative forms of assistance among men who avoid counseling. *Journal of Counseling Psychology, 39*(2), 240–246.

Robinson, E. J., & Whitfield, M. J. (1985). Improving the efficiency of patients' comprehension monitoring: A way of increasing patients' participation in general practice consultations. *Social Science and Medicine, 21*(8), 915–919.

Rosenstock, I. M. (1990). The Health Belief Model: Explaining health behavior through expectancies. In K. Glanz, F. M. Lewis, & B. K. Rimer (Eds.), *Health behavior and health education: Theory, research, and practice.* San Francisco: Jossey-Bass.

Roter, D. L., & Hall, J. A. (1997). *Doctors talking with patients/patients talking with doctors: Improving communication in medical visits.* Westport, CT: Auburn House.

Rothspan, S., & Read, S. J. (1996). Present versus future time perspective and HIV risk among heterosexual college students. *Health Psychology, 15*(2), 131–134.

Rubin, L. B. (1983). *Intimate strangers.* New York: Harper & Row.

Rule, W. R., & Gandy, G. L. (1994). A thirteen-year comparison in patterns of attitudes toward counseling. *Adolescence, 29*(115), 575–589.

Saurer, M. K., & Eisler, R. M. (1990). The role of masculine gender role stress in expressivity and social support network factors. *Sex Roles, 23*(5–6), 261–271.

Savage, I. (1993). Demographic influences on risk perceptions. *Risk Analysis, 13,* 413–420.

Sawyer, R. G., & Moss, D. J. (1993). Sexually transmitted diseases in college men: A preliminary clinical investigation. *Journal of American College Health, 42*(3), 111–115.

Scarce, M. (1999). *Smearing the queer: Medical bias in the health care of gay men.* New York: Haworth Press.

Schinke, S., Cole, K., Williams, C., & Botvin, G. (1999). Reducing risk taking among African American males. In L. E. Davis (Ed.), *Working with African American males: A guide to practice* (pp. 103–112). Thousand Oaks, CA: Sage.

Sharpe, M. J., & Heppner, P. P., (1991). Gender role, gender role conflict, and psychological well-being in men. *Journal of Counseling Psychology, 38,* 323–330.

Sharpe, M. J., Heppner, P. P., & Dixon, W. A. (1995). Gender role conflict, instrumentality, expressiveness, and well-being in adult men. *Sex Roles, 33*(1–2), 1–8.

Spigner, C., Hawkins, W., & Loren, W. (1993). Gender differences in perception of risk associated with alcohol and drug use among college students. *Women and Health, 20*(1), 87–97.

Stapley, J. C., & Haviland, J. M. (1989). Beyond depression: Gender differences in normal adolescents' emotional experiences. *Sex Roles, 20*(5–6), 295–308.

Stone, A. A., & Neale, J. M. (1984). New measure of daily coping: Development and preliminary results. *Journal of Personality and Social Psychology, 46*(4), 892–906.

Strube, M. J. (Ed.). (1991). *Type A behavior.* Newbury Park, CA: Sage.

Sutkin, L., & Good, G. (1987). Therapy with men in health-care settings. In M. Scher, M. Stevens, G. Good, & G. A. Eichenfield (Eds.), *Handbook of counseling and psychotherapy with men* (pp. 372–387). Thousand Oaks, CA: Sage.

Taggart, L. P., McCammon, S. L., Allred, L. J., Horner, R. D., & May H. J. (1993). Effect of patient and physician gender on prescriptions for psychotropic drugs. *Journal of Women's Health, 2,* 353–357.

Tannen, D. (1990). *You just don't understand: Women and men in conversation.* New York: Ballantine.

Taylor, S. E. (1986). *Health psychology.* New York: Random House.

Taylor, S. E. (1990). Health psychology: The science and the field. *American Psychologist, 45*(1), 40–50.

Thomas, C., & Kelman, H. R. (1990). Gender and the use of health services among elderly persons. In M. G. Ory & H. R. Warner (Eds.), *Gender, health, longevity: Multidisciplinary perspectives* (pp. 25–37). New York: Springer.

Thompson, E. H., Grisanti, C., & Pleck, J. H. (1985). Attitudes toward the male role and their correlates. *Sex Roles, 13*(7–8), 413–427.

Unruh, A. M. (1996). Gender variations in clinical pain experience. *Pain, 65*(2–3), 123–167.

Unruh, A. M., Ritchie, J., & Merskey, H. (1999). Does gender affect appraisal of pain and pain coping strategies? *Clinical Journal of Pain, 15*(1), 31–40.

U.S. Department of Health and Human Services. (1996). Report of final mortality statistics, 1994. *Monthly Viral Statistics Report, 45*(3, 2 Suppl.).

U.S. Department of Health and Human Services. (1998a). *Vital and health statistics: Current estimates from the National Health Interview Survey, 1995* (DHHS Publication No. PHS 98-1527). Hyattsville, MD: Author.

U.S. Department of Health and Human Services. (1998b). *Health, United States, 1998: Socioeconomic status and health chartbook* (DHHS Publication No. PHS 98-1232-1). Hyattsville, MD: Author.

U.S. Preventive Services Task Force. (1996). *Guide to clinical preventive services* (2nd ed.). Baltimore: Williams & Wilkins.

Verbrugge, L. M. (1980). Sex differences in complaints and diagnoses. *Journal of Behavioral Medicine, 3*(4), 327–355.

Verbrugge, L. M. (1982). Sex differences in legal drug use. *Journal of Social Issues, 38*(2), 59–76.

Verbrugge, L. M. (1985). Gender and health: An update on hypotheses and evidence. *Journal of Health and Social Behavior, 26*(3), 156–182.

Verbrugge, L. M. (1989). The twain meet: Empirical explanations of sex differences in health and mortality. *Journal of Health and Social Behavior, 30*(3), 282–304.

Waisberg, J., & Page, S. (1988). Gender role nonconformity and perception of mental illness. *Women and Health, 14*(1), 3–16.

Waitzkin, H. (1984). Doctor-patient communication: Clinical implications of social scientific research. *JAMA, 252*(17), 2441–2446.

Waitzkin, H. (1985). Information giving in medical care. *Journal of Health and Social Behavior, 26*(2), 81–101.

Wallen, J., Waitzkin, H., & Stoeckle, J. D. (1979). Physician stereotypes about female health and illness: A study of patients' sex and the information process during medical interviews. *Women and Health, 4*(2), 135–146.

Weinstein, N. D. (1987). Unrealistic optimism about illness susceptibility: Conclusions from a community-wide sample. *Journal of Behavioral Medicine, 10*(5), 481–500.

Weissfeld, J. L., Kirscht, J. P., & Brock, B. M. (1990). Health beliefs in a population: The Michigan Blood Pressure Survey. *Health Education Quarterly, 17*(2), 141–155.

Wells, K. B., Lewis, C. E., Leake, B., & Ware, J. E. (1984). Do physicians preach what they practice? A study of physicians' health habits and counseling practices. *JAMA, 252*(20), 2846–2848.

Williams, D. G. (1985). Gender, masculinity-femininity, and emotional intimacy in same-sex friendship. *Sex Roles, 12*(5–6), 587–600.

Woolf, S. H., Jonas, S., & Lawrence, R. S. (Eds.). (1996). *Health promotion and disease prevention in clinical practice.* Baltimore: Williams & Wilkins.

Zilbergeld, B. (1992). *The new male sexuality.* New York: Bantam Books.

Zuckerman, M. (1994). *Behavioral expressions and biosocial bases of sensation seeking.* New York: Cambridge University Press.

CHAPTER THREE

Consulting with Men in Business and Industry

Hope I. Hills
Aaron Carlstrom
Margaret Evanow

James Autry, the president of the Meredith Corporation, said: "Work can provide the opportunity for spiritual and personal, as well as financial growth. If it doesn't, we're wasting far too much of our lives on it" (Autry, 1991, p. 13). Companies that recognize the truth of Autry's statement are actively working to create environments that support the growth and development of their employees and are recognized as the leaders in their industries. This leadership is measured by decreased turnover, increased job satisfaction, more effective product development, quicker response time, increased profitability, and more citations on listings of the best places to work as compared with other companies. Many use the help of consulting psychologists who employ executive coaching, team building, and other leadership development tools to support the changes that are necessary for success.

As scientist practitioners, consulting psychologists can promote changes that are based on solid theory and research and measure the efficacy of their efforts through the many records kept as normal business practice. At the same time, they can help their clients develop scientific and strategic approaches to decision making and leadership. When business clients discover the basic set of beliefs (theory) they hold about leading their organizations (and themselves) and recognize the effects of these beliefs on their company's productivity, they are often motivated to take the personal risks inherent in changing their outmoded beliefs. They can become "scientist practitioners of leadership" and thus become successful at choosing and testing the strategies needed for success in the ever-changing business environment.

Many business leaders are becoming aware of the need to recognize and change the dysfunctional aspects of old leadership paradigms built around the masculine gender role. New approaches to leadership that incorporate the positive aspects of both gender roles are being tried and tested. As leaders try these new strategies, incorporating more cooperation and attention to the needs of their followers and less autocratic decision making that consciously includes the input of those affected by the decisions, they find that the results support the new theory behind these changes.

CHANGES IN CONTEMPORARY ORGANIZATIONS

To be profitable, businesses are flattening their organizations, becoming involved in the global marketplace, creating team-oriented cultures, intensifying their customer focus, and increasing the inclusion of women and minorities in the management ranks. The byword of contemporary business environment is *change*. To be successful in this constantly changing environment, leaders must develop open, flexible, and inclusive leadership styles. Paul Wieand was one of the banking industry's youngest-ever chief executive officers (CEOs) but was fired from that post because of his rigid leadership style. The experience changed his life and career path. He is now a psychologist who works with executives. He said:

> In today's free-flowing team environment, leaders have to have a strong core (values that they remain true to) but they also have to be adaptive. To achieve a flexible-yet-resilient identity, you have to be willing to look inward. (Kruger, 1999, p. 124)

But looking inward is clearly not something that most men readily choose. Men still underutilize traditional counseling services and underreport their difficulties in living, even if they do seek help (Robertson & Fitzgerald, 1992). The consulting psychologist is in a perfect position to help business leaders take this inward journey, in the context of becoming better leaders, able to create more productive business environments.

This inner journey toward increasing flexibility while maintaining a strong inner core could be a description of counseling and therapy (especially for those who espouse interpersonal theory). Whatever the reason may be for enhancing flexibility, whether productive business relationships and profit or effective personal relationships and happiness, these changes are likely to affect every area of life. If a man becomes more interpersonally effective, he will probably become both a better leader and a better friend, father, and partner.

Approach to Coaching and Consulting

In this chapter we outline an approach to consulting and the individually focused activity of coaching that looks at the early experiences and resulting beliefs about self, others, and the world that are affecting the ability to productively lead in the present. The process very often results in profound changes in self-concept, relationships, and leadership style, very similar to the objectives in therapy and counseling. There are, however, some reasons to clearly distinguish between coaching (or consulting) and counseling (or therapy).

Consulting psychologists use various techniques to help organizations increase productivity and profit by focusing a trained strategic eye on the human system and then working with key leaders and teams to most effectively create the needed changes. The purpose of consulting interventions, whether individual coaching or team facilitation and development, is to increase the productivity of the organization, not to increase the mental health of an individual. The relationship that a consultant develops with a leader in an organization is much different than the more narrowly defined relationship between a therapist and a client. Although it is critical to maintain clear ethical boundaries, the business consultant may meet with an executive to report on a project that the executive assigned on one day and the next day spend time with that same executive in a coaching mode exploring the underlying experiences of childhood that make it difficult to be assertive. The course of a coaching intervention is very different from the regularly scheduled weekly sessions one expects throughout a therapy or counseling relationship. While necessarily moving through the similar stages of establishing a trusting relationship, exploring and challenging beliefs, and then helping the individual strengthen new behaviors as in therapy, these stages may be the result of a variety of both individual and group interactions with the leader. Individual coaching (which looks most similar to counseling or therapy) may take place each time the consultant visits the company, or it could happen only once or twice, with other interventions then supporting the desired change. And very critically, whereas a therapy client pays for therapy and therefore "owns" the process, in consulting and coaching the company pays, with the expectation that whatever changes are made will benefit the company. This reality makes defining confidentiality with all interested parties and maintaining those trust agreements a complex and pivotal issue that affects the viability of the consultant's practice throughout the organization. It is also important to cast the work consultants do not as therapy but as coaching, for the very reasons Robertson and Fitzgerald (1992) would predict. Most business leaders see therapy or counseling as an option only if one has mental health problems, not business or leadership concerns. Coaching, even when focused on early childhood experiences, does not carry this stigma and so arouses less of the resistance that many men would experience.

Starting at the Top

This book is focused on the treatment of varied personal and relational problems that the masculine roles engender. The men whom a business consultant works with look like they have mastered society's demands and have become successful. Some are enormously successful by the external standards of money and status. Mental health professionals typically do not focus on the upper management ranks as a place where many are in need of help. However, there are many painful examples of men who have broken under this set of rigid expectations, revealing the very real and often extreme dysfunction hidden under the successful facade. News reports of outwardly successful men "suddenly" killing family members or themselves are just the tip of the iceberg of the underlying pain. Wealth and power can be a great camouflage for tremendous pain, confusion, and loneliness. Men are caught in a double bind, because the masculine gender role also makes it unacceptable to ask for help (Robertson & Fitzgerald, 1992).

Researchers and practitioners in both psychology and business have recognized that the behaviors prescribed by this culture's masculine roles can interfere with men's inner peace, family relationships, sexual fulfillment, and physical health (Meth, 1990). Because most businesses are still run by men, this gender role is mirrored in the generally accepted models of leadership behavior, which affects the peace, relationships, enjoyment, and financial health of entire organizations. Consulting with organizations offers a tremendous opportunity to work with men who would not otherwise seek to look inward for the answers to their own life dilemmas and the organizational dilemmas that mirror those personal dilemmas. Managers and executives have generally been successful at pointing the finger elsewhere. But opportunity knocks when their position or the positions of their companies are threatened. This is often the point of "optimum pain" when the stakes are high enough to motivate action but not so high that the individual feels that failure is the only possible outcome.

Coaching executives and their teams can be an extraordinary opportunity that can improve the lives of the executives as well as those of everyone in the organization and often the customers and partners (for example, vendors and distributors) of the organization. Working with the CEO or president of a multinational corporation offers the very real possibility of supporting changes that could touch the world. When a man in this position chooses to look inward and learn to care for himself and those around him more effectively, that new approach can reshape the leadership paradigm of the entire organization (Tobias, 1995).

The necessity of remaining profitable creates the demands for measurable and strategic changes in the ways that people lead organizations and for consultants who can help leaders to make those changes. For the consulting psychologist trained to look at systems, this bottom-line imperative is not the enemy. Seen from the human systems perspective, enhancing the bottom line can be the motivation to create humane environments in which to work.

In this chapter we describe a consulting practice based on an integrated theoretical approach (interpersonal theory). The executive coaching examples focus on two men with rigid but very different leadership styles. One was dominant and critical, and the other was more modest and nurturing. To reach their personal and business goals, each of them had to face the experiences, beliefs, and values that had created the need to rigidly use their interpersonal styles at work (as well as at home). As they faced these issues, they both broke through the barriers to their personal growth, happiness, and success as well as the success of their corporation.

CONSULTATION WITH ORGANIZATIONS

Despite the fact that "women held 46% of executive, administrative, and managerial positions in 1998, up from 34% in 1983" (Farrell, 1999, p. 35), the power brokers of most modern corporations and organizations continue to be men. Male leaders who continue to avoid conventional contact with psychologists because of their attitudes toward success, power, and restricted emotionality (Robertson & Fitzgerald, 1992) are being faced with a market-driven need to loosen their rigid leadership paradigms or face individual or corporate extinction. Organizational consultation and executive coaching are powerful means of providing men with the opportunity to examine their own maladaptive patterns and change. These changes can create humane, flexible, and diverse corporations capable of responding successfully to the fast-paced marketplace.

Historically, American organizations have been patriarchal hierarchies run by white men. As such, American corporations tend to mirror both the functional and dysfunctional sides of this culture's masculine gender stereotypes. The dysfunctional side clearly reflects a rigid, defensive style. Such organizations resist change, have rigid attachments to "successful" product lines, are reluctant to introduce change into the organizational culture, and reflect an in-group narcissism (Byrne, Diepke, Verity, Neff, Levine, & Forest, 1991; Levinson, 1994). A leading authority on corporate leadership indicates that most companies underestimate their external market threats and overestimate their internal power or abilities, a mirror of the narcissist's approach to the world (Taylor, 1999).

Facing today's global marketplace, with its increasingly complex demands, more diverse business partners, managers, and employees, and faster and more chaotic changes, is like rafting in "permanent white water" (Vaill, 1989). To stay afloat, leaders must recognize that inflexible personal and corporate beliefs and myths create a corporate "personality disorder." Recognition of this rigidity is the first step in changing to an open, flexible, and functional approach.

However, just as Robertson and Fitzgerald (1992) would predict, most executives do not recognize how their own psychological dynamics affect their organizations. If they have attended a workshop that has focused on self-awareness (a key to leadership success in the current business literature [Bridges, 1991; Covey, 1990; Farr, 1997; Lundin & Lundin, 1993; Rosen, 1996; Schutz, 1994; Senge, 1990]), they tend to cling to the personal value they experienced but, unless consistently coached to recognize it, do not readily see the parallel psychological dynamics at work in their organizations. They continue to cling to financial strategies, operational plans, and technological advances as prime targets for increasing organizational productivity and shareholders' value. But it is the focus on human dynamics, the very work that they resist, that could ensure the maximum competitive edge. Indeed, "There is a very compelling business case for this idea: Companies that manage people right will outperform companies that don't by 30% to 40%" (Webber, 1998, p. 154).

APPLICABLE MENTAL HEALTH SKILLS

Mental health workers who understand and empathize with the damage that gender role stereotypes have done to men, women, and whole organizations have the basic knowledge and skill level to work successfully in organizations. In addition, as scientist practitioners, they need to recognize the importance of working from a theoretical base that is consistently questioned, measured, and revised. With programs such as Total Quality Management (TQM), managers already see the value of following an accepted approach to the production system that is then measured to check its validity. As the consultant helps them to recognize the parallel process involved in recognizing, questioning, and measuring the effectiveness of their theory—their underlying belief system—about the human system, leaders can become scientist practitioners of leadership.

The conscious commitment to a clear ethical standard is another essential ingredient for success in this field. The questions of "Who is the client?" and "What will you share with others?" accompany consulting psychologists wherever they go in an organization (Newman, 1993; Newman & Robinson, 1991; Tobias, 1990). To remain effective, we must clearly outline our confidentiality agreements in every setting and follow up on any possible mistrust.

Training in learning, motivation, systems, and therapy provides a working knowledge and skill base to support change in organizations. A crucial ingredient for success is a sense of humility and continual solicitation of honest feedback from the businessmen and businesswomen who have poured their minds, hearts, and lives into the organizations they lead. This approach is also modeling good leadership skills.

INTERPERSONAL THEORY

As the core of this consulting model, interpersonal theory (see Figure 3.1) has been an exceptionally valuable tool not only to help clients recognize the effects of their personal interactions and style but also to shed light on corporate strategies, attitudes, and direction. In this section we briefly outline the theory (the references cited are excellent sources for further understanding) and some examples of its application in organizations.

The initial research into interpersonal theory took place under the auspices of the Kaiser Foundation. Timothy Leary and his colleagues, following the ideas of Harry Stack Sullivan (1953), studied the interpersonal behaviors of groups of subjects with various psychiatric diagnoses. They hypothesized that each disorder might have a discernible interpersonal pattern that then produced reactions from others that reinforced the pattern. They found that the map of these behaviors took the shape of a circumplex (Guttman, 1966) called the interpersonal circle (Figure 3.1), on which similar behaviors are close to each other and differing behaviors are on the opposite side of the circumplex (Leary, 1957). What interpersonal theory offers is a concrete operational definition, a behavioral map, of the very predictable actions and reactions among people. Understanding the dynamics of interpersonal behavior as defined by interpersonal theory can help anyone clarify the often mystifying reactions we experience in our daily lives.

Complementarity

The primary pattern seen in most interactions among people is called complementarity. There are two attributes to this pattern. The first is that one person's dominance (top half of the circle) will predictably pull, or evoke, submission from the other (bottom half of the circle). Just as powerfully, submission will evoke dominance. The second attribute is that when one person is hostile (the left half of the circle), it is most likely that the other will respond in kind. If the interaction is initially friendly (the right half of the circle), it is likely that the response will be friendly as well. When integrated, we see that behaviors from the dominant hostile quadrant of the circle will provoke submissive hostile behaviors, and submissive hostile behaviors will just as powerfully arouse dominant hostile reactions. Similarly, dominant friendly behavior is highly likely to pull a submissive friendly reaction, and submissive friendly behavior will attract dominant friendly reactions.

Other patterns are variants of complementarity. *Anticomplementary* interactions can be seen when one of the parties realizes at some level that the complementary pattern is not useful. For instance, he or she may not wish to be submissive hostile and would like to get the other person to stop being dominant hostile. The most powerful place to come from on the circle will then be dominant friendly, which would attract the other to be friendly and submissive. A way to think about this pattern is to recognize what outcome is desired for the interaction and then move to the place on the circle that will pull the other person to the place desired. Although this approach seems manipulative, it is actually something we all do without recognizing it.

The last basic pattern is *acomplementarity.* This, of course, is every other interactional pattern. One that is very damaging but is an almost automatic response is when a submissive hostile interaction pulls a dominant friendly response, usually a nurturant one. The first person claims, from the submissive hostile quadrant, that he or she is not good enough or some other self-critical statement. The almost automatic response is, "No, you are fine" (from the nurturing octant of the dominant friendly quadrant). Unfortunately, this response just reinforces the submissive hostile person's means of getting a nurturing response; it is likely that on the private level the nurturer feels resentful and critical and eventually will respond from this quadrant. When managers recognize this pattern, they immediately realize how frequently they fall into this trap and begin to try the anti-complementary response instead.

When managers are trained to recognize these patterns, they regularly report that they are becoming much more successful as leaders. One of the most startling revelations to most of them is that to create the environment for employees to act empowered, the most effective stance for the leader is submissive friendly. It is necessary to have a new definition of power to recognize that being submissive friendly is the most effective way to empower. This definition is that true power is creating a situation so that the desired outcome is achieved. To have true power, then, leaders must develop flexibility.

Flexibility

The key to effective functioning from the perspective of interpersonal theory and research (Benjamin, 1996; Kieser, 1996; Leary, 1957; Strong et al., 1988) and the theory and research on leadership and management (Hersey & Blanchard, 1988; Kruger, 1999; Vaill,

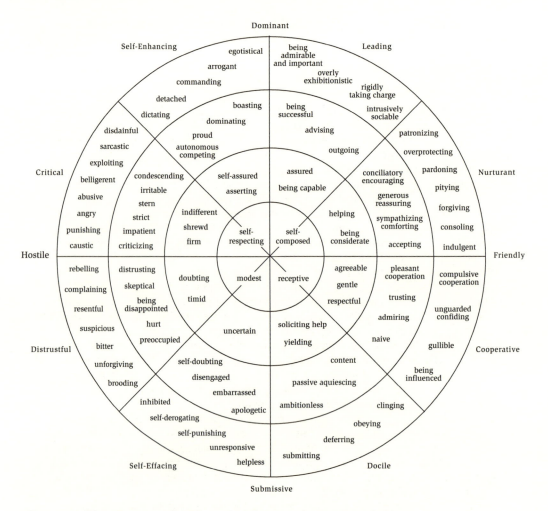

Figure 3.1. The Interpersonal Circle, a Classification of Interpersonal Behavior.

Source: Adapted from Strong and Hills, 1986.

1989) is flexibility. Paul Weiand's definition of the effective leader as having a "flexible yet resilient identity with a strong inner core" (Kruger, 1999, p. 124) is an excellent place to start.

A person who is flexible is able, in interpersonal terms, to move around the circle as the situation demands. So, rather than always needing to be dominant if he or she is a leader, the truly powerful and flexible leader could comfortably be modest or seek help from his or her followers without losing face. The result would be empowered and helpful employees, often eager to be able to take the lead from someone who is not actually giving up his or her authority.

INTERPERSONAL THEORY AND THE MASCULINE ROLE

In light of this theoretical perspective, it becomes clear why the masculine gender role sets men up for the eventual failure of many relationships in all areas of their lives. Mahalik (1999; see also Chapter Twenty-six) outlined the interpersonal behaviors seen in men who adhere rigidly to this society's expected male role (O'Neil, 1981a, 1981b, 1982). These men are dominant, emotionally distant, inflexible in their interpersonal behaviors, and unwilling to seek help from others. As expected, these attributes are also part of the accepted management style in many companies.

According to interpersonal theory, truly functional people are able to successfully use behaviors from any octant on the interpersonal circle (Strong & Hills, 1986) to get what they want or need without losing their sense of personal identity (see Figure 3.1). According to Mahalik's description, men who experience gender role conflict restrict themselves to operating their lives primarily from the critical and self-enhancing octants. These octants also define the leadership style of the majority of men who are struggling with their performance as managers and executives.

The theory predicts that those with whom these men interact will also feel restricted. They will be powerfully pulled to react primarily from the behaviors outlined in the distrustful and self-effacing octants. This submissive hostile profile is unfortunately prevalent in the subordinates of these men. The effects of this restricted profile can be recognized in most of the complaints that managers lodge about employees (for example, that they are resistant to change, are not self-starting, and only do the minimal job required to avoid getting fired). The double bind is obvious: set someone up to act in a certain way, then complain about the results.

Even if leading and perhaps nurturant are added to round out the currently practiced manager or leader profiles, leaders still have only half of all the available interpersonal strategies needed to be truly effective with all their employees. All of the dominant octants pull submissive behavior, not the dominant, empowered behavior that is needed from experienced workers.

Other leadership models, mirroring the hypotheses outlined in interpersonal theory, recommend that managers assess the needs of their employees and respond appropriately and flexibly. One such example that is used in many training programs for managers is the Situational Leadership Model (Hersey & Blanchard, 1988).

The Situational Leadership Model outlines how, as an employee becomes more task mature (for any task, from flipping hamburgers to the multifocused task of being the president), the supervisor must vary his or her leadership style from an initial telling mode that is very task oriented to an eventual delegating mode when the employee may actually have more expertise at the job than the supervisor has. Unfortunately, delegation is a skill that many managers have not developed. When they do delegate well, they will have much more committed and mature employees. This model fits neatly into a consulting practice that is based on interpersonal theory. It has been the basis of management training in many companies; the material Hersey and Blanchard have designed clearly demonstrates the importance and value of letting go of unidimensional leadership styles.

INTERPERSONAL PROCESS IN CONSULTING AND COACHING

Inflexible and restricted behavioral repertoires have very real effects on productivity and leadership effectiveness. Consultants must hone the ability to initially notice how a person pulls them and then have the self-confidence to disengage without withdrawing from the other. This task is actually much harder than it seems, especially when a person is new to the field of consulting. Leaders often question the seemingly "soft stuff" consultants bring into organizations. Until consultants gain experience and confidence in the concrete and measurable value of this work, they might feel that this critical reaction has merit and, caught in their own defensive maneuvers, may not recognize that this response may also be the leaders' defensive pattern signifying their real fear of change.

STAGES OF COACHING

We now discuss the three stages of coaching—social, asocial, and authentically social.

Stage 1: Social

Just noticing how one is pulled is the first step in the consulting process, which is clearly parallel to Kieser's (1988) description of therapy. Initially, it is important to notice the pattern before making any changes. During this social stage the consultant is building the trust needed for real change and may do things that create first-order change. In corporations, this stage is filled with many activities, which may include leadership training; consulting with leaders to solve various problems with employees, human resources programs, or personal issues; strategic planning and facilitation of team-building programs; succession-planning meetings; and staff meetings.

Stage 2: Asocial

Once an individual relationship with an executive is solid (the timing itself indicating the person's ability to trust and connect) the consultant would advance to the asocial stage, meaning that he or she would no longer respond to the complementary pull and instead respond from a different part of the interpersonal circle and actively pull for different behaviors. Over time, as the consultant remains "unhooked" from the old patterns, the client develops a healthy style and can move around the circle flexibly.

As leadership development in organizations becomes a planned strategy with increased productivity as its goal, some powerful change interventions are possible. The consultant can involve supervisors, peers, and subordinates in creating new "interpersonal worlds" for an individual. Through retreats and team meetings designed to share personal leadership plans that involve real change in leadership style, leaders can make agreements with various groups to change their patterns of responding. This strategy is extraordinarily powerful; it encircles the individual with new reactions and reinforces a new style. Some companies and leaders also include spouses and families in the process to complete the circle. These opportunities give the consultant tools to support the change process that are unavailable to most therapists.

Stage 3: Authentically Social

At the authentically social stage, the consulting psychologist notices that he or she is comfortable, does not feel as manipulated, and looks forward to being with the client. Reactions to one another move flexibly around the interpersonal circle. The consultant notices that many people find it easier to argue with, agree with, support, or question the leader. If the consulting psychologist were acting as a personal therapist, he or she would be close to termination. In a consulting practice, it is likely that the leader would now have much more success with his or her various relationships and support the consulting psychologist's work with other leaders and teams to further enhance the productivity of the organization.

These three stages vary in length, much as in the therapy process. If an organization is rigidly hierarchical and dominated by the masculine gender role leadership style, the length of the stages is likely to be extended. A leader with years in such an organization, especially one who is high in the organizational hierarchy, may never be willing to truly transform his or her style, given the reinforcers that are in place to support the status quo. Often the desire is there, and such a leader may be able to change the personally damaging style in retirement, perhaps even working with the consultant to facilitate the process. The following story demonstrates that consultants must be flexible and willing to build trust for perhaps years before there is a chance to support real change.

THE STORY OF VICTOR

One of my (Hills) first experiences with "Victor" was in a training meeting with the officers in his company. He sat apart, but even if he had been in the circle, his critical demeanor would have set him apart. It was early in my consulting career, and I remember very clearly thinking that I would never be able to connect with him. His disdain for leadership training was palpable, and I had to work to maintain my composure with the group. I did not know the real history of how other consultants had operated with this group until later (an important piece of information, like finding out a client's past experience with therapy). Once I did, it was clear why Victor had reacted as he had. The last consultant operated very clearly out of the dominant hostile quadrant, and Victor was just much more obvious about his distrust than the others. But the CEO was committed to leadership development, so I continued to work within the company and with the officers every month.

It was more than two years before Victor and I had the opportunity to break through his resistance and move to the second stage. During the first period, I had the chance to help many people in his organization learn effective management strategies, demonstrated by increased productivity and improved employee retention. By the time we had the chance to work together in a coaching mode, he had softened his opinion of me. This process and variety of roles demonstrate the very real differences in therapy and consulting. As a vice president, Victor was responsible for contracting with me for various assignments and then giving me feedback on the outcome. I needed to maintain my flexibility to respond to his sometimes negative feedback authentically and also be able to become his coach. Sometimes this task was very challenging. I am sure that there were times that I may have pulled his critical attacks on me as he may have sensed my insecurity and task immaturity. However, more times than not, the outcome was positive.

The CEO decided to make some changes in the organization and consulted with me about ways to pave the way for that change. We planned a multiphase process to help the officers become more of a team. Each officer met with me to explore his "lifeline" for answers to ongoing problems in his approach to leadership. This process can take from three to six hours or more, during which we use a piece of newsprint to graphically show the person's life history. Family history, test scores, and dreams for the future are all included in the basic format. Various themes that become apparent are noted at the bottom of the page. For the first time, an hour or two into our exploration, Victor found some answers that surprised him. He had long been criticized for his very dominant and critical leadership style but was able to "make things happen" so he had consistently moved up the ladder. He was in a group of three peers being considered for president, and his style stood in his way. He was at the point of optimum pain. He had been to a self-awareness workshop and valued the increased care he had for himself and his family but had not made the crucial connections to his unyielding leadership flaws.

I have found that, for most of the men I have coached, the initial place to look for the keys to their leadership behavior is in their relationship with their fathers. As we explored this relationship, it became very apparent that Victor's father's ever critical and punitive treatment had created a set of beliefs and defenses that drove him to mirror the same style while at the same time feeling insecure, distrusting, and fearful of men in authority over him. I always frame these early decisions as very valid "safety measures" a child would take to care for himself. He needed to honor that early decision and, in the present, discover other ways to deal with men in authority over him, as well as find new ways to express his own authority.

At a two-day retreat at which the officers shared their lifelines with each other, he shared his story. His tears surprised him and evoked tears from almost all of the other men. It was a pivotal moment not only for him and his colleagues but for the company as a whole. When men cry together over their pain and loss, nothing can be quite the same again. The change was not immediate. Masculine roles are strong. But others' defenses were markedly softer, much less intense, and there were many more invitations to reopen the doors after this experience.

His boss recognized the parallels between Victor's relationship with his father and Victor's relationship with him and began to change his reactions. The change in their relationship was hard won, because Victor's boss was also very critical. I call my client Victor (not his real name) because he did not stop his quest with these experiences. He used my support with him and his direct reports to do similar interventions in his organization. He also continued to challenge my leadership, helping me to grow at the same time, for which I will always be grateful.

He also became the president. As with anyone with a long-standing pattern, his "natural" first response often is critical. But he catches himself, often checking the interpersonal circle he keeps in a prominent place behind his desk to remind himself of more productive responses.

KEY PRACTICES

In this section we examine key business and consulting practices. More specifically, we discuss return on investments, ongoing consultation to executives, succession planning, team building, and leadership training.

Return on Investments

Whether we would normally use this language or not, we are all interested in a return on our investments. Indeed, "the continuous improvement of productivity is one of management's most important jobs" (Drucker, 1974, p. 111). If consultants recognize and honor this primary function of leaders and can help them fulfill it more effectively, leaders will be much more open to hearing consultants' proposals. The more clearly consultants understand that the purpose of being in business is to make a return on investments and frame the work they do in those terms, the greater the consultant's return on investments will be. Assessment is not the primary purview of this chapter, but it is important to explore the many measures that are useful for gauging the organization's baseline in order to guide initial planning and measure eventual results, the company's return on investment from the consultant's services.

Ongoing Consultation to Executives

It is critical for consultants to have ongoing approval and support from the highest possible level, preferably the CEO or president. One way to accomplish this objective is to have regularly scheduled meetings with the CEO or president to keep him or her abreast of the consultant's work, observations, and recommendations. Initially, this relationship may be simply a courtesy, but as the consultant's insights become valuable, the relationship can become one of a confidant to the executive, who often feels very alone. Notice the stages apparent in this statement from a retired CEO:

> I would characterize our relationship [between the CEO and consultant] as one that was guarded by me initially, and then grew to a warm, trusting one over a very few meetings. The trust that I developed in you was based on your clear, honest but compassionate analysis of our management situation. It was especially important to me that I had a knowledgeable, intelligent individual to exchange ideas with when there was no one else in the organization with whom I could fully discuss the bank's human problems. You were very helpful in demonstrating to our whole management team that inclusion went a long way further than maintaining individual fiefdoms. (Bill Viklund, personal communication, April 3, 1999)

Succession Planning

One of the most important responsibilities that managers and leaders have at all levels of an organization is career counseling or succession planning. Failure to select and develop leaders at every level is detrimental and costly (Bobo, 1999). Over the past ten years there has been an estimated 50 percent failure rate among corporate executives (DeVries, 1992; Sloan, 1994). If all the costs of this failure rate were calculated, it would begin to explain Webber's (1998) statement that companies that manage people right will outperform those that do not by 30 to 40 percent. Consultants, especially those with training in career assessment and planning, can play a pivotal role in helping executives to assess and plan for the leadership development of their managers and critique the clarity with which they outline the path to various kinds of success in their organizations.

Team Building

Because "teams outperform individuals acting alone or in larger organizational groupings" (Katzenbach & Smith, 1994, p. 9), many companies want to take advantage of this opportunity for greater productivity. However, the seemingly commonsense logic behind creating high-performing teams is difficult to successfully apply. The consultant must be keenly aware of both cultural and psychological issues that impact the successful productivity of teams. In those cultures, like the United States, that glorify individual effort, many revolt against the communal focus of teams. Working in teams may also create situations in which old family patterns are reenacted, confusing the seemingly clear business objective. Helping teams to recognize these issues and move beyond them is an exciting challenge.

There are many opportunities for consultants to help organizations learn to create high-performing teams. It is very important, though, to begin by helping leaders understand what it takes to make teams work in their environment. They must understand that high-performing teams depend on having clear direction and purpose (Katzenbach & Smith, 1994). If they autocratically demand that teams be the new "way" and do not invest time and money in the process, the teams will fail and become just another program of the day.

The Myers-Briggs Type Indicator is a good initial step in the team-building process. It is a step into self-disclosure and learning styles that will enable the leaders to work together effectively. It also begins to support the need to value diversity but in a mode that is not the threat that other kinds of diversity training can be for a company that has not addressed these issues. Many aids to this process are available.

Leadership Training

The consultant needs to develop and constantly fine-tune a set of models and collateral materials to use consistently with various individuals and groups. This set of models must be congruent with the consultant's own core theoretical approach and have research support. However, the models need to be in language that connects with the business world. People need to be able to remember a catchy phrase or an amusing image that reminds them of their new skills and models when they are under pressure to perform. Using the same handouts in various situations takes advantage of the learning value of repetition. The goal is to train scientist practitioners of leadership who eventually can rely on a solid theory of behavior, not an inconsistent set of skills learned at various quickie workshops.

Leadership training needs to be integrated into almost any meeting. Periodic workshops in which large groups learn about a certain topic are an excellent way to introduce and practice leadership theory and skills. Team-building sessions and retreats provide events at which the models can be used to help the team understand its dynamics as well as each other. Strategic planning retreats present the opportunity to help executives see that solid theory can be a practical tool when applied to the whole system. Whether they are planning employee succession, setting goals, or evaluating operations, a good theory will help to strengthen their assessment of the current state, clarify predictions about the future state, and improve the planning on how to get there. Meetings with problem employees and their supervisors provide powerful practice, in which using the models will improve their chances of understanding and resolving their issues. Executive coaching sessions offer the perfect opportunity for leaders to use the leadership training on themselves to create a new and self-affirming understanding of their current performance problems.

HENRY'S STORY

Victor's story outlines the basic format of the executive coaching model I (Hills) have developed over time. In 1998, after facilitating an in-depth succession-planning retreat, the officers of one firm contracted to put seven of their managers through an intensive program focused on dealing with their long-standing leadership issues. These seven individuals were seen as possible future officers. It was a critical juncture in the life of this company, and the officers wanted to see if these seven would make use of this program and change.

One of the seven had just been elevated to the human resources manager. He filled the function of a retired vice president and realized the statement it made about his leadership that he was not given the title of vice president. This, for him, was a point of optimum pain. The opportunity to participate in the intensive program of executive coaching finally brought him to do his lifeline, which he had now put off for seven years.

Most people in the company had valued "Henry" throughout his career for his caring, confidential, and growing professionalism in human resources. His former boss had been a micromanager in the extreme, so it had been difficult to truly ascertain what part of some ongoing feedback was a result of his place under this man or his own style. Now that the boss was gone, it was clear that Henry continued to appear less assertive and proactive than would be expected of someone who could be an officer in the company. He realized that he had always "hung back" from the pressure of confronting some people and had constructed his life so that he was comfortable with his back-seat role. But at this point, he was no longer comfortable and was ready to change.

His lifeline offered an answer to the long-standing feedback that has changed his self-appraisal and his leadership since that day. I noticed, as I explored his lifeline, that he did not say anything about his early childhood. I knew he came from an intact family and had lived in the community all his life. I finally asked what the blank was around his birth. His response shocked me. "Oh, I was a twin, actually a triplet, but the other two were dead. That has not had any effect on me, though." I told him that the deaths had not only affected him, but it was probably in this area of his life that we would discover the answers he sought.

We then reconstructed how his mother must have reacted to him and found that, of course, she had protected him and worried about his health much more than she had worried about the health of his siblings. We discussed how she must have felt during his first years, having lost two children, and what impact being the survivor could have on his sense of self. He saw very quickly how this situation had affected his willingness to risk and had created many beliefs about his own weaknesses. Once he had felt the impact and recognized how the many other deaths in his life had reinforced these beliefs, he was able (because he had truly worked on his self-awareness and leadership diligently for years) to make some remarkable changes rather quickly.

The next step in the process was to share his lifeline (which is on a newsprint sheet, written in a fashion that only the person could actually decipher its contents, which keeps the subject in control of what is said to others) with his boss, a person who had long questioned his ability to be an officer. He was able (in a three-way meeting with me) to share his insights and set challenging and clear agreements with his boss. He went on to share his lifeline and agreements in retreats with his peers and subordinates, as well as with his wife and children privately.

The change in Henry's energy level, demeanor, and personal expectations was dramatic. He became much more clear and forceful in his proposals about his area of responsibility. People began to comment on the change. The company merged with another similar chain, and Henry was in charge of all the processes involved in merging the human resources systems of the two. He is now the vice president of a much larger and more complex corporation.

His appraisal is that he was able, because of the lifeline and other meetings, to recognize that he had always avoided confrontation and then blamed others for the problems that resulted. He had protected others and rescued the weak (which he detested the most in others he counseled). But when he realized that he was no longer considered for the future he wanted it woke him up, and then the lifeline helped him to make changes from the position of understanding and caring for himself rather than criticism. He said he now works harder and smarter, even makes people angry at times with his challenges. He reports being "more at peace with who I am, and what I have to offer."

The men whose stories appear in this chapter came from very different early life experiences and therefore opposite public defenses. Victor was dominant and hostile, and Henry was more submissive and hostile. Both had been successful to a point. Then they had the chance to take a deep look at themselves and share their findings with other men, who also shared their findings. By sharing their insights and especially their emotions about these early experiences, as well as the results that had played out in their lives, they committed to new behaviors to replace the rigid ones that had held them back. The changes they made resulted not only in career advancement but also, and even more important to the two of them, in more authentic, warm, and satisfying relationships.

Consulting with businesses provides an amazing opportunity to affect the lives of many people by affecting the lives of a few. For those who decry the negative effects of rigid adherence to the masculine and feminine role stereotypes, the time is perfect for challenging the status quo. The chance to help leaders question their basic beliefs and theories about life and leading is exhilarating, challenging, fun, and profitable.

References

Autry, J. A. (1991). *Love and profit: The art of caring leadership.* New York: Morrow.

Benjamin, L. S. (1996). *Interpersonal diagnosis and treatment of personality disorders.* New York: Guilford Press.

Bobo, J. (1999). The care and feeding of our leaders. *National Underwriter* (National Underwriter Company, Cincinnati) 103(8), 19–20.

Bridges, W. (1991). *Managing transitions: Making the most of change.* Reading, MA: Addison-Wesley.

Byrne, J., Diepke, D. A., Verity, J., Neff, R., Levine, J. B., & Forest, S. A. (1991, June 17). IBM. *Business Week,* p. 25.

Covey, S. R. (1990). The 7 habits of highly effective people: Powerful lessons in personal change. New York: Simon & Schuster.

DeVries, D. L. (1992). Executive selection: Advances but no progress. *Issues & Observations* (Center for Creative Leadership) *12*(4), 1–5.

Drucker, P. F. (1974). *Management: Tasks, responsibilities, practices.* New York: Harper Business.

Farr, J. (1997, September). Leadership vs. management: Do you know the difference? *Business Leader,* p. 9.

Farrell, C. (1999, August 9). Women in the workplace: Is parity finally in sight? *Business Week,* p. 35.

Guttman, L. (1966). Order analysis of correlation matrixes. In R. B. Cattell (Ed.), *Handbook of multivariate experimental psychology.* Chicago: Rand McNally.

Hersey, P., & Blanchard, K. H. (1988). *Management of organizational behavior: Utilizing human resources* (5th ed.). Englewood Cliffs, NJ: Prentice Hall.

Katzenbach, J. R., & Smith, D. K. (1994). *The wisdom of teams: Creating the high-performance organization.* New York: HarperBusiness.

Kiesler, D. J. (1988). *Therapeutic metacommunication.* Palo Alto, CA: Consulting Psychologists Press.

Kiesler, D. J. (1996). Contemporary interpersonal theory and research: Personality, psychopathology, and psychotherapy. New York: Wiley.

Kruger, P. (1999, June). A leader's journey. *Fast Company, 25,* 116–129.

Leary, T. (1957). Interpersonal diagnosis of personality: A functional theory and methodology for personality evaluation. New York: Ronald Press.

Levinson, H. (1994). Why the behemoths fell: Psychological roots of corporate failure. *American Psychologist, 49,* 428–436.

Lundin, W., & Lundin, K. (1993). *The healing manager: How to build quality relationships and productive cultures at work.* San Francisco: Berrett-Koehler.

Mahalik, J. R. (1999). Interpersonal psychotherapy with men who experience gender role conflict. *Professional Psychology: Research and Practice, 30,* 5–13.

Meth, R. L. (1990). The road to masculinity. In R. Meth & R. Pasick (Eds.), *Men in therapy: The challenge of change* (pp. 3–34). New York: Guilford Press.

Newman, J. L. (1993). Ethical issues in consultation. *Journal of Counseling and Development, 72,* 148–156.

Newman, J. L., & Robinson, S. E. (1991). In the best interests of the consultee: Ethical issues in consultation. *Consulting Psychology Bulletin, 43,* 23–29.

O'Neil, J. M. (1981a). Male sex-role conflicts, sexism, and masculinity: Psychological implications for men, women, and the counseling psychologist. *Counseling Psychologist, 9,* 61–81.

O'Neil, J. M. (1981b). Patterns of gender role conflict and strain: Sexism and fear of femininity in men's lives. *Personnel and Guidance Journal, 60,* 203–210.

O'Neil, J. M. (1982). Gender role conflict and strain in men's lives: Implications for psychiatrists, psychologists, and other human service providers. In K. Solomon & N. B. Levy (Eds.), *Men in transition: Changing male roles, theory, and therapy* (pp. 5–44). New York: Plenum.

Robertson, J. M., & Fitzgerald, L. F. (1992). Overcoming the masculine mystique: Preferences for alternative forms of assistance among men who avoid counseling. *Journal of Counseling Psychology, 39,* 240–246.

Rosen, R. H. (1996). *Leading people: Transforming business from the inside out.* New York: Viking.

Schutz, W. (1994). *The human element: Productivity, self-esteem, and the bottom line.* San Francisco: Jossey-Bass.

Senge, P. M. (1990). *The fifth discipline: The art and practice of the learning organization.* New York: Doubleday/Currency.

Sloan, E. B. (1994). Assessing and developing versatility: Executive survival skill for the brave new world. *Consulting Psychology Journal, 46*(1), 24–31.

Strong, S. R., & Hills, H. I. (1986). *Interpersonal Communication Rating Scale.* Richmond: Virginia Commonwealth University.

Strong, S. R., Hills, H. I., Kilmartin, C. T., DeVries, H., Lanier, K., Nelson, B. N., Strickland, D., & Meyer, C. W., III. (1988). The dynamic relations among interpersonal behaviors: A test of complementarity and anticomplementarity. *Journal of Personality and Social Psychology, 54,* 798–810.

Sullivan, H. S. (1953). *The interpersonal theory of psychiatry.* New York: Norton.

Taylor, W. C. (1999). The leader of the future. *Fast Company, 25,* 130–142.

Tobias, L. L. (1990). *Psychological consulting to management: A clinician's perspective.* New York: Brunner/Mazel.

Tobias, L. L. (1995). Eleven ideas that have influenced my practice of psychological consulting. *Consulting Psychology Journal: Practice and Research, 47,* 56–63.

Vaill, P. B. (1989). *Managing as a performing art.* San Francisco: Jossey-Bass.

Webber, A. M. (1998, November). Danger: Toxic company. *Fast Company, 19,* 152–161.

CHAPTER FOUR

Counseling Men in College Settings

John M. Robertson

D o universities make people think? In a word, yes. More than that, most students actually change the way they think. Attitudes, values, morals, ideas, relational patterns—all are subject to change.

The evidence is abundant. Pascarella and Terenzini (1991) reviewed hundreds of studies about college life, then used an effect size strategy to estimate the change that occurs between the first and last years of college. When expressed as standard deviation units, an effect size can be converted to an estimate of the percentile point change. Using this technique, they provided strong evidence that young people change in college. For example, students show an improvement in their ability to communicate. Increases are seen in their verbal skills (+21 percentile points), their written communication skills (+19), and their oral communication skills (+22). Stronger changes are seen in their ability to think. Critical thinking improves (+34), as does their ability to use reason and evidence to address problems (+34) or to deal with conceptual complexity (+38). In short, students gain more than a knowledge base in their major fields of study. They learn thinking skills and begin to apply them to various questions they face.

Attitudes and values change as well. Students become interested in art, music, literature, and history. In general, their views broaden. They become aware of freedoms, inclusiveness, complexity, and tolerance. By the time they graduate, students are likely to have changed their relational views. They have become more autonomous (+36), less authoritarian (−81), and less ethnocentric (−45) over the course of their college years. They also are better adjusted psychologically (+40), and their views of religion and gender have become more flexible (Pascarella & Terenzini, 1991).

Although cautions may be offered about these findings (for example, group differences may hide individual differences, college may not actually cause these changes, or these shifts may represent development not change), the overall difference is unmistakable. During the years that young people are in college, they modify the way they communicate, think, value, and relate. These trends have been consistent for decades (Bowen, 1977; Corey, 1936; Jacob, 1957; Feldman & Newcomb, 1969; Pascarella & Terenzini, 1991) and do not therefore seem confined to a particular era. These findings are also consistent with what theorists have argued for quite some time (see Chickering, 1969; Perry, 1970); that is, people change (evolve, mature, develop) during their college years as they form an identity and think more carefully about the world in which they live.

It is not surprising, therefore, that many college students seek counseling. With so much change in the air, with so many new influences, ideas, and people in their lives, the challenges can become intense. Talking with someone about these issues becomes appealing to many students. Magoon's (1999) annual summary of information about university counseling centers tracks utilization patterns. Counseling centers at large universities (with more than ten thousand students) in a typical year see about nine hundred students for emotional or social problems and another two hundred students for educational or vocational questions. Many more students are seen in workshops, theme groups, outreach presentations, and guest lectures in classes. A conservative estimate is that campus counseling centers serve no less than 10 percent of the student body in any given year. Some campuses conduct exit surveys of seniors that ask about the services they have used during their educational careers. Results indicate that around 40 percent of graduating seniors at some universities report some contact with counseling staff at the counseling center while getting their degree (*Survey Results,* 1997).

HOW MEN USE COLLEGE COUNSELING CENTERS

Although college men may be reluctant to seek counseling, they do find their way to campus counseling centers. The most frequently presented questions address their relationships, their careers, their moods, and their use of alcohol and other drugs.

Rates of Psychological Services Utilization

Men do not visit counselors as frequently as do women. The ratio in North America is about one to two, with one male visit for every two or more female visits (Cheatham, Shelton, & Ray, 1987; Newton, 1999; Vessey & Howard, 1993). This pattern has not changed for many years (see Shueman & Medvene, 1981). The use rates do not mean that men have fewer problems than women; evidence indicates very similar levels of distress in men and women (Robins et al., 1984). In fact, men appear to have even higher rates of risk for some issues. Although younger boys and girls have similar rates of suicide, by the time they are in college (between the ages of twenty and twenty-four) men are actually six times more likely to commit suicide than are women (U.S. Department of Health and Human Services, 1992). This pattern continues throughout adulthood, as four of every five suicide deaths in North America are men (U.S. Department of Health and Human Services, 1992).

Another potential explanation for the differential rates of using counseling services is that referral sources might have a bias toward referring women. This explanation, however, does not appear to have much support. One study (Lott, Ness, Alcorn, & Greer, 1999) presented analogue cases (students, staff, and faculty) to potential referral sources on three college campuses and did not find that women were referred at higher rates than men. It is interesting to note, however, that this same study found that men were less likely than women to make referrals of students for counseling. Even as referral sources, men are less likely to think about counseling options than are women.

If men do not have fewer or less severe problems than women or are not referred less frequently than women, other explanations for their lower utilization rates can be considered. Several have suggested that the difference is related to male gender role socialization (see, for example, Wilcox & Forrest, 1992). Somehow, the desire to "be a man" may steer men away from counselors (Good & Wood, 1995). Several studies have found that traditional men do indeed have negative ideas about the traditional counseling process (Johnson & Brock, 1988; J. M. Robertson & Fitzgerald, 1992; Sipps & Janeczek, 1986). These negative attitudes about counseling seem to correlate with a general unwillingness to seek psychological help (Wisch, Mahalik, Hayes, & Nutt, 1995). Men also may be reluctant because they may hear on campus about some of the vast social problems that involve male oppression, male violence, or male sexual assault. Some may conclude that there is something bad or wrong with being male. Some have argued that it may seem that therapists treat masculinity as a pathology (Heesacker & Pritchard, 1992; Kelly & Hall, 1992). Traditional male behaviors have even been described as "chronic, terminal, and without redeeming value" (Long, 1987, p. 316).

Traditional counseling requires that men set aside much of their masculine socialization simply to get through the door and ask for help. Once they start talking with a counselor, they may discover other expectations that are difficult to meet. They are supposed to be verbal, expressive, and open. Counselors may want them to be emotionally aware, to acknowledge problems and uncertainty, and to think about their inner lives. Men are likely to feel less independent in such settings, less successful, and less in control. For many traditional men, these factors make counseling feel awkward and unfamiliar. Strong evidence now links these two variables—masculine socialization and a reluctance to seek psychological assistance. Good, Dell, and Mintz (1989) found that traditional attitudes about the male role, concern about expressing emotions, and a concern about expressing affection toward other men were all related to a negative attitude toward seeking counseling.

Reasons for Seeking Counseling

Many men in college begin counseling with the hope that they will be given direction and good advice. It is not uncommon for a man to start a session with, "Well, I came here to get some answers" or "I hope you've got some suggestions, because I've run out of them." Men often see their problems as situational rather than internal. They know they feel badly inside, but they tend to look for explanations in the situations around them. If a change might be made in the external world, then they will feel better inside. As a result, men are more likely than women to feel cautious about opening up and talking about their vulnerabilities and uncertainties. This perspective can change as counseling proceeds, but these expectations and feelings are often present at the outset.

In some ways, these tendencies in men are reinforced by some aspects of the academic environment. Classes teach men about the value of hypothesis testing, sequential thinking, and logical analysis. Professors and textbooks explain solutions to problems. For many classes, the focus is on external elements—cells and chemicals, numbers and treaties, blueprints and structures. Not many classes require men to consider their internal emotional states, their skills at communicating, or their personal limitations.

A taxonomy of presenting issues seen at university counseling centers (Chandler & Gallagher, 1996) suggests that most concerns cluster into only four or five categories: relationship issues, career concerns, mood difficulties, substance misuse, and, perhaps, eating disorders. It may be useful to consider briefly some of these presenting issues in college counseling centers, noting how strongly they are influenced by male gender role attitudes and expectations.

Relationship Issues. First, a primary concern for men in college is relationships. For heterosexual men, the questions are many. Because gender role expectations now vary, norms are unclear. Men must think through their own values on a wide range of gender issues. What sort of relationship does the man want? How does he want to address such issues as decision making, task allocation, and sexual behavior? What appeals to him in the women he meets? Independence? Strong career goals? Sexual assertiveness? Given the overall changes he is likely experiencing in his life (in communication and critical-thinking skills, for example), these questions may not have immediate and compelling answers for him. He may find himself experimenting in these areas, as he "tries on" various possibilities. This concern with relationships is central for many men. At many counseling centers, it is the most common presenting issue for men. It is not unusual for male-female couples to present themselves for couples counseling. The presenting issues must be taken seriously (for example, "we argue too much" or "we don't see each another enough"), but the underlying questions about gender role behavior are always close to the surface. Questions about sexuality may occur in this context as well. Making decisions about one's sexual behavior can be fraught with uncertainty, socialized pressures, and an awareness of health risks. These factors can lead men to ask for help in sorting out questions about sexual expectations, sexual practices, and sexual dysfunctions.

For gay and bisexual men, questions about relationships are also common, though shaped by additional challenges. It is still true that gay and bisexual men are harassed on campus. They face verbal insults hurled from windows of residence halls and fraternities, physical threats, and exclusion from social groups. This treatment leads some men to hide their sexuality for fear of discrimination. The fact that they may possess numerous skills and intelligence does not eliminate the reality in which they must live—a campus or community environment that can present an unexpected challenge or threat at any moment. These factors make the development of relationships a particular challenge for gay and bisexual men on campus. How does a gay or bisexual man meet other men? Should he attend a campus group of gay, lesbian, and bisexual students? If so, others will know about his sexual orientation, and he might be reluctant to make such a public statement while still in college. More manageable for some men is the experience of a support group for gay and bisexual men, provided by either the campus counseling center or an active group in the community. In this more supportive and private setting, he might begin the process of making friends and developing closer relationships.

Another relationship issue is the ongoing process of individuation from parents. A primary developmental concern for boys is creating a sense of independence from their parents. The awareness that they are being pushed away from a nurturing parent can begin early and can be traumatizing (Pollack, 1995). This early separation is consistent with what many men are socialized to idealize as adults—autonomy. Men do not easily give up this idealization of autonomy. They believe others expect them to be independently successful. Theorists have long noted this tendency in men (David & Brannon, 1976; Pleck, 1987).

In college, men face individuation issues very directly. They begin college as teenagers, with all the financial and emotional dependence implied in that role. They are expected to graduate as adults, fully ready to assume a productive and financially independent role in society. Along the way, men must redefine their familial and personal relationships. This can be exceedingly painful work, both for men and for their parents and siblings. Parents are not always eager to stop being parental. Drawing new boundary lines can be a formidable task for men.

Career Concerns. A second set of male presenting issues at campus counseling centers is the collection of career concerns. It is nearly axiomatic in this culture: able men must work. Although the number of male homemakers is increasing (U.S. Department of Commerce, 1992), virtually all men in college expect to work. It is often the primary reason for attending college. Men believe (and with reason) that a college degree increases their income potential. Enormous pressure is experienced when a man cannot answer the simple question, "What's your major?" It is a question asked early in nearly every conversation with a new person on campus. Much depends on this choice: his identity, his sense of himself, his economic future. Men who do not have a major field of study risk being thought of as indecisive and confused. If by some chance he should actively consider leaving college to become a full-time homemaker, he would be violating traditional definitions of masculinity. Criticism would follow (Bose, 1980, J. M. Robertson & Verschelden, 1993), and if he ends up talking with a counselor about his life he runs the risk of being given a more severe diagnostic label based only on his nontraditional choices (J. M. Robertson & Fitzgerald, 1990). The importance of career aspirations for college men can hardly be overestimated.

It is no wonder, then, that many men begin counseling by presenting career-related questions. It is familiar and socially appropriate for men to talk about occupational issues in college. They may inquire about testing to see what career might be best for them or begin by reporting difficulties sustaining an interest in a core class.

It should be noted, however, that career uncertainties often accompany personal difficulties. For example, a man may be struggling with external pressures to choose a certain career. A romantic partner or a parent may want him to consider a different career. The other person may criticize his choice ("You can't make any money with a music major" or "You'd make a great architect"). These challenges may lead to questions about his interactions with others. Is his partner correct? Will the relationship end if he remains a music major? Will his parents withdraw their financial support if he does not change his major? These questions are not hypothetical for men, because the threats can be very real. In the counseling center, a man may begin to struggle with such issues as developing his own autonomy, how he might become more assertive with his family, or how to be more expressive of his own needs in a romanticrelationship.

Regional and economic factors can shape these career issues. In the Midwest, for example, male students may come from a family farming background that stretches back one hundred years or more. When the family tells him that he is next in line to take over the farm, the pressure to major in some aspect of agriculture or the animal sciences can be intense. If he wants to leave the farm and pursue a career in some other field, the issue is no longer simply a career decision. It is a personal crisis about his male role in the family and the meaning of his life. Similar illustrations of the connection between career and personal issues can be found in other regions of the country and within various religious traditions or ethnic groups. The intergenerational conflict within families over career decisions can be intense.

Mood Difficulties. A third cluster of presenting issues involves moods, especially depression. For about twenty-five years, researchers have been exploring differences in the ways men and women experience depression. Empirical studies have demonstrated that women experience crying spells and feelings of dislike, whereas men tend to withdraw from their worlds and do so without as many tears. Men also tend to somaticize their depression (Funabiki, Bologna, Pepping, & Fitzgerald, 1980; Oliver & Toner, 1990). A particularly notable difference is that many men with depression do not talk about their distress. This theme has appeared in popular literature as well. Note the success of the book by Real (1997), *I Don't Want to Talk about It: Overcoming the Legacy of Male Depression;* Real described this pattern as "male covert depression." This factor may account for much of the difference in reporting rates, with men reporting depressive symptoms only half as often as women (Amenson & Lewinsohn, 1981). Men simply do not talk about mood disorders as readily as do women.

College men do get depressed, whether they report it as readily as women do or not. One factor that has been shown to be related to the depression and psychological distress of college men is traditional masculinity (Good & Mintz, 1990; Good et al., 1995). And the stronger the beliefs in the traditional male gender role, the more likely men are to withdraw socially and to somaticize their depression (Oliver & Toner, 1990). For a long time, it has been noted that college men have difficulty expressing their emotions with words (J. G. Allen & Haccoun, 1976; Pillemer, Krensky, Kleinman, & Goldsmith, 1991). Girls cry; boys do not. Girls talk about their feelings; boys do not. Two decades ago, this tendency of males to avoid things feminine was called a "fear of femininity" (O'Neil, 1981).

In many ways, this avoidance is experienced as positive. An unemotional style in business creates a reputation of being "on top of things" or not being "ruled by his heart." Men who can gather data and make impersonal judgments based on information are praised. Nevertheless, while in college, many men find that women want them to talk more, share more, feel more. It is no longer uncommon for men to actually present this issue to counselors at the beginning of their work. "What does my girlfriend mean when she says to me, 'Tell me about your feelings?' "

One exception to the general reluctance to express emotions is college men's experience with anger. It is not unusual for college men to be required to seek counseling for anger. Typically, this request follows an incident that has gotten the man in trouble with his residence hall, fraternity, athletic department, or the law enforcement community. This issue presents particular difficulties for university counseling centers, because most staff members see themselves as supportive, not punitive. Some counselors refuse to work with mandated cases, noting that their overall goals are educational or that they do not have time to participate in the legal proceedings that might be required. Students may be referred off campus to agencies in the private sector that provide this service rather readily.

Substance Misuse. A fourth group of issues involves the misuse of alcohol and the illegal use of other drugs. Substance abuse continues to be a significant problem on college and university campuses. Exactly how big the problem is can be difficult to quantify. Surveys and other studies use different methods and designs, but they all conclude that substance use is a troublesome problem on campuses in North America. One of the largest studies about the scope of the problem collected information from more than fifty-six thousand students on seventy-eight campuses (Presley & Meilman, 1992). Results showed that about 85 percent of all college students report drinking at least once during the previous year and about 66 percent report drinking at least once during the previous thirty days. Other studies have found similar rates of drinking, ranging from about 80 percent to more than 95 percent of all college students (Meilman, Stone, Gaylor, & Turco, 1990; Wiggins & Wiggins, 1987).

The total amount of alcohol consumed by college students in a single year is staggering. Eigen (1991) has calculated that students consume 430 million gallons of alcohol a year. That is enough to fill an Olympic-sized swimming pool thirty-five hundred times. If the empty beer cans were stacked end to end, they would reach the moon and continue for another seventy thousand miles.

Not surprisingly, most of the alcohol-related problems come with heavy drinking. The percentage of heavy drinkers has remained constant at about 20 percent for many years (Engs & Hanson, 1988). A heavy drinker is usually defined as someone who has drunk an average of more than one ounce of absolute alcohol a day for the previous thirty days.

Even more striking is the level of binge drinking, defined for men as drinking five or more drinks in a row at least once in the two weeks prior to the survey. Using this definition, the Harvard School of Public Health College Alcohol Study (Wechsler, Dowdall, Maenner, Gledhill-Hoyt, & Lee, 1998) found that nearly half of all college men (48 percent) are binge drinkers. Most college men (58 percent) drink to get drunk, and about one-third get drunk three or more times a month. Similar results have been found in others studies (Douglas, Collins, & Warren, 1997; Johnston, O'Malley, & Bachman, 1997; Presley, Meilman, Cashin, & Lyeria, 1996). A consistent finding in these studies is that college men are more likely than college women to use alcohol, although that gap appears to be narrowing. This difference remains evident even when correcting for body weight. More than twice as many male students as female students drink daily. Men also drink larger quantities when they drink, drink more frequently, are less likely to be abstainers, and have more problems related to alcohol than do women. Most of the differences appear to be found in the heavy drinker category. In one study of first-year students in Massachusetts (Wechsler & Isaac, 1992), about 20 percent of underage men drank at least ten times a month, but only 9 percent of women drank that often. One curious pattern is that college men drink more heavily than noncollege men. College students report higher levels of alcohol use than other young people on virtually all measures (Prendergast, 1994).

For a long time, it has been true that men in fraternities are more likely to drink than other men in college (Canterbury, Gressard, & Vieweg, 1991; Globetti, Stem, Marasco, & Haworth-Hoeppner, 1988; Werner & Greene, 1992). The most recent studies (for example, Wechsler et al., 1998) indicate that four of every five members of a fraternity are binge drinkers.

Binge drinking results in serious problems for men. The Harvard study (Wechsler et al., 1998) asked students to report on the consequences of their drinking. The most frequent problems were having study or sleep interrupted (61 percent), missing a class (65 percent), blackouts (56 percent), getting behind in schoolwork (48 percent), arguing with friends (47 percent), and engaging in unplanned sexual activity (45 percent). Another 29 percent reported being insulted or humiliated. Other studies have found additional consequences, many of them tragic: driving and boating accidents, falls, suicides while intoxicated, criminal behavior including assault and rape, and physical discomfort from drinking too much (Prendergast, 1994). Academically, first-year college men who drink heavily are more likely than those who do not to be on probation, earn lower grade point averages, and drop out of college during their first year (Eigen, 1991). In all, nearly four of every five students reported at least one significant negative consequence related to their drinking.

For counselors of college men, alcohol abuse raises the question of motivation for drinking. Prendergast (1994) reported that college students give several reasons for using alcohol. Some reasons are personal, such the desire to escape or forget problems or to deliberately induce a mood change. Other reasons include the desire to be more social with others or simply to get drunk. It is unfortunate, but many initiation rituals in college involve excessive drinking. These customs, norms, and traditions are difficult to break. Add to the mix the heavy promotion of alcohol to college students at athletic events by the alcohol industry, and it is easy to see why so many college men drink at such high rates.

Illegal drugs are used at various levels. Again, the self-report estimates vary, depending on age, how the questions are asked, region of the country, and so forth. Nationally, the percentage of those who have used marijuana in the past year is about 30 percent; during their college years, about 70 percent try it at least once. Other drugs (hallucinogens, amphetamines, heroin, tranquilizers, inhalants, and cocaine) are used by 6 percent or fewer students (Prendergast, 1994). Men show higher rates of usage of these drugs than do women, although the differences are generally slight (Johnston, O'Malley, & Bachman, 1993).

Knowing about a particular man's motivation for using alcohol or illegal drugs and the specific problems he is facing as a result provides an insight into his story that might point to other psychological or social issues that need to be addressed. Although alcohol itself can become a problem in college, it is also possible that the use of alcohol is experimental, and so exploring the reasons and problems associated with drinking can open up other areas of his life for discussion. Because men become old enough to use alcohol legally while they are students, their earliest experimenting occurs while they are making decisions about many values.

This list of major presenting issues for college men (relationships, careers, moods, and substance abuse) certainly is not exhaustive. Rather, it summarizes the arenas in which most of the common problems presented by college men are found and also highlights the significance of gender role issues in thinking about these concerns.

HELPING COLLEGE MEN

As noted earlier, college men seek counseling less frequently than do college women (Kirk, 1973; Nadler, Maler, & Friedman, 1984; Newton, 1999; M. F. Robertson, 1988), and the role of masculine gender role socialization appears to be a significant deterrent for many men in seeking counseling.

Making Therapy More Appealing to Men

The initial challenge for counselors of college men is to find ways to make it easier for men to seek and experience help (Dickstein, Stein, Pleck, & Myers, 1991; J. M. Robertson & Fitzgerald, 1992). Counselors must thus develop alternative approaches based on the socialization of men, with an awareness of the social and cultural influences that make traditional therapy unappealing (Kilmartin, 1994). Sher (1990) argued that counseling cannot be effective unless the gender role context in which a man seeks therapy is considered. To consider this context, several authors have suggested that new approaches be developed for men, approaches that are more congruent to masculine socialization (J. A. Allen & Gordon, 1990; Brooks, 1998; Levant, 1990; Prosser-Gelwick & Garni, 1988). In general, these approaches suggest that rather than change men to make them comfortable in therapy, it may be more effective to change the traditional therapy model itself (J. M. Robertson & Fitzgerald, 1992; Wilcox & Forrest, 1992).

There is now evidence that when attention is given to this issue, college men's unwillingness to seek help might change. When men are given a choice about the type of help they might receive, their attitudes toward help seeking change. For example, Wisch et al. (1995) found that undergraduate men with increased levels of conflict about gender roles became more open to counselors after viewing a videotape that described cognitive approaches than they did after viewing a videotape about emotional approaches. Hurst (1997) found similar results when college men were given a choice about various types of available help, including solution-focused and cognitive approaches. These results are consistent with the general notion that men are more comfortable when they can think their way to solutions and less comfortable when asked to rely on their emotions or intuition.

J. M. Robertson and L. F. Fitzgerald (1992) found that traditional college men preferred descriptions of help offered in workshops, classes, seminars, and library materials. Similar suggestions have been made by Wilcox and Forrest (1992), who recommended developing psychoeducation groups and individual therapy with a focus on problem solving, action, and cognition. Similarly, Kelly and Hall (1992) presented a model that emphasizes focusing on men's strengths, affirming that what they bring to therapy is positive, addressing the need for active interventions in their personal networks, and avoiding blaming men for not seeking help sooner.

Taken together, these notions suggest that counseling approaches to traditional college men might be more appealing when they are congruent with masculine socialization. That is, if counseling does not require men to set aside their sense of independence, their comfort with goals, tasks, and activities, or their preference of developing an understanding of a situation, then the idea of seeking help might be more appealing. When thinking about providing therapy to both women and men, it is no longer tenable to assume that "one size fits all" (Hurst, 1997). Thinking about therapy for college men from this perspective does indeed make them a "special population" that deserves attention based on social and cultural norms (Heppner, 1995).

Individual Counseling with College Men

Consistent with the previously mentioned themes, a few guidelines for one-on-one counseling of traditionally socialized men can be offered. First, it may be helpful to acknowledge the strength implied when a college man asks for help. Deciding to walk into the counseling room may have taken much time and effort. He is countering much of what he has been socialized to believe about himself just by sitting in the chair. If the counselor can acknowledge this step in some comfortable way and then frame his decision as a strength rather than as an admission of failure, then the man will experience the counseling atmosphere as positive at the outset.

Second, the counselor can experiment with language. The use of language familiar to traditionally socialized men may make the counseling room feel more familiar. Words such as *success, improvement, goals, agreements, progress, tasks, skills, homework, measurable differences,* and *baseline* are all familiar to college men. These concepts are also congruent with traditional socialization. Other words may be less familiar or appealing: *feelings, vulnerability, self-awareness, exploration, internalize, weakness,* and *expressiveness.* The use of familiar words may be helpful at the outset of therapy, when a man is feeling his way (so to speak) in a new environment.

Naturally, over time the therapist can begin to introduce new ideas and define them for male clients. Although talking about cognition and activities may be more comfortable for men, counselors need not avoid introducing ideas related to emotions, systemic relationships, or interactive processing. It helps to define these concepts clearly as they are introduced into the conversation. In the long run, widening his repertoire of skills to include emotional expressiveness, comfort with intimacy, and willingness to share power and resources is very important work for counselors. Rather than think of these issues as either/or (that is, counseling must focus on either masculine-congruent or masculine-incongruent themes), it may be more inclusive and promising to think of both/and. Counselors might begin with masculine-familiar themes and ideas and move toward a broader exploration of more nontraditional tendencies, such as expressiveness, inclusion, and intimacy.

Third, it may help to move slowly when working with emotional issues. The counselor can watch for expressions of anxiety and fear and normalize them. He or she can facilitate rather than push for the expression of affect and recognize that although men want relief from emotional pain, they find vulnerability to be extremely uncomfortable. They may be afraid that they will say too much and then be regarded as weak, unsuccessful, or foolish. They may feel a risk of being exploited, even by the warm and caring therapist. Although many men may deliberately withhold information about affect, it is often more likely that they simply do not have the language to describe their experiences. And so they can try to guess at what they "should" feel, which is often inaccurate. It can be relieving simply to acknowledge this frustration at trying to find that right word to describe an emotion. Supplying men with a list of words used to express common feelings can be helpful. When given such a list, many men actively consult it during sessions, looking for the right word to describe how they are feeling.

Another approach is to suggest to college men that emotions have a purpose, a function. They are not mere interruptions or distractions that get a man off course. Emotions can be described as tools to aid in understanding his personal strengths, his agenda for self-improvement, or his environment. This understanding may be experienced as giving him an edge in meeting various goals and objectives.

When working with men along these lines, I often provide a male-friendly definition of the word *emotion* to make sure we are speaking the same language. I explain that an emotion begins as a response to an Antecedent event (say, meeting a bear on the trail in the Sierras). As soon as the problem is identified, physiological Arousal occurs (for example, changes in heart rate, skin temperature, and pupil size). The purpose of this Arousal is to focus our attention on the event that needs to be addressed. As we survey the scene (quickly, in this case), we Appraise the situation and consider various options that might address the problem of the bear (fleeing, fighting, or freezing). When we make our choice, we then Act to solve the problem that the emotion identified for us in the first place. This whole experience can be given a name (such as fear or panic). For many men, this simple definition of an emotion in the form of a mnemonic (Antecedent, Arousal, Appraisal, Action) allows them to see emotions as significant and adaptive, not simply as "something women do." Far from leaving men feeling weak and vulnerable, emotions give them a sense of being adaptive and constructive (Plutchik, 1980; J. M. Robertson & Freeman, 1995).

It is important for counselors to be aware of their own emotions as they work with college men. Being willing to talk about their emotions at appropriate times may provide a model for men, especially when the therapist is male. It is not always easy to work with men who are beginning to experience intense emotions that have been blocked for years. Counselors who monitor their own levels of comfort in working with these issues are likely to avoid pitfalls associated with their own issues related to intimacy or power.

Fourth, counselors must take rationalizations seriously. Men can become rather skilled in offering plausible reasons and explanations for their behavior. In many college classes, men are rewarded when they think carefully, logically, analytically. And when they have finished college, they hope to be paid well for being incisive in their analysis of a problem. But to engage in exclusively cognitive discussions about problems makes therapeutic progress difficult. In some ways, responding to rationalizations requires a balancing act by counselors. On the one hand, it can be useful to avoid criticizing the tendency to look for rational explanations of a problem, given that society often sees such explanations as strengths for men. On the other hand, it is also helpful to broaden the scope of inquiry, so that men can include more affective, relational, and systemic elements in their work as clients.

Fifth, counselors can give men an opportunity to practice new patterns. College men are familiar with the ideas of homework, labs, and practice sessions. Extending this notion into the personal domain is familiar and reasonable for many college men. Conducting "little experiments" as men try a new approach to a problem gives them the impression that they are actually doing something, trying something. The variety of options for homework is virtually endless. Both counselor and client can participate in the creation of assignments outside the counseling hour. Although this approach may seem to represent a preference for cognitive-behavioral therapy, it does not need to be limited to that approach.

Groups and Workshops for College Men

Even though many counselors believe that men are seeking individual psychotherapy in greater numbers (see, for example, Betcher & Pollack, 1993; Meth & Pasick, 1990), many men are still highly resistant to the idea of one-on-one counseling. The idea is too threatening, too bewildering, or too confusing for them consider. For these treatment-resistant men, Brooks (1996) has argued that the all-male group is the best alternative. In a similar vein, Andronico (1996) suggests that "men are more familiar" with groups "than with any other type of format that is currently used for interpersonal growth and change" (p. xviii).

Brooks (1996) has noted that the group format offers several specific benefits to men. Groups provide a familiar terrain to men who have been in groups all their lives—sports, scouting, work groups, and so forth. Because the idea of talking about important issues in groups is already familiar, it is relatively easy to imagine using a group or class to gain information about personal questions as well. Groups also decrease men's social isolation. Even though men participate in other groups in their lives, the focus typically is on the sharing of activities, such as hunting, car repairs, and sports (Brehm, 1985). As a result, men can experience a social isolation and loneliness that groups can directly address. Brooks (1996) further argues that groups help men counter an overdependence on women, provide opportunities for self-disclosure, instill hope, help men discover emotional connections, and help men improve communication skills.

Numerous protocols have been developed for working with groups. McKay and Paleg (1992) and Andronico (1996) have edited volumes filled with practical ideas on running various theme and therapy groups. Andronico's book is designed specifically for male groups. Although counselors likely have their own preferences for organizing and developing groups, these resources offer many ideas. Group leaders have written about a wide variety of issues that have implications for men. Examples of group themes from just these two collections include shyness, depression, anger, assertiveness, incest offenders, addictions, male mentoring, gay issues, fathering, noncustodial fathering, parenting, sexual abuse survival, and men who batter.

Many of these groups present a workshop format, which offers a specific focus for men. These workshops or classes usually meet for a specified number of sessions and limit their focus to the announced topic. It is common for groups to consider various activities and exercises outside the group session. The purpose of the homework is to facilitate continuity during the week and to increase the rate of change. Written protocols are detailed (McKay & Paleg, 1992) and include such issues as screening and selection of group members, time and duration, structure, and goals. On college campuses, workshops are experienced somewhat like classes. They meet at the same time every week and have an informal syllabus that describes the group's purpose and focus.

Other groups focus less on given topics and more on therapy. As such, the intervention strategies are more broadly stated. For example, Jolliff and Horne (1996, pp. 65, 66) list twenty such strategies, including "teach clients the skills of authenticity and self-disclosure," "focus always on empowering the client," "normalize and encourage self-care," "model spontaneity, emotional expression, and self-disclosure," and "communicate affection, warmth, and gentleness."

The absence of women in these groups can offer several benefits. When heterosexual men do not have the opportunity to interact with women in a group, they cannot flirt. They may become more genuine and self-reflective than when they are with women. Men then tend to be more expressive, more relaxed, and more talkative. They seem to share their feelings with each other more easily. Men are socialized to talk about emotions more with women than with men. With no women present, they must turn to each other for support. The result is greater closeness with other men. They develop friendships with other men that are open, trusting, and caring. They can express feelings and thoughts in an all-male group that they would be reluctant to address in a mixed group. For example, they can talk openly about sexual questions and relationship issues. They can be expressive of anger without worrying about how a woman might interpret the rage. Techniques that have been tried in therapy groups for men include storytelling, genograms, role playing, unsent letter writing, poetry, and many more (see Jolliff & Horne, 1996).

McPhee (1996) recommends that therapy groups for men begin with a brief check-in at the beginning of the session, during which each member talks for one to two minutes about his week and what he wants from the group. He also suggests that the group end with closing statements, during which each member summarizes his experience in that particular session. Most groups emphasize confidentiality and develop policies for members missing meetings.

Men's Clinics on Campus

Some campuses are organizing clinics that coordinate medical and counseling services directed toward men (Stevens, 1998). Team members include psychologists or other counselors, physicians, physician assistants, and health educators. Together, this group forms the staff in the clinic, sometimes with health center space devoted to examination and interview rooms. These teams tend to be interested in offering proactive activities, such as presentations in fraternities, residence halls, and classrooms. They may participate in a panel at a public meeting in the student union. Presentation topics include sexually transmitted diseases, general health questions related to the genitals (for example, circumcision, contraception, urination, and testicular cancer), alcohol and recreational drug use, and sexual behavior.

Those who staff these clinics report that it is important to create a strong media awareness of their presence on campus. Men are more likely to use services that are well advertised and seem readily available (L. Moeller, personal communication, September 13, 1999; Stevens, 1998). Plans can be developed to market the clinic through posters, campus newspaper advertising, and public service announcements on the campus radio or low-power television station. The content of the advertisements not only announces the clinic's services but also focuses attention on particular health-related issues that the health team staff addresses.

Several themes have emerged in working with men in these settings (Stevens, 1998). Practitioners have discovered that many college men feel especially concerned about removing their clothing during an exam. Health team members have noted several explanations, including concerns that some men have about the appearance or responsiveness of their genitals. Homophobia appears to be an additional concern. Many men also seem uneasy about the possibility of being judged by their practitioners, especially with regard to sexual behavior. Initial questions are often tentative and asked indirectly. When they feel safe and are given permission to ask questions, most college men will talk about difficult issues. They may appear eager or even obsessive in their questioning. Perhaps this eagerness should not be surprising, because for many of these men, these conversations are the first they have had with anyone about these issues. It is not unusual to find that after men have presented their initial concern, they will then have questions about other personal matters, such as sexual identity, sexual compulsions, relationship interactions, prostitution, or other health matters. Given the psychological nature of many of these questions, the idea of working as a team is quite appealing to many physicians.

Other ideas associated with a men's clinic include the use of assessments and inventories to highlight concerns, a resource library for private reading, and a Web page that offers information of particular interest to men. Folders can be developed and distributed to men in groups on campus; the folders may include brochures on a variety of health topics such as testicular self-exams; the use of nicotine, alcohol, and other substances; rape awareness; anger management; and sexually transmitted diseases.

Using Media to Help College Men

Given the masculine socialization themes described earlier in this chapter and elsewhere in this book, it is not surprising that the use of media to convey information to men can be quite effective. I highlight three ideas in this section. The first is the social norms approach to drinking behavior on campus. The staff at Northern Illinois University began an experiment in 1990 that has been effective for more than a decade (Haines, 1998). Over that time, campus officials have measured a reduction in binge drinking of 44 percent. Other universities have started similar projects based on the same research and have found similar reductions. The approach is based on research (Berkowitz, 1991; Perkins & Berkowitz, 1986) that found that college students generally overestimate the amount of alcohol their classmates consume. They called this impression a "false norm." Other research indicates that social norms have a powerful influence on behavior. The staff at Northern Illinois University put these two ideas together and used the media to inform students about the actual social norms on campus. At Northern Illinois, the media campaign was built around stating a simple fact over and over again: "Most Northern Illinois students drink zero to five drinks when they party." The first year after introducing this campaign, binge drinking went down 18 percent, and the trend has continued every since. The same approach has been used at several other campuses, each time with a measurable reduction in binge drinking. This approach has been much more effective than media campaigns based on fear or campaigns that emphasize the harm that can come from abusive drinking. The typical student is portrayed as a moderate drinker, not an abusive drinker. In addition to advertisements in the campus newspaper, the campaigns include a weekly column, regular press releases, and other stories about normal drinking. Posters and leaflets are displayed in various locations. Although this approach may not seem like counseling in the traditional sense, counseling centers can participate in such activities with a strong expectation that the drinking behavior of men who would never come to counseling might be altered. Counselors can also refer to social norms data from the campus in talking directly with students in counseling.

A second example is the use of campus radio stations. Many campuses have radio stations that offer programming to students. Radio station personnel are often interested in the perspectives of staff members at the counseling center. In addition to providing interviews on topics of interest in the news, counselors can be creative in their use of this medium. Radio spots have been used on college campuses to provide psychological information directly to students on such issues as study skills, relationship issues, diversity, and holiday concerns (Wendt & Johnston, 1987). Brief dramatizations have also been used to illustrate common problem situations for students (Godin et al., 1986).

An interactive use of radio is also possible. At Kansas State University, a physician and a psychologist from the counseling center have teamed up to produce a call-in talk show on the topic of sexuality. The purpose of the show is "to provide information about sexually related issues to the students" on campus (Van Haveren, Blank, & Bentley, 1999, p. 5). Each program opens with the physician and psychologist providing information about a given topic and then inviting listeners to join the conversation by calling in with their questions. Common topics include date rape, sexually transmitted diseases, how to talk with partners about sexual behavior, alcohol and sexual responsiveness, birth control issues, sexual etiquette, and relationship issues. It is interesting to note that men are quite willing to call the show and actually do so at much higher rates than they visit counselors. Callers can remain anonymous. In fact, a caller can leave a question with the producer and not go on the air at all. Even though conversation is not private (thousands are listening), the caller can remain anonymous. This approach is consistent with the finding that men with traditional values are drawn to services that offer information directly to them (J. M. Robertson & Fitzgerald, 1992).

A third idea is to make men aware of self-help resources. Simply making information available so that men can find it without having to set up an appointment to talk with a counselor makes it easier for many men to inform themselves. The full range of media can be used: print, the Internet, radio, and television. With regard to written resources, counseling centers and other campus offices may cooperate in the development of posters, space ads in the campus newspaper, or a campus-specific Web site. Counseling centers around the country have coordinated their efforts and put many of their handouts and brochures on the Web. Men can simply look up a topic and do some initial reading on their own. An address that contains many of these psychoeducational "handouts" is the Counseling Center Village (http://ub-counseling.buffalo.edu /ccv.html). The site contains self-help information on about twenty-five topics. Although these resources are not intended to be exhaustive or to take the place of psychotherapy, they provide men with introductory information. If they make an appointment, men are more likely to come with questions raised by the brochures.

The use of media by counselors may seem different from "doing therapy" with men. And yet the purpose is very similar—to provide men with assistance in addressing significant problems. Developing alternatives to the one-on-one counseling relationship clearly brings more men into contact with helping professionals and is respectful of the socialization still experienced by traditional men.

Men undergo many changes while in college. They modify many of their attitudes, values, morals, ideas, and relationship styles. They improve their ability to think critically and to communicate their ideas. They become more autonomous, less authoritarian, and more flexible about gender roles.

Given the breadth of these changes, it is not surprising that college men seek counseling. Yet they seek help only half as frequently as do women. One widely regarded explanation for this gender difference is that masculine socialization simply makes individual therapy unappealing.

When they do ask for help, men commonly present issues about relationships, career concerns, mood disorders, and substance use problems. All of these issues are heavily colored by gender role expectations and themes. Suggestions for working with these issues in one-on-one counseling include acknowledging the strength involved in asking for help, using masculine-congruent language, working slowly with emotional issues, describing emotions as functional and adaptive, taking rationalizations seriously, and providing ample opportunity for men to act on the insights they are gaining in therapy.

Structured workshops and open-ended groups provide a setting for men that is comfortable and familiar. Groups seem especially helpful to college men otherwise resistant to individual therapy. In addition, campus counselors may want to explore the development of a men's clinic with medical staff or consider a creative use of campus media to reach men.

The college years are critical in the development of a man's life story. He trains for a career. He looks for a primary relationship. He develops his own values and goals for life. Counselors who work with men during this phase of their lives are given both an enormous opportunity and an awesome responsibility.

References

Allen, J. A., & Gordon, S. (1990). Creating a framework for change. In R. L. Meth & R. S. Pasick (Eds.), *Men in therapy: The challenge of change* (pp. 131–151). New York: Guilford Press.

Allen, J. G., & Haccoun, S. M. (1976). Sex differences in emotionality: A multidimensional approach. *Human Relations, 29,* 711–722.

Amenson, C. S., & Lewinsohn, P. M. (1981). An investigation into the observed sex differences in prevalence of unipolar depression. *Journal of Abnormal Psychology, 90,* 1–13.

Andronico, M. P. (1996). *Men in groups: Insights, interventions, and psychoeducational work.* Washington, DC: American Psychological Association.

Berkowitz, A. D. (1991). Following imaginary peers: How norm misperceptions influence student substance abuse. In G. Lindsay & G. Rulf (Eds.), *Project direction* (Module No. 2). Muncie, IN: Ball State University.

Betcher, R. W., & Pollack, W. S. (1993). *In a time of fallen heroes: The re-creation of masculinity.* New York: Atheneum.

Bose, C. (1980). Social status of the homemaker. In S. F. Berk (Ed.), *Women and household labor* (pp. 69–87). Beverly Hills, CA: Sage.

Bowen, H. (1977). *Investment in learning: The individual and social value of American higher education.* San Francisco: Jossey-Bass.

Brehm, S. (1985). *Intimate relationships.* New York: Random House.

Brooks, G. (1996). Treatment for therapy-resistant men. In M. P. Andronico (Ed.), *Men in groups: Insights, interventions, and psychoeducational work* (pp. 7–19). Washington, DC: American Psychological Association.

Brooks, C. (1998). *A new psychotherapy for traditional men.* San Francisco: Jossey-Bass.

Canterbury, R. J., Gressard, C. F., & Vieweg, W.V.R. (1991). Alcohol abuse among college freshmen in Greek societies. *Virginia Medical Quarterly, 118*(3), 171–172.

Chandler, L. A., & Gallagher, R. P. (1996). Developing a taxonomy for problems seen at a university counseling center. *Measurement and Evaluation in Counseling and Development, 29*(1), 4–12.

Cheatham, H. E., Shelton, T. O., & Ray, W. J. (1987). Race, sex, causal attribution, and help-seeking behavior. *Journal of College Student Personnel, 28*(6), 559–568.

Chickering, A. (1969). *Education and identity.* San Francisco: Jossey-Bass.

Corey, S. (1936). Attitude differences between college classes: A summary and criticism. *Journal of Educational Psychology, 27,* 321–330.

David, D. S., & Brannon, D. (1976). *The forty-nine percent majority: The male sex role.* New York: Random House.

Dickstein, L. J., Stein, T. S., Pleck, J. H., & Myers, M. F. (1991). Men's changing social roles in the 1990s: Emerging issues in the psychiatric treatment of men. *Hospital and Community Psychiatry, 42*(7), 701–705.

Douglas, K. D., Collins, J. L., & Warren, C. (1997). Results from the 1995 National College Health Risk Behavior Survey. *Journal of American College Health, 46,* 55–66.

Eigen, L. D. (1991). *Alcohol practices, policies, and potentials of American college and universities: An Office for Substance Abuse Prevention White Paper.* Rockville, MD: U.S. Department of Health and Human Services, Alcohol, Drug Abuse, and Mental Health Administration.

Engs, R. C., & Hanson, D. J. (1988). University students' drinking patterns and problems: Examining the effects of raising the purchasing age. *Public Health Report, 103,* 667–673.

Feldman, K., & Newcomb, T. (1969). *The impact of college on students.* San Francisco: Jossey-Bass.

Funabiki, D., Bologna, N., Pepping, M., & Fitzgerald, K. (1980). Revisiting sex differences in the expression of depression. *Journal of Abnormal Psychology, 89,* 194–202.

Globetti, G., Stem, J. T., Marasco, F., & Haworth-Hoeppner, S. (1988). Student residence arrangements and alcohol use and abuse: A research note. *Journal of College and University Student Housing, 18*(1), 28–33.

Godin, S., Angevine, J., Asher, M., Clorez, S., Combs, B., Jacobson, S., Juskowski, R., & Miller, R. (1986). A psychoeducational prevention program for college radio stations. *Journal of College Student Personnel, 27,* 87–88.

Good, G., Dell, D., & Mintz, L. (1989). Male roles and gender-role conflict: Relationships to help-seeking in men. *Journal of Counseling Psychology, 3,* 295–300.

Good, G. E., & Mintz, L. B. (1990). Gender role conflict and depression in college men: Evidence for compounded risk. *Journal of Counseling and Development, 69,* 17–21.

Good, G. E., Robertson, J. M., O'Neil, J. M., Fitzgerald, L. F., Stevens, M., DeBord, K. A., & Bartels, K. M. (1995). Male gender role conflict: Psychometric issues and relations to psychological distress. *Journal of Counseling Psychology, 42*(1), 3–10.

Good, G. E., & Wood, P. K. (1995). Male gender role conflict, depression, and help seeking: Do men face double jeopardy? *Journal of Counseling and Development, 74*(1), 70–75.

Haines, M. P. (1998). Social norms: A wellness model for health promotion in higher education. *Newsletter of the National Wellness Association, 14*(4), 1, 8.

Heesacker, M., & Pritchard, S. (1992). In a different voice, revisited: Men, women, and emotion. *Journal of Mental Health Counseling, 14*(3), 274–290.

Heppner, P. P. (1995). On gender role conflict in men: Future directions and implications for counseling. *Journal of Counseling Psychology, 42*(1), 20–23.

Hurst, M. A. (1997). *The best fit in counseling men: Are there solutions to treating men as the problem?* Unpublished doctoral dissertation, Ball State University, Muncie, IN.

Jacob, P. (1957). *Changing values in college: An exploratory study of the impact of college teaching.* New York: Harper & Row.

Johnson, R., & Brock, D. (1988). Gender-specific therapy. *Journal of Psychology and Christianity, 7*(4), 50–60.

Johnston, L. D., O'Malley, P. M., & Bachman, J. G. (1997). *National survey results on drug use from the Monitoring the Future Study, 1975–1992: Vol. 2. College students and young adults* (NIH Publication No. 93–3598). Rockville, MD: National Institute on Drug Abuse.

Jolliff, D. L., & Horne, A. M. (1996). Group counseling for middle-class men. In M. P. Andronico (Ed.), *Men in groups: Insights, interventions, and psychoeducational work* (pp. 51–68). Washington, DC: American Psychological Association.

Kelly, K. R., & Hall, A. S. (1992). Toward a developmental model for counseling men. *Journal of Mental Health Counseling, 14*(3), 257–273.

Kilmartin, C. T. (1994). *The masculine self.* New York: Macmillan.

Kirk, B. A. (1973). Characteristics of users of counseling centers and psychiatric services on a college campus. *Journal of Counseling Psychology, 20,* 463–470.

Levant, R. (1990). Psychological services designed for men: A psychoeducational approach. *Psychotherapy, 27*(3), 309–315.

Long, D. (1987). Working with men who batter. In M. Sher, M. Stevens, G. Good, & G. A. Eichenfield (Eds.), *Handbook of counseling and psychotherapy with men* (pp. 306–320). Newbury Park, CA: Sage.

Lott, J. K., Ness, M. E., Alcorn, J. S., & Greer, R. M. (1999). The impact of gender and age on referrals to psychological counseling. *Journal of Counseling Psychology, 46*(1), 132–136.

Magoon, T. M. (1999). *College and university counseling center directors' 1998–1999 data bank: Analysis by enrollment.* (Available from Thomas M. Magoon, University of Maryland, College Park, MA 20742)

McKay, M., & Paleg, K. (1992). *Focal group psychotherapy.* Oakland, CA: New Harbinger.

McPhee, D. M. (1996). Techniques in group psychotherapy with men. In M. P. Andronico (Ed), *Men in groups: Insights, interventions, and psychoeducational work* (pp. 21–34). Washington, DC: American Psychological Association.

Meilman, P. W., Stone, J. E., Gaylor, M. S., & Turco, J. H. (1990). Alcohol use among undergraduates: Current use and 10-year trends. *Journal of Studies in Alcohol, 51,* 389–395.

Meth, R. L., & Pasick, R. S. (1990). *Men in therapy: The challenge of change.* New York: Guilford Press.

Nadler, A., Maler, S., & Friedman, A. (1984). Effects of helper's sex, subject's androgyny, and self-evaluation on males' and females' willingness to seek and receive help. *Sex Roles, 10,* 327, 339.

Newton, F. (1999). *Annual report of university counseling services.* (Available from University Counseling Services, 232 Lafene Student Health Center, Manhattan, KS 66503–3301).

Oliver, S. J., & Toner, B. B. (1990). The influence of gender role typing on the expression of depressive symptoms. *Sex Roles, 22,* 775–790.

O'Neil, J. M. (1981). Male sex role conflicts, sexism, and masculinity: Psychological implications for men, women, and the counseling psychologist. *Counseling Psychologist, 9*(2), 61–80.

Pascarella, E. T., & Terenzini, P. T. (1991). *How college affects students: Findings and insights from twenty years of research.* San Francisco: Jossey-Bass.

Perkins, H. W., & Berkowitz, A. D. (1986). Perceiving the community norms of alcohol use among students: Some research implications for alcohol education programming. *International Journal of the Addictions, 21,* 961–976.

Perry, W. (1970). *Forms of intellectual and ethical development in the college years: A scheme.* New York: Holt, Rinehart & Winston.

Pillemer, D. B., Krensky, L., Kleinman, S. N., & Goldsmith, L. R. (1991). Chapters in narratives: Evidence from oral histories of the first year in college. *Journal of Narrative and Life History, 1*(1), 3–14.

Pleck, J. H. (1987). *The myth of masculinity.* Cambridge, MA: MIT Press.

Plutchik, R. (1980). *Emotion: A psychoevolutionary synthesis.* New York: Harper & Row.

Pollack, W. S. (1995). Deconstructing dis-identification: Rethinking psychoanalytic concepts of male development. *Psychoanalysis and Psychotherapy, 12*(1), 30–45.

Prendergast, M. L. (1994). Substance use and abuse among college students: A review of recent literature. *College Health, 43,* 99–113.

Presley, C. A., & Meilman, P. W. (1992). *Alcohol and drugs on American college campuses: A report of college presidents.* Carbondale: Southern Illinois University, Student Health Program Wellness Center.

Presley, C. A., Meilman, P. W., Cashin, J. R., & Lyeria, R. (1996). *Alcohol and drugs on American college campuses: Use, consequences, and perceptions of the campus environment: Vol. 4. 1992–1994.* Carbondale: Southern Illinois University.

Prosser-Gelwick, B., & Garni, K. F. (1988). *Counseling and psychotherapy with college men. Changing roles for men on campus.* New Directions for Student Services, No. 42. San Francisco: Jossey Bass.

Real, T. (1997). I don't want to talk about it: Overcoming the legacy of male depression. New York: Scribner.

Robertson, J. M., & Fitzgerald, L. (1990). The (mis)treatment of men: Effects of client gender role and life-style on diagnosis and attribution of pathology. *Journal of Counseling Psychology, 37*(1), 3–9.

Robertson, J. M., & Fitzgerald, L. F. (1992). Overcoming the masculine mystique: Preferences for alternative forms of assistance among men who avoid counseling. *Journal of Counseling Psychology, 39*(2), 240–246.

Robertson, J. M., & Freeman, R. (1995). Men and emotions: Developing masculine-congruent views of affective expressiveness. *Journal of College Student Development, 36*(6), 606, 607.

Robertson, J. M., & Verschelden, C. (1993). Voluntary male homemakers and female providers: Reported experiences and perceived social reactions. *Journal of Men's Studies, 1*(4), 383–402.

Robertson, M. F. (1988). Differential use by male and female students of the counseling service of an Australian tertiary college: Implications for service design and counseling models. *International Journal of the Advancement of Counseling, 11,* 231–240.

Robins, L. N., Heltzer, J. E., Weissman, M. M., Orraschel, H., Gruenberg, E., Burke, J. D., & Reiger, D. A. (1984). Lifetime prevalence of specific psychiatric disorders in three sites. *Archives of General Psychiatry, 41,* 949–958.

Sher, M. (1990). Effect of gender role incongruities on men's experience as clients in psycho-therapy. *Psychotherapy, 27*(3), 322–326.

Shueman, S. A., & Medvene, A. M. (1981). Student perceptions of appropriateness of presenting problems: What's happened to attitudes in 20 years? *Journal of College Student Personnel, 22,* 264–267.

Sipps, G. J., & Janeczek, R. G. (1986). Expectancies for counselors in relation to subject gender traits. *Journal of Counseling Psychology, 33*(2), 214–216.

Stevens, M. A. (1998). *Men's health team at the University of Southern California.* Symposium conducted at the meeting of the American Psychological Association, San Francisco.

Survey results summary for University Counseling Services. (1997). Unpublished manuscript, Kansas State University, Manhattan.

U.S. Department of Commerce, Bureau of the Census. (1992). *Current Populations Reports, Series P-20, No. 458, Household and family characteristics: March, 1991.* Washington, DC: U.S. Government Printing Office.

U.S. Department of Health and Human Services, National Center for Health Statistics. (1992, January 7). *Monthly Vital Statistics Report, 40* (Suppl. 2).

Van Haveren, R. A., Blank, W. J., & Bentley, K. W. (1999). *Lafeneline: Promoting sexual health through college radio.* Manuscript submitted for publication. (Available from Rick Van Haveren, Counseling Center, Georgia State University, Atlanta, GA 30303)

Vessey, J. T., & Howard, K. I. (1993). Who seeks psychotherapy? *Psychotherapy, 30,* 546–553.

Wechsler, H., Dowdall, G. W., Maenner, G., Gledhill-Hoyt, J., & Lee, H. (1998). Changes in binge drinking and related problems among American college students between 1993 and 1997: Results of the Harvard School of Public Health College Alcohol Study. *College Health, 47,* 57–67.

Wechsler, H., & Isaac, N. (1991). *Alcohol and the college freshman: Binge drinking and associated problems. A report to the AAA Foundation for Traffic Safety.* Boston: Harvard School of Public Health, Youth Alcohol-Drug Program.

Wendt, K. F., & Johnston, P. G. (1987). "60 seconds to think about": Radio announcements for college counseling centers. *Journal of College Student Personnel, 28,* 91–92.

Werner, M. J., & Greene, J. W. (1992). Problem drinking among college freshmen. *Journal of Adolescent Health Care, 13*(6), 487–492.

Wiggins, J. A., & Wiggins, B. B. (1987). Drinking at a southern university: Its description and correlates. *Journal of Studies in Alcohol, 48*(4), 319–324.

Wilcox, D. W., & Forrest, L. (1992). The problems of men and counseling: Gender bias or gender truth? *Journal of Mental Health Counseling, 14*(3), 291–304.

Wisch, A. F., Mahalik, R., Jr., Hayes, J. A., & Nutt, E. D. (1995). The impact of gender role conflict and counseling technique on psychological help-seeking in men. *Sex Roles, 33*(1–2), 77–89.

CHAPTER FIVE

Issues of Males with Physical Disabilities in Rehabilitation Settings

Irmo D. Marini

The impact of a sudden traumatic disability to any individual often has profound and lasting implications in relation to his or her socialization, employment outlook, and basic independent functioning. Research findings pertaining to the psychosocial adjustment of persons who sustain a paralyzing trauma such as spinal cord injury, myocardial infarction, or stroke generally describe stages of adjustment (Livneh, 1991b; Shontz, 1975) or an ongoing recurrent model of adaptation (Kendall & Buys, 1998). Although statistically these specific disabilities are sustained more often by males (for example, 80 percent of all spinal cord injuries affect men), there is scant focus on the particular disability-related issues of what males endure. Before exploring the psychosocial adjustment issues for males with severe physical disabilities and subsequent therapeutic treatment strategies, I would like to share my own experience sustaining a disability.

A PERSONAL ACCOUNT OF DISABILITY

On February 10, 1981, while playing in a varsity hockey game for Lakehead University in Thunder Bay, Ontario, Canada, I was propelled headfirst into the end boards, immediately rendering me with C5 tetraplegia at age twenty-three, paralyzed from the chest down. My entire life drastically changed within the blink of an eye. During the ensuing three weeks, I lay in traction without the ability to feed myself, move my head, or tend to my own hygiene needs. I was then flown one thousand miles from home to Toronto, Ontario, with the comforting support of my girlfriend and younger sister at my side. While in Toronto, I underwent surgery to fuse and stabilize the vertebrae in my neck. The operation went well; however, my lung collapsed the following evening. I went into cardiac arrest and after my resuscitation was placed on a respirator, where I remained for the next thirty days. During this time, I was fed through a tube, could not speak, had a halo vest screwed into my skull to immobilize my head and neck, and lost forty-five pounds of muscle I had worked hard to develop from body building since age twelve. After three months of being confined to a bed, I sat up for the first time and was wheeled in front of a mirror. I was devastated by my rapid loss of muscle mass after eleven years of body building. It had all been erased in ninety days. Up until this point, I had denied the severity and permanency of my injury despite my physician's prognosis that I would not be able to walk again. The reality of my situation left me despondent and depressed. The multitude of questions that had been racing through my head were more pronounced now than ever. Would I be able to have sex and father a child? Would I be able to work or was I to collect disability for the rest of my life? How would others relate to me? How often would I be sick and rehospitalized? Would I have to live in a nursing home? Who would take care of me? How could I replace my interest and love of playing sports? What was I going to do now that I was no longer able to do anything?

On December 6, 1981, after ten months of acute hospitalization and rehabilitation, I returned home with my girlfriend Darlene. The oddity of returning home in a wheelchair and seeing people who had last seen me standing or going to local places where I used to play hockey or golf left me with a surreal feeling. Being out in the community in a wheelchair and seeing firsthand just how inaccessible and segregating certain places were was frustrating and disheartening and a reminder that I was now disabled. Some friends and acquaintances who once enjoyed my company now appeared visibly uncomfortable in my presence. Strangers sometimes pitied me or offered me assistance when I did not ask for it. A year or more after the injury, some people still responded to me as though I were depressed . . . or should be. I suppose they rationalized that if this type of thing had happened to them, they would surely be depressed and perhaps suicidal. However, because I seemed to be OK and was going back to school, well, then, I was admired for being so strong and courageous. I began to resent the fact that society expected me to act a certain way with this disability (for example, helpless and dependent), and I began to think about how I was going to bring back some manhood and dignity to my life.

Now, nineteen years after the injury and having counseled numerous persons with severe physical disabilities, I am better able to understand some of the issues I went through and better able to appreciate some of the same issues my male clients face with their disabilities. Many of my initial fears and worries, however, have passed. Since earning my master's degree in clinical psychology in 1985, I have always been employed and subsequently earned a Ph.D. in rehabilitation in 1992. Today, I am a professor and coordinate a graduate program in rehabilitation counseling. My once girlfriend Darlene has been my wife since 1982, and we feel closer than most couples we know because of the experience we both endured. Although I have been physically capable of having sex since my injury, Darlene and I elected not to have children because of ejaculatory problems. I also have never been rehospitalized or become seriously ill since my injury, and I retain the same personality and attitude toward living that I once had. Overall, to some degree, one's disability is only as severe as one makes it.

The purpose of this chapter is to explore the unique experience of males who sustain a sudden traumatic physical disability, with a focus on the multitude of issues they may present during the acute rehabilitation phase. To fully appreciate the possible origins of these issues, I address several relevant dynamics. From a sociological perspective, I discuss societal views of masculinity and what it means to be male in Western society. Relatedly, I examine empirical findings regarding societal views and attitudes toward persons with disabilities. This examination is followed by a discussion of the impact of disability on male masculinity. I next review psychological adjustment to traumatic physical disability, with primary attention given to stage versus recurrent models of adjustment. Finally, I discuss some of the unique concerns and reactions males present in rehabilitation settings and recommend therapeutic and counseling points of discussion for male patients.

SOCIETAL VIEWS OF MASCULINITY

The concept of masculinity and masculine traits is well documented elsewhere and is only briefly addressed here (Bem, 1974, 1993; Brannon, 1976; Gerschick & Miller, 1995, 1997; Herek, 1986; Sprecher & Sedikides, 1993; Tepper, 1997; Zilbergeld, 1992). Zilbergeld (1992) claims that by age seven, most lessons about male socialization have been learned. He and earlier researchers have defined masculinity and masculine behavior as reflecting a cluster of male competency traits including strong, self-reliant, successful, having sexual interest and prowess, active, independent, tough, not prone to tears, aggressive, dominant, stoic, persistent, self-confident, athletic, assertive, and unexpressive of emotions (Bem, 1974; Herek, 1986; Spence, Helmreich, & Stapp, 1974).

The origin of gender-polarized traits is conditioned or programmed from various societal influences as projected by culture, the media, family influences, and religion. The North American culture embraces the "body beautiful" concept that focuses on youth, health, physical or personal appearance, athletic prowess, and wholeness (Roessler & Rubin, 1982; Wright, 1983; Zilbergeld, 1992). Television and movies portray successful persons as having many of the successful traits described.

Several empirical studies lend support to the notion of masculinity traits. Sprecher and Sedikides (1993) found that men express less emotion than women in close relationships, which the authors attribute to male social role expectations of self-control, toughness, and autonomy. These authors concluded that men have problems asking for support and responding to such questions as "How do you feel?" Relatedly, Belle (1987) found that, compared with women, men tend to provide and receive less social support and are less likely to seek social support. Other researchers have noted that many males do not seek social support because doing so signifies weakness and dependence or they find self-disclosure to be inversely related to trait masculinity (Butler, Giordano, & Neren, 1985; Winstead, Derlega, & Wong, 1984). As I describe in more detail later in this chapter, when a male incurs a severely disabling condition, his identity becomes conflicted because of the virtual loss of all of his perceived masculine traits.

SOCIETAL ATTITUDES TOWARD DISABILITY

Having reviewed the masculine traits typically used to describe the "real" man in Western society, I turn now to a brief review of traditional societal views toward persons with disabilities. There are a plethora of empirical and theoretical studies relating to the investigation of attitudes toward persons with disabilities (Anthony, 1972; Belgrave, 1984; Belgrave & Mills, 1981; Comer & Piliavin, 1975; Donaldson, 1980; English, 1971; Evans, 1976; Fichten, Robillard, Tagalakis, & Amsel, 1991; Marini, 1992; Yuker, 1988). Chubon (1982), however, in a critical review of the literature regarding attitudes toward disablement, found that only 60 of 102 studies reviewed were empirical in nature. The remaining studies were conceptual, with little or no empirical basis.

In the 1991 Lou Harris poll of one thousand able-bodied Americans concerning their attitudes toward persons with disabilities, results indicated that persons with disabilities are generally thought of as objects of pity or admiration and perceived to be fundamentally different from nondisabled persons (Harris, 1991). Lyons (1991) adds that our society perceives persons with disabilities as helpless, incapable, and inferior. Gething (1991) notes how societal attitudes can affect how people react toward a perceived minority.

These perceptions can subsequently affect the quality of life, opportunities, and extent to which members of the stigmatized group can reach their potential.

Numerous studies have explored whether the sentiment Western society has toward persons with disabilities is positive, negative, or simply ambivalent (English, 1971; Evans, 1976; Havranek, 1991; Makas, 1988; Marini, 1992; Wright, 1960; Yuker, 1988). The answers to such questions are, however, much too complex for any one researcher to make global generalizations from. In his extensive literature review on attitudes toward disability, Yuker (1988) noted that of the studies pertaining to contact and disability, 51 percent showed a positive attitude change, 31 percent were inconclusive, and 10 percent reported a more negative attitude resulting from contact.

The literature indicates that many nondisabled persons become anxious or tense because they do not know what to say or how to behave around someone with a disability (Albrecht, Walker, & Levy, 1982; Belgrave & Mills, 1981; Evans, 1976; Marinelli & Kelz, 1973; Yuker, 1988). Albrecht et al. (1982) found that 83 percent of their nondisabled sample reported that ambiguity or uncertainty in not knowing how to behave was the major reason for social avoidance of persons with disabilities. The Harris (1991) poll confirms this sentiment; nondisabled Americans report feeling awkward around persons with disabilities. However, the same poll also suggests that previous positive familiarity with a person with a disability creates more favorable attitudes.

Another factor related to contact pertains to what Donaldson (1980) refers to as "equal status" of the person with a disability. Specifically, the likelihood of a positive attitude change toward disability increases when the person with a disability possesses a similar education, socioeconomic status, and vocational status and is roughly the same age as the nondisabled person.

Livneh (1991a) classified the origins of negative attitudes toward disability into thirteen categories: (1) psychodynamic mechanisms, (2) childhood influences, (3) aesthetic aversion, (4) minority group comparability, (5) sociocultural conditioning, (6) punishment for sin, (7) disability as a reminder of death, (8) prejudice-inviting behaviors of persons with disability, (9) threats to body image integrity, (10) anxiety-provoking unstructured situations, (11) disability-related factors associated with negative perceptions (for example, functional or organic causality, level of severity, and visibility), (12) demographic factors (for example, sex, age, socioeconomic status, and educational attainment), and (13) personality variables associated with attitudes. Each origin is empirically or theoretically supported in the literature. Although it is beyond the scope of this chapter to fully address all the origins of negative attitudes, I address two.

Dembo, Leviton, and Wright (1975) describe "psychodynamic mechanisms" as pertaining to societal beliefs that if a person does not feel badly about the disability, he or she must be in denial. This expectation of having to mourn the loss poses a problem for males, who typically attempt to hide their emotions (Bem, 1993). A related mechanism, the spread phenomenon, refers to society's belief that a disability affecting one aspect of an individual (that is, paralysis) spreads and affects all other aspects such as mental abilities and emotional stability. This belief, of course, becomes problematic for males who want to return to work and are perceived by employers as being incapable both mentally and physically of performing the job.

The concept of "anxiety-provoking situations" refers to the body of literature examining the anxiety nondisabled persons feel when interacting with someone with a disability (Albrecht et al., 1982; Cloerkes, 1981; Kleck, 1968; Marinelli & Kelz, 1973). Findings suggest that in novel encounters with visibly disabled persons, nondisabled persons fear saying something that may upset the person with a disability (for example, telling a wheelchair user you enjoy jogging, then realizing he or she cannot walk and therefore may become upset). Marini (1992) noted that nondisabled persons cognitively weigh the pros and cons of a possible interaction with someone who is disabled and decide the anticipatory anxiety and discomfort over having to guard what one should or should not say ultimately leads to avoidance.

Such findings begin to describe the potential fears, insecurities, and related difficulties some males with disabilities may feel in their attempts to attract a partner. It does not take a trained observer to notice when one is being ignored or avoided. Men with disabilities will begin to question their sexual prowess and may lose self-esteem if others continually avoid them at social gatherings. Marini (1992) and others note that it therefore becomes critical for the individual with a disability to be able to develop the social skills and strategies to be able to quickly place others at ease and convey an "I'm-OK-with-my-disability" type of attitude (Evans, 1976).

Overall, societal views of disability are somewhat similar to attitudes reserved for other minority groups. Specific to disability, however, are popular sentiments of either pity or admiration and perceptions of those with disabilities as being sick, incapable, and needing to be cared for. When surveyed, those without disabilities claim to feel awkward and anxious around persons with disabilities. These factors begin to set the stage for the identity crisis males experience after sustaining a severe physical disability.

DISABILITY IMPACT ON MASCULINITY

The assault of a physical disability on a man's sense of masculinity compromises virtually all of the traits typified by society for the male gender. Two sets of social dynamics men struggle with are, on the one hand, dealing with pressures of being masculine, while, on the other hand, trying to disprove society's perception of them as passive, dependent, pitiful, sick, and incapable (Gerschick & Miller, 1995, 1997).

From her interviews of men with chronic disabilities, Charmaz (1995) found that some males attempt to preserve aspects of there predisability selves by maintaining qualities or attributes that previously defined their self-concept. As they come to adapt to their disability, males "preserve self" by limiting the impact of the disability in their daily lives and develop strategies to minimize the limiting aspects of the disability.

Charmaz (1995) found that other males with disabilities attempt to "recapture" all aspects of their past selves by ignoring their limitations. When these men realize it is not possible to ignore their disabilities, they become despondent and depressed. Wright (1983) defines this approach as "as-if" behavior, whereby an individual denies his or her limitations by acting as if he or she does not have a disability.

Finally, Charmaz found that still other males with disabilities attempt to preserve their public predisability identity and conceal their private disability identity. These males strive to preserve the same strong public persona as they had in the past but privately at home maximize the sick, dependent role. It is important for these men to maintain their masculine image outwardly to the public. This type of male is illustrated in Hugh Gallagher's (1994) book, *FDR's Splendid Deception*. Gallagher describes President Roosevelt, who was born with polio, as having totally denied his disability, never speaking to anyone including his wife and mother about his disability. Roosevelt was adamant about never being filmed or photographed in public with his leg braces on or while sitting in his wheelchair. He feared he would be perceived as a weak and incapable leader if the public ever learned of his secret.

Gerschick and Miller (1995) conducted ten in-depth interviews using an analytic induction approach with men who sustained either paraplegia or tetraplegia (Katz, 1988). They noted three patterns of coping that interviewees with disabilities used in dealing with the dominant masculinity standards. The first pattern, reformulation, characterized males who redefined idealized masculine traits to conform to their new abilities. Males who needed a personal attendant to assist in performing activities of daily living (for example, grooming and dressing) still viewed themselves as independent because they controlled the actions of the personal attendant. They also defined the term *self-reliant* as meaning earning capacity and the ability to work and support oneself.

The second pattern of coping, defined as reliance, characterized those males who relied heavily on the masculine ideals of strength, independence, and sexual prowess. These males were deeply bothered by the fact that they could not live up to their ideals. Some attempted to function independently even when they needed assistance and refused to ask for help. Others became involved in risk-taking behavior or played wheelchair sports to remain competitive, and still others viewed wheelchair sports as not being the "real" thing and therefore did not participate.

The third pattern of coping Gerschick and Miller (1995, 1997) described was rejection of the masculine ideals. This group of men with disabilities rejected the traditional notion of what made the "real" man. They tended to create an alternative masculine identity, identifying themselves as "persons," and believed that mental ability was superior to physical strength. In all cases, those in this group attempted to come to terms with their disability in different ways.

There are essentially two views as to how individuals adjust or adapt to traumatic disability. The first is the stage model of adjustment, in which an individual progresses through a series of stages over time, and the second is the recurrent adjustment model, which asserts that individuals gradually become less distressed over time with adjustment being ongoing, experiencing periodic times of sorrow or despair.

STAGE MODEL OF ADJUSTMENT

In any stage model of adaptation to loss, there are certain consistently reported observations of which to be aware. First, adjustment to a traumatic disability is a dynamic and not a static process (Kahana, Fairchild, & Kahana, 1982). An individual may experience a regression in stages, progress through one stage only to revert back again later, or skip a stage altogether. Second, there is no predetermined time limit for any one stage or stages, and not all persons go through all stages. Third, some persons may never reach what might be considered an end stage and essentially become "stuck" at an earlier phase. Fourth, each defined stage carries with it certain behavioral, emotional, and cognitive correlates indicative of that stage. Finally, involvement in various stages is usually temporary and transitional in nature (Livneh, 1991b). After reviewing more then forty different stage of adjustment models, Livneh (1991b) synthesized five distinct stages, which I briefly outline in the following sections.

Initial Impact

In relation to the time the traumatic injury occurs, the period of initial impact generally involves immense anxiety and shock immediately following the bodily insult and may last for hours, days, or even weeks. During this period, the injured person (if alert) and his or her family often psychologically deal with the catastrophe using an "emotion-focused" coping response (Lazarus & Folkman, 1984). Emotion-focused coping allows affected individuals to deal with the incapacitating anxiety and stress by maintaining hope and keeping up morale through prayer. During such periods, the shock persons experience often impairs the ability to concentrate, problem solve, or make rational decisions. Interestingly, this idea is in contrast to findings by Stone and Neale (1984), who suggest that males tend to use problem-solving coping strategies more often than do women.

Defense Mobilization

Bargaining and denial are the two major components of the next stage, defense mobilization (Livneh, 1991b). Once the injured loved one is off the critical list, the situation may become awkward when the family and injured person begin to hope and pray for full recovery. Bargaining is perhaps a focal spiritual time period when the injured person and his or her family offer some trade-off to a higher power for complete recovery. Throughout this process, there often remains a strong wall of denial in the person injured, but the family may slowly begin to realize and reluctantly accept the imminent situation. Denial continues from the initial impact stage and occurs concomitantly with bargaining, except now the focus of denial involves healing the disability and complete recovery. It is not denying so much the injury itself but rather the permanency of its disabling effect.

Initial Realization

Mourning of the loss, possible reactive depression, and internalized anger over one's situation primarily mark the stage of initial realization. At this stage the injured person begins to fully realize the implications of his or her injury. Livneh (1991b) describes mourning (grief) as being short-lived, with a focus on the loss of a body part and past lifestyle. The reactive depression, when it occurs, tends to be longer in duration, with a focus on the consequences of the disability. Although it is generally believed that everyone mourns loss in some way, there are conflicting study findings as to whether depression is always involved (Trieschmann, 1988). Nevertheless, a traumatic, severe disability often leaves the injured person with thoughts of hopelessness and helplessness, feelings of despair and sadness, and a desire to initially avoid social contact. Also sometimes evident at this stage is internalized anger (Livneh, 1991b), marked by feelings of self-blame and guilt over what has happened. The individual searches and often finds reasons (no matter how insignificant) as to why God has justifiably punished him or her (Hohmann, 1975). Suicidal ideation and verbalizations are also common at this stage.

Retaliation

During the retaliation stage, the injured person turns his or her anger and frustration outward, sometimes lashing out at significant others and medical staff. He or she begins to displace blame for the injury away from the self and may direct fault to medical personnel perceived as incompetent, persons related to the accident itself, or God, with overt behavioral outbursts. A less overt sign of rebellion is not cooperating with the prescribed treatment regimen for rehabilitation. The patient may demand special privileges, test hospital rules, or manipulate others.

Reintegration

Livneh (1991b) subdivides this final stage into three successive substages. The first is that of acknowledgment, in which the injured person is able to realize the final implications of his or her situation. The perceived impact on social, vocational, and familial roles is met with some trepidation. Acceptance is described as the second of three substages. It is an affective assimilation of the disability and the development of a new emotional self-concept. At this stage, the individual feels that it is essentially OK to be disabled despite the inherent societally imposed attitude barriers of having a disability. Final adjustment represents the last stage. This stage is characterized by a person who feels positive, confident, and content about his or her capabilities (Shontz, 1975). The client knows his or her limitations but focuses on remaining or new strengths.

RECURRENT ADJUSTMENT MODEL

The other model of adjustment is referred to as the recurrent adjustment model of disability. B. H. Davis (1987) and others have argued that although stage models of adjustment describe the linear progression of adjusting, they do not account for the ongoing, recurrent nature of adjustment over time. The recurrent adjustment model accounts for the ongoing, reemerging periods of sorrow or despair persons with traumatic disabilities experience (Kendall & Buys, 1998). It is based on Beck and Weishaar's (1989) cognitive theory concept of cognitive schemata development. Cognitive schemata are our beliefs and assumptions of self, others, and how our environment works.

After an injury, an individual attempts to continue working from his or her preinjury schemata. Wright (1983) refers to this approach as the "as-if" behavior noted earlier. When these older schemata no longer work, the individual may experience anxiety, helplessness, hopelessness, and despair. As time goes on, the individual begins to gradually develop new schemata to function in the environment with the disability. Modification of new schemata is guided by three themes: (1) the search for meaning in this new life with a disability; (2) the need for mastery and control over the disability, environment, and one's future; and (3) the effort to protect and enhance the disability. Development of new schemata can be positive ("I can do this") or negative ("I'm a failure"), and individuals often fluctuate in their adjustment over time, analogous to a pendulum that gradually slows to center (Kendall & Buys, 1998).

MALE ISSUES IN REHABILITATION SETTINGS

Regardless of which adjustment theory one subscribes to, it is clear that persons who sustain a severe physical disability must deal with bodily function changes and with immediate and drastic changes to their past lifestyles. When a physical disability is sustained, both genders are immediately thrust into minority group status. As Gerschick and Miller (1997) indicate, men with disabilities are marginalized and stigmatized in American society. The connotations of disability in Western society are in stark contrast with societal views as to what defines a "real" man in America.

The majority of issues men experience when faced with a disabling injury most often relate either directly or indirectly to losses of their masculine identity traits. Males are unfortunately placed in a paradoxical situation when injury occurs. As Zilbergeld (1992) explains, even though men with traumatic disabilities have numerous fears and concerns, they often feel the need to conceal them and not express their despair because of the perception that revealing emotions would further diminish their manhood. Some males continue to project a stoic, tough, no-sissy-stuff, no-crying demeanor while inwardly attempting to deal with numerous concerns and fears on their own. In these situations, therapists have to initiate common topics of concern such as sexuality, employability issues, finances, feelings of helplessness and dependence, and patients' inability to express fear and frustration.

Life-Cycle Development Issues

The issues males present in an acute rehabilitation setting vary depending on their age. Although there is some overlap of concerns regardless of the age at which the injury is sustained, different stages of life bring somewhat different priorities of concern for the involved male. Teenage males who sustain a physical disability, for example, have several primary concerns. During a period when they are beginning sexual experimentation, preparing for college or work, and contemplating moving out on their own to test their independence, the impact of a severe disability temporarily or permanently compromises all these desires.

Simmons and Rosenberg (1975) found that adolescents are more concerned about changes to their physical appearance than they are about changes to any other aspect of themselves. Older adolescents are typically concerned with developing intimate relationships, dating, having sex, and bonding with their peer group (S. E. Davis, Anderson, Linkowski, Berger, & Feinstein, 1991). Several researchers have found that adolescents with disabilities expressed great concern about their social relationships, were fearful of rejection, and expressed loneliness and a sense of isolation (Blum, 1983; Minde, 1978). Because adolescence is also a time when males participate in sports and go out often, adolescent males with a physical disability are often forgotten or unable to participate in these activities, thus creating the sense of isolation noted earlier. Adolescent males may also encounter difficulties in developing vocational maturity (Brolin, 1980). Not knowing one's present abilities and not being sure of one's future ability to earn a living are additional areas of concern, especially with societal pressures for males to be breadwinners. The inability to make a living affects other issues such as ability to attract a mate, quality of life, and where and how one will live.

For males sustaining a disability in early adulthood or midlife, major concerns include career constraints, sexuality, and family role (Power, Hershenson, & Schlossberg, 1991). Depending on the severity of the disability, husbands may face reversal of traditional gender roles, in which they are no longer the independent, strong, breadwinning head of the household but rather a dependent, unemployed, insecure, and anxious person who requires personal assistance to complete simple everyday tasks. Anxiety and fear over how one will support one's family are primary concerns, as are deep-seated fears of abandonment by the spouse.

Sexuality Issues

Tepper (1997) disclosed his experience as a twenty-year-old male with tetraplegia. Although his major concerns focused on his sexual capabilities and ability to father a child, he found that the medical staff would not acknowledge his sex concerns. Indeed, research indicates that many medical professionals feel uncomfortable in discussing sex with patients. Gill (1988) discovered that although 79 percent of the rehabilitation staff in a Boston hospital stated that sexual adjustment was important to patients' recovery, only 9 percent reported feeling comfortable discussing these issues with patients. Of this sample, 51 percent reported they would discuss the topic only if the patient initiated the conversation.

Zilbergeld (1992) cited the many myths Western society has regarding male sex performance and sexuality. Sentiments such as "a real man isn't into the sissy stuff like feelings and communicating" (p. 44), "all touching is sexual and should lead to sex" (p. 45), "a man is always interested in and always ready for sex" (p. 47), "a real man performs in sex" (p. 48), "good sex requires orgasm" (p. 55), and "good sex is spontaneous with no planning and no talking" (p. 59) all perpetuate the myth. Males who attempt to conform to such pressures ultimately will have many questions regarding their sexuality.

Tepper (1997) states that treatment for males with physical disabilities should include medical staff–initiated questions and education regarding the physiological changes in sex function with a spinal cord injury. It should also include dispelling sexual myths and education on positioning, establishing sexual relationships, dating issues, and fathering. Milligan and Neufeldt (1998) found that the major concern for males with spinal cord injuries related to their capacity to succeed in present or future intimate relationships, sexual performance concerns, sexual identity, and others' perceptions of them as asexual. Overall, sexuality is a primary issue for males of all ages who have sustained physical disabilities.

Dealing with Humility and Helplessness

As a practitioner and someone with a severe physical disability, I have experienced and observed other males also struggle with the frustration of having to relearn basic activities we typically learn at age four such as relearning how to dress, eat, brush, write, and deal with the loss of bowel and bladder functions. As previously noted, because males are socialized not to express their feelings and because they must already depend on medical staff and family for physical assistance, many men perceive that it would be even more embarrassing and burdensome to then admit to having psychological problems. To suddenly and forcibly relinquish being independent, autonomous, self-reliant, dominant, and in control becomes overwhelming for many males, but that they are overwhelmed often remains their best-kept secret. It is a humbling experience that virtually all humans ultimately will grieve and may or may not become clinically depressed over (Trieschmann, 1988). Grief is related to loss of body function as well as loss of previous lifestyle and may last several weeks or months.

With a sense of helplessness may come an almost intolerable boredom due to the sudden and abrupt loss of a previously active lifestyle. A typical day in therapy rotates between physical therapy (muscle strengthening) and occupational therapy (relearning basic activities). If weekend home visits or recreational outings are nonexistent during treatment, an individual may begin to slip into depression.

RECOMMENDATIONS FOR THERAPISTS

The issues men face after sustaining a debilitating, permanent physical injury challenge the very essence of their male identity and often create an identity crisis. Because gender role expectations for males include not expressing emotions, many men continue to convey an outwardly stoic front of toughness while inwardly struggling with numerous unresolved issues. In Western society, "real" men are perceived as tough, independent, stoic, athletic, self-reliant, self-confident, strong, and in control. Conversely, persons with disabilities are viewed as passive, pitiful, incapable, dependent, and needing to be cared for. An obvious contradiction and paradox exists for males who become disabled.

The primary issue for males with disabilities in rehabilitation settings is sexuality and reproductive in nature and includes perceived loss of sexual prowess, sexual performance fears, concerns about the ability to father a child, fears about the ability to attract a mate, and loss of ability for spontaneous sex. A second major issue pertains to loss of control of bodily functions and to the surrounding medical environment because patients have to comply with hospital rules and are passive recipients of services. A third issue males may struggle with relates to finances and future employability. Concerns revolve around the ability to financially support family, job alternatives and marketability, perceived employer discrimination, and perceived social status as a poor, unemployed person with a disability. Such issues contradict the male identity of self-reliance, success, and independence. A final major issue relates to the immense frustration of having to relearn basic human functions we generally acquire by age four. Having been previously strong and independent, many males may struggle with childlike feelings of dependency and perceive having to ask for assistance to complete the simplest of tasks as embarrassing and shameful. I discuss specific counseling strategies to deal with these issues in the following sections.

Cognitive Reframing of Societal Views of Disability

The first recommendation is that therapists have a thorough understanding of Western societal views of masculinity and disability. This knowledge base provides for a solid framework and foundation from which to work. Many clients harbor some unresolved issues relating to the contradiction between masculinity and disability. As noted in the recurrent model of adjustment, many males initially strive to hold on to their preinjury schemata as if they do not have a disability (Kendall & Buys, 1998; Wright, 1983). As injured individuals continue to realize that these old schemata no longer work, they may experience anxiety and helplessness. Therapists should assist clients to reframe old schemata and build new schemata to function in the environment with the disability. Kendall and Buys (1998) recommend modifying or reframing positive new schemata around three themes: (1) the search for meaning in this new life with a disability; (2) the need for mastery and control over the disability, the environment, and one's future; and (3) the effort to protect and enhance the disability. Developing a can-do attitude while offering practical suggestions to make positive changes relative to these three themes becomes important (Kendall & Buys, 1998). For example, in working with the need to master or control one's environment, discussions centering on gaining independence in the home, in the community, or at work may include purchasing adaptive driving equipment, employing personal care attendants, furthering one's education to enhance employment marketability, and taking an assertiveness-training course.

Another aspect to cognitive reframing relates to Albert Ellis's (1973) rational emotive therapy and challenging clients' irrational beliefs that their future is predetermined. Clients who are not depressed but rather despondent and feeling hopeless or helpless about their situation could be questioned about what they believe their future holds. Those who feel their life is over should be tactfully challenged about what proof they have regarding their assertion. Therapists should be prepared beforehand, however, to back up their own arguments that an individual's life is not over. For example, persons with paraplegia who believe they will never work, marry, or have children should be shown examples of persons with paraplegia who have accomplished these activities.

The appropriate use of humor in certain instances can also be quite effective in assisting clients to view their situation from a different perspective. Again, therapists can be challenged by clients who are not clinically depressed but who make self-deprecating statements such as "Who will want me like this?" The cognitive technique of paradoxical intent described by Frankl (1967) can be effective when clients unwittingly feed their negative self-talk about their being unattractive to a potential mate. If a therapist's best attempts to convince a client that he is still attractive fail, the therapist may consider paradoxical intent. With this technique, for example, the therapist may finally agree with the client and attest as to just how ugly the client really is. The therapist might then proceed further and ask the client to exaggerate his "ugliness" by hunching over, moaning, and acting like a monster. At some point, the client will begin to see that he is really not as unattractive as the therapist claims he is and perhaps begin to view his situation from a more positive or lighter perspective. The therapist could then proceed to discuss concrete ways the client could improve his self-image (for example, by dress, hygiene, and social skills).

Initiating Talking Points with Clients

A second suggestion relates to the idea that therapists will likely have to initiate discussions regarding the issues noted earlier. For resistant clients who continue to assert that everything is fine, therapists must differentiate denial from masking what one really feels. Livneh's (1991b) five-stage adjustment theory holds that denial is common during the defense mobilization stage. If, however, clients know the implications of their situations but still claim everything is OK, therapists should begin to initiate talking points with the clients. Therapists should openly address the notion of clients not wanting to burden others with their problems so as to grant clients permission to do so. Because they know many of the most commonly cited concerns for males with severe disabilities, therapists can touch on each concern and gauge their clients' responses to various topics such as sex, abandonment, health, career, financial, and other issues. If clients see that therapists already know and empathize with the fear and anxiety they are feeling over these issues, clients may begin to open up and discuss their worries and perhaps experience their first catharsis.

In empowering clients to finally talk about their fears, therapists are better able to assist clients in problem-solving approaches geared toward alleviating uncertainties and developing strategies to concretely do something about their fears. Clients who cannot return to a former physical labor job and are concerned about how they will support their family can be assisted in exploring advanced education or specialized training for sedentary jobs that pay well. Relatedly, concerns about sexuality might be addressed by exploring the myths and misconceptions of male performance and methods for enhancing performance (for example, medications and implants).

Addressing Inappropriate Coping Mechanism Issues

The third recommendation pertains to addressing inappropriate ways of dealing with stress such as alcohol or substance abuse, avoidance, and reckless behavior. Statistics regarding persons with physical disabilities indicate that as many as 68 percent of persons who sustain traumatic injuries have been under the influence of substances. In many cases, substance abuse continues after the injury, not only because of preinjury use but also to mask the pain experienced from the disability (Heinemann, 1993). In extreme cases of addiction, referral to a substance abuse program is warranted. Ironically, drinking tolerance may be considered as macho or masculine behavior for some males and thus perceived as a way to hold on to some of their masculinity.

Avoidance and isolating oneself from others may be another type of inappropriate response observed in clients. Again, being embarrassed or ashamed can lead clients into avoiding significant others who could help bring meaning back to their lives. Therapists can help clients explore and challenge their concerns regarding the differences between a person's physical appearance and who he or she is as an individual. If therapists question their clients as to what traits they like about others, clients become aware that significant others are loved for who they are, not what they look like.

Another area to observe and discuss is a client's mental status, especially pertaining to suicidal ideation. The rate of suicide in males with spinal cord injury is about twice as high as that in the general population (Geisler, Jousse, Wynne-Jones, & Breithaupt, 1983). Death from unintentional injury and suicide are the leading causes of death for persons with spinal injury six months after injury (Brown, 1998). As such, reckless behavior or suicidal ideation is another area that therapists need to explore during acute care rehabilitation.

Regarding Livneh's (1991b) five stages of adjustment, suicidal ideation may be common during the retaliation stage because of feelings of despair and frustration with one's perceived situation. It is beyond the scope of this chapter to provide detailed recommendations regarding therapeutic treatment of suicidal ideation, but consulting with treating physicians for appropriate medication prescriptions and having knowledge of clinical depression and crisis intervention become essential.

Understanding Disability-Specific Physiology

A fourth suggestion is for therapists to become thoroughly familiar with the physiological changes of specific disability populations with which they are working. Aside from reading about the limitations, therapists can talk to treating therapists and physicians about individuals' functional limitations. From this information, therapists are able to educate clients about sexual myths and functioning as well as health and wellness practices regarding taking care of oneself (for example, managing stress, nutrition, drug or alcohol use, exercise, and so forth). Knowledge of psychoneuroimmunology or behavioral medicine and relevant practice of healthy habits can help clients in minimizing the frequency of rehospitalization. For persons with tetraplegia, for example, weight gain can severely compromise independence and increase the potential for pressure sores, which are not only costly but can be deadly. Long hospitalizations can also affect job status and quality of life.

Introducing Clients to Role Models with Disabilities

Finally, despite nondisabled therapists' best efforts, nothing compares with recruiting successfully adjusted persons with disabilities for clients to interact with and from whom they can see firsthand that a quality life can still be pursued and enjoyed after a disabling injury. Role models can be introduced individually or as part of group counseling, which is particularly effective. Therapists should be cautious, however, to always first ask clients if they would like to meet and talk to someone who has lived with the disability. Most newly injured persons have a certain period (usually right after injury) during which their denial of the long-term prognosis is so great that they will resent and be unwilling to meet another person with a disability. Therapists should be prepared to broach the topic occasionally until clients are finally ready to meet the individual. In addition, it is important, of course, to locate good role models who are married, working, or otherwise have positively moved on with their lives.

Today, persons with severe physical disabilities are living longer and healthier lives thanks to advances in medicine, assistive technology, empowering legislation (for example, the Americans with Disabilities Act), and pharmacological developments. As such, the quality of life for this population continues to improve, with exciting new advances on the way. Sperm extraction and fathering a child for males with spinal cord injury, for example, had a less than 15 percent success rate fifteen years ago. With today's medical advances, the success rate now stands at over 90 percent in this regard. Physical barriers in the community and with transportation continue to be eliminated, opening the once closed doors of engaging in activities such as attending a movie or sporting event, going to restaurants, or taking a train ride. Riding the wave of the growing numbers of aging baby boomers who want alternative options to living in nursing homes, many states now allow persons with severe disabilities to live independently in their homes with the aid of personal attendants. These are all exciting changes that not only enhance the quality of life for persons with disabilities but also improve their overall mental health. Once the task of working with males with disabilities was getting them to accept their plight of living in an unfair world that functioned mainly for able-bodied people.

Psychotherapists today must still be able to address the many issues described here but can now assure clients that many barriers of the past no longer exist. Indeed, perhaps the greatest remaining barriers are the sometimes negative attitudes not only of others but also of those with disabilities themselves.

References

Albrecht, G. L., Walker, V. G., & Levy, J. A. (1982). Social distance from the stigmatized. *Social Science Medical, 16,* 1319–1327.

Anthony, W. A. (1972). Societal rehabilitation: Changing society's attitudes toward the physically and mentally disabled. *Rehabilitation Psychology, 19*(3), 193–203.

Beck, A. T., & Weishaar, M. (1989). Cognitive therapy. In A. Freeman, K. M. Simon, L. E. Beutler, & H. Arkowitz (Eds.), *Comprehensive handbook of cognitive therapy* (pp. 21–36). New York: Plenum.

Belgrave, F. Z. (1984). The effectiveness of strategies for increasing social interaction with a physically disabled person. *Journal of Applied Social Psychology, 14*(2), 147–161.

Belgrave, F. Z., & Mills, J. (1981). Effects upon desire for social interaction with a physically disabled person after mentioning the disability in different contexts. *Journal of Applied Social Psychology, 11,* 44–57.

Belle, D. (1987). Gender differences in the social moderators of stress. In R. C. Barnett, L. Biener, & G. K. Baruch (Eds.), *Gender and stress* (pp. 257–277). New York: Free Press.

Bem, S. L. (1974). The measurement of psychological androgyny. *Journal of Consulting and Clinical Psychology, 42*(2), 155–162.

Bem, S. L. (1993). *The lenses of gender: Transforming the debate on sexual inequality.* New Haven, CT: Yale University Press.

Blum, R. W. (1983). The adolescent with spina bifida. *Clinical Pediatrics, 22,* 331–335.

Brannon, R. (1976). The male sex role: Our culture's blueprint of manhood, and what it's done for us lately. In D. David & R. Brannon (Eds.), *The forty-nine percent majority* (pp. 1–45). Reading, MA: Addison-Wesley.

Brolin, D. E. (1980). *Vocational preparation of persons with handicaps* (2nd ed.). Columbus, OH: Merrill.

Brown, W. J. (1998). Current psychopharmacologic issues in the management of major depression and generalized anxiety disorder in chronic spinal cord injury. *SCI: Psychosocial Process, 11*(3), 37–45.

Butler, T., Giordano, S., & Neren, S. (1985). Gender and sex-role attributes as predictors of utilization of natural support systems during personal stress events. *Sex Roles, 13,* 515–524.

Charmaz, K. (1995). Identity dilemmas of chronically ill men. In D. Sabo & D. Gordon (Eds.), *Men's health and illness: Gender, power, and the body* (pp. 266–291). Thousand Oaks, CA: Sage.

Chubon, R. A. (1982, Winter). An analysis of research dealing with the attitudes of professionals toward disability. *Journal of Rehabilitation, 48*(1), 25–30.

Cloerkes, G. (1981). Are prejudices against disabled persons determined by personality characteristics? *International Journal of Rehabilitation Research, 41*(1), 35–46.

Comer, R. C., & Piliavin, J. A. (1975). As others see us: Attitudes of physically handicapped and normals toward own and other groups. *Rehabilitation Literature, 36*(7), 206–221.

Davis, B. H. (1987, June). Disability and grief. *Journal of Contemporary Social Work,* pp. 352–357.

Davis, S. E., Anderson, C., Linkowski, D. C., Berger, K., & Feinstein, C. F. (1991). Development tasks and transitions of adolescents with chronic illness and disabilities. In R. P. Marinelli & A. E. Dell Orto (Eds.), *The psychological and social impact of disability* (3rd ed., pp. 70–80). New York: Springer.

Dembo, T., Leviton, G., & Wright, B. (1975). Adjustment to misfortune: A problem of social psychological rehabilitation. *Rehabilitation Psychology, 22,* 1–10.

Donaldson, J. (1980, April). Changing attitudes toward handicapped persons: A review and analysis of research. *Exceptional Children, 46,* 504–514.

Ellis, A. (1973). *Humanistic psychotherapy: The rational-emotive approach.* New York: Julian Press.

English, R. W. (1971). Correlates of stigma toward physically disabled persons. In R. P. Marinelli & A. E. Dell Orto (Eds.), *The psychological and social impact of physical disability* (3rd ed., pp. 162–182). New York: Springer.

Evans, J. H. (1976). Changing attitudes toward disabled persons: An experimental study. *Rehabilitation Counseling Bulletin, 19,* 572–579.

Fichten, C. S., Robillard, K., Tagalakis, V., & Amsel, R. (1991). Causal interaction between college students with various disabilities and their nondisabled peers: The internal dialogue. *Rehabilitation Psychology, 36,* 3–20.

Frankl, V. E. (1967). Paradoxical intention: A logotherapeutic technique. In V. E. Frankl (Ed.), *Psychotherapy and existentialism.* New York: Washington Square Press.

Gallagher, H. G. (1994). *FDR's splendid deception.* Arlington, VA: Vandamere.

Geisler, W. O., Jousse, A. T., Wynne-Jones, M., & Breithaupt, D. (1983). Survival in traumatic spinal cord injury. *Paraplegia, 21*(6), 364–373.

Gerschick, T. J., & Miller, A. S. (1995). Coming to terms: Masculinity and physical disability. In D. Sabo & D. Gordon (Eds.), *Men's health and illness: Gender, power, and the body* (pp. 183–204). Thousand Oaks, CA: Sage.

Gerschick, T. J., & Miller, A. S. (1997). Gender identities at the crossroads of masculinity and physical disability. In M. Gergen & S. Davis (Eds.), *Toward a new psychology of gender* (pp. 455–475). New York: Routledge.

Gething, L. (1991). Generality vs. specificity of attitudes towards people with disabilities. *British Journal of Medical Psychology, 64,* 55–64.

Gill, K. M. (1988). *Staff needs: Assessment data.* Unpublished manuscript.

Harris, L. (1991). *Public attitudes towards people with disabilities.* New York: Louis Harris & Associates.

Havranek, J. E. (1991). The social and individual costs of negative attitudes toward persons with physical disabilities. *Journal of Applied Rehabilitation Counseling, 22*(1), 15–21.

Heinemann, A. W. (1993). An introduction to substance abuse and physical disability. In A. W. Heinemann (Ed.), *Substance abuse and physical disability* (pp. 3–10). Binghamton, NY: Haworth Press.

Herek, G. M. (1986). On heterosexual masculinity. *American Behavioral Scientist, 29*(5), 563–577.

Hohmann, G. W. (1975). Psychological aspects of treatment and rehabilitation of the spinal cord injured person. *Clinical Orthopedics, 112,* 81–88.

Kahana, E., Fairchild, T., & Kahana, B. (1982). Adaptation. In D. J. Mangen & W. A. Peterson (Eds.), *Research instruments in clinical gerontology: Vol. 1. Clinical and social psychology* (pp. 145–193). Minneapolis: University of Minnesota Press.

Katz, J. (1988). A theory of qualitative methodology: The social system of analytic fieldwork. In R. Emerson (Ed.), *Contemporary field research: A collection of readings* (pp. 127–148).

Kendall, E., & Buys, N. (1998, Summer). An integrated model of psychosocial adjustment following acquired disability. *Journal of Rehabilitation, 64*(3), 16–20.

Kleck, R. (1968). Physical stigma and nonverbal cues emitted in face-to-face interaction. *Human Relations, 21,* 19–28.

Lazarus, R. S., & Folkman, S. (1984). Stress, appraisal, and coping. In R. L. Atkinson, R. C. Atkinson, E. E. Smith, & D. J. Bem (Eds.), *Introduction to psychology.* New York: Harcourt Brace Jovanovich.

Livneh, H. (1991a). On the origins of negative attitudes toward people with disabilities. In R. P. Marinelli & A. E. Dell Orto (Eds.), *The psychological and social impact of disability* (3rd ed., pp. 181–196). New York: Springer.

Livneh, H. (1991b). A unified approach to existing models of adaptation to disability: A model of adaptation. In R. P. Marinelli & A. E. Dell Orto (Eds.), *The psychological and social impact of disability* (3rd ed., pp. 111–138). New York: Springer.

Lyons, M. (1991). Enabling or disabling? Students' attitudes toward persons with disabilities. *American Journal of Occupational Therapy, 45*(4), 311–316.

Makas, E. (1988). Positive attitudes toward disabled people: Disabled and nondisabled persons' perspectives. *Journal of Social Issues, 44*(1), 49–61.

Marinelli, R. P., & Kelz, J. W. (1973). Anxiety and attitudes toward visibly disabled persons. *Rehabilitation Counseling Bulletin, 16*(4), 198–205.

Marini, I. (1992). The use of humor in counseling as a social skill for disabled clients. *Journal of Applied Rehabilitation Counseling, 23*(3), 30–36.

Milligan, M. S., & Neufeldt, A. H. (1998). Postinjury marriage to men with spinal cord injury: Women's perspectives on making a commitment. *Sexuality and Disability, 16*(2), 117–132.

Minde, K. K. (1978). Coping styles of 34 adolescents with cerebral palsy. *American Journal of Psychiatry, 135,* 1344–1349.

Power, P. W., Hershenson, D. B., & Schlossberg, N. K. (1991). Midlife transition and disability. In R. P. Marinelli & A. E. Dell Orto (Eds.), *The psychological and social impact of disability* (3rd ed., pp. 81–104). New York: Springer.

Roessler, R., & Rubin, S. E. (1982). *Case management and rehabilitation counseling.* Austin, TX: PRO-ED.

Shontz, F. C. (1975). *The psychological aspects of physical illness and disability.* New York: Macmillan.

Simmons, R., & Rosenberg, M. (1975). Sex, sex roles, and self-image. *Journal of Youth and Adolescence, 4,* 229–258.

Spence, J. T., Helmreich, R. L., & Stapp, J. (1974). The personal attributes questionnaire: A measure of sex-role stereotypes and masculinity-femininity. *JSAS Catalog of Selected Documents in Psychology, 4,* 127.

Sprecher, S., & Sedikides, C. (1993). Gender differences in perceptions of emotionality: The case of close, heterosexual relationships. *Sex Roles, 28*(9–10), 511–530.

Stone, A. A., & Neale, J. M. (1984). New measure of daily coping: Development and preliminary results. *Journal of Personality and Social Psychology, 46*(4), 892–906.

Tepper, M. S. (1997). Living with a disability: A man's perspective. In M. Sipski & C. Alexander (Eds.), *Sexual function in people with disability and chronic illness* (pp. 131–146). Gaithersburg, MD: Aspen.

Trieschmann, R. (1988). *Spinal cord injuries.* New York: Demos.

Winstead, B. A., Derlega, V. J., & Wong, P.T.P. (1984). Effect of sex-role orientation on behavioral self-disclosure. *Journal of Research in Personality, 18,* 541–553.

Wright, B. A. (1960). *Physical disability: A psychological approach.* New York: Harper & Row.

Wright, B. A. (1983). *Physical disability: A psychosocial approach* (2nd ed.). New York: Harper & Row.

Yuker, H. E. (1988). *Attitudes toward persons with disabilities.* New York: Springer.

Zilbergeld, B. (1992). *The new male sexuality.* New York: Bantam Books.

CHAPTER SIX

Counseling and Psychotherapy for Male Military Veterans

Gary R. Brooks

When one speaks of health care services to U.S. military veterans, one is primarily speaking of services delivered through the Department of Veterans Affairs (VA). This federally administered organization is the largest health care provider in the world and employs more counselors and therapists than any other organization.

Historically, the VA has paid little overt attention to the gender of its treatment population. In the 1990s, however, the VA experienced a dramatic rise in the number of female veterans, causing gender to emerge as an important topic of interest. According to Weiss (1995), projections call for women to make up 11 percent of the veteran population by 2040. In response to this trend, the VA has begun offering new programs to women and established the Women Veterans Program Office in 1994.

Ironically, it has been the appearance of a large number of female veterans that has helped the VA realize that it must pay greater attention to gender and must become more aware of the differential needs of male and female veterans. Dr. Kenneth Kizer, then the national VA medical director, stated that "excellence in customer service" requires that the VA "tailor the care environment" to the particular needs of special populations of patients (Kizer, 1996, p. 43). Because female veterans were identified as one of these special groups, gender could no longer be overlooked as a critical variable affecting the veteran population.

As is often the case, the appearance of a new group stimulates awareness of issues previously invisible. Because the VA treatment population has been predominantly male, most practitioners were able to ignore masculinity as a relevant aspect of their clients' lives. Much as fish are unaware of the existence of water, the VA has been relatively gender blind—that is, inattentive to how men's socialization into masculinity has affected their lives.

This chapter will further this process of creating greater gender awareness in the treatment of male military veterans. In particular, it will supplement the new literature on female veterans' special mental health needs and offer ideas about the corollary mental health needs of male veterans. I briefly review the general problems of male socialization and then focus on how military experience powerfully reinforces the most traditional aspects of this masculinity socialization and makes veterans especially susceptible to gender role strain. Informed by this information, I finally elaborate on the core elements of successful therapy with veteran men.

HOW MILITARY SOCIALIZATION EXACERBATES GENDER ROLE STRAIN

Although men have long enjoyed the political and economic benefits granted by a patriarchal culture, they have also carried substantial costs that have only recently received broad recognition. Pleck's "gender role strain paradigm" (1981, 1995) challenged previous ideas about masculine identity and pointed out that socially constructed gender roles create problems for women and for men. In many ways these gender roles are inconstant, impossible to fully satisfy, inherently dysfunctional in their expectations, and unforgiving when their rigid standards are violated. As has been extensively reported in other chapters of this volume, men have paid the price of masculinity in terms of damage to both physical and emotional well-being. From their decreased life expectancy to their common experiences of loneliness and personal powerlessness, many men have ultimately realized that the "privileged" status of manhood has multiple liabilities.

Long before they enter the military, young men have already been exposed to a rigorous and relatively unforgiving course of gender socialization. Pollack (1995) and Levant (1996) have been leading advocates of the position that the normative developmental course for young men is highly problematic. Pollack (1995) noted that this process is characterized by premature psychic separation from both maternal and paternal caregivers and by "traumatic abrogation of their early holding environment" (p. 44). Levant (1996) described this process as the "ordeal of emotion socialization" (p. 262).

In adolescence, the "male chorus" (Pittman, 1993) exerts further pressure on young men to conform to narrow ideas of manliness. This male chorus, composed of all a young man's comrades, rivals, buddies, bosses, male ancestors, and cultural heroes pushes the adolescent to "sacrifice more and more of his humanity for the sake of his masculinity" (p. 42).

The sacrifices, ordeals, and traumas of normative male socialization take on new and unimagined dimensions when the young man enters military basic training. The single most urgent mission of this training is to take a select group of immature young men and turn them into "warriors and fighting machines" (Egendorf, 1985, p. 23; see also Dunning, 1996; Wikler, 1980). Although this military socialization process provides many benefits in the national interest, it does so at a sizable cost to the young men who undergo it. In brief, the military has a principal mission of creating warriors who, if they survive the combat for which they are being prepared, must ultimately reenter a larger civilian culture in which warrior values are minimally adaptive. Let us turn to a closer examination of these warrior values.

Violence

Wartime military experience is inherently about violence, and soldiers become conditioned to its pervasive presence. To prepare for war a new recruit is exposed to a value system in which (1) violence is central, (2) the world is divided into allies and enemies, and (3) enemies are depersonalized as justifiable targets of violent impulses (Carlson, 1987).

Because wars are typically imbued with moral rationale, soldiers must adopt a value system in which violence becomes a highly legitimate mechanism, a means to serve moral goodness (Egendorf, 1985). At times, combat situations create the extremes of what Laufer (1985) calls "abusive violence." According to Laufer, this type of violence involves systematic or intentional killing when one's life is not threatened. Laufer found that one-third of his sample of Vietnam veterans had been exposed to abusive violence. One-tenth had participated in the episodes.

Emotional Insensitivity

Because soldiers do not have the luxury of emotional sensitivity, emotional suppression is an essential component of military life. Lifton (1973) described "psychic numbing" as endemic to Vietnam soldiers. Shatan (1978) noted that from the beginning of their basic training soldiers are taught to suppress their compassion by dehumanizing the enemy and ultimately distorting their own humanity.

> After consistently anesthetizing their empathic reactions and cutting themselves off from ordinary sensory experiences under fire, many ex-combatants find it painful and difficult to have humane feelings for other people—difficult because they are frozen in a state of "emotional anesthesia," painful because thawing out their numbed reactions to the evil and death which enveloped them in combat is unsupportable. . . . Frequently they find inner peace only by devising a "dead space" in their psyches where memories live on, cut off from their enduring emotional impact. The price of this peace—alienation from feelings in general—creates a powerful obstacle to the formation of close relationships. (p. 49)

Dunning (1996) noted that because the Persian Gulf conflict relied so heavily on call-ups of reserve and National Guard members, the situation was unique and less conducive to this common psychological defense.

Paranoia and Distrust of Others

Based on their work with male soldiers and their families, Keith and Whitaker (1984) referred to the military as the "paranoid edge of the culture" (p. 150). Because paranoia is an intrinsic part of soldiering, the paranoid component is extremely difficult to displace. Hendin and Haas (1984) noted that because veterans tend to see civilian life as an extension of the wartime situation, "paranoid adaptation" is a common residual effect for combat veterans. They characterized this paranoid stance as incorporating "eternal vigilance in dealing with others, an expectation that any argument is a prelude to a violent fight, and a need to fight first in the face of potential aggression. . . . [T]he veteran perceives civilian life as an extension of the war" (p. 88).

In terms of combat-induced paranoia, special mention must be made of the plight of Vietnam veterans. The later years of Vietnam combat featured a counterinsurgency fighting style and an invisible enemy who fought sporadically through sniping, booby traps, and mines. Because the North Vietnamese and Vietcong frequently enlisted civilian support, U.S. soldiers commonly generalized their fear and antipathy toward all Asians and developed broad patterns of racial hatred toward all "gooks" (*gooks* being the pejorative term applied to all Asians) (Leventman & Camacho, 1980).

Additionally, the prolonged stress of the "unwinnable" war generated major disruptions among American soldiers. Hostilities and violence ("fraggings") within U.S. ranks reached epidemic proportions during the later phases of the Vietnam conflict (Moskos, 1980). Those who had been involved in the war only a short time distanced themselves from new arrivals, and "grunts" were resentful of rear-echelon support troops; senior sergeants were viewed as lifers and, as such, took on the negative characteristics relegated to the "brass" of earlier wars.

As if the numerous internal tensions were not enough to generate severe interpersonal distrust and a paranoid life stance, the Vietnam veteran returned to a painfully divided country. The well-documented antipathy that greeted the returning Vietnam veteran only worsened his deeply felt paranoia and distrust. Family, friends, the VA, the media, and the government were commonly lumped together as part of the distrusted civilian world. Eventually, many Vietnam veterans came to believe that only Vietnam veteran comrades could be trusted (Carlson, 1987).

Substance Abuse

The military has a long history of tacit (sometimes relatively overt) support for alcohol use as a coping mechanism (Stanton, 1980). In Vietnam, as in many other military environments, the serviceman's club, with inexpensive and readily available alcohol, was the primary recreational outlet. Jelinek and Williams (1982) charged that the military has encouraged the use of alcohol for stress reduction and used alcohol as a reward for successful combat operations. In Vietnam, alcohol use was supplemented heavily by reliance on marijuana (Bey & Zecchinelli, 1970). Even when discouraged from doing so by official policies, soldiers commonly have learned to use chemicals to cope with stresses and human problems.

To some extent, soldiers' use of alcohol and illicit drugs is related to the type of warfare they undergo. In high-intensity ground wars (such as the Persian Gulf conflict) there are likely to be more anxiety- and conversion-related disorders. War situations that include periods of prolonged stress (Vietnam War and World War II) are likely to produce higher rates of substance abuse (Koshes, 1996).

Problematic Relations with Women

Although recent scandals may have provoked certain changes, the military has historically been considered by many observers to be a bastion of male dominance and misogyny. Egendorf (1978) noted that "the military world denigrates women and treats sex as a commodity even more blatantly than the civilian world does" (p. 240). Numerous authors have commented on the military's suppression of sexuality as an important part of preparing young men for military combat (Egendorf, 1985; Tanay, 1982; VanDevanter, 1982).

But the problem is larger than sexual deprivation, because the sexual denial has commonly been accompanied by highly misogynistic views of women and sexuality. Hickman (1987) described these negative views in both mild and severe forms. The milder instances have included references to women as fickle and disloyal, as represented in the omnipresent references to "Jody" (Jody is the mythical civilian man who would take advantage of a soldier's absence and steal his girl and his job). The most serious instances of misogyny have been those in which women are routinely portrayed as "harlots, hussies, and whores" (Hickman, 1987, p. 195).

Prostitution not only is common around military settings but is considered by many to be deeply woven into the military lifestyle. In general, the military too rarely encourages the view of sex as part of a loving relationship and too commonly encourages the view of it as "a bodily indulgence to be paid for or ripped off to get your rocks off" (Egendorf, 1978, p. 241).

Work Compulsion

If obsession with work and career is considered a big problem for the civilian man, then it is a huge problem for the military man. For the soldier all else is considered secondary to his principal mission of fighting wars and completing the mission (Ridenour, 1984). Keith and Whitaker (1984) noted that all families within the military are indoctrinated with the ethos that loyalty to military duties is paramount. Dunning (1996) quoted the oft-heard military maxim, "if the military had wanted you to have a family, it would have issued you one" (p. 198).

IMPLICATIONS FOR CLINICAL TREATMENT OF MALE VETERANS

Before veterans can be assimilated into or reenter a civilian culture that has undergone substantial shifts in expectations of men and women, these veterans must be helped to understand the culture's conflict with the most anachronistic aspects of military culture.

To offer culturally sensitive clinical services to male veterans, we must recognize the powerful socializing forces that shape men, as well as the primary values or "dominant discourses" (Hare-Mustin, 1994) of both civilian culture and military culture.

Previously, I argued that treatment programs for Vietnam veterans would not be optimally successful until clinicians understood male gender role strain and viewed male veteran clients as men as well as veterans (Brooks, 1990). More recently I have described a gender-sensitive model of psychotherapy with traditional men (Brooks, 1998a, 1998b). For convenience, I use the acronym MASTERY to represent the core components of the model. In the remainder of this chapter, I briefly describe the components of this model and illustrate its applicability with male veterans through a case illustration.

Luis: Anguish of Combat Veterans

Luis was a thirty-eight-year-old divorced, Mexican American, unemployed bricklayer, who, as a Vietnam combat veteran, was eligible for services at the Temple (Texas) VA Hospital. Prior to admission he had been suicidal and homicidal in reaction to separation from his girlfriend Rose (age thirty-five). Rose had broken off the relationship after becoming impatient with Luis's moodiness and temper outbursts, usually directed at her and her three children from an earlier marriage.

When seen for the initial triage meeting with the psychiatry inpatient staff, Luis appeared angry and frustrated, though not overtly depressed. He clearly was upset about the breakup of his relationship with Rose, but bitterness and anger were his most prominent affects. In the initial meeting he was observed to be a neat, clean-shaven man, with impeccable grooming, dressed in blue jeans and a denim shirt. He was short and muscular, with a dark complexion, and had thick black hair. He had several military-theme tattoos on his arms, with the letters "L-O-V-E" on the knuckles of his left hand and "H-A-T-E" on the right. His general demeanor was marked by emotional intensity. Luis seemed to be a deadly serious man of powerful emotions. Although Luis was obviously bitter and hypervigilant, he was also fearful and desperate. He very much wanted help, yet was confused by the help-seeking process, defensive about self-revelation, and suspicious of the helping community.

As we collected information about Luis's history, we became even more uncomfortable with him. We learned that after a military career that had included two Vietnam combat tours, Luis had begun having major adjustment problems. Unable to cope with his memories of Vietnam combat, he had begun abusing alcohol and heroin and lived on the streets, literally fighting to survive. He eventually was arrested for a variety of criminal acts and spent several years in prison. During his incarceration, Luis was divorced by his first wife and became estranged from his two children.

After leaving prison, Luis began to "go straight." He quit drug and alcohol use and began work with his father as an apprentice bricklayer. In the early 1980s, he met Rose, a divorced mother of three. Luis saw Rose as a "good" woman, who was loving, supportive, and moral. He was interested but was troubled because she seemed to be from a higher social class. Of even greater concern to him was the realization that she was not at all like other women he had known. Rose was intelligent, educated, independent, assertive, socially competent, and politically active (as a barrio organizer of a Latino political action group).

An impassioned and conflictual relationship developed. Rose was drawn to Luis's strength, work ethic, and loyalty yet fearful of his intensity and moodiness. Luis was drawn to Rose as someone who not only excited his manly passions but also could understand him, soothe him, and exorcise his demons. Although he could never fully reveal the extent of his combat trauma, he nevertheless sensed that she knew and accepted his anguish. When he had experienced the sudden flashbacks, wrenching nightmares, and anguished guilt that are hallmarks of posttraumatic stress disorder, he had relied on Rose to provide comfort and compassion. Rose had been the only person who could get inside his macho facade and could tease and joke, allowing access to a playful side he had never recognized.

At the same time, however, Luis was becoming deeply fearful of the dependency he was developing on Rose. Never particularly comfortable with emotional intimacy, he was terrified that he might lose her. As his fears increased he became more possessive and sought to control her. Not surprisingly, Rose resented Luis's controlling behaviors. Intense conflicts ensued, with bitter fights, threats, separations, and impassioned reconciliations. Over the years, Rose had grown increasingly weary of Luis's insecurities yet could not imagine how to end the cycle. Luis was also tired of it but knew how to express his fears only through his rage. Although he had never become violent, he was deeply fearful of losing control.

Overview of Psychotherapy with Luis

Over the next several months I worked intensively with Luis. For a number of reasons I have explicated elsewhere (Brooks, 1996), I opted initially for intensive exposure to a men's therapy group. Luis immediately benefited from this environment through a greater sense of connection with other men in distress and a greater appreciation of potential benefits of seeking help. Because his Vietnam issues were so pressing, I referred Luis to an intensive posttraumatic stress disorder program. There he confronted the horrors of his Vietnam combat experiences and his significant survivor guilt. Although he realized that his Vietnam experiences had made permanent changes in his approach to life, he returned with a commitment to make the best accommodation he could. At this point he seemed far better prepared to begin working on his relationship with Rose and seek a marital relationship more in keeping with Rose's needs and changing times.

THE MASTERY MODEL: CONCEPT AND APPLICATION

In the remainder of this chapter I describe the conceptual basis of the MASTERY model and illustrate how it was effectively applied in psychotherapy with Luis (and Rose).

Monitor Personal Reactions to Men and Male Behavior Styles

Before describing my work with Luis, I first describe the conceptual basis of this initial step of my MASTERY model. I then illustrate its application with Luis.

Concept. Empathy, the capacity to understand the world from the perspective of a client, has long been accepted as a critical component of successful psychotherapy. One of the most respected principles of psychotherapy is that clients are more likely to entertain change when they feel they have been understood, appreciated, valued, or esteemed. In the case of therapy with traditional men, empathy is especially important because of the many ways that these men make themselves difficult to value or understand. Brooks and Silverstein (1995) noted that the "dark side of masculinity" includes a wide range of negative behaviors—violence, alcohol and drug abuse, sexual excess, emotional flight or withdrawal, sexism, and inadequate behavior as relationship partners—that frequently appear in populations of traditional men.

Therapists working with the victims of men's dark-side behavior are quite likely to have strong negative reactions to the perpetrators. These reactions are fully understandable and, to the extent that they alert therapists to the need to protect vulnerable parties, they are functional. However, in some extreme cases of dark-side behavior, men are likely to evoke unnecessarily strong reactions and be labeled as "wife beaters," "winos," "dead-beat dads," or "male chauvinist pigs." At other times, therapists must struggle to avoid generalizing their negative reactions to some male perpetrators onto all men—that is, to the entire male gender.

Already angry or defensive about entering the therapy situation, many of these men can be expected to be quite sensitive to therapist disapproval and may quickly exit if they sense it. Some men may adopt a supplicant and self-condemning stance, heaping blame and guilt on themselves while idealizing loved ones whom they have mistreated. Others may present as overwhelmed, confused, or emotionally anesthetized. Regardless of the type of client presentation, the therapist faces a significant challenge.

To establish therapeutic rapport the therapist must find a way to get behind aversive features of the male client's pretherapy behavior and highlight the client's positive or ennobling characteristics. In brief, the capacity to monitor personal reactivity and to value traditional men is one of the core elements of treatment.

Application. From the moment I first encountered Luis, I realized that I would need to monitor my affective reactivity to him. His strength and physical power were apparent. His muscular torso was barely hidden by his T-shirt and jeans. He exuded emotional intensity through his confrontational glare and tense posture. The atmosphere felt oppressive as he sat forward in his chair, clenching and unclenching his fists in an effort to cope with his discomfort. My discomfort was not helped by my recognition of his history. Because this man had been in Vietnam combat and had been in prison, he probably had become accustomed to dealing with his distress in some pretty scary ways. To work with him, I might eventually need to confront some things and/or set limits. Could I overcome my fear of him to do that?

But fear was not the only source of discomfort. In many ways, Luis was clearly different from me. He had grown up in an impoverished, ethnic minority environment. When he had gone to school, he had attended inferior ones, with less qualified teachers. Most of his "education" came on the streets. When I was attending college and protesting the Vietnam War, he had been a frontline "grunt" in the Vietnam jungles. When I was completing graduate training, he had been battling drugs and incarceration. When I began my cerebral and emotion-focused career as a psychologist, he had been sweating and enduring the rigors of physical labor. In many ways my life was going well and I was a "success." Luis was on the edge. By some traditional standards of masculinity, he was a "loser."

These realities created a number of additional affective reactions that I needed to monitor very closely. Would I be susceptible to subtle feelings of superiority and condescension in the face of this unsuccessful man? On the other hand, would I be subject to feeling inadequate in the company of a man who exuded intense physical masculinity and had minimal regard for "shrinks"? What about guilt and social justice? Luis was a member of a minority group and been raised in a culture that granted no advantages to Mexican Americans. Luis had served his country in Vietnam, while I had bettered myself in college and graduate school.

Obviously, my therapy with Luis would depend on my capacity to recognize and manage my affective reactivity to him. Over the past twenty years, I have worked assiduously to do exactly that—to recognize my multiple reactions to traditional men and their (our) methods of coping with distress. Although this is a continual struggle, I believe that I am far more empathic and realistic than when I first entered the VA system.

In the most general terms, I have found that to work successfully with male veterans, I must be both realistic and compassionate. I must not be awed or overly honoring of them (even if they are celebrated and decorated war heroes). When they run into trouble, I must find a way to develop noble ascriptions of them. Sometimes, a veteran's war injuries provide visible evidence of his victimization. At other times, however, a man's injuries are not apparent and I must recognize the less obvious wounds, whether they are from actual combat or from the more brutalizing aspects of masculinity socialization.

Sometimes I have found it necessary to curb my negative reactions to certain men and search for their more noble aspects—for example, their loyalty to their provider, protector, and family leadership roles. In the specific case of veterans, it becomes critical to put aside any lingering hatred of wars and respect the sacrifices and loyalty of the individual warriors.

Assume the Male Client Is Feeling Pain

The second step of the MASTERY model calls for attention to the emotional anguish implicit in traditional masculinity socialization. I first address this step at the conceptual level and then illustrate it in my work with Luis.

Concept. When one reviews the newly emerging men's studies literature, a critical realization emerges about the lives of contemporary men: Although there are many benefits of the traditional model of manhood, there are also many penalties. This, of course, is the heart of the gender role strain model described earlier in this chapter and throughout the handbook.

Although many men are leading very fulfilling lives, most men suffer in many areas. Most men are plagued with a degree of anxiety about whether they are "man enough"— that is, do they measure up to the next guy or to unrealistic public images of male heroes? Almost all men are susceptible to a range of health problems that are related to the way men are taught to treat their bodies. Many men die prematurely. Many men have satisfying sex lives, but a great many others are dissatisfied with the quantity or quality of their sexual activities or the physical appearances of their partners. Finally, many feel emotionally isolated and yearn for closer connections with others.

Application. Because he exuded anger and frustration, it was easy to see that Luis was in pain. But behind his enraged exterior lay the far deeper suffering that had triggered much of his dark-side behavior.

The breakthrough came in a particularly intense group session when Luis tearfully and haltingly told the group of his loss of a "normal boyhood." "I didn't have no childhood, man. . . . They needed me. . . . Somebody had to be the man of the family!" With anguish he related his efforts as a twelve-year-old boy to provide food for his mother and siblings after his father had abandoned them. He described both his humiliation and his pride at searching through garbage cans to ensure family survival. From that reverie, Luis moved to his painful memories of Vietnam—of his failure to save a comrade who had run across a field of fire to reach a departing chopper. Luis had reached down and caught the bloodied wrist of the panicked man but had lost his grip as the chopper ascended. Luis needed more than thirty minutes to describe his years of self-recrimination and vivid nightmares in which he would reexperience the images and screams of a man about to face death or torture.

Traditional working-class men are subject to intense emotional states that they poorly comprehend and rarely express directly and appropriately. Luis was no exception, as therapy began in earnest when Luis was able to access his considerable psychic pain.

See the Male Client's Problems in Gender Context

The third step of the MASTERY model calls for therapists to be gender sensitive, in both their case conceptualizations and their therapeutic interventions.

Concept. Culturally sensitive therapy adjusts its diagnostic formulations and intervention style to the dominant value system of clients. When it comes to therapy for traditional men, it follows that masculinity should come under the microscope. Solomon (1982) proposed that most men benefit from "gender role psychotherapy," in which gender role issues are explicitly agreed on as a major focus of therapy. Many others have argued for "gender-sensitive" or "gender-aware" therapies—that is, those that make gender an integral aspect of counseling and that view client problems within their social context (Good, Gilbert, & Sher, 1990; Philpot, 1991).

At their heart, these context-aware therapies urge men to see themselves in social context—that is, as products and sometimes victims of their upbringing in a gendered culture. This challenge to men's usual attribution system usually provides immense subjective relief. Men often benefit when they see their failures as less personal and as more the product of a severe and unforgiving socialization process. When they recognize that they have suffered because they have been loyalists to an anachronistic masculine code, they cannot help but experience a dramatic decrease in excessive self-blame. This process not only provides substantial comfort for many anguished men but also may generate enough energy for them to begin the corollary investigation of how socialization pressures have limited women.

Application. A special emphasis of all my men's groups is that of examining the members' problems through a gendered lens and elucidating the manner in which rigid role definitions contribute to situational problems. Repeatedly, I define the group as one that would examine the stresses we all shared as men.

With Luis, one therapeutic focus was that of his obsession with work performance as the only meaningful evidence of masculine worth. As a blue-collar male, he was realistic about the survival value of work, but he had additionally incorporated unrealistic aspects of the work ethic. For example, his rigid work ethos allowed for no possibility that he could be assisted by Rose's work, because that would be interpreted as further evidence of his failure as a male breadwinner. His capacity for providing Rose with practical help and emotional support was negated as unworthy of a man. Ironically, one of Luis's traditional ideas about male-female relationships—women are drawn to the highest-performing men—was a basic source of his insecurity with Rose.

Over the course of the therapy group, Luis was able to grasp what had formerly been in the background—his strong ideas about proper male conduct. Although that new awareness alone did not produce answers to his situational problems, it did provide a measure of subjective comfort. What he had formerly seen as a complete personal failure he could now see, in part, as a product of a changing culture, with its revolutionary ideas about what is suitable for women and men.

Transmit Empathy and Understanding

The fourth step of the MASTERY model calls for the therapist to communicate to the male client that his struggles and pain are recognized.

Concept. If hidden emotional pain is the shameful secret of traditional men, then it is especially critical that therapists establish therapeutic connection by recognizing and validating men's psychic pain. When they are not translating their vulnerable emotions into rage, men typically experience any psychic pain as humiliating weakness. Psychic pain can be so terrifying that men will go to great lengths to hide from it. Rage and frustration, because they are "manly" emotions, are the primary affective states men allow themselves. McLean (1996) stated that "the process of turning boys into men has, historically, been one of systematic abuse, both physical and emotional, designed to teach boys not to show most emotions, except in certain ritually prescribed situations, and if possible, not to feel them" (p. 21).

For growth to occur, men's pain cannot remain hidden or misunderstood. For that pain to come into the open, an environment of empathy and acceptance must be established. Before significant therapeutic change can take place, therapists must understand the dimensions of men's psychic pain and they must convince men that it is safe to encounter it. Often, a man will not feel safe unless he realizes that he is not alone, that other men also hide similar emotional burdens. As a result therapy must be conducted in a fashion that maximizes the possibility of men becoming more self-disclosing. In my experience, this self-disclosure is most likely to occur in the relative safety of a men's group, although it can certainly occur with a skillful therapist in other therapy formats.

Previously I have noted that men's groups help men reveal their pain because "participative self-disclosure" allows them to feel a sense of "universality" with other men (Brooks, 1996, 1998a, 1998b). Many times I have heard a troubled man say "*these* men can understand me because they have been there, they have walked in my shoes."

This process is also helpful because it frequently instills hope in a troubled man. Group members can bear witness and offer testimony about the benefits of therapy and the potential for therapeutic growth.

Even when groups are not feasible, this critical step of transmitting compassion and understanding can be accomplished. A therapist who has worked extensively with men can reach a troubled man by describing his or her past encounters with men in similar straits. A male therapist can, to some extent, describe his own struggles and fears. A female therapist can describe her experiences with important men in her life and demonstrate her empathic connection with these struggles.

Application. Luis had lost touch with a male reference group. Although he shared the common gender role problems of most traditional men and carried around the omnipresent and invisible psychic "male chorus" (Pittman, 1990), he had become socially and emotionally isolated from other men. He fully experienced the negative aspects of the male chorus in that he was always evaluating himself negatively against other men who seemed to be problem free. At some deep level, he truly felt that he alone was experiencing the common problems and failures of contemporary men.

Once he realized he was not alone, Luis experienced a rush of relief and enthusiasm. In the words of a fellow group member, "Luis, you're just like us." The new excitement of shared struggles allowed Luis entrée into the most positive and healing aspects of the male community through loyalty, supportive interactions, and a sense of belonging. Within a brief period of time, Luis became a central figure in the group, elevating his personal morale and injecting new energy into the group milieu.

Luis had been demoralized by his seemingly vulnerable position and confused by the vagaries of the psychotherapy process. But when he started group therapy he was buoyed by the testimonials of more experienced group members. Group veterans extolled the benefits of the group environment, describing it as a psychological haven that had enabled them to regain a sense of control over their lives. These testimonials, though overblown at times, were particularly helpful in relieving Luis's fear about the shameful or "feminizing" effects of psychotherapy.

Empower Men to Change

The fifth step of the MASTERY model calls for the therapist to push the male client not to settle for subjective relief but to make more substantial life changes.

Concept. As I noted earlier, men are likely to experience considerable subjective relief and gain substantial self-respect as they recognize the universality of these struggles among men—that is, "I am not alone in this." They may realize tension reduction through their cathartic expression of intense negative feelings. But, although these accomplishments are quite important, they are not sufficient. This is the point at which my approach to men differs markedly from that of certain others. Let me elaborate.

From Robert Bly's *Iron John* (1990) and John Gray's *Men Are from Mars, Women Are from Venus* (1996) to the controversial work of sociobiologists and evolutionary psychologists, there have been many calls for greater understanding of men's behavior and more acceptance of male modes of being. These works are helpful yet in my view are highly disappointing, even counterproductive, when they espouse essentialist philosophies and call for nothing more than improved understanding of men's behavior. It is my fervent belief that therapists cannot settle for mere understanding of men; we must also have complete commitment to helping men change. The subjective relief experienced by our male clients is a critical first step, but therapy cannot stop there. Men must be challenged to initiate a major reevaluation of their gender role values and assumptions in an effort to bring themselves into greater harmony with a changing world.

Application. Luis had made immense progress though his work in the men's group. For the first time in years, he was able to function without the constant support and emotional validation he had demanded from Rose. A crisis generated a brief relapse but also a major spurt of relational growth.

Rose was due to come to the hospital to pick up Luis for a weekend pass. One day earlier, she had called with unsettling news. To her horror, she had learned that, many years before, her oldest daughter, Marie (age twenty-two), had been sexually assaulted by her stepfather (Rose's second husband). Although tormented by Marie's pain, Rose was terrified to tell Luis. "He'll go crazy," she said. "He'll either kill the bastard or fall all to pieces." I agreed to try to help Rose talk with Luis.

Our conjoint session was superficial and uneventful, because Rose stayed clear of the troubling issue. As the hour neared an end, I suggested we needed to prepare to stop. Rose became frantic: "No! We can't stop yet." Luis was shocked and perplexed.

I asked her to talk more, but she could not. I asked her to keep trying. As the silence wore on, Luis became increasingly unnerved. "What the hell is it?" he demanded.

Rose tried but still could not speak. That was it for Luis. "Well, to hell with this, let me get to hell outta here. You've met a man haven't you? Don't bother telling me. . . . I can see it. . . . Let's get a goddamn divorce!"

Rose became even more distraught when she saw that Luis was totally misreading her messages. She looked to me in near panic: "Can you help?"

I turned to Luis. "Luis, relax. You are way off the mark . Rose needs to tell you something . . . but it's very hard for her. . . . She needs your help and support."

Luis could not let it go. "Support! I'll give her support. She can pack her damn bags and hit the road. . . . Let that other dude give her support!"

I continued to try to reach him. "Luis, it's not about divorce, . . . it's about something entirely different." That calmed him. He turned to Rose and asked in a far more tender voice, "What is it?"

Eventually Rose was able to tell him. Luis was taken completely by surprise and was awkward in trying to comfort Rose. I coached him to sit beside her. He began to get it.

Slowly his put his arm around Rose, who then began wailing. Luis nearly panicked and ran to get her water. He returned and began pacing the floor. I urged him to move back beside Rose. Emboldened by my encouragement, he resumed holding Rose. For several minutes he held and rocked her, and she painfully confronted her guilt and described her fears for her daughter.

Luis had been so preoccupied with losing Rose that he could imagine only one reason for Rose to be upset. Lacking any other substantive relationships or sources of emotional support, he had become obsessed with Rose's nurturance and reassurances. He had been intensely overreactive to any interruptions in her attentions and often paralyzed by fears that she might abandon him for a worthier man.

Fortunately, in the group environment Luis had felt understood and had begun to broaden his circle of emotional support. He had become more confident of his personal assets and less needy of Rose's constant comforting. At times he was able to recognize the irrational aspects of his abandonment fears. Yet in a crisis his first response had been to panic and regress to a more dependent state.

As this vignette illustrates, the compassion and empathy of gender-sensitive therapy can provide a critical step in helping a traditional man to change. But the process should not stop at that point. The subjective relief of early therapy should be used as an inspiration for men to launch fundamental changes in their lives. Men should not only recognize the distress caused by gender role strain but also be encouraged to actually challenge the narrow and limiting masculine code that has constrained them. They need to be empowered to broaden their life options beyond those of warriors and providers to become better friends, fathers, and relational partners.

Respect Resistance and Yield Some Control to the Larger System

The final step of the MASTERY model calls for therapists to be persistent yet realistic in their efforts to help men change.

Concept. There are many metaphors from which to choose: Rome wasn't built in a day. The longest journey begins with a single step. You can only eat an elephant one bite at a time. It is my belief that the first therapy contact, whether in a men's group or in gender-sensitive individual therapy, is only one step in the therapy journey of traditional men. As a systems therapist I believe that families and larger social systems are rule governed. Therefore, any attempt to change the beliefs, attitudes, and behaviors of one person will be met with a "change-back" reaction, homeostatic pressures to return to more customary patterns. For this reason, I commonly envision the initial contacts as a critical step that prepares the way for more systematic change in the form of eventual family therapy and, for some, men's movement activism. Men are shaped by their families and by the larger culture. At the same time, they themselves contribute to creating that culture. Change needs to occur at both the individual and the societal level.

Despite my belief in the ultimate convergence of psychotherapy and social action, I recognize that many men will take only small steps. Not all traditional men will take on the larger project of reforming the culture. Most will approach therapy itself in a tentative and cautious fashion. If they feel understood and the overall experience is positive, they will return. For this reason, I consider it essential that therapists develop a high degree of respect for men's reluctance to embrace change and a high level of patience for change in the larger social system.

Application. Patience and respect were especially critical in my work with Luis and Rose. Luis had seemed greatly relieved to recognize the value of confronting some aspects of the rigid male code. At the same time, however, traditional masculinity was deeply ingrained in him and he was deeply ambivalent about even minimal change. His gender role journey would be slow and episodic, requiring continual guidance and support from an understanding therapist.

Not long after Luis entered therapy, I made contact with Rose to lay the groundwork for couples therapy and family therapy. Rose had been in therapy herself and had been impatient for Luis to become more psychologically minded. The session described here provided a marvelous springboard to family therapy that continued intermittently for the next two years.

Luis did not change every aspect of his value system or his traditional masculinity. He certainly did not become a men's movement activist. In many ways, I would have liked to have seen him change more than he did. At the same time, however, I was pleased to see that he had become far more comfortable in and had made a far better accommodation to his life circumstances. He may not have radically changed his beliefs about masculinity, but he had incorporated more flexibility and broadened his ideas about how men and women can interact.

OVERVIEW OF THERAPY WITH LUIS AND MALE VETERANS

Luis received considerable benefit from the gender-sensitive therapy he experienced in the men's group. An environment was created in which he was able to interact meaningfully with other traditional men in similar straits—a male healing group. He became less distrustful of psychotherapy and gained markedly in self-respect from the recognition that his problems were common among other men. He realized tension reduction through cathartic expression of intense painful feelings.

However, this was not enough. When he left the group he reentered a world undergoing major cultural changes. To maximize Luis's ability to cope with this world and to facilitate more flexible role functioning in his marital and family life, further work was necessary. Luis had been made comfortable in therapy because he had been understood and validated. Discovering other struggling men had increased his comfort. Ultimate progress, however, depends on the therapist's ability to challenge men to make still further changes.

In working with veterans and other traditional men, therapists are challenged to persuade them that whatever their negative feelings about the changing culture, it is their responsibility to make appropriate accommodations in themselves. The seemingly idyllic world of yesterday will not return. Although they may consider it more masculine to be the ram that keeps buttin' that dam, they can be assured that, in most cases, this only produces dented dams and dead rams.

To accomplish its mission of "excellence in customer service," the VA needs to continue the vitally important process of refining the health care services it delivers to its veteran clients, including the innovative programs for female veterans. But the VA should not stop there. With the newly emerging findings about gender as a critical mediating variable in health, special attention must be given to how the needs of women and men are similar yet different. Health care givers in the VA must avail themselves of the information being developed in the newly emerging fields of women's studies and men's studies. In these rapidly changing times, compassionate, thoughtful, and gender-aware psychotherapists offer unique hope for the many male and female veterans who seek help in the VA health care system.

Compassionate, thoughtful, and gender-aware psychotherapists offer unique hope for challenging men to reach out to each other, to interact sensitively with women, to challenge regressive institutions, and to mentor the next generation of men. These therapies offer hope for developing couple relationships characterized by feminist principles of mutual respect and empowerment. Psychotherapists must be continually alert to the destructive potential of the darkest aspects of traditional masculinity and yet hold utmost confidence in the potential of men—men who desperately want a better deal for themselves, their culture, and their loved ones. Therapists are uniquely positioned to provide leadership in the painful but ultimately exhilarating process of helping traditional men discover realistic and compassionate masculinities, helping couples develop egalitarian relationships, and helping family systems empower women and men.

References

Bey, D. R., & Zecchinelli, V. A. (1970). Marijuana as a coping device in Vietnam. (USARV Pamphlet 40). *USARV Medical Bulletin, 22,* 21–28.

Bly, R. (1990). *Iron John: A book about men.* New York: Vintage Books.

Brooks, G. R. (1990). Post-Vietnam gender role strain: A needed concept? *Professional Psychology: Research and Practice, 21,* 18–25.

Brooks, G. R. (1996). Treatment for therapy-resistant men. In M. Andronico (Ed.), *Men in groups: Realities and insights* (pp. 7–19). Washington, DC: APA Press.

Brooks, G. R. (1998a). *A new psychotherapy for traditional men.* San Francisco: Jossey-Bass.

Brooks, G. R. (1998b). Group therapy for traditional men. In W. S. Pollack & R. F. Levant (Eds.), *New psychotherapy for men* (pp. 83–96). New York: Wiley.

Brooks, G. R., & Silverstein, L. B. (1995). Understanding the dark side of masculinity: An integrative systems model. In R. F. Levant & W. S. Pollack (Eds.), *A new psychology of men* (pp. 280–333). New York: Basic Books.

Carlson, T. A. (1987). Counseling with veterans. In M. Scher, M. Stevens, G. Good, & G. Eichenfield (Eds.), *Handbook of counseling and psychotherapy with men* (pp. 343–359). Newbury Park, CA: Sage.

Dunning, C. M. (1996). From citizen to soldier: Mobilization of reservists. In R. J. Ursano & A. E. Norwood (Eds.), *Emotional aftermath of the Persian Gulf War: Veterans, families, communities, and nations* (pp. 197–225). Washington, DC: American Psychiatric Press.

Egendorf, A. (1978). Psychotherapy with Vietnam veterans: Observations and suggestions. In C. R. Figley (Ed.), *Stress disorders among Vietnam veterans* (pp. 231–253). New York: Brunner/Mazel.

Egendorf, A. (1985). *Healing from war: Trauma and transformation after Vietnam.* Boston: Houghton Mifflin.

Good, G., Gilbert, L. A., & Sher, M. (1990). Gender aware therapy: A synthesis of feminist therapy and knowledge about gender. *Journal of Counseling and Development, 68,* 376–380.

Gray, J. (1996). *Men are from Mars, women are from Venus.* New York: HarperCollins.

Hare-Mustin, R. (1994). Discourses in the married room: A postmodern analysis of therapy. *Family Process, 33,* 19–35.

Hendin, H., & Haas, A. P. (1984). *Wounds of war: Psychological aftermath of combat in Vietnam.* New York: Basic Books.

Hickman, P. (1987). But you weren't there. In T. M. Williams (Ed.), *Post-traumatic stress disorder: A handbook for clinicians* (pp. 193–208). Cincinnati, OH: Disabled American Veterans.

Jelinek, J. M., & Williams, T. (1982). Post-traumatic stress disorder and substance abuse. In T. Williams (Ed.), *Post-traumatic stress disorder* (pp. 103–118). Cincinnati, OH: Disabled American Veterans.

Keith, D. V., & Whitaker, C. A. (1984). C'est la guerre: Military families and family therapy. In F. W. Kaslow & R. I. Ridenour (Eds.), *The military family: Dynamics and treatment* (pp. 147–166). New York: Guilford Press.

Kizer, K. W. (1996). *Prescription for change.* Washington, DC: Department of Veterans Affairs.

Koshes, R. J. (1996). The care of those returned: Psychiatric illnesses of war. In R. J. Ursano & A. E. Norwood (Eds.), *Emotional aftermath of the Persian Gulf War: Veterans, families, communities, and nations* (pp. 393–414). Washington, DC: American Psychiatric Press.

Laufer, R. S. (1985). War trauma and human development: The Vietnam experience. In S. M. Sonnenberg, A. S. Blank, & J. A. Talbot (Eds.), *The trauma of war* (pp. 31–56). Washington, DC: American Psychiatric Press.

Levant, R. F. (1996). The new psychology of men. *Professional Psychology: Research and Practice, 27,* 259–265.

Leventman, S., & Camacho, P. (1980). The "gook" syndrome: The Vietnam war as racial encounter. In C. R. Figley & S. Leventman (Eds.), *Strangers at home* (pp. 5–44). New York: Praeger.

Lifton, R. (1973). *Home from the war.* New York: Simon & Schuster.

McLean, C. (1996). The politics of men's pain. In C. McLean, M. Carey, & C. White (Eds.), *Men's ways of being* (pp. 11–28). New York: Westview Press.

Moskos, C. (1980). Surviving the war in Vietnam. In C. R. Figley & S. Leventman (Eds.), *Strangers at home* (pp. 71–86). New York: Praeger.

Philpot, C. L. (1991). Gender-sensitive couples therapy. *Journal of Family Psychotherapy, 2,* 19–40.

Pittman, F. (1990). The masculine mystique. *Family Therapy Networker, 14*(3), 40–52.

Pittman, F. (1993). Man enough: Fathers, sons, and the search for masculinity. New York: Perigee.

Pleck, J. H. (1981). *The myth of masculinity.* Cambridge, MA: MIT Press.

Pleck, J. H. (1995). The gender role strain paradigm: An update. In R. F. Levant & W. S. Pollack (Eds.), *A new psychology of men* (pp. 11–32). New York: Basic Books.

Pollack, W. S. (1995). No man is an island. In R. F. Levant & W. S. Pollack (Eds.), *A new psychology of men* (pp. 33–67). New York: Basic Books.

Ridenour, R. I. (1984). The military service families and the therapist. In F. W. Kaslow & R. I. Ridenour (Eds.), *The military family: Dynamics and treatment* (pp. 1–17). New York: Guilford Press.

Shatan, C. F. (1978). Stress disorders among Vietnam veterans: The emotional content of combat continues. In C. R. Figley (Ed.), *Stress disorders among Vietnam veterans* (pp. 43–56). New York: Brunner/Mazel.

Stanton, M. D. (1980). The hooked serviceman. In C. R. Figley & S. Leventman (Eds.), *Strangers at home* (pp. 279–292). New York: Praeger.

Tanay, E. (1982). The Vietnam veteran—Victim of war. In W. E. Kelley (Ed.), *Post-traumatic stress disorder and the war veteran patient* (pp. 29–42). New York: Brunner/Mazel.

VanDevanter, L. M. (1982). The unknown warriors: Implications of the experiences of women in Vietnam. In W. E. Kelley (Ed.), *Post-traumatic stress disorder and the war veteran patient* (pp. 148–169). New York: Brunner/Mazel.

Weiss, T. W. (1995). Improvements in VA Health Services for women veterans. *Women and Health, 23,* 1–12.

Wikler, N. (1980). Hidden injuries of war. In C. R. Figley (Ed.), *Stress disorders among Vietnam veterans* (pp. 87–108). New York: Brunner/Mazel.

SECTION TWO

TREATING MEN'S PROBLEMS

CHAPTER SEVEN

Assessing and Treating Depression in Men

Sam V. Cochran

For many years clinicians and researchers alike have assumed that about half as many men as women experience depression. This assumption has led many to conclude that men experience fewer and less severe symptoms of depression and that men do not seek help for depression. In general, scientific studies tended to confirm these assumptions (Nolen-Hoeksema, 1987). Recently, however, increasing attention has been directed to the problem of undiagnosed and untreated depression in men in both professional venues (see Cochran & Rabinowitz, 2000; Pollack, 1998) and popular venues (see Lynch & Kilmartin, 1999; Real, 1997). These authors argue for greater sensitivity on the part of psychotherapists to the insidious and often deadly effects of depression on men.

Epidemiological studies have found that in certain population samples men experience depression just as frequently as women do. In some samples, such as the elderly, rates of depression may even be greater in men than in women (Bebbington et al., 1998). Furthermore, the course of depressive disorders is remarkably similar for both men and women diagnosed with depression (Simpson, Nee, & Endicott, 1997). In addition, conditions related to depression, such as alcohol and substance abuse, have been found to be more prevalent in men than in women (Fava et al., 1996). Finally, data on suicide indicate that men of all ages and races commit suicide at rates from four to fifteen times that of women in comparable groups (Moscicki, 1997). In light of these reports, it now appears that the commonly referenced epidemiological findings asserting that women experience depression at twice the rate that men do encourage oversimplified interpretations that simply do not capture the full reality of depression as it may be experienced by many men.

In this chapter I provide an overview of recent epidemiological findings on major depression and suicide as well as psychotherapy outcome studies that report results of investigations examining the treatment of depression. Attention is directed toward what these findings tell us about depression in men. In addition, I present practical guidelines for the assessment and treatment of depression in men that are linked to these empirical findings. Indeed, the outlook is improving for men who experience depression. Increasing numbers of therapists are becoming sensitized to the problem of undiagnosed and untreated depression in men. Well-tested treatments and new, innovative therapies provide relief for men who come forward and seek treatment for their depression.

SEX, GENDER, AND DEPRESSION

Depression was long considered a woman's malady. For many years, demographic data on hospital admissions and from treatment settings were interpreted to confirm that compared with men women tended to be depressed in greater numbers and tended to have more lengthy and severe episodes of depression. Because many more women than men were treated in institutions and outpatient settings this conclusion appeared warranted.

With the development of empirically based diagnostic criteria for various mental and physical conditions, rigorous epidemiological studies on the incidence and prevalence of mental disorders, including depression, could be undertaken. One of the first large-scale investigations of this kind, the Epidemiological Catchment Area study (Robins & Reiger, 1991), found that in a sample of almost twenty thousand persons drawn from five sites in the United States the incidence and prevalence of both major depression and dysthymia were greater for women than for men. In this study lifetime prevalence estimates for major depression and dysthymia for men were 2.6 and 2.2 percent, respectively, compared with 7.0 and 4.1 percent, respectively, for women. These estimates were confirmed in a later investigation, the National Comorbidity Survey (Kessler et al., 1994). In this survey, which used a stratified sample of more than eight thousand adults from the United States, the lifetime prevalence estimates for major depression and dysthymia for men were 12.7 and 4.8 percent, respectively, and the comparable rates in women were 21.3 and 8.0 percent, respectively. Differences in prevalence estimates between the two studies were attributed to the probing life review section of the interview protocol included in the National Comorbidity Survey methodology. Although the addition of this life review section to the methodology to counter the "forgetting" effect that the investigators believed might skew the results in the direction of higher rates for women, the ratio of prevalence estimates for the depressive disorders was still two to one. In both epidemiological surveys women were approximately twice as likely as men to develop a depressive condition at some point in their lifetimes.

At about the same time that these two landmark epidemiological studies appeared, several other investigations found notable divergences from the typical two-to-one female-to-male ratio of prevalence estimates of mood disorders. One of these, the Old Order Amish study reported by Egeland and Hostetter (1983), found that in a small community of Amish in Pennsylvania the rates of bipolar disorder and unipolar depression were practically identical in men and women. Another investigation that examined the rates of depression in a community of Orthodox Jews living in London found no significant differences in rates of depression between 157 men and 182 women (Loewenthal et al., 1995). An investigation of 1,747 Chinese Americans in Los Angeles reported equivalent rates of both depression and dysthymia in low-acculturation samples but found the common two-to-one female-to-male ratio in subjects with higher levels of acculturation (Takeuchi et al., 1998). Other studies that have examined populations of Atlantic Canadians (Murphy, Olivier, Monson, Sobol, & Leighton, 1988), New Zealanders (Wilhelm & Parker, 1994), and elderly persons (Girling et al., 1995) found that under certain circumstances men in these samples experience depression at rates equal to or greater than those of women.

What might be the common factor in these studies in which the men have been found to experience depression in numbers comparable to those of women? Some investigators have hypothesized that the cultural norms of these select samples are such that the men tend to suppress alcohol abuse, drug abuse, and sociopathy, thus permitting a more direct manifestation of depression. This hypothesis is plausible for the communities with strong religious and spiritual roots such as the Amish community in Pennsylvania and the Orthodox Jewish community in London.

Consistent with this hypothesis, a model of depression that has been termed the depressive spectrum disease model proposes that alcoholism and antisocial behavior disorders are a masculine expression of an underlying genetically based depressive disorder (Winokur, 1997). Hence, in populations in which these behaviors are discouraged a greater rate of depression would be expected in some of the men.

In addition to the suppressing effect that certain cultural norms might exert on atypical depressive symptoms, two of these studies used what the investigators considered more "gender-fair" criteria for defining depression within the samples (Murphy et al., 1988; Wilhelm & Parker, 1994). When alternative criteria that might be more likely to detect depression in the men were used, the rates of depression in both the men and the women in these investigations converged to nearly identical values. These findings demonstrate that our culturally derived definitions of depression, the criteria by which we designate depression in a person, have a distinct influence on who is included in the final tally.

The results from the study sampling the Chinese American community further highlight the important role that culture plays in the manifestation of depression. In this study, investigators found that the more acculturated (that is, more like Americans) the subjects were, the more likely the women were and the less likely the men were to show depression. On the other hand, the less acculturated (that is, less like Americans, more like traditional Chinese) the subjects were, the greater the likelihood of finding an even ratio of rates of depression in these men and women.

Taken together, these findings demonstrate the critical importance cultural forces (implicit and explicit behavioral norms about appropriate masculine behavior, for example) have as intervening variables in the manner in which depression is defined and manifest in the populations studied (Manson, 1995). Indeed, research on masculinity-related psychological distress has tended to confirm that gender role–related conflicts in men are correlated with high levels of distress in general (Good, Robertson, Fitzgerald, Stevens, & Bartels, 1996) and with depression in particular (Good & Wood, 1995). Reported sex differences in rates of depression are certainly influenced by gender-related (that is, cultural) variables. Clinicians can no longer ignore the implications of culturally derived gender role values in the case definition, experience, manifestation, assessment, and treatment of depression in men.

GENDER AND SYMPTOMS OF DEPRESSION

Interestingly, studies that have evaluated symptom profiles of subjects with depression have found that the actual manifestation of clinical depression is very similar in men and women (see Young, Scheftner, Fawcett, & Klerman, 1990). By and large, men with depression report the same symptoms as women with depression. For both men and women, dysphoria is reported most commonly, followed by death thoughts, changes in appetite and sleep patterns, fatigue, concentration problems, guilt, psychomotor changes, and loss of interest (Weissman, Bruce, Leaf, Florio, & Holzer, 1991). This similarity of symptom profiles appears to hold even for those subjects with chronic depression, defined as a major depression lasting at least two years without antecedent dysthymia (Kornstein et al., 1996).

In addition to studies that have detailed the symptoms of depression in men and women, studies examining the clinical progression of depression have found that women and men are very similar in terms of the course and chronicity of the disorder (see Simpson et al., 1997). The number of symptoms reported, the time elapsed between diagnosis and recovery, and the length of time between episodes all appear to be very similar in both men and women. For practical purposes the actual clinical manifestation of depression is very similar in men and women.

In contrast to the studies that have found similarities between men and women with depression, a number of investigations have reported sex-related patterns of comorbid conditions in subjects with depression. Most important, compared with women with depression, men with depression have been found to have more comorbid alcohol and other drug abuse and dependence (Fava et al., 1996; Hanna & Grant, 1997). Men with depression are also more likely than women with depression to show increased incidence of antisocial personality traits (Black, Baumgard, & Bell, 1995), masculine gender role strains (Good & Wood, 1995; Heifner, 1997), compulsive personality characteristics, and defensive or exaggerated assertions of autonomy (Frank, Carpenter, & Kupfer, 1988).

For purposes of assessment it is important for clinicians to recognize that although men show many of the same symptoms of depression that women show there are important masculine-specific patterns of behavioral and emotional expression that uniquely characterize the male experience of depression. These patterns include significant alcohol- and drug-related comorbidity, behaviors characterized as compulsive and antisocial, and increases in interpersonal conflict such as anger, withdrawal, and defensive assertions of autonomy. Sensitive assessment of depression in men must recognize the overlap between these expressions, which may appear inconsistent with a clinical picture of depression and the likely presence of depression in the men who exhibit them.

CASE EXAMPLES

Because depression is so frequently underdiagnosed in men, in this section I present some clinical examples that illustrate issues involved in assessment and treatment. These case examples demonstrate the wide variety of triggering events and clinical presentation the clinician encounters in working with men. A follow-up to the presentations given here is provided later in the chapter as a means of illustrating some of the treatment process issues that can arise in working with depression in men.

Case I. Tim scheduled an appointment for evaluation and possible psychotherapy at the urging of his spouse, to whom he had been married less than a year. He had become increasingly withdrawn from her over recent months and spent more time at work and at the golf course with friends. When his spouse questioned him about his distance and seeming lack of interest in joint activities, he often responded by becoming argumentative and would withdraw further, sometimes stomping out of the house in anger. His evaluation with a therapist revealed an intense dissatisfaction with his current employment, sadness over having given up his "last chance" to become a professional golfer, and questioning of his commitment to his marriage and relationship with his spouse. He met the criteria for a depressive episode and was offered individual psychotherapy.

Case II. Roger was required to seek psychotherapy by his employer, a city transit office. He had tested positive for drugs and alcohol at a random drug screen that was a requirement in his workplace. He reported to his initial evaluation with an uncommon openness as he revealed his history of serious alcohol abuse, lack of friendships and relationships, and long-standing symptoms of depression. He had smoked some marijuana at a bar the night before the drug screen, and residue had remained in his system. He said he was actually glad to finally have an opportunity to discuss his current unhappiness, which he said he had felt at least since high school. He met diagnostic criteria for alcohol abuse and dysthymia. He continued in individual psychotherapy with his therapist for a year beyond his required attendance.

Case III. Robert and Arlene sought couples therapy at Arlene's behest. After his retirement, Robert had shown an initial interest in working on some projects around the house. Now, one year into his retirement, he spent most of his days watching television or reading. When Arlene asked him what was wrong, he responded, "Oh, nothing." Arlene knew better. Robert simply was not his old, cheerful, outgoing self. Together they described to their therapist that Robert had eagerly anticipated his retirement. However, one of his best friends had died unexpectedly shortly after they both had retired. Robert played a significant part in the memorial ceremony and even delivered a moving eulogy. Shortly afterward, however, Robert began to feel sad and tired and lost interest in many of the activities he had enjoyed prior to his retirement. A number of these activities he and his friend had planned to enjoy together.

These three case examples illustrate the wide range of triggering events and clinical presentations of depression in men. In the first case, the transition from bachelorhood to married life triggered withdrawal, overinvolvement with work, and anger. In the second case, the overlap of alcohol and substance abuse with depression is evident. And in the third case, the impact of loss on a man is expressed through sadness and withdrawal. In both the first and third cases an intimate partner is instrumental in motivating the man to seek help for his depression.

MASCULINE-SPECIFIC ASSESSMENT OF DEPRESSION

Clinicians must balance three tasks in assessing depression in men. First, a thorough assessment of symptoms of depression based on the diagnostic criteria outlined in the *Diagnostic and Statistical Manual of Mental Disorders (DSM-IV)* (American Psychiatric Association, 1994) must be completed. Second, because there is significant gender-specific comorbidity of depression with various depression-related disorders in many men, a thorough evaluation of the potential contribution of these comorbid disorders is warranted. Finally, because important culturally derived influences shape the experience and expression of depression across many settings and communities, a careful consideration of the contribution that these influences make to the manifestation of depression in men is essential.

The *DSM-IV* outlines nine symptoms of a major depressive episode, including (1) depressed mood, (2) decreased interest or pleasure in most activities, (3) weight loss or gain, (4) insomnia or oversleeping, (5) psychomotor retardation or agitation, (6) fatigue, (7) feelings of worthlessness or guilt, (8) trouble concentrating, and (9) thoughts of death or suicide. A man must manifest at least five of these criteria over a two-week period, and at least one of these five criteria must be either depressed mood or decreased interest or pleasure in most activities. Many men presenting for evaluation or treatment report a number of these common symptoms of depression. With patient, gender-sensitive listening and gentle coaxing many men often reveal enough symptoms to warrant an outright diagnosis of major depression.

In addition to assessing for the presence of the standard diagnostic criteria for depression, a therapist must also carefully assess the masculine-specific symptoms and comorbid conditions that are related to depression in men. Symptoms commonly associated with depression in men include alcohol and substance abuse, increased interpersonal conflict, work-related concerns and difficulties, and increased impulsive, self-destructive behavior. These symptomatic manifestations of depression in men are often rooted in important cultural and community norms that must also be considered when assessing a man for depression. Exhibit 7.1 outlines important features of a masculine-specific assessment of depression. By combining traditional diagnostic criteria with culturally sensitive inquiry into other possible manifestations of depression rather than focusing only on the traditional diagnostic criteria, a clinician is much more likely to detect and diagnose depression in men.

SUICIDE RISK IN MEN WITH DEPRESSION

Suicide is now recognized as a major public health concern that warrants national attention. Because men commit suicide at high rates compared with women, death from suicide is a significant mortality risk for men with depression. Consequently, any therapist working with men must devote time to assessing the potential risk for suicide, especially when working with men with depression (Cochran & Rabinowitz, 2000).

Suicide rates in men have been estimated to be between approximately twenty deaths per one hundred thousand for men between fifteen and twenty-four years of age and approximately seventy deaths per one hundred thousand for men over eighty years of age (Buda & Tsuang, 1990). These suicide rates for men range from seven to fifteen times the suicide rates for women of comparable ages. Because fewer men than women seek treatment for depression and because untreated depression greatly increases the risk of suicide, men who may be depressed are at significantly increased risk for death due to suicide.

Thoughts of death and suicide are not uncommon in depression. In fact, one of the *DSM-IV* diagnostic criteria for a major depressive episode is recurrent thoughts of death or suicide or a suicide attempt or plan for committing suicide. The specificity of suicidal ideation and a detailed plan that would be carried out with accessible means are significant risk factors in suicide assessment. In addition to these commonly identified factors that elevate suicide risk, recent alcohol or drug intoxication or antisocial behaviors, recent health-related problems, and interpersonal loss coupled with access to a firearm have been associated with completed suicides in men (Fowler, Rich, & Young, 1986; Isometsa et al., 1994).

Increased age further exacerbates suicide risk in men (Osgood & Thielman, 1990). Whether due to advanced age, the gradual accrual of the impact of deaths of friends and family, or increasing physical ailments, an alarming number of elderly men commit suicide. Assessment of depression in elderly men must directly address the issue of suicide, including the availability of lethal means for completing suicide (Adamek & Kaplan, 1996).

TREATING DEPRESSION IN MEN

Even though men are often not counted in the tally of rates of depression, there is clear evidence that many men experience depression. Furthermore, when this depression is left undiagnosed and untreated, the risk of suicide in men is exacerbated. Suicide remains a major mortality risk for men of all ages and all races. In light of possible risk of suicide and the lost productivity and negative impact on communities and families that result from not treating depression in men, gender-sensitive therapists are now beginning to recognize the importance of assessing and treating depression in the men who consult them for help.

Exhibit 7.1. Masculine-Sensitive Assessment of Depression.

1. Assessment of *DSM-IV* criteria for major depressive episode
2. Identification of important comorbid conditions
   - Alcohol abuse and dependence
   - Substance abuse and dependence
   - Related personality features (antisocial, compulsive, and narcissistic traits)
3. Masculinity-related symptom expression
   - Somatic or physical complaints
   - Increases in interpersonal conflict
   - Work-related difficulties and conflicts
   - Wounds to self-esteem (job loss or relationship loss)
4. Culturally influenced manifestations of emotional distress
   - Class and race considerations regarding emotional expressivity
   - Level of awareness and acceptance of traditional male gender roles
   - Family of origin role models and norms regarding emotional expressivity
5. Suicide and homicide risk assessment
   - Ideation, plan, means, access, and intent
   - Alcohol or drug intoxication
   - Psychotic or delusional features
   - Capacity for cooperation with clinician

In spite of the increased visibility of clinical and research findings pertaining to depression in men, fewer men than women schedule appointments with psychotherapists. However, once men come for an initial appointment, they are just as likely as women to continue with psychotherapy (Vessey & Howard, 1993). For men who persevere with treatment, research has demonstrated the efficacy of many types of psychotherapy used to treat depression in men.

Empirical evaluations of psychotherapeutic treatments for depression have demonstrated positive results with men. The National Institute of Mental Health Treatment of Depression Collaborative Research Program (Elkin et al., 1989) assessed the efficacy of two well-known psychosocial treatments—cognitive-behavioral and interpersonal psychotherapy. These treatments were compared with a standard, proven effective pharmacological treatment (imipramine). This investigation found the psychological treatments to be as effective as the drug treatment for most patients. The gender of the subject was not a significant predictor of outcome in this investigation. Subsequent reports from this and other randomized, controlled trials that assessed either interpersonal or cognitive-behavioral therapy have found that men respond positively to both of these treatments (see Thase et al., 1994, 1997). In addition to these individual treatments, group treatments that have yielded positive results with men experiencing depression have been reported (Kelly et al., 1993). Couples therapy approaches have also been demonstrated effective when working with men with alcohol or substance abuse problems along with concurrent relationship difficulties (Fals-Stewart, Birchler, & O'Farrell, 1996).

Taken as a whole, these studies demonstrate that men benefit from the standard psychotherapies that have been subjected to empirical testing. In most outcome studies, the gender of the subject has not been a significant predictor of outcome. Men have even re-covered more quickly than women in some cases (see Frank et al., 1988). Findings from these and other investigations offer good news for men with depression in that they clearly establish the effectiveness of psychotherapy in helping men recover from episodes of depression.

In addition to these empirically verified treatments, several innovative, gender-sensitive approaches for treating depression in men have been proposed. Pollack (1998) describes a psychodynamic approach to psychotherapy with men that integrates self-psychology with psychoanalytic developmental psychology. Early relational and emotional trauma, derived from child-rearing practices based on stereotypical norms about appropriate mas-culine behavior, creates in many men a core emotional landscape that consists of feelings of loss, depression, and sadness. By using a therapeutic stance of empathic attunement, a therapist working from this perspective helps a man gain awareness of the impact of these traumatic losses on his life and to change his patterns of behavior.

Cochran and Rabinowitz (1996) describe an approach that emphasizes the integration of early childhood experiences of relational discontinuity and loss with other experiences of loss that accrue over a man's life span that are related to gender role strains and con-straints. Many men experience failure to meet society's unrealistic and unhealthy norms about masculinity as real or symbolic loss. Full realization of these loss experiences may precipitate depression in men who are vulnerable or predisposed to mood disturbances.

These conceptualizations of psychotherapy for depression in men parallel the self-in-relation model of recovery from depression in women formulated by Stiver and Miller (1997). In this model, a core therapeutic task is the differentiation of feelings of depres-sion from those of sadness. Depression is viewed as a clinical syndrome, whereas sad-ness is viewed as a natural response to experiences of loss. In women, such losses are often relational. In men, losses may also be symbolic and based on the perceived failure to meet culturally defined expectations of masculinity. For both men and women, recov-ery from depression is in part based on the recognition of the losses that have precipi-tated a depressive episode. In women, recovery involves a movement away from depression and into sadness over these losses. For men, an additional step in the process may include recognition of the roles that anger, interpersonal conflict, and withdrawal play as prominent defenses against both depression and sadness.

In addition to the approaches that address specific issues clinicians encounter when working with men with depression, Good, Gilbert, and Scher (1990) outline tenets of gender-aware therapy that explicitly incorporate elements of masculine gender role strain into the conceptualization of client problems. Brooks (1998) describes innovative approaches to dealing with men for whom therapists perceive traditional psychothera-peutic venues as inappropriate. Although not specifically designed to address depression in men, these approaches introduce important gender-sensitive values into psychother-apy with men. Such values underscore the restrictive, detrimental impact that rigid adherence to traditional masculine gender role behaviors and values can have on men. Because masculine gender role strain has been associated with increased levels of depres-sion in samples of men, gender-sensitive approaches that openly invite men to consider the negative impact of the constraining influence of traditional gender roles on their lives are important innovations.

Both empirically verified treatments and new, innovative treatments offer proven effectiveness and enhanced potential for improving the diagnosis and treatment of depression in men. Exhibit 7.2 summarizes the available treatments that have been described and tested in the psychological and psychiatric literature. There are many and

Exhibit 7.2. Psychotherapies Used to Treat Depression in Men.

1. Empirically verified treatments
   - Cognitive-behavioral therapy (Beck, Rush, Shaw, & Emery, 1979)
   - Interpersonal therapy (Klerman, Weissman, Rounsaville, & Chevron, 1984)
   - Integrative behavioral-couples therapy (Christensen, Jacobson, & Babcock, 1995)
   - Group therapy (Kelly et al., 1993)
   - Behavioral therapy (Lewinsohn & Gotlib, 1995)

2. Innovative treatments
   - Psychodynamic therapy (Pollack, 1998)
   - Loss-focused integrative therapy (Cochran & Rabinowitz, 1996)
   - Gender-aware therapy (Good et al., 1990)
   - Psychotherapy for traditional men (Brooks, 1998)

varied possibilities available for therapists who wish to increase their effectiveness in detecting and treating depression in men.

CASE EXAMPLES

In Case I, Tim revealed in an early session that he was having difficulty adjusting to his recent marriage. He had been married about ten months, and he related much of his unhappiness to his difficulty in getting "settled in" to married life. His treating therapist decided to use an interpersonal approach (Klerman, Weissman, Rounsaville, & Chevron, 1984) enhanced with gender-aware insights to treat his depression. Tim's core conflicts were cast in terms of interpersonal disputes (conflict with his spouse over priorities, time spent together, and planning of mutual activities) and role transition (mourning the loss of single adulthood status, adjustment to new married man status, and acceptance that he would not become a professional golfer). By couching Tim's depression in terms of these changes in his life, his therapist was able to help Tim to step back and gain some perspective on his current situation. His therapist also emphasized Tim's struggle with adjusting to his shifting expectations about the meaning of manhood (for example, settle down and get serious, give up your dreams, and do not play with old buddies). Tim was able to learn to express some of his pent-up anger to his spouse more directly and to work through the frustrations he was experiencing with having to accept the limitations of his current employment situation. He met for a total of eighteen sessions and terminated treatment with a greatly improved mood and increased satisfaction with both his marriage and his new married man status.

Roger, described in Case II, was treated for approximately one year with weekly individual psychotherapy that combined the psychodynamic approach of Pollack (1998) and the loss-focused therapy of Cochran and Rabinowitz (1996). Although Roger had never sought treatment before, he quickly and eagerly took to the weekly meetings with his therapist. It was almost as if he had wanted an excuse to talk to someone about his difficult life experiences.

Roger was the older of two boys, raised in a family in which his father was a laborer who held two jobs to support the family and his mother was a homemaker. He related many instances of feeling misunderstood, rejected, and abandoned by both his mother and his father. His father was always working and never seemed to have time for him or his brother. His mother, who was a religious fundamentalist, was involved in reading the bible, attending study groups, and imposing strict, rigid rules of living on Roger and his brother based on her religious beliefs. Roger recounted feeling intensely alone, isolated, and sad during most of his grammar school and high school years. He did not have many friends and tended to keep mostly to himself. He was expected to take care of his younger brother much of the time. He felt he never related to the traditional boyhood activities in which he saw many of his peers involved.

After graduating from high school, he enlisted in the army and spent two years in active duty, one of which was spent in two tours of duty in Vietnam. He returned to the United States and enrolled in college, took a number of different courses, and finally graduated with a degree in English literature. He had intended to continue to study creative writing but needed to work to support himself and obtained employment as a subway train driver. He quickly advanced in seniority and salary and soon found his income too high to warrant jumping to another career or entering a graduate writing program. Underneath his easy-going exterior, he felt trapped, unable to pursue his dreams. He began to abuse alcohol and marijuana as an escape from his feeling of being trapped. He was frustrated that he had not been able to "make anything more" of himself even though he earned a substantial salary with excellent benefits. He had always had a dream of making something better of himself, which for him meant something better than what his father had attained as a laborer. Roger did not believe he had done any better than his father and felt his life was becoming what his father's life had been—"work, work, work."

Over the months, a theme emerged in therapy with Roger—that he had been forced to abandon his dreams and resign himself to a marginal and "second-rate" life. He progressively uncovered many layers of feelings about himself and his life. He was angry at his situation yet did not know whom to hold accountable. He was depressed and felt helpless and hopeless about ever accomplishing anything different from what he had already accomplished. He did not like his life but was unable to formulate any concrete strategies to change it. And toward the end of his therapy, he felt sad that his life had been what it was and mourned his failure to fulfill many of his dreams. Yet in the midst of this sadness he discovered a deep, lasting, spiritually based acceptance of his life on which he based a number of plans for changing his life within the context of "what it had turned out to be."

Robert and Arlene, described in Case III, came to a total of six sessions with their couples therapist. At the beginning, Robert exhibited many symptoms of depression, including withdrawal and loss of interest in activities he had previously enjoyed, sad and depressed mood, fatigue, and loss of energy. Robert's therapist put Robert's symptoms into the context of a normal grieving process and, with Arlene's support, helped Robert to acknowledge his feelings of loss for his close friend. In addition to grieving the loss of his close friend, Robert also recognized that he needed to grieve the loss of what he had anticipated during his retirement. He was not going to be able to share activities with his old friend. Naming and openly acknowledging these losses and Robert's feelings about them moved him quickly from his depression into a deep sadness. This sadness was acknowledged as signifying the importance of this relationship to Robert, and he was supported in his efforts to "move on" as he was sure his old friend would wish for him to do. The couples sessions ended with Robert having gained a new perspective on his emotional responses to his recent losses, decreased depressive symptoms, and a new, optimistic determination to look to the future and revise his retirement plans.

In these three cases, three different approaches are used to treat the men's depression. In the first, in which Tim is involved in adjusting to marriage, interpersonal psychotherapy with a gender-aware emphasis is used. Addressing Tim's failures to live up to his culturally based expectations of himself as a man plays an important role in this treatment. In Roger's case, the impact of early childhood neglect and trauma is integrated into the treatment and combined with addressing his "failure" to live up to his dream of surpassing his father's accomplishments. Finally, Robert and Arlene represent a common presentation for depression in a man who is prompted into treatment at the suggestion of a concerned partner. The loss of his friend had triggered a depressive episode in Robert that he did not know how to manage. Identifying and naming his emotional reactions to his friend's death released him to move on and plan his retirement in a positive and constructive fashion.

SUMMARY

Undiagnosed and untreated depression is a serious health problem for many men. Suicide rates and levels of alcohol and substance abuse in men indicate that men with depression often slip through the net of our mental health system undetected until it is too late. Gender role–related strains further compound men's depression by contributing to feelings of failure and loss as many men are unable to meet their own or society's expectations of success and achievement. By increasing awareness of the manifestations of depression and depression-related conditions in men and by emphasizing the availability of effective treatments, more men with depression may be identified and treated.

References

Adamek, M., & Kaplan, M. (1996). Firearm suicide among older men. *Psychiatric Services, 47,* 304–306.

American Psychiatric Association. (1994). *Diagnostic and statistical manual of mental disorders* (4th ed.). Washington, DC: American Psychiatric Association.

Bebbington, P., Dunn, G., Jenkins, R., Lewis, G., Brigha, T., Farrell, M., & Leltzer, H. (1998). The influence of age and sex on the prevalence of depressive conditions: Report from the National Survey of Psychiatric Morbidity. *Psychological Medicine, 28,* 9–19.

Beck, A., Rush, J., Shaw, B., & Emery, G. (1979). *Cognitive therapy of depression.* New York: Guilford Press.

Black, D., Baumgard, C., & Bell, S. (1995). A 16- to 45-year follow-up of 71 men with antisocial personality disorder. *Comprehensive Psychiatry, 36,* 130–140.

Brooks, G. (1998). *A new psychotherapy for traditional men.* San Francisco: Jossey-Bass.

Buda, M., & Tsuang, M. (1990). The epidemiology of suicide: Implications for clinical practice. In S. Blumenthal & D. Kupfer (Eds.), *Suicide over the life cycle: Risk factors, assessment, and treatment of suicidal patients* (pp. 17–38). Washington, DC: American Psychiatric Press.

Christensen, A., Jacobson, N., & Babcock, J. (1995). Integrative behavioral couples therapy. In N. Jacobson & A. Gurman (Eds.), *Clinical handbook of couples therapy* (pp. 31–64). New York: Guilford Press.

Cochran, S., & Rabinowitz, F. (1996). Men, loss, and psychotherapy. *Psychotherapy, 33,* 593–600.

Cochran, S., & Rabinowitz, F. (2000). *Men and depression: Clinical and empirical perspectives.* New York: Academic Press.

Egeland, J., & Hostetter, A. (1983). Amish Study, 1: Affective disorders among the Amish. *American Journal of Psychiatry, 140,* 56–61.

Elkin, I., Shea, M., Watkins, J., Imber, S., Sotsky, S., Collins, J., Glass, D., Pilkonis, P., Leber, W., Docherty, J., Fiester, S., & Perloff, M. (1989). National Institute of Mental Health Treatment of Depression Collaborative Research Program. General effectiveness of treatments. *Archives of General Psychiatry, 35,* 971–982.

Fals-Stewart, W., Birchler, G., & O'Farrell, T. (1996). Behavioral couples therapy for male substance-abusing patients: Effects on relationship adjustment and drug-using behavior. *Journal of Consulting and Clinical Psychology, 64,* 959–972.

Fava, M., Abraham, M., Alpert, J., Nierenberg, A., Pava, J., & Rosenbaum, J. (1996). Gender differences in Axis I comorbidity among depressed outpatients. *Journal of Affective Disorders, 38,* 129–133.

Fowler, R., Rich, C., & Young, D. (1986). San Diego Suicide Study, 2: Substance abuse in young cases. *Archives of General Psychiatry, 43,* 962–965.

Frank, E., Carpenter, L., & Kupfer, D. (1988). Sex differences in recurrent depression: Are there any that are significant? *American Journal of Psychiatry, 145,* 41–45.

Girling, D., Barkley, C., Paykel, E., Gehlhaar, E., Brayne, C., Gill, C., Mathewson, D., & Huppert, F. (1995). The prevalence of depression in a cohort of the very elderly. *Journal of Affective Disorders, 34,* 319–329.

Good, G., Gilbert, L., & Scher, M. (1990). Gender aware therapy: A synthesis of feminist therapy and knowledge about gender. *Journal of Counseling and Development, 68,* 376–380.

Good, G., Robertson, J., Fitzgerald, L., Stevens, M., & Bartels, K. (1996). The relation between masculine role conflict and psychological distress in male university counseling center clients. *Journal of Counseling and Development, 75,* 44–49.

Good, G., & Wood, P. (1995). Male gender role conflict, depression, and help-seeking: Do college men face double jeopardy? *Journal of Counseling and Development, 74,* 70–75.

Hanna, E., & Grant, B. (1997). Gender differences in DSM-IV alcohol use disorders and major depression as distributed in the general population: Clinical implications. *Comprehensive Psychiatry, 38,* 202–212.

Heifner, C. (1997). The male experience of depression. *Perspectives in Psychiatric Care, 33,* 10–18.

Isometsa, E., Henriksson, M., Aro, H., Heikkinen, M., Kuoppasalmi, K., & Lonnquist, J. (1994). Suicide in major depression. *American Journal of Psychiatry, 151,* 530–536.

Kelly, J., Murphy, D., Bahr, R., Kalichman, S., Morgan, M., Stevenson, Y., Koob, J., Brasfield, T., & Bernstein, B. (1993). Outcome of cognitive-behavioral and support group based therapy for depressed, HIV-infected persons. *American Journal of Psychiatry, 150,* 1679–1686.

Kessler, R., McGonagle, K., Zhao, S., Nelson, C., Hughes, M., Eshelman, S., Wittchen, H., & Kendler, K. (1994). Lifetime and 12-month prevalence of DSM-III-R psychiatric disorders in the United States: Results from the National Comorbidity Survey. *Archives of General Psychiatry, 51,* 8–19.

Klerman, G., Weissman, M., Rounsaville, B., & Chevron, E. (1984). *Interpersonal psychotherapy of depression.* New York: Basic Books.

Kornstein, S., Schatzberg, A., Yonkers, K., Thase, M., Keitner, G., Ryan, C., & Schlager, D. (1996). Gender differences in presentation of chronic major depression. *Psychopharmacology Bulletin, 31,* 711–718.

Lewinsohn, P., & Gotlib, I. (1995). Behavioral theory and treatment of depression. In E. Becker & W. Leber (Eds.), *Handbook of depression* (pp. 352–375). New York: Guilford Press.

Loewenthal, K, Goldblatt, V., Gorton, T., Lubitsch, G., Bickness, H., Fellowes, D., & Sowden, A. (1995). Gender and depression in Anglo-Jewry. *Psychological Medicine, 25,* 1051–1063.

Lynch, J., & Kilmartin, C. (1999). *The pain behind the mask: Overcoming masculine depression.* Binghamton, NY: Haworth Press.

Manson, S. (1995). Culture and major depression; Current challenges in the diagnosis of mood disorders. *Psychiatric Clinics of North America, 18,* 487–501.

Moscicki, E. (1997). Identification of suicide risk factors using epidemiological studies. *Psychiatric Clinics of North America, 20,* 499–517.

Murphy, J., Olivier, D., Monson, R., Sobol, A., & Leighton, A. (1988). Incidence of depression and anxiety: The Stirling County Study. *American Journal of Public Health, 78,* 534–540.

Nolen-Hoeksema, S. (1987). Sex differences in unipolar depression: Evidence and theory. *Psychological Bulletin, 101,* 259–282.

Osgood, N., & Thielman, S. (1990). Geriatric suicidal behavior: Assessment and treatment. In S. Blumenthal & D. Kupfer (Eds.), *Suicide over the life cycle: Risk factors, assessment, and treatment of suicidal patients* (pp. 341–379). Washington, DC: American Psychiatric Press.

Pollack, W. (1998). Mourning, melancholia, and masculinity: Recognizing and treating depression in men. In W. Pollack & R. Levant (Eds.), *New psychotherapy for men* (pp. 147–166). New York: Wiley.

Real, T. (1997). *I don't want to talk about it: Overcoming the secret legacy of male depression.* New York: Simon & Schuster.

Robins, L., & Reiger, D. (1991). *Psychiatric disorders in America.* New York: Free Press.

Simpson, H., Nee, J., & Endicott, J. (1997). First-episode major depression: Few sex-differences in course. *Archives of General Psychiatry, 54,* 633–639.

Stiver, I., & Miller, J. B. (1997). From depression to sadness in women's psychotherapy. In J. Jordan (Ed.), *Women's growth in diversity* (pp. 217–238). New York: Guilford Press.

Takeuchi, D., Chung, R., Lin, K., Shen, H., Kurasake, K., Chun, C., & Sue, S. (1998). Lifetime and twelve-month prevalence rates of major depressive episodes and dysthymia among Chinese Americans in Los Angeles. *American Journal of Psychiatry, 155,* 1407–1414.

Thase, M., Greenhouse, J., Frank, E., Reynolds, C., Pilkonis, P., Hurley, K., Grochocinski, V., & Kupfer, D. (1997). Treatment of chronic depression with psychotherapy or psychotherapy-pharmacotherapy combinations. *Archives of General Psychiatry, 34,* 1009–1015.

Thase, M., Reynolds, C., Frank, E., Simons, A., McGeary, R., Fasiczka, A., Garamoni, G., Jennings, R., & Kupfer, D. (1994). Do depressed men and women respond similarly to cognitive behavior therapy? *American Journal of Psychiatry, 151,* 500–505.

Vessey, J., & Howard, K. (1993). Who seeks psychotherapy? *Psychotherapy, 30,* 546–553.

Weissman, M., Bruce, M., Leaf, P., Florio, L., & Holzer, C. (1991). Affective disorders. In L. Robins & D. Reiger (Eds.), *Psychiatric disorders in America* (pp. 53–80). New York: Free Press.

Wilhelm, K., & Parker, G. (1994). Sex differences in lifetime depression rates: Fact or artefact? *Psychological Medicine, 24,* 97–111.

Winokur, G. (1997). All roads lead to depression: Clinically homogeneous, etiologically heterogeneous. *Journal of Affective Disorders, 45,* 97–108.

Young, M., Scheftner, W., Fawcett, J., & Klerman, G. (1990). Gender differences in the clinical features of unipolar major depressive disorder. *Journal of Nervous and Mental Disease, 178,* 200–203.

CHAPTER EIGHT

Treating Substance Abuse in Men

Carl Isenhart

When I was first asked to write this chapter for this handbook, I was struck with a sense of irony about writing a chapter about men's issues in substance abuse treatment. Because most of the substance abuse literature in general and the treatment outcome literature in particular involves male subjects, it would be reasonable to ask why this chapter is needed.

But there are some very good reasons. First, men have more significant alcohol abuse and alcohol-related problems, become intoxicated at an earlier age, and experience more alcohol-related legal and other social problems than do women (Dawxson, 1996; Fillmore et al., 1997).

Second, there are gender differences in substance abuse treatment outcomes. Some reviews have found mixed or contradictory results (Moos, Finney, & Cronkite, 1990; Toneatto, Sobell, & Sobell, 1992), but Beckman (1993) suggested that women may have a slightly better outcome than men. Project MATCH (Project MATCH Research Group, 1997) results indicated that of the patients in an aftercare group men had fewer days of abstinence than did women and that being male, along with other variables, predicted more alcohol consumption during drinking days. Moos et al. (1990) noted that being male, along with having more psychiatric symptoms, was associated with increased alcohol use as length of time increased during the follow-up period.

Third, men either do not seek medical or psychological services or do so later than they should (Helgeson, 1995). This masculine reluctance to seek health care in general implies that men will be reluctant to seek substance abuse services in particular.

Consequently, there are some good reasons to address male gender issues in substance abuse treatment. Because the research has focused mostly on alcohol use rather than other drug use, alcohol abuse and its treatment are the focal points of this chapter. However, before going any further, I offer three caveats.

First, to describe what a male role is implies what a female role is not and vice versa. Obviously it is not as simple as that. Both sexes have a mix of gender expectations. There may be clusters of gender role expectations, some attributable more to men and others attributable more to women but nonetheless attributable to some extent to both sexes. Therefore, it is simplistic to think in terms of either-or; a more realistic way to think about this topic is to what extent expectations apply to both sexes and within each individual.

Some of the literature cited in this chapter (for example, Kaplan & Marks, 1995) references levels of femininity and masculinity in both women and men. Within the sexes, many men (depending on age, social status, education, and region) display some features that would traditionally be described as feminine, and many women display some features that would traditionally be described as masculine. Therefore, in this chapter I discuss issues related to masculinity with the assumption that they apply in greater proportion to men. However, clearly some of these issues do not apply to some men and may apply to some women.

The second caveat is that nothing in this chapter is intended to reduce the responsibility of men's decision to use substances and to be accountable for the resulting consequences. Men may be under pressure to comply with masculine role expectations, but everyone is under pressure to fulfill and live up to many other role expectations: father, mother, spouse, and so forth. It is up to everyone to fulfill his or her roles in ways that are beneficial to the person, his or her immediate social network, and society in general.

The third caveat is that substance abuse treatment services have been helpful to many people, and I review some relevant literature in this chapter. Consequently, it is not my intent in this chapter to dismiss those accomplishments but rather to show that there is room for improvement; toward that aim, this chapter may provide some guidance.

I describe common expectations of the traditional male role and how many of these expectations encourage alcohol use. These expectations encourage alcohol use because (1) alcohol use is associated with the traditional masculine role and (2) men use alcohol to better fit into the traditional masculine role and to better manage the stress associated with living up to the traditional masculine role. Williams and Ricciardelli (1999) referred to these styles as confirmatory and compensatory drinking, respectively. The review of the masculine role expectations is also important because such expectations may lead to conflicts with treatment and recovery expectations. Such conflicts may interfere with men's participation in alcohol abuse treatment services.

I review research describing the impact of male role expectations on health care use, both medical and psychological, to provide a context in which to understand men's health care–seeking behavior, including services for alcohol abuse. Given this background, I describe the stages of change model and motivational interviewing as strategies to address men's issues in treatment. Also, because traditional treatment may be contradictory to the traditional male role, I explore the treatment outcomes research to demonstrate that a number of treatment options are available to staff and patients. Such options provide therapists and clients flexibility in developing treatment goals and strategies. The implication is that services can be tailored to meet the patient's needs rather than wasting time trying to force a patient to adopt a particular philosophy that is inconsistent with his masculine identity.

TRADITIONAL MASCULINE GENDER ROLE EXPECTATIONS

The traditional masculine role expectations provide a backdrop against which to better understand men's substance use and behavior in treatment. As mentioned earlier in this handbook, David and Brannon (1976) identified four male role expectations: "No Sissy Stuff," "The Big Wheel," "The Sturdy Oak," and "Give 'Em Hell."

If men perceive these expectations as mandates for behavior, then stress will result when men perceive their behavior as inconsistent with or falling short of these expectations. Two concepts have been used to address the relationship between the masculine role and stress associated with that role. It should be noted that stress as referred to in this discussion relates to stress associated with fulfilling masculine role expectations and not to using alcohol to cope with stress in general. Cooper, Frone, Russell, and Peirce

(1997) reported that stress or coping style could not account for gender differences in alcohol abuse.

The first concept is masculine gender role stress (Eisler & Skidmore, 1987). A man experiences masculine gender role stress in two circumstances: when he feels unable to live up to the expectations of the traditional male role or when he perceives himself as being expected to behave in ways that are inconsistent with the traditional male role. The authors identified five classes of stressful situations that constitute masculine gender role stress: (1) inadequate physical performance, (2) having to express emotions, (3) subordinating to women, (4) inferior intellectual performance, and (5) overall performance failure.

The second concept is gender role conflict and strain (O'Neil, 1982; O'Neil, Good, & Holmes, 1995; Pleck, 1995), which may result from the conflict resulting from attempting to comply with the "masculine mystique." O'Neil (1982) described the masculine mystique as a set of rigid expectations and attitudes about masculinity that prescribes the rejection of any thoughts, feelings, attitudes, or behaviors that others may see as feminine. Specifically, men traditionally have aversions to anything feminine, strive to be masculine, inhibit emotional expression, and keep emotional and physical distance from other men. The conflict and strain set up six patterns of conflict: (1) restricted emotionality; (2) homophobia; (3) behavioral demonstrations of power, control, and competition; (4) limited expression of sexual and affectionate behaviors; (5) overemphasis on achievement and success; and (6) avoidance of seeking health care.

Use of Alcohol to Meet Gender Role Expectations

Williams and Ricciardelli (1999) described compensatory drinking as individuals using alcohol to "heighten their sense of masculinity or femininity" (p. 324). In this section I review how traditional masculine role expectations promote alcohol use as a way for a man to better fit in to the masculine role and also as a way to manage the stress associated with not fitting into the role. Williams and Ricciardelli found that, for both men and women, high scores on alcohol use were associated with high scores on "negative masculinity" (for example, "being bossy") and low scores on "positive femininity" (for example, "loves children").

Blazina and Watkins (1996) reported a significant relationship between success, power, and competition and college men's admission of increased alcohol use. McCreary, Newcomb, and Sadava (1999) maintained that the more men held traditional attitudes, the more alcohol they consumed. They found that high masculine gender role stress and alcohol use were associated with alcohol problems; however, high masculine gender role stress was not associated with alcohol consumption.

In a study by Isenhart (1993), men dependent on alcohol participating in a substance abuse treatment program with high scores on selected masculine gender role stress scales had high scores on the Enhancement scale of the Alcohol Use Inventory—Revised (AUI-R) (Horn, Wanberg, & Foster, 1990). This finding would suggest that high masculine gender role stress scores were associated with using alcohol to improve social, emotional, cognitive, and interpersonal functioning. Patients with high masculine gender role stress also experienced more alcohol-related disruptions and more concern about their alcohol use than men with low masculine gender role stress scores.

Finally, McClelland, Davis, Kalin, and Wanner (1972) found that when their male subjects consumed small or moderate amounts of alcohol, the subjects reported increased fantasies of "socialized" or "altruistic" control over others. Such control is represented by acts of teaching or helping others. However, when the subjects consumed larger amounts of alcohol, the fantasies changed to "personalized" or "self-aggrandizing" control over others. This kind of control is represented by acts that are sexual or aggressive in character. McClelland and coworkers' research supports the line of reasoning in the previous paragraphs that men use alcohol to augment their ability to fulfill gender role expectations associated with power, dominance, and control.

Alcohol and "Manliness"

Alcohol use can be a major part of what defines a man socially. This idea is important because, given this relationship between alcohol and masculinity, when a man is asked (or told) to give up alcohol, he may feel like he is also giving up part of his masculine identity. Williams and Ricciardelli (1999) described confirmatory drinking as alcohol use that reinforces gender stereotypes. In this section, I review literature that shows that alcohol use has been inextricably integrated into the masculine role for many years. Pursch (1976) provided one description about the relationship between men and alcohol use:

> the hard drinking, two-fisted, pioneering frontiersman; the hard-charging tiger of an aviator who can drink all night and fly all day; the ruggedness of the guy who can hold his liquor like a man; and the notion that you can't trust a man who won't drink (p. 1656)

Lemle and Mishkind (1989) outlined how alcohol has been symbolic of being male and how alcohol use has been associated with personality features that are consistent with male role expectations: questioning authority, challenging convention, and being uninhibited. Lemle and Mishkind (1989) nicely summarized their argument: "Alcohol is the only drug which is part of the male sex role, the only mood altering drug which society overtly promotes as manly" (p. 217).

One major way in which society promotes the connection between the male role and alcohol use is through the media. Postman, Nystrom, Strate, and Weingartner (1987) concluded that beer was associated with traditionally masculine pursuits and leisure activities that required strength, endurance, and risk. Beer was presented as a source of group cohesiveness, identity, and membership, and it was a symbol for acceptance, friendship, and affection.

Also, beer was shown as a way to enhance the romantic relationships between men and women via lowered inhibitions and the creation of an amorous mood. Wallack, Breed, and Cruz (1987) found that 74 percent of beverages consumed during a sample of prime-time shows were alcoholic and that the frequency of consumption by men was twice that by women. The impact of these ads is significant. For example, Grube and Wallack (1994) reported that in a sample of fifth- and sixth-grade children, recognition of televised beer commercials was associated with positive drinking attitudes and heightened intentions to use alcohol as an adult.

ISSUES OF MEN'S UTILIZATION OF HEALTH CARE

The preceding sections suggest that the traditional masculine role has clear expectations for behavior, that alcohol use can be used to comply with those expectations, and that alcohol in itself is a part of the masculine identity. In this section I review how these expectations influence men's health care utilization. Helgeson (1995) reported that men are less likely than women to follow standard health procedures, consult physicians, and report symptoms. Kaplan and Marks (1995) found that men with high measures of femininity displayed higher levels of health concern than men with low femininity scores.

Field, Kockey, and Small (1997) reported that men avoid help-seeking behavior because it is traditionally feminine, and men are expected to be self-reliant and to minimize illness. However, these authors cautioned that such explanations are made out of context of other variables, such as age and social class. Waldron (1995) reported other cautions; she acknowledged that women seek medical care more often then men but for conditions that do not typically result in death. For example, women wait just as long or longer than men to seek services for many types of cancer and for heart disease.

Men's reluctance to seek services goes beyond medical interventions and includes seeking psychological services as well. Helgeson (1995) reported that redivorced men, when compared with redivorced women, reported twice as much depression but sought treatment for the depression less frequently. She also noted that men with depression are viewed more negatively than women with depression. Good, Dell, and Mintz (1989) reported similar findings. They found that traditional male role attitudes were associated with negative attitudes about obtaining psychological services and noted that

> The need to dispel the popular yet restrictive image of men as the "strong and silent type" appears warranted. Indeed, for men who hold traditional attitudes toward the male role, a reframing of the stigma of seeking counseling appears necessary. (Good et al., 1989, p. 300)

Helgeson (1995) attributed these findings to a gender role that dissuades men from admitting to problems and concerns and from seeking health care services. This kind of behavior is seen as inconsistent with being strong, invulnerable, and self-reliant. Eisler (1990) stressed that some men may see obtaining help as feminine, and consequently obtaining help may threaten their sense of independence. He added that the expectation of disclosing vulnerabilities and giving over power and control to others could also be stressful. He concluded: "the role we require male clients to perform in traditional counseling runs counter to the coping techniques that men have learned as essential in maintaining their sense of values as men" (p. 57).

Researchers have examined men's behavior specifically in substance abuse treatment. Beckman (1993) reported that women are more likely to be aware of their alcohol abuse problem, whereas men are more likely to experience conflicts, particularly with those in authority positions, that result in them being involuntarily referred to substance abuse treatment. Blazina and Watkins (1996) postulated a curvilinear relationship between alcohol use and masculinity: although masculinity is associated with increased alcohol consumption, after the point when the man loses control over his alcohol use (that is, manifests lower levels of success, power, and competition) perceived masculinity may be reduced. Lemle and Mishkind (1989) made a similar point: a man's ability to "hold his liquor" is consistent with the male role and not being able to do so (that is, experiencing signs of dependency and alcohol-related problems) is inconsistent with the male role. Therefore, the admission of alcohol-related problems, let alone seeking help, is patently inconsistent with the traditional masculine role.

One reason to consider substance abuse treatment options (and why this issue is reviewed later in this chapter) is that some of the expectations associated with the traditional, Alcoholics Anonymous–based treatment philosophy may be inconsistent with traditional masculine roles. Beckman (1993) reported that one reason Women for Sobriety was established was because Alcoholics Anonymous was perceived as not meeting women's needs. The same may be true for men. Because of masculine role expectations, men may find it difficult to admit to powerlessness and turn over power and control, disclose weaknesses and "character defects," and unconditionally accept a set of tenets (particularly if they are inconsistent with decades of socialization).

Moos et al. (1990) reported a significant positive correlation between men's alcohol consumption at follow-up and the level of staff control within the substance abuse treatment programs. They interpreted this relationship between staff control and outcome to be consistent with the male gender expectation of maintaining power and control. They suggested that poorer outcome may be the result of a treatment environment that is perceived as being too controlled and that promotes a feeling of powerlessness on the part of the participants. In their study, women also reacted negatively to perceptions of increased staff control in the form of more depression and less social activity. Finally, DiClemente (1993) noted that Alcoholics Anonymous–based services may not be appropriate for particularly ambivalent patients in general because of the prominence of turning over power and control to a higher power, the declaration of oneself as being an alcoholic, and the emphasis on abstinence as the only goal.

APPROACHES TO ADDRESSING MEN'S ISSUES IN SUBSTANCE ABUSE TREATMENT

I have reviewed some of the variables that influence men's use of alcohol and health care services in this chapter: the masculine role is closely affiliated with heavy alcohol use to fit in and to manage the stress associated with not living up to these expectations, seeking help is inconsistent with the traditional male role, and men do not routinely seek out health care in general (and they show very low adherence rates to any recommended or prescribed interventions). In addition, many substance abuse services and interventions require men to behave in ways that are inconsistent with the traditional male role and that are counter to decades of socialization. With this background, I review intervention services that may be more appropriate for the treatment of men with substance abuse problems.

Ambivalence

One of the greatest challenges of working with those with substance abuse problems or any clients considering change is the reluctance and ambivalence they exhibit about making changes. The typical response by treatment staff is to attribute that ambivalence to denial, and clients are expected display less denial and become motivated for change as treatment progresses. Thus, motivation has been traditionally perceived as a dichotomy: a patient is either motivated or is not motivated.

However, this traditional attitude misses the fact that ambivalent behavior is consistent with the traditional masculine role of maintaining power and control and questioning convention and authority. Staff members' attribution of ambivalence to denial also ignores any interventions they can make to decrease this resistance, and, just as important, it minimizes the role staff members may have in increasing resistance. The net result is that men become frustrated and at best marginally participate or at worst leave treatment; these actions only reinforce staff members' beliefs about denial, which results in less effective treatment.

Readiness for Change

Studies have demonstrated inconsistencies and contradictions with this model of motivation and have supported new perspectives (Miller, 1985, 1995, 1998; Miller & Rollnick, 1991); these new perspectives have led to innovations for working with clients with substance abuse problems. For example, studies of "self-changers" (people who have changed behavior without professional intervention) have shown that ambivalence or doubt about making changes is normal and natural in the change process (Cohen et al., 1989; Orford, 1985). Previous research by McConnaughy, Prochaska, and Velicer (1983) and McConnaughy, DiClemente, Prochaska, and Velicer (1989) identified stages of change through which patients proceed during psychotherapy: (1) precontemplation, (2) contemplation, (3) determination, (4) action, and (5) maintenance.

In *precontemplation,* the individual perceives that there is no problem and consequently sees no reason to change. A person at the *contemplation* level begins to consider the possibility that there may be a problem and begins to experience some ambivalent feelings about the possibility of change. In *determination,* the individual acknowledges the presence of a problem and makes a decision to initiate changes to address that problem in the future. The individual takes steps to implement change to address the problem behavior while in the *action* level. And a person in *maintenance* strives to establish conditions to maintain their changes.

These concepts have been applied to substance abuse and have demonstrated that people experience varying levels of motivation to change their addictive behavior (Prochaska, DiClemente, & Norcross, 1992); that is, like most change, addressing one's addictive behavior involves progressing and regressing through a range of readiness-for-change levels. Although these concepts are discussed as stages, more accurately they represent points along a continuum where one point imperceptibly merges with the next point.

Also, this view means not only that there is overlap and no clear demarcation between stages but also that clients may experience features associated with different stages simultaneously. For example, even while a client is taking action, he or she may continue to have feelings of ambivalence, which are associated with contemplation. Consequently, instead of referring to stages of change, many clinicians refer to this process as readiness for change. The term implies that change is not dichotomous and that people do not simply go from not being motivated to being motivated to change; change involves a complex and dynamic continuum that is greatly influenced by the environmental conditions in which change is being considered.

For men, one source of this ambivalence can be the perceived contradictions between treatment expectations and social role expectations regarding alcohol use. The implications of these concepts is that men are at different levels of readiness for change regarding their alcohol use. For a number of reasons that I have already addressed (for example, using alcohol to be more manly or reluctance to seek help because it is counter to traditional men's socialization), some men may be unwilling to consider change, others may be considering but not yet ready to take action, and still others may be ready to take action.

Prochaska et al. (1992) provided strategies for working with clients at different levels of motivation. These strategies work well when integrated with motivational interviewing, which I discuss in the next section. When working with a man who is precontemplative, one goal would be to increase his consciousness about his alcohol use. One strategy might be to examine the relationship between alcohol use and the man's feelings of masculinity, sense of independence and control, and how alcohol may help him manage feelings and feel dominant and confident in social situations. This process can lead to the man's increased awareness that he may be using alcohol as an artificial support and how this use of alcohol has led or can lead to problems.

Once a man is aware of his alcohol use and the potential problems, he may become contemplative—that is, ambivalent—about his alcohol use. The strategy now is to have the man generate the positive and negative past consequences and future expectations associated with both maintaining and changing his current alcohol use pattern. Acknowledgment on the part of the therapist regarding alcohol's benefits and the downside of making changes communicates acceptance and respect for the client's perspective. This acknowledgment and respect increase the likelihood that the patient will begin discussing the negative consequences of alcohol use and be willing to admit to problems and concerns. The goal is to have the client generate his own list of problems rather than have the therapist outline them for him. This approach allows the man to maintain a sense of control and not feel subordinate to the therapist.

A client within the determination range of the continuum has decided that he has a problem but has not yet initiated behavior changes. The goal would be for him to begin considering action steps to change his alcohol use. This consideration can be facilitated by discussing how seeking such services may be inconsistent with masculinity: it may feel "unmanly" to sit in a group and discuss problems, going to others for help may feel like giving up control and is inconsistent with being strong and independent, and such activities may not allow the man to engage in achievement- or success-oriented activities (for example, work at a job or take advantage of possible career opportunities). Once these distortions are identified and verbalized, the client can be encouraged to dispute them: it is OK for men to discuss problems, control can be maintained in treatment by allowing the male to state the direction and timing of services, and engagement in such services may actually facilitate achievement and success by addressing any alcohol-related career problems.

A man within the action and maintenance ranges is ready to engage in new behaviors to change his alcohol use and to maintain those changes and prevent relapse, respectively. This is where the strategies typically associated with substance abuse treatment (for example, brief interventions and mutual-help groups) are instituted. However, even these interventions need to be initiated within a therapeutic relationship and environment that addresses the masculinity issues that have been mentioned so far. For example, not requiring the man to refer to himself as an alcoholic may facilitate his admission to having "problems" with his alcohol use and consequently make him more willing to seek services.

Overall, rather than attempting to engage all patients in action-oriented strategies (because by doing so the therapist establishes the context to intensify resistance), the therapist needs to listen and understand the patient's perspective about his problems and goals, negotiate a plan for realistic change, and solicit from the patient strategies to achieve those goals. This does not mean that the therapist has to agree with these goals or strategies; I discuss constructive ways for the therapist to express his or her concerns about the patient's plans later in this chapter.

Motivational Interviewing

This process of working with clients is embodied in motivational interviewing. Miller (1985, 1995, 1998) has reported that patients' ambivalence is not a personality trait but rather a dynamic interaction between patients and their environment (including the relationship with the therapist). Also, it has been found that the type of intervention and counselor style influences whether the ambivalence (and consequently motivation) increases or decreases (Luborsky, McLellan, Woody, O'Brien, & Auerbach, 1985; Miller, Benefield, & Tonigan, 1993). Consequently, motivation can be increased (or decreased) through the therapeutic relationship, and one aspect of that relationship involves addressing clients' masculinity issues.

Miller and Rollnick (1991; Rollnick and Morgan, 1995) have developed the concept of motivational interviewing as a client-centered style that establishes an atmosphere in which the client can openly discuss his mixed feelings about change, verbalize the benefits and costs of changing and staying the same, and review possible strategies to initiate and maintain any change. Motivational interviewing is a directive approach that encourages the client to decide whether change will occur, to what degree, according to what time frame, and by what means. Although motivational interviewing has strategies and techniques, more than anything it is a therapeutic attitude or philosophy about engaging the client and establishing a therapeutic relationship.

The motivational interviewing approach is conducive to working within the context of masculine role expectations. For example, this approach encourages a man to discuss his concerns about not appearing to be masculine and his reservations about taking advice or discussing vulnerabilities. Specifically, the client retains control by directing the treatment focus, goals, and expectations. This approach supports the client's self-reliance and independence, and it allows the client to make his own decisions. The traditional power gradient is minimized, and the client is not likely to be seen as being in a "one-down" position. The client is truly allowed to maintain responsibility for the direction of his treatment. This strategy supports and encourages a questioning and critical attitude when assessing what is best for the client. The client is encouraged to do what he thinks is in his best interest rather than doing what is traditional.

Miller and Rollnick (1991) discussed five principles of motivational interviewing: (1) express empathy, (2) develop discrepancies, (3) avoid argumentation, (4) roll with the resistance, and (5) support self-efficacy.

A definition of these principles and an example of a therapeutic response follow. *Express empathy* by maintaining and demonstrating an acceptance of (though not necessarily an agreement with) the patient's perspective of the problem: "I understand that you have been getting a lot of messages for a lot of years to use alcohol; it must be tough to consider not drinking." *Develop discrepancies* by generating cognitive dissonance between where the patient currently is and where he aspires to be: "It is difficult to open up and talk about problems, but your being here tells me that you do want some help." *Avoid argumentation* and the use of confrontational dialogue in which the client will feel the need to defend himself: "You're right, there are other ways to look at this." *Roll with the resistance* instead of confronting it directly by using other strategies such as reframing (reflecting the client's statements with an added different perspective) the client's resistance to invite or volunteer a new perspective: "Yes, it is frustrating to be out of control and to have your family telling you what to do, but it sounds like they really care about you." And *support self-efficacy* and build up the individual by recognizing and highlighting past accomplishments and strivings to achieve current goals (no matter how small): "It must have been difficult for you to decide to come in and ask about our services."

Motivational interviewing uses a number of processes to engage these principles. Five opening strategies are used to initiate contact with clients (Miller & Rollnick, 1991): (1) ask open-ended questions: "How does alcohol help you feel more manly?"; (2) listen reflectively: "It sounds like you are giving up control and giving in to others if you stop drinking"; (3) affirm the client: "It takes real strength to admit to having those kinds of problems"; (4) summarize: "You're getting tired of being told what to do, you don't like being treated like a patient, and you'd just like to get all this over with"; and (5) elicit self-motivational statements: "You seem to question how things are typically done in this program; how has this helped you in the past to make changes?" Although these sound like basic interviewing strategies (and they are), they are scarce even in well-trained and seasoned staff.

Motivational interviewing also involves increasing a therapist's awareness of "counseling traps"; these traps may be particularly detrimental when working with men with high masculine expectations. Examples of counseling traps include premature focus and the expert trap. Premature focus occurs when the therapist focuses on an apparent problem before the client is ready to do so; it frequently results in increased resistance. The expert trap involves the therapist having all the answers and giving little encouragement or support for the client to generate alternatives for himself. Both of these traps take away control from the client, place him in a subordinate position, and inhibit a questioning attitude, all of which run counter to masculine role expectations. Although motivational interviewing readings are included in the reference list, this approach is best learned by participation in an experiential training session with a qualified motivational interviewing trainer. Additional information, including how to contact a trainer, can be found on the motivational interviewing Web site (www.motivationalinterview.org).

TREATMENT OPTIONS

It is critical for therapists to be aware of the treatment options available to clients experiencing substance-related disorders. This awareness is particularly important in relationship to the traditional male role, which expects the man to question standard procedures, consider alternatives, and make independent decisions. The studies discussed in this overview include men and women, although more men than women are represented in such studies. The idea that there are alternatives to traditional (that is, Alcoholics Anonymous–based substance abuse programs) was supported by the results of Project MATCH. That study compared the impact of Alcoholics Anonymous–based, cognitive-behavioral, and motivational enhancement interventions on those who abuse alcohol. The results suggested that all three interventions were equally effective and that no particular client characteristic was a better match for one intervention over the other.

Miller, Andrews, Wilbourne, and Bennett (1998) critically evaluated the alcohol treatment outcomes literature. They identified a number of different interventions that had empirical support for reducing alcohol consumption and alcohol-related problems. These interventions included brief interventions and motivational enhancement, coping and social skills training, and the community reinforcement approach. Therefore, rather then engage a client in a debate over a particular program or treatment philosophy, particularly a man who has been encouraged to maintain and demonstrate power and control and who is reluctant to seek services anyway, the therapist can help the client to explore service alternatives and encourage him to identify which strategies to try, how they will be implemented, and for what goals.

Miller et al. (1998) stressed, however, that whatever the treatment service, clients' success depends on the relationship they have with their therapists: "Clients show better short-term and long-term drinking outcomes when treated by therapists who display high levels of client-centered counseling skills" (p. 213). Client-centered counseling is the foundation of motivational interviewing and a main theme of this chapter; therapists who are aware of men's issues in treatment, who meet patients where they are at motivationally, and who incorporate the kinds of philosophies and strategies espoused by motivational interviewing (for example, reflective listening) develop strong therapeutic relationships with the clients with whom they work.

CONCLUSION

Alcohol abuse and dependence are complex disorders, and it would be naive to suggest that the use of the concepts and strategies discussed in this chapter can make these problems any less complex. However, increased awareness of these issues can enhance the quality of the therapeutic relationship, which consistently has been shown to affect treatment outcome. A therapist who communicates an awareness that alcohol is a part of the masculine identity and that alcohol is used to comply with those identity expectations builds the foundation for a strong therapeutic relationship. Also, this relationship is further enhanced if the therapist is sensitive to how seeking alcohol abuse treatment can be inconsistent with male role expectations and may require engaging in behavior that is inconsistent with the male role; this sensitivity can help a male client accept treatment and minimize any reservations or resentments associated with seeking services. Services that match the client's level of motivation will help engage him and avoid overwhelming him. Motivational interviewing strategies will allow the client to identify and prioritize problems, generate strategies, and formulate the timetable to address the problems. The therapist is in a position and has the ability to create an atmosphere that allows for the development of a truly collaborative and client-centered therapeutic relationship that considers a variety of empirically supported treatment opportunities to facilitate behavior change.

References

Beckman, L. J. (1993). Alcoholics Anonymous and gender issues. In B. S. McCrady & W. R. Miller (Eds.), *Research on Alcoholics Anonymous* (pp. 233–248). New Brunswick, NJ: Alcohol Research Documentation.

Blazina, C., & Watkins, E. (1996). Masculine gender role conflict: Effects on college men's psychological well-being, chemical substance usage, and attitudes toward help-seeking. *Journal of Counseling Psychology, 43*, 461–465.

Cohen, S., Lichtenstein, E., Prochaska, J. O., Rossi, J. S., Gritz, E. R., Carr, C. R., Orleans, C. T., Schoenbach, V. J., Biener, L., Abrams, D., DiClemente, C. C., Curry, S., Marlatt, G. A., Cummings, K. M., Emont, S. L., Giovino, G., & Ossip-Klein, D. (1989). Debunking myths about self-quitting: Evidence from 10 prospective studies of persons quitting smoking by themselves. *American Psychologist, 44*, 1355–1365.

Cooper, M. L., Frone, M. R., Russell, M., & Peirce, R. S. (1997). Gender, stress, coping, and alcohol use. In R. W. Wilsnack & S. C. Wilsnack (Eds.), *Gender and alcohol* (pp. 199–224). New Brunswick, NJ: Alcohol Research Documentation.

David, D. S., & Brannon, R. (1976). *The forty-nine percent majority: The male sex role.* Reading, MA: Addison-Wesley.

Dawson, D. (1996). Gender differences in the risk of alcohol dependence: United States, 1992. *Addiction, 91*, 1831–1842.

DiClemente, C. C. (1993). Alcoholics Anonymous and the structure of change. In B. S. McCrady & W. R. Miller (Eds.), *Research on Alcoholics Anonymous* (pp. 79–97). New Brunswick, NJ: Alcohol Research Documentation.

Eisler, R. M. (1990). Gender role issues in the treatment of men. *Behavior Therapist, 13*, 57–60.

Eisler, R. M., & Skidmore, J. R. (1987). Masculine gender role stress: Scale development and component factors in the appraisal of stressful situations. *Behavior Modification, 11*, 123–136.

Field, D., Kockey, J., & Small, N. (1997). Making sense of differences: Death, gender, and ethnicity in modern Britain. In D. Field, J. Kockey, & N. Small (Eds.), *Death, gender, and ethnicity* (pp. 1–28). New York: Routledge.

Fillmore, K. M., Golding, J. M., Leino, E. V., Motoyoshi, M., Shoemacker, C., Terry, H., Ager, C. R., & Ferrer, H. P. (1997). Patterns and trends in women's and men's drinking. In R. W. Wilsnack & S. C. Wilsnack (Eds.), *Gender and alcohol* (pp. 21–48). New Brunswick, NJ: Alcohol Research Documentation.

Good, G. E., Dell, D. M., & Mintz, L. B. (1989). Male role and gender role conflict: Relations to help seeking in men. *Journal of Counseling Psychology, 36*, 295–300.

Grube, J. W., & Wallack, L. (1994). Television beer advertising and drinking knowledge, beliefs, and intentions among schoolchildren. *American Journal of Public Health, 84*, 254–259.

Helgeson, V. S. (1995). Masculinity, men's roles, and coronary heart disease. In D. Sabo & D. F. Gordon (Eds.), *Men's health and illness: Gender, power, and the body* (pp. 68–104). Thousand Oaks, CA: Sage.

Horn, J. L., Wanberg, K. W., & Foster, F. M. (1990). *Guide to the alcohol use inventory.* Minneapolis, MN: National Computer Systems.

Isenhart, C. E. (1993). Masculine gender role stress in an inpatient sample of alcohol abusers. *Psychology of Addictive Behaviors, 7,* 177–184.

Kaplan, M. S., & Marks, G. (1995). Appraisal of health risks: The roles of masculinity, femininity, and sex. *Sociology of Health and Illness, 17,* 206–220.

Lemle, R., & Mishkind, M. E. (1989). Alcohol and masculinity. *Journal of Substance Abuse Treatment, 6,* 213–222.

Luborsky, L., McLellan, A. T., Woody, G. E., O'Brien, C. P., & Auerbach, A. H. (1985). Therapist success and its determinants. *Archives of General Psychiatry, 42,* 602–611.

McClelland, D. C., Davis, W. N., Kalin, R., & Wanner, E. (1972). *The drinking man: A theory of human motivation.* New York: Free Press.

McConnaughy, E. A., DiClemente, C. C., Prochaska, J. O., & Velicer, W. F. (1989). Stages of change in psychotherapy: A follow-up report. *Psychotherapy, 26,* 494–503.

McConnaughy, E. A., Prochaska, J. O., & Velicer, W. F. (1983). Stages of change in psychotherapy: Measurement and samples profiles. *Psychotherapy: Theory, Research, and Practice, 20,* 368–375.

McCreary, D. R., Newcomb, M. D., & Sadava, S. W. (1999). The male role, alcohol use, and alcohol problems: A structural modeling examination in adult women and men. *Journal of Counseling Psychology, 46,* 109–124.

Miller, W. R. (1985). Motivation for treatment: A review with special emphasis on alcoholism. *Psychological Bulletin, 98,* 84–107.

Miller, W. R. (1995). Increasing motivation for change. In R. K. Hester & W. R. Miller (Eds.), *Handbook of alcoholism treatment approaches: Effective alternatives* (2nd ed., pp. 89–104). Boston: Allyn & Bacon.

Miller, W. R. (1998). Enhancing motivation for change. In W. R. Miller & N. Heather (Eds.), *Treating addictive behaviors* (2nd ed.). New York: Plenum.

Miller, W. R., Andrews, N. R., Wilbourne, P., & Bennett, M. E. (1998). A wealth of alternatives: Effective treatments for alcohol problems. In W. R. Miller & N. Heather (Eds.), *Treating addictive behaviors* (2nd ed., pp. 203–216). New York: Plenum.

Miller, W. R., Benefield, R. G., & Tonigan, J. S. (1993). Enhancing motivation for change in problem drinking: A controlled comparison of two therapist styles. *Journal of Consulting and Clinical Psychology, 61,* 455–461.

Miller, W. R., & Rollnick, S. (1991). *Motivational interviewing.* New York: Guilford Press.

Moos, R. H., Finney, J. W., & Cronkite, R. C. (1990). *Alcoholism treatment: Context, process, and outcome.* New York: Oxford University Press.

O'Neil, J. M. (1982). Gender-role conflict and strain in men's lives: Implications for psychiatrists, psychologists, and other human-service providers. In K. Solomon & N. B. Levy (Eds.), *Men in transition: Theory and therapy* (pp. 5–44). New York: Plenum.

O'Neil, J. M., Good, G. E., & Holmes, S. (1995). Fifteen years of theory and research on men's gender role conflict: New paradigms for empirical research. In R. F. Levant & W. S. Pollack (Eds.), *A new psychology of men* (pp. 164–206). New York: Basic Books.

Orford, J. (1985). *Excessive appetites: A psychological view of addictions.* New York: Wiley.

Pleck, J. H. (1995). The gender role strain paradigm: An update. In R. F. Levant & W. S. Pollack (Eds.), *A new psychology of men* (pp. 11–32). New York: Basic Books.

Postman, N., Nystrom, C., Strate, L., & Weingartner, C. (1987). *Myths, men, and beer: An analysis of beer commercials on broadcast television, 1987.* Falls Church, VA: Foundation for Traffic Safety.

Prochaska, J. O., DiClemente, C. C., & Norcross, J. C. (1992). In search of how people change: Applications to addictive behaviors. *American Psychologist, 47,* 1102–1114.

Project MATCH Research Group. (1997). Matching alcoholism treatments to client heterogeneity: Project MATCH posttreatment drinking outcomes. *Journal of Studies on Alcohol, 58,* 7–29.

Pursch, J. A. (1976). From Quonset hut to naval hospital: The story of an alcoholism rehabilitation service. *Journal of Studies on Alcohol, 37,* 1655–1666.

Rollnick, S., & Morgan, M. (1995). Motivational interviewing: Increasing readiness for change. In A. M. Washton (Ed.), *Psychotherapy and substance abuse: A practitioner's handbook* (pp. 179–191). New York: Guilford Press.

Toneatto, A., Sobell, L. C., & Sobell, M. B. (1992). Gender issues in the treatment of abusers of alcohol, nicotine, and other drugs. *Journal of Substance Abuse, 4,* 209–218.

Waldron, I. (1995). Contributions of changing gender differences in behavior and social roles to changing gender differences in mortality. In D. Sabo & D. F. Gordon (Eds.), *Men's health and illness: Gender, power, and the body* (pp. 22–45). Thousand Oaks, CA: Sage.

Wallack, L., Breed, W., & Cruz, J. (1987). Alcohol on prime-time television. *Journal of Studies on Alcohol, 48,* 33–38.

Williams, R. J., & Ricciardelli, L. A. (1999). Gender congruence in confirmatory and compensatory drinking. *Journal of Psychology, 133,* 323–331.

CHAPTER NINE

Male Survivors of Trauma

David Lisak

It is a measure of change that *The New Handbook of Psychotherapy and Counseling with Men* includes a chapter on male survivors of trauma. No such chapter appeared in the *Handbook of Counseling and Psychotherapy with Men* published in 1987. The inclusion of this chapter is not the result of a sudden increase in the prevalence of trauma among men. Men—as boys, adolescents, and adults—have been experiencing trauma for as long as there have been humans on this planet. Rather, the change represented by inclusion of this chapter is one of collective consciousness.

In the years since the publication of the first edition of this book, what was a fledgling new field of men's studies has grown into a dynamic and rapidly expanding discipline. Psychology's corner of it is now represented in the American Psychological Association by the Society for the Psychological Study of Men and Masculinity (Division 51). Three scholarly journals publish the growing body of work associated with this new discipline. The discipline of men's studies serves both as a vanguard for changing consciousness and as a reflection of broad-based cultural changes that are beginning to occur.

Included among these changes is a new and still fledgling awareness that men can indeed experience trauma and its long-term effects in unique ways that are determined by men's unique patterns of gender socialization. The emergence of this awareness has been slow because it challenges many of the core assumptions about men that were not questioned until very recently. Chief among those assumptions was perhaps the most basic of them: that men are synonymous with masculinity, that masculinity is somehow an intrinsic property of maleness. When we free ourselves of this assumption, we become capable of seeing masculinity as a kind of ideology, a set of powerfully held beliefs. Masculinity is a unique ideology in that it is exalted to the status of a gender identity: men are forced to internalize the ideology until they experience it as an intrinsic part of their being—indeed, often the very core of their personal identities. Because the essential features of masculine ideology are toughness, fearlessness, and the denial of vulnerability, it is not surprising that men and the culture that surrounds them have been slow to acknowledge that men can indeed be victimized and that like all victims they suffer.

Our culture's blindness to the suffering of male survivors of trauma can be understood as the result of clashing schemata. The schema of men as essentially synonymous with masculinity is still well entrenched. It is therefore very difficult for people to hold in consciousness the clashing view of men as tough and invulnerable on the one hand and hurt and suffering on the other. How can a man be both at the same time?

An example of this clash of schemata can be seen in some of the best writing from the field of trauma studies. In Judith Herman's excellent book *Trauma and Recovery* (1992) she uses the feminine pronoun to refer to generic victims and the masculine pronoun to refer to generic perpetrators. This usage is interesting because many of the victims discussed in the book, including war veterans and holocaust survivors, are men. The schema that men are perpetrators and women are victims was even more baldly revealed in a recent published study of victimization among navy recruits (Merrill et al., 1998). The abstract, quoted in part, speaks for itself:

> U.S. Navy recruits (n = 3,776) were surveyed for premilitary histories of adult sexual assault. They completed a survey designed to estimate rates for experiences as victims (women) and perpetrators (men) of attempted and completed rape since the age of 14.

The assumption—quite explicit in this case—is plainly that the only thing relevant about men and sexual assault is whether and how often they have perpetrated it. The possibility that they may have been victims of it never seemed to have entered the researchers' minds.

Many individual men have also experienced the clash of these schemata, although more directly and more painfully. More than once male survivors of sexual assault have told me that they were turned away by rape crisis centers. The worst example is a male victim who was told that the crisis center did not have the staff to treat perpetrators. Again, it never entered the staff member's mind that the caller was not a perpetrator but rather a victim of sexual violence.

Fortunately, the changing cultural consciousness about men and masculinity has created a new openness to studying and understanding male survivors of trauma. This development is important for three reasons. First, the evidence now makes it clear that vast numbers of men have suffered traumatic experiences. Second, although men's response to trauma is in part simply a generic human response, it is also in part shaped by their gender socialization, by their internalization of masculine ideology. Thus, the treatment of male trauma survivors must incorporate an understanding of the interaction between trauma and masculinity. Finally, the evidence also makes clear that male survivors of trauma are not only a risk to themselves, in the form of self-destructive behaviors, but also to those around them. Male survivors of trauma are more likely than women to externalize their pain, resulting in the perpetration of interpersonal violence and the tragic continuation of the cycle of pain.

COMMON FORMS OF MALE VICTIMIZATION

Men can experience trauma in an infinite number of ways. However, clinicians are likely to encounter particular forms of traumatic experience, including those described in the following sections.

Childhood Physical Abuse

Estimates of the lifetime prevalence of childhood physical abuse among men, mainly derived from self-reports of college student samples, range from 10 to 20 percent (Briere, 1992; Graziano & Namaste, 1990). Wolfner and Gelles (1993) reported rates of "minor violence" of 65 percent and "severe violence" of 12.6 percent based on responses to the Conflict Tactics Scale (Straus, 1979). Estimates of the incidence of physical abuse of children range from 3.5 to 5.7 cases per 1,000 when based on documented cases to 110 cases per 1,000 when based on surveys of households (Kolko, 1992).

From a clinical perspective, underreporting of childhood physical abuse by men is a chronic problem. Men pervasively downplay the severity of the abuse they experienced and tend to describe it the context of nonabusive discipline. Nevertheless, physical abuse is associated with a wide array of potentially long-term problems, including developmental delays, neurological impairment, disturbances in attachment, impaired self-esteem, decrements in cognitive functioning and school achievement, school discipline problems, difficulties in childhood peer relations, and a greater tendency toward physical aggression and externalizing behaviors, alcoholism, and substance abuse (Crittenden, 1998; Dembo et al., 1987; Dodge, Bates, & Pettit, 1990; Kaufman & Cicchetti, 1989; Kolko, 1992; Lisak & Luster, 1994; Salzinger, Feldman, Hammer, & Rosario, 1991; Schaefer, Sobieraj, & Hollyfield, 1988).

Childhood Sexual Abuse

Once considered a rarity, sexual abuse of males is now beginning to receive the attention it has always deserved. It has been difficult to pin down the prevalence of sexual abuse—that is, the percentage of adult men who experienced sexual abuse at some point during their childhood—but increased research over the past decade has provided some solid estimates. Holmes and Slap (1998) reviewed 166 studies in which the prevalence estimates ranged from 4 to 76 percent. These estimates vary because of differences in sampling and survey techniques, but there has been a narrowing in the range of estimates. Perhaps the best indicators are studies of nonclinical samples in which standardized survey techniques and roughly equivalent abuse definitions have been used. Among these studies, the range of estimates narrows to the neighborhood of 15 to 20 percent (see Finkelhor, Hotaling, Lewis, & Smith, 1990; Fromuth & Burkhart, 1989; Lisak, Hopper, & Song, 1996).

Childhood sexual abuse is associated with an array of long-term negative consequences, although here too there is a great range in the diversity and severity of the impact. In male samples, a history of childhood sexual abuse has been associated with disrupted intimate relationships (Dimock, 1988; Hunter, 1990; Lew, 1988; Lisak, 1994; Lisak & Luster, 1994), substance abuse (Krug, 1989; Lisak & Luster, 1994; Rogers & Terry, 1984), sexual problems (Lisak, 1994; Rogers & Terry, 1984), and an array of psychiatric symptoms (Briere, Evans, Runtz, & Wall, 1988; Fromuth & Burkhart, 1989), including suicidal impulses and attempts (Darves-Bornoz, Choquet, Ledoux, Gasquet, & Manfredi, 1998; Garnefski & Arends, 1998; Lisak, 1994). Gartner (1999) and Mendel (1995) provide summaries and analyses of this literature.

Witnessing Parental Violence

It is extremely difficult to obtain reliable data on the number of children who have witnessed violence between their parents, let alone a breakdown of those numbers according to the sex of the child. Studies of the prevalence of domestic violence rarely query about the presence of children or whether children witnessed the acts described. Further, it has been shown that parents' accounts of their children's exposure are not reliable (O'Brien, John, Margolin, & Erel, 1994). Nevertheless, it is estimated that between 3.3 and 10 million American children each year are witnesses to acts of violence between their parents (Margolin, 1998). The effects of exposure to domestic violence are potentially diverse and long lasting for children and may include depression, impaired social competence and empathic abilities, and aggression. Retrospectively, witnessing violence has been associated with an increased risk among men of committing dating violence and marital violence (Margolin, 1998).

Witnessing Community Violence

For many children, violence is a pervasive feature of the landscape outside their homes. Growing up in such environments is a chronic stressor, is a threat to safety, and can have important long-term effects. Several studies in the 1990s have documented the prevalence of exposure to community violence among particular at-risk groups. For example, Bell and Jenkins (1993) reported that approximately 30 percent of African American children between seven and fifteen years of age who live in Chicago had witnessed either a shooting or a stabbing. Among slightly older children, the proportions increased to more than a third, and 23 percent had by then witnessed a killing. Although there is variability in the reported effects of such exposure, it is generally associated with increased distress, depression, symptoms of posttraumatic stress disorder, and acting-out behavior (Horn & Trickett, 1998).

Combat

Until quite recently, war was the exclusive province of men. It still is a predominantly male endeavor. At the end of the twentieth century, America could look back on two world wars, two protracted regional wars (in Korea and Vietnam), and countless other more contained or brief military engagements. There are currently about 25 million veterans, about 80 percent of whom served during a period of active hostility or war. Of these, a significant number, from senior citizens to young adults still launching their lives, have experienced combat. Many of these men—hundreds of thousands—have symptoms of trauma related to those experiences.

It is probably safe to say that without the Vietnam War there would be no official diagnosis of posttraumatic stress disorder. There certainly would be a much smaller body of literature on the cognitive, emotional, medical, and neurobiological consequences of trauma, because the study of Vietnam veterans has produced the single largest body of research of any type of trauma. As Herman (1992) noted, the antiwar movement provided veterans with the political muscle they needed to force society to acknowledge the psychological impact of combat and ultimately to change the very institutions of society. The suffering of Vietnam veterans has been well documented and has inspired scores of books and movies. The trauma of the Vietnam veteran has become part of America's national consciousness.

This focus has provided a much-needed corrective. The traditional view of the heroic warrior served society's purposes by laying the groundwork for the next generation of young men who would be needed to fight the next war and by salving the consciences of those who stay behind, those who vote to send those young men off to war. But war has always been hell, and it has always scarred its participants. The Vietnam War may have finally exposed the nation to the toll that war exacts from those who survive it, but it was not unique in exacting that toll. Eric Dean, in his book *Shook over Hell* (1999), uncovered evidence of the psychological toll of the American Civil War on its veterans. Similarly, the Korean War, World War I, and World War II caused untold suffering among their veterans, many of whom suffered in isolation because society provided no language, no diagnosis, and no opening for them to speak about the legacy of their experiences.

A colleague of mine treated a World War II veteran for more than two years, the final two years of this man's life. He had survived Normandy, the Battle of the Bulge, the liberation of two concentration camps, and an unimaginable sequence of daily horrors. The seventy-year-old man had never been diagnosed with posttraumatic stress disorder, even though he had suffered a variety of psychiatric symptoms for decades. It was his wife who finally revealed the true scope of his posttraumatic symptoms when she described the decades of nightmares and flashbacks that both of them had endured. For the final two years of his life, this World War II veteran recounted horror after horror, all long stored in his memory and never before revealed. To the end he told his therapist that he would spare her the worst of it, and he did.

Many hundreds of thousands of war veterans suffer in isolation and silence, some because they cannot or will not speak and others because they have never been asked to.

Assault

It is (hopefully) standard practice now when conducting a psychological assessment to inquire about traumatic childhood experiences. If the client is a woman, inquiring about possible sexual assaults would be equally advisable. It ought to be similar standard practice to inquire of men whether they have been victims of assault or other forms of violence.

According to statistics compiled by the Bureau of Justice Statistics, a branch of the U.S. Department of Justice, men outnumber women as victims of violent crime in the United States (*National Crime Victimization Survey,* 1994). In 1994, the most recent year for which a breakdown by sex is available, more than six million American males experienced some form of violent assault, as follows:

Homicide	17,448
Rape/sexual assault	32,900
Robbery	857,300
Aggravated assault	1,658,700
Simple assault	4,012,500

These are the numbers for a single year. Clearly, the odds are excellent that a male client experienced a violent victimization at some point during his lifetime.

Masculinization

I am not simply trying to make a political point by including masculinization in the list of common traumas experienced by men. Nor am I asserting that all men experience their gender socialization as traumatic. However, many men have had profoundly negative and traumatic experiences in the course of their socialization into masculinity, experiences that have branded them and that shape and distort their personalities in much the way that other forms of trauma do. Very often, the most traumatizing masculinization experiences are those that come at the hands of peers—vicious taunting, humiliation, rejection, and degradation. Such experiences become etched in the memories of their victims in much the way that other traumas do, so it behooves therapists to conduct sensitive assessments, both to unearth information and to help their clients understand the enduring impact of these experiences on their behavior.

INTERACTION OF TRAUMA AND MASCULINE SOCIALIZATION

Masculine ideology was in all likelihood constructed over thousands of generations to capitalize on a couple of relatively minor differences between human males and females. Human males tend to have a larger muscle mass and to be more predisposed to aggressive action. A culture that takes these characteristics and dramatically amplifies them would garner an advantage in any conflict with competing human groups or simply in the struggle to survive in harsh environments. By creating an ideology of masculinity and through various traumatic socialization practices forcing males to internalize that ideology, a culture would produce an entire class of humans who struggle mightily to reject within themselves any semblance of vulnerability, any sign or feeling of fear, and who certainly never manifest externally any sign of those dreaded internal experiences. Such a class of humans would be extraordinarily useful as fighters or as scavengers of prey, because they would do very dangerous things despite their fear—that is, they will have been trained to disregard the biologically ingrained fear signals that tell them to run and would instead move forward into the maw of the beast.

The primary function of the ideology of masculinity has always been to confront particular aspects of human biology and quell them—to train individuals to disregard their biological signals to run in fear or to cry in grief and pain. And so one can easily see what this ideology is likely to do to the human male who is unfortunate enough not only to be subjected to such a socialization but also to suffer some other form of victimization, such as childhood physical or sexual abuse. The experience of victimization produces intense biological states of fear, grief, and distress, the very states that masculine ideology was designed to expunge. So the man who experiences abuse is subjected to an apparently irresolvable conflict between his biology and the ideology of masculinity he has internalized.

What do men who are caught in this vicious vise do? Most simply suffer, squeezed by two opposing and converging forces—masculine ideology and the emotional legacy of victimization. Men who have experienced abuse are for the most part destined to feel internally branded by the experience, not intrinsically by the fear and grief it evoked but rather by the inevitable conclusion they must come to that because they most definitely have and continue to experience intense states of fear and vulnerability they can never truly possess what masculinity ideology offers—the identity of being men. To be men under the dictates of this ideology, they cannot experience the vulnerability that is forever the legacy of their victimization.

Branded internally as nonmale, they feel insecure and inferior, and they bring these handicaps with them into many of their life endeavors, relational and occupational. They may spend many decades being productive, raising children, and supporting their community and all the while internally feel themselves to be frauds who at any moment will be discovered as such and exposed as nonmen in a world of true men.

For victimized men who spend long decades in this vise, squeezed between the psychobiological legacy of trauma and masculinity, the only escape is through breaking one of the two jaws of the vise. Which one? Well, there is no choice. They cannot break their biology or erase the psychological legacy of trauma. So their only choice is to break the jaw of masculinity. They must recognize and confront their internalization of that ideology, reconnect with their human biological heritage, and with the heat and energy of that confrontation force open the jaws of the vise sufficiently to make their escape.

Unfortunately, there is another method of escape from the vise, but it is only an apparent escape, not a real one, and the consequences are tragic for men and often for those around them. Some victimized males, squeezed between their biological heritage and masculinity, attempt to renounce biology. They attempt to deny the fear and powerlessness and vulnerability that are essential, biological parts of them, because through such a renunciation they can clutch at the "I am a man" identity offered to them by the ideology of masculinity. It is a classic deal with the devil. In exchange for the cherished object—the masculine identity—victimized males give up so much of what makes them human that they are left profoundly distorted. Emotionally and empathically crippled, they are unable to relate meaningfully to other humans.

And as in all stories about dealing with the devil, the cherished object too turns out to be tainted. The masculine identity garnered through such a deal is a brittle shell founded on illusion. The devil may promise that fear and vulnerability will disappear, but it is not a promise that can be kept. Those vulnerabilities, intrinsic human qualities that they are, will forever haunt their hosts, as biology is wont to do, and so the hosts will forever strain to hold them at bay.

Men who attempt to bury their victimization in this way are likely to react harshly, even violently, when they are confronted externally by the ghosts of their own vulnerability. So when they see vulnerability in their children they will lunge at it in fear and hatred, because it evokes the ghosts of their own. Because their culture bombards them with messages that women as a group are vulnerable and weak, they will hate them, too, and they may attack the vulnerability they see in women.

IMPLICATIONS FOR TREATMENT

Male survivors of trauma are best conceptualized as suffering from dual and interacting traumas. They have been socialized, often traumatically, into an ideology of masculinity that in many cases has severely limited the resources with which they live their lives. In addition, they have suffered a traumatic experience that while leaving its own legacy also tends to massively complicate the legacy of their masculine socialization. The implication of this conceptualization is that the treatment of male survivors of trauma should in most cases proceed on two fronts: (1) confronting the trauma and its legacies and (2) confronting masculinization and its legacies.

Although this conceptualization may seem abstract, it has very concrete implications. Consider some of the likely interactions between men's gender internalizations and the basic work of trauma-focused therapy. No matter which therapeutic school the therapist is anchored in, treatment of trauma includes, typically as its primary component, the active emotional processing of traumatic memories. Trauma therapists routinely work in creative ways to help their clients feel sufficiently safe to approach traumatic memories, to expose themselves to them, and to integrate their cognitive and emotional components. For many male trauma survivors, these basic avenues for healing are partially or wholly blocked by the proscriptive dictates of masculine ideology. To render themselves open and vulnerable to such extreme emotional states, to such states of pain and vulnerability, is to flagrantly violate the norms of masculinity. Any therapist who embarks on such a treatment strategy with a male trauma survivor had better be cognizant of this added impediment to treatment.

At the core of most traumatic experiences are overwhelming states of fear, helplessness, and vulnerability. These are extremely difficult states for anyone to deal with, but they carry an added message and burden for male trauma victims. Most men carry around some degree of scarring resulting from their masculinization experiences. Virtually all men feel to some degree that they do not measure up to the standards of masculine ideology; this "failure" is a certainty because the standards literally defy men's basic humanity. Therefore all men carry with them underlying insecurities about their identity as men, insecurities that almost certainly will be enormously exacerbated by any attempt to approach the emotional legacy of victimization experiences.

Consequently trauma therapy with male victims must incorporate an active effort to treat the legacies of masculine socialization. Those legacies stand like a giant roadblock on the path toward healing from trauma; without actively confronting the legacies, the roadblock will remain.

Treating gender internalizations is essentially the same process as treating any other type of internalization that a therapist perceives to be destructive to clients. For example, clients who were psychologically abused as children would very likely retain many internalized messages from that abuse. They would likely feel themselves to be inferior, bad, spoiled, selfish—whatever the particular words and messages their emotionally abusive parents conveyed to them. A therapist would need to confront those internalizations by identifying them when they crop up, giving them labels, and helping clients trace them back to their source. And the therapist would take an active rather than neutral stance. It is hard to imagine a therapist saying, in effect, "Maybe your parents were right, maybe they were wrong." Rather, few therapists would hesitate to actively challenge such negative internalizations and label them as internalized distortions.

A similar stance is required when confronting the negative, distorting internalizations that result from masculine socialization. The therapist must be prepared to challenge the ideology of masculinity, including its rigid prescriptions and proscriptions and its distorting norms and dictates. Consider the following simple example: When a male trauma client finally approaches the threshold of tears and automatically pulls himself back from "the brink," the therapist must actively identify the full meaning, the consequences, and the roots of that choice. Often, it is helpful to incorporate large measures of psychoeducation in the process, teaching the client the biology of emotions and the role of emotions in human evolution and adaptation. Such lessons in human evolution and biology carry both explicit and implicit messages. Explicitly, they familiarize the client with his emotional systems and help demystify them. Implicitly, they begin to erode his identity as a man and supplant it with an identity as a human.

CONFRONTING THE SCARS OF ABUSE

Paul was a successful investment banker with a six-figure income, an expensive car, a high-priced home in the suburbs, and a work week that typically spanned dawn until dusk six days per week. He was also married and the father of three young children. The superficial indicators of success in his life—his career, financial well-being, and family— actually belied deep undercurrents of fear, insecurity, and profound feelings of inferiority. Virtually no one in Paul's life was aware of those undercurrents, although he was and always had been conscious of them. He simply kept them under tight wraps and compensated for them with a zealous devotion to his work.

Paul's adaptation is not unusual among male survivors of childhood abuse. Although he was profoundly scarred by sexual abuse perpetrated by an uncle throughout his early childhood, Paul sealed away the overt signs of his pain and buried his fears and insecurities to survive the gauntlet of masculine socialization. He emerged from it with at least a superficial hold on the masculine identity he viewed as absolutely crucial to his existence. He was by no means hypermasculine. His gender persona was designed not to flaunt his masculinity but rather to display just enough of it to ward off the critical gaze of other men. It was not that other men saw through him or gave him any reason to doubt himself. Rather, Paul's own feelings of inferiority were so vivid and pervasive that he was constantly vigilant about how other men perceived him, always fearing that they judged him to be less than a man. No matter how successfully he managed his career, no matter how much money he earned, Paul—in the classic manner of male survivors of sexual abuse—felt himself to be branded internally by the abuse, a man who was less than a man.

There was of course a great cost to Paul's adaptation to his trauma and gender socialization, and it was this cost that ultimately forced him to seek treatment. The great seal he placed over his childhood pain—the wall he built to contain all those overwhelming emotions—also walled him off from his capacity to connect emotionally to his wife and children. Thus, with the birth of each child Paul drifted further and further into a one-sided existence, a drift that was virtually preordained by the constraints instilled in him by his abuse history and his experiences of abuse. His disconnection was so great that his wife's threat of separation if he did not seek treatment hit him like a blow from a phantom punch. He had not had a clue that she was that much in despair.

This scenario is not unusual for the initiation of treatment of a male client, and, not surprisingly, Paul was skeptical, guarded, and evasive. He professed genuine bafflement at his wife's desperation about the state of their relationship. Such initial sessions with male clients present therapists with a difficult choice. Do you hold back, shy away from confrontation, and try to establish a degree of trust in an effort to delay what often feels like the man's inevitable judgment that psychotherapy is meaningless? Or do you use the opposite strategy: move in quickly and show the skeptic that things can really happen in the space of one hour?

There can be no rigid rule about such choices, but I almost always choose the latter strategy. I try to quell my fears about scaring the male client away by telling myself that he is already halfway out the door anyway. It is my job to pull him in, not to simply avoid a mistake that hastens his departure.

After Paul's opening remarks I made a deliberately provocative comment. I told him that he was certainly not the first man to sit in that chair without a clue about why his life was about to crash and burn around him and that if he was genuinely interested in figuring out what had happened to him and perhaps avoiding the disaster I was there to try to help him. I also told him that it did not seem as though we had much time and that he had better make a decision quickly. Paul was predictably taken aback by my remarks and was genuinely frightened by them. So I apologized for scaring him, but I did not back off. By the end of the hour we had established a relationship; it was not warm and fuzzy, but it was a relationship built around a job we had to do.

Paul did not disclose his history of sexual abuse to me until the third session. It was by then painfully clear that he was holding back something and becoming unbearably uncomfortable with the strain. Partway through the session I interrupted him and simply asked him to tell me what was scaring him. It was all the prompt he needed.

With the secret out, our work began to take shape. Within a few sessions, we invited Paul's wife to join us so that he could tell her about the abuse and begin to talk about the fears he had been masking for so many years. From then on, couples work became an integral part of the treatment.

I also began giving Paul homework, in the form of readings. He began with *Victims No Longer* (Lew, 1988), a book for male sexual abuse victims. As I began to actively challenge his internalized masculine ideology, he became curious about the language I was using, terms such as *masculinization* and *gender conformity*. So he started reading men's studies texts and was soon immersed in a new universe of ideas that served to validate the changes that he was facing within himself. To help offset the erosion of his former masculinized identity, I gave him LeDoux's book *The Emotional Brain* (LeDoux, 1996). The new discoveries about the neurobiology of emotions, the information about the long evolutionary development of the human repertoire of emotions, and the links between humans and other animal species all served to underscore his more essential identity as a human being, an identity rooted in his biology and one that could eventually supplant the rigid masculinity that he had for so long clung to.

Of course this description does not convey the hard slugging of such treatment—the moments of despair and the impulses to retreat to familiar ground, the ill-timed interpretations and the inevitable misunderstandings. Nevertheless, Paul persevered. He began to meet and experience the emotional legacy of his abuse, simultaneously stretching and eventually breaking the bonds of masculine ideology. His newfound emotional life was a stormy one, and he found himself at times overcome by strange tides of rage, at other times awash in unexpected tears. Had these been the only consequences of his new emotional openness he might well have retreated. But there was an enormous benefit that soon made itself felt: Paul discovered his love for his wife and children, and his emotional connection to them was reciprocated. He soon found himself chafing at the demands of his job, regretting the time spent away from his family. As Paul altered his fundamental adaptation to life as a man who had been abused, he found that the life he had built no longer matched his altered self, and he began looking for ways to make further changes.

There are hopeful signs that men are beginning to challenge masculine ideology, to alter their views of themselves and thereby to alter the way society views them collectively, as a gender. One of the immediate consequences of this change is an increase in the number of men who are seeking treatment, and among these men are many who have experienced psychological trauma. The psychological community must prepare itself to meet these men; mental health professionals must be well informed and capable of providing the treatment these men need and deserve.

However, these emerging changes are part of a much broader cultural change that has immense social and political implications. Further, recent history suggests that for such fundamental—and personal—changes to be successful, individual men need the support and validation of a movement. Heroic individuals can sometimes overcome the tidal forces of culture independently and provide the rest of us with an example and an inspiration. But for such changes to reach the many, we need more than heroism. We need a movement that can provide its own tidal force, one that can create the new language forms and the new ideas that serve to liberate the many millions of men who are increasingly ready to abandon the maladaptive tenets of masculine ideology.

References

Bell, C. C., & Jenkins, E. J. (1993). Community violence and children on Chicago's Southside. In D. Reiss, J. E. Richters, M. Radke-Yarrow, & D. Scharff (Eds.), *Children and violence* (pp. 46–54). New York: Guilford Press.

Briere, J. (1992). *Child abuse trauma.* Newbury Park, CA: Sage.

Briere, J., Evans, D., Runtz, M., & Wall, T. (1988). Symptomatology in men who were molested as children: A comparison study. *American Journal of Orthopsychiatry, 58*(3), 457–461.

Crittenden, P. M. (1998). Dangerous behavior and dangerous contexts: A 35-year perspective on research on the developmental effects of child physical abuse. In P. K. Trickett & C. J. Schellenbach (Eds.), *Violence against children in the family and the community* (pp. 11–38). Washington, DC: American Psychological Association.

Darves-Bornoz, J. M., Choquet, M., Ledoux, S., Gasquet, I., & Manfredi, R. (1998). Gender differences in symptoms of adolescents reporting sexual assault. *Social Psychiatry and Psychiatric Epidemiology, 33*, 111–117.

Dean, E. T. (1999). *Shook over hell.* Cambridge, MA: Harvard University Press.

Dembo, R., Dertke, M., La Voie, L., Borders, S., Washburn, M., & Schmeidler, J. (1987). Physical abuse, sexual victimization, and illicit drug use: A structural analysis among high risk adolescents. *Journal of Adolescence, 10,* 13–33.

Dimock, P. T. (1988). Adult males sexually abused as children: Characteristics and implications for treatment. *Journal of Interpersonal Violence, 3*(2), 203–221.

Dodge, K. A., Bates, J. E., & Pettit, G. S. (1990). Mechanisms in the cycle of violence. *Science, 250,* 1678–1683.

Finkelhor, D., Hotaling, G., Lewis, I. A., & Smith, C. (1990). Sexual abuse in a national survey of adult men and women: Prevalence, characteristics, and risk factors. *Child Abuse and Neglect, 14,* 19–28.

Fromuth, M. E., & Burkhart, B. R. (1989). Long-term psychological correlates of childhood sexual abuse in two samples of college men. *Child Abuse and Neglect, 13,* 533–542.

Garnefski, N., & Arends, E. (1998). Sexual abuse and adolescent maladjustment: Differences between male and female victims. *Journal of Adolescence, 21,* 99–107.

Gartner, R. B. (1999). *Betrayed as boys.* New York: Guilford.

Graziano, A. M., & Namaste, K. A. (1990). Parental use of physical force in child discipline: A survey of 679 college students. *Journal of Interpersonal Violence, 5,* 449–463.

Herman, J. L. (1992). *Trauma and recovery.* New York: Basic Books.

Holmes, W., & Slap, G. (1998). Sexual abuse of boys: Definition, prevalence, correlates, sequelae, and management. *Journal of the American Medical Association, 280,* 1855–1862.

Horn, J. L., & Trickett, P. K. (1998). Community violence and child development: A review of research. In P. K. Trickett & C. J. Schellenbach (Eds.), *Violence against children in the family and the community* (pp. 103–138). Washington, DC: American Psychological Association.

Hunter, M. (1990). *Abused boys.* Lexington, KY: Lexington Books.

Kaufman, J., & Cicchetti, D. (1989). Effects of maltreatment on school-age children's socioemotional development: Assessments in a day-camp setting. *Developmental Psychology, 25,* 516–524.

Kolko, D. J. (1992). Characteristics of child victims of physical violence. *Journal of Interpersonal Violence, 7,* 244–276.

Krug, R. S. (1989). Adult male report of childhood sexual abuse by mothers: Case descriptions, motivations, and long-term consequences. *Child Abuse and Neglect, 13,* 111–119.

LeDoux, J. (1996). *The emotional brain.* New York: Simon & Schuster.

Lew, M. (1988). *Victims no longer.* New York: Nevraumont.

Lisak, D. (1994). The psychological consequences of childhood abuse: Content analysis of interviews with male survivors. *Journal of Traumatic Stress, 7,* 525–548.

Lisak, D., Hopper, J., & Song, P. (1996). Factors in the cycle of violence: Gender rigidity and emotional constriction. *Journal of Traumatic Stress, 7,* 507–523.

Lisak, D., & Luster, L. (1994). Educational, occupational, and relationship histories of men who were sexually and/or physically abused as children. *Journal of Traumatic Stress, 7,* 507–523.

Margolin, G. (1998). Effects of domestic violence on children. In P. K. Trickett & C. J. Schellenbach (Eds.), *Violence against children in the family and the community* (pp. 57–101). Washington, DC: American Psychological Association.

Mendel, M. P. (1995). *The male survivor.* Thousand Oaks, CA: Sage.

Merrill, L. L., Hervig, L. K., Newell, C. E., Gold, S. R., Milner, J. S., Rosswork, S. G., Koss, M. P., & Thornton, S. R. (1998). Prevalence of premilitary adult sexual victimization and aggression in a navy recruit sample. *Military Medicine, 163,* 209–212.

National Crime Victimization Survey. (1994). Washington, DC: U.S. Department of Justice, Bureau of Justice Statistics.

O'Brien, M., John, R. S., Margolin, G., & Erel, O. (1994). Reliability and diagnostic efficacy of parents' reports regarding children's exposure to marital aggression. *Violence and Victims, 9,* 45–62.

Rogers, C. M., & Terry, R. (1984). Clinical intervention with boy victims of sexual abuse. In I. R. Suart & J. G. Greer (Eds.), *Victims of sexual aggression: Treatment of children, women, and men* (pp. 91–104). New York: Van Nostrand Reinhold.

Salzinger, S., Feldman, R. S., Hammer, M., & Rosario, M. (1991). Risk for physical child abuse and the personal consequences for its victims. *Criminal Justice and Behavior, 18,* 64–81.

Schaefer, M. R., Sobieraj, K., & Hollyfield, R. L. (1988). Prevalence of childhood physical abuse in adult male veteran alcoholics. *Child Abuse and Neglect, 12,* 141–149.

Straus, M. A. (1979). Measuring intrafamily conflict and violence: The Conflict Tactics (CT) Scales. *Journal of Marriage and the Family, 41,* 75–88.

Wolfner, G. D., & Gelles, R. J. (1993). A profile of violence toward children: A national study. *Child Abuse and Neglect, 17,* 197–212.

DEVELOPMENTAL ISSUES OF BOYS AND MEN

CHAPTER TEN

The Crises of Boyhood

Ronald F. Levant

Boys today are in crisis even though many appear to be doing just fine on the surface. Over the past decade we have become aware of how difficult it is to grow up female in U.S. society and of the major crisis many girls experience in adolescence, manifested in a dramatic loss of self-confidence and self-esteem. We are less aware of the problems for boys. In fact, we have a cultural blindness to the problems of boys, in part because of our assumption that males should be self-sufficient and in part because boys are required to keep their problems to themselves. However, recent work in the new psychology of boys and men indicates that boys suffer from not one but two crises: the first at the point of entrance into school (between the ages of five and seven) and the second in adolescence.

The first crisis is actually several years in the making and is fundamentally the result of how we socialize our sons' emotions. Because of widespread beliefs in U.S. society about how boys and men ought to behave (what I call the "code of masculinity"), we tend to get swept up in a process of shaping and channeling boys' expression of emotions so that, although boys start out life more emotional than girls, they wind up much less so. By the time a boy enters school he has learned to hide and feel ashamed of two important sets of emotions: those that express vulnerability in one way or another (fear, sadness, loneliness, hurt, shame, and disappointment) and those that express neediness, caring, or connection to others. As a result boys become deeply alienated from themselves and from those closest to them, from whom they feel they must hide their shameful sense of vulnerability and neediness (Levant & Kopecky, 1995; Levant & Pollack, 1995). Thus boys enter school with a fragile personality, which—interacting with the stress of the school situation—manifests itself in an array of problems. Hence, the problems that boys manifest at the start of school are but the tip of the iceberg of deeper-lying difficulties that will not only profoundly influence boys' subsequent development but will also give boys' adolescent crisis its unique character.

THE FIRST CRISIS: SCHOOL DAZE

Quite apart from these underlying problems, boys are vulnerable at the point of entry into school because of the state of their maturation. They are less able than girls to adapt to the school environment; they are slower to learn to read and write, have greater needs for large-muscle activity, and have much less ability to sit quietly and listen to the teacher. The school environment simply has not been planned to accommodate boys' needs. Schools that are doing away with recess may exacerbate this problem for boys.

Boys' Symptoms

Boys also have more symptomatic behavior than girls. At the onset of the school experience boys begin to express more symptoms than girls—in learning, behavior, and emotions. Boys are twice as likely as girls to be diagnosed with learning disabilities. Although girls are diagnosed with dyslexia (a specific learning disability that affects the ability to read) nearly as frequently as are boys, they are more likely to overcome it so that after intervention girls' rates drop to 25 percent that of boys. In terms of behavior, compared with girls, boys are five times more likely to have conduct problems, three times more likely to be enrolled in special education classes, and six times more likely to be diagnosed with attention-deficit/hyperactivity disorder. Of the one million children taking Ritalin for attention-deficit/hyperactivity disorder, 75 percent are boys. In terms of emotions, although girls are eight times more likely to attempt suicide, boys are four times more likely to complete it (Bushweller, 1994; Kiselica & Horne, 1999; Pollack, 1998).

Why do boys have so many problems at the point of entry into school? Partly because of differing rates of maturation of physical and cognitive abilities of boys and girls, such that girls are simply more ready for school than boys, a problem that could be remedied by redesigning the primary grades to take into account boys' needs. But the difference in maturation rates only explains part of the problem. There is a deeper level that is harder to see, hidden as it is by our assumptions about how boys ought to behave. This deeper level concerns the way our sons' emotions and behavior are molded. Just as we discourage our daughters from being too aggressive and (when they are older) too sexual because of our beliefs about how girls ought to behave, we discourage our sons from expressing a whole set of needs and emotions that we consider inappropriate for boys: dependency, vulnerability, and even caring and affection. The net effect of this discouragement is that we inadvertently compound our sons' slower maturation, creating emotional difficulties and vulnerability to symptom formation.

"Snips and Snails and Puppy Dog Tails": Our Beliefs About Boys

I have been studying our beliefs about how boys and men ought to behave for the past decade and have found that the major beliefs in our society are that males must (1) be independent and self-reliant, (2) not express their emotions (particularly those that show vulnerability or their attachment to another person), (3) be tough and aggressive, (4) seek high social status, (5) always be ready for sex, (6) avoid all things "feminine" lest there be any confusion about their masculinity, and (7) reject homosexuality. Together these beliefs make up the code of masculinity—which is quite a demanding set of behaviors, at once stoic and heroic (Levant et al., 1992).

To put these beliefs in context, the code of masculinity fits best with harsh social conditions, such as those that occurred in the United States from the period of industrialization through World War I, the Great Depression, and World War II. In such conditions certain male traits such as toughness, self-reliance, and lack of awareness of emotions are likely to be more adaptive.

Although the code is waning, it still holds sway and in fact profoundly affects how we raise our sons. It is interesting that the code is more strongly endorsed by males than by females and shows differential endorsement in different ethnocultural subgroups in U.S. society (Levant & Fischer, 1998; Levant & Majors, 1997; Levant, Majors, & Kelley,

1998; Levant, Wu, & Fischer, 1996). Nonetheless, we all get caught up in the code, whether we explicitly endorse it ourselves, carry it as a set of unexamined assumptions, or have it forced on us by others (for example, our spouses, other children acting on their parents' views, teachers, coaches, or the culture at large). The net result is that it has a profound influence on the shaping of our boys' emotional lives.

Boys' Emotional Shaping: Birth to Six Years

In this section, we discuss the emotion socialization of boys, showing that, although boys start out more emotionally expressive than girls, they wind up much less so due to their socialization by parents and peers. This emotion socialization process is aimed at curbing boys' expression and ultimately their awareness of both their caring and connection emotions (such as affection, fondness, etc.) and their vulnerable emotions (like fear, sadness, etc.). However, as we shall see, anger and aggression are permitted and even encouraged.

Boys' emotional beginnings. One interesting biological difference between the sexes is that boys seem to be more emotional than girls at birth and remain so until at least one year of age. A review of twelve studies (eleven of which were of neonates, studied just hours after birth) found that boys cry more often and more intensely, but they also coo, gurgle, and smile more often, and they fluctuate more rapidly between emotional states than do girls (Haviland & Malatesta, 1981). Another study found that infant boys were judged to be more emotionally expressive than were infant girls, even when the judges were misinformed about the infants' actual sex, thus controlling for the effects of gender role stereotyping on the part of judges (Cunningham & Shapiro, 1984, cited in Brody & Hall, 1993). Finally, boys remain more emotional than girls at least until six months of age; compared with girls, they exhibit "more joy and anger, more positive vocalizations, fussiness, and crying, and more gestural signals directed toward the mother" (Weinberg, 1992, p. vii).

Crossover in emotional expression. Despite this initial advantage in emotional expressivity, boys learn to tune out, suppress, and channel their emotions, whereas the emotional development of girls encourages their expressivity. These effects become evident with respect to verbal expression by two years of age and with respect to facial expression by six years of age. One study found that two-year-old girls refer to feeling states more frequently than do two-year-old boys (Dunn, Bretherton, & Munn, 1987). Another assessed the ability of mothers of four- to six-year-old boys and girls to accurately identify their children's emotional responses to a series of slides by observing their children's facial expressions on a television monitor. The older the boy, the less expressive his face, and the harder it was for his mother to tell what he was feeling. This researcher found no such correlation among the girls: their mothers were able to identify their emotions no matter what their age. The author concluded that between the ages of four and six years, "boys apparently inhibit and mask their overt response to emotion to an increasing extent, while girls continue to respond relatively freely" (Buck, 1977, p. 234).

Socialization and how it works. What would account for this "crossover in emotional expression" such that boys start out more emotional than girls and wind up much less so? The socialization influences of mother, father, and peer group combine to result in the suppression and channeling of male needs and emotions and the encouragement of female emotionality. These influences are wrought through (1) selective reinforcement, modeling, and direct teaching of desired behavior; (2) the different kinds of experiences that boys and girls have with parents and peers; and (3) punishment for breaking the code of masculinity. These matters were treated in greater detail in another publication (Levant & Kopecky, 1995); hence I simply present a brief overview here.

In infancy, mothers work hard to manage their more excitable and emotional male infants. They smile more when their sons are calm, thus reinforcing calm, inexpressive behavior when they play with their sons. In fact, mothers may go to special lengths to ensure that their sons are contented. Mothers also control their own emotional expressivity to avoid "upsetting their sons' more fragile emotional equilibria" (Haviland & Malatesta, 1981, p. 202). In contrast, mothers expose their infant daughters to a wider range of emotions than they do their sons (Malatesta, Culver, Tesman, & Shephard, 1989).

In the toddler years, fathers take an active interest in their children. This interest becomes apparent in the thirteenth month of life, and from that point on fathers tend to interact with their toddler sons and daughters along gender-stereotyped lines (Lamb, 1977; Lamb, Owen, & Chase-Lansdale, 1979). Fathers interact more with infant sons than they do with infant daughters (Lamb, 1977). With older children, fathers engage in more verbal roughhousing with sons and tend to speak more about emotions with daughters (Greif, Alvarez, & Ulman, 1981; Schell & Gleason, 1989). Fathers also express more disapproval to sons who violate the code of masculinity by engaging in doll play or expressing emotions such as neediness, vulnerability, and even attachment (Langlois & Downs, 1980). Many adult men whom I have counseled recall experiences in which their fathers made them feel deeply ashamed of themselves for expressing vulnerable emotions such as sadness or fear or attachment emotions such as caring, warmth, or affection.

Both parents participate in the development of language for emotions, differentiated along the lines of gender. Parents discourage their sons from learning to express vulnerable emotions; although they encourage their daughters to learn to express their vulnerable and attachment emotions, they discourage their daughters' expression of anger and aggression. It should be noted that females' language superiority also plays a role in their greater ability to express emotions verbally (Brody & Hall, 1993). One investigative team found that mothers used more emotion words when speaking with daughters than with sons (Dunn et al., 1987). Another found that mothers spoke more about sadness with daughters than with sons and only spoke about anger with sons. With daughters, mothers discussed the experience of emotions, whereas with sons they discussed the causes and consequences of emotions, which would serve to help sons learn to control their emotions (Fivush, 1989). A third study had parents "read" stories to their children using wordless books and videotaped and transcribed their conversations. Mothers talked about anger twice as frequently with sons as with daughters (Greif et al., 1981). Finally, another team of researchers found that school-age sons expected their parents to react negatively to the expression of sadness, whereas school-age daughters expected their mothers to react more positively to the expression of sadness than they would to the expression of anger (Fuchs & Thelen, 1988).

Sex-segregated peer groups complete the job. Young girls typically play with one or two other girls, and their play consists of maintaining the relationship (by minimizing conflict and hostility and maximizing agreement and cooperation) and telling each other secrets, thus providing experiences that foster their learning skills of empathy, emotional self-awareness, and emotional expressivity. In contrast, young boys typically play in larger groups in structured games—experiences in which they learn skills such as how to play by the rules, teamwork, stoicism, toughness, and competition (Lever, 1976; Maccoby, 1990; Paley, 1984). One study found that boys experience direct competition in their play half of the time, whereas girls experience it very infrequently (less than 1 percent of the time) (Crombie & Desjardins, 1993, cited in Brody, 1996). Boy culture is also notoriously cruel to boys who violate male role norms, such as expressing vulnerable emotions, showing affection, or being unwilling to fight (Krugman, 1995).

Hardening of boys' hearts. Many adult men recall that their first experiences with limitations on expressing caring emotions actually occurred in the context of their relationships with their fathers, for, in the typical postwar family, hugs and kisses between father and son came to an end by the time the boy was ready to enter school. In addition to whatever messages boys hear at home, they also get the message from their peers that it is not socially acceptable to be affectionate with their mothers (lest they be a "mama's boy"), girls (for fear of being teased by friends), or boys (where anything but a cool, buddy-type relationship with another boy can give rise to the dreaded accusation of homosexuality). Childhood experiences of this type set up powerful barriers to the overt expression of attachment and caring emotions, which thus get suppressed (Levant & Kopecky, 1995).

Overdevelopment of aggression. Through a similar process boys become ashamed of expressing vulnerable emotions such as fear, sadness, loneliness, or hurt, so that they lose touch with their ability to express these emotions as well. On the other hand boys are allowed to feel and become aware of emotions in the anger and rage part of the spectrum, as prescribed in the toughness dimension of the male code. As a result males express anger more aggressively than do females (Brody & Hall, 1993; Campbell, 1993; Eagly & Steffen, 1986; Frodi, Macaulay, & Thome, 1977). The aggressive expression of anger is in fact one of the very few ways boys are encouraged to express emotion; as a consequence, the outlawed vulnerable emotions, such as hurt, disappointment, fear, and shame, get funneled into the anger channel. This rechanneling of emotions has been called "the male emotional funnel system," the final common pathway for all those shameful vulnerable emotions that are too unmanly to express directly (Long, 1987). Some boys learn to actively transform these vulnerable emotions into anger, rage, and aggression, as when a boy is pushed down on the playground and knows that it is expected that he come back up with a fistful of gravel rather than a face full of tears. This facility to transform vulnerable emotions into aggression is learned in boy culture and accounts for the fact that many adult men get angry when their feelings are hurt. It may also have played a role in the school killings by adolescent boys in Jonesboro, Arkansas, Pearl, Mississippi, and Paducah, Kentucky.

The Net Result

These socialization experiences not only prevent boys from being able to express a wide band of the spectrum of human emotions but also make them feel very ashamed of themselves for even having these emotions. Because aggression is encouraged, it becomes boys' only outlet and as a result overdevelops.

This socialization creates a tremendous burden for boys, who come to feel that parts of themselves are unacceptable and even shameful and that they dare not let others see these parts of themselves. Hence boyhood socialization puts boys at odds with parts of themselves and cuts them off from other people, thus creating low self-esteem and a self-imposed isolation. Although this isolation is socially sanctioned, it is also destructive because boys have many needs and feel many vulnerable and caring emotions. As a consequence boys must live a lie and learn to deaden themselves to it.

When you combine these results of socialization with boys' biologically based preference for large-muscle motor activity and later development of reading and writing skills, is it any wonder that our boys are having so many problems when they enter school? However, as already noted, the problems that boys manifest at the start of school are but the tip of the iceberg of deeper-lying difficulties that will not only profoundly influence the boys' subsequent development but also give boys' adolescent crisis its unique character.

THE SECOND CRISIS: TEEN YEARS

Whereas girls experience their major crisis in early adolescence, boys actually have two crises: the school crisis discussed previously and the crisis of adolescence. Boys' adolescent crisis revolves around issues that all children share, such as independence versus dependence, identity, self-confidence, and sexuality. However, it has a particular character because of boys' early training to hide and feel ashamed of their caring and vulnerable emotions, their resultant feelings of being at odds with parts of themselves and unable to go to others for emotional support, their often problematic relationships with their fathers, and the influence of boy culture and the culture at large. These unique effects are seen in such problematic areas as sexuality, alcohol and drug use, risky behavior, and finding a direction in life.

Problematic Sexuality

The way we have traditionally raised our sons to be strong, competitive, and emotionally stoic fosters a problematic sexuality. In adolescence, when interest in sexuality dawns thanks to the combined effects of hormones and culture, boys' caring and connection emotions and their more vulnerable counterparts are nowhere to be found because of boys' earlier emotional training. Hence the basis for letting oneself be vulnerable, for exchanging emotional intimacy, and for the integration of emotional with physical intimacy is simply not there.

Rather, prevailing images in our society of females as sex objects encourage boys to view girls as vehicles for the release of their sexual urges. Acting on messages from their peers and the culture at large, adolescent boys also develop the need to prove their manhood by "scoring" with girls. As a result sexuality for boys becomes nonrelational and self-centered, in contrast to girls' greater emphasis on relational intimacy (Brooks, 1995; Levant & Brooks, 1997). In support of these differing views of sexuality by gender, recent research has found that only half as many males as females reported that affection for their partner was the reason for having sexual intercourse for the first time (Michael, Gagnon, Laumann, & Kolata, 1994).

Some research that I and colleagues have recently conducted on the major concerns of adolescent boys today is relevant to this discussion (Levant, Brooks, & Pitta, 2000). The question teachers (confederates in the study) posed to the boys was, "If you had the chance to have a private and confidential conversation with an expert with a great deal of knowledge and understanding about the concerns of adolescent boys today, what would you want to ask him or her? Please write down six questions about anything at all that is on your mind." Well over 90 percent of the responses concerned sex. Hence sexuality for teenage boys seems to be a looming, every-minute type of obsession.

Why does sex loom so large for boys? For basically the same reasons that anger, rage, and aggression serve as proxies for boys' more vulnerable emotions such as hurt, disappointment, sadness, shame, and loneliness: namely, that boys have been trained to so thoroughly suppress the expression of caring, attachment, neediness, and dependency that these emotions can only emerge in a very disguised, certainly unacknowledged, form hidden in the sexual experience. Like being angry when you are hurt, being lustful when you are needy is the only acceptable way a teenage boy trained under the code of masculinity can behave: powerful, dominant, aggressive, and self-sufficient and in no way vulnerable or needy. Teenage boys are rarely able to articulate this subterranean expression of caring emotions in their overt sexuality, but adult men have acknowledged to me how truly close and intimate they can feel with their wives during the act of sex.

With regard to the specific research results, boys had a lot of questions about sex. Some of these questions concerned anatomical aspects of genitalia, mechanical aspects of intercourse, sexually transmitted diseases, birth control, pregnancy, impotence, premature ejaculation, virginity, homosexuality and what causes it, how to know if you are gay, masturbation, oral sex, the experience of sex (many questions), and girls and how they think about, desire, and experience sex. This long list of questions highlights boys' isolation and underscores how difficult it is for them to talk to adults (parents and teachers) about things that matter a lot to them.

Influence of Popular Culture

For aeons parents have had to battle the influence of popular culture in their attempts to raise their children. Recently, malignant elements that foster misogyny and debasement of sex, as seen in the lyrics of contemporary rap music and MTV shows, have entered into the culture. One result is predatory sex, such as in the infamous "spur posse" (a gang of well-to-do boys who competed by victimizing girls), the "whirlpool" phenomenon (in which a group of boys surround a girl in a public swimming pool, swim around her to create a diversion, and then pull off her swimsuit or worse), "wilding" (in which a group of boys went on a rampage in Central Park, New York, assaulting women), and the like. In addition, the Internet offers too easily accessible XXX-rated pornography and provides pedophiles with a powerful means by which to lure children. These dangers are very real, and parents struggle to know what to do about them.

Alcohol and Drugs

The need to keep the communication channels open becomes even more important in relation to alcohol and drugs. Many teenage boys are involved with drugs of various sorts. Surveys conducted by the National Institute of Drug Abuse indicate that more than 60 percent of high school students have smoked cigarettes at least once, 90 percent have drunk alcohol at least once, and 44 percent have smoked marijuana at least once (Witters, Venturelli, & Hanson, 1992).

Peer pressure plays a large role in substance use. But drugs and alcohol have a particular appeal to teenage boys because they can have the effect of temporarily deadening boys' sensitivity to their emotional turmoil—the struggle between their needs and emotions (if these are not yet fully suppressed) and their beliefs about how boys are supposed to behave. In addition some drugs can temporarily assuage adolescents' bitter feelings of low self-esteem and embarrassment and shame about natural parts of themselves that violate the masculine code.

Because of boys' isolation from self and others and their need to appear self-sufficient, parents may miss the opportunity to discuss these matters at a time when it might make a difference. Many boys who use drugs have reported that there were periods of confusion and ambivalence, when having a way to talk to an empathic and concerned adult might have made a difference in their choice to use drugs.

Lack of Adult Supervision

Drugs, sex, and other problematic teen behaviors are aided and abetted by the lack of adult supervision that is widespread in U.S. society. Many changes in the family and neighborhood have taken place in the space of a generation. When the baby boom generation grew up, only a handful of mothers were in the workforce while children were small, and there were always adults around in the neighborhood after school. Children appear to have been more adequately supervised then. Now 75 percent of mothers are in the workforce, and the typical middle-class neighborhood is bereft of adults from 2 to

6 P.M. on school days. We became aware of this problem in the 1980s and termed the children "latchkey" or "self-care," as if giving them a label somehow dealt with the problem. However, we did not deal with the problem, and it has gotten much worse. For example, violent crime committed by juveniles soars during the 2 to 6 P.M. time slot. And of course, this is prime time for nonrelational sex. In the 1950s there were many obstacles to teen sex, which usually took place in the back seat of a car. Today it happens in the comfort of the child's home—usually the boy's. Once again this is a very difficult problem. Parents need guidance on what they can do to ensure that their children are adequately supervised during this highly vulnerable time.

Finding a Direction in Life

As has been noted, boys often have a problematic relationship with their fathers, which profoundly affects their ability to find a sense of direction in life and to visualize themselves as adult men. The father's role tends to vary a great deal today, from highly involved coparent to traditional breadwinner in two-parent homes, from custodial parent to visitation father to disengaged noncustodial parent in divorced families, and the role of stepfather in remarried families. However, three themes tend to recur with a high degree of consistency.

The first theme is that fathers tend to be the transmitters and chief enforcers of the code of masculinity. As noted, men tend to endorse the code to a much higher degree than do women. Furthermore, fathers believe that it is their job to "make men" out of their sons and as a consequence tend to deliver the shaming message that "big boys don't cry" or that males do not express affection to each other.

The second theme is that fathers tend to remain somewhat emotionally distant from the family, either by staying on the periphery or by focusing on the instrumental rather than the interpersonal and emotional aspects of family life.

The third theme is that fathers, like the men Henry David Thoreau described, "lead lives of quiet desperation." Themselves the servants of the code of masculinity, fathers tend to be breadwinners, or at least think of themselves that way, even when their wives earn half or more of the family income. They often approach their work as joyless duty, something that must be done to "put bread on the table and a roof over their heads."

IMPLICATIONS FOR COUNSELORS AND THERAPISTS

The dominant myths that males should be tough and stoic made more sense when social conditions were harsh, such as in the United States from the period of industrialization through World War I, the Great Depression, and World War II. However, in today's world emotional intelligence and the ability to balance one's own perspective with that of others—to be relational instead of nonrelational—is vitally important. Hence we need to debunk the myths and construct new, more flexible images of manhood. The women's movement succeeded in expanding women's adult roles, so that a woman can be both an aggressive marketer and a loving mother. We have yet to do the equivalent for men. We seem to fear that men will lose their essential manhood if they are not tough enough.

Counselors and psychologists are in a unique position to help boys, their parents, and their teachers respond to these crises. However, to do so requires developing a gender-aware perspective on boys and their emotional development, such as has been offered in this chapter and elsewhere (Pollack, 1998), and applying this perspective to the boys in counseling, their parents, and their teachers.

With regard to counseling boys, it is important to not take a boy's apparent self-sufficiency and emotional disengagement at face value. The counselor should also work at developing a relationship that will allow the boy to feel a strong and trusting bond, a sense of safety, and a secure knowledge that he will not be made to feel ashamed of himself, so that he can begin to explore his feelings of vulnerability and shame. Some adolescent boys have already been so thoroughly socialized that they are unable to experience and express their emotions. These boys could be considered mildly alexithymic and might benefit from my psychoeducational program designed to enhance males' emotional self-awareness (see Chapter Twenty-one).

As a family psychologist, I generally prefer to see the child in the family context. In addressing the problems of boys, parents are in great need of guidance for how to raise their sons in what many parents perceive as a sea of trouble. They need help on a range of matters such as (1) how to help their sons succeed in school (for example, addressing complaints or concerns voiced by teachers about their sons' performance or behavior, including blunt statements that the boy has "attention-deficit/hyperactivity disorder and needs an evaluation," which a teacher made to a family I counseled); (2) how to deal with the cruelty of boy culture (including how to handle bullies); (3) how to deal with peer pressure and the influence of other parents who may have different standards (for example, one couple I counseled was fairly strict and needed help in dealing with their son's complaints that "all the other boys get to do X"); (4) how to deal with the influence of the culture at large (including television, popular music, film, and of course the Internet); (5) how to find adult supervision during the vulnerable after-school period; and (6) for older children, how to deal with sex, alcohol, and drugs.

Finally, counseling professionals could have a significant influence on these problems (above and beyond the help they provide in the consulting room) by offering talks, workshops, and in-service training programs to groups of parents and teachers designed to raise their level of awareness of the influence of the code of masculinity and how it affects our boys.

References

Brody, L. (1996). Gender, emotional expression, and parent-child boundaries. In R. Kavanaugh, B. Zimmerberg-Glick, & S. Fein (Eds.), *Emotion: Interdisciplinary perspectives* (pp. 139–170). Hillsdale, NJ: Erlbaum.

Brody, L., & Hall, J. (1993). Gender and emotion. In M. Lewis & J. M. Haviland (Eds.), *Handbook of emotions* (pp. 435–460). New York: Guilford Press.

Brooks, G. R. (1995). *The centerfold syndrome.* San Francisco: Jossey-Bass.

Buck, R. (1977). Non-verbal communication of affect in preschool children: Relationships with personality and skin conductance. *Journal of Personality and Social Psychology, 35*(4), 225–236.

Bushweller, K. (1994). Turning our backs on boys. *American School Board Journal, 181,* 20–25.

Campbell, A. (1993). *Men, women, and aggression.* New York: Basic Books.

Dunn, J., Bretherton, I., & Munn, P. (1987). Conversations about feeling states between mothers and their children. *Developmental Psychology, 23,* 132–139.

Eagly, A. H., & Steffen, V. J. (1986). Gender and aggressive behavior: A meta-analytic review of the social psychological literature. *Psychological Bulletin, 100*(3), 309–330

Fivush, R. (1989). Exploring sex differences in the emotional content of mother child conversations about the past. *Sex Roles, 20,* 675–691.

Frodi, A., Macaulay, J., & Thome, P. R. (1977). Are women always less aggressive than men? A review of the experimental literature. *Psychological Bulletin, 84*(4), 634–660.

Fuchs, D., & Thelen, M. (1988). Children's expected interpersonal consequences of communicating their affective state and reported likelihood of expression. *Child Development, 59,* 1314–1322.

Greif, E. B., Alvarez, M., & Ulman, K. (1981, April). *Recognizing emotions in other people: Sex differences in socialization.* Paper presented at the meeting of the Society for Research in Child Development, Boston.

Haviland, J. J., & Malatesta, C. Z. (1981). The development of sex differences in nonverbal signals: Fallacies, facts, and fantasies. In C. Mayo & N. M. Henly (Eds.), *Gender and nonverbal behavior* (pp. 183–208). New York: Springer.

Kiselica, M. S., & Horne, A. M. (1999). Preface: For the sake of our nation's sons. In A. M. Horne & M. S. Kiselica (Eds.), *Handbook of counseling boys and adolescent males* (pp. xv–xx). Thousand Oaks, CA: Sage.

Krugman, S. (1995). Male development and the transformation of shame. In R. F. Levant & W. S. Pollack (Eds.), *A new psychology of men.* New York: Basic Books.

Lamb, M. E. (1977). The development of parental preferences in the first two years of life. *Sex Roles, 3,* 475–497.

Lamb, M. E., Owen, M. J., & Chase-Lansdale, L. (1979). The father daughter relationship: Past, present, and future. In C. B. Knopp & M. Kirkpatrick (Eds.), *Becoming female* (pp. 89–112). New York: Plenum.

Langlois, J. H., & Downs, A. C. (1980). Mother, fathers, and peers as socialization agents of sex-typed play behaviors in young children. *Child Development, 51,* 1217–1247.

Levant, R. F., & Brooks, G. R. (Eds.). (1997). *Men and sex: New psychological perspectives.* New York: Wiley.

Levant, R. F., Brooks, G. R., & Pitta, P. (2000). [The concerns of adolescent boys.] Unpublished raw data.

Levant, R. F., & Fischer, J. (1998). The Male Role Norms Inventory. In C. M. Davis, W. H. Yarber, R. Bauserman, G. Schreer, & S. L. Davis (Eds.), *Sexuality-related measures: A compendium* (2nd ed., pp. 469–472). Newbury Park, CA: Sage.

Levant, R. F., Hirsch, L., Celentano, E., Cozza, T., Hill, S., MacEachern, M., Marty, N., & Schnedeker, J. (1992). The male role: An investigation of norms and stereotypes. *Journal of Mental Health Counseling, 14,* 325–337.

Levant, R. F., & Kopecky, G. (1995). *Masculinity reconstructed.* New York: Dutton.

Levant, R. F., & Majors, R. G. (1997). An investigation into variations in the construction of the male gender role among young African American and European American women and men. *Journal of Gender, Culture, and Health, 2,* 33–43.

Levant, R. F., Majors, R. G., & Kelley, M. L. (1998). Masculinity ideology among young African American and European American women and men in different regions of the United States. *Cultural Diversity and Mental Health, 4,* 227–236.

Levant, R. F., & Pollack, W. S. (Eds.). (1995). *A new psychology of men.* New York: Basic Books.

Levant, R. F., Wu, R., & Fischer, J. (1996). Masculinity ideology: A comparison between U.S. and Chinese young men and women. *Journal of Gender, Culture, and Health, 1,* 207–220.

Lever, J. (1976). Sex differences in the games children play. *Social Work, 23*(4), 78–87.

Long, D. (1987). Working with men who batter. In M. Scher, M. Stevens, G. Good, & G. A. Eichenfield (Eds.), *Handbook of counseling and psychotherapy with men* (pp. 305–320). Newbury Park, CA: Sage.

Maccoby, E. E. (1990). Gender and relationships: A developmental account. *American Psychologist, 45,* 513–520.

Malatesta, C. Z., Culver, C., Tesman, J., & Shephard, B. (1989). The development of emotion expression during the first two years of life. *Monographs of the Society for Research in Child Development, 50* (1–2, Serial No. 219).

Michael, R. T., Gagnon, J. H., Laumann, E. O., & Kolata, G. (1994). *Sex in America: A definitive survey.* Boston: Little, Brown.

Paley, V. G. (1984). *Boys and girls: Superheroes in the doll corner.* Chicago: University of Chicago Press.

Pollack, W. S. (1998). *Real boys: Rescuing our sons from the myths of boyhood.* New York: Random House.

Schell, A., & Gleason, J. B. (1989, December). *Gender differences in the acquisition of the vocabulary of emotion.* Paper presented at the annual meeting of the American Association of Applied Linguistics, Washington, DC.

Weinberg, M. K. (1992). *Sex differences in 6-month-old infants' affect and behavior: Impact on maternal caregiving.* Unpublished doctoral dissertation, University of Massachusetts, Amherst, MA.

Witters, W., Venturelli, P., & Hanson, G. (1992). *Drugs and society.* Boston: Jones & Bartlett.

CHAPTER ELEVEN

Addressing the Implications of Male Socialization for Career Counseling

Mary J. Heppner
P. Paul Heppner

A curious irony exists in the literature on the career development of men. In some ways, most of the history of the field has been male centered. Frank Parsons, who is widely regarded as the father of career development, began this field in the early part of the twentieth century by emphasizing the importance of "matching men and jobs." Throughout the century, researchers and theorists have continued to emphasize men in their longitudinal research and in their development of vocational assessment measures, career theories, and normative work patterns. As Leona Tyler (1977) argued, "much of what we know about the stages through which an individual passes as he [sic] prepares to find his [sic] place in the world of work might appropriately be labeled 'The Vocational Development of Middle Class Males' " (p. 40). Given that history, it is rather amazing how little is actually known about the influence of male gender role socialization in various facets of career development for contemporary American men.

The irony is that much of the foundational work in the area of career development was conducted at a time when men were viewed as homogeneous. The men studied were, as Tyler noted, typically white and middle class. Their career development patterns were studied at a time when most men followed what today would be labeled a traditionally masculine gender role pattern. During this time researchers and practitioners gave little attention to differences among men, particularly in terms of gender role socialization. No one thought much about the gender socialization context of a man's chosen career path or about the psychological or physical consequences created by living the career pattern of the traditional male. Even in the early twenty-first century, we find that men's career development has not been extensively studied within a gendered perspective.

The purpose of this chapter is twofold. First, we highlight ten critical issues that we perceive emerging from both the new psychology of men literature (Levant, 1996) and our own experience in counseling men; it is particularly important for counselors to understand these issues in counseling male clients about career choices. Second, using a model of the career counseling process (Gysbers, Heppner, & Johnston, 1998), we illustrate how these themes often emerge in actual career counseling sessions. Throughout this final section, we provide numerous case examples from the lives of men that portray the lived experiences of men as they struggle with career issues.

Before we proceed we offer two caveats: First, it is important to underscore that providing career counseling for men is similar in many respects to providing career counseling in general; however, special gender dynamics often arise that can either facilitate or hinder the career counseling process. Gender issues do not always affect the career counseling process, but we conceptualize these gender dynamics as an additional set of variables (among many) that can affect the career counseling process (see Heppner & Gonzales, 1987). Second, because there are virtually no empirical data on gender-related career counseling with men, the information and suggestions provided in this chapter are based largely on our own experience and observations from the professional litera-ture. Thus, until empirical data emerge, it is important to realize that it is unclear to what extent these observations are generalizable. We know from our experience that men dif-fer greatly in how they respond to the various suggestions we make. For example, although reinforcing a man's strength for coming into counseling may feel validating to one man, it may seem condescending to another. Thus, the suggestions and observa-tions that follow are not meant to be a foolproof recipe but rather a list of possible potent ingredients that the individual counselor will need to sensitively apply given the unique-ness of each individual man's experience.

TEN CRITICAL ISSUES IN CAREER COUNSELING WITH MEN

In examining the literature and thinking about our own counseling experiences when working with men, a host of issues could be addressed. Here we highlight ten that we consider to be the most important for counselors to understand to work effectively with men in career counseling.

Relationship Between Men's Life Goals and Their Male Socialization

Perhaps the most overarching issue is the importance of placing gender awareness at the core of career counseling with men. At each step of the career counseling process, it is important to understand how a man's early and current gender role socialization may have influenced the man in the past and may continue to affect his life choices. For exam-ple, some men might be unaware of the impact of early messages they received about what it is to be a boy (for example, strong, resilient, unexpressive emotionally, and aggressive) on choices they are now making about careers. Other men might be unaware of the pres-sure they experience from working multiple jobs to obtain a certain lifestyle for their fam-ily. Thus, the counselor might discuss how early attitudes about sex-appropriate and sex-inappropriate occupations were formed (Gettys & Cann, 1981). Often by the time boys or men seek career counseling, the socialization process affects all parts of the process, including whether they seek career services at all, how they interact with the counselor, how open or closed they are in discussing their problems, what career fields they may be considering, and their willingness to engage with the process that career counseling entails.

In short, it is helpful to continually seek to understand the many facets of a male client's life goals in terms of his prior socialization as a male; such a perspective often is helpful in understanding the psychological dynamics (that is, cognitions, affect, and behaviors) related to the man's motivation and career choices and development. More-over, gender role constructs may well affect the type of psychological problems that exist, their associated symptoms, and how people respond to problems (Cook, 1990; Eisler & Blalock, 1991). For example, research indicates that strong adherence to particular stan-dards and expectations within a man's gender role ideology may have both negative physical and negative psychological effects (Pleck, 1995). In addition, research has indi-cated that men use different ways of coping with stress than women use during some stressful career transitions (Heppner, Cook, Strozier, & Heppner, 1991). Thus, under-standing the career issue within the broader gender socialization context gives the coun-selor a much more complete picture of the male client's process.

Critical Role of Work in Most Men's Lives

Men often define who they are in the world through work. As Skovholt (1990) poignantly expressed, "Painting a picture of men's lives often results in a work-dominated land-scape" (p. 39). For example, Keen (1991) described the first job as a rite of passage into manhood. At this point work often begins to influence a man's identity, either directly or indirectly, to the point that work and self become inseparable for many men. To be a man is to be successful in one's career, to achieve, to make money, and to be able to afford possessions that also become symbols of a man's worth (David & Brannon, 1976). "Whether the job is loved, hated, intrinsically satisfying, or boring, is much less relevant than the expectation that a man will work. A long term non-working male adult violates this strong male principle and is usually shunned or rejected" (Skovholt, 1990, p. 42). It is not surprising, given the importance of the role of work for many men, that there is often an imbalance between the amount of time a man devotes to work and the amount of time he devotes to leisure activities and even personal relationships and fam-ily life (O'Neil, 1981). O'Neil and his colleagues have found that conflict between work and family relations is a major source of gender role conflict in men (see O'Neil, Good, & Holmes, 1995). Thus, it is important for the counselor to understand how central the role of work is to many men and that it often means a great deal more than earning a living; it is really about earning a self. It is thus important to understand the role of work in a male client's life, how work affects other aspects of his life, and how career-related decisions affect the man's physical and psychological well-being.

Variations Among Men: Individual Differences That May Influence Men's Career Development

It is critical that career counselors not continue to subscribe to the homogeneity myth that all men are alike. Men in need of career services are a diverse group and differ in all sorts of individual areas, including racial and ethnic minority status, age and devel-opmental stage in the career planning process, sexual orientation, and physical stature and appearance, all of which contribute to how they view themselves as men and the career paths they may want to pursue. Moreover, men differ on a multitude of person-ality variables such as self-esteem, need for control, locus of control, and problem-solv-ing style and have acquired a unique set of values. Thus, it is critically important that career counselors be sensitive, aware, and skillful in working with a diverse range of male clients and not be biased in their assumptions and myths about men in general.

Recent career texts have devoted considerable attention to the unique needs of various groups (Gysbers et al., 1998; Leong, 1995). Today's career counselors need to continue to review current research on specific groups and ways of meeting their career planning needs most effectively. This knowledge can include such varied competencies as understanding how racial and ethnic identity development may influence the career development process (Helms, 1990; Helms & Piper, 1994) and becoming knowledgeable of the guidelines of the Americans with Disabilities Act of 1990 and the amendments of 1992 and how these guide-lines influence the career options of clients with disabilities. As is probably evident, this knowledge base is large; highly skilled professionals are needed to serve the unique career development needs of an increasingly varied clientele (and in this case a varied clientele of men). Thus, it is important for counselors not only to be knowledgeable about male gender role socialization and its many intragroup variations but also to continually check the accuracy of assumptions and conclusions we draw about a particular client, preferably in dialogue with the client.

Assessment of Male Gender Role Attributes and Traditional Career Assessments

Assessment is an important, ongoing process in career counseling and can consist of both formal and informal assessment methods (see Gysbers et al., 1998). Moreover, a number of formal assessment measures are designed to specifically assess aspects of the male gender role. These assessments can be used along with traditional career interest assessments (such as the Strong Interest Inventory [Harmon, Hansen, Borgen, & Hammer, 1994] and the Self-Directed Search [Holland, 1985]) to provide a more complete picture of the issues facing contemporary men. It may also be useful for counselors to take the assessments to evaluate their own gender role socialization, which may affect the efficacy of their work with clients (see Heppner & Gonzales, 1987).

Thompson and Pleck (1995) reviewed the available instruments on men and masculinity-related constructs. Four of the most used and researched instruments are (1) the Gender Role Conflict Scale (O'Neil, Helms, Gable, David, & Wrightsman, 1986), (2) the Masculine Gender Role Stress Scale (Eisler & Skidmore, 1987), (3) the Male Roles Scale (Brannon & Juni, 1984; Fischer, Tokar, Good, & Snell, 1998; Thompson & Pleck, 1986), and (4) the Gender Role Journey measure (O'Neil, Egan, Owens, & McBride, 1993). As assessment tools, these four instruments provide a context in which and a language with which to discuss the complex issues of gender and career planning. Counselors can use them with male clients to introduce gender role constructs and incorporate these constructs as integral parts of the career counseling process. Used in concert with more traditional career planning measures, gender-informed formal assessments can help male clients understand their career development process. In addition, informal assessment of clients' cognitions, affect, and behaviors is equally important to understand the messages particular clients have received or incorporated into their worldviews about being men, particularly related to the world of work. Thus, useful information about male clients can be obtained through formal assessment or by asking clients throughout the counseling process about their beliefs, thoughts, feelings, and actions related to male gender role socialization.

Integration of Psychological Adjustment with Issues of Career Choice or Adjustment

An unfortunate dichotomy of separating career adjustment from issues of psychological adjustment has existed in the field of career development for years (see Hackett, 1993). This dichotomy has led to some serious problems for clients in that most if not all career concerns are intertwined with psychological issues. Research indicates that most adult clients seeking career services also have psychological adjustment issues (such as depression or anxiety) (Multon, Heppner, Gysbers, Zook, & Ellis, 1998). Because work tends to be such a vital part of men's lives, chances are very good that when men seek counseling for psychological problems, their problems relate to their work life or their psychological distress affects their work life. Thus, it is critical that career counselors use a holistic approach to working with men and see career as just one part, albeit a very important part, of a broader picture of how male clients are functioning. This holistic approach would also include examining the role of relationships with family and friends, exercise, and leisure activities. Again, the integration of psychological adjustment with career issues emphasizes the need for a broad, thorough, and careful assessment.

Strengths That Male Socialization Often Develops

Oftentimes only the negative aspects of the male role are discussed. For example, men in general have been described as tending to be emotionally restrictive (see O'Neil, 1981), unaware of their own feelings or the feelings of others (see Heppner & Gonzales, 1987), and often requiring control and dominance (Farrell, 1975). Although considerable evidence suggests that male gender role socialization and subsequent gender role conflict are linked to a host of problems for many contemporary men (see Cournoyer & Mahalik, 1995; Good et al., 1995; O'Neil, Good, & Holmes, 1995; Sharpe & Heppner, 1991), focus on only these potentially negative aspects of the male role may leave men feeling stripped of any redeeming characteristics. It is vitally important that counselors recognize and affirm strengths related to male gender role socialization. For example, male socialization is typically linked to a myriad of skills such as the ability to persist in difficult situations until problems are resolved; the ability to strategize, think logically, take risks, and stay calm in the face of danger; willingness to sacrifice personal needs to provide for others; willingness to withstand hardship to protect others; and ability to express love through action, or doing things for others (Levant, 1996). It is helpful for counselors to not only emphasize and bring into clients' awareness these and other skills related to problem solving in particular but also to draw on these skills in developing career paths with clients. In short, affirming these and the other strengths that many men possess can be very helpful in the career counseling process and instrumental in achieving the desired career planning outcomes.

Men and the Difficult Art of Help Seeking

The constellation of self-reliance, emotional restrictiveness, and the need for control defines the traditional male gender role (David & Brannon, 1976). To be able to take care of oneself, to not need others, and to be independent are all well-socialized characteristics for many men. Thus, to seek counseling services goes against the very core of many contemporary men (Good & May, 1987; Good, Dell, & Mintz, 1989). It is not surprising that compared with women, men underuse all forms of social services, including career counseling services (Gysbers et al., 1998). It is often very difficult for men to admit not only to others but even to themselves that they need assistance to solve a problem. As Scher (1979) noted, "his pride will be suffering" (p. 253). Thus, counselors should consider the cost to the self-esteem of men who have to admit they cannot deal with their lives and must enlist the aid of others to resolve their problems (Heilbrun, 1961). It is also important for counselors to recognize that when men actually seek counseling, they are likely to be experiencing a fair amount of distress in some aspect of their lives. Often it is useful for counselors to acknowledge the strength it takes to come to counseling and that the male clients have taken an important first step in improving their life situation. Moreover, some men who seek psychological assistance find it difficult to complete counseling and thus end counseling prematurely. Thus, we have found it helpful to occasionally process with clients how they are experiencing counseling and if they are progressing in the intended manner.

Men, Relationships, and the Formation of the Working Alliance

The importance of building a strong working alliance with clients to achieve successful outcome has been well documented in the literature (Beutler, Machado, & Nuefeldt, 1994; Meara & Patton, 1994). Meara and Patton described the alliance as the part of counseling that can be characterized as mutuality, collaboration, and cooperation of two individuals working together toward common goals through a mutual bond. Research has also indicated that this alliance needs to be formed early in the counseling relationship and that in most counseling the alliance is either firmly in place (or not) by the third session (Eaton, Abeles, & Gutfreund, 1988). Building a strong working alliance with male clients can pose some challenges. Much has been written about the traditional male socialization process with regard to interpersonal relationships (see Goldberg, 1976; Lewis, 1978), but surprisingly little has been written about how best to establish a strong working alliance with different types of men. Because of the traditional male socialization process, building a relationship with male clients may sometimes be difficult. For example, if the counselor is male, the male client may feel vulnerable, competitive, or uncomfortable with this unfamiliar intimacy with another man (see Heppner & Gonzales, 1987). If the counselor is a woman, the client may feel more or less comfortable, defensive, or resistant, depending on his past relationships with women (see Carlson, 1987).

It is important that the client perceive that the counselor understands and accepts his situation. Appreciating the pride of the man and empathizing with his discomfort and inadequacy may be important for the formation of a working alliance. Self-disclosure of relevant and appropriate information from the counselor's own life may help model the appropriate expression of emotion and assist in building the bond. As the counselor begins building the working alliance he or she can also reinforce client strengths; such reinforcement may be especially important because the client may feel he has few strengths left if he has reached the point of coming for help.

Intricate Dance Between Taking Action and Focusing on the Process

The process of career counseling with many men involves a delicate balance between the push to take action and the pull to focus on issues of self-awareness. In general, men tend to be problem focused and are typically inclined to take action to solve their problems (see Scher, 1979). However, many men are less interested or comfortable with a discussion of how their feelings or socialization may have influenced their career development (see Heppner & Gonzales, 1987). Some men use a variety of techniques to avoid dealing with their feelings about themselves as men. For example, one man said quite directly, "I don't care about this touchy-feely stuff; I am here to find a new job." Others simply intellectualize the issue away. Sometimes men are simply unaware of their feelings, whereas other times fear and anxiety drive this avoidance. Thus, the counselor needs to achieve a balance between problem solving and taking action, on the one hand, and identifying important psychological issues related to the process that some men would rather not talk about, on the other hand. During the dance between process and action, the counselor needs to monitor whether the male client has sufficient self-knowledge and occupational knowledge to make these critical life choices.

The Changing Job Market and Skills Requirements

The contrast between the workplace of the current generation and the workplace of previous generations is vast. In essence, the changes that are currently taking place raise questions about the very basic assumptions of what it is to be a worker and what it is to have a career. Specifically for men, the personal characteristics so important to the last generation such as competitiveness, ability to rise within a hierarchical structure, longevity, and stability are not necessarily the most valued traits in today's workforce. In many of today's companies, individual accomplishment is no longer highly valued because workers function primarily as part of a larger group brought together to work as a team on specific projects (Feller & Waltz, 1995). This team structure requires far different skills than those needed in the traditional, more individualistic structure. For example, interpersonal skills become paramount in these kinds of organizations; one must be able to work with diverse people (including both men and women and people of diverse races and social backgrounds), have excellent verbal skills, and be able to disagree or express conflict in appropriate ways. For some men, this new marketplace requires skills they have not developed. They are being asked to be interdependent with their team, to cooperate for the good of the team, to express their thoughts and feelings by using interpersonal skills, and to collaborate on resolving problems. This changing work environment can create new stresses for some men. For the counselor, it may be especially important to address these differences and to help the client find ways of enhancing his skills to better meet the changing needs of today's marketplace.

INTEGRATING ISSUES OF MALE GENDER ROLE SOCIALIZATION INTO THE CAREER COUNSELING PROCESS

It is often difficult to take an intellectual understanding of a topic such as male gender role socialization and apply it to your own work with career clients. Thus, we provide a model of the career counseling process developed by Gysbers and his colleagues (1998) and then discuss examples of integrating the issues relevant to the gendered context for men into this structure. The Gysbers et al. (1998) model proposed a number of activities within the career counseling process, which for clarity are identified chronologically as phases and subphases. Although Gysbers et al. presented these phases in a linear fashion, they emphasized the nonlinear nature of the career counseling process and the need to return to various phases and subphases as counseling progresses.

The first phase is client goal or problem identification, clarification, and specification, which includes the subphases of (1) opening and forming the working alliance, (2) gathering client information, and (3) understanding and hypothesizing about client behavior. The second phase is client goal or problem resolution, which includes (1) taking action, (2) developing goals and plans of action, and (3) evaluating results and closing the relationship. We describe these phases and subphases in the following sections, along with particular aspects of the male gender role that might be important in each phase. Although we selected issues that often occur in a particular phase of career counseling, any of the ten issues previously described can be important throughout the counseling process.

First Phase of Treatment

The first major phase of the career counseling process is one of defining and building the relationship, gathering and evaluating client information, and using this information to understand and hypothesize about client behavior.

Opening. The opening phase of career counseling has as its central goals (1) identifying the client's goals or problems and the internal thoughts and feelings that might be involved, (2) beginning to form the working alliance, and (3) defining and clarifying the client-counselor relationship and responsibilities.

Given that most men tend to avoid career counseling, some men may feel threatened in some way if they seek assistance. Thus, as the initial counseling session begins, it is often useful to affirm the man's strength in seeking counseling. A subtle reassurance concerning the wisdom and courage he is exhibiting, such as the following statement, may be helpful to some men:

> Many men stay in jobs they hate for their whole working lives. Other men, like you, are clear that they want something better for themselves and their families. I am glad that you have taken an important first step by coming here today.

In addition, the working alliance begins to form in this first session. As we have indicated, building a strong alliance with men requires sensitivity to what will build and conversely what will diminish this alliance. For example, although self-disclosure by the counselor is often seen as a positive way of emphasizing communality with the client, such strategies can backfire, as a client of ours recently stated:

> Yes, I was in counseling once before, but the guy I worked with kept telling me how his parents had never let him cry and how he is less able to express himself than he would like. . . . I thought the guy was a flake and maybe needed more help than I did.

Our suggestion is to take the lead from the client. For example, if the man tends to be task oriented, then the counselor can communicate that he or she is willing to work with him on the tasks and goals that are most important to him at this time in his life. In this way, the counselor can communicate caring in a way that some men are better able to receive.

Another example of communicating understanding of a male client might relate to the close link between work and self. Although a career change, job layoff, or firing can begin to seem a normative and routine experience for many career counselors, it is often critical for the counselor to communicate understanding about the importance of these events to the individual man. It can be helpful to build a working alliance by communicating that the counselor really understands how hard it can be to lose a job, for example.

Another important part of building the working alliance in this early phase is identifying and acknowledging that each man has developed strengths that will be helpful to him at this time. For example, as the counselor learns more about his or her client's career history, the counselor may search for skills such as the client's ability to persist in difficult situations, to work on problems until they are resolved, or to think logically (see Levant, 1996). For purposes of career counseling, the skills associated with male gender role socialization can be strengths for the career planning process. Recognizing and affirming them can also help to build the working alliance, as a recent client emphasized in a closing session:

> I don't know, when I came in here, I was at an all-time low. I kind of felt like a dinosaur. . . . Like who I was, and the way I was raised wasn't good enough. My wife kept telling me I needed to communicate with her and tell her I loved her more and express my feelings. While I definitely know I do need to work on being more open, you helped me see that I do communicate love, only in a different way than she does, and that I do have strengths, I just need to—what did you call it?—"expand my repertoire."

As the relationship grows with the individual, the counselor might start helping the client examine his goals through a gender filter (for example, "Which of your goals are motivated from your upbringing as a man?" or "Which of your difficulties are the result of environmental pressures and a need to prove some aspect of the traditional male role?") The counselor might also note to what extent the client tends to express emotions freely and honestly, even if they include feelings of vulnerability or fear. Does the client appear to be setting authentic goals based on a full knowledge of relevant information? If relevant, the counselor can openly discuss these questions with the client.

With some clients, the counselor may need to approach the questions later and less directly. It may also be important to make explicit that the goal of such exploration is to help the client make more life-affirming choices about his work life.

Greg's situation is a good example. Greg was in his late forties when he came in for counseling, had held a variety of jobs in business, and had worked his way up to a very comfortable and high-status position. But he reported being unhappy in his work. The counselor noted that even though all of Greg's formal jobs had been within conservative financial firms, Greg's Daydreams list on Holland's Self-Directed Search indicated he had dreamed of being a social worker, a Peace Corps volunteer, and a minister at earlier times in his life. However, it seemed difficult for him to talk about the inconsistency between his dream jobs and his real jobs, and so the counselor provided the following type of rationale:

> Greg, it seems like you are telling me that you have a position that pays well and has a great deal of status in your firm and yet you feel unhappy. I see that you had earlier dreams of becoming a social worker, Peace Corps volunteer, or minister. It seems important to explore how it was that you left that socially oriented path and followed the business path you did. By understanding more about some original dreams, we may be better able to help you decide what path might be most beneficial for you right now.

This initial phase is also a time for clarifying the counselor-client relationship and responsibilities. Counselors whose philosophy includes working together in a collaborative manner with the client need to clarify this orientation from the start. Some men view the counselor as an "answer dispenser." Their expectations are to go in and get fixed, not to work in a collaborative relationship that emphasizes self-awareness. Also the counselor and client may need to discuss the role of the environment in shaping the individual. In essence, the client has a right to be informed in his choice of a career counselor. The counselor's philosophical base is important information in making that choice.

Gathering client information. The clarification and information-gathering subphase of the career counseling process has as its central goal learning more about the client. Any of the assessments discussed earlier in this chapter can be used to supplement any other standardized or nonstandardized career-related assessment measures. The Gender Role Conflict Scale, Masculine Gender Role Stress Scale, Male Role Norms Scale, and Gender Role Journey are all effective assessment measures to gather information about experiences that may affect the client's career planning process. If a counselor uses one of these measures with a client, it is important to discuss the rationale for doing so. The counselor might say something like the following:

> I think it would be helpful for you to take a series of instruments to help us both get a better picture of where you are in your life right now. A couple of these will be instruments that assess your career interests and values. Another one relates to how you view yourself as a man and how that may be influencing your career planning.

Assessment instruments such as those mentioned can also be used in creative ways, perhaps as a stimulus for journal writing. For example, the counselor might ask the male client to take one of the gender role instruments and then write in a journal to help explore the various themes further. For example, the following was a portion of a client's journal entry after taking the Male Role Norms Scale:

> When I was growing up, I was always critical of my dad for being so materialistic. He was never with us, because he was always out there trying to earn a buck. Now that I have my own family, I am struck with how much like him I have become. Partly I understand

more the pressures he was facing, but partly I also want to achieve a better balance in my own work and family life.

Combining both traditional career measures such as Holland's Self-Directed Search and gender role measures such as the Gender Role Journey measure by O'Neil and his colleagues can provide a comprehensive assessment of what would be most helpful to the client. For example, Don had what would be considered a very low, flat profile on the Self-Directed Search, with only high scores in the Realistic area (indicating that the client was expressing interests in working independently, primarily with his hands, on very tangible kinds of products). Don's scores on the Gender Role Journey measure indicated that he was at the gender role stage characterized by gender role ambivalence, confusion, anger, and fear. By talking through the antecedents of his ambivalent feelings, it became clear that he wanted to be more open to different occupations but felt confused about whether he could be involved in more interpersonally oriented occupations and still feel like a man.

Understanding and hypothesizing about client behavior. The specification subphase of the career counseling process has as its central goal understanding clients more fully and hypothesizing about their unique dynamics and the psychological and environmental reasons behind their actions. Thus, in this phase it may be appropriate to examine how a male client's psychological adjustment may be influencing his career adjustment. It may also be an appropriate place to discuss how the environmental changes in today's labor force might have changed which characteristics are valued in some workplaces and how these changes may be affecting the individual. Thus, in this phase the counselor is trying to probe deeper and understand more about how the client is making meaning out of himself and his occupational world.

During this phase the counselor may assess the psychological adjustment of the client, either formally or informally, and determine how psychological adjustment may be influencing career adjustment. For example, James came into career counseling at the urging of his wife. He had lost his job when his company downsized and had been unable to find work for the past six months. As he talked, the counselor noted his flat affect and slow speech. She began hypothesizing that James was depressed, perhaps clinically. It was clear that he had been unable to conduct an active and successful job search, due in large part to his depression. When he went for interviews, he presented himself as a low-energy person with little zest for the position. Thus, in this case both formal and informal assessments provided useful information to the counselor and client and altered the course of counseling.

In this phase it may also be appropriate to assess how environmental change such as the changing culture of the workplace may be influencing an individual client. The following scenario occurred after the counselor noted that the client was having difficulty interpersonally in the workplace:

COUNSELOR: You said you feel uncomfortable at work, like you don't fit in. Can you say more about that?

CLIENT: I don't know. . . . It just seems like I used to know the rules. I came up with an idea, I brought it to my boss, and if he liked it I ran with it. . . . Now everything goes through my team. I have to sell my idea to eight other people, some of whom I don't get along with at all. I don't know, I was always able to talk to my boss—and we would see eye to eye most of the time—but some of those people on my team, particularly the two ladies, . . . we just don't seem to be on the same wavelength.

This type of interchange helps the counselor understand more about the interpersonal dynamics of the client and what strategies might be effective in helping him.

In this phase the counselor may hypothesize about and understand how unique aspects of the man such as his race, ethnicity, sexual orientation, or physical stature may be influencing his career choices. This process can take many forms; for example, it may be a time to talk with a gay client about how his sexual orientation may be influencing his career planning process. It might also be important that the client understand the phenomenon of internalized homophobia and recognize whether he has internalized society's heterosexist messages and beliefs. It may be a time to talk to an African American client about his own black racial identity and how this identity may be influencing his career choice or adjustment. For example, he may be at the immersion-emersion status, which is characterized by high racial saliency and idealization of black standards and denigration of white standards (Helms, 1990). If so, his racial identity as an African American may be influencing many facets of his career, including where he feels comfortable working and with whom he wants to work. Thus, these individual difference variables may be important influences on the career planning process and ones that need in-depth exploration at this phase.

Second Phase of Treatment

The second major phase of the career counseling process is one of action taking. In this phase counseling moves from gathering and evaluating information to actually taking steps to act on this information. Getting to this phase means that the counselor and client have examined all the major aspects of the client's situation and the client is in a position to make an authentic life decision based on as complete a set of information about himself and the world of work as possible.

Taking action. Taking action is sometimes an easier phase of the counseling process than earlier ones for many men because it typically is consistent with their gender role training. Nonetheless, it is important to be sure men have the necessary self-knowledge and occupational knowledge to make career decisions before proceeding with the action phase. Consider the following example of a midcareer man, Bill, who came to a career planning center and began speaking rapidly, in an authoritative tone:

> Well, you could say I am in a bit of a mess. I just lost my job—was fired for what my idiot boss described as "insubordination"—and then my wife decides "we have grown too far apart" and moves out, all in the course of one week. I need to get a job and fast. I heard you people could help people find a job. Where can I begin looking?

Even from this short introduction, it is easy to determine there are many issues here and most likely a great deal of pain. Underneath the assertive exterior, the man is probably very scared, hurt, and angry, and yet his main goal is action—to get a job quickly. This man's situation is a good example of when being able to do the dance between taking action and staying with the process becomes important. Thus, even though this man's life is difficult, it is important to help him slow down a bit and live with the ambiguity inherent within the career transition to increase the probability of making good choices.

Developing career goals and plans of action. Individualized career plans are particularly important when the counselor is helping a male client incorporate parts of his gender role ideology into the career planning process. It can be very helpful to a client to carefully examine each step of the plan of action in terms of how he is likely to handle the particular action steps given his gender role upbringing. For example, if a counselor is helping a man who may likely come off as arrogant when interviewing with women, building the client's awareness about the consequences of various interpersonal styles might be helpful. If one is helping a gay man apply for positions in an employment setting that may not be open to gay men, discussing each choice point he has in the job application and interview process is often important (Hedgepeth, 1979/1980). In essence, many times it is useful to role-play and strengthen various skills or thoroughly discuss choice points to increase the probability of the client's action plan being successful and producing long-term satisfaction.

Evaluating results and closing the relationship. The closing sessions are a time to examine whether goals have been met and what the process was like for the counselor and the client. When examining the closure sessions through a gender filter, several issues are often important.

The counselor and client can reflect on the journey the career counseling process has taken. For some men this may have been the first time that they identified the need for help and sought counseling. It is sometimes very important for the counselor to reflect on and again reinforce the courage of that act. It may be helpful to the client to see the experience of asking for help as a sign of strength rather than a sign of weakness.

It is also sometimes helpful to reflect on the entire counseling process to examine whether new things can be learned from the process. For example, is there anything to be learned from how the working alliance developed? Or if there were tears in the working alliance, is there anything to be learned from how they were mended? How are both the counselor and client feeling about termination of the counseling? In short, it can be helpful to talk about how the counseling relationship developed, how communication became more honest, and other important events that might be transferable to other situations or relationships in the man's life.

The counselor may want to encourage the client to return for additional sessions or just to update the counselor on the client's progress. It is often especially important for men to know that the support system that was provided during counseling will remain if they meet with difficulties after counseling has closed.

Although the field of career counseling has focused since its inception at the turn of the twentieth century primarily on understanding men, much more information is needed about being effective in career counseling with contemporary men in the twenty-first century. In this chapter we have highlighted some aspects of the male gender role socialization process that seem to affect the career counseling process with men. Helping clients understand how their male gender role socialization might affect their life path is an important but complex goal for counselors. We hope that future researchers will investigate this important issue and provide the next generation with much-needed data to inform the career counseling process with contemporary men.

References

Beutler, L. E., Machado, P. P., & Nuefeldt, S. A. (1994). Therapist variables. In A. E. Bergin & S. L. Garfield (Eds.), *Handbook of psychotherapy and behavior change* (pp. 229–269). New York: Wiley.

Brannon, R., & Juni, S. (1984). A scale for measuring attitudes toward masculinity. *JSAS Catalog of Selected Documents in Psychology, 14,* 6 (MS No. 2012).

Carlson, N. L. (1987). Woman therapist: Male client. In M. Scher, M. Stevens, G. Good, & G. A. Eichenfield (Eds.), *Handbook of counseling and psychotherapy with men* (pp. 39–50). Newbury Park, CA: Sage.

Cook, E. P. (1990). Gender and psychological distress. *Journal of Counseling and Development, 68,* 371–375.

Cournoyer, R. J., & Mahalik, J. R. (1995). Cross-sectional study of gender role conflict examining college-aged and middle-aged men. *Journal of Counseling Psychology, 42,* 11–19.

David, D. S., & Brannon, R. (1976). *The forty-nine percent majority: The male sex role.* Reading, MA: Addison-Wesley.

Eaton, T. T., Abeles, N., & Gutfreund, M. J. (1988). Therapeutic alliance and outcome: Impact of treatment length and pretreatment symptomatology. *Psychotherapy, 25,* 536–542.

Eisler, R. M., & Blalock, J. A. (1991). Masculine gender role stress: Implications for the assessment of men. *Clinical Psychology Review, 11,* 45–60.

Eisler, R. M., & Skidmore, J. R. (1987). Masculine gender role stress: Scale development and component factors in the appraisal of stressful situations. *Behavior Modification, 11,* 123–136.

Farrell, W. T. (1975). *The liberated man.* New York: Random House.

Feller, R., & Walz, G. R. (1995). *Optimizing life transitions in turbulent times: Exploring work, learning, and careers.* Greensboro, NC: ERIC Clearinghouse on Counseling and Student Services.

Fischer, A. R., Tokar, D. M., Good, G. E., & Snell, A. F. (1998). More on the structure of male role norms: Exploratory and multiple sample confirmatory analyses. *Psychology of Women Quarterly, 22,* 135–155.

Gettys, L. D., & Cann, A. (1981). Children's perceptions of occupational sex stereotypes. *Sex Roles, 7,* 301–308.

Goldberg, H. (1976). *The hazards of being male: Surviving the myth of masculine privilege.* New York: Nash.

Good, G. E., Dell, D. M., & Mintz, L. B. (1989). Male roles and gender role conflict: Relationships to help seeking in men. *Journal of Counseling Psychology, 3,* 295–300.

Good, G. E., & May, R. (1987). Developmental issues, environmental influences, and the nature of therapy with college men. In M. Scher, M. Stevens, G. Good, & G. A. Eichenfield (Eds.), *Handbook of counseling and psychotherapy with men* (pp. 150–164). Newbury Park, CA: Sage.

Good, G. E., Robertson, J. M., O'Neil, J. M., Fitzgerald, L. F., Stevens, M., Debord, K. A., Bartels, K. M., & Braverman, D. G. (1995). Male gender role conflict: Psychometric issues and relation to psychological distress. *Journal of Counseling Psychology, 42,* 3–10.

Gysbers, N. C., Heppner, M. J., & Johnston, J. A. (1998). *Career counseling: Process, issues, and techniques.* Boston: Allyn & Bacon.

Hackett, G. (1993). Career counseling and psychotherapy: False dichotomies and recommended remedies. *Journal of Career Assessment, 1,* 105–117.

Hedgepeth, J. M. (1979/1980). Employment discrimination law and the rights of gay persons. *Journal of Homosexuality, 5*(12), 67–78.

Heilbrun, A. B. (1961). Male and female personality correlates of early termination in counseling. *Journal of Counseling Psychology, 8,* 31–36.

Helms, J. E. (1990). *Black and white racial identity: Theory, research, and practice.* New York: Greenwood Press.

Helms, J. E., & Piper, R. E. (1994). Implications of racial identity theory for vocational psychology. *Journal of Vocational Behavior, 44,* 124–136.

Heppner, P. P., Cook, S. W., Strozier, A. L., & Heppner, M. J. (1991). An investigation of coping styles and gender differences with farmers in career transition. *Journal of Counseling Psychology, 38,* 167–174.

Heppner, P. P., & Gonzales, D. S. (1987). Men counseling men. In M. Scher, M. Stevens, G. Good, & G. A. Eichenfield (Eds.), *Handbook of counseling and psychotherapy with men* (pp. 30–38). Newbury Park, CA: Sage.

Keen, S. (1991). *Fire in the belly: On being a man.* New York: Bantam Books.

Leong, F.T.L. (1995). *Career development and vocational behavior of racial and ethnic minorities.* Mahwah, NJ: Erlbaum.

Levant, R. F. (1996). Masculinity reconstructed. *Independent Practitioner, 16,* 1. American Psychological Association, Division 42, Bulletin of the Division of Independent Practice.

Lewis, R. A. (1978). Emotional intimacy among men. *Journal of Social Issues, 34,* 108–121.

Meara, N. M., & Patton, M. J. (1994). Contributions of the working alliance in the practice of career counseling. *Career Development Quarterly, 43,* 161–177.

Multon, K. D., Heppner, M. J., Gysbers, N. C., Zook, C. E., & Ellis, C. (1998). Relationship of personal adjustment outcomes to process in career counseling. In D. Luzzo (Chair), *Career counseling process and outcome research.* Symposium conducted at the annual meeting of the American Psychological Association, San Francisco.

O'Neil, J. M. (1981). Male sex-role conflicts, sexism, and masculinity: Psychological implications for men, women, and the counseling psychologist. *Counseling Psychologist, 9,* 61–81.

O'Neil, J. M., Egan, J., Owens, S. V., & McBride V. (1993). The gender role journey measure: Scale development and psychometric evaluation. *Sex Roles, 28,* 167–185.

O'Neil, J. M., Good, G. E., & Holmes, S. (1995). Fifteen years of theory and research on men's gender role conflict: New paradigms for empirical research. In R. F. Levant & W. S. Pollack (Eds.), *The new psychology of men* (pp. 164–206). New York: Basic Books.

O'Neil, J. M., Helms, B. J., Gable, R. K., David, L., & Wrightsman, L. S. (1986). Gender Role Conflict Scale: College men's fears of femininity. *Sex Roles, 14,* 335–350.

Pleck, J. H. (1995). The gender role strain paradigm: An update. In R. F. Levant & W. S. Pollack (Eds.), *The new psychology of men* (pp. 11–32). New York: Basic Books.

Scher, M. (1979). On counseling men. *Personnel and Guidance Journal, 58,* 252–253.

Sharpe, M. J., & Heppner, P. P. (1991). Gender role, gender-role conflict, and psychological well-being in men. *Journal of Counseling Psychology, 38,* 323–330.

Skovholt, T. M. (1990). Career themes in counseling and psychotherapy with men. In D. Moore & F. Leafgren (Eds.), *Men in conflict* (pp. 39–53). Alexandria, VA: American Association for Counseling and Development.

Thompson, E. H., & Pleck, J. H. (1986). The structure of male role norms. *American Behavioral Scientist, 29,* 531–543.

Thompson, E. H., & Pleck, J. H. (1995). Masculinity ideology: A review of research instrumentation on men and masculinity. In R. F. Levant & W. S. Pollack (Eds.), *A new psychology of men* (pp. 129–163). New York: Basic Books.

Tyler, L. E. (1977). *Individuality.* San Francisco: Jossey-Bass.

CHAPTER TWELVE

Psychotherapy with Men Navigating Midlife Terrain

Sam V. Cochran

For many years social and behavioral scientists considered middle age the "latency" period of adulthood, paralleling the latency of childhood in which little active development was thought to be occurring. Psychoanalytic theorists viewed childhood as formative, and the years after puberty received scant attention from most scientific and psychological writers in the first half of the twentieth century. Two notable exceptions were Carl Jung and Erik Erikson. Unlike Freud, who believed that psychological structures and functions were fixed by childhood experiences, Jung believed that psychological changes occurred throughout life and that important transformations occurred in particular at midlife (see Jung, 1969). Erikson (1956) outlined the tasks of ego and identity development from childhood through adulthood. His model of development contributed important understandings to issues that are activated in midlife and beyond.

Psychological inquiry focused on sex differences related to midlife has occurred more recently. Since 1980, several groundbreaking investigations that charted the developmental and psychological challenges that men experience in adulthood have been reported (see Farrell & Rosenberg, 1981; Levinson, Darrow, Klein, Levinson, & McKee, 1978; Vaillant, 1977). Several issues that characterize men's experiences at midlife have emerged from these studies. Men navigating midlife terrain struggle with issues of commitment to family and work, personal and psychological integrity, real and symbolic loss, and mortality.

In this chapter I review current psychological perspectives on midlife or middle age in men and integrate these perspectives with a new psychology of men. Attention is paid to several important empirical investigations of men that have tended to shape our psychological understanding of the challenges men face at midlife. In addition to these empirical reports, a number of clinical reports have further documented the various issues that men navigating midlife terrain encounter. A perspective that integrates these empirical and clinical viewpoints yields an empathic and depth-oriented understanding of men and provides groundwork for suggestions for psychotherapy with men as they navigate this midlife terrain.

DEFINING MIDLIFE IN MEN'S LIVES

Definitions of midlife or middle age tend to be inconsistent and highly variable. This variability most likely reflects the difficulty scholars, scientists, and clinicians have had in clearly outlining the parameters of middle age for both men and women. Several perspectives can be used to define the boundaries of midlife or middle age. Biological perspectives rely on actuarial estimates of expected life span as well as predictable timetables for natural biological processes associated with aging to play out over the life span. Role transition perspectives emphasize expected changes in typical social and occupational roles as individuals grow older and progress through roles of worker, parent, and family and community member. Life stage perspectives seek to chart the various developmental stages from childhood through young adulthood, middle adulthood, and old adulthood and to describe the developmental challenges encountered as an individual passes through each stage.

Biological Perspectives

The average life expectancy for a man born in 1950 is 65.6 years. For a man born in 1960 the life expectancy increases one year to 66.6 years. Medical advances and changes in personal life style have extended the life expectancy for many men since that time. In 1996, a white man who was forty years old could expect to live for seventy-six years, whereas a forty-year-old African American man could expect to live for sixty-seven years. Based on these average life expectancies, middle age for most American men would be somewhere between thirty-three and thirty-eight years of age (National Center for Health Statistics, 1998).

Physiological change occurs rapidly at birth, in adolescence, and in old age. Although physiological changes continue in middle age, for most people this time is characterized by relative stability, in contrast to the rapid changes of other periods of life. Perhaps the most significant naturally occurring physiological process of middle age is menopause in women. Some investigators have suggested that men may experience a similar sex hormone–based process. Age-associated testosterone decline in men has been noted as a contributing factor to many problems in men that appear to be associated with advancing age (Sternbach, 1998). Manifestations of this normal decline in male hormone levels may include depression, anxiety, irritability, insomnia, weaknesses, decreased libido, impotence, poor memory, reduced muscle and bone mass, and reduced sexual body hair. Such changes would be expected to garner a reaction in most men as they enter middle age, especially if they have based aspects of their identity on traditional definitions of masculinity that emphasize physical and sexual prowess, strength, and vigor.

Social Role Perspectives

Analysis of social roles has also proved to be a useful approach to studying midlife. Moen and Wethington (1999) emphasize how men's and women's roles shift as the requirements of certain social roles change and evolve over time. For men, for example, the requirements of the social role of provider may shift as economic requirements of supporting a family evolve. In addition, men at midlife may experience family roles in a much different manner than women at midlife.

Huyck (1999) summarizes the differential impact of gender roles on the experience of middle age in women and men. Family relationships, work relationships, and community relationships are the most important domains in which men's and women's roles are defined throughout adulthood. In comparison to women, men's midlife role transitions have been found to be more closely connected to shifts in work, career, and men's perceived role as the family provider (see Levinson et al., 1978). In addition to these shifts, other investigators have found an increased sense of commitment to family relationships (see Farrell & Rosenberg, 1981) and work and community relationships (see Weiss, 1990) and an increased valuing of the parental role in men (see Guttman, 1987).

Life Stage Perspectives

Another perspective that has proved useful in studying changes over the life cycle is a perspective that views these changes as occurring at distinct stages. Erikson (1956) was one of the first developmental theorists to define the tasks of adult (male) development, including negotiating intimacy in young adulthood and, later, generativity and integrity. Neugarten (1968) detailed personality changes that paralleled chronological age in adults and located distinct shifts in perspective in the fifth decade of life that resulted in greater reflection and introspection.

Results of Levinson and colleagues' (1978) investigation confirmed that men passed through definable stages, or "eras," of life. Levinson and his colleagues were able to identify distinct transitions from young adulthood, during which the early aspects of a life structure (occupation and family) are put in place, into middle adulthood, during which the elements of this life structure are reviewed and revised. In addition to this finding with American men, Guttman (1976) confirmed the existence of a midlife transition period or "crisis" in five different cultural groups that included men from urban American, American Indian, Middle Eastern Druze, and lowland and highland Mayan samples.

Although these and other studies have yielded important findings that have helped to define the midlife terrain for men, developmental stage approaches have also been controversial. Feminist researchers have challenged developmental stage models for their reliance on exclusively male samples from which conclusions are drawn (see Gilligan, 1982). Nonetheless, in terms of studying a specific segment of the population, these findings provide convenient markers or signposts that designate the challenges and tasks many men encounter at various points across the life cycle.

Are there unique, masculine-specific challenges that arise in midlife? I examine two perspectives that have illuminated many important midlife issues for men. Empirical studies that have used longitudinal and cross-sectional methodologies have defined the issues men encounter in midlife (see Ciernia, 1985; Cournoyer & Mahalik, 1995; Farrell & Rosenberg, 1981; Levinson et al., 1978; Vaillant, 1977). In addition to these empirical findings, clinical case reports have also contributed to an understanding of the midlife challenges that at times become so severe as to overwhelm coping resources and bring men to therapy (see Braverman & Paris, 1993; Cochran & Rabinowitz, 1996; Kernberg, 1985; Rabinowitz, 1998). In general, these findings converge to point to the importance of four separate but interrelated issues as important for men at midlife: work, health, family relationships, and death awareness.

MEN AT MIDLIFE: EMPIRICAL FINDINGS

In this section I explore the empirical findings about men at midlife. In particular, I describe research investigating the seasons of a man's life, men's adaptation to life, men and midlife, and staying the course.

The Seasons of a Man's Life

Levinson et al. (1978) studied forty men from diverse backgrounds representing four different occupational groups: hourly workers, executives, academic scientists, and novelists. These men were between the ages of thirty-five and forty-five and were studied using a qualitative-quantitative methodology. Levinson and his colleagues' specific purpose in this investigation was to examine the middle years and to explore what was considered to be an important life transition that the investigators hypothesized occurred in men around age forty. Results of this study identified a distinct process of transition from that segment of the life span that was characterized as the early adult era into the middle adult era. They called this entry into middle age the "midlife transition" to imply that it is a transition between early adulthood and the settling-down phase that characterized middle age.

The tasks of middle age include revising "the dream" and resolving the four polarities of life. Revision of the dream entails measuring actual occupational achievement against childhood dreams and fantasies that provided a sense of identity and purpose for a young boy. Often, midlife conflict can occur in relation to discrepancies between the persistent force of the dream of boyhood and the reality of occupational accomplishment in adulthood. For some men, too great a discrepancy may result in despair and frustration at midlife and beyond. These sentiments may give rise to a "midlife crisis" in some men.

Resolution of the four polarities of life involves reconciliation of conflicts related to age (old versus young), purpose or direction (destructiveness versus creativity), identity (masculinity versus femininity), and intimacy (attachment versus separateness). Interestingly, a number of men in the four cross-sectional samples experienced a period of tumult or struggle around the midlife transition. This period of tumult was revealed in questions concerning the life plan or life accomplishments and feelings of anger and recriminations against the self and significant others. Faced with the challenges of resolving life polarities, the men in this study found that they must either choose a new path or modify the old one. For some men, this challenge was met with relatively little upheaval; for others, it amounted to a midlife crisis that resulted in considerable disruption in family and work relationships.

Adaptation to Life

Vaillant (1977) reported the results of a longitudinal study of 268 men who were chosen as exemplars of health and promise as college students. These men, like those in the Levinson et al. (1978) report, were studied using a quantitative-qualitative methodology over a span of thirty years. The purpose of the study was to explore how individuals adapt to the challenges that life presents over a period of time. One of the main findings of this study was that maturity of psychological defenses was the strongest predictor of an individual's capacity to manage life challenges. The use of immature defenses (such as projection, acting out, and denial) tended to ensure marginal adjustment over the life span regardless of age. Use of mature defense mechanisms (such as sublimation, altruism, and humor) tended to be associated with better adjustment over the life span. In regard to men's use of immature defense mechanisms, Mahalik, Cournoyer, Cherry, and Napolitano (1998) identified the associations between immature coping mechanisms and masculine-specific gender role strain. They found that men who experienced greater strain related to issues of power and competition, expression of emotions, and expression of affection to other men tended to also use immature psychological defense mechanisms. The persistent use of such defense mechanisms would be expected to increase the likelihood of unsuccessful coping with various developmental crises over the life span.

Men at Midlife

Farrell and Rosenberg (1981) studied a total of 433 men in two age groups, a younger group of men between twenty-five and thirty years of age and an older group of men between thirty-eight and forty-eight years of age. The purpose of their investigation was to examine men's responses to midlife challenges and to verify differences in responses that might be related to the age differences of the two groups. For both age groups Farrell and Rosenberg identified four general types of response styles: the antihero or dissenter, the transcendent-generative, the pseudodeveloped man, and the punitive-disenchanted-authoritarian type. In Farrell and Rosenberg's study, the men of both age groups evidenced dramatic variation in how they responded to middle age stresses. In general, this investigation found that men tended to avoid the stresses and pressures of middle age.

Staying the Course

As the subtitle of the book indicates, Weiss (1990) and his colleagues studied the emotional and social lives of eighty men who were considered to be successful at work. Although the study was not designed to investigate midlife, the subjects in this study were between thirty-five and fifty-five years—ages generally considered to encompass the midlife years. This study used a cross-sectional or contemporaneous design, permitting in-depth analysis of the men's lives at a given point in time.

Not surprisingly, one of the main findings of this particular study is that work plays a significant role as the foundation of successful men's lives. For the men in this sample, a successful career established a place within the community and was the basis of respect, self-worth, and identity. Success in the community enabled these men to function happily and effectively at home as spouses and parents.

Paradoxically, for most of the men in this study family relationships and commitments were always viewed as more important than work. There was a synergistic effect between these two domains: success and pride derived from each tended to facilitate success in the other. Success at work enabled the men to feel positive about themselves as providers, parents, and spouses. Success at home as providers, spouses, and fathers tended to provide additional value and meaning to the sacrifice and effort endured at work.

Consistent with the findings of these studies, Cournoyer and Mahalik (1995) found that compared with college-aged men, middle-aged men experienced less masculine-specific gender role conflict in issues of power, success, and competition but experienced greater conflict in issues related to balancing work and family. This finding confirms that for middle-aged men, issues of commitment to family and work are highly salient and can be a significant source of stress. In contrast to this finding, Stillson, O'Neil, and Owen (1991) failed to discover differences in levels of gender role conflict among three different age groups of men. However, it is possible that their sample did not contain a wide enough age spread for the hypothesized conflicts to emerge because they used men between the ages of twenty-two and thirty-nine compared with a range of thirty-six to forty-five years of age in Cournoyer and Mahalik's sample.

MEN AT MIDLIFE: CLINICAL FINDINGS

Clinical work with men at midlife has uncovered the meaning men attribute to the life changes they may be experiencing that have brought them to seek the assistance of a psychotherapist. Cochran and Rabinowitz (1996) underscore the importance of attending to issues of loss in the lives of men at all points in the life span. Men often experience the realities of middle age as losses—losses of physical strength, deaths of family members and friends, loss of children as they leave home, and loss of relationship for those men who experience separation and divorce. Cultural prohibitions against the experience of sadness, loss, and grief in men make the open acknowledgement of these experiences difficult. Braverman and Paris (1993) view midlife challenges as a reflection of a narcissistic vulnerability in some men that is secondary to childhood neglect. Their perspective views the midlife crisis in men as a reactivation of an unresolved depressive response that occurred because of inadequate childhood emotional supplies. Both Cochran and Rabinowitz (1996) and Braverman and Paris (1993) suggest an open engagement with the emotional content of this depressive response to loss that middle age is prone to activate in many men.

Another consistent theme in these and other reports based on clinical work with men at midlife is the increasing awareness of mortality that results in a confrontation with death anxiety. Yalom (1980), Jacques (1965), Cochran and Rabinowitz (1996), Erikson (1956), Kernberg (1985), and Braverman and Paris (1993) all emphasize the importance of facing this reactivation of the "depressive position" associated with increased awareness of personal mortality. With the prospect of a finite life span, deaths of parents and children, and the limitations of creativity, men at midlife are presented with both a challenge and an opportunity as they come to terms with the meaning of death in their lives.

A major challenge for men at midlife is to embrace this death awareness and anxiety and the ensuing depression fully, to experience the grief and loss that attends this awareness, and to bear the painful affect states that are activated in this process. Men who are willing to persevere with their own emotional work on this issue have an opportunity to reconcile the ultimate polarities of life. These men may genuinely achieve a sense of resolution and serenity in the face of the prospect of death and may finally be ready to fully recommit to the remaining years of life with a renewed sense of perspective, appreciation, and wisdom.

Both empirical inquiry and clinical inquiry have contributed to an increased understanding of the issues and emotional challenges that men face at midlife. As they navigate midlife terrain men experience shifts in roles, reevaluations of commitments, and the challenge of facing inevitable losses and working through death awareness. For many men midlife challenges reawaken earlier conflict-laden aspects of development. However, with the added perspective of maturity and life experience, many men are also able to positively navigate this terrain and enter older adulthood with an enhanced sense of perspective on their lives.

CLINICAL PRESENTATION OF MIDLIFE ISSUES

From the empirical and clinical reports it is clear that men vary widely in their experiences of midlife. Clinical presentation may yield direct evidence of midlife issues. However, it is more likely that a man in midlife will present with a number of various and seemingly unrelated issues from which the psychotherapist, through careful listening, may discover the theme of midlife challenge. The following case presentation illustrates the manner in which midlife issues may be activated and presented in a man seeking psychotherapy.

Bill consulted a therapist for help "coping with stress." Bill was a successful forty-two-year-old education professional. He was married and had two children, a daughter age twelve and a son age nine. His spouse worked as a nurse in the local hospital. Bill and his spouse had moved several states away from their hometown area for Bill's career at the time of their oldest child's birth. Since then, Bill had advanced in his career and was now a popular and successful superintendent of the local school district.

At the time Bill scheduled his appointment he had been having a number of physical problems that concerned him. He was finding he experienced a noticeable shortness of breath as he played his usual pickup basketball game over the lunch hour with his friends. He had various pains in his chest and had been having an increasing number of headaches throughout the day at work. He had consulted his family physician, who found no physical problems. His physician suggested that stress might be at the bottom of Bill's physical problems and recommended a consultation appointment with a therapist.

As Bill and his therapist explored the various aspects of Bill's life that were stressful, Bill disclosed that his mother had died about ten months ago. He told his therapist that his mother's death was unexpected and was quite a shock for him. She was sixty-five years old and had died quite suddenly from a cerebral hemorrhage. Bill remembered the phone call when his father told him of his mother's death. "I knew something was wrong, and when he said Mom had passed away I felt this awful, sinking feeling in my stomach. I just knew then that my life would never be the same. It was terrible."

Sensing the obvious emotional intensity of this event, Bill's therapist invited Bill to talk more about his mother. "She was always there for me, was one of my biggest supporters. She gave me totally unconditional love. I feel like a part of me is gone now."

"I'm so sorry," Bill's therapist responded. "This sounds like a profound loss. How have you coped with it since then?"

"I've been pretty busy, I guess. The service and the wake were very emotional, but I felt like I really was able to let go and get all my emotions out." Bill paused. "I don't know. Do you think that has something to do with how I'm doing now?"

As Bill and his therapist explored his reactions to his mother's death and how he had coped with it several themes emerged. Bill's general emotional state had been mainly sad, and he attributed it to his mother's death. But as he and his therapist talked, his sadness extended to a number of other areas of his life, too. He had feelings of sadness and loss over his decline in physical strength and well-being over the past few years. "I'm just not my old self," Bill lamented to his therapist as he discussed the limitations he perceived in his physical endurance and strength.

He felt sad as he worked to reestablish a closer relationship with his father, who now relied on him more and more for emotional support. Bill found himself thinking about his father's death as their visits increased in frequency. He felt sad at times when he found himself contemplating his own death and how he would miss his spouse and his children.

In addition to Bill's sad mood, he reported feeling bored and at times frustrated with his work. He felt he was "solving the same old problems over and over" yet could not just quit and move somewhere else for the sake of a new challenge. "I have devoted a lot of my life to this community. My kids are well established. We know a lot of people. It wouldn't be fair to them. And I know, too, the grass is rarely greener."

Over a period of six months of weekly therapy sessions, Bill and his therapist explored what began as grief work over his mother's death but quickly branched out to encompass a number of areas of his life. Bill noticed how several of the issues he discussed were related to an increasing awareness of his own mortality. The impact of his mother's death was the most obvious of these issues. But his reflections on his father's advancing age and increasing reliance on Bill as a caregiver and support system brought Bill in touch with questions about how his father would probably need more attention and support as he got older. And then, finally, Bill's increasing awareness of his own aging process, played out on the basketball court at lunchtime with his buddies, brought him face-to-face with his own mortality. As Bill and his therapist explored the interrelations of all these issues, Bill gradually developed an increased sense of acceptance of his mother's death, the aging of his father, and ultimately his own aging process.

At forty-two years of age, Bill was beyond the statistical definition of midlife. If Bill were to live out his expected life span he would in fact be past middle age by at least five years. Bill's initial visit to his therapist was based on a referral from his physician. Physical concerns and symptoms had initially set the wheels in motion for Bill to seek help. It is not uncommon for middle-aged men to notice the effects of advancing age, as was apparent in Bill's concerns over shortness of breath and decreased physical endurance.

Bill's stress and his attention to his declining physical health signified for him a transition to a different stage in his life. At several points in his sessions with his therapist he engaged in comparisons that highlighted that he believed his physical strength and conditioning had changed from when he was a younger man. His workouts with his buddies on the basketball court served as daily reminders of the vulnerability of his body to the aging process. These changes also heightened his awareness of his own mortality and the evolution of his own place in the life cycle.

In Bill's situation, the death of his mother dramatically altered his role as his mother's son. The role of dutiful, responsible son who worked hard for his mother's love and approval was now challenged because his mother was dead. The comforts and support he had internalized were still in him, but the real person who had provided those vital supplies was no longer living. This shift for Bill catapulted him into examining the nature of his role not only as his mother's son but also as his father's son and as a father himself. As noted, he experienced a sense of sadness and loss as he examined these shifts in the roles he had played for such a long time. Bill's therapist expressed interest and empathy for this emotional aspect of Bill's situation and focused on Bill's feelings of grief and loss.

IS MIDLIFE A CRISIS?

The term *midlife crisis* has been applied to both men and women. But for men there exists an unfortunate stereotype popularized through media portrayals. This particular narrative involves a middle-aged man who suddenly and inexplicably plunges into a despairing crisis, leaves his spouse and children, quits his job, buys a sporty red convertible, and races off into the sunset accompanied by a voluptuous younger woman. Of course, such depictions are nothing more than negative stereotypes of men behaving badly when faced with this so-called midlife crisis. In general, research has failed to confirm the existence of such a crisis for men.

Although they worked with a highly select sample, Vaillant (1977) and his colleagues did not find compelling evidence for a midlife crisis in the men they studied. Vaillant speculated that the middle years are not without challenge but reports that the notion of a midlife crisis is simply a creation of the popular press and was rarely observed in the men in his sample. Similarly, after reviewing several longitudinal and cross-sectional studies Nydegger (1976) found little evidence for a midlife crisis in middle-aged men. Her conclusion was that the years between age forty and age fifty are characterized more by stability than by upheaval. Farrell and Rosenberg (1981) also did not find any evidence of a crisis response in the men they studied. Instead, they found that a common response style was to avoid or deny the issues of midlife. Weiss (1990), in his study of successful middle-aged men, found an occasional instance of a man who engaged in an extramarital affair or a man who became frustrated and discouraged at his place of work. These reports are consistent with Vaillant's (1977) conclusion that "divorce, job disenchantment, and depression occur with roughly equal frequency throughout the adult life cycle" (p. 223).

In summarizing their perspective on middle age, Reid and Willis (1999) conclude that the notion of a midlife crisis that has been popular since the 1970s or 1980s has been overdramatized. They, too, find midlife characterized by a period of reevaluation, reflection, introspection, and prioritization. Some men respond to this challenge with vigor and perspective, whereas others are demoralized and dejected by it. Optimally, an emerging sense of perspective and reflection is a by-product of successful navigation of these years.

In recognizing the limitations of conclusions drawn from group-derived data, Rosenberg, Rosenberg, and Farrell (1999) suggest a shift to a personal narrative conceptualization of midlife crisis. The personal narrative perspective is based on the application of narrative psychology to the experience of midlife. Narrative psychology proposes that individuals construct narratives, or stories, of their lives that give meaning and coherence to their lived experience. For Rosenberg et al. (1999), a narrative perspective can give meaning to what may be experienced as a chaotic, tumultuous midlife crisis. The midlife crisis construct can be invoked to account for dramatic shifts in an individual's life narrative that may occur at various points in the life span. This shift is particularly notable in the fourth and fifth decades of life, as narratives of stability and achievement may be revised to include an element of tragedy, romance, or decline.

In contrast to these findings that question the validity of the midlife crisis construct, Ciernia (1985) reported results of a study that found that a large percentage of men (70 percent of his sample) did in fact experience a midlife crisis. This study questioned 227 businessmen about their experiences of midlife crisis and the extent that death awareness played a part in this crisis. In general, the older subjects reported they had experienced a midlife crisis and that a concern over their mortality had been a central aspect of this crisis.

In spite of this single study that lends some support to the validity of this construct, empirical findings do not support the notion that most men experience a crisis as they navigate midlife terrain. The construct may be helpful for some men as they adjust to changes in their lives and are faced with the challenge of revising their life narrative (see Rosenberg et al., 1999). Some men, such as those in Vaillant's (1977) study, most likely experience crisis as a result of immature coping strategies. However, generalizations about men's midlife crises are not warranted from the existing data.

CLINICAL PERSPECTIVES ON WORKING WITH MEN AT MIDLIFE

Three themes emerge from the clinical and empirical literature regarding midlife developments that are relevant for clinical work with men navigating the midlife terrain. First, there is a heightened awareness of evolving roles and relationships at work, in the community, and with intimate others including family of origin and family of choice. Second, there is an emerging awareness of individual mortality and a confrontation with the reality of death. This awareness occurs not only through the individual growth, maturation, and change that reinforce the decline of physical health but also through the death and disability of close friends and family members. Finally, the opportunity that midlife reflection affords for revision of aspects of a man's identity can be both liberating and daunting. If midlife is indeed a crisis for some men, then the Chinese character for crisis as both danger and opportunity is an appropriate representation for this stage of life.

Shifts in Male Roles at Midlife

A number of studies have pointed to the importance of shifts in roles that occur at midlife. For men, these shifts occur mainly in the context of family relationships and work relationships. Changes in family relationships can be triggered through separation and divorce, deaths of parents, and shifting roles of other family members such as spouse, partner, or children. Old assumptions and expectations concerning self and others must be reexamined as men face increasing demands for equality from women and as children leave home and strike out on their own. Divided allegiances may require reconciliation as conflicts between work and family relationships emerge (see Cournoyer & Mahalik, 1995). In addition, changes in health status of parents and ultimately parental death significantly affect how a man views himself and his relationships with family members (see Kernberg, 1985). Renewed commitments to family are commonly reported outcomes of having navigated the midlife terrain (see Farrell & Rosenberg, 1981; Guttman, 1987; Levinson et al., 1978).

Shifts in work roles, responsibilities, and interests occur as men advance in their careers. Sometimes new challenges emerge that require a revision of the original motive or impetus for pursuit of a particular career path. Career stagnation or career failure can also serve as a jarring precipitant for reexamination of the meaning of a man's job and the intrinsic value it continues to hold for him and his identity. Revision of "the dream" (Levinson et al., 1978) affords men an opportunity to examine the childhood fantasy of integrity and purpose that is established through a meaningful work role. This examination, when measured against actual occupational accomplishments, results in either a shift in occupational direction or a recommitment to an already established occupation.

Social roles, which were often seen as relatively simple and straightforward in the early adulthood years, are now viewed as more complicated and tinged with considerable ambivalence. This ambivalence is often unsettling for men who have been socialized to be decisive and in control. Such ambivalence is frequently experienced as a loss and may trigger a depressive episode that might lead to a visit to a therapist (see Cochran & Rabinowitz, 1996). Increasing commitments to other roles (such as career and family) frequently trigger a reexamination of priorities and an assessment of the ultimate value of the various roles in a man's life.

Managing Death Anxiety in Middle Age

Jacques (1965) constructs a model of midlife crisis around the impact of confrontation with death and mortality. For him, midlife begins around age thirty-five and is initially characterized by an increasing awareness of the reality of death. Yalom (1980) points out the subtle ways that individuals experience (and deny) the existence of death as an integral issue in their lives. This realization is particularly heightened in middle age as awareness of individual physical decline and the death of parents and peers begin to occur with increased frequency. Cochran and Rabinowitz (1996) also highlight the significance of death awareness for men and recommend the use of an existential approach to psychotherapy with men that focuses on the meaning of actual and symbolic losses at various points over the life span.

Kernberg (1980) views the confrontation with loss and death as one of the main developmental tasks of middle age. Through this confrontation, triggered by decline in health and the deaths of parents and peers, it is possible to work through both the real and anticipated losses while maintaining a sense of hope and generativity. The existence of adequate inner resources (sufficient internalized self and object representations) is a key element in a man's capacity to manage the mourning that is required in navigating midlife terrain.

Through their clinical experience with successful middle-aged men Braverman and Paris (1993) discovered a common theme of struggle with a depressive position in middle age that was thought to be secondary to the parental neglect the men experienced and that left them with a deficit in the self. The therapeutic tasks for these men often revolved around assisting the men to develop a healthy sense of generativity as a substitute for the wish for acquiring the supplies that were not provided in childhood. Awareness of these deficits and a shift from reparation to generativity often were accompanied by an increased awareness of personal mortality.

Overall, increased awareness of the reality of death can lead to an increased appreciation of a man's individual contribution to children, family, community, and profession. For men, a shift of values often occurs in midlife. This shift is reflected in increased time spent with those with whom a man feels close attachments, a desire to value work and achievement in greater perspective, and an increased interest in passing on gifts to the succeeding generation. Guttman (1987) emphasizes the importance of this shift in middle age, because men from a number of cultures were found to exhibit an increased valuing of the parental role.

Existential Psychotherapy: Facing Midlife Challenges

The changes characteristic of midlife activate issues that resonate deeply in many men. Changes in relationships at work and in the family, increased awareness of mortality, reconciliation of dreams with actual accomplishments, and renewed commitments in various domains of life are all highlighted as men navigate the midlife terrain. Levinson et al. (1978) identified the importance of the four polarities of life that are activated in midlife: age, purpose and direction, identity, and intimacy. An existential approach to psychotherapy (see Cochran & Rabinowitz, 1996; Yalom, 1980) directly addresses these concerns. Loss and death (age), isolation and connection (intimacy), meaning and values (identity), commitment (purpose and direction), and responsibility are core themes in the existential approach to psychotherapy. The existential approach reaches directly into these core elements of the midlife terrain and offers empathic understanding and perspective on these universal human challenges.

Existential psychotherapy focuses directly on the emotional dimension and the meaning of these core issues. As normative changes unfold over the course of a man's life, he is faced with both the emotional content of these changes and their meaning. For example, the death of a parent triggers strong emotional reactions as well as a reflection on the reality of death for everyone. The experience of reaching a career plateau forces an examination of both emotional reactions to this common occurrence and a rededication to a chosen career or a shift to another career pathway.

One inclusive theme that characterizes these and other elements of midlife challenges is the theme of examining and affirming or revising elements of a man's identity. Choices of work, family, values, leisure, and friends all accrue over the life span to constitute elements of a man's identity. As he examines and weighs the value of these elements as a result of midlife changes, a man has the opportunity to affirm a clearer sense of his own identity, meaning, and purpose in life. Existential approaches to psychotherapy directly address the personal meaning of these many facets of individual identity and invite revision as warranted.

Deficits in self and identity, failure of psychological defenses to contain anxieties associated with change and increased awareness of mortality, and lack of enduring relationships to family, friends, and community may combine to yield a sense of despair and depression for some men at midlife. In contrast, most men successfully navigate midlife terrain and emerge with renewed appreciation for the fullness of the life cycle and sensitivity to their own and others' place within it. For these men, there is a deep sense of satisfaction and resolution of the conflicts that may have been activated by midlife changes. Such resolutions set the stage for entry into the subsequent life stages.

EXAMINING LIFE AT MIDDLE AGE

A common element of clinical reports of men who are facing midlife is the challenge of examining the meaning of choices and commitments and how they contribute to a sense of fulfillment or failure in a man's life. Often, a crisis precipitates such an examination and sometimes leads to a sense of despair and depression. The following case example illustrates how a crisis can often be a point of departure for examining a number of aspects of a man's life.

Barry was a forty-five-year-old man who was referred by his work supervisor for anger management therapy. Barry had been reprimanded on two occasions for slamming doors and kicking a hole in the wall of the warehouse building where he was employed. One more outburst would jeopardize his job. He readily accepted a referral from his supervisor for counseling. At his initial session he and his therapist discussed what these angry outbursts meant for him.

"It's like a frustration. It just builds up and then I explode," Barry said as he attempted to explain what had happened.

"Hmmm. Like a frustration. I'm not sure I follow what you mean here, Barry," his therapist responded.

"You know, it's like a frustration. Something doesn't go the way I want it to go. Or I do something that I look back on and realize is a mistake or is stupid."

"You get angry if you make a mistake or look stupid?"

"Yeah."

"I don't follow the connection there. Why does doing something that is what you think is a mistake or that looks stupid make you angry?" his therapist continued.

"I guess these situations make me realize that I've done some stupid things, or that I'm not really very confident or happy with myself. So I get mad, and BAM I just lash out," Barry replied.

"Not very confident or happy with yourself. That sounds like an important connection here. What do you mean by that?"

"I've been working this same old job for over twenty years now. I've had some administrative duties and a chance at a promotion but I guess I couldn't handle those. They never worked out. Then I look back at my divorce. I never really have felt very confident of myself since then. I blame myself for that. It's just a lot of things that have gone wrong over the last twenty or so years, and they have all built up, and sometimes it just gets to be too much and I get frustrated and angry and I lash out."

In Barry's next session, he and his therapist discussed his feelings of dissatisfaction with his life and what he could do to improve his sense of self-worth and happiness. Barry looked back over the past twenty years of his life and reflected, "I have done a lot of things that I'm not happy with. The divorce really threw me. I started drinking a lot after that. And I got into some trouble."

"Got into some trouble? Like what?"

"Well, I got arrested for drunk driving. And I got into some fights with some guys when I was drinking. Just stupid stuff."

Barry's therapist picked up on the replay of the word *stupid.* "You keep referring to yourself and to the things you have done as 'stupid.' What's that about?"

"I guess I've never felt like I've accomplished much. And here I am, forty-five years old, working at the same old job and not taking advantage of any advancements that come my way. I just go to work and come home and plop down on the couch. I don't do anything for myself. I'm divorced. I don't really have much contact with my daughter anymore. She's eighteen now and that's when my custody payments end. So I don't know if we will ever see each other again. Doesn't that sound like stupid to you?"

Barry paused. His therapist sat in silence with him, then probed, "Barry, what's it like to be talking about yourself in this way?"

"It's sad. Like my life hasn't really amounted to much. Like it may never really amount to much. This is what gets me frustrated and why I lash out with anger."

"You feel sad. It sure sounds like you've had to contend with a lot of disappointments with yourself."

"Yeah."

In subsequent sessions Barry and his therapist explored Barry's deep sense of sadness and despair at the state of this life. They discussed how his anger outbursts appeared to be a wake-up call for Barry to begin to make some decisions about how he was conducting his life.

Barry introduced the term *midlife crisis* to describe his experiences at work and to convey his sense of frustration and disappointment in himself. He conscientiously attended his therapy sessions, and over time he began to activate aspects of himself that had been dormant for many years. He rediscovered his interest in music and began to attend local meetings of a folk music club. He began to view his employment as providing him material comforts and the opportunity to engage in some self-improvement activities. He returned to exercise as he had done during his years in the service and prior to his divorce. He lost some of his "excess baggage," his term for the forty pounds he had gained over the past ten or so years and that he attributed to just sitting in front of the television in his spare time.

Barry's case contains several themes that are identified in clinical writings on working with men at midlife. His relationships at work were deteriorating, and he was faced with a threat of loss of employment. Although he had been divorced for several years, he still struggled with what the divorce meant for him and held to the notion that he had failed in his marriage and family. Barry struggled with feeling isolated and disconnected from these important relationships both at work and with his own ex-spouse and daughter. He expressed considerable discomfort and shame as he recounted how he felt responsible for these disconnections. He felt "stuck" as he considered what he might do to repair these relationships. These concerns all represented an increased sensitivity to his isolation and his fears that his own "stupidity" and "badness" were to blame for this situation.

He was also concerned with his state of health. As a younger man he had been an athlete in high school and had been in good shape in military service. He had gained considerable weight after his divorce and perceived himself as a "couch potato" who spent his free time sitting in front of his television "wasting away." He expressed feelings of loss and sadness as he recounted his previous state of well-being and how that contrasted with how he now felt about himself physically.

His general mood state was depressive, although his therapist focused on this depression as a natural reaction to the losses he had accumulated in adulthood and the fact that as he looked back on his life he concluded that he had failed at most things he had tried. His sense of despair over his perceived failures at work was found to be directly related to his increasing awareness of his advancing age and the limited time he felt he had left to make changes if he was going to do so. As Barry and his therapist discussed his options, Barry's awareness of a limited, finite number of years left in his work life and his life in total left him feeling depressed. He disclosed that he frequently spent time contemplating whether "life was even worth it." In the depths of his despair he said that because he had failed so badly at his work and at his marriage and because there was no time left to really make any meaningful changes, perhaps death was not such a bad option after all. At other times, he found meaning in working, attending antique shows, and playing the piano.

Barry's situation represents how a man who faces midlife challenges can plunge into despair and depression. The accumulation of losses and perceived failures may finally break through the defenses and produce a deep sense of failure, shame, and sadness that can be paralyzing and can inhibit working through the conflicts that produce these feelings. In Barry's case, he found a therapist who was sensitive to his pain and grief but who was also willing to offer him a positive, supportive, empathic relationship. The therapist helped Barry to recognize and repair his damaged sense of self and to pick up the pieces and move on with his life. Barry made significant progress in his efforts to relieve some of his sense of failure by examining the meaning of some of his perceived failures. He decreased some of his feelings of depression by facing the reality of the losses he had accrued over his life and by constructing realistic and positive plans for engaging in meaningful activities. By learning to accept himself and his "failures" more fully, he became less angry with himself for having failed and found himself less prone to angry outbursts at work or in social settings.

Midlife can present significant challenges as well as opportunities for men. Research has confirmed that men experience common themes as they navigate midlife terrain, including shifts in social, familial, and occupational roles and relationships, increases in awareness of mortality and death anxiety, and increases in opportunities to reconcile unresolved conflicts that may have been repressed at earlier ages. Most men face these challenge and move through the midlife terrain with little difficulty. However, a few men may experience the midlife terrain as particularly rocky and may experience this time of life as a crisis.

There is little empirical evidence to support the universality of the midlife crisis. Stability and perseverance are characteristic of midlife for most men. However, some men do plunge into despair and depression as they face losses that become evident in middle age. Combined with increased anxiety about what to make of the little time that is left in life, these losses can indeed create a crisis situation.

Psychotherapy that focuses on the core constituents of midlife terrain can assist men in working through the complex feelings associated with their own mortality, deaths of family and friends, and shifts in roles at work and in their families. An existential approach to these concerns may prove beneficial for most men because this approach directly addresses these concerns in the context of death anxiety, isolation, meaning and values, responsibility, and commitment.

References

Braverman, S., & Paris, J. (1993). The male mid-life crisis in the grown-up resilient child. *Psychotherapy, 30,* 651–657.

Ciernia, J. (1985). Death concern and businessmen's mid-life crisis. *Psychological Reports, 56,* 83–87.

Cochran, S., & Rabinowitz, F. (1996). Men, loss, and psychotherapy. *Psychotherapy, 33,* 593–600.

Cournoyer, R., & Mahalik, J. (1995). Cross-sectional study of gender role conflict examining college-aged and middle-aged men. *Journal of Counseling Psychology, 42,* 11–19.

Erikson, E. (1956). The problem of ego identity. *Journal of the American Psychoanalytic Association, 4,* 56–121.

Farrell, M., & Rosenberg, S. (1981). *Men at midlife.* Boston: Auburn House.

Gilligan, C. (1982). *In a different voice.* Cambridge, MA: Harvard University Press.

Guttman, D. (1976). Individual adaptation in the middle years: Developmental issues in the masculine mid-life crisis. *Journal of Geriatric Psychiatry, 9,* 41–59.

Guttman, D. (1987). *Reclaimed powers: Toward a new psychology of men and women in later life.* New York: Basic Books.

Huyck, M. (1999). Gender roles and gender identity in mid-life. In S. Willis & J. Reid (Eds.), *Life in the middle: Psychological and social development in middle age* (pp. 209–232). New York: Academic Press.

Jacques, E. (1965). Death and the mid-life crisis. *International Journal of Psychoanalysis, 46,* 502–514.

Jung, C. G. (1969). *The structure and dynamics of the psyche. The Collected Works of C. G. Jung* (Vol. 8). (R. F. C. Hull, Trans.). Princeton, NJ: Princeton University Press.

Kernberg, O. (1985). *Internal world and external reality.* New York: Aronson.

Levinson, D., Darrow, C., Klein, E., Levinson, M., & McKee, B. (1978). *The seasons of a man's life.* New York: Knopf.

Mahalik, J., Cournoyer, W., Cherry, M., & Napolitano, J. (1998). Men's gender role conflict and use of psychological defenses. *Journal of Counseling Psychology, 45,* 247–255.

Moen, P., & Wethington, E. (1999). Midlife development in a life course context. In S. Willis & J. Reid (Eds.), *Life in the middle: Psychological and social development in middle age* (pp. 3–24). New York: Academic Press.

National Center for Health Statistics, Centers for Disease Control. (1998). *National Vital Statistics Report, 47*(13).

Neugarten, B. (1968). Adult personality: Toward a psychology of the life cycle. In B. L. Neugarten (Ed.), *Middle age and aging* (pp. 137–147). Chicago: University of Chicago Press.

Nydegger, C. (1976). Middle age: Some early returns—a commentary. *International Journal of Aging and Human Development, 7,* 137–141.

Rabinowitz, F. (1998). Psychotherapy with depressed middle-aged men: A grief based model. *Bulletin of the Society for the Psychological Study of Men and Masculinity, 3*(3), 16–17.

Reid, J., & Willis, S. (1999). Middle age: New thoughts, new directions. In S. Willis & J. Reid (Eds.), *Life in the middle: Psychological and social development in middle age* (pp. 275–280). New York: Academic Press.

Rosenberg, S., Rosenberg, H., & Farrell, M. (1999). The midlife crisis revisited. In S. Willis & J. Reid (Eds.), *Life in the middle: Psychological and social development in middle age* (pp. 47–73). New York: Academic Press.

Sternbach, H. (1998). Age-associated testosterone decline in men: Clinical issues for psychiatry. *American Journal of Psychiatry, 155,* 1310–1318.

Stillson, R., O'Neil, J., & Owen, S. (1991). Predictors of adult men's gender-role conflict: Race, class, unemployment, age, instrumentality-expressiveness, and personal strain. *Journal of Counseling Psychology, 38,* 458–464.

Vaillant, G. (1977). *Adaptation to life.* Boston: Little, Brown.

Weiss, R. (1990). *Staying the course: The emotional and social lives of men who do well at work.* New York: Free Press.

Yalom, I. (1980). *Existential Psychotherapy.* New York: Basic Books.

THERAPEUTIC APPROACHES AND MODALITIES

CHAPTER THIRTEEN

"Masked Men"

New Psychoanalytically Oriented Treatment Models for Adult and Young Adult Men

William S. Pollack

Who was that masked man?
—"The Lone Ranger"

B oys will be boys," we are told: a certainty passed down from generation to generation, held up as a model in our culture, and too often unwittingly allowed to invade not only the approach to the boys in our care but also the clinical interventions provided to men and teenage young men in our consulting rooms. And what does this unquestioned, so-called natural truth suggest? That boys, and therefore men, are likely to get into trouble because they are born that way. That where there are boys and men there is testosterone and where there are male hormones there will always be a thirst for aggression, violence, and lustful sex without commitment. It is just something we will have to accept. In my research on men's development and their psychological and psychiatric treatment (Pollack, 1990, 1992, 1995, 1998a, 1998b) and the more recent McLean Hospital–Harvard Medical study *Listening to Boys' Voices,* reported in part in my books *Real Boys: Rescuing Our Sons from the Myths of Boyhood* (1999) and *Real Boys' Voices* (2000), I outline the pain this toxic view of men generates. It illustrates what I believe to be the silent crisis of masculinity extant in America. I have been shocked to find that this belief—one that I consider a particularly detrimental myth about men—continues to hold sway over America. It is still embraced not only by some of the lay public and media but even by some so-called experts and psychotherapists. So, as we try to unravel the complex reasons for boys' and men's apparently aggressive tendencies, tragically murderous acts, difficulty in expressing empathy or feelings in words, and proclivity to noncommitted, intimacy-phobic sexuality, we are still plagued by practitioners with oversimplified, outmoded psychodynamic theory about men or elementary so-called evolutionary truths that inform their treatment model, causing untold harm to the men under their care—at least those who do not flee because of "lack of compliance." And yet there is not a shred of scientific evidence to support these negative biological myths about men and no positive outcome data to suggest that their therapeutic implementation is salubrious or curative.

In fact, as I attempt to demonstrate and illustrate in this chapter, it is the loss of men's emotional voice in boyhood that puts them at risk for a hollow and stiff sense of self, covered over by a mask of false bravado and sexualized enactments, meant to unconsciously assuage their inner sense of emptiness and sadness or depression. This, in turn, is due to premature loss of emotional connection and society's encasement of their later development in a gender straitjacket that yields the significant cause of the pain we see in the men we treat. I also show that an empathic psychodynamic treatment model, based on a modified form of psychoanalytic relational–self-psychological theory (and when appropriate state-of-the-art psychopharmacology), is what is required to bring about the breadth and depth of change necessary to free men from these invisible psychic chains of loss and shame. Specifically addressed are my theory that historical, cultural, and economic forces have affected parenting styles so as to make it likely that boys will suffer a traumatic disruption of their early holding environment, a premature psychic separation from both maternal and paternal caregivers. This loss is a normative male, gender-linked loss, a trauma of abandonment for boys that may show itself later in adult men through symptomatic behavior and characterological defense (Pollack, 1995).

As a result of the unconscious sense of shame accompanying this frightening sense of deficit, many men seek treatment only reluctantly and under pressure from significant others. Often they present with empathic disruptions in their relationships (love-desire splits in romance or an inability to commit) as an attempt to unconsciously protect against further loss, restricted emotionality with an inability to tolerate feelings of vulnerability or to express and bear sadness, and consequently an impingement in the capacity to grieve, to mourn, and to change. Such a combination of defenses is often incorporated into a syntonic character armor that blocks the overt expression of all strong feelings except anger and may be consciously maintained—indeed, valued—as (false) self-sufficiency, a process I have described elsewhere as *defensive autonomy* (Pollack, 1990).

THEORY OF TREATMENT

The psychoanalytic community continues to view healthy masculine development either as Oedipally based unrequited desire and problematic aggression or as pre-Oedipal struggles to master separation and to achieve independence. Indeed, the achievement of autonomy has become so central a construct in our conceptualization of the normal tasks of early male development that we have actually created an extra hurdle of separation for boys to jump through—the so-called disidentification stage (Greenson, 1968). Within this model (and I believe it is a model still embraced in many quarters today) the pre-Oedipal boy is required to disidentify with his maternal caretaker to move psychically closer to the father, thereby achieving a more secure male gender identity. Modern feminist theorists (including Chodorow, 1978, 1989) have also noted this extra separation stage for young boys, reframing it as the fault line on which adult male identity precariously rests. From this perspective, boys and men are constantly fending off the psychic sense of feminine identification for fear of being pulled back into a symbiotic union with the mother and thereby losing their masculine sense of self.

My own clinical work with men and research on fathering and its effects on child development suggest a significantly different view (Betcher & Pollack, 1993; Pollack, 1990, 1995, 1998b). There is no question that Oedipal conflicts emerge in the men we see in treatment. And we see many men in treatment who have felt forced to distance themselves at an early age from their mothers to create protomasculine, nascent autonomous selves. But such events are rarely remembered as part of a sequence of healthy development. Rather, if one listens empathically (free from the bias of a disidentification or separation model), a different affective experience emerges. Unearthed from beneath layers of repression and anger, a deep sadness often comes forward, a delayed mourning for a tragic loss. This premature push for separation in boys is not a healthy form of self-differentiation but rather a traumatic disruption of their early holding environment. Indeed, I argue that we may be seeing a developmental basis for a normative male-gender-linked trauma (or impingement)—a life-cycle loss in boys that may show itself later in adulthood in symptomatic behavior and characterological disturbance. Many men who seek treatment present with empathic disruptions in relationships; restricted emotionality and an inability to commit (often as an attempt to protect against loss); an inability to tolerate feelings of vulnerability, especially to express sadness or to grieve and mourn; and a type of syntonic character armor blocking the expression of strong emotional feeling, *a mask of masculinity* (Pollack, 1998b), a false self-sufficiency, which I have called defensive autonomy (Pollack, 1990).

In retrospect, it is striking that we have never stopped to wonder what it must feel like for a young boy to lose his connection to his mother and be shamed to suppress his "voice" of human vulnerability and tears, replacing it with the only acceptable protomale affect: anger. Such an enforced separation from the most cherished, admired, and loved person in his life (and the psychic loss of half of the feeling self) must come as a terrible loss—all the more so in a family structure in which girls of the same age are encouraged to remain bonded and in which fathers are often unable or unwilling to assuage their son's fall from the maternal safety net with an equally nurturing form of caregiving. Men's traumatic experience of abandonment in boyhood, though not consciously remembered, forever casts a shadow on their relationships. It is sadness without a name, a yearning without clear object. It cannot be remembered, not only because it occurs so early in life and is repressed nor merely because of the traumatic nature of the loss but also because of the shame and humiliation that unrequited love elicits. Without the capacity for conscious awareness, men are unable to grieve, to mourn this psychic disruption, and often are never able to face or bear it directly.

Later, adult heterosexual relationships are likely to revive in men deeply repressed yearnings for the earliest mother. The result may be the creation by many men of transitional object or self-object relationships with women who function unconsciously as mother substitutes in a manner meant to both repair and assuage the unspeakable hurt of premature traumatic separation while allowing men to consciously deny the loss of or need for a relational bond. In their unconscious yearning for closeness, men may often seek out women who meet these repressed needs, only to deny such women any mutually empathic response. This behavior occurs not because these men are "immature" or "bad" or fear symbiotic reunion but because they need to protect themselves from the danger of reexperiencing the repressed pain, sadness, or covert (hidden) depression that the new affiliation threatens to evoke and that they feel unable to mourn or to tolerate. Such men, as we know, maintain that they are self-sufficient while they are in the midst of a deeply dependent or interdependent connection. Following is a summary of a normative false self-development and typical symptom picture in later male adolescents and adult men:

Disorder of the Self: Male Type

- Partial affective-intellectual split
- Anger prominence, rage, or repression personality

- Walling off of vulnerable core self: "mask of masculinity"
- Phobic avoidance or denial of interdependent object relations: sexualized self-object yearnings
- Shame sensitive or shame phobic
- Action blunting of empathic recognition
- Incapacity to translate feelings into language: alexithymia
- Harsh unconscious self-criticism, sometimes projected onto others
- Perfectionistic need to master; workaholism
- Inability to grieve or mourn
- Vulnerability to substance abuse and depression (male type)

This paradoxical situation may lead to the misunderstanding that we see in traditional intimate relationships between men and women and perhaps may account for much of the pain experienced by the two genders as they attempt to listen to and interpret each other's "voice." It may also begin to explain the apparent resistance that men show in unmodified forms of dynamic psychotherapy and the preponderance of the diagnosis of narcissistic personality disorder and atypical depressions among men. Relational psychoanalytic treatment theories and models best respond to such psychological pain in our "everyman." Following Modell (1976), I believe that dynamic treatment must pay close attention to the requirement for creating a symbolic re-creation of the early holding environment in the treatment of so-called narcissistic issues. Kohut's (1971, 1977) understanding of the need for facilitating and maintaining (for long periods of time) a stabilizing self-object transference arrangement— of either a mirroring or an idealizing type—may broaden our capacity for empathic connection with patients—often men— conflicted about the treatment relationship itself. (For a more complete rendition of this complex argument, see Pollack, 1995, 1998a, 1998b.)

NATURE AND NURTURE

One of the most confused and least productive debates about men's psychological pain and characterological disturbance has been the debate between what I believe is a false distinction between nature and nurture. It is important, however, to parse out both biological proclivities and social interactions that affect men's boyhood—consciously and unconsciously—in a manner to create traditional psychopathology, so that we can shed additional light on its treatment. In addition to my argument for powerful unconscious sequelae (stemming from premature separation) in the functioning of adult men are two influences on the developmental psychology of men: (1) the historically insidious, psychoeducationally oriented, skill-based, gender-tracked role socialization models in schools and homes (see Pollack, 1999) and (2) the biological pre-disposition to male expressivity in infancy and its psychosocial repression throughout the life cycle of men.

Gender-Bifurcated Role Socialization

The systems of gender-bifurcated role socialization that feminist scholars have strongly criticized for stifling girls' voice and for tracking girls into doll play and sibling care and away from assertion and mathematics skills have been equally devastating and limiting for little boys in their developmental pathways. David and Brannon (1976) have delineated four stereotyped male ideals or admonitions through which we have historically socialized boys into manhood. The injunction to become a "sturdy oak" refers to men's stoicism and our teaching little boys not to share pain or to openly grieve. The "give 'em hell" stance of our sports coaches creates the false self of daring, bravado, and love for violence, whereas the ideal of being a "big wheel" stresses the need to achieve status and power at any cost. But perhaps the most traumatizing, straitjacketing social role training is that of "no sissy stuff"—the condemnation of the expression in boys of any strong, dependent, or warm feelings or urges, which are seen as "feminine" and therefore totally unacceptable or taboo. These roles combine with our admonitions to boys as young as four or five years old to "cut Momma's apron strings," "be a little man," and "stand on your own two feet," inculcating an impossible and hurtful "boy code." Male youngsters who fail to live up to these impossible expectations are teased and experience tremendous shame, beginning the process of creating the false mask of male bravado or masculinity (Pollack, 1999). The Mommy track for women and its equally destructive counterpart, the Daddy without feeling, work-'til-you-drop track for men, begin long before the career ladder is in view. It is the fruition of our early, rigid gender-bifurcated socialization systems—systems internalized into early models of boys' intrapsychic engendered ideal selves.

Pleck (1981, 1995) has argued that men are ground down trying to live up to such inhuman standards of masculinity, or what he calls "gender role strain." Indeed, the Fox Indians of Iowa refer to the ritualized achievement of manhood status as "The Big Impossible" (Gilmore, 1990). Levant has pointed cogently to the skill deficits these gender-based training experiences in boyhood create in men. He notes in particular a severe inability of men to identify, express, and describe their own feeling states, especially those of warmth, caring, sadness, or pain. He links this inability to the psychological disorder of *alexithymia*—the inability to connect words with feelings that leaves men with a vague "buzz" of undifferentiated affect rather than a clear or articulate emotional message of caring and love to convey to their loved ones (Levant & Kopecky, 1995).

Biological Imperatives

Although it is difficult to parse out the distinct contributions of nature versus nurture in gender differentiation, some infancy research data are telling in this regard. A critical review of the developmental and biological data concerning the differences between female and male babies reveals evidence significant enough to support the claim that at birth male infants are more expressive and emotive than female infants (Haviland & Malatesta, 1981).

Brody (1993, 1996) argues that gender dimorphic, biologically based (and socially reinforced) temperamental predispositions in infants, in combination with specific caretaker interactions, lead to radically different affective socialization for boy and girl babies. Following from Cunningham and Shapiro (1984) and Weinberg (1992), Brody (1996) states that, Infant boys are more emotionally expressive than are infant girls, and hence their expressions are easier for parents to read.

Supported by her interpretation of the findings by Tronick and colleagues (Tronick, 1989; Tronick & Cohn, 1989) that mothers and their infant sons have an easier time matching their emotional interactive states, Brody suggests that, "Both mothers and daughters may have to work harder to read each other's emotional signals than do mothers and sons" (Brody, 1996). The result may be the beginning of a long journey toward affective bonding for mothers and their daughters and an increasing emotional inexpressiveness and disconnection for parents and their young sons:

Working harder may translate into talking more to daughters about feelings, as well as in displaying a wider range of feelings to daughters. . . For females, this may eventually result in both amplified facial expressiveness in order to communicate more clearly, as well as in better emotional recognition abilities. In contrast, in adapting to their sons' higher emotional intensity, parents may respond with more constraint and a de-emphasis on emotional expressiveness. These types of socialization patterns also represent conformity to the cultured gender role stereotype that girls should be more emotionally expressive and that boys should be more emotionally constrained. (Brody, 1996)

The empirical findings on differential socialization of emotion language for young boys and girls do not disappoint us in this regard. It has been shown that mothers appear to use more words about emotions when they speak to their young daughters than when they speak to their sons (Dunn, Bretherton, & Munn, 1987; Fivush, 1989) and tend to speak more about sadness with girls and more about anger with boys (Fivush, 1989). By the time they are of school age, little girls are expecting more positive reaction from mothers for the expression of sadness than for anger, and their little boy counterparts are expecting negative reactions from both parents if they express sadness (Fuchs & Thelen, 1988).

Fathers have been especially active in promulgating such gender-bifurcated socialization models of the expression of emotion. They have been found to use more emotion-laden words with their daughters than with their sons and to engage in more negative teasing or aggressive verbal jousting with their sons than with their daughters (Gleason & Greif, 1983; Schell & Gleason, 1989).

Perhaps now we have a better developmental understanding of why anger has always been the favorite son of men's limited family of emotions. Through anger—the final common pathway for all their other strongly repressed affects—boys and later men express their vulnerability, powerlessness, and pain in their search for safety. Anger is the stepchild of men's repression of their vulnerability in their search for legitimate authority. Its true parentage—the earlier trauma of abandonment—remains too shameful to face; hence, men exhibit poorly defined responses of violence and rage, by which they hope to achieve what is in essence the unachievable.

As to the issue of testosterone receptors and other neurotransmitters, we now have important evidence that brain growth is highly influenced in the first three years after birth, and the physical loving and cooing we provide or withhold from our male infants affects not only their personalities but also the laying down of neurological functions and proclivities. The nurture of our sons—or its lack thereof—has profound biological implications for their later functioning as men, making nurture more powerful than we have lately given it credit for (in development or treatment) and the atavistic distinction between nature and nurture a debate, hopefully, to be abandoned early in the twenty-first century (see Pollack, 1999, 2000).

Biological predisposition, then, combines with cultural and social patterns to foster an earlier and potentially more hurtful separation paradigm between boys and their parents. Added to the thesis arguing for the unconscious trauma of loss, such an integrated biopsychosocial model becomes a powerful hermeneutic for a new psychoanalytic psychology of men and their dynamic treatment in psychotherapy.

If this argument is correct, then, what would a man who as a boy sustained such gender-bifurcated socialization and early unconscious psychological hurt look like? In all likelihood, he would be obsessive about maintaining a rigidly independent self and have a matrix of intrapsychic defenses, such as unconscious anger or rage toward women, defensive condescension of anyone in a caretaking role, overvaluation of independence (defensive autonomy), devaluation of the need for connectedness or interdependence, stoic denial of sadness or pain with an inability to grieve loss or to mourn, a walling off of a vulnerable but hidden core self, a proclivity to externalize inner conflict, a relative incapacity to put feelings into words (alexithymia), and the need to take refuge in impulsive action to avoid anxiety. Interestingly enough, this description is remarkably similar to that of a prototypic so-called narcissistic character structure.

In addition, one would expect that any overt sense of "dependency"—especially on women—would be quite frightening for men because it would threaten a repetition of the "undependable" earlier tie, which had been disrupted. Simultaneously, however, there would be the conflicted need to be mirrored and to connect with an idealized soothing object, side by side with the terror of sustaining such a connection for fear of its disruption. If this is indeed men's dilemma, from whence comes the resolution?

Here, I am beginning to suggest that so-called healthy traditional masculine gender identity (replete with rigid differentiation from femininity) is at least in part a false self-construction and rests on two faulty biopsychic foundations: (1) an identification with the absent aggressor "bogeyman" father (Mitscherlich, 1963), creating a harsh, self-critical, and perfectionistic superego that demands never-ending proof through workaholic, production-oriented successes to fend off rageful states of depressed self-esteem, and (2) an impinged-on, enfeebled, depleted core self shamed into hiding its prematurely disrupted sense of needing to be held, hiding behind a false self, a mask of angry defiance and pseudoindependence. I also suggest that the psychological consequence of such a faulty foundation is the vulnerability of men to a traditionally gender-specific disorder of the self, as outlined previously in the section "Theory of Treatment" (see also Pollack, 1998a, 1998b).

TREATMENT

To help men to become more empathic, we must in turn become more empathic toward men. In psychotherapy we see many men who are frightened about some aspect of their work or love life that they cannot master. These men are most afraid of the very fact that they are afraid. They have been brought up to believe that a man must not seek help at a time when he needs it most. So they deny their dependence on the therapy or the therapist. If pushed prematurely to face the truth they will resort to more drastic protection of their fragile self, their "independence": they will flee from treatment or devalue the therapy or the therapist. If, however, the therapist remains calm and does not criticize in return, if he or she recognizes and supports men's need to save face when receiving help, then internal changes of great consequence may occur. We must be sensitive to men's shame and not further shame them in psychotherapy (Pollack, 1994).

Winnicott (1974) wrote that one should never ask, "Did you conceive of this or was it presented to you from without?" If we can sustain the process of change without putting demands on men before they can accept them, transformation can occur. This concept is not very different from the theory of how to get a "good idea" accepted by an organization. Consultants know that the best way to help others is to enable them to believe that they have come to the "good idea" themselves. They can then "own" it and empower its implementation.

With many men I have treated, I have found it necessary to modify psychoanalytic psychotherapy not so much in its frequency (intensity), duration, or self-reflective associative model but rather in the arena of supporting the patient's need to believe, for long periods of time and without interpretation or challenge to his denial, that both the therapy and therapist are almost unimportant to him. In this way my approach is similar to Modell's (1976) understanding of the cocoon transference necessary for the maintenance of what he calls the "illusion of self-sufficiency" within the early holding environment of psychoanalysis—a background of safety that is required for mutative change in the treatment of narcissistic personality disorder. It differs, however, in that it does not require a confrontation of the reality of separateness and thereby falls closer to Kohut's (1977) concept of the creation of stabilizing, idealizing self-object transference.

We may thank Heinz Kohut (1971, 1977) specifically for his treatment strategy of intervention when the self-object line of development, the so-called narcissistic line, is traumatized or derailed. He argued that the appropriate response is an empathic or "experience-near" understanding of the individual's needs to take in and use the other— that is, the self-object—in a manner that silently performs missing functions within the self without necessarily acknowledging these significant external contributions. In other words, Kohut accepted that certain people might need to be highly dependent on others to fulfill deficits or tolerate conflicts and traumas in their earlier lines of self-development while never consciously acknowledging such dependency. Consequently, he advised against disrupting such a stable transference constellation until it could be interpreted from within the patient's own perspective rather than therapists imposing their own external "maturity morality," because of their countertransference needs for recognition and authority. I find such advice, such a modification of the modern relational aspect of dynamic treatment to bring it into line with boys' and men's unique dilemmas, invaluable in the depth psychological treatment of men.

Sometimes, as in Eric's case (described next), the early phase of the treatment may be conceptualized—by patient and therapist alike—along the lines of an "extended consultation" in which the patient's defensive independence and fear of connection are neither interpreted nor confronted. Rather, in this case, as in many others, the associations often begin in the work arena with discussions of disappointments in competitive expectations and interpersonal conflicts with coworkers without requiring any acknowledgment of the patient's need for support for extended periods.

STORY OF ERIC

Eric had sought a consultation with the therapist because he was concerned about the ethics of his work in a prestigious and sophisticated legal firm. In addition, he had vague but deeply painful feelings that "something is terribly wrong in my life." He had observed the therapist during a seminar on business leadership and felt comfortable with him.

The "consultation" developed first into once-weekly psychotherapy. During the first few sessions, which consisted of Eric responding to the therapist's request to talk about his history, several traumas from his early life emerged. However, Eric saw no connection at the time between these painful events and his present-day anxieties. When the therapist floated a trial balloon to make such a connection, Eric looked frightened and launched into a discussion of his work, his leadership capacities, and his guilt.

Rather than interpreting this response as a defense or trying to confront Eric's apparent "denial," the therapist felt strongly that Eric was doing his best to maintain his sense of dignity while developing a new form of dependent relationship with the therapist. He continued to listen to Eric's work concerns and helped him to cope with a number of competitive struggles with senior partners. The patient appeared to become more comfortable and was complimentary of the help he received. But he was often careful to say that this was a "consultation" in which he was putting his own "spin" on what the therapist offered. He also had numerous "scheduling" difficulties and managed to be away from therapy often because of "important business matters."

In the second phase of the treatment, Eric began to hesitantly describe difficulties in his marriage and in parenting. Over time, the therapist observed that although Eric often felt "angry" at times he also appeared to be very sad. As Eric began to feel that "it's OK to have needs," he also seemed to develop a more complex understanding of his wife's concerns and had greater empathy for her. He stopped blocking her effort to find a couples therapist and started to feel that "maybe this marriage needs help."

As a result of what Eric was learning about his marriage, he realized that some of the issues he was struggling with as an adult were frighteningly similar to those from his early life. Even some of his work conflicts began to remind him of situations in his family while he was growing up. He asked somewhat sheepishly, "Isn't this what some people do in psychotherapy?" and whether he and the therapist could explore these connections in the sessions.

The therapist concurred and outlined the basic model of free association and the interpretive stance to be taken, reminding Eric that in the very first sessions he had talked about his premature separation from his family because of a childhood hospitalization for a serious illness. Eric became tearful and by the end of the session was discussing the effects of this trauma on his development, a linkage that the therapist had alluded to two years earlier but had held in abeyance until the time was right. Eric continues in twice-weekly treatment with positive alliance and excellent results.

COVERT ABANDONMENT DEPRESSION

As became evident in Eric's treatment, issues of self-protection from an abandonment-based depressive syndrome, covered by what are sometimes dubbed narcissistic defenses but are most empathically understood as maintaining the mask of masculinity, bring covert depression to the center of many men's treatments. Much rage is really strait-jacketed tears yearning to be set free. Although in Eric's case the depression was mild to moderate, many other men display more extreme versions of a "male-type" depression that all too often goes unnoted and untreated because the signs and symptoms differ from those of the *Diagnostic and Statistical Manual of Mental Disorders* (DSM-IV) (American Psychiatric Association, 1994) model, better suited to women's expression of affective illness. I have explicated this syndrome in greater detail elsewhere (Pollack, 1998a), but it may be of use to delineate my model of male depression before briefly summarizing and illustrating a more extensive new psychoanalytically male-oriented psychotherapy. Following are symptoms of major depressive disorder–male type (Pollack, 1998a, 1999, 2000):

Major Depressive Disorder: Male Type

- Increased withdrawal from relationships (may be denied by patient)
- Overinvolvement with work activities; may reach a level of obsessional concern, masked by comments about stress (burnout)
- Denial of pain
- Increasingly rigid demands for autonomy

- Avoiding the help of others: the "I-can-do-it-myself" syndrome
- Shift in the interest level of sexual encounters; may be either a decrease or an increase (differentiate from mania)
- Increase in intensity or frequency of angry outbursts
- New or renewed interest in psychoactive substance self-administration to create self-numbing tension relief states without classic dissociative mechanisms
- A denial of any sadness and an inability to cry
- Harsh self-criticism, often focusing on failures in the arenas of provider and protector
- Impulsive plans to have loved ones cared for in case of patient's death or disability: "The wife and kids only need me for the money"
- Depleted or impulsive mood
- Concentration, sleep, or weight disorders

Providing experience-near empathic treatment for a range of disorders in men requires the following elements: (1) recognition of the gender-specific syndrome (for example, male-type depression or so-called narcissistic, self-protective "masking functions") as a bona fide defensive structure (at times with biological proclivities) without recourse to moralistic judgment or critical misunderstanding by the therapist; (2) a sensitivity to men's shame, exacerbated by the expression of help-seeking behavior and the manifestation of "gender weakness," attempting to actively interpret and diminish patients' harsh self-criticism and be ever vigilant to not further shame male patients, while hiding behind a mask of "neutrality" or "therapeutic confrontation"; (3) the creation of a therapeutic "holding environment" or "cocoon" (Modell, 1976) that simultaneously sustains enfeebled male patients while allowing them to save face and deny their dependence on the therapist if necessary, providing the opportunity to form a stabilizing self-object transference (Kohut, 1971, 1977) that understands narcissistic defense as a thwarted need to grow and reinstitutes the human growth-enhancing developmental environment (see Pollack, 1990, 1995, 1998b); and (4) an integration of biological interventions (when appropriate) with depth psychological approaches prescribed in a mutually alliance-building approach between patient and therapist.

MR. Q'S STORY

Mr. Q called to inquire as to whether the therapist had any available treatment time, because his couples therapist had suggested he needed a specialist in "men's problems." During their first meeting he confided that the reason he felt that couples therapy was not yielding any improvement in his marriage of three years was his hidden affairs with other women, which he had kept secret from not only his wife but his other therapist as well. He wondered aloud with some sadness whether anything could really be done, because he thought he suffered from what he somewhat mockingly referred to as "president's addiction"—alluding to the proclivity of certain males in positions of authority to engage in extramarital affairs. "Maybe it's just biological," he explained with a sadness on his face (and the therapist believed in his heart) that he appeared not to notice himself.

The therapist explained that although he could not ethically guarantee any particular outcome, he had a hunch that no matter what role biology played in this situation, there were many deeper feelings of Mr. Q's own that had yet to be explored and that working together in facing these—including Mr. Q's willingness to talk about any "blocks" caused by shame or negative experiences he might have about the therapist understanding him—could well help to free him from what he referred to as his "sexual addiction."

After agreeing to this approach (perhaps as much out of exasperation as out of any sense of hope), Mr. Q launched into a discussion about his early experiences with his mother. When, after listening quietly for a period, the therapist asked why the topic of his mother had come up, Mr. Q remarked immediately: "I thought that's what you guys think about, that Oedipus stuff!" The therapist suggested that the best approach would be to stick with what was most pressing on Mr. Q's own mind, and he began to defend his mother, explaining that she was always close to him, made him his favorite foods as a child, and still doted on him as a married adult. "You couldn't think of a sweeter woman," he explained.

After being informed of an upcoming interruption in the work because of the therapist's family needs, the patient appeared to have no response for a long period. When finally the therapist could tolerate what appeared to be the client's defensiveness no longer, he gingerly offered an interpretation about avoidance of feelings of being left behind. "What are you talking about, Doc?" Mr. Q exclaimed. "I hate to tell you but it's like a vacation for me. You always think these things that happen here have to do with you and me. But I just don't see it. It's like I'm driving my Jeep and you're running alongside trying to jump in, but there's no room for you."

The therapist had received his wake-up call. Defensive or not, Mr. Q's need to see the therapist as unnecessary and his absence as the relief of a burden was part and parcel of his need "not to be crammed in by others, like all those women." First it needed to be respected as legitimate and only then analyzed. So the therapist responded, "Tell me about your fantasy about those weeks I'll be gone." Quickly Mr. Q replied, "It will be like being on a camping trip all on my own, no wife or therapist to nag—pure pleasure." "Sounds like I misunderstood about my being away," the therapist responded, and Mr. Q appeared relieved from the relational burden the therapist had been imposing. But then the therapist added: "Too bad there's no room in the Jeep for the two of us." At that moment the patient began to fall asleep.

The therapist waited quietly, and Mr. Q soon awoke with a start, apologizing for dozing off. The therapist reiterated previous discussions about self-criticism and suggested they avoid blame or "duty" and try to understand what had transpired between them. "It's funny, you know. You were saying something about being in the car together, and I had like a minidream about being a small boy, left all alone in a big car." As he associated, an early memory—never completely repressed so much as ignored—came to mind of how his parents would often leave him alone when shopping and with neighbors on the weekends when their economic needs forced them to take second jobs. "It's not like they didn't love me or anything, or they were abandoning me; they were just trying to make ends meet." "Of course," the therapist replied, "but to a little boy it would still have been quite scary." "They told me to act 'like a big boy' and understand and I guess I did, 'til now." Tears began to well up, which Mr. Q did his best to suppress.

When the therapist returned from his absence, the patient seemed calm, almost happy to see him. "I'm still not having sex with Dorothy, but just last night, I had this thought when I looked in my appointment book and saw we'd be meeting today. Sex really is a very close thing. You could get let down by someone you love . . . hurt." "You could even get left alone by someone you need, like your therapist, and that would make being intimate pretty scary," the therapist replied. Mr. Q smiled. "Maybe I ought to add another seat in that Jeep," he said, and asked if they could begin to meet more frequently in treatment.

What could easily have been prematurely confronted as Oedipal defense or narcissistic character was dealt with quite differently. The therapist's knowledge of male-specific, developmentally oriented empathic therapeutic responsiveness allowed the patient to begin to recover his (pre-Oedipal) abandonment depression, grapple with its sexualized enactment, and form a mutual treatment alliance. All this could occur once the therapist threw out the classic rule book and used our growing body of knowledge of boys' and men's early pain and stereotypic defenses of bravado that must be respected before they can be successfully deconstructed and eventually exchanged for relational interaction and comfortable intimacy.

CONCLUSION

From boyhood onward, men are encased in a gender straitjacket, prematurely and psychically separated both from the loving connection of their mothers and from their inner "voice" of the warm and vulnerable parts of themselves. Shamed by a "Boy Code" to renounce such open empathic expression of feeling, they are pushed toward the one "carrier" emotion of anger, away from intimate commitments and toward denial of life's emotional interdependence and love's need for intimate mutuality. But men are not true "Lone Rangers," disconnected, independent beings. Like the rest of the species they are yearning for connection but remain unconsciously frightened of the revived sense of abandonment, depression, and traumatic premature separation such bonding may rekindle. Nowhere is this male conundrum more salient than in both the real and transference relationship that forms the heart of psychoanalytically oriented depth psychotherapy. Recognized for its true source, such pain can become the basis of lasting personal change (even at times the beginning of the lifting of a covert depression). But if it is misapprehended in a nonempathic fashion as mere narcissism or sexual addition, therapists may run the risk of retraumatizing an already hurt man, because his mask of false bravado hoodwinks them.

While maintaining appropriate boundaries therapists must reach out to the men under their care and, without forcing them to admit the frailties that make them feel unmasculine, lend a helping hand out of the psychic cold into which we thrust them as boys; in doing so, therapists help create a broader sense of what it means to be a man or, for that matter, a person. And given the great suffering of men around us, and the pain it causes their loved ones, therapists must do it with alacrity. Perhaps they should be guided on their new therapeutic journey with men by the balanced wisdom of the medieval Jewish sage Hillel, who advised: "If I am not for myself, who will be for me? But if I am for myself alone, then what am I? If not now, then when?" Indeed, for the men entrusted to our therapeutic care: If not now, then when?

References

American Psychiatric Association. (1994). *Diagnostic and statistical manual of mental disorders* (4th ed.). Washington, DC: American Psychiatric Association.
Betcher, R. W., & Pollack, W. S. (1993). *In a time of fallen heroes: The re-creation of masculinity.* New York: Atheneum.

Brody, L. R. (1993). On understanding gender differences in the expression of emotion. In S. Ablon, D. Brown, J. Mack, & E. Khantazian (Eds.), *Human feelings: Explorations in affect development and meaning* (pp. 87–121). Hillsdale, NJ: Analytic Press.

Brody, L. R. (1996). Gender, emotional expression, and the family. In R. Kavanaugh, B. Zimmerberg-Glick, & S. Fein (Eds.), *Emotion: Interdisciplinary perspectives.* Hillsdale, NJ: Erlbaum.

Chodorow, N. (1978). *The reproduction of mothering.* Berkeley and Los Angeles: University of California Press.

Chodorow, N. (1989). *Feminism and psychoanalytic theory.* New Haven, CT: Yale University Press.

Cunningham, J., & Shapiro, L. (1984). *Infant affective expression as a function of infant and adult gender.* Unpublished manuscript, Brandeis University, Waltham, MA.

David, D., & Brannon, R. (1976). *The forty-nine percent majority: The male sex role.* Reading, MA: Addison-Wesley.

Dunn, J., Bretherton, I., & Munn, P. (1987). Conversations about feeling states between mothers and their children. *Developmental Psychology, 23,* 132–139.

Fivush, R. (1989). Exploring sex differences in the emotional content of mother-child conversations about the past. *Sex Roles, 20,* 675–691.

Fuchs, D., & Thelen, M. (1988). Children's expected interpersonal consequences of communicating their affective state and reported likelihood of expression. *Child Development, 59,* 1314–1322.

Gilmore, D. D. (1990). *Manhood in the making.* New Haven, CT: Yale University Press.

Gleason, J. B., & Greif, E. G. (1983). Men's speech to young children. In B. Thorne, C. Kramarae, & N. Henley (Eds.), *Language, gender, and society* (pp. 140–150). London: Newbury House.

Greenson, R. (1968). Disidentifying from mother. *International Journal of Psychoanalysis, 49,* 370–374.

Haviland, J. J., & Malatesta, C. Z. (1981). The development of sex differences in nonverbal signals: Fallacies, facts, and fantasies. In C. Mayo & N. M. Henly (Eds.), *Gender and nonverbal behavior.* New York: Springer-Verlag.

Kohut, H. (1971). *The analysis of the self.* New York: International Universities Press.

Kohut, H. (1977). *The restoration of the self.* New York: International Universities Press.

Levant, R., & Kopecky, G. (1995). *Masculinity reconstructed.* New York: Dutton.

Mitscherlich, A. (1963). *Society without the father.* New York: Harcourt.

Modell, A. H. (1976). The "holding environment" and the therapeutic action of psychoanalysis. *Journal of the American Psychoanalytic Association, 24,* 285–308.

Pleck, J. (1981). *The myth of masculinity.* Cambridge, MA: MIT Press.

Pleck, J. (1995). The gender role strain paradigm: An update. In R. Levant & W. S. Pollack (Eds.), *A new psychology of men* (pp. 11–32). New York: Basic Books.

Pollack, W. S. (1990). Men's development and psychotherapy: A psychoanalytic perspective. *Psychotherapy, 27*(3), 316–321.

Pollack, W. S. (1992). Should men treat women? Dilemmas for the male psychotherapist: Psychoanalytic and developmental perspectives. *Ethics and Behavior, 2,* 39–49.

Pollack, W. S. (1994). Engendered psychotherapy: Listening to the male and female voice. *Voices, 30*(3), 43–47.

Pollack, W. S. (1995). No man is an island: Toward a new psychoanalytic psychology of men. In R. Levant & W. S. Pollack (Eds.), *A new psychology of men* (pp. 33–67). New York: Basic Books.

Pollack, W. S. (1998a). Mourning, melancholia, and masculinity: Recognizing and treating depression in men. In W. S. Pollack & R. F. Levant (Eds.), *New psychotherapy for men* (pp. 147–166). New York: Wiley.

Pollack, W. S. (1998b). The trauma of Oedipus: Toward a new psychoanalytic psychotherapy for men. In W. S. Pollack & R. F. Levant (Eds.), *New psychotherapy for men* (pp. 13–34). New York: Wiley.

Pollack, W. S. (1999). *Real boys: Rescuing our sons from the myths of boyhood.* New York: Henry Holt.

Pollack, W. S. (2000). *Real boys' voices.* New York: Random House.

Schell, A., & Gleason, J. B. (1989, December). *Gender differences in the acquisition of the vocabulary of emotion.* Paper presented at the annual meeting of the American Association of Applied Linguistics, Washington, DC.

Tronick, E. (1989). Emotions and emotional communication in infants. *American Psychology, 44,* 112–119.

Tronick, E., & Cohn, J. (1989). Infant-mother face-to-face interaction: Age and gender differences in coordination and the occurrence of miscoordination. *Child Development, 60,* 85–92.

Weinberg, M. K. (1992). Boys and girls: Sex differences in emotional expressivity and self-regulation during early infancy. In L. J. Bridges (Chair), *Early emotional self-regulation: New approaches to understanding developmental change and individual differences.* Symposium conducted at the International Conference on Infant Studies, Miami, FL.

Winnicott, D. W. (1974). *The maturational processes and the facilitating environment.* New York: International Universities Press.

CHAPTER FOURTEEN

Cognitive Therapy for Men

James R. Mahalik

Cognitive therapy is a reality-testing and problem-solving model of psychotherapy in which the cognitive therapist often acts as a teacher or ally against illogical thinking, uses a broad range of directive techniques that modify a client's maladaptive schemata, and promotes a rational-empirical method in everyday life (Beck & Weishaar, 1995). Although cognitive psychotherapy is equally applicable to both men and women (see Davis & Padesky, 1989, for a description of how cognitive therapy can incorporate gender issues for women), Levant (1995) notes two consequences of masculine socialization that may make cognitive therapy an especially useful way to approach treatment with men.

First, Levant (1995) describes the phenomenon of alexithymia—taken from the Latin and literally meaning "without words for feelings"—among men whereby they have difficulty identifying and describing their own and others' feelings. For men who experience difficulty in identifying and describing feelings, therapy that focuses primarily on exploring and expressing emotions is likely to feel frustrating and uncomfortable. Although emotions are a central part of the work that goes on in cognitive therapy, its focus on the importance of thoughts is likely to feel more congruent for men who conform to traditional gender roles regarding emotional expression.

Supportive of this idea is preliminary empirical evidence suggesting that masculine gender role conflict (that is, the rigid enactment of traditional masculine gender roles that leads to interpersonal and intrapersonal conflict; see O'Neil, 1981a, 1981b, 1982) is associated with preference for a cognitive focus in treatment. Specifically, in a study examining men's preferences for cognitive-focused or emotion-focused counseling, men who experienced less gender role conflict were equally positive about emotion-focused and cognition-focused treatment, whereas men who reported higher levels of gender role conflict preferred a counseling approach that was cognition focused (Wisch, Mahalik, Hayes, & Nutt, 1995).

A second consequence of masculine socialization that I believe makes cognitive therapy a useful intervention in working with men is Levant's (1995) observation about men's tendency to develop "action empathy." He describes action empathy as the ability to take another person's perspective and know what that person will do. This ability is understood as useful for teaching emotional empathy because a person can be taught to reframe his or her reference from what the person is likely to do to focus on what the person is likely to feel. Consistent with this approach, Levant capitalizes on this ability to take action in prescribing a psychoeducational style to working with traditionally socialized men that uses data-gathering techniques (for example, an emotional response log) to develop the skill of emotional awareness (Levant, 1993; Levant & Kelly, 1989). Thus, Levant capitalizes on these men's strengths (that is, action-oriented skills) to build additional skills helpful to them in living (that is, emotional empathy skills).

It is in these two ways that cognitive therapy may be especially congruent with traditional men's socialization toward emotional restriction and the tendency toward action. Specifically, compared with expressive or insight-oriented treatments, cognitive therapy's focus on cognitions and its problem-solving approach may be more congruent with the action skills of traditionally socialized men.

A therapist who wants to use a cognitive therapy approach in working with a traditionally socialized man has to decide whether to use this approach as the primary therapeutic intervention in treatment or as a type of "bridging" technique (Lazurus, 1981). This latter approach would encourage the therapist to tune into the traditionally socialized male client's preference for focusing on cognitions at the beginning of the work before moving to other areas. In this case, the therapist may believe that he or she will be more effective in the long run if the work moves away from a cognition and problem-solving focus but recognizes the importance of starting with the client's strengths or what feels comfortable for him before bridging into other approaches.

VIEWING COGNITIVE THERAPY THROUGH THE LENS OF MASCULINE SOCIALIZATION

As a basis for viewing cognitive therapy from a gendered perspective, one needs to understand that the center of the cognitive therapy process is the assessment and treatment of self-defeating messages that cause a client's psychological distress (Beck, 1963, 1964; Beck et al., 1990; Beck, Rush, Shaw, & Emery, 1979). Specifically, the foundational premise of cognitive therapy is that when a person experiences psychological disturbance, there is a selective bias in the way he or she processes information:

> Thus, an individual whose thinking selectively synthesizes themes of loss or defeat is likely to be depressed. Similarly, in anxiety there is a systematic shift toward selectively interpreting themes of danger, in paranoid conditions the dominant shift is toward indiscriminate attribute of abuse or interference, and in mania the shift is toward exaggerated interpretations of personal gain. (Beck & Weishaar, 1995, pp. 229–230)

Viewed from the lens of gender role development, one sees men's (and women's) cognitive structures built through the process of gender role socialization wherein men (and women) are shaped to conform to societal gender norms. To understand the process by which these gender-related cognitive structures are formed, leading gender role scholars (for example, Bem, 1981, 1983; O'Neil, 1981a, 1981b, 1982; Pleck, 1981) note that males and females learn masculine and feminine shoulds and musts from important persons and are encouraged to adopt traditional gender role attitudes (such as "big boys don't cry" or "a woman's place is in the home").

For example, O'Neil and Egan (1992) note that throughout the life span, but especially in early childhood and adolescence, persons are socialized by "family, schools, peers, and society where attachment and early bonding with mothers and fathers, gender-related preferences for companions and toys, peer acceptance and rejection, and developing intimacy and sexual preference are all potential psychosocial events affecting gender role development" (p. 311). Bem (1981) posits a cognitive theory in which cultural forces shape an individual's development of gender role schemata of "maleness" and "femaleness." As a result of this process of shaping, gender role schemata form in response to society's external standards, expectations, and norms about masculine and feminine behavior through social forces such as family, schools, peers, and the media (Meth, 1990; Pleck, 1981, 1995).

Indeed, Beck's description of how cognitive structures develop early in life from personal experiences, identification with others, and reinforcement (Beck & Weishaar, 1995) is very similar to how others describe gender role schemata developing (Bem, 1981; Levant & Pollack, 1995; Meth, 1990; O'Neil, 1981a, 1981b, 1982; Pleck, 1981, 1995). Specifically, both cognitive theorists and gender role theorists posit that all persons are shaped from early experiences with important persons in their lives to internalize shoulds and musts that govern their feelings and behaviors.

Pleck (1981, 1995) notes, however, that the shoulds and musts are more rigidly applied to men than to women. Specifically, he observes that although violating gender roles has negative consequences for both men and women, the negative consequences are more severe for men than for women for violating these norms. This finding would suggest that the shoulds and musts may be more strongly internalized in men through socialization pressures and that observers in society may apply these shoulds and musts more strongly to men than to women, thereby making deviation from traditional gender roles more costly for men than for women.

Although some positive elements come from traditional masculine socialization (see Antill & Cunningham, 1979; Whitley, 1983, 1985), research suggesting that traditional masculinity messages contribute to psychopathology in men is mounting quickly. For example, research on masculine gender role conflict reports the conflict to be associated with low self-esteem (Cournoyer & Mahalik, 1995; Davis, 1988), low capacity for intimacy (Cournoyer & Mahalik, 1995; Sharpe & Heppner, 1991), high anxiety and depression (Cournoyer & Mahalik, 1995; Davis, 1988; Good & Mintz, 1990; Sharpe & Heppner, 1991), abuse of alcohol (Blazina & Watkins, 1996), rigidly dominant and hostile interpersonal behaviors (Mahalik, 2000a), aggressive-projective psychological defenses (Mahalik, Cournoyer, DeFranc, Cherry, & Napolitano, 1998), and high levels of general psychological symptomatology (Good et al., 1995). Also, research on masculine gender role stress (that is, men's stress resulting from their appraisal of failing to live up to traditional masculinity standards; Eisler & Skidmore, 1987) reports the stress to be related to anger and hostility (Eisler, Skidmore, & Ward, 1988; Watkins, Eisler, Carpenter, Schechtman, & Fisher, 1991), social fears (Arrindell, Kolk, Pickersgill, & Hageman, 1993), and type A behavior, elevated blood pressure, and high-risk health habits (Eisler et al., 1988; Watkins et al., 1991).

These findings would suggest that something associated with traditional masculinity is causing psychological distress for men. A cognitive therapist views a client's self-defeating thoughts, or cognitive distortions, as the source of his or her problems in living (Beck, 1963, 1964; Beck et al., 1979, 1990). Thus, the findings that gender role strain is related to pathology would suggest that specific cognitive distortions are associated with masculine gender role strain.

As a first order of business, the cognitive therapist would be interested in finding out what specific distorted cognitions are causing distress for the client. Masculinity scholars have helped to identify a number of these distortions by noting the shoulds and musts associated with traditional masculinity (David & Brannon, 1976; Eisler & Skidmore, 1987; Levant et al., 1992; O'Neil, 1981a, 1981b, 1982). In the earliest work on masculine ideology,

David and Brannon (1976) identified four masculine injunctions of traditional masculinity: (1) "no sissy stuff," (2) "the big wheel," (3) "the sturdy oak," and (4) "give 'em hell." These injunctions are associated, respectively, with messages to men that they should avoid anything that might be remotely feminine (for example, expressing feelings, experiencing vulnerability, and being nurturing); they should strive to defeat others and achieve status by climbing to the top; they should never show weakness and should have the ability to endure difficulties without relying on others for help; and they should actively seek out adventure and risk, even responding with violence if necessary.

In more recent years, Levant and his colleagues (1992, 1996) identified seven dimensions of traditional masculine ideology that also highlight the shoulds and musts of masculine norms. They identify masculine socialization as telling men that they should avoid all things feminine (for example, not doing housework), restrict their emotional life (for example, not crying in public), act tough and aggressive (for example, taking risks even if it means getting hurt), be self-reliant (for example, never counting on others for help), emphasize achieving status above all else (for example, sacrificing personal relationships for career advancement), be nonrelational and objectifying in their attitudes toward sexuality (for example, always being ready to perform sexual relations), and fear and hate homosexuals (for example, not continuing a friendship with another man once he finds out that his friend is homosexual).

When enacted flexibly these messages may be adaptive for persons who do not overconform to them (for example, who does not want to win and succeed?). However, when these messages are enacted rigidly in a way that reflects overconformity to gender norms (such as doing anything that it takes to win regardless of the cost), it is likely that the individual is selectively synthesizing themes related to masculinity messages that produce interpersonal rigidity (Mahalik, 2000a) and interpersonal problems (including conflictual relationships) and intrapersonal distress (including depression and anxiety).

Thus, through the lens of the gender role strain paradigm, then, one sees masculine gender role socialization as contributing to gender-related cognitive distortions for men who are overcommitted to regulating their behavior according to masculine prescribed behavior. With this framework as a backdrop, in the next part of the chapter I identify how specific gender-related cognitive distortions may arise through nine injunctions of traditional masculinity. These nine areas were determined by reviewing the literature on masculine gender roles and identifying overlapping constructs from several of the most authoritative sources (that is, David & Brannon, 1976; Eisler & Skidmore, 1987; Harris, 1995; Levant et al., 1992; O'Neil, 1981a, 1981b, 1982). Although it is not intended to be an exhaustive listing of all masculinity messages that men receive in U.S. society, it is extensive, and I believe each theme has clinical relevance for practitioners working with male clients. Specifically, I discuss messages that men receive from socialization forces organized around the following themes: winning, emotional control, risk taking, violence, playboy, self-reliance, primacy of work, disdain of homosexuals, and physical toughness.

Winning

Men are told throughout their lives that it is important to win and be competitive to get status, respect, recognition, and admiration, especially in work and sports settings (David & Brannon, 1976; Eisler & Skidmore, 1987; Harris, 1995; Levant et al., 1992; O'Neil, 1981a, 1981b, 1982). Men are socialized to try to "get ahead" at work and win in the games and sports competitions in which they actually—or vicariously—participate. They have difficulty and feel open to attack when they fail or do not excel. They give little time and energy to relationships that do not help advance their status and feel uncomfortable when they are not moving ahead. Men who overconform to this socialized gender role may endorse ideas such as making money is part of being a successful man, "winning isn't everything, it's the only thing," and the best way to attain happiness is to be successful. Cognitive distortions associated with winning might include "I must defeat others to be happy and fulfilled" and "I must win against others to be worthwhile."

Emotional Control

Men are told that it is important to be in control of oneself emotionally and are socialized to be stoic and not to show emotions, especially vulnerable ones (David & Brannon, 1976; Eisler & Skidmore, 1987; Harris, 1995; Levant et al., 1992; O'Neil, 1981a, 1981b, 1982). They are taught to neglect or repress the feminine parts of themselves and are afraid of feelings that seem womanly. Men who rigidly adhere to this masculine identity tend to have difficulty telling others they care about them, disclosing and discussing vulnerabilities, and finding words to describe their feelings. As such, these men give little time and attention to their emotional or inner lives, feel uncomfortable being demonstrative or taking care of their children, and feel that if they express their strong feelings they will be open to attack by other people (Harris, 1995). They usually endorse such ideas as "big boys don't cry." Cognitive distortions associated with restrictive emotionality may include "If I share my feelings with others, people will think I am a sissy," "I cannot express my feelings because others will see me as weak," and "Important others will think I am falling apart if I cry."

Risk Taking

Men are told it is important to be aggressive, take risks, be adventurous, and use violence if necessary (Brooks & Silverstein, 1995; David & Brannon, 1976; Harris, 1995). They are taught that it is important to appear brave even when frightened or nervous and that they should be ready to risk their lives or face death if called on. Men often have difficulty and feel open to attack when others recognize that they are afraid. They endorse such ideas as it is important to handle dangerous situations without showing fear or doubt and "never let them see you sweat." Potential cognitive distortions include "A real man isn't afraid of anything," "People will think I'm a wimp if they know I'm scared," and "If I don't do this dangerous thing, people will think I'm gutless."

Violence

Men are told that they should always be ready to be violent. Boys are socialized to roughhouse, fight, and play sports such as football and wrestling (David & Brannon, 1976). Later in life, men are encouraged to go into the military service, during which time they are taught how to kill in defense of their country. Men are taught that they should respond with violence to perceived humiliations to avoid looking like a "punk" or being seen as weak. If a little boy gets beat up on the playground and goes home, his mother or father is likely to tell him to "go back and give him as good as you got." Men who overconform to this gender role endorse ideas such as a real man knows how to fight and may have cognitive distortions that include "If you don't fight back you're a sissy."

Playboy

Men are told through messages from advertising, television and the movies, and their peers that their sexual relations are supposed to be recreational and with multiple partners (Harris, 1995). They are socialized to be adventurous in their sexuality, spend little time developing relationships that are intimate beyond physical intimacy, and feel open to attack when partners want their relationships to be more than recreational. They endorse such ideas as a man's worth is based on how many sexual partners he has and men are not biologically set up to be monogamous and avoid ideas such as sex is a part of a nurturing relationship based on trust and intimacy. Cognitive distortions include "Without many sexual partners, I won't feel fulfilled" and "If I don't or can't seduce many partners it means that I am unworthy or that people won't respect me."

Self-Reliance

Men are told it is important not to look for help from anyone other than oneself and are socialized to do things alone and not rely on others (Harris, 1995). They are taught that it is important to take care of your own problems and that a man does not let others tell him what to do. Men often have difficulty with asking for help or admitting that they do not know or cannot do something and feel uncomfortable with taking charity or getting help from others when they are having difficulty. Men who overconform to this gender role endorse such ideas as a man should always stand on his own two feet and "if you want things done right you had better do them yourself." Cognitive distortions include "If I can't do it myself, people will think I'm inept," "Asking for help is a sign of weakness," and "I must always be able to do everything by myself."

Primacy of Work

Men are told in many subtle and not so subtle ways that work is the most important part of their identity (Harris, 1995; Meth, 1990). They are socialized to put their work goals ahead of their personal relationships with family and are shown models from other men—often their own fathers—that it is necessary to sacrifice family relationships to get ahead. Consequently, men have difficulty with family members making demands on their time and energy that take away from work goals and give little time to their own physical or familial well-being (Meth, 1990). Men often feel uncomfortable when attending to family matters because they worry about how it will affect their jobs and feel open to attack when family members or important others question their absence or noninvolvement in their families. Men who overconform to this gender role endorse ideas such as their personal identity and work identity are synonymous and "I am what I do." The cognitive distortions associated with this factor include "Work must take priority over my family and all other commitments or I'll never be successful" and "If I spend time with my family I will not advance in my career."

Disdain of Homosexuals

Men are socialized to believe that sexuality must be heterosexual and they cannot be perceived as homosexual (David & Brannon, 1976; Levant et al., 1992; O'Neil, 1981a, 1981b, 1982). Because many men are socialized to be wary of friendly male overtures, they often avoid the expression of tender feelings toward the males they care for and stay away from being very personal with other men. These men have difficulty demonstrating caring toward other men without getting anxious about the homosexual meaning that may be attributed to such expressions. Many men give little time to developing friendships with other men and feel uncomfortable when other men initiate emotional or physical closeness. They feel open to attack when their behaviors or associations might be considered homosexual and believe intimacy with other men leads to homosexuality or that "homos" deserve to be assaulted (that is, they support "gay bashing"). As such, men who internalize this socialization message may have cognitive distortions such as "I cannot be close to other men or people will think I'm homosexual."

Physical Toughness

Men are given messages that they have to be physically tough and able to take a lot of punishment "like a man." They are socialized to endure physical and emotional hardships without making a fuss. Consequently, they are reluctant to tell other people when they are experiencing either physical or emotional pain. This message produces barriers to help seeking similar to the self-reliance message described earlier. However, whereas the self-reliance message suggests that persons who seek help are not competent, the physical toughness message suggests that the person who seeks help "can't take it." Men who internalize this socialization message may have cognitive distortions such as "If I'm not a tough guy, everyone will push me around" and "If I give in to pain, it means I'm a wimp."

WORKING WITH MALE CLIENTS' GENDER-RELATED COGNITIVE DISTORTIONS

The nine examples provided are meant to illustrate how messages men receive about masculinity might lead to gender-related cognitive distortions. The clinical agenda for therapists working with clients who endorse these types of gender-related cognitive distortions is to first help clients monitor these distortions, then help them understand the connections between their cognitions, feelings, and behaviors (Beck et al., 1979). For example, clients who find the gender-related distortions of winning messages to be salient need to develop awareness that messages such as "Winning isn't everything, its the only thing" affect how they feel about themselves and how they live their lives. Clinicians need to help clients make connections between such messages about winning and feelings of depression, anxiety, or poor self-esteem in men (Cournoyer & Mahalik, 1995; Davis, 1988; Good & Mintz, 1990; Sharpe & Heppner, 1991).

Clients also need to become aware of the connections between their gender-related cognitive distortions and behaviors that result from these distortions. Again, in examining the messages associated with winning, male clients need to develop awareness about how these messages may relate to workaholic, type A behavior (Eisler et al., 1988; Watkins et al. 1991), their unavailability to their partners and children (Mintz & Mahalik, 1996), or problematic behaviors such as drug and alcohol abuse (Blazina & Watkins, 1996; Eisler et al., 1988; Watkins et al., 1991). In addition, therapists can help their male clients by exploring with them how these problematic behaviors may be in response to feelings of depression, anxiety, or poor self-esteem when they fail to live up to internalized ideals of being, for example, "a winner."

Intervening to modify these biased interpretations involves (1) searching for disconfirming evidence of clients' cognitive distortions from past experience, (2) helping clients see the illogicalness of current cognitive distortions, and (3) helping clients conduct personal experiments to gather data about whether their cognitive distortions are accurate. From a cognitive therapy perspective, change is produced by substituting more rational responses for the cognitive distortions.

Table 14.1 presents examples of cognitive distortions related to each of the masculine injunctions reviewed earlier and rational responses that might address those cognitive distortions. Therapists can teach these rational responses to clients by using the same three approaches that cognitive therapists use generally. That is, first, therapists can help clients search for disconfirming evidence of their cognitive distortions by examining past

Table 14.1. Sample Masculine-Gender-Related Distortions and Potential Rational Responses to Nine Masculinity Injunctions.

Masculine Injunction	Masculine-Gender-Related Cognitive Distortion	Potential Rational Response
Winning	Winning isn't everything, it's the only thing.	*History review:* Although it feels good to win, I've lost a lot of friends and alienated a lot of people in the process. *Illogicalness:* Does it make any sense to have to win all the time when I can never relax and enjoy it? *Personal experiment:* Try to support other people in their efforts on the playing field or in the workplace and see how I feel about helping someone else instead of trying to beat him or her.
Emotional control	If I share my feelings with others, people will think I am a sissy.	*History review:* By controlling my emotions I protect myself from hurt, but I usually feel isolated and lonely. *Illogicalness:* Everybody has feelings. Does it make sense to ignore such an important part of myself? *Personal experiment:* As soon as I get home at night I'll try sharing some affection with my partner and children. After a couple of weeks, I'll see how they view me.
Risk taking	Taking dangerous risks helps me to prove myself.	*History review:* Taking dangerous risks in the past has led to significant physical and financial costs. *Illogicalness:* Does it make sense to put the most important things in life (such as health) in jeopardy for no good reason? *Personal experiment:* Try out some prosocial risky behavior that challenges me but doesn't risk life and limb (such as speaking out for a cause I believe in).

| MViolence | If you walk away from a fight, you are a coward. | History review: There certainly have been times in the past that I've been involved in violence and regretted it.

Illogicalness: Does it make sense to risk jail because I'm angry at someone right now?

Personal experiment: Talk to friends I respect who do not get into fights and check out how they deal with things when they are angry. |
| Playboy | Without many sexual partners, I won't feel fulfilled. | Historical review: Although I feel excitement when I am out at bars trying to seduce new partners, it becomes tiresome always trying to "score."

Illogicalness: It does not make sense to be working so hard at maintaining my playboy reputation when I feel no real future, security, or satisfaction in moving from one partner to another.

Personal experiment: I might try staying with a partner who makes me feel good about myself and shares similar values or try talking to persons without trying to seduce them. |

Table 14.1. Sample Masculine-Gender-Related Distortions and Potential Rational Responses to Nine Masculinity Injunctions (*continued*).

Masculine Injunction	Masculine-Gender-Related Cognitive Distortion	Potential Rational Response
Self-reliance	Asking for help is a sign of failure.	*History review:* I've helped others and not thought them inept. It has also saved me a lot of time, energy, and frustration when I have gotten help in the past. *Illogicalness:* It is not practical to put such pressures on my time and energies to do everything myself. Also, it isolates me from my significant others (for example, partner and children). *Personal experiment:* Approach others whom I have some trust in to share the work. Work on some mutual tasks or chores. Approach others for help and see the effect that receiving help has on interpersonal and work effectiveness.
Primacy of work	Work must take priority over family and all other commitments or I'll never be successful.	*History review:* I remember my father working all the time and feeling that I'd rather have him home more than have another car. *Illogicalness:* I try to take care of my family and be the good provider by working long hours, but is it worth it when I feel like a stranger with my significant others? *Personal experiment:* Leave work-related issues at work, especially on Friday evenings, and spend weekends with family activities. Set aside time for activities with significant others such as evening school events or special occasions.

	I cannot be close to other men or people will think I am homosexual.	*Historical review:* I shared chum experiences and friendships with childhood male friends and my family valued them.
Disdain of homosexuals		*Illogicalness:* It is not rational to view my close male friendships as being abnormal when they help and support me in times of need and crisis.
		Personal experiment: Try to remain rational about my male relationships and not distort the warm feelings I might have for these important men in my life.
Physical toughness	I should always be tough as nails.	*Historical review:* Sometimes it would have been better for me to have seen a doctor than to "tough it out."
		Illogicalness: Sure I don't want to cry over every bump and bruise, but does it make sense to have to take every physical blow that comes my way?
		Personal experiment: Try treating my body more carefully and see if it performs better for me.

experiences. They can do so by having clients examine experiences in their own lives, noticing how others react to certain behaviors in men, and recalling how they have reacted to behaviors of important men in their lives, especially their own fathers. For example, in looking at winning, therapists could help clients examine evidence of times in their lives when they did not win or were not successful but remember being happy. Related to self-reliance, clients might examine how internalizing this message sharply isolates them from others. Last, examining messages related to playboy, therapists could help male clients examine their own reactions to seeing other men coldheartedly seducing women or being unfaithful to their partners.

A second strategy from a cognitive therapy framework is helping clients to see the illogicalness of current cognitive distortions by helping them weigh whether the work involved in living up to a certain ideal is worth the often minimal payoff. For example, in examining messages related to the primacy of work, therapists could help clients question whether it makes any sense to be working themselves into an early grave. Therapists could also ask clients how they might view other men who engaged in the same sort of behavior. For example, for self-reliance, therapists could help clients question whether they considered a man who was toiling futilely at an important task without asking for help to be admirable or stupid.

Last, conducting personal experiments to test whether clients' gender-related cognitive distortions are accurate might also be a useful cognitive therapy exercise. In this case clients might be asked to stop a behavior (such as isolating themselves or making everything a contest) or start a behavior (such as sharing more of themselves with their partners or coming home instead of working late) and examine their own reactions and others' responses to this new behavior. For example, in addressing self-reliance, clients could try asking for help with a difficult task and see whether they are humiliated or relieved. Similarly, in addressing winning, therapists could ask clients to observe people's reactions to them when they are not competing all the time. Clients may discover that others view them as more likeable and that they have "won" some new friends when they stop making everything a competition.

Case Illustrations

To illustrate some of the clinical issues in working with men's cognitive distortions, consider the cases of Joe and John. Joe is in his midforties and has had a "perfect" life. He had an Ivy League education, an attractive wife and two kids, a very successful business, and a beautiful home but always felt empty inside, as if all of this was still not enough. Throughout his life Joe had internalized winning and playboy messages, and these messages affect his behavior in that he always strives for "one more victory," whether through defeating a rival or womanizing. These gender-related cognitive distortions also affect Joe's evaluation of himself because he measures himself primarily based on the scholarships, contracts, the attractive woman he married, and the attractive women he seduces. Although Joe saw everything in his marriage as "fine," his wife complained that he is always argumentative and badgering her and the children about their shortcomings such that there is great resentment between Joe and his wife and children. She finally starts divorce proceedings when she discovers his infidelities. Joe sees himself losing everything by which he measures himself (that is, his woman, half his money and business, and his house), feels depressed, and wants help winning back his wife.

In this short description of Joe's complaints and experiences, one can see the interpersonal and marital problems arising from and being maintained by gender-related cognitive distortions. For example, his emphasis on winning always places him in the position of rival with others. This position is likely to lead to interpersonal isolation, resentment from others, and only feeling that he has worth when he achieves measurable accomplishments. Joe may be telling himself that "if others defeat me or I don't achieve, then I won't be happy." His emphasis on defeating others also seems to extend to his relationships with his wife and children. Joe may be telling himself that "if I don't prevail in family decisions, I'll look like a weak husband or father." In looking at his infidelities tied to the playboy messages that he has internalized, Joe may be telling himself that "it proves that I am worthwhile because I get women to sleep with me."

A second case example is that of John, who is married and has teenage boys and a demanding job. Although he experiences a lot of misgivings about seeking professional help, John decides to talk to a therapist about long-standing feelings of depression. John's presenting complaints focus on feeling isolated and alone and under a lot of pressure at work. John describes his wife as complaining that he is emotionally unavailable to her. John complains that she wants to know how he is feeling all the time, but most of the time he does not know how he feels himself. When he is overwhelmed and alone he reports that he is uncomfortable with asking for support and affection from his wife, and he does not think he can talk to his male friends about his problems. Although work is full of pressure for him, he often finds it easier to "throw himself into his work" and resents his wife and kids at times because their needs take time and energy away from achieving at work.

In this short description of John's complaints and experiences, one can understand John's depression and interpersonal problems as arising from or being maintained by gender-related cognitive distortions. For example, his emotional unavailability to his wife and himself may be tied to messages of emotional control. John may be telling himself that "if I share my feelings with my wife, she will think I'm falling apart" or "if I am emotionally available to her, her feelings will overwhelm me." In looking at his reluctance to ask for help from his wife and friends and his ambivalence about seeking professional help, one might assess that these reactions are tied to messages of self-reliance. John may be telling himself that "asking for help is a sign of weakness" or that if he talks to his male friends about his problems they will think he is a "wussy." His need to throw himself into work and resentment of family for taking energy away from work are likely tied to messages about success and the primacy of work. He may be telling himself that "once I am successful then I will be happy" or "if I spend time with my family I'm not going to get ahead at work."

Opportunities for male clients to modify these gender-related cognitive distortions and understand the social context in which they were formed can come from therapists helping male clients to first notice these self-defeating messages, then reflect on the sources of these beliefs. For example, the therapist might say to Joe, "It sounds like you feel everything is a contest. Where did you learn that lesson?" Similarly with John, the therapist might say, "It sounds like you feel that you have to do everything yourself. I wonder how you came to believe that?" Such an intervention prompts the client to explore the sources of these messages (for example, messages from father, mother, teachers, and coaches). This type of intervention also helps male clients see themselves in a sociocultural context whereby they may "learn to view themselves as products of, and sometimes victims of, their upbringing in a 'gendered' culture" (Brooks, 1998, p. 83).

From a cognitive therapy framework, once the gender-related cognitive distortions are identified, the therapist helps male clients modify these distortions as described in the preceding section. Research on Beck's cognitive therapy provides strong empirical support that modifying biased interpretations leads to reductions in symptomatology (Blackburn, Bishop, Glen, Whalley, & Christie, 1981; Evans et al., 1992; Rush, Beck, Kovacs, & Hollon, 1977). Thus, modifying gender-related cognitive distortions should lead to reductions in the type of symptoms noted earlier that are associated with gender role conflict and stress.

For Joe, searching for disconfirming evidence of his cognitive distortions from past experiences might focus on times that he had extramarital affairs but felt guilty and ashamed, not worthwhile. In examining the illogicalness of current cognitive distortions, the therapist could help Joe see if it makes any sense to win and dominate his family when he creates such resentment and ill will. The therapist might also help Joe test his gender-related cognitive distortions through personal experiments in which he supports (rather than defeats) other people in their efforts to get ahead and sees how he feels about himself and how others react to him. Finally, the therapist would work to help Joe substitute a more rational response for the cognitive distortion (for example, "There are a lot of ways I can feel worthwhile about myself without having to hurt so many people").

These three concrete ways of trying to substitute more rational responses for gender-related cognitive distortions could be applied to the case of John also. For example, John and the therapist might search for disconfirming evidence of his cognitive distortions from past experiences (for example, "I remember when we were first married and talked all the time and how good I felt about sharing my life with her"), see the illogicalness of current cognitive distortions (for example, "What's the good of being successful and having money if I have no one to share it with?"), and conduct personal experiments about whether his cognitive distortions are accurate (for example, John might talk to one of his male friends about his feeling pulled by work and family responsibilities and see how he feels and how his friend reacts). John may then be able to substitute a more rational response for the cognitive distortions (for example, "Talking to my wife about my feelings might feel awkward at first, but I usually feel less isolated and depressed afterward").

Adaptive Versus Maladaptive Schemata

Traditional men experience many of the gender-related cognitive distortions identified in this chapter as adaptive rather than costly. For example, traditional men who believe that "winning isn't everything, it's the only thing" may react negatively to therapists who challenge this view as a cognitive distortion. Thus, therapists need to recognize that messages associated with traditional masculinity are often adaptive to boys, adolescent males, and adult men on a number of levels (for example, by conforming to them men avoid the disparagement that comes from violating gender norms; see Mahalik's [2000b] Model of Conformity to Masculinity Norms). Therapists need to walk the line between acknowledging how these messages have been helpful and good for such clients on one level while exploring with them how these rigidly held messages may also be costing them. For example, "You know it's clear to me, John, how great the promotions and career advancement have been for you and your family. You are able to send your kids to the best schools and give your wife the things she deserves. I wonder, though, if we could take a look at what type of effect your seventy-hour work weeks have had on your time with the kids or maybe your feelings of isolation. I remember you talking about your father working those same long hours and how you just really wanted to have him around more."

Given that cognitive therapy is a learning model of psychotherapy, if male clients are able to learn the skills to modify their gender-related cognitive distortions, they may be able to generalize these techniques from therapy to situations in daily living (Beck et al., 1979). That is, after learning the connections between gender-related cognitive distortions and their feelings and behaviors and testing those schemata, male clients may begin to ask themselves questions such as "What's the evidence that people will love me more if I stay late and work?" "How problematic is it really that I didn't get the promotion when it means more headaches and seeing my family much less?" "What degree of harm to me is it really if a stranger thinks I'm a 'chicken'?" or "What will I lose if I'm more available emotionally to important people in my life?" Such questioning of internalized masculine gender role schemata that clients discover cause distress in their lives is a way to avoid the "thoughtless thinking" (Beck et al., 1979, p. 5) that occurs when people are bound by stereotyped automatic patterns.

CONCLUSION

By incorporating gender role analyses into psychological assessment (see Brown, 1986) and treatment with male clients, clinicians should be better able to work effectively with a group that is hesitant to use and quick to leave psychotherapy. Specifically, clinicians who can appreciate the contribution of gender role socialization to men's cognitive distortions will be better able to understand contributing factors to men's presenting problems, respond more empathically to their male clients, and anticipate the types of messages male clients internalize that may contribute to their depression, anxiety, and rigid self-defeating interpersonal relationships (see Mahalik, 1999). Such gender-informed interventions might help reduce gender role strain in clients and break some of the connections between societal gender role stereotypes and men's feelings of adequacy and self-worth.

References

Antill, J. K., & Cunningham, J. D. (1979). Self-esteem as a function of masculinity in both sexes. *Journal of Consulting and Clinical Psychology, 47,* 783–785.

Arrindell, W. A., Kolk, A. M., Pickersgill, M. J., & Hageman, W. J. (1993). Biological sex, sex role orientation, masculine sex role stress, dissimulation, and self-reported fears. *Advances in Behaviour Research and Therapy, 15,* 103–146.

Beck, A. T. (1963). Thinking and depression, I: Idiosyncratic content and cognitive distortions. *Archives of General Psychiatry, 9,* 324–333.

Beck, A. T. (1964). Thinking and depression, II: Theory and therapy. *Archives of General Psychiatry, 10,* 561–571.

Beck, A. T., Freeman, A., & Associates (1990). *Cognitive therapy of personality disorders.* New York: Plenum.

Beck, A. T., Rush, A. J., Shaw, B. F., & Emery, G. (1979). *Cognitive therapy of depression.* New York: Guilford Press.

Beck, A. T., & Weishaar, M. E. (1995). Cognitive therapy. In R. J. Corsini & D. Wedding (Eds.), *Current psychotherapies* (pp. 229–261). Itasca, IL: Peacock.

Bem, S. (1981). Gender schema theory: A cognitive account of sex typing. *Psychological Review, 88,* 354–364.

Bem, S. (1983). Gender schema theory and its implications for child development: Raising gender aschematic children in a gender schematic society. *Signs, 8,* 598–616.

Blackburn, I. M., Bishop, S., Glen, A.I.M., Whalley, L. J., & Christie, J. E. (1981). The efficacy of cognitive therapy in depression: A treatment trial using cognitive therapy and pharmacotherapy, each alone and in combination. *British Journal of Psychiatry, 139,* 181–189.

Blazina, C., & Watkins, C. E., Jr. (1996). Masculine gender role conflict: Effects on college men's psychological well-being, chemical substance usage, and attitudes toward help-seeking. *Journal of Counseling Psychology, 43,* 461–465.

Brooks, G. R. (1998). *A new psychotherapy for traditional men.* San Francisco: Jossey-Bass.

Brooks, G. R., & Silverstein, L. B. (1995). Understanding the dark side of masculinity: An interactive systems model. In R. F. Levant & W. S. Pollack (Eds.), *The new psychology of men* (pp. 280–336). New York: Basic Books.

Brown, L. S. (1986). Gender role analysis: A neglected component of psychological assessment. *Psychotherapy, 23,* 243–248.

Cournoyer, R. J., & Mahalik, J. R. (1995). Cross-sectional study of gender role conflict examining college-aged and middle-aged men. *Journal of Counseling Psychology, 42,* 11–19.

David, D. S., & Brannon, R. (1976). *The forty-nine percent majority: The male sex role.* Reading, MA: Addison-Wesley.

Davis, D., & Padesky, C. (1989). Enhancing cognitive therapy with women. In A. D. Freeman, K. M. Simon, L. E. Beutler, & H. Arkowitz (Eds.), *Comprehensive handbook of cognitive therapy* (pp. 535–557). New York: Plenum Press.

Davis, F. (1988). Antecedent and consequents of gender role conflict: An empirical test of sex-role strain analysis (Doctoral dissertation, Ohio State University). *Dissertation Abstracts International, 48*(11), 3443.

Eisler, R. M., & Skidmore, J. R. (1987). Masculine gender role stress: Scale development and component factors in the appraisal of stressful situations. *Behavior Modification, 11,* 123–136.

Eisler, R. M., Skidmore, J. R., & Ward, C. H. (1988). Masculine gender-role stress: Predictor of anger, anxiety, and health-risk behaviors. *Journal of Personality Assessment, 52,* 133–141.

Evans, M. D., Hollon, S. D., DeRubeis, R. J., Piarceki, J. M., Grove, W. M., & Garvey, M. J. (1996). Differential relapse following cognitive therapy and psychopharmaco-therapy for depression. *Archives of General Psychiatry, 49,*802–808.

Good, G. E., & Mintz, L. B. (1990). Gender role conflict and depression in college men: Evidence for compounded risk. *Journal of Counseling and Development, 69,* 17–21.

Good, G. E., Robertson, J. M., O'Neil, J. M., Fitzgerald, L. F., Stevens, M., DeBord, K. A., Bartels, K. M., & Braverman, D. G. (1995). Male gender role conflict: Psychometric issues and relations to psychological distress. *Journal of Counseling Psychology, 42,* 3–10.

Harris, I. M. (1995). *Messages men hear: Constructing masculinities.* Bristol, PA: Taylor & Francis.

Lazurus, A. A. (1981). *The practice of multimodel therapy.* New York: Guilford.

Levant, R. F. (1993). *Men and psychotherapy: Assessment and treatment of alexithymia in men.* Paper presented at the annual convention of the American Psychological Association, Toronto, Canada.

Levant, R. F. (1995). Toward the reconstruction of masculinity. In R. F. Levant & W. S. Pollack (Eds.), *A new psychology of men* (pp. 229–251). New York: Basic Books.

Levant, R. F., Hirsch, L. S., Celentano, E., Cozza, T. M., Hill, S., MacEachern, M., Marty, N., & Schnedecker, J. (1992). The male role: An investigation of contemporary norms. *Journal of Mental Health Counseling, 14,* 325–337.

Levant, R. F., & Kelly, J. (1989). *Between father and child.* New York: Viking.

Levant, R. F., & Pollack, W. S. (1995). *The new psychology of men.* New York: Basic Books.

Levant, R. F., Wu, R., & Fischer, J. (1996). Masculinity ideology: A comparison between U.S. and Chinese young men and women. *Journal of Gender, Culture, and Health, 1,* 207–220.

Mahalik, J. R. (1999). Interpersonal psychotherapy with men who experience gender role conflict. *Professional Psychology: Theory, Research, and Practice, 30,* 5–13.

Mahalik, J. R. (2000a). Men's gender role conflict in men as a predictor of self-ratings of behavior on the Interpersonal Circle. *Journal of Social and Clinical Psychology, 19,* 276–292.

Mahalik, J. R. (2000b). A theory of conformity to masculine norms. In J. R. Mahalik (Chair), *Conformity to masculine norms: Theory, research, and practice.* Symposium conducted at annual convention of the American Psychological Association, Washington, DC.

Mahalik, J. R., Cournoyer, R., DeFranc, W., Cherry, M., & Napolitano, J. (1998). Men's gender role conflict and use of psychological defenses. *Journal of Counseling Psychology, 45,* 247–255.

Meth, R. L. (1990). The road to masculinity. In R. L. Meth & R. S. Pasick (Eds.), *Men in therapy: The challenge of change* (pp. 3–34). New York: Guilford Press.

Mintz, R., & Mahalik, J. R. (1996). Gender role orientation and conflict as predictors of family roles for men. *Sex Roles, 34,* 805–821.

O'Neil, J. M. (1981a). Male sex-role conflicts, sexism, and masculinity: Psychological implications for men, women, and the counseling psychologist. *Counseling Psychologist, 9*, 61–81.

O'Neil, J. M. (1981b). Patterns of gender role conflict and strain: Sexism and fear of femininity in men's lives. *Personnel and Guidance Journal, 60*, 203–210.

O'Neil, J. M. (1982). Gender role conflict and strain in men's lives: Implications for psychiatrists, psychologists, and other human service providers. In K. Solomon & N. B. Levy (Eds.), *Men in transition: Changing male roles, theory, and therapy* (pp. 5–44). New York: Plenum.

O'Neil, J. M., & Egan, J. (1992). Men's gender role transitions over the life span: Transformations and fears of femininity. *Journal of Mental Health Counseling, 14*, 305–324.

Pleck, J. H. (1981). *The myth of masculinity.* Cambridge, MA: MIT Press.

Pleck, J. H. (1995). The gender role strain paradigm: An update. In R. F. Levant & W. S. Pollack (Eds.), *The new psychology of men* (pp. 11–32). New York: Basic Books.

Rush, A. J., Beck, A. T., Kovacs, M., & Hollon, S. (1977). Comparative efficacy of cognitive therapy and imipramine in the treatment of depressed outpatients. *Cognitive Therapy and Research, 1*, 17–37.

Sharpe, M. J., & Heppner, P. P. (1991). Gender role, gender role conflict, and psychological well-being in men. *Journal of Counseling Psychology, 38*, 323–330.

Watkins, P. L., Eisler, R. M., Carpenter, L., Schechtman, K. B., & Fisher, E. B. (1991). Psychosocial and physiological correlates of male gender role stress among employed adults. *Behavioral Medicine, 17*, 86–90.

Whitley, B. E. (1983). Sex role orientation and self-esteem: A critical meta-analytic review. *Journal of Personality and Social Psychology, 44*, 765–785.

Whitley, B. E. (1985). Sex role orientation and psychological well-being: Two meta-analyses. *Sex Roles, 12*, 207–225.

Wisch, A. F., Mahalik, J. R., Hayes, J. A., & Nutt, E. A. (1995). The impact of gender role conflict and counseling technique on psychological help-seeking in men. *Sex Roles, 33*, 77–89.

CHAPTER FIFTEEN

Interpersonal Psychotherapy for Men

James R. Mahalik

Our interpersonal relationships with others are shaped from the very first interactions we have with caretakers. As infants we rely on caretakers—usually our mothers—to meet all of our physical and emotional needs. This reliance helps form our attachments to caretakers and serves as the foundation on which we learn to form relationships with others (Ainsworth, 1989; Bowlby, 1969). Specifically, attachments from our early relationships help us to be able to connect to others, to experience intimacy, and to rely on other persons during rocky times.

One central experience that complicates the formation of attachments to caretakers and the subsequent development of all later relationships is the process of gender role socialization (DeFranc & Mahalik, 1999; Fischer & Good, 1998). That is, from an early age girls and boys are shaped by parents, teachers, and peers such that girls and women are encouraged to make interpersonal connections whereas boys and men are shaped to disconnect from others and be self-sufficient (Gilbert & Scher, 1999). Specific to infants and young boys, Levant and Kopecky (1995) observe that mothers try to control the expression of their more excitable and emotional male infants, fathers tend to push toddlers toward gender-stereotypic behavior, and both parents tend to discourage boys from expressing vulnerability in interpersonal relationships (for example, tell their sons that "big boys don't cry") and instead encourage their boys to be self-sufficient and aggressive.

This detached and dominant interpersonal style continues to be reinforced by societal messages that encourage boys and men to follow the (1) "no sissy stuff," (2) "big wheel," (3) "give 'em hell," and (4) "sturdy oak" injunctions of masculinity (David & Brannon, 1976). These injunctions are associated, respectively, with messages to men that they (1) should avoid anything feminine (for example, being dependent or vulnerable), (2) should strive to defeat others and achieve status by getting to the top, (3) should actively seek out adventure and risk, responding with violence if necessary, and (4) should never show weakness and should endure difficulties without relying on others for help. Thus, boys and men are presented with messages from parents, peers, and other societal agents influencing them to act disconnected and dominant in their relationships.

Although there are large intragroup differences among men, research supports these observations about how masculine gender role socialization affects men's interpersonal behavior. Specifically, in terms of being disconnected in relationships, men are reported to be more hostile, mistrusting, cold, detached, inhibited, aloof, and introverted than women (Tracey & Schneider, 1995; Wiggins & Holzmuller, 1978, 1981); coldness, mistrust, hostility, and detachment are related to masculine gender role conflict (Mahalik, 2000). Related to being dominant in relationships, research reports men as more dominant, arrogant, quarrelsome, and competitive than women (Tracey & Schneider, 1995; Wiggins & Holzmuller, 1978, 1981); dominance and control in interpersonal relations are related to masculinity (Johnson & Brems, 1989; Portello & Long, 1994; Sayers, Baucom, & Tierney, 1993) and masculine gender role conflict (Mahalik, 2000).

Masculinity scholars have identified some presenting issues associated with these detached and dominant interpersonal patterns. For example, detachment in men contributes to reduced paternal involvement and marital success (Pleck, 1985; Snarey & Pleck, 1993), interpersonal disconnection (Pollack, 1990, 1995), restrictive affectionate behavior (Bergman, 1995; Eisler & Skidmore, 1987; O'Neil, 1981a, 1981b, 1982; O'Neil, Helms, Gable, David, & Wrightsman, 1986), and alexithymia (Levant, 1992). Similarly, masculinity scholars have identified presenting issues associated with dominance and control in men to include aggressiveness (Doyle, 1989; Krugman, 1995; Levant, 1992; Levant et al., 1992; Mosher & Sirkin, 1984), including sexual aggressiveness (Kaplan, 1992; Kaplan, O'Neil, & Owen, 1993; Widom, 1984), anger management (Campbell, 1993; Eisler, 1995; Eisler, Skidmore, & Ward, 1988; Levant, 1995; Pollack, 1995), violence (Levant, 1995; Spence, Helmreich, & Holahan, 1979), power over women (Bergman, 1995), and fear of subordination, inferiority, or failure (Eisler & Skidmore, 1987).

Given these types of issues identified by masculinity scholars, counselors and therapists can expect these issues to contribute to presenting problems, as well as the client's level of psychological distress, his significant personal relationships, and the therapeutic relationship. For example, consider the client seen in individual therapy who describes intense feelings of depression and loneliness. He describes wanting to be in a supportive and emotionally intimate relationship, yet he seems to become automatically detached emotionally and competitive when involved with others. This type of experience leaves him feeling more isolated and lonely with less hope of things changing. In this case, the client's detached and dominant interpersonal style contributes to both the type of presenting issue he has and the intensity of his distress.

As another example of how traditional socialization may contribute to interpersonal presenting issues, consider the man seen in couples counseling because his partner complains he is emotionally unavailable and their relationship is unsatisfying. She further complains that when she talks to him about problems or concerns in their relationship he starts to "take charge" of the problem rather than listen to her. In this example, the client's distant and dominant interpersonal style contributes to the couple's presenting issues but in different ways than in the first example.

Finally, consider how this interpersonal style may affect the counseling relationship. For example, a male client with this interpersonal style may have difficulty talking about his feelings or experiences with the therapist because he feels he will then be open to attack. As a result he may withdraw during sessions or become defensive and irritated with the therapist for not "fixing" the problem quickly. He may also treat his and others' feelings as irrelevant to his problems or become competitive with the therapist, trying to prove he is right and convince the therapist to work differently or do things his way.

Clinicians working with men who experience these types of presenting problems in their relationships might consider using a therapeutic framework that addresses issues of interpersonal rigidity. Interpersonal psychotherapy (Kieser, 1983; Leary, 1957) may be particularly well suited to address the psychological distress men experience and cause for others related to masculine socialization because it places assessment of rigid maladaptive interpersonal patterns at the center of treatment planning. Thus, in the remainder of this chapter I describe the framework of interpersonal psychotherapy and then examine relationship and therapeutic issues for traditionally socialized men from an interpersonal psychotherapy framework.

INTERPERSONAL PSYCHOTHERAPY

Interpersonal psychotherapy is based on conceptualization of the client in terms of the Interpersonal Circle (Carson, 1969; Kieser, 1983; Leary, 1957; Wiggins, 1982). (See Figure 15.1 for Kieser's 1982 version of the Interpersonal Circle.) On the Interpersonal Circle, all interpersonal actions represent a blend of two motivations: the need for control (that is, power and dominance) and the need for affiliation (that is, love and friendliness). From the interpersonal framework, persons interacting with each other are "continually negotiating how friendly or hostile they will be with each other and how much in charge or control each will be in their encounters" (Kieser, 1988, p. 10). This relationship between these two tasks is represented on the Interpersonal Circle by placing control (that is, the dominance-submission dimension) and affiliation (that is, the friendliness-hostility dimension) along the vertical and horizontal axes of the circle, respectively. The Interpersonal Circle is composed of three sets of circles, with the innermost circle representing a dimension of interpersonal behavior (for example, dominance), the second circle representing mild to moderate interpersonal behavior on that dimension (for example, controlling), and the outer circle representing extreme interpersonal behavior on that dimension (for example, dictatorial).

A central component to interpersonal psychotherapy is examining the complementarity of interpersonal behavior between two persons. Most broadly described, complementarity refers to the notion that

> interpersonal acts are designed to invite, pull, elicit, draw, entice, or evoke restricted classes of reactions from those with whom we interact, especially from significant others. Reactions by others to these acts are not random, nor are they likely to include the entire range of possible reactions. Rather, they tend to be restricted to a relatively narrow range of interpersonal responses. At mostly automatic levels, our actions are designed to push or force others to respond in ways complementary to our acts so as to confirm our self-definitions and self-presentations; however we are mostly unaware that we are doing so. (Kieser, 1988, p. 10)

More specifically defined in relation to the Interpersonal Circle, interactional complementarity takes place when interpersonal behavior is reciprocal along the control dimension (that is, dominance "pulls" submission, submission "pulls" dominance) and corresponding along the affiliation dimension (that is, hostility pulls hostility, friendliness pulls friendliness). As Figure 15.2 illustrates, the hostile-dominant interaction pulls for the hostile-submissive response, the friendly-dominant interaction pulls for the friendly-submissive response, the hostile-submissive interaction pulls for the hostile-dominant response, and the friendly-submissive interaction pulls for the friendly-dominant response.

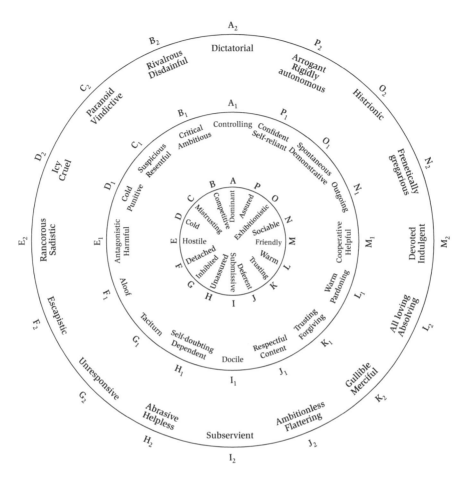

Figure 15.1. The Interpersonal Circle.

Source: Kieser, 1983, p. 189. Copyright © 1983 by the American Psychological Association. Reprinted with permission.

INTERPERSONAL PATHOLOGY
AND RIGID TRADITIONAL MASCULINITY

From an interpersonal framework, maladjusted behavior in persons reflects recurring, inflexible, and self-defeating interpersonal actions (Carson, 1969; Kieser, 1983; Leary, 1957). The disturbed individual "consistently broadcasts a rigid and extreme self-presentation and simultaneously pulls for a rigid and constricted relationship from others" (Kieser, 1988, p. 17). Those with maladjusted behavior are either unwilling or unable to change their interpersonal transactions even though the people they interact with are not responding with complementary behavior. For example, the emotionally detached man who is rigid and extreme in his self-presentation will not respond with

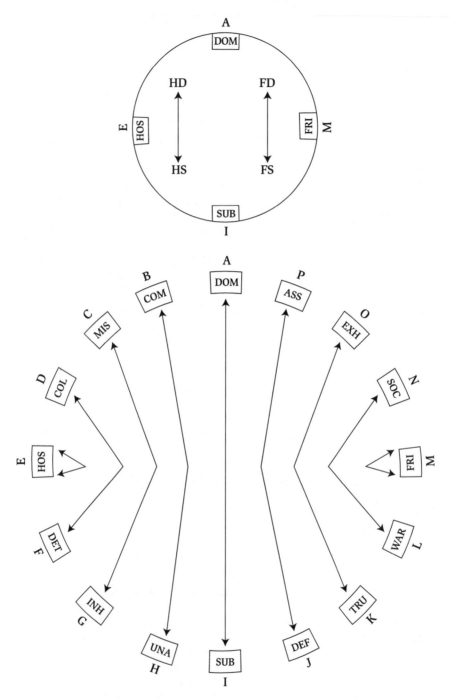

Figure 15.2. Complementary Quadrants and Segments from the 1982 Interpersonal Circle.

Source: Kieser, 1983, p. 202. Copyright © 1983 by the American Psychological Association. Reprinted with permission.

emotional support regardless of the frequency or intensity of this pull from those around him. In Leary's (1957) words, the disturbed person "tends to overdevelop a narrow range of one or two interpersonal responses. They are expressed intensely and often, whether appropriate to the situation or not" (p. 126).

As described at the beginning of this chapter, the process of masculine socialization contributes to the type of interpersonal pathology men display and is characterized by the dominant and hostile quadrant of the Interpersonal Circle in Figure 26.1.[1] In looking at hostile behavior on the Interpersonal Circle, one is likely to observe the male client withdrawing from connection to others and neglecting or repressing his emotional self. For example, he may have difficulty telling others that he cares about them, knowing what he feels, and expressing vulnerabilities. At home he is unlikely to show affection to family members or be able to ask for support and affection. For example, he may expect that his partner and children "know" what he feels for them even when he may himself have difficulty being able to name or experience his feelings. Also, he may expect that his partner be able to know when he needs support and is feeling bad even if he has difficulty knowing what he is feeling. In raising sons, one might expect his relationship to his boys to be undemonstrative and distant for fear of modeling "queer" behavior or making them "soft." Thus, he perpetuates a model for his sons of how men are to be emotionally distant from each other. At both home and work settings, he is likely to form relationships with other males that are task focused, or he may be suspicious of other men who try to get close to him. At the workplace, he may withdraw into himself when faced with disappointments or frustrations (such as being passed over for promotion).

Dominant behavior would likely include having to "be in charge," be smarter or physically stronger than other men, and be powerful and defeat others. This quality may show up in a range of interpersonal behaviors at home or in the workplace. At home he may try to control his partner and children. This behavior may include needing to dominate his partner by keeping tabs on where the partner has been, whom the partner has seen, and how his partner dresses or looks, for example. He may also insist that his partner and children be "perfect" or "winners" so as to reflect well on him. In the workplace he may try to succeed at others' expense by pushing over them for recognition or promotion, berating their performance, or insisting that people with whom he works do things his way. The need to be successful may also lead to difficulty in asking for help either at work or at home because he would have to admit that he is doing poorly. Also, he may experience resentment toward family members who need his emotional support and time because they take away from achievement at work. His need to be "successful," usually measured by money and power, often interferes with family relationships.

CASE OF JOHN SMITH

To illustrate interpersonal therapy in a more concrete way, I describe the case of John Smith. Although the illustration is meant to be a caricature to demonstrate issues in men's interpersonal relationships and the therapeutic relationship, I believe many of the elements of the case will ring familiar to clinicians who work with men in individual, couples, and family therapy.

Let us assume that John Smith has undergone a traditional masculine gender role socialization experience. As a result of this socialization, he tends to be emotionally distant and act dominant in his interpersonal relationships. Specifically, because of his fear of being or appearing feminine—ingrained in him from family, peers, and the media— John tends to act out stereotypical male roles in a rigid and extreme way. As a result,

John tends to be domineering and controlling of his partner and children. His explicit and implicit messages to them communicate that they must reflect well on him. John's partner and children describe him as withdrawn emotionally and having difficulty attending to his own, his partner's, and his children's emotional lives. John finds it uncomfortable to ask for or give support and affection to his partner and children; he finds it easier to avoid their needs by investing himself in work. Consequently, he expects his partner and children not to place emotional demands on him, and he resents their needs because of the time and energy it takes away from achieving at work. He models for his sons to be emotionally distant and act "manly" and relates to his family mainly through tasks that they accomplish together.

In the workplace John works hard to beat his competitors (colleagues, coworkers, or others with whom he feels he needs to compete). When he experiences difficulty at work, John feels he must handle it himself and cannot ask for help. In addition to coworkers experiencing him as either cutthroat, emotionally distant, or both, if John were to find a coworker's performance lacking or if a coworker showed strong feelings at the workplace, John would be likely to evaluate that person harshly.

By using an interpersonal therapy approach and understanding the influence of traditional male socialization, we can make three predictions about the types of interpersonal problems one would expect John Smith to experience. First, because of the rigid enactment of traditional male gender roles, John is going to use only a very narrow range of interpersonal behaviors. Those behaviors are likely to be limited to the dominant and hostile quadrant in Figure 15.1. This means that regardless of what type of interpersonal situation John faces, he only has behaviors that are competitive and detached to drawn on. This pattern probably works well in situations in which the need for competition and emotional disconnection are useful (such as when he is trying to meet a deadline for a task-oriented project). However, John is likely to feel he does not have the tools to handle interpersonal situations in which he needs emotional connection, cooperation, or to go along with others.

In working with men, I like to use a tool metaphor to illustrate how interpersonal therapy views the interpersonal issues of men who are rigidly distant and dominant. To begin the metaphor, let us assume that each person has an interpersonal toolbox that helps him or her in the different types of interpersonal interactions he or she faces each day. An interaction with one person may require one tool (for example, supporting a friend or partner), whereas a different interpersonal interaction will likely require a different tool from the interpersonal toolbox (for example, taking charge in a crisis). If they bring the right interpersonal "tool" to the right interpersonal "job," people tend to have positive relationships with each other. Conversely, using the wrong tool for a particular interpersonal project tends to lead to problems in that relationship.

To make use of this analogy in the current context, the man who has been socialized to respond to all situations with distant and dominant interpersonal behavior is able to use only one interpersonal tool in his relationships with other people (for example, he is only able to use the hammer). The problem for John, then, is that when another interpersonal tool would be more productive (such as being emotionally available or asking for help), he only feels comfortable and skilled in using the hammer (that is, being detached and dominant).

The second prediction we can make using interpersonal therapy with traditionally socialized men is that John is likely to enact those dominant-hostile behaviors on the Interpersonal Circle in an extreme way. Recent research supports the notion that gender role conflict in men is related to more extreme behavior on the Interpersonal Circle (Mahalik, 2000).

Several socialization influences are likely to contribute to this phenomenon. First, the gender labels of masculine and feminine are typically viewed as dichotomous, giving little flexibility for males to engage in anything other than "masculine" behavior. Second, the "masculine mystique" that O'Neil (1990) identifies as pervasive in U.S. society maintains that masculinity is superior to femininity, that power and control are essential to prove masculinity, and that vulnerability and intimacy are to be avoided because they are feminine. Third, violating traditional gender roles has been shown to produce more negative consequences for men than for women (Pleck, 1981, 1995), and when men fail to live up to gender roles, they are likely to compensate by overconforming to traditional roles (Pleck, 1981, 1995).

As such, one would expect John Smith to enact behaviors from the outer circle of the Interpersonal Circle in Figure 15.1. That is, the greater rigidity John experiences around male gender roles, the more likely he will act dictatorial instead of dominant, escapist instead of detached, and antagonistic instead of hostile. To continue the tool analogy from earlier in this section, beyond the burden of having only a hammer to work with interpersonally, John has a very big and heavy hammer that he brings to all his interpersonal "projects."

The third prediction we can make about John is that he will pull from important others a limited range of behaviors (see Figure 15.2) that will eventually create alienation in their relationships with him (Carson, 1969; Kieser, 1983; Leary, 1957). Because John has only emotionally withdrawn and dominant interpersonal behaviors on which to rely (that is, the hostile-dominant quadrant in Figure 15.2), he is only able to interact with people using these types of interpersonal behaviors. Despite significant others trying to enact a wide range of behaviors with John (for example, those with which he might be supportive or emotionally available), these significant others would be consistently pulled to respond to John with a very narrow range of their behaviors in return. In such a case, people in John's life will often feel pulled into a pattern of interaction with him that they do not want and that does not change over time, despite trying to engage him differently. As a result either John will have relationships in which the other person is submissive and emotionally distant or people will withdraw from being in relationship with him. To continue the tool metaphor, John will be able to continue relationships only with persons who have heavy-duty "nails" in their interpersonal toolbox. Given that most people want to stay out of relationships with persons who are always hammering them, we can expect that the people in John's life will eventually disconnect themselves from him.

USING INTERPERSONAL THERAPY WITH JOHN

Given the interpersonal dynamics described and the predictions made concerning John Smith and his interpersonal relationships, some issues are salient for the clinician to understand in working with John Smith and other traditionally socialized men. Kieser (1988) describes the therapist's most important task in psychotherapy as disrupting the "vicious cycle of self-defeating action" (p. 22) that the client continually enacts. He specifies five principles derived from knowledge of the dynamics of the Interpersonal Circle that help guide the therapist in his or her work. From the earlier illustrations describing the interpersonal patterns of men who experience gender role conflict, we can readily see this "vicious cycle of self-defeating action" that Kieser describes as interpersonal pathology. Using his model of interpersonal psychotherapy, I will describe each of the five principles that Kieser (1988) outlines as the framework for interpersonal psychotherapy, then illustrate each as they apply to working with the man who experiences gender role conflict.

Principle One: Reduce Interpersonal Extremeness and Increase Interpersonal Repertoire

"The goal of therapy is to facilitate an increased frequency and intensity of interpersonal acts with significant others from segments on the Circle OPPOSITE those that define the patient's pattern of maladaptive interpersonal behavior" (Kieser, 1988, p. 23). Goals for work with the client entail reducing the extremeness of the interpersonal behavior and increasing the interpersonal repertoire of the client (Kieser, 1988). If the therapist is able to help the client meet these two goals, the client is likely to act more appropriately in different interpersonal situations. In John's case, the goal of counseling would be to reduce the intensity of his interpersonal behaviors in the hostile-dominant quadrant of the Interpersonal Circle and help John use interpersonal behaviors from other quadrants of the Interpersonal Circle. Specifically, in terms of reducing the intensity of his interpersonal behaviors, the goal for him might be to talk others into doing what he wants (that is, act dominant) instead of insisting that others do things his way (that is, act dictatorial), for example. In terms of using behaviors from other quadrants, the goal of therapy for him might be to confide in others, offer help to others, or follow another's lead. That is, the goal would be to have him use behaviors from the friendly and submissive parts of the Interpersonal Circle.

Principle Two: Anticipate Being Hooked into Complementary Responses

"In early therapy sessions especially, the patient will evoke or pull covert and overt responses from the therapist that are precisely characterized at segments of the Circle COMPLEMENTARY to those that define the patient's maladaptive interpersonal style" (Kieser, 1988, p. 23). Figure 15.2 shows the complementary interpersonal stances that the therapist can anticipate getting pulled into when working with clients who are rigid in their interpersonal style. In the case of working with John or other men who experience gender role conflict, from whom one expects a hostile and dominant interpersonal style (Mahalik, forthcoming), therapists should anticipate being initially hooked into complementary responses that are hostile and submissive.

Typical in-session interactions with John based on our knowledge of gender role conflict patterns and behaviors from the hostile-dominant quadrant of the Interpersonal Circle include the following (see Figure 15.1): John is likely to attack the therapist for not "fixing" the problem quickly (E-Hostile), blame others for problems (D-Cold), be suspicious of the therapist or therapy process and fearful that he may be judged unfairly (C-Mistrusting), work hard to prove he is right about others causing his problems (B-Competitive), and try to convince the therapist to work differently or do things his way (A-Dominant).

Given these sets of John's behaviors, the therapist is likely to be pulled into complementary behavior with John (see Figure 15.2). Such complementary in-session interactions may include the therapist disputing John's criticism for not fixing his problems (E-Hostile complementary to E-Hostile), being slow to respond or support him when he blames others (F-Aloof complementary to D-Cold), being carefully deliberate before speaking when John acts suspicious of the therapist (G-Inhibited complementary to C-Mistrusting), fumbling with his or her words when John is trying to prove others are causing his problems (H-Unassured complementary to B-Competitive), and giving into John when he wants to work differently (I-Submissive complementary to A-Dominant), for example.

Getting pulled into these complementary responses is inevitable for the therapist because the client "is more adept and more expert in his or her distinctive game of interpersonal encounter" (Kieser, 1988, p. 23). Although the therapist often experiences this situation as initially disconcerting, he or she is experiencing the different feelings, action tendencies, thoughts, and fantasies of important others in the client's life. This experience of being pulled into complementary responses with the man who experiences gender role conflict often serves as a reference point for the therapist in understanding his impact on important others.

Principle Three: Identify What the Client Pulls for and Disengage from That Automatic Response

"The first therapeutic priority is for the therapist to DISENGAGE from the complementary covert and overt responses being pulled by the patient" (Kieser, 1988, p. 24). After being hooked into a complementary response, the therapist's task is to identify what the client is pulling for and disengage from that automatic response. For the therapist working with John or other men who are interpersonally distant and dominant, the task is to break the pattern of hostile-submissive responding that the client pulls for from the therapist. In this stage of the work, the therapist needs to notice and label the behavior that is being pulled. By doing so, the therapist regains options in the therapeutic repertoire for more varied responses with John, thus helping him face "tuned-out" parts of his experience in a supportive way (Kieser, 1988).

Because clients engage therapists in ways that pull them into their most practiced interpersonal patterns, therapists need to be interpersonally aware of how they are influenced by clients. Part of this awareness in working with traditionally socialized men is identifying how therapists' own gender role patterns interact with clients' gender roles. As such, both male and female therapists should anticipate issues related to working with male clients who experience gender role conflict. Because male therapists are also influenced by masculine socialization, male clinicians might experience competition and struggling for control of the session with John. Female therapists who have been socialized into traditionally feminine gender roles may find themselves conspiring with the client to preserve his rigid gender-related behaviors; female therapists who are aware of the negative influence of traditional male roles on women's lives may find themselves reacting with resentment toward John when he enacts rigid male gender roles.

After identifying the repetitive pattern of the client in his interpersonal relationships and the therapeutic relationship and after the therapist has begun to disengage from the complementary pattern of interacting with the client, principles four and five of interpersonal therapy are useful to help the client broaden his interpersonal repertoire. In working with John, both principle four and principle five ask the therapist to move away from responding to John's hostile-dominant behaviors with the complementary relationship pattern of hostile-submissive behaviors. In doing so, the therapist will start to pull for John to act differently in the therapeutic relationship and help him develop a range of other interpersonal tools useful for relationships with important others.

Principle Four: Elicit "Beneficial Uncertainty"

"The therapist can produce cognitive ambiguity and uncertainty for the patient, as the first step toward disrupting the patient's maladaptive style, by shifting from complementary to therapeutic ASOCIAL responses" (Kieser, 1988, p. 24). With the awareness of how the therapist has been pulled into acting with the client, the therapist now needs to begin to act differently. If the therapist has been pulled to be defensive with John, he or she needs to become more open. If the therapist has been pulled to be hostile with John, he or she needs to become more friendly. If the therapist has been pulled to be submissive with John, he or she needs to take more leadership in the therapeutic relationship. When the therapist does not respond to the client in the usual way that he has come to expect, the client experiences a sense of "beneficial uncertainty" (Beier, 1966) because the client's usual interpersonal style does not bring about the expected interpersonal reactions from the therapist.

Principle Five: Experiment with Different Interpersonal Behavior Within the Therapeutic Relationship

"In later sessions, the therapist can exert the greatest pressure for change in the patient's interpersonal behavior (for increasing the frequency and intensity of actions from opposite segments of the circle) by initiating responses that are ANTICOMPLEMENTARY on the Circle to the patient's maladaptive interpersonal style" (Kieser, 1988, p. 26). When the therapist acts in an anticomplementary fashion, he or she is rejecting both components of the client's interpersonal behavior (Kieser, 1988). In the case of John the therapist is acting in a nonreciprocal way along the control axis (that is, responding with dominance to dominance) and affiliation axis (that is, responding with friendliness to hostility). Kieser (1988) notes that if this therapeutic stance were used early in therapy the client would likely reject therapy and terminate work. However, if a sufficiently strong working alliance is in place, the client may be able to tolerate the anticomplementary responses of the therapist and experiment with different interpersonal behavior within the therapeutic relationship.

Consistent with the goal of having the client develop aspects of himself from different parts of the Interpersonal Circle, the anticomplementary response of the therapist pulls for the client to respond with interpersonal behaviors that are in the quadrant opposite of those that are most strongly ingrained in the client. In John's case, when the therapist responds with in-session behavior that is from the friendly-dominant quadrant of the Interpersonal Circle, John has the opportunity to respond with behavior that is friendly-submissive. Specifically, if the therapist can disengage from the hostile-submissive behavior patterns being pulled for by John and engage in asocial or anticomplementary patterns such as taking control, being assured, being demonstrative, being outgoing, being helpful, being warm, pardoning, being trustful, and being respectful (that is, behaviors from different parts of the Interpersonal Circle than the ones he or she was using with John), John has the opportunity to begin to use different interpersonal behaviors with the therapist that are likely to be warm and nurturing, trusting, outgoing, spontaneous, and demonstrative.

These new behaviors encouraged by the therapist's use of asocial and anticomplementary responding are behaviors that are typically viewed as "feminine." In helping the client who has overdeveloped a set of detached and dominant interpersonal behaviors, the interpersonal therapist is trying to help the client unlearn some of the messages of masculine socialization. Specifically, whereas the masculine socialization process encourages developing a sense of self through renouncing "femininity," interpersonal psychotherapists can help traditionally socialized men integrate parts of themselves that have been underdeveloped. Whereas the "masculine identification processes stress differentiation from others, denial of affective relation," and approaches that "tend to deny the relationship" (Chodorow, 1978, p. 176), therapists using an interpersonal framework can help clients move toward relationships with others and integrate an emotional life into men's sense of self.

In the therapeutic relationship, specifically, the therapist has the opportunity to reinforce John's fledgling attempts at emotional expression with feedback that supports his new behaviors. This support is in contrast to how John likely experienced punishment from family and peers for expressing his emotional needs. Therapists can also provide reinforcement and support instead of punishment and derision for men who express feelings such as "I need to be close," "I'm lonely," or "I'm feeling overwhelmed and I need your help." In the case of John, for example, the therapist can give feedback such as how much more likable and approachable he seems when he lets others know how he feels.

Given our current understanding of how masculine gender roles can contribute to greater psychopathology and compromised well-being for men, their families, and society, more attention on integrating the effects of gender role socialization into treatment seems necessary. This chapter is an illustration of how one therapeutic framework that addresses interpersonal rigidity can help counselors and therapists understand the effect of gender role socialization on men and how psychotherapists might respond to help male clients develop less conflictual and more rewarding interpersonal relationships.

Note

1. One point about the interpersonal model deserves some clarification in discussing distant or dominant interpersonal behavior in men. From an interpersonal therapy framework, the problem is not that a man acts distant or dominant. Rather, the difficulty is that these distant and dominant interpersonal behaviors happen automatically whether or not they are appropriate to a given situation or a particular relationship. It is this lack of flexibility in the behavioral repertoire that is problematic in a man's relationships, not the distancing or dominant behavior per se.

References

Ainsworth, M.D.S. (1989). Attachment beyond infancy. *American Psychologist, 44,* 709–716.

Beier, E. G. (1966). *The silent language of psychotherapy.* Chicago: Aldine.

Bergman, S. J. (1995). Men's psychological development: A relational perspective. In R. F. Levant & W. S. Pollack (Eds.), *The new psychology of men* (pp. 68–90). New York: Basic Books.

Bowlby, J. (1969). *Attachment and loss.* New York: Basic Books.

Campbell, A. (1995). *Men, women, and aggression.* New York: Basic Books.

Carson, R. C. (1969). *Interaction concepts of personality.* Chicago: Aldine.

Chodorow, N. (1978). *The reproduction of mothering.* Berkeley and Los Angeles: University of California Press.

David, D. S., & Brannon, R. (1976). *The forty-nine percent majority: The male sex role.* Reading, MA: Addison-Wesley.

DeFranc, W., & Mahalik, J. R. (1999). Examining a model of male gender role strain, perceived paternal gender role strain, and maternal and paternal attachment. In J. M. O'Neil & G. E. Good (Cochairs), *Gender role conflict research: Expanding empirical research in men's studies.* Symposium conducted at the annual meeting of the American Psychological Association, Boston.

Doyle, J. A. (1989). *The male experience* (2nd ed.). Dubuque, IA: W. C. Brown.

Eisler, R. M. (1995). The relationship between masculine gender role stress and men's health risk: The validation of the construct. In R. F. Levant & W. S. Pollack (Eds.), *A new psychology of men* (pp. 207–225). New York: Basic Books.

Eisler, R. M., & Skidmore, J. R. (1987). Masculine gender role stress: Scale development and component factors in the appraisal of stressful situations. *Behavior Modification, 11,* 123–136.

Eisler, R. M., Skidmore, J. R., & Ward, C. H. (1988). Masculine gender role stress: Predictor of anger, anxiety, and health-risk behaviors. *Journal of Personality Assessment, 52,* 133–141.

Fischer, A. R., & Good, G. E. (1998). Perceptions of parent-child relationships and masculine role conflicts of college men. *Journal of Counseling Psychology, 45,* 346–352.

Gilbert, L. A., & Scher, M. (1999). *Gender and sex in counseling and psychotherapy.* Boston: Allyn & Bacon.

Johnson, M. E., & Brems, C. (1989). Differences in interpersonal functioning as related to sex-role orientation. *Psychology: A Journal of Human Behavior, 26,* 48–52.

Kaplan, R. (1992). *Normative masculinity and sexual aggression among college males.* Unpublished doctoral dissertation, University of Connecticut, Storrs, CT.

Kaplan, R., O'Neil, J. M., & Owen, S. (1993). Sexist, normative, and progressive masculinity and sexual assault: Empirical research. In J. M. O'Neil (Chair), *Research on men's sexual assault and constructive gender role interventions.* Symposium conducted at the annual meeting of the American Psychological Association, Toronto.

Kieser, D. J. (1983). The 1982 interpersonal circle: A taxonomy for complementarity in human transactions. *Psychological Review, 90,* 185–214.

Kieser, D. J. (1988). *Therapeutic metacommunication.* Palo Alto, CA: Consulting Psychologists Press.

Krugman, S. (1995). Male development and the transformation of shame. In R. F. Levant & W. S. Pollack (Eds.), *The new psychology of men* (pp. 91–126). New York: Basic Books.

Leary, T. (1957). *Interpersonal diagnosis of personality.* New York: Ronald Press.

Levant, R. F. (1992). Toward the reconstruction of masculinity. *Journal of Family Psychology, 5,* 379–402.

Levant, R. F. (1995). Toward the reconstruction of masculinity. In R. F. Levant & W. S. Pollack (Eds.), *The new psychology of men* (pp. 229–251). New York: Basic Books.

Levant, R. F., Hirsch, L. S., Celentano, E., Cozza, T. M., Hill, S., MacEachern, M., Marty, N., & Schnedecker, J. (1992). The male role: An investigation of contemporary norms. *Journal of Mental Health Counseling, 14,* 325–337.

Levant, R. F., & Kopecky, G. (1995). *Masculinity reconstructed.* New York: Dutton.

Mahalik, J. R. (2000). Men's gender role conflict in men as a predictor of self-rating of behavior on the Interpersonal Circle. *Journal of Social and Clinical Psychology, 19,* 276–292.

Mosher, D. L., & Sirkin, M. (1984). Measuring a macho personality constellation. *Journal of Research in Personality, 18,* 150–163.

O'Neil, J. M. (1981a). Male sex-role conflicts, sexism, and masculinity: Psychological implications for men, women, and the counseling psychologist. *Counseling Psychologist, 9,* 61–81.

O'Neil, J. M. (1981b). Patterns of gender role conflict and strain: Sexism and fear of femininity in men's lives. *Personnel and Guidance Journal, 60,* 203–210.

O'Neil, J. M. (1982). Gender role conflict and strain in men's lives: Implications for psychiatrists, psychologists, and other human service providers. In K. Solomon & N. B. Levy (Eds.), *Men in transition: Changing male roles, theory, and therapy* (pp. 5–44). New York: Plenum.

O'Neil, J. M. (1990). Assessing men's gender role conflict. In D. Moore & F. Leafgren (Eds.), *Problem solving strategies and interventions for men in conflict* (pp. 23–38). Alexandria, VA: American Counseling Association.

O'Neil, J. M., Helms, B., Gable, R., David, L., & Wrightsman, L. (1986). Gender Role Conflict Scale: College men's fear of femininity. *Sex Roles, 14,* 335–350.

Pleck, J. H. (1981). *The myth of masculinity.* Cambridge, MA: MIT Press.

Pleck, J. H. (1985). *Working wives, working husbands.* Beverly Hills, CA: Sage.

Pleck, J. H. (1995). The gender role strain paradigm: An update. In R. F. Levant & W. S. Pollack (Eds.), *The new psychology of men* (pp. 11–32). New York: Basic Books.

Pollack, W. S. (1990). Men's development and psychotherapy: A psychoanalytic perspective. *Psychotherapy, 27,* 316–321.

Pollack, W. S. (1995). No man is an island: Toward a new psychoanalytic psychology of men. In R. F. Levant & W. S. Pollack (Eds.), *The new psychology of men* (pp. 33–67). New York: Basic Books.

Portello, J. Y., & Long, B. C. (1994). Gender role orientation, ethical and interpersonal conflicts, and conflict handling styles of female managers. *Sex Roles, 31*, 683–701.

Sayers, S. L., Baucom, D. H., & Tierney, A. M. (1993). Sex roles, interpersonal control, and depression. *Journal of Research in Personality, 27*, 377–395.

Snarey, J., & Pleck, J. H. (1993). Midlife consequences of paternal generativity for fathers themselves. In J. Snarey (Ed.), *How fathers care for the next generation* (pp. 84–118). Cambridge, MA: Harvard University Press.

Spence, J. T., Helmreich, R. L., & Holahan, C. T. (1979). Negative and positive components of psychological masculinity and femininity and their relationships to self-reports of neurotic and acting out behaviors. *Journal of Personality and Social Psychology, 37*, 1673–1682.

Tracey, T.J.G., & Schneider, P. L. (1995). An evaluation of the circular structure of the Checklist of Interpersonal Transactions and the Checklist of Psychotherapy Transactions. *Journal of Counseling Psychology, 42*, 496–507.

Widom, C. S. (1984). *Sex roles and psychopathology.* New York: Plenum.

Wiggins, J. S. (1982). Circumplex models of interpersonal behavior in clinical psychology. In P. C. Kendall & J. K. Butcher (Eds.), *Handbook of research methods in clinical psychology* (pp. 183–221). New York: Wiley.

Wiggins, J. S., & Holzmuller, A. (1978). Psychological androgyny and interpersonal behavior. *Journal of Consulting and Clinical Psychology, 46*, 40–52.

Wiggins, J. S., & Holzmuller, A. (1981). Further evidence on androgyny and interpersonal flexibility. *Journal of Research in Personality, 15*, 67–80.

CHAPTER SIXTEEN

Integrative Therapy for Men

Glenn E. Good
Laurie B. Mintz

Contemporary psychotherapists overwhelmingly endorse an integrative-eclectic theoretical orientation. Indeed, the integrative-eclectic orientation is the most widely endorsed therapeutic orientation by all types of U.S. psychotherapists, including psychologists, psychiatrists, counselors, and social workers (Prochaska & Norcross, 1999). The popularity of the integrative-eclectic approach is likely due to a number of factors, including pressure from managed care companies for more time-efficient interventions and the availability of empirically supported integrative approaches (see Beitman & Yue, 1999). The popularity of the integrative-eclectic approach signals that therapists are increasingly responding to the unique needs of their clients rather than to their allegiance to a particular theoretical orientation. Integrative-eclectic therapists view theories and techniques as tools to draw from rather than as "banners to ride under" (Shoben, 1962, p. 621), enabling them to better match interventions to clients' needs.

Although psychotherapy integration is growing rapidly, this is the first attempt to incorporate the theory and research associated with the new psychology of men into an integrative psychotherapy framework. We selected the integrative framework proposed by Beitman and Yue (1999) because it is highly compatible with the clinical and research literature on men's issues. In this chapter we provide an overview of how therapists may approach their work with male clients from this integrative perspective. More specifically, we discuss in this chapter the following aspects of this integrative approach to therapy with men:

- Engagement: forming effective, collaborative working alliances with men

- Recognizing men's maladaptive patterns

- Incorporating strategies to facilitate change

- Determining readiness to change and addressing resistance

- Addressing transference and countertransference issues

- Termination: supporting continued growth and maintenance of progress

It is our hope that this chapter will improve the ability of gender-aware therapists to optimally address the concerns of their male clients (Good, Gilbert, & Scher, 1990).

ENGAGEMENT: FORMING EFFECTIVE, COLLABORATIVE WORKING ALLIANCES WITH MEN

Few researchers or clinicians would disagree that the therapy relationship is the building block on which successful therapy rests. Indeed, research suggests that the strength of the therapeutic "working alliance" is highly correlated with therapeutic outcomes (Gelso & Carter, 1985; Horvath & Greenberg, 1989; Moras & Strupp, 1982). Indeed, meta-analytic studies indicate that at least 7 percent of variance in therapeutic outcome across various treatments is associated with the working alliance (Wampold, 2000). Although many conceptions of the working alliance have been developed, Bordin's (1979) concept of the working alliance continues to receive wide acceptance by researchers and practitioners. Bordin's conceptualization emphasizes collaboration between the therapist and client and defines three components: goals, tasks, and bonds.

Goals

Goals (or outcomes) are the objectives of the therapeutic interventions. In other words, goals might be thought of as "what" we are going to work on in therapy. Some men come to their first scheduled session with a clear idea of "what they want to fix"; others, perhaps those prodded into therapy by a partner, have a harder time knowing what they want to change. The first step of therapy is for the client and counselor to mutually agree on goals for treatment. This step is important because strong working alliances are characterized by therapist and client mutually endorsing and valuing shared goals of their work together. Paul serves as an illustration of the importance of mutually agreed on goals.

Paul came to therapy after his wife (Rose) had been seen for two sessions. Although Rose's initial goal for therapy was to decide whether she wanted to divorce her husband or learn to live with an unhappy situation, the therapist suggested a possible third goal of improving the marriage. Rose decided that improving the marriage was indeed her goal, and to this end she brought Paul to therapy. Paul initially stated that he was there because his wife asked him to be. However, after meeting twice with the therapist alone, Paul and the therapist were in agreement concerning Paul's goals for therapy: to be happier in his marriage—specifically, to feel closer to his wife and to resume the sexual relations that had ended over a year ago.

Tasks

Tasks refer to in-therapy behaviors and cognitions that form the substance of the therapy process. Tasks are the "what" or "how" (tools) the therapist and client are using together to reach the client's goals. When therapy is going well, both the therapist and the client believe that the "how" of therapy is relevant and useful, and both are fully engaged in the work of therapy.

In Paul's case (described previously) tasks associated with reaching his goal included both tasks of individual work and tasks of couple work. Individual tasks included examining his childhood models of relationships and how they were influencing his current behaviors, learning to identify his feelings through the use of a feeling list and journal, and learning to communicate his feelings. Couple tasks included additional communication skills training, joint bibliotherapy (that is, reading a book on relationship skills together), and engaging in both in-session and out-of-session couple exercises such as those in *Getting the Love You Want* (Hendrix, 1988).

Bonds

Bonds consist of the connection and attachment felt by both the client and the therapist; effective bonds include acceptance, mutual trust, and confidence (Beitman & Yue, 1999; Horvath & Greenberg, 1989). Bonds are how the client and therapist are going to relate and feel toward each other—the meaning of their relationship. From our perception, the bonds component is often the most delicate issue therapists must address when seeking to establish effective working alliances with male clients.

Men have good reason to be ambivalent about letting their therapist into their inner world and about allowing their therapist to become emotionally important to them. Men's past experiences have typically taught them that they should seek to be self-sufficient in important aspects of their lives and immune from interpersonal vulnerability (that is, counterdependent or defensively autonomous; Good & Mintz, 1990; see Chapter Twenty-four of this handbook). Men's ambivalence about bonding is depicted in Chapter Twenty-four, in which a male client describes his ambivalence about allowing the therapist to metaphorically "get into his Jeep with him" (that is, allowing his therapist to join him in his life journey). (See also Chapters Thirty-three and Thirty-four for additional elaboration about men's issues concerning bonding.) In our opinion, it is typically helpful for therapists to normalize the cultural and familial socialization process that taught the male client to strive for invulnerability. It is also helpful for therapists to reflect the issues and feelings their clients are reporting, to comment on the legitimacy of their clients' concerns, to acknowledge the strength shown by seeking to resolve the issues, and to find ways to make interpersonal contact with them.

In Paul's case, the therapist talked with him about how many men raised in his era (the 1950s) had learned to not show their feelings to others. The therapist reflected Paul's fear and awkwardness at learning a new skill at age fifty, as well as his embarrassment the first time he cried in session. The therapist also made meaningful contact with Paul by sharing genuine reactions with him. The therapist told Paul of being touched by his struggles and of feeling closer to him when he shared his feelings. The therapist also expressed the belief that Paul was exhibiting great strength to embark on this new learning and openness to his feelings and his relationship.

Paul's case illustrates something else we have noticed in our work with men: for some men, the bond is itself a task. In other words, whereas Bordin's (1979) model delineates goals, tasks, and bonds, for some male clients, the task of allowing another person to form a bond with them is indeed the most challenging and ultimately therapeutic task of therapy. This process of allowing another person (their therapist) to accompany them as copilot on such an intimate segment of their life journey is transformative for many male clients in and of itself. Indeed, many men have been so used to trying to do it all on their own—to be "big boys" who need (and allow) no one to know their inner world—that they become joyful and giddy about not being alone in the world anymore. They also may begin sharing intimate details of their lives and interactions in spontaneous and often unconventional ways. For example, one therapist has had several male clients spontaneously forward him copies of lengthy and intimate e-mail exchanges between them and their lovers or close friends. These clients sent their therapist such uncensored interpersonal exchanges because the clients see these exchanges as illustrative of what they are working on in therapy—struggling to understand their primary relationships and themselves. Clearly, the clients' sharing of such information and exchanges illustrates trust and openness. These men are willing to share both their own perceptions and the unfiltered reactions of others in their lives to the issues that they are dealing with. These e-mails seem to be a way for the male clients to say, "We have a deep bond and I am seeking your help by sharing this with you."

Of course, things do not always "click" well between clients and their therapists. Sometimes an initially poor working alliance can be improved, and studies of poor working alliances point to several concrete suggestions for improvement. Specifically, studies report that working alliances that started off poorly were improved by the therapist exhibiting a positive attitude; being more challenging; being more here-and-now oriented; addressing clients' defenses, guilt, and problematic feelings in relation to the therapist; and linking the problematic feelings with the therapist to clients' defenses (see Forman & Marmar, 1985; Kivlighan, 1990; Kivlighan & Schmitz, 1992). Similarly, clients who are highly reactant (rebel against direction from others) may be best engaged through empathic understanding, therapist self-revelation, and gentle questioning, whereas less reactant clients may be more directly engaged by direct guidance, questioning, and possibly confrontation (see Beitman & Yue, 1999).

RECOGNIZING MEN'S MALADAPTIVE PATTERNS

Many times when a client presents for one or two issues, as therapy progresses, the therapist and client are able to connect these issues to an overall rather fixed or well-formed pattern of reacting or acting in the world. In the integrative therapy model we are presenting and adapting for male clients, pattern recognition and subsequent change are key elements of therapy (Beitman & Yue, 1999).

Therapists should be on the lookout for patterns in their male clients, because discovering these patterns may be a prerequisite for helping people change. The goal is to identify patterns of thoughts, feelings, and behaviors that are within the client's ability to influence and that if changed lead toward a desirable outcome (Beitman, 1987). Sometimes patterns are clear to clients and therapists, and little guesswork and inductive reasoning are needed. Most other times, therapists need to use the iterative process of inductive reasoning to help clients discern patterns. In this process, therapists notice specific pieces of perhaps seemingly unrelated information and then generalize from these specific bits of information to patterns that persist across situations.

Gender-aware therapists are also able to place these patterns in a broader context. For example, using their knowledge of the masculine role socialization process, such therapists may notice a pattern of emotional constriction that the client exhibits regardless of the place, person, or event he is describing. Gender-aware therapists would help the client recognize this pattern and to place it within its appropriate societal or familial learning context. Therapy can then focus on altering this maladaptive, learned pattern. For example, just as many women with mild depression benefited from assertiveness training in the 1970s, many men benefit greatly from a little "emotional competence training" in the twenty-first century. It is not necessary for men who are a bit out of touch with their emotional lives to complete a graduate degree in men's studies that enables them to place their problems within the most accurate context. Instead many men benefit from support and encouragement for affective awareness and expression as just one aspect of their therapeutic experience.

Once the client agrees that the pattern should change, one possible next step is to help him explore the reasons he has not changed it thus far. This process may clarify his typical coping and problem-solving strategies, the barriers to the changes he is seeking, and the optimal choice of change strategies discussed later in this chapter.

We are certainly not the first authors to recommend that therapists look for and help clients to change maladaptive patterns. Dysfunctional patterns have been described at differing degrees of detail, from very general to very specific (Beitman & Yue, 1999). The most general level includes descriptions of "personality traits" and provides a general picture of clients (for example, aggressive, impulsive, avoidant, subassertive, or withdrawn). Although the most general level descriptions of patterns are beyond the influence of a particular theoretical orientation, a second level of specificity encompasses "school-based patterns." These conceptions of dysfunctional patterns are based in the various therapeutic orientations. Examples include lack of healthy ego functioning (ego psychology), poor object relations (object relations), conditions of worth (person-centered therapy), dysfunctional beliefs (cognitive therapy), and skills deficits (behavior therapy). These school-based dysfunctional patterns are readily applied to men's psychological issues and concerns. In Chapter Twenty-four of this handbook, Pollack describes shame and defensive autonomy resulting from traumatic disruption of the early holding environment—clearly a maladaptive pattern derived from psychodynamic therapy. Likewise, Mahalik (in Chapters Twenty-five and Twenty-six) notes men's gender-related cognitive distortions (cognitive therapy) and their rigid enactments of gender roles (interpersonal therapy). In short, in identifying maladaptive patterns of male clients, it may be helpful for therapists to use notions derived from schools of therapy.

The third and most specific level is client-relevant dysfunctional patterns. These are specific descriptive patterns of individuals that can be observed both clinically and in daily life and that provide sufficient detail to point the way toward change. These patterns, or parts of them, usually appear in therapists' reflections and restatements of what their clients say. Once a client-relevant maladaptive pattern is identified and understood, we find that it is often useful to give it a name; this name helps both the client and the therapist have a powerful way of speaking about the pattern. The case of William illustrates the concept of pattern recognition and naming.

William, a successful professional in his midforties, entered therapy at the recommendation of his employer's employee assistance program. He was becoming increasingly distraught and distracted. He was married for a second time, had children, and was in the midst of an increasingly complicated extramarital affair. In the course of therapy, he described wanting others to like him—and generally being quite successful at fulfilling this desire over the course of his life. However, in his marriages, his pattern of concealing his wants and resentments from his spouse was causing him repeated problems. Because of his desire to be approved of—and concomitant desire to not risk rejection or shame by making his wants and feelings known in his primary relationship—William would seek approval and affection from women who accepted him less conditionally than his spouse could. Over the course of therapy, William and his therapist identified this pattern and began referring to it as his "pleasing-others facade."

In William's case, what was named as his pleasing-others facade was his individual, client-specific pattern. This specific pattern can also be analyzed at the two other more global levels of patterns. At the most general level, this pattern can be described as a criticism-avoidant personality style. Similarly, at the school-based level, both interpersonal and skills deficits can be seen (that is, his difficulty expressing his needs and desires). All of the issues William faced can also be tied back to the broader social environment that teaches men to be strong and to not express vulnerability to others (that is, his masculinity and shame-based reluctance to directly express his wants, needs, anger, and hurt).

The ability of therapists to recognize dysfunctional patterns and to name them is important to therapy with men; effective gender-aware therapists will be able to discern and understand patterns at several levels of specificity and to tie them to the broader social environment.

INCORPORATING STRATEGIES TO FACILITATE CHANGE

After trust is established and the therapist and client have identified maladaptive patterns (that is, what needs to be changed), therapy can focus on change. Change involves active collaboration between the therapist and the client to do what is in the client's best interest. Change may mean stopping, decreasing, initiating, modifying, altering, or increasing specific feelings, thoughts, behaviors, and interaction patterns.

It is far beyond the scope of this chapter to present details concerning all the available strategies to help clients change. Such specific change strategies can be found in writings on specific schools of therapy, and strategies drawn from specific schools are also summarized and discussed by integrative therapists such as Beitman and Yue (1999). Hence, rather than present specific techniques (such as the empty chair technique or the thought-stopping technique), in this section we suggest and illustrate some overarching organizational schemata that therapists can use to facilitate change. First, we provide a five-focus way of viewing the areas that clients may need to change. Second, we present a three-step way of thinking of the process of changing dysfunctional patterns. Third, we suggest the use of empirically supported treatments. Fourth, we present the capitalization hypothesis as a guiding tool for choosing specific change techniques. Finally, we present psychoeducation as useful in assisting men in the change process.

Five Interacting Foci of Change

Change strategies may be organized by their area of primary focus: emotions, cognitions, behaviors, interpersonal relationships, and systems (ECBIS) (Beitman & Yue, 1999). Although there is of course some overlap across the five areas, we nevertheless find it useful to examine each area separately.

1. Emotions. Strategies focused on emotions typically aim to encourage clients to attend to and intensify their emotional experience. The expression of emotions can be healing in and of itself. In addition, the expression and intensification of emotions in therapy can also lead to a discovery, understanding, and changing of maladaptive emotional schemata and ways of reacting. We describe such an emotion-based intervention for a client named Jim.

Jim came to couples therapy at his wife, Mary's, insistence because of their escalating marital and sexual issues. Jim was a powerfully built former marine currently employed as a blue-collar professional. He was prone to erupting in anger. For example, he had recently thrown a chair through a window at a work party. At one point in the session, Jim's wife described her distaste at his repeated descriptions of a scene in an X-rated video he had viewed. When he heard this, Jim immediately became enraged: his jaw clenched, his faced turned red, he pointed his finger in his wife's face, and through gritted teeth yelled, "I told you not to embarrass me!" He then moved forward in his chair—preparing to walk out of the session and out of his marriage.

At this point, the therapist told Jim that despite being very upset it would be best if he would hang in there and stay both in the room and with the feelings. The therapist pointed out that Jim was at an important crossroads—and that he could stay and work through the feeling and likely improve his marriage or he could leave the room and hence avoid the emotion temporarily yet likely make things worse in his life and in his marriage. Jim chose to stay, and the therapist reinforced this behavior, complimenting the courage and strength it took to stay. The therapist then shared her perception of his emotions and her own emotional reaction. She told Jim that he seemed extremely angry and that when he reacted in that way she felt afraid of him and wondered if his wife felt the same. Mary admitted to feeling afraid, despite the fact that Jim had never hit her and she trusted that he never would. The therapist stayed with the emotion, exploring it with Jim until he was able to realize and admit that behind his anger was extreme embarrassment and humiliation. He was afraid of what the therapist would think of his use of pornography and wondered if he was normal. He felt vulnerable. As Jim got in touch with his vulnerability, he was able to recognize more deeply a pattern that had previously been identified in therapy: when he felt embarrassed, humiliated, or vulnerable, he tended to erupt in anger (an anger that further alienated those who cared about him). Jim was able to develop a plan in which he would try to honor his embarrassment and vulnerability and share these feelings with his wife rather than erupt in anger. By the end of the session, with tears in his eyes, he was able to reach over, hug his wife, and apologize for scaring her. He was able to more deeply understand his wife's views and reactions to pornography, and they reached a marital agreement about its use. In short, the therapist focused on Jim's feeling of rage, reacted to his expression of rage, and was thus able to help Jim change a maladaptive way of dealing with humiliation.

2. Cognitions. Change strategies focused on cognitions seek to identify both maladaptive, often automatic thoughts and the broader dysfunctional cognitive schemata in which these thoughts are often embedded. In other words, cognitive interventions seek to modify both dysfunctional thoughts and deeper schemata (Beck, 1995). Ellis and Dryden's (1987) ABC technique is an example of this technique. *A* is the activating event, *B* is the beliefs (cognitions), and *C* is consequence (subsequent feeling or behavior). The faulty cognition (B) is identified and modified, hence resulting in a change in C. Cognitive interventions have been found to be particularly effective in treating depression (see Chapters One and Ten).

3. Behaviors. Behavioral change strategies typically seek to develop and reinforce more adaptive behaviors, desensitize phobic avoidance, and improve contingency management. Behavioral change strategies are focused on changing behaviors and often include modeling, practicing, and reinforcing desired behaviors. Assertion training, desensitization, relaxation training, and other psychoeducational interventions often fall into this category. The case of William described earlier illustrates cognitive and behavioral change strategies.

After naming his pleasing-others facade William quickly identified his dysfunctional thoughts about "needing others' approval" and noted that he was "an approval addict." With a bit of in-session rehearsal of more adaptive self-talk (such as "Linda's getting upset does not mean that our marriage is over nor that I must agree with her"), William was able to put his more adaptive thoughts to use. During a disagreement with Linda the subsequent week, he consciously used his new thoughts, stayed in touch with his feelings and views, shared them with Linda without catastrophizing, and was able to successfully resolve their conflict much more effectively than he had ever been able to in the past.

4. Interpersonal relationships. Interpersonal and psychodynamic change strategies focus on the identification and alteration of maladaptive interpersonal schemata and responses. Examples of techniques in this area include understanding deep-rooted patterns (psychodynamic) and identifying the client's interpersonal patterns within the therapeutic relationship and experiencing corrective emotional experiences in session (interpersonal). An example of psychodynamic and interpersonal change strategies in action is the case of Bob.

Bob came to therapy for grief issues concerning his father's death and what was initially unexplained anger at his brother. In working with the grief and anger, Bob was able to see that his anger stemmed from his having been his father's sole caretaker while his brother did nothing to help. Further igniting his anger was that his brother had asked Bob for some of their father's possessions, including ones that held great sentimental value for Bob. Bob wanted these possessions but nevertheless relinquished them to his brother. The therapist and Bob identified a deeper schema, developed through childhood experiences. Bob consistently gave selflessly to others, ignoring his own needs, and then became angry at these others for their selfishness—yet he never gave others the chance to give to him, because he was reluctant to ask for anything. Through the process of discovering this way of interacting, understanding its childhood roots, and trying new ways of interacting, Bob was able to change his way of relating to others.

Another example of an interpersonal change strategy in action is William, the client mentioned earlier whose maladaptive pattern was named his pleasing-others facade.

At one point in therapy, William described having "gone along" (agreed) with something Linda had suggested without sharing his true reaction with her. A bit later in the same session—but on a different topic—he inquired about the therapist's reaction to what he had been discussing. The therapist shared his reluctance to express his reaction out of concern that William would "go along" with it and not share his true reaction with the therapist either. William burst out with a deep laughter and recognized how his pattern of attempting to please others robbed both him and others of honest communication and the opportunity for authentic interpersonal encounters with others.

5. Systems. Systems approaches typically seek to identify factors that maintain undesirable homeostatic patterns, determine the most available and effective entry points for change, and then induce a change deemed most likely to cascade the system into a more desired homeostasis. Examples of techniques with this focus include genograms, enactments, paradox, task setting, and changing enmeshed boundaries.

Changing Patterns

A maladaptive pattern can be composed of any of the five foci described earlier, either singly or in combination. As an example, a maladaptive pattern may be emotional or cognitive or interpersonal; more commonly, it will have aspects of all of these. Although the specific intervention may be tailored to the problematic area (for example, cognitions or interpersonal), the actual process of changing the overall pattern can be viewed as having three components.

1. Relinquishing dysfunctional patterns is the first component. Examples of this component of change could include less substance abuse, less externalizing of distress, less restriction of emotions, less interpersonal isolation, less workaholic behavior, or fewer passive responses to one's spouse.

2. Developing more functional patterns and increasing their duration, intensity, or frequency is the second component. Examples of this component include greater comfort in experiencing and expressing a full range of emotions, greater skills for negotiating and resolving interpersonal conflicts, greater use of health-enhancing coping strategies such as exercise and social support, greater involvement with one's children, greater disclosure with male friends, and greater recognition and countering of dysfunctional thought patterns.

3. Maintaining new functional patterns is the final component of the change process. Change in psychological issues rarely progresses in a straightforward manner. Instead, clients often make a few steps forward and then may backslide a bit. This component involves helping clients incorporate, deepen, and generalize the changes they desire so that obstacles and minor setbacks do not result in relapse. Effective maintenance often involves therapists being able to accurately identify and anticipate the issues that clients are likely to experience in the future. Therapists can help their clients anticipate and prepare for the likely problematic scenarios in advance. Doing so will ensure that clients are less likely to be caught unaware ("blindsided") by situations that might otherwise have resulted in them resorting to their previous dysfunctional patterns.

One common situation that illustrates the importance of the maintenance stage involves male clients becoming more emotionally competent as an aspect of their therapeutic work. Therapists can help clients anticipate that some people in their lives will react negatively to their newfound emotional awareness and expressiveness. (This reaction results in part because societal views about appropriate masculine behavior are in transition—expectations for both the traditional "strong, silent type" and the "emotionally available type" are present.) Therapists may warn clients that some individuals in their lives may seek to restore them to their former and more familiar emotionally restricted style (that is, homeostasis). Even wives who have wanted their husbands to become more emotionally expressive for decades may have some misgivings when their husbands finally become expressive. In one case, a wife initiated therapy because she wanted her husband to be more emotionally expressive and later admitted that she had wanted more expression of affection and love but had not anticipated that this additional expressiveness would also include "unpleasant" feelings such as doubt, anger, fear, and insecurity. The more that men can anticipate and prepare for some of these reactions to the changes they are making, the more likely that the changes can become permanent. The importance of this cannot be underestimated; helping men to maintain new functional patterns, even when faced with challenges, is a critical component of effective therapy with men.

Empirically Supported Interventions

As described in Chapter One, knowledge of empirically supported interventions for specific problems (such as depression, anxiety, and sexual dysfunction) allows integrative therapists to select interventions that have the greatest chance of leading to successful outcome for their clients' concerns (Nathan & Gorman, 1998). We also believe that gender-aware therapists' incorporation of clients' specific masculinity-related issues into the empirically supported interventions will improve the effectiveness of such interventions for male clients. Chapters Twenty-five and Twenty-six, by Mahalik, provide excellent examples of ways in which empirically supported interventions and knowledge of the psychology of men can be integrated for improved efficacy.

Capitalization Hypothesis

The capitalization hypothesis is the finding that interventions are typically more effective if they capitalize on clients' preexisting strengths rather than attempting to directly ameliorate clients' deficits (Cronbach & Snow, 1977). In other words, the capitalization hypothesis suggests that therapists should use men's effective resources and coping strategies to address their concerns rather than seeking to directly compensate for men's weaknesses. For example, when working with a male client with depression, the therapist may contemplate whether to begin with an interpersonal or a cognitive-behavioral intervention, both of which have empirical support for their effectiveness in treating depression. The capitalization hypothesis suggests that male clients with depression who have more solid cognitive schemata would respond better to cognitive-behavioral therapy because it capitalizes on their existing strengths. Likewise, a male client with depression who has a good social support would likely respond favorably to interpersonal therapy (Sotsky et al., 1991).

Psychoeducation

Research has identified many ways in which individual men's beliefs about the appropriate thoughts, feelings, and behaviors for men in general are linked to the problems they experience (Eisler, 1995; Good et al., 1995; Good, Robertson, Fitzgerald, Stevens, & Bartels, 1996; Good, Wallace, & Borst, 1994; O'Neil, Good, & Holmes, 1995; see also Chapter One of this handbook). Although the readers of this handbook are likely aware of this relation, male clients are often far less so. Hence, we have found that it is often helpful to supplement traditional psychotherapy with psychoeducational interventions. Fortunately, now that the new psychology of men and masculinity is catching the public's interest, there are many resources with which to supplement men's work in therapy. Popular books, movies, community lectures, and magazine and newspaper articles can all be used to help men recognize and normalize their issues and struggles. Similarly, we have also found it helpful to prepare special psychoeducational handouts on both masculinity-related issues and the process of therapy in general. For example, we have developed handouts that describe the value of emotions, reasons people learn to suppress emotions, skills associated with emotional competence, and stages of change. These personalized handouts can accompany traditional out-of-session activities, such as journals, feeling sheets, and the cognitive-behavioral therapy triple-column activity. We have found that supplying educative interventions increases the rate at which men change in therapy. Such a focus on education and information may be especially useful for male clients in that it is in keeping with the capitalization hypothesis; it plays into the stereotypical male strength of rationally examining information.

DETERMINING READINESS TO CHANGE
AND ADDRESSING RESISTANCE

Resistance. The term alone raises the frustration and stress level of many therapists. Missed sessions, unpaid bills, crossed arms, silence, anger, "yes, but," and "forgotten" assignments are but a few of the ways in which clients manifest resistance. Why would male clients possibly resist the helpful and insightful efforts of their talented and well-intentioned therapists?

One potential explanation is that these clients are not yet ready to change. This lack of readiness to change can sometimes be seen in the early stages of therapy. Alternatively, it can come after a solid relationship has been formed and the therapist and client bump up against some difficult or scary material in their work. For the former type of resistance (which we call stage-related resistance), Prochaska and DiClemente's (1982) model is informative. For the latter type (which we call issue-related resistance) we find principles from Gestalt therapy quite useful.

Stage-Related Resistance

The stages of change model of Prochaska and DiClemente (1982) is useful to consider when dealing with resistant clients, especially early in therapy. This model outlines five states of change: precontemplative, contemplative, preparation, action, and maintenance. Although it is beyond the scope of this chapter to explore every implication of this model to the treatment of men and their issues, it is important to note that appropriate interventions vary widely according to a client's readiness to change.

Most therapists are comfortable treating motivated clients (that is, clients in the action and maintenance stages). However, male clients in the precontemplative and contemplative stages (for example, a man who is court mandated for treatment after repeatedly abusing alcohol and battering his wife) are typically viewed as far less pleasant. Such clients do not perceive a problem and are likely only in treatment because of pressure from others. The primary task of the therapist for clients in the precontemplative and contemplative stages of change is to help clients recognize and acknowledge the problem and to increase their awareness of the negative aspects of the problem.

Motivational interviewing has been found to be effective in eliciting the need for change from the client (J. Miller, 1998). This approach allows therapists to avoid the classic dysfunctional confrontation between therapists and unmotivated clients, in which therapists attempt to persuade clients of their need for change. By using motivational interviewing, the therapist maintains a warm and empathic stance that permits clients to explore ambivalent feelings about changing. Clients' resistance is channeled into open exploration, with the aim of developing a "motivational discrepancy" between clients' present behaviors (real self) and their desired goals (more ideal self). Research indicates that this discrepancy provides motivation that triggers subsequent change (W. R. Miller & Rollnick, 1991). Hence, with motivational interviewing, therapists reinforce the client-generated reasons for concern and for change and use resistance as something to explore rather than as something to fight against.

Issue-Related Resistance

At times, clients who at one point seemed to be quite motivated for change begin to resist that change. Male clients' resistance represents an excellent opportunity (note the reframe) for gender-aware therapists to step back and reflect on male clients' experience. For some reason, they are experiencing ambivalence or internal conflict about changing. The task of therapists is to identify the source or sources of the tension. Clients may fear loss of personal control. They may feel that they need to change (afraid) or that they are unable to change (helpless). Indeed, they may also be aware of some potential negative consequences of changing (such as greater expectations from others, with subsequent loss of personal power and freedoms). A colleague of ours (Rebecca V. DeGraaf) describes numerous strategies for dealing with resistance that she has drawn from Gestalt principles, including honoring the resistance, "dancing" with the resistance, moving around the resistance, and going with the resistance.

1. Honoring resistance. Acknowledging with the client that resistance exists is one way of honoring resistance. This act of communication strengthens the relationship by acknowledging the reality of this aspect of the therapeutic relationship. Acknowledging resistance might be as simple as saying, "I am aware that you did not do the homework that we agreed on last session. Maybe you are trying to tell me something?"

Describing resistance is another way of honoring resistance. Describing resistance seeks to have the client become more aware of his internal experiences. If the therapist offered some comment to which the client replied "yes, but . . ." the therapist may say, "Let's replay this interaction, and you pay particular attention to your internal world." The therapist then gives his or her same spiel again but pauses at the point that the client said "yes, but." The client is then asked, "What are you aware of internally?" "Do you feel any tension?" or "What stands out for you?" These awareness exercises based in Gestalt interventions may help bring internal tensions into greater awareness.

2. Dancing with resistance. Often male clients are "stuck." They want to change on the one hand, and they are not able to change on the other. Splitting ("I'm so torn I can't decide"), ambivalence or polarities ("The two parts of me want different things"), and unfinished business ("I'm mad at my [deceased] father for abandoning me when I was a child") are forms of resistance that lend themselves to exploration via "split work." The client is encouraged to explore the polarities or unfinished business in greater depth (for example, via the Gestalt empty chair technique).

3. Moving around the resistance. At times, male clients have had such emotionally traumatic experiences, especially those that occurred early in their lives, that they have difficulty accessing the core emotional schemata underlying their fears. Their fixed core beliefs (for example, "If I let anyone get close to me I will hurt again") are often fused with painful feelings such as abandonment, terror, and vulnerability. Because even accessing the belief touches on the concomitant unprocessed raw feelings, it is understandable that men would avoid addressing the core emotional schemata. In such cases, healing can frequently be accomplished via the use of healing metaphors or stories that have a message parallel to that with which the client is wrestling. Metaphors and stories allow clients to take in the message in a less threatening way. Sometimes the intervention offers a new way of viewing the issue, a perspective that is a bit more objective, or a different emotional attachment. In this way, it is sometimes possible to "slide around" the point at which clients are otherwise stuck. As they progress further in other areas, clients may come back to this particular issue to seek further resolution at a later time.

4. Going with the resistance. Sometimes male clients may be so deeply stuck that change seems impossible. When more collaborative approaches are ineffective, it is sometimes necessary to "go with the resistance." Going with the resistance typically involves paradoxical interventions such as prescribing clients' symptoms. Prescribing the symptoms means instructing the client to do exactly what he is already doing or even to increase the undesired behavior. The usual outcome of this behavior is that clients realize that they do have control of their behavior. For example, after repeated (unsuccessful) collaborative attempts to alter Jim's severe depression associated with overwhelming grief about the loss of a loved one who had died a year earlier, the suggestion that he should seek to feel the grief more intensely during the coming week successfully broke his ruminative cycle.

Reframing the resistance is another way to shift the meaning of clients' behavior. Reframing is useful for both issue-related resistance and for clients who are in a stage of lack of readiness to change (that is, stage-related resistance). The case of James illustrates reframing the resistance.

James, a bright but troubled male adolescent, was having multiple problems. He had dropped out of high school, was socially isolated, was abusing alcohol and drugs, and was not maintaining steady employment. He was in therapy at his mother's strong recommendation. (Family therapy was not an option because of other family issues.) Although he always arrived early for his appointments (dressed in black, with body-piercing jewelry displayed), he tended to be surly and showed little effort to become less depressed or isolated. Indeed, when shown a cartoon-style diagram of the stages of change, he indicated that he was between "precontemplative" and "contemplative." Not surprisingly, efforts to facilitate change using more straightforward collaborative approaches yielded little progress. However, when the therapist reframed James's problematic behaviors as reflecting his desire to anger his parents and wondered aloud if there might be other ways that he could let them know that he was angry with them without hurting himself, James smiled reflexively and got more interested in the therapeutic process.

ADDRESSING TRANSFERENCE
AND COUNTERTRANSFERENCE ISSUES

Therapists (and therapeutic orientations) differ in the degree of importance accorded to transference and countertransference.

Transference

In essence, transference refers to clients' feelings, beliefs, wishes, and intentions from other relationships that they "transfer" onto their therapists. In the case of positive transference, these feelings are positive in nature (for example, "You are the most loving, caring, understanding, attractive, best therapist ever"). In the case of negative transference, the feelings are negative (for example, "You are the most rigid, mean, unhelpful, selfish, worst therapist ever"). Although therapists are more likely to recognize the latter, it is helpful that both types of reactions be examined to determine the extent to which they contain transference material and the extent to which they may be related to clients' goals in therapy.

Countertransference

Countertransference refers to all the feelings and reactions that therapists experience toward their clients. Sometimes therapists' feelings and reactions stem from client-originated issues (that is, "objective" countertransference: most people have this reaction to the client). At other times, countertransference arises from therapists' issues ("subjective" countertransference). For example, if a therapist's male client, his issues, or his way of being reminds the therapist of his or her father, friend, relative, bully, enemy, or any other person with whom the therapist has significant issues, countertransference would likely arise. Recognizing this type of countertransference is particularly important for effective therapy and is one of the values of engaging in self-observation, professional consultation, peer supervision, and personal therapy.

It is not unusual for both objective and subjective countertransference to occur. For example, if a male client in couples therapy suddenly turns from calm silence to seething rage, most people will typically feel tense, apprehensive, or afraid (objective countertransference). Additionally, most therapists (as people) have had their own experiences at the hands of angry males (for example, a bully, father, or friend), and thus the male client's anger may also bring up feelings that are associated with the therapist's unique situation. Depending on the particular client and his concerns, it is likely to be useful to address some aspect of the objective countertransference in therapy. Typically, the therapist's subjective countertransference should be addressed outside of the therapy session.

TERMINATION: SUPPORTING CONTINUED GROWTH
AND MAINTENANCE OF PROGRESS

Male clients are frequently uncomfortable with termination of therapy and may want to just skip this phase of integrative therapy. After all, if the "tasks are accomplished" and the "work is done," then what is there left to talk about? They might say, "I've reached my goals so this is the last session." However, therapy termination is often more complex than most men are aware. More specifically, three general foci of termination are solidifying gains and preparing for future issues, processing the ending, and leaving with good feelings about the experience.

Solidifying Gains and Preparing for Future Issues

As mentioned earlier, in the section "Incorporating Strategies to Facilitate Change," it is typically very helpful for therapists to apply their knowledge of gender roles in their clients' culture and interpersonal world to help clients anticipate and prepare for likely bumps on their future journey. Also, given that the time spent in therapy is relatively brief compared with the decades of life outside of therapy, insights and changes that occur in therapy can be fragile; their persistence after therapy ends is somewhat tenuous. Consequently, it is often helpful for termination of therapy itself to be gradual. As an example (because like all aspects of therapy, termination should be tailored to the client's needs and issues), counseling sessions can be tapered to every two weeks and then to once per month so that both the client and the therapist can determine whether change has been maintained. Another alternative is for the client to schedule a "check-in" session four to six weeks after the problems have been resolved to ensure that issues have indeed remained resolved and to troubleshoot any unanticipated issues that may arise. Finally, it is also important to educate clients that a recurrence of issues or pain at any future point does not necessarily mean a total backslide. In the context of termination of therapy, it is critical to educate clients that issues may resurface in a similar or different form and that rather than meaning therapy was a failure, this relapse may simply indicate that it is time to return to therapy for a session or two or even more. In this vein, therapy and therapists can be presented as analogous to medical checkups and family physicians, respectively; it is perfectly acceptable to return for checkups and preventive or remedial treatment as needed.

Processing the Ending

In general, termination of therapy is an opportunity to look forward, to look back, and to discuss the meaning and impact of therapy and the client-counselor relationship. Many of the chapters in this book discuss men's ambivalence about bonding with others—with allowing others to become emotionally important to them. After all, the position taken by good adherents to traditional masculinity is to need no one (that is, defensive self-sufficiency). Hence, for many men, making an honest interpersonal connection with another person is a new experience. Many men find that their therapists become very important to them. They let down their facades and become known by another. Hence, the ending of this relationship can be a time of great ambivalence and discomfort. Clients may want to jump into action to avoid feeling the sense of loss. However, we believe that effective gender-aware therapists help their clients recognize that it is healthy to embrace these feelings of loss and sadness. Healthy men allow themselves to experience a full range of emotions. The bond has been real, and the feelings associated with ending it are just as real.

Leaving with Good Feelings About the Experience

The work done with male clients is a potential template for healthier interpersonal relationships in the future. Additionally, although clients may not be finished with therapy (from therapists' perspectives) when they terminate therapy, leaving with good feelings about the therapeutic experience this time may keep the door open to return for further development in therapy at a later time.

Men enter therapy, with male and female therapists, alone or as part of a family, for a wide range of reasons and under a wide range of situations. No one technique or school of therapy will work for all men, with all therapists, and for all problems. Thus, integrative psychotherapy integration coupled with knowledge of the new psychology of men is likely to be a very effective way to approach work with male clients. To this end, we have adapted one integrative therapy framework (Beitman & Yue, 1999) for gender-aware use with male clients. In this male-oriented integrative framework, engagement is a first and primary step. Another key element is the recognition of men's maladaptive patterns. Specific change strategies are tailored to the client and his issues. Transference, countertransference, and resistance are all addressed. Finally, termination of therapy is handled in a growth-enhancing manner. We hope that this framework will serve to guide and help both therapists and the male clients they serve.

References

Beck, J. S. (1995). *Cognitive therapy: Basics and beyond.* New York: Guilford Press.

Beitman, B. D. (1987). *The structure of individual psychotherapy.* New York: Guilford Press.

Beitman, B. D., & Yue, D. (1999). *Learning psychotherapy: A time efficient, research-based, and outcome measured psychotherapy training program.* New York: Norton.

Bordin, E. S. (1979). The generalizability of the psychoanalytic concept of the working alliance. *Psychotherapy: Theory, Research, and Practice, 16,* 252–259.

Cronbach, L. J., & Snow, R. E. (1977). *Aptitudes and instructional methods.* New York: Irvington.

Eisler, R. M. (1995). The relationship between masculine gender role stress and men's health risk: The validation of the construct. In R. F. Levant & W. S. Pollack (Eds.), *A new psychology of men* (pp. 207–225). New York: Basic Books.

Ellis, A., & Dryden, W. (1987). *The practice of rational-emotive therapy.* New York: Springer.

Forman, S. A., & Marmar, C. R. (1985). Therapist actions that address initially poor therapeutic alliance in psychotherapy. *American Journal of Psychiatry, 142,* 922–926.

Gelso, C., & Carter, J. A. (1985). The relationship in counseling and psychotherapy: Components, consequences, and theoretical antecedents. *Counseling Psychologist, 13,* 155–243.

Good, G. E., Gilbert, L. A., & Scher, M. (1990). Gender aware therapy: A synthesis of feminist therapy and knowledge about gender. *Journal of Counseling and Development, 68,* 376–380.

Good, G. E., & Mintz, L. B. (1990). Depression and the male gender role: Evidence for compounded risk. *Journal of Counseling and Development, 69,* 17–21.

Good, G. E., Robertson, J. M., Fitzgerald, L. F., Stevens, M. A., & Bartels, K. M. (1996). The relation between masculine role conflict and psychological distress in male university counseling center clients. *Journal of Counseling and Development, 75,* 44–49.

Good, G. E., Robertson, J. M., O'Neil, J. M., Fitzgerald, L. F., DeBord, K. A., Stevens, M., Bartels, K. M., & Braverman, D. G. (1995). Male gender role conflict: Psychometric properties and relations to distress. *Journal of Counseling Psychology, 42,* 3–10.

Good, G. E., Wallace, D. L., & Borst, T. S. (1994). Masculinity research: A review and critique. *Applied and Preventive Psychology, 3,* 3–14.

Hendrix, H. (1988). *Getting the love you want: A guide for couples.* New York: Harper Perennial.

Horvath, A. O., & Greenberg, L. S. (1989). Development and validation of the working alliance. *Journal of Counseling Psychology, 36,* 223–233.

Kivlighan, D. K. (1990). Relationship between counselor use of intentions and clients' perception of the working alliance. *Journal of Counseling Psychology, 37,* 27–32.

Kivlighan, D. K., & Schmitz, P. J. (1992). Counselor technical activity in cases with improving working alliances and continuing-poor working alliances. *Journal of Counseling Psychology, 39,* 32–38.

Miller, J. (1998). The enemy inside: An exploration of the defensive processes of introjecting and identifying with the aggressor. *Psychodynamic Counselling, 4*(1), 55–70.

Miller, W. R., & Rollnick, S. (1991). *Motivational interviewing: Preparing people for change.* New York: Guilford Press.

Moras, K., & Strupp, H. H. (1982). Pretherapy interpersonal relations, patient's alliance, and outcome of brief therapy. *Archives of General Psychiatry, 39,* 405–409.

Nathan, P. E., & Gorman, J. M. (1998). *A guide to treatments that work.* New York: Oxford University Press.

O'Neil, J. M., Good, G. E., & Holmes, S. (1995). Fifteen years of theory and research on men's gender role conflict: New paradigms for empirical research. In R. F. Levant & W. S. Pollack (Eds.), *A new psychology of men* (pp. 164–206). New York: Basic Books.

Prochaska, J. O., & DiClemente, C. C. (1982). Transtheoretical therapy: Toward a more integrative model of change. *Psychotherapy: Theory, Research, and Practice, 19,* 276–288.

Prochaska, J. O., & Norcross, J. C. (1999). *Systems of psychotherapy: A transtheoretical analysis* (4th ed.). Pacific Grove, CA: Brooks/Cole.

Shoben, E. J. (1962). The counselor's theory as a personal trait. *Personnel and Guidance Journal, 40*(7), 617–621.

Sotsky, S. M., Glass, D. R., Shea, M. T., Pilkonis, P. A., Collins, J. F., Elkin, I., Watkins, J. T., Imber, S. D., Leber, W. R., Moyer, J., & Oliveri, M. E. (1991). Patients' predictors of response to psychotherapy and pharmacotherapy: Findings in the NIMH Treatment of Depression Collaborative Research Program. *American Journal of Psychiatry, 148,* 997–1008.

Wampold, B. E. (2000). Outcomes of individual counseling and psychotherapy: Empirical evidence addressing two fundamental questions. In S. D. Brown & R. W. Lent (Eds.), *Handbook of counseling psychology* (4th ed., pp. 711–739). New York: Wiley.

CHAPTER SEVENTEEN

Group Therapy for Men

Fredric E. Rabinowitz

Although men have been reluctant participants in all forms of psychotherapy (Vessey & Howard, 1993), they have been socialized to be active members in various types of all-male groups (Andronico, 1996). From hunting parties in early civilization to Cub Scouts, Little League, fraternities, and work in modern life, men have often found themselves in the company of each other. In these same-sex groups, they have competed as well as supported and worked with each other toward common goals such as hunting for food, winning a game, bringing success to a company, or fighting a war. Survival, competition, and winning have often defined the motives for men's actions in groups.

A significant but less emphasized by-product of the all-male group experience has been the camaraderie, support, and defense against existential isolation that men in groups have shared. Technological automation, long-distance commuting to work, the breakdown of traditional family and social structures, and the introduction of significant numbers of women into the workforce have left many men displaced from the benefits of naturally occurring men's groups, leaving them discouraged and isolated. Since the 1970s, group therapy for men has developed as a useful treatment modality to address the needs of disaffected men.

EMERGENCE OF MEN'S GROUPS

Group therapy for men emerged in the early 1970s as an outgrowth of the women's consciousness-raising movement and often involved men supportive of the cause of women's equality (see Bradley, Danchik, Foger, & Wodetzki, 1971; Pleck & Sawyer, 1974). In these groups, men challenged their assumptions about what it meant to be a man and tried to change their behavior to be more in line with egalitarian values.

Also during this period, returning veterans from the Vietnam War who sought psychological treatment in Veterans Administration hospitals were exposed to group treatment. In these all-male groups, men were often encouraged to talk about their traumatic experiences in the supportive atmosphere of others who had been there. Posttraumatic stress, drug addiction, depression, and anxiety could often be addressed in the group setting through sharing experiences and confrontation of defensive behavior (see Brooks, 1996, 1998b; Catherall & Shelton, 1996).

In the 1980s, all-male mythopoetic retreat groups were formed to assist men who felt alienated and isolated in reconnecting with each other. Myths, stories, and poems were integrated into the group work to help men identify with their roots in male culture and rebuild some of the sense of male value and strength deconstructed by patriarchal critiques and a strong societal focus on the strengths and values of women (see Bliss, 1992; Liebman, 1991).

The devastating effects of the acquired immunodeficiency syndrome (AIDS) epidemic in the mid-1980s forced many gay and bisexual men into therapy situations to deal with their fears of death, grief, and changes in lifestyle and behavior (see Frost, 1996, 1997; Norsworthy & Horne, 1994). For these men, the all-male therapy group seemed to be a facilitative therapeutic environment for sharing experiences, gaining support, and rebuilding community.

Group therapy for men who had committed acts of domestic violence also became a treatment of choice in the mental health and legal fields. The group setting has provided male participants with anger management skills, support, and confrontation to assist in changing behavior (see Caplan & Thomas, 1995; Haraway & Evans, 1996; Palmer, Brown, & Barrera, 1992).

In the twenty-first century, male therapy groups continue in all of these venues, as well as for adolescent boys, who have been identified as particularly vulnerable to the harming effects of our culture, especially in the realms of violence, depression, and substance abuse (see Millian & Chan, 1991).

In addition, more men who have been physically and sexually abused as children are coming forth (Lisak, 1994). Groups have been created to help these men deal with the feelings of anger, betrayal, fear, isolation, shame, and humiliation that they have often kept hidden (see Friedman, 1994; Gartner, 1997; Harrison & Morris, 1996; Thomas, Nelson, & Sumners, 1994).

WHAT MAKES MEN'S GROUPS WORK

The attractiveness and success of group therapy for men have been built on the foundation that the group situation is a better fit than individual psychotherapy for men (Brooks, 1998b). Most men who consider seeking psychological help are in desperate psychological distress or have been instructed by family or threatened by legal entities to seek treatment or face severe consequences. Individual therapy has been criticized because it exposes a man to an interpersonal situation that he has not been particularly trained for, that of patient or the weak one (Krugman, 1998; Osherson & Krugman, 1990). For many men it is a situation likely to bring up discomfort, shame, and defensiveness because it runs counter to traditional male socialization that encourages men to be independent, strong, stoic, and private about personal foibles or needs (Scher, 1990).

Male Support

A significant but less acknowledged function of all-male groups has been the emotional and psychological support men give each other during especially hard times. This supportive function has typically been seen as the major benefit of women gathering together but as only a secondary side effect in all-male work groups.

Men's therapy groups build on the support that men can uniquely give each other. Because they share similar physical bodies, similar socialization, and similar relational perspectives, men often feel a different kind of support with men than with women. One man in a weekly therapy men's group said it this way: "I have always gone to women for emotional support to my tender and expressive side. With my male friends, I tended to relate about sports, school, and work and not burden them with the stuff I would tell my mother or girlfriend. I felt like I couldn't be completely real with either women or men. In the men's group I have found out that most men feel this way. It has been such a feeling of a burden lifted to realize I can be totally myself here—gentle, aggressive, compassionate, wild, or competitive—and still be accepted by these guys, whom I initially thought were going to judge and reject me."

Male Trust

Men's groups help men trust other men again. In our competitive culture, it is not uncommon for men to be pitted against each other at work or even at play. The buddies one might have had growing up are more difficult to find in the adult world. Many men find that the pressures of work and family take most of their energy and time. It is easy to lose touch with one's emotional self by trying to obey the social rules in each aspect of life. In a men's group, it is expected that each man will talk about who he really is, not just his work or social persona. Because of rules of confidentiality and through honest sharing, men learn they are not alone and in the process build trust with each other at a personal level.

Action Orientation

Men's therapy groups often tend to be action oriented rather than purely conversational. In natural settings, much male friendship is built around activities rather than interpersonal sharing (Caldwell & Peplau, 1982). Shared activity can help men feel more comfortable and trusting in group and set the groundwork for later interpersonal risk taking. Activities may include structured exercises that reduce ambiguity, provide a task that can be accomplished, and give men a familiar way to relate with difficult or potentially shaming topics. For example, in pairs, men might be asked to generate a list that describes the way they have been inhibited by the traditional male gender role in their behavior toward other men and share this list with the rest of the group. Depending on the male subculture norms, physically interactive exercises, guided imagery meditations, mask making, drawing, voice exercises, drumming, role playing, making rounds, and talking sticks may also be introduced as group activities (see Heppner, 1983; Jolliff & Horne, 1996; McPhee, 1996; Rabinowitz & Cochran, 1994). Exercises and activities can alter the social role–bound consciousness of the men entering group to one of reflection, honesty, and emotional self-awareness (McDargh, 1994).

Hope and Confidence

Men's groups give hope and rebuild confidence in members. In very few settings do men actually verbalize and show each other support, respect, and care. The men who initially come to group are often emotionally isolated and discouraged and receive very little positive support from relationships or work (Rabinowitz, 1998). Often they are in the midst of a personal crisis, such as divorce or other significant loss, or they are in a situation in which they must change to avoid family dissolution or incarceration. Some are recovering from addictions to drugs, sex, gambling, or work. The common thread is that they feel like their lives are out of control and that they see little hope in turning their lives back around.

Self-disclosure of impotent feelings and expressions of anger, frustration, and sadness are usually met by supportive comments, sharing of similar experiences, and even physical holding in certain cases (Rabinowitz, 1991). A man may begin to feel less alone and find hope from the support found in group.

Dealing with Discomfort

Men who depend on women for initiating interpersonal conversation and giving them social validation often find the men's group challenging. Although some men's groups have female leaders, the all-male group situation brings up a different set of dynamics for men than a mixed group of both male and female members. Competition centers not on the need to posture for female attention, as is common in mixed groups, but on personal insecurity and inadequacy (Wallach, 1994).

Without women, men are forced to deal with their discomfort with each other, including learned homophobia (Rabinowitz & Cochran, 1987). Introjected anger toward other men may also be a source of discomfort, stemming from unexpressed resentment toward the father (Osherson, 1986) and socialized distrust of other men (Pleck, 1995). The men's group may provide a corrective emotional experience for men who have been culturally alienated from each other (Brooks, 1996).

Dealing with Interpersonal Conflict

Men's groups challenge men to constructively deal with interpersonal conflict. Many men have been socialized to avoid conflict through distracting activities, intellectual rationalization, rage, or silence (Philpot, Brooks, Lusterman, & Nutt, 1997). It is not uncommon for heated exchanges to arise in a men's group. Depending on the stage of the group, men will respond to these interpersonal challenges with varying effectiveness.

In the early stages of a group, conflict is typically ignored to focus on commonality among members. Although this focus allows for early trust building, it also sets the stage for conflict later in the group process. Once initial trust has been established through mutual sharing and self-disclosure, group members will begin to tire of being "nice" to each other. If allowed to go on for too long, niceness will become a group norm that supports safety but not challenge.

For a men's group to work, it must provide a challenging psychological atmosphere (Brooks, 1998a). Group leaders must encourage and model both interpersonal confrontation and support for men. Learning to deal with confrontation can help participants acknowledge their own feelings, value interpersonal feedback, and understand the projective nature of many confrontational remarks. These interpersonal skills can be used in relationships in the world outside of the group to facilitate intimacy and connection.

Emotional Safety

Men's groups allow for the safe expression and containment of strong emotion. Many men have been taught that expressing strong feeling makes them vulnerable. Because they are socialized to keep feelings to themselves, many men find that they are unable to speak, even under safe conditions such as a confidential group. Some men have unlearned how to identify their feelings, and others have very few distinctions between emotional states.

For men who are detached, unassertive, or depressed, anger-releasing exercises may encourage an openness to feeling in the body, leading to more emotional honesty. In domestic violence groups, it may be more important for men to learn strategies to control their anger and identify other emotions such as fear, sadness, and hurt that often have been overridden by expressions of rage.

Family-of-Origin Issues

Men's groups allow men to reexplore their family-of-origin roots. Through the process of storytelling, interpersonal encounter, and strong emotional expression, the story of one's earlier life often emerges. Memories about mother, father, siblings, friends, and others who had a significant influence on one's life are often rekindled. It is not unusual for a man to recall something his father said or did when he was a boy or to reflect on the interactions with siblings that helped shape his views on trust, masculinity, or sense of self. The past unlocks some of the mystery of current interpersonal problems and allows for a reframing of current emotions, reactions, and behaviors (Yalom, 1985).

Although it is useful to know from where one's life has emerged, the past is not to be used as an excuse to rationalize behavior. Once a member becomes aware of his behavior, leaders and other members encourage him to deal with the emotional core but not use it to avoid dealing with current life issues.

Existential Issues

Finally, men's groups work because they address the existential predicaments of life. In the presence of his peers, a man can face his fears of the unknown. Often group discussion centers on the willingness to take risks. Ultimately this focus is based on the assumption that life is finite and that if one is to make the most of his time here, he must be willing to risk leaving the safety of the familiar and move toward the potential unknown (Yalom, 1980). Men may come to group intellectually ready to leave a job or let go of a dysfunctional relationship, but they are often deeply frightened of risking life change. The group uniquely encourages men to take the risk.

The voices from a well-functioning group often counter internalized society, family, and work messages that say "don't change" or "just be a man and suck it up." Although it is up to each man to decide what, when, and how to risk, all members know that the group will accept them no matter what choices they make. This knowledge gives group members the impetus to leap and trust that if all else fails their comrades in the group will be there with them in their failure or triumph.

HOW THE MEN'S GROUP PROCESS UNFOLDS

Regardless of the reason an individual man comes to a group, the group itself usually follows a fairly predictable process as it incorporates the themes and issues of its members (see Corey & Corey, 1997; Rabinowitz & Cochran, 1987; Yalom, 1985). The nature of the group and how the therapists or leaders manage the group process determine its speed, intensity, and depth.

Groups that are time limited may travel more quickly through the stages of group process but with less intensity and depth. Ongoing groups with open membership or high absenteeism have difficulty managing trust issues, slowing the group process, and keeping intensity and depth consistent.

Long-term groups with closed membership and consistent attendance likely have the greatest cohesiveness, have the most consistent norms for doing psychological work, and encourage the most emotional risk taking. These groups travel at a moderate pace, with increasing intensity and depth, provided that the leadership is willing to provide challenge rather than just safety and comfort (Yalom, 1985).

Initial Ambivalence

The initial stage of the long-term group with closed membership is often marked by emotional ambivalence. Despite assurances by group leaders of confidentiality and safety, group members question whether the group and its leaders can be trusted. Many men find few situations in the world outside of therapy in which confidences are kept or vulnerability is not exploited. Sharing of personal information in this stage is often superficial and tentative. Early disclosures, regardless of their quality or relevance, are often met with verbal acceptance but nonverbal neutrality by the group.

The group leaders' task is to help men feel included by encouraging each member to speak. Through empathic verbalizations, the leaders model support and show the members that they will actually be trustworthy and not exploitative of their vulnerability.

Some literature has suggested that men's groups should use a structured format to reduce the interpersonal discomfort among men and to build trust in this anxiety-producing arena (see Crews & Melnick, 1976; Heppner, 1983; Washington, 1979). Others have found that structure may lead to member passivity and excessive reliance on the leaders for direction (see Lieberman, Yalom, & Miles, 1973; Rabinowitz & Cochran, 1987). The type of structure provided is a significant element to encouraging active participation and readying men for depth emotional work.

Leaders can facilitate men in reconnecting with their emotions by introducing exercises in the early stages of group that focus on the body. Based on the theories of Reich (1949), Lowen (1975), and Perls (1969), these exercises soften ego defenses and increase access to emotion stored in muscle memory while engaging men in an ambiguity-reducing structured activity. Techniques that encourage men to become aware of their breathing and body rigidity and that promote physical movement and vocal expression seem to result in integration of feelings and verbal content during the group sessions (Rabinowitz, 1998).

Conflict Stage

Once group members have become comfortable with the group's structure, format, and membership, they can start being more open to the content and implied messages of member disclosures. A successful group in the early stage is characterized by members who feel secure and safe.

This stage is then replaced by a period of restlessness and a return of ambivalence as the men are faced with the reality that they must deal with the conflicting emotional material being raised by increased disclosure. For instance, some members may find it uncomfortable to continue to give unconditional support to someone in the group who is annoying or negative. If group members are not challenged to take risks to speak honestly about their feelings about others and themselves, there is a high potential for some membership dropout.

One man in group said during this period, "I came here to learn about myself and be challenged. Right now I feel like we are just sitting around being supportive and safe and it is boring. I don't really want to confront anyone in particular, though, because I don't want to single anyone out or get attacked." These words are an indication that the leaders need to personalize the process by encouraging group members to verbalize feelings about specific people in the group. Leaders might also need to open themselves up to any negative feelings about the group or its leaders, demonstrate a willingness to handle criticism, and model an openness to conflict.

The conflict stage of group is often both exciting and frightening. Dynamic issues include challenges to leadership, resistance to exercises, disagreements about interpretations of interpersonal behavior, confrontation of quieter or more talkative members, and the formation of norms about risk taking. Group members often thrive on the emotional "charge" of trying to be honest but are also fearful that what they say will be taken the wrong way.

When all group members feel accepted, they begin to loosen their censorship on honest reactions and engage in some blaming or criticism of other members. Leaders should encourage honesty but help members interpret their actions. Both the projector and the receiver of a critical comment will benefit by expressing their immediate reactions and then processing their feelings. This processing can be done in the context of what the comment has stirred up from a man's past or current life situations. In the process, the projector is encouraged to reown his projection and realize that the man he has confronted probably characterizes an aspect of himself that he has depreciated. The one being confronted often learns about how others are seeing him and can practice differentiating the feedback from his own insecurities and fears about himself (Corey & Corey, 1997).

Work Phase

By the time the group has established norms about confrontation and honesty, it has reached the work phase. As each man's dynamic issues are revealed, leaders can personalize exercises, psychodrama activities, and interventions to facilitate each man in working on his own psychological issues in the group.

Supportive participation from other group members is common. Group members not only give and receive feedback about current behavior but also often participate in a member's psychodramatizations of past conflicts, playing roles as his parents, children, or other significant figures. More intense and spontaneous emotional expression, including rage, deep sadness, and even belly laughter, is not unusual during this stage of the group.

Closure

As the group comes to a close, there is a need for review, feedback, and closure. The group leaders must be cognizant of interpersonal distancing and an absence of risk taking in the group and encourage men to discuss their ambivalence about the group ending.

For many men, the group has become a stable, consistent part of their lives in which honesty and genuineness have been valued, something that often feels lacking in their work and outside relationships. Expressions of apprehension and frustration that group is ending are common. The final group sessions often center on reviewing and celebrating the year's work. It is important for the men to give each other feedback about what they value and what they could continue to address in their lives. An ending ritual is usually introduced in the final session to ensure closure.

WORKING THROUGH ISSUES IN A MEN'S GROUP

The center of the circle in our men's group has been nicknamed "the pit." It is symbolic of the intense inner work that is played out in the middle of the group that brings men face-to-face with their fears, vulnerability, anger, grief, and shame. Often the psychological work is drawn out by a thematic group exercise and encouraged by the other members, who play psychodramatic roles in each man's encounter at the pit.

The leaders and, on several occasions, experienced group members serve as "pit guides," keeping the man in the center focused on his movements, body expressions, voice quality, and felt emotion as he faces significant people, frightening images, and projections of himself that are often avoided in everyday life. The leaders monitor the observing group members to notice reactions and encourage participation.

Following a pit encounter, leaders make sure that the event is given a cognitive framework for the benefit of the man who has worked, as well as those who have participated and observed. Leaders elicit feedback from the observers and give the man who has had an encounter time to speak. It is not uncommon to move into another encounter when the issues raised spark an inner movement in one of the other group members.

The following case study illustrates how the group atmosphere of trust, risk encouragement, and support facilitated self-awareness and emotional expression in a man who was struggling with issues of self-doubt and unexpressed anger and resentment. Initially unassertive and unexpressive, this member of the group used a group exercise about the "shadow" geared toward finding the passionate aspect of himself as a vehicle for becoming more assertive in his relationships. In subsequent encounters inside and outside of the group over a period of six months, he used the imagery from the initial exercise to energize his movement from passivity to emotional aliveness.

Clint was a thin, fragile-appearing forty-eight-year-old man, living alone after the breakup of his marriage of twenty years. He had recently changed careers at his wife's suggestion. She had given him a list of demands that if fulfilled might lead to a chance at reconciliation. Even while separated, Clint turned his paycheck over to his wife, who gave him an allowance. This arrangement was made because she believed he was not responsible with money because his career as a businessman had landed them in bankruptcy court.

Before the bankruptcy, Clint, his wife, and their three children lived in the most desirable area of the city in a large house. His wife was currently in individual therapy to deal with her strong emotions toward a cold and unfeeling father. Clint had an intellectual awareness that she was projecting some of her anger and disappointment with her father onto him, but it did not seem to register at the emotional level.

He originally came to the group at his wife's suggestion and displayed passive behavior: speaking when called on, obediently following the introduced exercises, and rarely initiating conversation. The facilitators recognized the signs of disengagement and tried to encourage more spontaneous interaction when possible. The first breakthrough came approximately twelve sessions into the group.

Much of the conflict between group members was not being expressed directly. The members did not trust themselves to get angry or frustrated even when nonverbal behaviors clearly indicated that they had these feelings. Unexpressed emotion was certainly a core issue with Clint, who had specialized in not rocking the boat in his marriage and earlier in his family of origin. Clearly this style was not working, but Clint was frozen, fearful of expressing anger and asserting himself in relationships.

The facilitators had introduced the Jungian concept of the shadow, the part of the self that is unexpressed and unacceptable to the conscious ego. It often contains strong negative feelings that are taboo in the social world but also is a source of creativity, passion, and instinct (Jung, 1964). Each group member was asked to close his eyes and envision his shadow self. The men were directed to show the shadow through facial expression and body movement. They were then encouraged to face the other group members, as the shadow, and bring up any issues with the facilitators or other members that were not to their liking. After some initial hesitation, some of the men began to express episodes of feeling ignored or not understood, and a few leveled angry comments toward the leaders. Although Clint remained quiet during the session, he was clearly stirred.

At the start of the following session, Clint opened the group by verbalizing his desire to be his shadow again. To make the setting more dramatic, the leaders turned off all but one light and had Clint stand in front of it so he cast a rather large shadow. He was encouraged to speak to his shadow. Clint expressed fear of his shadow self and wondered if he was strong enough to take it on.

Directed to lie on the ground and be his shadow self and respond, Clint initially hesitated. As a religious person who had a strong belief in God, this exercise was clearly moving him toward a line he had rarely if ever crossed. Finally, he lay on the floor where his shadow had been cast. He was encouraged to feel the strength of the shadow and to respond to his conscious self. His voice became strong and clear: "I am powerful and you are weak. I know that you don't like being pushed around. I am angry that you don't stand up for yourself." He also let out a growl that contained a sense of animal passion. The dialogue continued, with Clint taking on the role of both his conscious self and shadow self. He emerged from the exercise with increased strength in his voice and clarity in his eyes. Other group members commented on the intensity of his shadow and their desire to see more of it in the group setting. Clint smiled and acknowledged a sense of feeling big and strong.

Over the next twelve sessions, Clint would slip back into his frozen self, but it was accepted that others could call him on it. Acknowledging the shadow element allowed him to connect with this aspect of himself periodically in group and outside of group, he reported. Around this time in his real life, his wife asked him to move back in with the family. Instead of following her wishes, he stated that he was not ready for that yet. He wanted to feel strong and able to combat his passivity more readily before he immersed himself in this volatile relationship again. It was apparent that Clint had made progress but he still seemed frozen and rigid when expressing disappointing or frustrating episodes from his life.

The next intervention at week twenty-four built on his growing awareness that he had trouble accessing the shadow on his own. His wife had told him that he would not be able to see his children unless he met more of her demands. Other group members were furious, but Clint did not seem to be connecting on the body level to his own feelings.

Four group members were instructed to hold on to Clint's legs as he was asked to imagine three other group members as his children, whom he could no longer see. He was instructed to try to get to them with the four men on his legs. To the group's surprise, Clint began to growl and scream. He remained stuck initially until some of the observing members began to take on his wife's voice, telling him he was not capable of being a good father to his kids.

Clint lunged forward, dragging the four men with him. Over a period of ten minutes he made his way toward the "kids." He collapsed onto some pillows and began to weep. The group members surrounded Clint and touched him at various places on his body from head to feet, giving physical support. He lay prone for several minutes.

Finally, Clint rose and was encouraged to make eye contact with the group. His face was visibly changed. It was softer in character and a rosy color, his eyes glistened, and he was shaking. His voice deepened as he said, "There is no way I am going to stay passive again. This feels so good to be feeling my emotions so strongly. I feel solid." He was in touch with feelings in his body that his intellect could not override. Clint still has a long path ahead of him, but he now has some vivid and strongly felt experiences he can access when he finds himself in his long-standing character position of feeling weak and paralyzed.

This case illustrates how a man used the group to experiment and take chances with new behavior and self-definition in a challenging yet supportive atmosphere. The encounters in group allowed Clint to face his fears and translate his emotional awareness into action in his life. The process-oriented nature of the group encouraged this man to engage his issues at his own pace and to build on earlier work he had done in the group. He seemed to benefit from the consistent therapeutic framework, which provided him with male support, trust, safety, and challenge. The ongoing encouragement from the facilitators for him to stay in touch with his emotions led to a breakthrough at both the cognitive and affective levels.

PRACTICAL ISSUES

Therapists must confront many practical issues when considering leading a men's group. Although I address some of these issues briefly here, the reader is encouraged to refer to earlier work by Rabinowitz and Cochran (1987) for more detail on these factors.

Purpose

Leaders of men's groups should be clear about their purpose. It is not enough to say they would like to work with men; instead, they should be specific as to the population or goal of the group. It is certainly easier to recruit members to a group that will provide incentive for individuals to attend.

Male populations that have been identified as problematic, such as men who have been charged with domestic violence offenses or male teens who have gotten in trouble with drugs, are more likely to attend if they know that participation will help them stay out of jail. If therapists are planning to work with men who have specific psychological issues such as anxiety, depression, or addiction, it is important to recognize that the group must be centered on these concerns for it to be attractive to potential members.

Before recruiting, potential men's group leaders should decide on the day and time of the sessions, as well as the setting in which sessions will be held. They should also make a decision about the number of sessions that the group will have. If the group is to be fewer than sixteen sessions, it is important that attendance be emphasized and rules established about missing sessions. Groups that do not allow new members after the first few sessions typically create better cohesion than groups that remain open.

The optimal setting for the men's group is a private, soundproof, comfortable room that is free of interruption. Comfortable chairs or pillows on the floor are likely to decrease the formality of the interactions and create a psychological space that seems casual and open. Because many men are uncomfortable with structureless situations, even a psychotherapy-oriented group should have some structure planned in the early sessions, with a reduced need for therapist-initiated topics as the group becomes more comfortable with generating its own topics from members' experiences.

Recruitment

Recruiting men for a group is wrought with difficulty. Men are less likely than women to seek out psychological help. Even though the group format is more desirable than traditional individual psychotherapy for many men, most traditional men who are not being coerced into treatment will still likely avoid a men's group.

It has been my experience that a descriptive flyer or letter describing the group, its goals, and ideal membership sent to private practitioners and community agency therapists will help get the word out that a men's group exists. Many current men's group members have been in individual therapy or previous self-help groups before coming to a specific group for men (Rabinowitz, 1998).

Once a leader has made contacts in the community and men begin to inquire about membership, it is important to have a screening interview. The screening interview allows the leader to explain the purpose of the group, share expectations, discuss confidentiality, and answer questions.

The interview also gives the therapist a chance to learn about the needs of the potential member to assess whether there is a match between the group goals and his goals. If not, the therapist can make a referral for a more appropriate modality. Getting a commitment of attendance from potential members in the screening interview is a significant part of establishing functional group norms. Some leaders ask for a deposit to cover the first eight sessions so that members are more likely to stick with the process.

Coleading

The decision of whether to have a coleader or to lead solo is also an important one. Coleading has its advantages. Coleaders can model effective and honest interpersonal behavior, provide supportive backup for the group when dealing with highly emotional issues with a group member, allow for processing before and after group of significant themes and issues, and facilitate the pacing and focus of the group process.

The disadvantages of coleading have to do with conflicts that may occur because of stylistic differences, competition, and unresolved personality issues (Rabinowitz & Cochran, 1987). Although coleading provides another perspective and set of eyes for the group, coleaders need to address and work through interpersonal differences to make it effective.

A female cotherapist in an all-men's group creates a highly different set of dynamics than an all-male therapist team (Bonds-White, 1996). Because of traditional gender role stereotyping of women by certain men, female therapists are more likely than male therapists to elicit defensiveness, sexual transference, and hesitation in revealing darker emotional expression (Potash, 1998). Although a female therapist can earn male trust, especially in working on issues related to significant women in their lives, the men in the group must work through their biases, fears, and projections for the leader to be effective.

Therapeutic Strategy

Men's group therapists are encouraged to be creative in their intervention strategies. Emotional risk taking can become an expected outcome when framing the men's group experience as an adventure or journey, appealing to a more stereotypical masculine perspective. Because men tend to relate better in action-oriented situations, each group session, especially in the beginning of a group, should have some activities that facilitate interpersonal interaction and body-oriented emotional awareness.

Group leaders must be vigilant in their observations in the group. Much of what happens occurs at the nonverbal level. For instance, a man who is speaking without much energy or passion may elicit bored looks from other members. Although he may not verbally acknowledge feeling hurt or rejected, it is important for the leader to make note of both his reaction and the group's so that the leader can effectively intervene at the appropriate time. It is important for the leader to have time to review what has happened in the previous session in order to anticipate themes and note the psychological progress of each man.

Regardless of the techniques used to elicit interaction or emotional honesty, the leader must both respect each man's defenses and facilitate each member's movement beyond these barriers. Self-disclosure by the therapist in terms of relevant, here-and-now emotional reactions is also an excellent way to model verbalizing feeling and to give permission for men to take risks.

Common Themes in Men's Groups

In a men's group, themes and issues recycle in various forms. Whereas in earlier stages themes might be spoken about in intellectual ways, in later group stages the themes have a personally relevant quality.

Themes and issues that might emerge during a men's group include trust, vulnerability, fear, shame, pride, rage, strength, weakness, the dark shadow self, warrior, father, fathering, male-male relationships, competition, mother, male-female relationships, boundaries, family of origin, friendship, sexuality, tenderness, disappointment, dominance, submissiveness, desire, love, hatred, dreams, pleasure, pain, grief, secrets, passion, will paralysis, obsessions, work, and death. Many of these themes can be stimulated by exercises or teachings introduced by the leaders and can be facilitated as they arise from a member's personal experience.

Attitudes Toward Men

To help men, it is important to have empathy for their life experiences (Cochran & Rabinowitz, 1996; Pollack, 1998). Before working with them therapeutically, therapists must deal with their own psychological issues and introjections about masculinity. Many typical male behaviors and emotional expressions push psychological buttons for therapists. Many traditionally socialized men show sexist and homophobic attitudes, have engaged in vulgar and degrading behavior toward men and women, and have very little emotional repertoire beyond anger in many cases (Brooks, 1998b).

Working with this population demands that therapists deal with their countertransference feelings. To identify with many men's issues, potential group leaders must be willing, in their own therapy or under supervision, to explore the "darker" aspects of self, including tendencies toward addiction, anger toward women, and resentments toward significant males in their lives.

Rarely in our culture except in war do men find themselves sharing an experience of inner emotional depth with each other. Although all men face intense emotional situations in their lives, often the opportunities for growth are missed by the excessive use of defenses designed to minimize pain and stay in control. Many men have been well programmed by Western culture to pursue power and control at the expense of emotional connection to each other (see Brannon, 1976; O'Neil, 1981). Other men are often seen as competitors, not to be trusted with doubts, fears, and emotions. Society teaches young men to be brave and courageous in the outer world, but it often does not give them permission to be brave and courageous in the emotional realm (Gurian, 1996).

Although more empirical studies need to be done on the most effective group interventions for men with varying concerns, research findings suggest that men's groups are an effective treatment alternative (see Babcock & Steiner, 1999; McRoberts, Burlingame, & Hoag, 1998). Many of the benefits of a men's group resemble Yalom's (1985) curative factors: altruism, group cohesiveness, universality, interpersonal learning, development of socializing techniques, catharsis, imparting of information, imitative behavior, family reenactment, instillation of hope, and existential awareness.

It has been my experience that a well-functioning men's group nurtures interpersonal trust, facilitates psychological awareness, encourages risk, and provides safe containment of strong emotions for its members. Men's group leaders should have a solid intellectual understanding of the developmental principles of the new psychology of men, a willingness to be creative in designing activities and interventions, and a strong empathic identification with what it means to be a man.

References

Andronico, M. P. (1996). *Men in groups.* Washington, DC: American Psychological Association.

Babcock, J. C., & Steiner, R. (1999). The relationship between treatment, incarceration, and recidivism of battering: A program evaluation of Seattle's coordinated community response to domestic violence. *Journal of Family Psychology, 13,* 46–59.

Bliss, S. (1992). What happens at a mythopoetic weekend? In C. Harding (Ed.), *Wingspan: Inside the men's movement* (pp. 95–99). New York: St. Martin's Press.

Bonds-White, F. (1996). Working with men in groups: A female therapist's perspective. In M. Andronico (Ed.), *Men in groups* (pp. 181–191). Washington, DC: American Psychological Association.

Bradley, M., Danchik, L., Foger, M., & Wodetzki, T. (1971). *Unbecoming men.* New York: Times Change Press.

Brannon, R. (1976). The male sex role: Our culture's blueprint of manhood, and what it's done for us lately. In D. David & R. Brannon (Eds.), *The forty-nine percent majority: The male sex role* (pp. 1–45). Reading, MA: Addison-Wesley.

Brooks, G. R. (1996). Treatment for therapy resistant men. In M. Andronico (Ed.), *Men in groups* (pp. 7–19). Washington, DC: American Psychological Association.

Brooks, G. R. (1998a). Group therapy for traditional men. In W. S. Pollack & R. F. Levant (Eds.), *New psychotherapy for men* (pp. 83–96). New York: Wiley.

Brooks, G. R. (1998b). *A new psychotherapy for traditional men.* San Francisco: Jossey-Bass.

Caldwell, M., & Peplau, L. (1982). Sex differences in same-sex friendship. *Sex Roles, 8,* 721–732.

Caplan T., & Thomas, H. (1995). Safety and comfort, content and process: Facilitating open group work for men who batter. *Social Work with Groups, 18,* 33–51.

Catherall, D. R., & Shelton, R. B. (1996). Men's groups for post-traumatic stress disorder and the role of shame. In M. Andronico (Ed.), *Men in groups* (pp. 323–337). Washington, DC: American Psychological Association.

Cochran, S. V., & Rabinowitz, F. E. (1996). Men, loss and psychotherapy. *Psychotherapy, 33,* 593–600.

Corey, M. S., & Corey, G. (1997). *Groups: Process and practice* (5th ed.). Pacific Grove, CA: Brooks/Cole.

Crews, C. Y., & Melnick, J. (1976). Use of initial and delayed structure in facilitating group development. *Journal of Counseling Psychology, 23,* 92–98.

Friedman, R. M. (1994). Psychodynamic group therapy for male survivors of sexual abuse. *Group, 18,* 225–234.

Frost, J. C. (1996). Working with gay men in therapy groups. In M. Andronico (Ed.), *Men in groups* (pp. 163–179). Washington, DC: American Psychological Association.

Frost, J. C. (1997). Group psychotherapy with the aging gay male: Treatment of choice. *Group, 21,* 267–285.

Gartner, R. B. (1997). An analytic group for sexually abused men. *International Journal of Group Psychotherapy, 47,* 373–383.

Gurian, M. (1996). *The wonder of boys.* New York: Jeremy Tarcher/Putnam.

Haraway, M., & Evans, K. (1996). Working in groups with men who batter. In M. Andronico (Ed.), *Men in groups* (pp. 357–375). Washington, DC: American Psychological Association.

Harrison, J. B., & Morris, L. A. (1996). Group therapy for male survivors of abuse. In M. Andronico (Ed.), *Men in groups* (pp. 339–355). Washington, DC: American Psychological Association.

Heppner, P. P. (1983). Structured group activities for counseling men. *Journal of College Student Personnel, 24,* 275–277.

Jolliff, D. L., & Horne, A. M. (1996). Group counseling for middle-class men. In M. Andronico (Ed.), *Men in groups* (pp. 51–67). Washington, DC: American Psychological Association.

Jung, C. G. (1964). *Man and his symbols.* Garden City, NY: Doubleday.

Krugman, S. (1998). Men's shame and trauma in therapy. In W. S. Pollack & R. F. Levant (Eds.), *New psychotherapy for men* (pp. 167–190). New York: Wiley.

Lieberman, M. A., Yalom, I. D., & Miles, M. B. (1973). *Encounter groups: First facts.* New York: Basic Books.

Liebman, W. (1991). *Tending the fire: The ritual men's group.* St. Paul, MN: Ally Press.

Lisak, D. (1994). The psychological impact of sexual abuse: Content analysis of interviews with male survivors. *Journal of Traumatic Stress, 7,* 525–548.

Lowen, A. (1975). *Bioenergetics.* New York: Penguin Books.

McDargh, J. (1994). Group psychotherapy as spiritual discipline: From Oz to the kingdom of God. *Journal of Psychology and Theology, 22,* 290–299.

McPhee, D. M. (1996). Techniques in group psychotherapy with men. In M. Andronico (Ed.), *Men in groups* (pp. 21–33). Washington, DC: American Psychological Association.

McRoberts, C., Burlingame, G. M., & Hoag, M. J. (1998). Comparative efficacy of individual and group psychotherapy: A meta-analytic perspective. *Group Dynamics: Theory, Research, and Practice, 2,* 101–117.

Millian, F., & Chan, J. (1991). Group therapy with inner city Hispanic acting-out adolescent males: Some theoretical observations. *Group, 15,* 109–115.

Norsworthy, K. L., & Horne, A. M. (1994). Issues in group work with HIV-infected gay and bisexual men. *Journal for Specialists in Group Work, 19,* 112–119.

O'Neil, J. M. (1981). Patterns of gender role conflict and strain: Sexism and fear of femininity in men's lives. *Personnel and Guidance Journal, 60,* 203–210.

Osherson, S. (1986). *Finding our fathers.* New York: Fawcett Columbine.

Osherson, S., & Krugman, S. (1990). Men, shame, and psychotherapy. *Psychotherapy, 27,* 327–339.

Palmer, S. E., Brown, R. A., & Barrera, M. E. (1992). Group treatment program for abusive husbands: Long term evaluation. *American Journal of Orthopsychiatry, 62,* 276–283.

Perls, F. S. (1969). *Gestalt therapy verbatim.* Moab, UT: Real People Press.

Philpot, C. L., Brooks, G. R., Lusterman, D., & Nutt, R. L. (1997). *Bridging separate gender worlds.* Washington, DC: American Psychological Association.

Pleck, J. H. (1995). The gender role strain paradigm: An update. In R. F. Levant & W. S. Pollack (Eds.), *A new psychology of men* (pp. 11–32). New York: Basic Books.

Pleck, J. H., & Sawyer, J. (1974). *Men and masculinity.* Englewood Cliffs, NJ: Prentice Hall.

Pollack, W. S. (1998). Mourning, melancholia, and masculinity: Recognizing and treating depression in men. In W. S. Pollack & R. F. Levant (Eds.), *New psychotherapy for men* (pp. 147–166). New York: Wiley.

Potash, M. S. (1998). When women treat men: Female therapists/male patients. In W. S. Pollack & R. F. Levant (Eds.), *New psychotherapy for men* (pp. 282–308). New York: Wiley.

Rabinowitz, F. E. (1991). The male-to-male embrace: Breaking the touch taboo in a men's therapy group. *Journal of Counseling and Development, 69,* 574–576.

Rabinowitz, F. E. (1998). Process analysis of a long term psychotherapy group for men. In F. Rabinowitz (Chair), *Researching psychotherapy with men: Findings and prospects.* Symposium conducted at the annual meeting of the American Psychological Association, San Francisco.

Rabinowitz, F. E., & Cochran, S. V. (1987). Counseling men in groups. In M. Scher, M. Stevens, G. Good, & G. Eichenfield (Eds.), *Handbook of counseling and psychotherapy with men* (pp. 51–67). Newbury Park, CA: Sage.

Rabinowitz, F. E., & Cochran, S. V. (1994). *Man alive: A primer of men's issues.* Pacific Grove, CA: Brooks/Cole.

Reich, W. (1949). *Character analysis* (3rd ed.). New York: Orgone Press.

Scher, M. (1990). Effects of gender role incongruities on men's experience as clients in psychotherapy. *Psychotherapy, 27,* 322–326.

Thomas, C. M., Nelson, C. S., & Sumners, C. M. (1994). From victims to victors: Group process as the path to recovery for males molested as children. *Journal for Specialists in Group Work, 19,* 102–111.

Vessey, J. T., & Howard, K. I. (1993). Who seeks psychotherapy? *Psychotherapy, 30,* 546–553.

Wallach, T. (1994). Competition and gender in group psychotherapy. *Group, 18,* 29–36.

Washington, C. S. (1979). Men counseling men: Redefining the male machine. *Personnel and Guidance Journal, 57,* 462–463.

Yalom, I. D. (1980). *Existential psychotherapy.* New York: Basic Books.

Yalom, I. D. (1985). *The theory and practice of group psychotherapy* (3rd ed.). New York: Basic Books.

CHAPTER EIGHTEEN

Family Therapy for Men

Carol L. Philpot

When family therapy first came on the scene in the 1940s, the theorists and therapists who led the field (Ackerman, 1966; Bowen, 1978; Haley, 1976; Minuchin, 1974) conceptualized families through a lens colored by a patriarchal value system. They were unaware of the impact of gender socialization on the families they saw and ignored the very real power differential between men and women in society at the time. As a result, early theorists adopted a male value system as the epitome of health and engaged in much mother bashing. They were taken to task in the 1970s and 1980s by feminist family psychologists (Avis, 1988; Goodrich, 1991; Luepnitz, 1988; McGoldrick, Anderson, & Walsh, 1989; Walters, Carter, Papp, & Silverstein, 1988), who pointed out flaws in their theories. For example, mothers who were overinvolved in their children's lives were labeled "enmeshed," whereas fathers who were essentially absent from child rearing were labeled "disengaged." Early theorists failed to acknowledge that the roles society assigned to mothers and fathers would quite naturally result in this "pathology." Likewise, because they were mostly male, early writers revered differentiation, individuation, autonomy, and rationality over affiliation and emotional expression, when in fact a more balanced perspective would value so-called feminine qualities as well.

Gender roles have changed since the 1970s, and now many men are confused about what determines maleness. In fact, in the media today, males are often portrayed as incompetent and backward. Psychologists (Brooks & Silverstein, 1995; David & Brannon, 1976; Lazur & Majors, 1995; Levant & Kopecky, 1995; O'Neil, Good, & Holmes, 1995; Pleck, 1981, 1995) have pointed out that traditional gender socialization has been detrimental to men as well as women, the details of which have been documented elsewhere in this book. Some authors (Meth & Pasick, 1990) have noted that psychotherapy, as it is usually conducted, is a more "female-friendly" treatment, requiring verbal expressivity, vulnerability, and emotional awareness, all skills that are difficult for males to acquire in our society. As a result men are less likely to engage in psychotherapy to get help for the problems they experience.

One solution to this problem is gender-sensitive family therapy. Gender-sensitive psychotherapy is therapy conducted with an awareness of the special issues of women and men that might facilitate or impede psychotherapy. Gender-sensitive therapists are (1) knowledgeable about the differing perceptions of reality for men and women; (2) familiar with the literature in women's studies, men's studies, and gender difference research; (3) unwilling to impose limits on the roles to be played by males or females; (4) not prone to view gender differences as intrapsychic pathology; and (5) likely to approach therapy from as androgynous a perspective as possible, as they maintain awareness of the special needs of men and women and of the techniques that will enhance treatment.

GENDER-SENSITIVE FAMILY THERAPY

For gender-sensitive family therapy to be effective, both therapists and clients must understand and accept several important concepts. First, therapists should recognize the existence of a *gender ecosystem*—a group of same-gender individuals who are indoctrinated with beliefs, attitudes, expectations, and behaviors that, despite overlap, are mostly different from those held by the other gender. Second, they should grasp the importance of *gender socialization*, including modeling, labeling, cognition, reward and punishment, and self-fulfilling prophecy, which works to shape the values, personality characteristics, and behaviors of each gender. Third, they should appreciate *androgyny*—the recognition that men and women have the capacity and freedom to adopt all human values and attributes. Fourth, they should seek *empathic knowing*—the ability to understand the experiential world of another without actually being a member of that world. Fifth, they should appreciate *gender coevolution*—the process by which men and women use reward and punishment to mold one another, ideally in a positive fashion. Finally, they should comprehend the *gender role journey* (O'Neil & Egan, 1992)—the metaphorical process of moving from unconscious compliance with rigid gender programming received in childhood through dissatisfaction, anger, and blame to empathic knowing and coevolution.

GENDER ISSUES IN FAMILIES

Because males and females are essentially socialized in different gender ecosystems, they often adopt different value systems, personality characteristics, communication styles, problem-solving skills, attitudes toward sexuality, and role assignments. Conflict and misunderstanding can result from these differences in the husband-wife dyad, between fathers and sons, and between fathers and daughters. Gender-sensitive family therapists are alert to the part gender socialization plays in the difficulties men experience in family relationships. I provide a few examples in the following sections.

Husband-Wife Dyad

Men are trained to value autonomy and self-reliance above affiliation and interdependency, whereas women are socialized to do the reverse. In fact, Pollack (1990) claimed that men suffer from defensive autonomy—a fear of engulfment that results in the well-known clinical pattern of male distancing. Because men fear a loss of masculine self-worth, they are prone to feel a need to control women (O'Neil, 1982). Husbands are also likely to view wives' requests (even legitimate ones) as attempts to control them. The perception of control seeking often causes men to refuse to comply or to become passive-aggressive, initiating a nagging-withdrawing marital pattern.

Because the developmental challenges of boys include powerful pressures to separate from mothers, boys routinely suffer a "traumatic abrogation of the holding environment" (Pollack, 1991). This process causes males to yearn for maternal attachment and to develop unconscious emotional dependence on their wives. This early trauma, plus the self-sacrifice required by the male role of protector and provider, may also contribute to the male sense of "destructive entitlement," male selfishness, and a belief that men deserve special treatment (Boszormenyi-Nagy & Ulrich, 1981). For example, a husband may feel justified to financially indulge his personal desires because he is the person who provides the greater share of the income. Or he may choose to refuse to help with housework and child care because he has worked hard all day (even if his spouse is also employed full time outside the home).

Boys are trained very young to be emotionally stoic and squelch all emotions other than anger. This process often results in alexithymia—the inability to identify and describe one's feelings in words (Krystal, 1982). Men experience unrecognized emotions as a "buzz" (Levant & Kelly, 1989), which they handle by distracting themselves, by exploding in anger, by going numb, or by expressing the emotion nonverbally. Women, on the other hand, are more likely to be in tune with their emotions and to be very adept at expressing themselves verbally. This mismatch in emotional awareness often leads to frustration on the part of women and discomfort for men. It also reduces the effectiveness of behavioral interventions such as communication training. Unless men can identify and talk about emotions other than anger, problems do not get resolved.

A second result of emotional stoicism is the devaluing of emotional responses and emphasis on rational solutions when problems arise. Although intellectual reasoning may indeed produce a quicker solution to a problem, women who have been taught to express emotion often feel unsatisfied and negated if their husbands provide an answer without soothing their emotions. In fact, the provision of a solution by the husband establishes a clear hierarchy in which the woman is one down, which further adds to her unhappiness.

Related to this difficulty is that men and women use communication for different reasons (Tannen, 1990). Women use language to provide understanding and support, give praise, validate experiences, listen attentively, and express empathy. They tend to be tentative and indirect in their speech patterns, qualify their statements, and deprecate their own contributions. All of these patterns reflect women's use of language to connect. Men, on the other hand, use language to provide solutions, offer advice, share information, impress others with their credentials and ideas, and criticize opponents, all of which establish their place in the hierarchy. Whereas female communication patterns encourage self-disclosure and serve as a vehicle to emotional intimacy, male patterns divert away from personal issues that might show weakness. Although the male style of communication may give men the advantage in business, it is ineffective in intimate relationships. Again, this style of communication is a source of frustration for women and a source of extreme discomfort for men.

Men's high appraisal of self-reliance leads to their inclination to think a problem through by themselves until they have found a solution. Women, in general, would prefer to talk about their problems with the hope that the listener will provide sympathy and understanding while facilitating their discovery of a solution. Women often feel rejected and shut out when their husbands refuse to share difficulties with them. They see such talk about troubles as intimacy enhancing. Men feel such talk lowers their self-esteem and makes them less of a man. Conflict and misunderstanding can easily result from these divergent perspectives.

Men frequently experience sexuality in a nonrelational way (Farrell, 1986); that is, they objectify women and view sex and women as rewards. Women, on the other hand, experience sexuality as an extension of emotional intimacy. Men's defensive autonomy, emotional restriction, and unconscious dependency on their wives create a complex approach to sexuality. At times men use women simply for sexual gratification, without consideration of their needs or feelings and with no intention of developing a relationship. At other times, men who have difficulty with emotional expression rely on sex as their only way of experiencing intimacy. Across the centuries, men have been expected to be sexually aggressive, ever ready and willing, regardless of their emotional state or their feelings toward their potential sexual partner. Women, however, have been charged with the thankless role of the sexual gatekeeper. Obviously, this polarization of approaches toward sexual activity sets the stage for major problems.

Men and women also differ markedly in their parenting styles. Fathers are more likely to emphasize competition and achievement (see later section), whereas mothers, trained to be nurturers, are more likely to be tuned in to their children's emotional needs (Biller, 1971; Gilligan, 1982; Miller, 1986). Husbands and wives sometimes get polarized on child-rearing issues—she feels he is too tough and detached; he feels she is overinvolved and too lenient. Specific father-child interactions are discussed in the following two sections.

Father-Son Dyad

Traditional fathers parent their sons in a manner designed to make them tough, self-reliant, and independent. Researchers have found that boys are subjected to more physical punishment than are girls (Hartley, 1974; Weitzman, Eifler, & Ross, 1972), are less likely than girls to receive comfort for a minor injury (Lambert, Yackley, & Hein, 1971), are more likely than girls to be left alone (Fagot, 1978), and are taught to stifle emotions that might make them appear weak or vulnerable (Choti, Marston, & Holston, 1987; Ross & Mirowsky, 1984). Fathers goad their sons, withhold praise, and punish tears because they do not want their sons to be too "soft" (Osherson, 1986; Wagenvoord & Bailey, 1978).

Fathers, more than mothers, are likely to enforce narrow gender role expectations that discourage sons' experimentation with other-gender behaviors, such as sewing or cooking (Lamb, 1986; O'Leary & Donahue, 1978; Pleck, 1981). Fathers, whose gender socialization tends to make them very competitive, often pressure their sons for achievement and success (Biller, 1971; Pleck, 1987). Men, because of their identification with the hierarchical worlds of the military, corporations, and sports settings, are accustomed to interactions characterized by the use of power, threat, and intimidation (Arkin & Dobrofsky, 1978; Doyle, 1994; Messner, 1992). Not surprisingly, fathers are more likely than mothers to be coercive, authoritarian, and power based in their parenting style (Jacklin, Dipietro, & Macoby, 1984; Pleck, 1987).

Father-Daughter Dyad

Men, who are taught the general roles of providers and protectors, are especially protective of their daughters, whom they tend to see as innocent and vulnerable. Daughters give fathers the opportunity to discover and express their "softer" characteristics of nurturance and compassion (Philpot, Brooks, Lusterman, & Nutt, 1997). And a daughter is often able to "wrap her father around her little finger" simply because she provides her father with a nonsexual intimacy he rarely encounters elsewhere. Because fathers are less likely to think of daughters as career oriented, they are more tolerant of passivity, laziness, or indifference in them (Fox, 1978). This attitude makes it difficult for young women to take themselves seriously and set high goals for themselves.

Furthermore, fathers are prone to be overprotective of their daughters. This overprotection becomes an issue during adolescent years, when fathers remember what they were like as teenage boys. The male tendency to objectify women and use them sexually (Brooks, 1995) provokes great anxiety in fathers of nubile young women. Daughters may experience this overprotection as smothering.

New Models of Fatherhood

Although new models of fatherhood have begun to replace the old (Pleck, 1987), fathers still struggle with a number of obstacles to their ability to be close to their children. First, prominent cultural institutions such as the workplace and the legal system interfere with fathers' capacity to play a major role in child care (Doyle, 1994; Kiselica, Stroud, & Rotzien, 1992). As a result, fathers have less time to spend with their children during a marriage and often find themselves estranged from their children after divorce.

Furthermore, because many men suffer from the alexithymia of normative male gender socialization, they lack key emotional skills to parent effectively (Balswick, 1988; Levant & Kelly, 1989). Finally, adolescent males have limited opportunities to practice child care, and as adults they commonly feel unprepared for the task. So in spite of the trend for young men to participate more in childbirth and infant care, many men still remain detached and uninvolved in the lives of their children in the succeeding years.

TECHNIQUES OF GENDER-SENSITIVE FAMILY THERAPY

The most important aspects of gender-sensitive family therapy are the therapist's attitude and knowledge of gender issues. At the same time, however, several techniques have been found to be particularly effective in conducting gender-sensitive therapy (Philpot, Brooks, Lusterman, & Nutt, 1997). These techniques include (1) validation and normalization, (2) psychoeducation, (3) uniting against the ecosystem as scapegoat, (4) reframing and translating, (5) empathic interviewing, and (6) gender inquiry. I discuss each of these techniques briefly in the following sections.

Validation and Normalization

Validation and normalization is the first step in the process because clients will not be able to entertain any notions about change until they feel heard and understood. It is important for the therapist to provide clients with the opportunity to share their painful experiences without blaming other members of the family. When an individual expresses a frustration that has clear gender roots, the therapist can normalize this experience as a product of gender socialization. When family members are polarized on an issue, frequently their positions can be understood in terms of what they have been taught as a man, woman, girl, or boy. The therapist validates that the particular issues or behaviors some family members find to be problematic may be the result of clashing gender expectations—how males and females construe the world or how they approach familial issues. The therapist emphasizes that on most issues there is no single right or wrong way to behave; instead, there are many different ways to view an issue.

Psychoeducation

After validation and normalization, the therapist can make a natural transition into explaining the process of gender socialization, including the concepts of the gender ecosystem, androgyny, gender coevolution, and the gender role journey. Stereotypical gender differences in value systems, family roles, personality characteristics, communication styles, problem-solving techniques, and attitudes toward marriage and sexuality can be addressed as applied to the specific situation. As clients begin to understand that the behaviors and attitudes of the other family members are frequently a result of the differing rules and regulations of the gender ecosystem, they can move beyond accusing and blaming toward understanding and accepting.

Uniting Against the Ecosystem as Scapegoat

The next step in the process is to unite family members against the real culprit at the root of their difficulties: rigid gender ecosystems that penalize family members for violating stereotypical and unhealthy gender expectations. Keeping the systemic perspective in mind, the therapist responds to those complaints and frustrations that have roots in gender socialization. The therapist explains the situation, "normalizing" the experience and demonstrating to the family that the larger culture and social system has victimized them. The therapist points out how family members have contributed to the socialization process and also suffered from it. In this way, family members can come to see how the traditional gender ecosystem, with its overly narrow expectations, is the actual enemy. In the natural evolution of this process, clients can "externalize the problem" (White, 1995). They direct their anger outward toward the larger system and form new partnerships to challenge outmoded conventions and make new rules for their family system.

Reframing and Translating

Next, the therapist acts as a "gender broker," essentially explaining the "male code" to female family members and the "female code" to male family members. The therapist serves as a communication mediator, a translator of the separate cultures and languages of the genders. The therapist decodes the message from one gender and puts it into the language of the other. Take, for example, the case of a husband who works long hours and seems to be always away from the home. Frequently, the wife is angry because she feels taken advantage of and has to deal with the children alone. In this common situation, the therapist can help the wife understand that the husband is doing exactly what he believes is expected of him—providing for his family through hard work and dedication to the good provider role. When she understands that his intent is good, she can then approach him from a more compassionate stance. She can correct any misconceptions he may have about her expectations of him and clarify exactly what she wants most. If she chooses, she can ask him to show his love and support in a different way. By reframing the husband's behavior in a positive way, the therapist opens the door for negotiation and change (although the behavior is not ignored or fully excused).

Empathic Interviewing

Next, this process can be greatly facilitated by "empathic interviewing" (Lusterman, 1989). Because a major goal of gender-sensitive family therapy is to create an atmosphere of empathy and understanding, it is often necessary to teach family members empathic communication techniques. These techniques include such skills as asking open-ended questions, using active listening skills, attending to emotions, repressing the urge to interrupt or defend oneself, resisting the desire to attack the other while describing the experience within oneself, monitoring body language and voice tone, using reflecting skills, and so on. The goal is to interrupt the negative patterns of accusation and defense and provide an opportunity for each gender to be heard and understood.

During this process, family members can begin to recognize that some of the concerns of the other gender are not ridiculous but a by-product of gender training. Family members can begin to recognize that another's unhappiness may not be as much a direct criticism of a deficiency within oneself as it is a product of frustration that should be directed at the rigidity of gender roles. In an atmosphere of empathy and understanding, family members can come to feel validated and emotionally closer. This process allows them to seek solutions to their problems as a team.

Gender Inquiry

"Gender inquiry" (Philpot et al., 1997) is a process based on a list of questions designed to stimulate conversation about the role of gender in people's lives and relationships. The gender inquiry is conducted when the therapist recognizes that gender issues are influencing a problem in the family. Although the questions are usually asked in a developmental order—that is, starting with messages received in childhood—it is not necessary to ask all questions. By distancing the family from the immediate situation, the gender inquiry, like the genogram, can provide insight into the experience of the respondent while reducing the tension associated with highly charged toxic issues.

The gender inquiry serves three primary purposes. First, it teaches family members that the gender ecosystem is at the core of many of the misunderstandings and dissatisfactions experienced by the family. In this way it helps to depersonalize much of the conflict. Second, the gender inquiry provides historical context. It demonstrates how persons of each gender in the family of origin have molded and influenced one another and have passed on this cultural shaping to future generations. Finally, this process expands the "cognitive maps" (Tomm, 1988) of the family members and thereby offers greater possibility for change. (The gender inquiry is found in Appendix B, at the end of this chapter.)

CARTALONE FAMILY

Angie Cartalone (name changed) was a forty-five-year-old police dispatcher who was married to a police officer and the mother of four children. She called for an appointment because her fourteen-year-old son, Tony, was in trouble in school. The Cartalone family consisted of Angie, Mark (age forty-eight), Jennifer (age eighteen), Barbara (age seventeen), Tony (age fourteen), and Debbie (age ten).

Mark, a lieutenant with twenty-five years of experience on the police force, was essentially an absentee father because of his long and unpredictable work hours. Angie was a dispatcher for the same police department and had been working full time for the past four years. Jennifer, a senior in high school, was a straight-A student, president of student government, and active in sports. She had been accepted to a state university for the following fall. In contrast, Barbara, a junior in the same high school, was overweight, withdrawn, and presented with a depressed appearance. She was getting C's and D's in school, had a small circle of friends, had no outside interests, and had recently begun a dating relationship with a boy who did not meet her parents' approval because "he was lazy."

Tony, the identified patient, was in the ninth grade and, according to his parents' report, hanging out with the wrong crowd. Tony cut school frequently, had a history of detentions for "mouthing off," and was recently suspended from school for taking his father's unloaded gun to school. Surprisingly, despite numerous absences, Tony's grades were B's and C's. Debbie was in the fifth grade, a "good little girl" and "the apple of her parents' eye." According to her parents, Debbie could do no wrong. Angie and Mark complained that Tony tormented all three of his sisters and made their life a "living hell" at home. Because she could not understand Tony's anger, Angie even wondered aloud whether he might be "possessed." It was immediately clear that Tony was the scapegoat child in this family.

Time alone with Tony gave the therapist more insight into his problems. Tony's father was a distant hero who was revered in the community. Although he risked his life on a daily basis for society, he rarely had time for his son. Tony admired his father but felt abandoned by him. Lately, the only interactions with his father were those of a disciplinary nature. He regularly heard the old threat, "Wait till your father gets home!"

Angie, the more available parent, had a different parenting style for her daughters and her son. She was nurturing, protective, and supportive of all of her daughters. Even Barbara, who was not achieving to her potential, was treated well. However, Angie used her sarcastic wit to discipline Tony. She rarely praised him and never accepted his affection. Angie minimized his complaints about his sisters and would not tolerate tears from him. In further listing of his distress, Tony described many times when his sisters instigated fights and he ended up as the only one punished. It was clear that Tony felt unloved and unwanted in this family. It was also clear that he saw many of his problems as the result of his being male.

A conjoint session with the parental dyad allowed the therapist time to explore relevant gender issues tracing back to the family of origin. Angie and Mark had both been raised in a poor, New York City Italian community. In their families of origin the male and female worlds were separate and very different. The women cooked, cleaned, shopped, and took care of children. The men worked and played together, coming home only to eat and sleep. Angie viewed men as different—tough, combative, demanding. Angie was competitive and had wanted to be part of the male world as a child. She learned to be rough and tough with her male friends. She learned well enough that she now could joke in the same style as her male coworkers at the police station. These interactions reinforced her belief that you had to be tough and insensitive with men.

As therapy progressed, Angie began to realize that she had treated Tony as she had treated her male childhood friends, and she had treated her daughters the way her mother had treated her. She admitted that she was unsure about how to raise a son, because she really believed males were strange creatures with secret rules about life.

This was a perfect opportunity to invite Mark to talk about his experience of growing up in New York City. Mark had played in the streets with the rest of the kids, had taken his share of teasing, and had felt the pressure of having to prove his manhood in sports, fights, car races, drinking, and seduction of women. He also recognized that experience as a developmental stage from which he "had emerged reasonably unscathed, Thank God!" He said that he had been lucky to have a father, uncles, and older male cousins who served as a support system and good role models for him.

Mark had a sentimental, softer side. He was thoughtful and philosophical. In fact, it was this part of him that had attracted Angie, that made him stand out from the rest of the men she knew. As he talked, it became clear that he and Tony had a great deal in common, but because he was so absent from Tony's life he was not aware of the pain his son felt in adjusting to adolescence. Mark had been attracted to police work because in his home environment police officers were often instrumental in helping teenagers stay out of trouble. Mark found it to be a painful irony that now that his own son was in trouble, he was uninvolved.

The session ended with a little psychoeducation about the world of adolescent boys. The therapist discussed these issues to help Angie understand that her son was going through some of the painful rituals of male socialization and was not possessed by some demon. His behavior, although recognized as a bit extreme, was normalized.

To help Tony feel validated and understood, the therapist conducted a session with the father-son dyad. Before the session began, the therapist coached Mark to listen to his son and use his own adolescent experiences to facilitate understanding of Tony's feelings. The therapist warned Mark that although he might be tempted to lecture, to defend, to admonish, or to take sides against Tony, he should resist so he could really get into Tony's world.

The therapist then led Tony through his story. As Tony talked, Mark recognized Tony's struggle to be accepted as a man among his peers. The incident with the gun, he realized, was an attempt to impress the other adolescent boys. As Mark shared with Tony some of his own experiences on the streets of New York, the therapist had a sense of being unnecessary, of eavesdropping on a male-bonding session. Tony left the session feeling more hopeful and less pathological than he had in some time. Mark left the session resolved to find time to spend with his son.

During the course of therapy, both parents became aware of their tendency to view their daughters as innocent and Tony as bad. Because of that awareness, they began to listen to Tony more and administer punishments more fairly. When the girls could no longer get away with blaming Tony for everything, the conflicts reduced substantially.

Now that they were less concerned about Tony, both Angie and Mark were free to shift some of their attention to Barbara, whose quiet depression had thus far gone unnoticed. Barbara was also having difficulty dealing with "favoritism" shown to her older sister. On hearing about this difficulty, Angie and Mark began to search for ways to bolster Barbara more.

Mark began to take time off to take his son fishing and camping and eventually got him involved in setting up sporting events for the Police Athletic League. Mark became a more present and realistic model for his son, a model that even allowed the expression of soft emotion. Angie worked at being more empathic and gentle with Tony, although it was not easy for her. She no longer ignored his occasional awkward attempts to show affection and began to reward the positive things he did with praise. As life with his family became more pleasant, Tony's conduct-disordered behavior diminished.

Gender issues were prevalent in this case. For example, this family illustrated common gender patterns of absent fathering, the differential treatment of boys and girls, and adolescent male trauma strain. Tony was particularly stressed because Angie, unlike many mothers, was not attending to his emotional needs any more than his father was. Tony was subjected to a demanding and coercive parenting style from both parents, while his sisters received all the parental nurturance. The therapist validated Tony's experience, normalized his behavior, provided psychoeducation about male gender issues, and used both the empathic interview and gender inquiry. In using this approach, the therapist helped the parents gain insight into their son's anger and behavior and began to ease the family suffering.

The therapist used many other interventions in addition to gender-sensitive psychotherapy to bring about change in this family, including such things as behavioral contracting and anger management. Nevertheless, the turning point came when father and son connected over the trauma of male adolescence and mother recognized her tendency to treat her son more harshly than her daughters. It was then that the emotional atmosphere in the family changed from that of the scapegoat child to one of empathy and understanding.

Gender-sensitive family therapy can be a powerful adjunctive tool for working with males in therapy. The therapist who brings a knowledge of the male and female gender ecosystems to the treatment room can use that information to form a therapeutic bond, to act as a gender broker, and to facilitate the resolution of problems stemming from rigid gender socialization. The gender-sensitive therapist encourages clients to approach one another with an attitude of curiosity rather than one of defensiveness. In this way, clients become interested to learn about the gender world of the other. This shift is instrumental in the development of the empathic knowing that produces profound positive changes in families.

References

Ackerman, N. (1966). *Treating the troubled family.* New York: Basic Books.

Arkin, W., & Dobrofsky, L. (1978). Military socialization and masculinity. *Journal of Social Issues, 34,* 151–168.

Avis, J. (1988). Deepening awareness: A private study guide to feminism and family therapy. In L. Braverman (Ed.), *A guide to feminist family therapy* (pp. 15–46). New York: Harrington Park Press.

Balswick, J. O. (1988). *The inexpressive male.* Lexington, MA: Lexington Books.

Biller, H. (1971). *Father, child, and sex role.* Lexington, MA: Lexington Books.

Boszormenyi-Nagy, I., & Ulrich, D. (1981). Contextual family therapy. In A. S. Gurman & D. P. Kniskern (Eds.), *Handbook of family therapy* (pp. 159–186). New York: Brunner/Mazel.

Bowen, M. (1978). *Family therapy in clinical practice.* New York: Aronson.

Brooks, G. (1995). *The centerfold syndrome: How men can overcome objectification and achieve intimacy with women.* San Francisco: Jossey-Bass.

Brooks, G., & Silverstein, L. (1995). Understanding the dark side of masculinity: An interactive systems model. In R. Levant & W. Pollack (Eds.), *A new psychology of men* (pp. 280–333). New York: Basic Books.

Choti, S., Marston, A., & Holston, S. (1987). Gender and personality variables in film-induced sadness and crying. *Journal of Social and Clinical Psychology, 5,* 535–544.

David, D., & Brannon, R. (Eds.). (1976). *The forty-nine percent majority: the male sex role.* Reading, MA: Addison-Wesley.

Doyle, J. A. (1994). *The male experience* (3rd ed.). Dubuque, IA: W. C. Brown.

Fagot, B. I. (1978). The influence of sex on parental reactions to toddler children. *Child Development, 49,* 459–465.

Farrell, W. (1986). *Why men are the way they are.* New York: McGraw-Hill.

Fox, G. L. (1978). "Nice girl": Social control of women through a value construct. *Signs, 2,* 805–817.

Gilligan, C. (1982). *In a different voice.* Cambridge, MA: Harvard University Press.

Goodrich, T. (Ed.). (1991). *Women and power: Perspectives for family therapy.* New York: Norton.

Haley, J. (1976). *Problem-solving therapy.* San Francisco: Jossey-Bass.

Hartley, R. E. (1974). Sex role pressures and the socialization of the male child. In J. Pleck & J. Sawyer (Eds.), *Men and masculinity* (pp. 7–13). Englewood Cliffs, NJ: Prentice Hall.

Jacklin, C. N., Dipietro, J. A., & Macoby, E. E. (1984). Sex-typing behavior and sex-typing pressure in child-parent interaction. *Archives of Sexual Behavior, 13,* 413–415.

Kiselica, M. S., Stroud, J., & Rotzien, A. (1992). Counseling the forgotten client: The teen father. *Journal of Mental Health Counseling, 14,* 338–350.

Krystal, H. (1982). Alexithymia and the effectiveness of psychoanalytic treatment. *International Journal of Psychoanalytic Psychotherapy, 9,* 353–378.

Lamb, M. (Ed.). (1986). *The father's role: Cross-cultural perspectives* (pp. 292–330). Hillsdale, NJ: Erlbaum.

Lambert, W., Yackley, A., & Hein, R. (1971). Child training values of English Canadian and French Canadian parents. *Canadian Journal of Behavioral Sciences, 3,* 217–236.

Lazur, R., & Majors, R. (1995). Men of color: Ethnocultural variations of male gender role strain. In R. F. Levant & W. S. Pollack (Eds.), *A new psychology of men* (pp. 337–358). New York: Basic Books.

Levant, R., & Kelly, J. (1989). *Between father and child.* New York: Viking.

Levant, R., & Kopecky, G. (1995). *Masculinity reconstructed.* New York: Dutton/Plume.

Luepnitz, D. (1988). *The family interpreted: Feminist theory in clinical practice.* New York: Basic Books.

Lusterman, D. D. (1989). Empathic interviewing. In G. Brooks, D. D. Lusterman, R. Nutt, & C. Philpot (Chairs), *Men and women relating: The carrot or the stick?* Symposium presented at the annual conference of the American Association of Marriage and Family Therapy, San Francisco.

McGoldrick, M., Anderson, C., & Walsh, F. (Eds.). (1989). *Women and families: A framework for family therapy.* New York: Norton.

Messner, M. (1992). *Power at play: Sports and the problem of masculinity.* Boston: Beacon Press.

Meth, R. L., & Pasick, R. S. (1990). *Men in therapy: The challenge of change.* New York: Guilford.

Miller, J. B. (1986). *Toward a new psychology of women* (2nd ed.). Boston: Beacon Press.

Minuchin, S. (1974). *Families and family therapy.* Cambridge, MA: Harvard University Press.

O'Leary, V. E., & Donahue, J. M. (1978). Latitudes of masculinity: Reactions to sex-role deviance in men. *Journal of Social Issues, 34,* 17–28.

O'Neil, J. M. (1982). Gender role conflict and strain in men's lives. In K. Solomon & N. Leng (Eds.), *Men in transition: Theory and therapy.* New York: Plenum Press. pp.5-44

O'Neil, J., & Egan, J. (1992). Men's and women's gender role journeys: A metaphor for healing, transition, and transformation. In B. R. Wainrib (Ed.), *Gender issues across the life cycle* (pp. 107–123). New York: Springer.

O'Neil, J., Good, G., & Holmes, S. (1995). Fifteen years of theory and research on men's gender role conflict: New paradigms for empirical research. In R. F. Levant & W. S. Pollack (Eds.), *A new psychology of men* (pp. 164–206). New York: Basic Books.

Osherson, S. (1986). *Finding our fathers: The unfinished business of manhood.* New York: Free Press.

Philpot, C. L., Brooks, G. R., Lusterman, D.-D., & Nutt, R. L. (1997). *Bridging separate gender worlds: Why men and women clash and how therapists can bring them together.* Washington, DC: APA Books.

Pleck, J. (1981). *The myth of masculinity.* Cambridge, MA: MIT Press.

Pleck, J. (1987). American fathering in historical perspective. In M. S. Kimmel (Ed.), *Changing men: New directions in research on men and masculinity* (pp. 83–97). Beverly Hills, CA: Sage.

Pleck, J. (1995). The gender role strain paradigm: An update. In R. F. Levant & W. S. Pollack (Eds.), *A new psychology of men* (pp. 1–32). New York: Basic Books.

Pollack, W. (1990). Men's development and psychotherapy: A psychoanalytic perspective. *Psychotherapy, 27,* 316–321.

Pollack, W. (1991, August). Can men love? In R. Levant (Chair), *Men, emotions, and intimacy.* Symposium conducted at the annual meeting of the American Psychological Association, San Francisco.

Ross, L., & Mirowsky, J. (1984). Men who cry. *Social Psychology Quarterly, 47,* 138–146.

Tannen, D. (1990). *You just don't understand: Women and men in conversation.* New York: Ballantine.

Tomm, K. (1988). Interventive interviewing, III: Intending to ask lineal, circular, strategic, or reflexive questions? *Family Process, 27,* 1–15.

Wagenvoord, J., & Bailey, J. (1978). *Men: A book for women.* New York: Avon Books.

Walters, M., Carter, B., Papp, P., & Silverstein, O. (1988). *The invisible web: Gender patterns in family relationships.* New York: Guilford Press.

Weitzman, L., Eifler, E., & Ross, C. (1972). Sex-role socialization in picture books for preschool children. *American Journal of Sociology, 77,* 1125–1150.

White, M. (1995). *Reauthoring lives: Interviews and essays.* Adelaide, South Australia: Dulwich Centre.

SPECIAL CONSIDERATIONS AND SKILLS FOR THERAPY WITH MEN

CHAPTER NINETEEN

Women Helping Men

Strengths of and Barriers to Women Therapists Working with Men Clients

Norine G. Johnson

Times are changing in therapy. Because more therapists are female and more clients are male, there has been a surge in the male client–female therapist dyad. Male clients of all ages are finding their way to therapy and are frequently choosing female therapists. In my own practice, approximately two-thirds of my clients are men, treated in individual, couples, or family formats.

Single male clients in their twenties and thirties are confused, depressed, and anxious about the changes in women and women's expectations of men. These men know that somehow the rules of all relationships have changed, whether in social, romantic, or work settings. These men are unsure of exactly how the relationships have changed and do not know what to do about their confusion.

Older men who are divorced, lonely, and angry commonly find that working all the time does not relieve the pain anymore. Because of my business background, I also see business and professional men who want to change the way they work—such as a successful small business owner who was also fighting with his male partner or a lawyer who could not get to sleep at night because he could not turn off his worries.

More therapists are now adopting familial and systems approaches. In part, the use of these approaches contributes to the trend for more men coming to therapy. Often, they are initiating the therapy and are choosing women therapists. More than half of the calls I receive for couples and family therapy come from men. This dramatic change has occurred over the past ten years and suggests that more men have come to understand the importance of relationships for their well-being.

Couples may seek out my services to improve their situation through marital enrichment or conflict-resolution interventions. Others may simply want to escape their marriages. Perhaps because I am a woman therapist, most of my referrals are of the first type. They may be determined to stay together but feel that the relationship needs to change. Or they may want to work through the strain of a marital infidelity.

Today there are also more divorced men or fathers who are single caretakers who want a better relationship with their children. I see a significant number of father-son dyads to help them develop a positive relationship, frequently for the first time. When I ask, "How may I help?" the most frequent response is, "I want a better relationship with my son than I had with my father."

SOME REPRESENTATIVE MEN

Over the past decade I have found that many types of men, in many situations, seek my help. In part, they have called because I am a woman therapist.

Fathers

Kevin (age forty-two) called and asked for an appointment for himself and his son (age twelve). Kevin's ex-wife had suggested therapy after their son refused court-ordered visits. Kevin had been in therapy before for issues about his failing marriage. He had previously seen a male therapist, but now he wanted a woman therapist because his son would not talk to him and he did not know how to open up the communication. He knew his son was angry with him. He had gotten angry in turn when his son refused to get in the car for their last visit.

Bachelors

Tony called, saying he was feeling some stress and wanted to make an appointment. He said he just was not himself recently after his girlfriend made him move out. He was having a particularly hard time now because he had seen her with another man. He said even his dad was on his case about his seeming down. He had never seen a therapist and was not sure what therapy was all about. But he knew he needed to do something or he might lose his job. Tony was thirty-one and lived at home with his parents. His dad drank most nights, and his mom took care of them and their home. He had a married sister. He said he called a woman therapist because he thought a woman could help him understand why the relationship busted up. Later, he admitted that he had hoped that a woman could tell him how to get his girlfriend back.

Husbands

Richard was fifty-five and owned his own business. His youngest child had just gone off to college. Richard's secretary called and asked me to wait while she got him on the phone. He asked for an appointment for his wife, Helen, and himself because *she* was unhappy. They had been referred by her male therapist. Richard said they had seen a male therapist seven years before, and they both decided to try a woman this time. He thought his wife would be more comfortable with a woman and, because she was the one who thought they needed therapy, he agreed. He said the appointment would have to be after 7 P.M. because his business frequently kept him late. The therapist only had a 6 P.M. opening, which he agreed to, for one time only.

WHY MEN MAY CHOOSE WOMEN THERAPISTS

Starting in the mid-1990s, I noticed male clients began explicitly stating why they chose a woman therapist. Safety, attribution of "special knowledge," and reputation are the reasons I hear most. Wanting a woman therapist is markedly different from twenty years ago. Early studies of this issue examined how unspoken gender stereotypes affected all elements of therapy, including the assignment of clients to same-sex therapists (American Psychological Association, 1975), the therapist's view of the client (Broverman, Broverman, Clarkson, Rosenkrantz, & Vogel, 1970), and the client's perceived satisfaction with therapy (Toomer, 1980). Although some of these studies later were found to be flawed, they stimulated the gender studies work that followed. Based on my understanding of previous research and my own clinical experience, it seems to me that men seek women therapists for a number of reasons.

Comfort Showing "Weakness"

Most men who specifically seek out a woman therapist for individual therapy expect her to provide a safe environment for emotional expression and to have expert knowledge about relationship issues. Many men, particularly men under age fifty, want a different type of relationship than they saw in their parents' generation, but they frequently do not have the skills to change and are afraid of intimacy. They feel they will be more comfortable showing their "weakness" to a woman therapist.

Because most men's relationships with other men are highly competitive, men are prone to see a woman therapist as someone who will be different and will not taunt or tease a man for his failures (real or imagined). They frequently hope that with a woman therapist they will be able to expose the vulnerable self they have hidden.

Seeing Women as More Sensitive and Relationship Oriented

Many men want more intimate relationships that include positive emotionality. Because they commonly believe that women have special expertise in understanding feelings and helping relationships, they are likely to seek individual therapy with a female therapist.

Insistence from a Female Partner

Sometimes a man wants he and his wife to go to therapy, but she will not go unless the therapist is a woman. Feminism has had a significant effect on women, including their expectations for equality within their intimate relationships. Contemporary women are less accepting of the limitations of traditional men's roles. They want their partners to be friends as well as providers and warriors. Also, today's women may be lonely. Working mothers and working women in relationships have less time to make the tight friendships that women enjoy. Many women are turning more to their husbands, to the men in their lives, for the type of friendship women used to get from other women. This means women want men to be able to listen to and to talk about feelings and relationship issues.

Today's women make demands on their partners for improved relations, and male partners look to therapy as a way to help resolve the issues. Men's workaholism or their relational problems at work may be affecting couples.

Whatever the cause of men's problems, most women are now less likely to accept the status quo. When they meet resistance from their male partners, they may become particularly insistent that the therapist be a woman.

Bad Experience with a Male Therapist

Some male clients and couple clients report having a bad experience with a male therapist. The complaints I hear the most are ones of not feeling heard or respected. Behavior such as taking phone calls during a session may be perceived by a male client as an entitlement or a power play. Or the male therapist sharing information on his own life may be misheard as competition—a message that the therapist is handling his life better than the client is.

Woman Therapist Recommended by Someone the Client Respects

Ninety percent of my male clients call because someone they respect recommended me. I can only think of a handful of men who called because of a referral from an anonymous source such as a managed care company or a physician. Interestingly many of my male clients are referred by female friends or female family members for whom they have deep respect and with whom they have shared some small part of their despair. A male client might also be referred by a member of his extended family who was seen in another context.

FEMINIST PRINCIPLES WHEN WOMEN THERAPISTS WORK WITH MEN

To be most effective with their male clients, women therapists must be knowledgeable about gender issues. One way to be knowledgeable is to study paradigms from feminist therapy, gender-sensitive therapies, and gender-aware therapies. The new psychology of men (Pollack & Levant, 1998) presents the most helpful understanding of men's issues today. The literature and research on men stress how the expectations for men make certain aspects of today's living difficult and may damage men's physical and emotional health. Also, the applications of feminist therapy principles and gender-aware therapy provide a powerful framework and constructive tools for women therapists helping men (Good, Gilbert, & Scher, 1990; Worell & Remer, 1992; Wyche & Rice, 1997).

Awareness of Context

Being knowledgeable about gender issues involves being aware of messages associated with traditional masculine roles and the "code of masculinity" (Allen & Gordon, 1990; Brooks, 1991; Meth & Pasick, 1990; Pollack, 1998, 2000; Pollack & Levant, 1998; Scher, 1990). When a woman therapist is able to view male clients' responses less as individual pathology and more as a product of male socialization, she will be better able to move into the world of men. In so doing, she will increase her sensitivity to the pressures that shape men's behavior. For a woman therapist to be successful in the treatment of men she must help them understand how emotions, thinking, and behavior have been shaped by societal expectations for men and that they have the power to change their views. A woman using feminist therapy will have knowledge of how context has shaped men's issues such as achievement striving, anger expression, sex versus intimacy, fear of being a "wuss," patriarchy, and avoidance of emotionality (Levant et al., 1992).

In assuming the mantle of manhood, men are expected to leave behind the world of women and the freedom to be comforted (Pollack, 1998). Often, they mourn the lost opportunity for closeness with their own fathers. As a woman therapist I hear men expressing father longing as one result of their own fathers' emotional entrapment by societal expectations.

Most men may have difficulty understanding, confronting, and expressing their emotions and can be considered to be alexithymic (Fisher & Good, 1997; Levant, 1992; Napier, 1991). Most therapists would understand a woman crying as she tells a story of loss or betrayal. At the same time, a woman therapist needs to understand that, in a similar situation, a man may display emotional stoicism or anger because of how he was taught to respond to his sadness.

Most men experience gender role strain, stress, or conflict resulting from conflicting socialization and cultural expectations for masculinity (Allen & Gordon, 1990; Eisler, 1995; O'Neil, Good, & Holmes, 1995; Pleck, 1980). Placing the male client within the context of male socialization means understanding the conflict between his workaholism or seeming overemphasis on the role of provider and his expressed desire to have more time with his family or for himself. Men also find conflict between their need for nurturance and the expectation that they be powerful and in control. One result of these conflicts can be seen in ambivalence toward women (Fisher & Good, 1997; Levant, 1992; Napier, 1991).

Women therapists working with men need to understand the interaction between masculinity and adult developmental stages (Levinson, 1978; Pollack, 1998). Recently, I have observed a number of new developmental themes in men's lives. I have encountered men in their twenties and early thirties who fear commitment. I have seen men in their midthirties to late forties who express difficulty balancing family and work similar to the role strain women experience. I have met men in their late forties to fifties who react to crises in health or relationships with anxiety and depression. And I have worked with older men who are confused about how to adjust to losses of identity, status, or loved ones.

Analysis of Power and Oppression

Therapists from a variety of orientations—psychodynamic, cognitive-behavioral, and family systems—have been influenced by the feminist emphasis on the social construction of gender and the role of power and oppression (Crites & Fitzgerald, 1980; Meth & Pasick, 1990; Shay & Maltas, 1998; Worell & Johnson, 1997). Cognitive therapy and short-term therapy appeal to many men because of the emphasis on defined tasks and goals. Using feminist therapy principles in working with male clients requires a willingness to talk about men's feelings of entitlement, the abuse of women, the effect of abuse on men and women, and the indisputable reality that women are exposed to hatred and fear by men.

For most women therapists it is certainly a lot easier to talk to a woman who has been or is being abused than it is to talk to the man who is abusing her. The abuse that occurs today ranges from very subtle putdowns that are like dripping water eroding a woman's self esteem to the deadly abuse of the obsessive stalker. When a woman therapist decides to work with male clients, she must be prepared to hear about the range of abuse. Therefore it is important that therapists know themselves and that they have, through their own therapy and continuing in peer consultation and supervision, continued to look at their attitudes and feelings about men's abuse and entitlement. This issue must be confronted in therapy, but how to confront it becomes a therapeutic issue.

The first step in knowing yourself is knowing where you draw the line. For example, I cannot and will not work with perpetrators. I have on occasion seen a perpetrator in a family session, but the goal of the session was clear and the perpetrator was informed ahead of time. For example, I was working with a female client who had been abused as a child by her grandfather. The grandfather agreed to a family session with my client and her parents. He knew the purpose of the session was for her to be able to confront him directly in a climate in which she felt safe. He valued his relationship with his son enough to come to the session, and he did apologize sincerely to her.

Emphasis on Strengths

Emphasizing strengths rather than deficits is a new trend in the psychotherapy literature (Seligman & Csikszentmihalyi, 2000). There are several reasons to focus on strengths, including increasing the male client's self-esteem, reducing resistance to therapy, increasing willingness to talk, destigmatizing therapy, and fostering adaptive strategies for coping (see Chapter Twenty-Seven; Levant, 1992; Shay & Maltas, 1998; Wyche & Rice, 1997). The "capitalization hypothesis" is a recent research finding that supports using clients' strengths to increase the effectiveness of interventions (see Chapter Twenty-Seven).

In my presidential address to the American Psychological Association Division of the Psychology of Women (Johnson, 1995) I proposed using the lens of strengths as a way of viewing women's lives. In that address, I focused on reconceptualizing women's strength as valuing enactment in addition to the more traditional value of endurance. Similar principles apply to conceptualizing men's strengths. One such list of men's positive attributes includes devotion to the other's well-being, physical affection and sexual intimacy, expression of positive feelings, sharing tasks of daily living, and practical assistance (Shay & Maltas, 1998, p. 105).

Increasing Father-Son Communication

Kevin and his son Keith sat at opposite ends of the therapy room. Keith had on hip-drop jeans, a baggy T-shirt, scruffy sneakers, no socks, and an eye-shading Red Sox baseball cap. Dad had on a suit, white shirt, shiny shoes, clipped hair, and a briefcase. I knew Keith was a gifted preteen with attention-deficit/hyperactivity disorder and minimal to moderate language-based learning difficulties. Dad quickly revealed that he too had attention-deficit/hyperactivity disorder and was empathetic of Keith's difficulties in school. But Dad was furious that Keith would not go cooperatively on their weekly visitations and that when Keith did go he was either silent or rude. I knew that Keith was a talented artist and decided to use this area of strength to begin letting these two alexithymic males learn to express their feelings of love and hurt in addition to the anger on which they were both so focused. I had them draw sketches, then complete each other's beginning sketches and tell a story about what they had drawn. Within a few sessions, Keith had communicated that he was angry with his dad for leaving home, abandoning his mother and the kids, and being with another woman.

He was also angry because his father never really did anything with him alone. The dad would bring all the children, including Keith's two older brothers, to an arcade, where the brothers would throw coins in the machines until it was time to go home. While they were doing that, their dad went somewhere—Keith was not sure where—and drank coffee. Kevin was able to talk about his own relationship with his father, who had been loving but harsh and distant. Gradually over the course of a year, these two learned to talk together about their mutual feelings of abandonment and shame over their disabilities.

Power Issues

Feminist therapy is based on the constant and explicit monitoring of the power balance between therapist and client and pays attention to the potential use and misuse of power within the therapeutic relationship. For the woman therapist and male client, achieving this balance is further complicated by the societal expectations that women will nurture men but men will retain the authority and the power. From the beginning of treatment, dealing with the issue of power imbalance is crucial for the success of therapy with a male client. One way to establish power equity is for the woman therapist to establish her credentials and credibility (Erickson, 1993). After all, have we really come so far that men, on entering therapy with a woman therapist, do not sometimes wish and wonder as did Professor Higgins, "Why can't a woman be more like a man?"

In couples therapy, balance of power issues may be played out in the "experts" the male client brings into the session. For example, in the 1990s there was significant emphasis on different gender styles of communication, including the well-known *Men Are from Mars, Women Are from Venus* (Gray, 1992). In my experience many men coming to couples therapy are familiar with Gray's approach. They have recited pat phrases such as "I'm in my cave . . . don't bother me" or "I'm just putting on my Mr. Fix It Hat now." Helping a couple move beyond these simplistic understandings of gender differences means the woman therapist will need to constantly be aware of the delicate power balance in sessions with a male client. She must balance between supporting his efforts to grow, which includes his tolerating feelings and learning a new language of relationships, while confronting his attempts to remain the same, which means staying silent about shameful feelings and holding to his assumptions regarding male power and privilege.

A woman therapist needs to remain acutely sensitive to abusing the power of her position as healer. Although the risks are greater in couples therapy than in individual therapy, they exist in both venues. Being mindful that men have been acculturated to expect women to nurture them, a woman therapist should attempt to provide an atmosphere of shared power within the sessions. Because of the powerful position of therapist, a woman therapist needs to be careful not to shame a male client, because shame is such a difficult feeling for men. It is also important not to blame the male client for attributes that are gender related such as difficulties dealing with emotions (Erickson, 1993).

Analysis of Cultural Values

Feminist therapy stresses the importance of deconstructing the gender, racial, class, and homophobic messages conveyed by society (Wyche & Rice, 1997). A woman therapist using feminist principles of therapy analyzes how these constructs are experienced within each male client. For example, the woman therapist needs to know the specific ways her client experiences the expectations that he will try to be a warrior, a provider, a good lover, and an emotionally stoic partner. Remaining up to date with the literature on the psychology of men helps women therapists understand current cultural expectations, as do reading and viewing pop culture. When a woman therapist develops a partnership with a man she helps him to deconstruct and then reconstruct concepts of what it means to be a man from his own perspective (Wyche & Rice, 1997).

A woman therapist who analyzes cultural values for men is able to be as effective as a male therapist, just as excellent coaches may not necessarily be good athletes. When I was ten, I was fortunate to have Jim Clark as a swim coach. Mr. Clark sent more young swimmers to the Olympics than any other coach of his time. Mr. Clark was overweight and could not swim. But he could inspire and he could teach because he understood kids, he understood swimming, and he understood what it took to win.

Personal Subjectivity

A woman therapist who is committed to feminist principles monitors her own biases related to the cultural, social, political, economic, and historical aspects of her male clients' experiences (Worell & Johnson, 1997; Wyche & Rice, 1997). Just as a woman therapist has empathy for the negative effects of societal expectations on women, so does she need to use empathic knowledge about how men have been affected and to be extremely careful regarding her own biases.

To manage possible biases, a woman therapist should include peer supervision with male colleagues who are knowledgeable of men's issues. In addition to my American Psychological Association contacts with leaders in men's psychology, I have attempted to explore my own biases through scholarly endeavors such as presentations at conventions and participation in peer-review activities.

Equally helpful have been two peer supervisory groups, both of which have men and women in various life stages of development with diverse psychotherapy training and orientation. Like Erickson (1993), I have found working with men to be highly charged. For that reason, I am especially careful to know my biases as a woman working with men.

When Male Clients Feel Unmasculine

Tony, the bachelor mentioned in the opening paragraphs of this chapter, came to the first several sessions with a list of what he wanted to talk about: relationship failures, his continuing obsession with Leslie (the woman who asked him to leave), and anger at his father for mistreating his mother. He was clearly in pain and thinking about these issues for the first time in his life. He said he knew I was a feminist and was concerned that I would not understand what it was like for him. Psychoeducation regarding how society constructs gender and the effect on men and women was integrated into the content of each session. And some time was spent in each of the earlier sessions talking about what it meant to Tony to have a woman therapist.

Tony started the eighth session by recounting an incident that had happened over the weekend. He had been driving by Leslie's house when she left with another man. Tony jumped out of the car and ran toward them. He said he doubled his fist to hit the guy and then noticed Leslie's face and her fright. He stopped, apologized, and went back to his car. Since then he had been replaying the scene in his head. What he said in therapy was, "I don't know what happened. In the past I would have hit him and felt ashamed afterward, but I looked at her face and knew she was scared and I couldn't do it. This therapy is making me feel like a 'wuss.' "

As Tony had begun to experience his emotions, talk about feelings, and become more sensitive, he began to fear that he was becoming a "wuss." Although I was feeling good about Tony's changes, he was becoming increasingly uncomfortable. As a result, I had to make a special effort to appreciate why my satisfaction was not matched by his. Then I had to help Tony recognize how his fears were a residual of his earlier way of thinking and were no longer realistic. Additionally, I spent considerable time helping him realize that sensitivity and relational skill were actually more functional (and appreciated) than anachronistic possessiveness and territorial rage reactions.

SPECIAL ISSUES FOR WOMEN TREATING MEN

To work successfully with men, women therapists should attend to several special issues.

Overcoming Stereotypes

Male clients are burdened by the stereotypes and narrow expectations that society holds for men. These stereotypes may be seen in both the content of the sessions and the process. Some examples of content are that women are more interested in relationships than work, that women are too emotional, that women are weak and need to be protected, that women need help, and that for women love is more important than sex. Therapy must include efforts to overcome these limitations.

In working with men, the woman therapist must address the common stereotype that men must be warriors and providers (Shay & Maltas, 1998). Although it is comforting to believe that this role is losing its saliency, this comfort is not warranted. To become more realistic, one has only to look out the window and see young boys tumbling with each other in the grass, watch the bully taking the bike and the smaller boy learning just the right tone to get him to back off, or just witness the content of the ever-popular hand-held video games used by the boys in our own waiting rooms.

For the male client to deal with his stereotype about himself as a warrior and a provider, he must find a balance between protecting those he loves and expecting his partner to share responsibility for the safety and security of the family. For the therapist, dealing with this stereotype also means finding a balance between helping a man celebrate the value of his work while still finding time for himself and his relationships. It means valuing the courage required of the protector role while not becoming so foolhardy as to needlessly risk health and safety.

Women have both recognized and challenged the role strain of contemporary societal expectations regarding work and family. As male and female partners have moved away from rigid role division into more egalitarian partnerships, each has had to confront the role strain of multiple demands. Because women therapists with families or partners face this task on a daily basis, they enrich therapy with their own experiences of role strain and management of multiple roles. The woman therapist recognizes the impossibility of perfect balancing and is uniquely able to empathize with the male client who is attempting to balance his multiple demands. In fact, she may even be able to help him by sharing successful techniques. Finally, women therapists must guard against some problematic gender stereotypes related to the processes of therapy (for example, women should take care of men's feelings, women should need and want the protection of men, women are unduly afraid of anger, women are too subjective and unable to be objective, and women cannot really understand men).

Recognizing Shame

Shame is one of the most powerful emotions men bring into therapy. It is crucial to the success of therapy that the woman therapist understand the role of shame in men's lives and that she understand that many men fear that a woman will shame them (Osherson & Krugman, 1990). The stereotype of the shrewish, henpecking wife is but one reflection of this stereotype. The male client's fear of shame, which may be present in his resistance to dealing with certain topics, can occur at any time during therapy. He may hear something the therapist says as chastising him or he may be relating a shameful encounter but underplay it in such a way that the woman therapist risks missing the shame experienced during the event.

For men shame is such a powerful emotion that it interferes with their expressing other feelings such as anger, sadness, love, or anxiety (Osherson & Krugman, 1990). Several writers on men's psychology have set the origins of men's shame in their relationships with their mothers (Osherson & Krugman, 1990; Pollack & Levant, 1998). A crucial therapeutic goal for men is to help them accept interdependency and intimacy as desirable and not a cause for shame (Erickson, 1993).

Shame is a particularly important component in the treatment of men who have been abused or who observed abuse in their families of origin. In my experience an important source of a man's shame is his relationship with his father. I find it tragic to witness how many men still experience significant shame from the verbal or physical abuse of their fathers. The feelings of vulnerability of oneself, and in some cases, one's mother, produce overwhelming shame. A woman therapist might miss the intensity of the shame because she is looking for another emotion such as anger, whereas her client is feeling the shame of the small boy.

I suspect that the majority of men over forty have experienced or observed some form of abuse in their family of origin. Male clients who have experienced abuse as a child or observed their mother being abused are a particular challenge for a woman therapist. It is very rewarding to help these men work through their experiences and strengthen their resolve to be a different type of man. As men explore the impact of abuse, they change their behavior and develop a different way of conceptualizing abuse significantly sooner than they are able to experience parallel emotional changes.

Men's feelings of shame about being weak may be projected on to their intimate partners. When men use this approach, the woman therapist needs to be particularly alert to understand that the man who is complaining about his too-dependent partner may actually be afraid that he will be unable to protect her. He then reexperiences shame when she is hurting, even if the hurt is emotional, not physical.

Dealing with Resistance

It is important to normalize men's resistance to therapy, because they have not been acculturated to the process. A woman therapist working with men may need to revisit the resistance issue in each session. Initially the woman therapist might bring up the issue in the context of overall gender socialization. Later resistance is apt to be more subtle and related to the male client's belief that a woman simply cannot understand certain aspects of his existence or the "code of masculinity" or that she is trying to turn him into a woman.

A couple was referred to me after unsuccessful treatment with another woman therapist. They had gone into therapy after the husband's discovery of his wife's infidelity. They specifically chose a woman therapist both times. The reason they gave was that they thought a woman would help them develop better relationship skills. However, the couple was resistant to dealing with the underlying relationship dysfunction because both were colluding in keeping the man in the role of provider and saving him from shame. It was easier for them to do the dance of anger in which he exploded and she withdrew rather than talk about the shame of his work difficulties and his seeming helpless in dealing with an unfair work situation that produced unbearable stress.

A woman therapist needs to be aware that when she sees progress in therapy, that may be a time when the male client wants to shut down or flee. It is common for female therapists to want to help men be more emotionally expressive. However, when a male client slowly begins to share his inner experiences, he frequently feels a rush of relief but then experiences anxiety with the release of suppressed emotion (Scher, 1990). A woman therapist must recognize that although it may be easier for a male client to express feelings to her, he does so by breaking out of the male tradition and probably will experience concern about loss of manliness.

Handling Transference and Countertransference

Transference and countertransference issues are more difficult when the therapist and client are different sexes than when they are the same sex. Transference has classically been understood as attributing qualities to the therapist from a client's past relationships with mother and father and others of particular importance. A woman therapist trained to conceptualize transference and countertransference in a traditional way needs to understand the impact of gender socialization on how the client feels about her and the feelings she might experience toward the client. A woman therapist treating men needs to understand that transference will also include the male client's stereotypes and expectations about proper female conduct.

Positive transference helps clients generalize to other relationships in their lives and may help them reduce their fear of intimacy. Negative transference most often leads to treatment failure. To reduce the negative effects of countertransference (which is defined as the therapist's attributions of the client based on her experiences and gender schema) and to be able to use the phenomena productively, a woman therapist must carefully understand and analyze the role of men in her life (Carlson, 1987). She must know the gender roles assigned to important women in her life. Each male client has the potential to bring new issues, and therefore she needs a continuous exploration of her own gender role socialization and her own gender schema.

In their interactions with men, all women therapists have experienced both the positive and negative aspects of men's socialization. The woman therapist might have been abused by her father, brother, male partner, or stranger. She might have been silenced. Her abilities may have been ignored or underestimated by teachers or even professors in graduate school. She might have grown up in a family with rigid gender roles, may have been indulged, or may have been abandoned. She might be in love or might be recovering from a bitter romantic disappointment. Whatever her gender experiences, she must make them a conscious part of her day-to-day working with her male clients.

The first client I saw while in graduate school was a woman in her twenties who was intensely anxious because of an ongoing abusive relationship. I would see her late at night in a building somewhat off campus. It was my supervisor's office, and frequently we were the only people in the building. During the course of her therapy she made the decision to terminate the relationship. One night during a session her former male friend came and pounded repeatedly on the door, shouting, "I know you are in there." For several interminable moments I was immobilized with fear. We called the campus police and talked to him under their watchful presence. Although I saw her for a year after that episode and the ending was positive, I am still haunted by the memory and carry it with me each time I hear a man talk about stalking his former girlfriend.

The male client frequently struggles with issues of power in regard to a woman therapist (Scher, 1990; Silverberg, 1986). When a female therapist works with a male client, it is common to encounter a power struggle. Frequently, the woman therapist who is sensitive to her own feelings regarding power and control will be able to use the evocation of the feeling of competition between her and the client to make an effective interpretation.

Just as transference and countertransference can be useful in understanding issues from the past that are still present today, they can also be useful in understanding the impact of societal expectations on the man's current functioning. Even the work of expressing feelings can provoke a man to feel that he has relinquished power to his therapist.

Women therapists may be seen as objects of desire. Women therapists may also be seen as "the special woman." They may be idealized as a blend of the man's early emotional connection to his mother and the social expectation of a forever loving, nurturing woman. Most men remember strong messages about the importance of separating from their mothers to become a man. Yet they retain the yearning to have that attachment (Betcher & Pollack, 1983). Some ways a therapist might see the negative effects of this longing for a special woman are the client's articulation of feelings of having married the wrong woman and an inability to be faithful, because there is a splitting of affectionate feelings and sexual desires into at least two separate women.

A woman therapist can also have sexual feelings for her male client. Obviously she must monitor these feelings. She needs to be careful that she is not interfering with the man's marriage or relationships. There is a risk that he might idealize the therapist and turn her into the special woman. The media's portrayal of women therapists treating men has often chosen the sexual feelings between them as the important dramatic element. In the first year of the television hit *The Sopranos*, much of the dramatic material included therapeutic material and the therapeutic relationship. In one episode the therapist brings up that the male client, Mr. Soprano, said in a previous session that he had feelings for her. The male client quickly says, "I said I love you." This is a significant improvement in showing competent women therapists from the novel and movie *Prince of Tides*, in which the therapist seduces the already sexually traumatized male patient and even gets him involved with her own family.

Using Peer Support Groups

In addition to keeping up with the literature on the new psychology of men, women therapists can continue knowing and growing by using a mixed-sex peer support group. The multiple perspectives on male clients can be invaluable in providing alternative perspectives of the male client's issues.

Setting Limits

When she sets a therapeutic limit with a male client, the woman therapist cultivates the ground for a power struggle. Nevertheless, limits must be set, because effective therapy requires a variety of nonnegotiable limits.

Who comes to sessions. Effective therapy requires that the therapist be in charge of participation in sessions. This issue is more frequently discussed in the modalities of couples and family therapy than in individual therapy. Most therapists doing family therapy and parent counseling require that when partners are living together they both come to the sessions. Family therapy's emphasis on the participation of fathers and husbands has helped to increase men's involvement in psychotherapy (Allen & Gordon, 1990). When the therapist is a woman, there is an increased probability of the father "playing the provider card" to make scheduling of the sessions difficult.

To reinforce limit setting, the woman therapist should state her rules of participation during the intake phone call and repeat them in the first session. It is equally important that she follow through on each session and not agree to any client-precipitated variations. Naturally, the therapist may sometimes wish to have individual meetings with either partner or some other combination of the family. However, in my experience, a woman therapist needs to be very careful if she desires to see a segment of the family without the father present. This decision on her part reinforces a continuing societal expectation that fathers are involved with their families only if the involvement has minimal effect on their work.

There are also family developmental patterns that require limit setting. About 90 percent of my clients with children under the age of five both want to come to therapy, so the rule of participation need only be set with a few parents. For parents of teen girls, it is more difficult to get the father's involvement. I think part of that resistance is the unspoken difficulty men have in knowing the appropriate level of intimacy with their teen girls. I am firm in the rule that I will not see a child or teen unless I meet first with both parents and unless both parents agree to be part of the therapy, as needed. During the initial session with parents of a teen girl I share the research on the importance of fathers for the girl's development and I go into detail about the positive benefits of his involvement with her throughout this state. I help the father from the first session forward to understand the difference between emotional support and closeness and sexuality.

Expressions of anger. To be effective in working with male clients a woman therapist must be able to help men verbally express their anger and rage within the sessions (Brooks, 1991). She must then help the men explore the myriad of emotions contained and hidden within the rage. However, it is also important that a woman therapist set limits on the physical expression of anger not just within but outside the session as well. In addition to the informed consent given and gone over with each client, a woman therapist must let her clients, male and female, know the limits on the expression of anger. This limit is particularly necessary when, under the rubric of "discipline," parents shake a child, tightly grasp a child's arm, pull an ear, slap a child's face, or put pepper on a child's tongue. The therapist notifies the family that violence is violence, regardless of the intended objective.

Another limit I set is to not work with parents, men or women, who hit their children, regardless of the name of the hitting (for example, "I only spank her when she needs it"). I share the literature about an increased risk of aggression in children who are hit or spanked and the research on modeling behaviors. I empathize with their own experiences of being hit when growing up. I understand that they are only trying to do their best. But I maintain the limit.

Threatening behaviors. Work with Tony illustrated another example of the potentially threatening behaviors that a woman therapist might see in a male client. I was concerned that Tony might be stalking his former girlfriend. Hearing that he was "driving by her home" made me anxious. When he told me about the incident, there was enough of a therapeutic relationship, and he had learned enough about exploring and describing his inner landscape, that he was able to see that he had been obsessively driving by her home. He was also able to explore what he was looking for in doing that and eventually to understand that to get on with his life he needed to stop all contact with her. She would call him if he had not called for a few days, and Tony realized he needed to ask her to stop calling and make a clean break. My responsibility as a therapist was to understand my anxiety about his potential for expressing anger so as to be able to deal directly with the stalking behavior while maintaining a therapeutic alliance with Tony.

Recognizing Power Imbalance in Couples Therapy

In using a feminist approach to couples work, one must be sensitive to the issues of power and power imbalances. Although issues regarding power are there from the beginning, they are most effectively addressed after the couple is communicating effectively and after both members have established a working relationship with the therapist. Richard and his wife, Helen, were such a couple.

As noted in the introduction to this chapter, Helen was the one who wanted therapy, but Richard was the one who made the call. The first indication of Richard's use of power (and perhaps his worldview of women) was that he had his secretary, a woman, initiate the call for an appointment, as she probably did with his other doctors. Helen was feeling somewhat depressed. She felt that they had lost touch with each other, and with their last child out of the home she was lonely. She was considering her own business and had hired a job coach. Richard supported her in this endeavor.

While exploring their family backgrounds, gender issues became clearer to both of them. There was a history of depression with angry outbursts from women in Richard's family. His father was somewhat removed and would come into the family interactions primarily to "soothe" the "emotional women." In Helen's family, her father was more involved and she saw her parents being loving with each other. However, her family also had a dark side. Her father would spank her in a derogatory and excessive way while her mother did nothing to protect her. Her father was also verbally abusive to her brother. Richard and Helen were able to see how some of their difficulty in communicating about difficult issues and the way they handled their anger had significant roots in the relational patterns of their families of origin.

They were working on alternative ways to handle anger. Helen opened a session by talking about an incident from the previous weekend. They were out to dinner with another couple, old friends, and Helen for the first time began openly and enthusiastically talking about her plans for her new business. The friends appeared interested and engaged in the conversation, but Richard interrupted by making a crack about Helen not even being able to balance her checkbook so how in the world did she imagine she could run a business. Helen was stunned and fell silent. Later, she exploded at home, to which Richard replied he was just kidding and everyone knew it, so what was the big deal?

In unraveling the episode, I felt that it was time to talk about male power and entitlement in this society. I also introduced information about how women's gender stereotypes create anxiety about work outside the home, particularly in a field that was not really a "woman's place." I explained male entitlement as a natural outcome of how our society has viewed men and that at the same time society has viewed women's place as in the home. I talked about the unease that both sexes feel when they strive for equality because of the undercurrent of societal pressures. By using positive statements such as, "Richard, you've been very supportive of Helen's trying this new venture. What feeling did you have prior to your comment?" and "Helen, you've been able to handle doubts about this work effort before; what threw you this time?" both were able to experience the feelings coming from their own uneasiness about the change in stereotyped gender roles happening in their family.

Richard owned that he had felt a little jealous at the attention Helen was getting. And Helen owned that despite her bravado she was feeling that she would probably fail and that everyone knew but they were placating her as had happened in school. By opening up the issue of patriarchy, Richard and Helen were able to reach another level of emotional honesty and intimacy in their relationship.

SPECIFIC SUGGESTIONS FOR TREATING MEN

Aside from the general issues I have already noted, I have found certain specific strategies to be effective in treating men.

Bibliotherapy

Using books and tapes to help educate men about gender issues is effective for many male clients. Being able to learn some of the concepts independently reduces the feelings of dependency and the possibility of feeling shameful about ignorance. Timing is all. I usually wait to introduce the idea of reading about men's issues or emotional expression until a client asks or an issue arises for which he expresses some curiosity. In this way I am responding to his request and am less likely to evoke the feeling that I am infantilizing him. I tailor the recommended readings for each man. For the man who resists reading, I have a list of audiotapes. If the man is highly resistant, I start him with an audiotape that encourages good listening skills but is geared to his work. Several good books and tapes by business "gurus" have borrowed heavily from gender psychology.

For women therapists interested in treating men in psychotherapy, in addition to this volume, there are many good references of the new psychology of men from which to choose (Allen & Gordon, 1990; Brooks, 1998; Erickson, 1993; Meth & Pasick, 1990; Philpot, Brooks, Lusterman, & Nutt, 1997; Pollack & Levant, 1998). Women therapists looking for additional resources in group work might want to consult Levant's article (1990) on psychological services designed for men.

Teaching Emotional Competence

It is highly recommended that therapy with men involve teaching them language to use in expressing feelings. In the beginning the woman therapist has the power from many perspectives, including that she knows the language of therapy. When a woman therapist teaches a male client language to use about feelings, the therapist is taking one step toward equalizing the power balance. Many approaches are described in the literature (Allen & Gordon, 1990; Levant & Kelly, 1989; Shay & Maltas, 1998). Therapists can develop an approach that fits their style and helps their male clients learn to label feelings.

Using Validating Feedback

Using positive feedback helps a man minimize shame and see the restrictive role shame-based behavior has played in his life. One of the biggest complaints I hear from men is, "She always finds something wrong. She never notices what I've done right." A therapeutic approach that focuses on the man's strengths and helps him develop competencies is experienced as supportive. Defining some of the therapy as coaching, which focuses on skill development, is another way of helping men learn new ways to deal with their emotions and relationships.

Using Storytelling, Metaphors, Drawing, and Journaling

Telling stories and using metaphors about men help male clients trust that the female therapist is knowledgeable about men's issues. Some of the stories I have found beneficial to my clients involve stories of men as adults telling their fathers what they would like from them at this point in their lives. Other stories involve scenarios of men relating differently with coworkers. The metaphor of a man pushing a very large stone up the hill only to have it roll back down again is effective with some men who are aware of the energy it takes to keep their emotions in check constantly. Asking men to talk about stories they remember that shaped their beliefs and asking them to write a different ending is another technique that appeals to some men.

Although I do not personally find drawing as effective with men as with women clients, I use it in father-son therapy. Drawing with this dyad can level the playing field in a way words do not.

A few male clients have found some success in keeping a journal. I have found it works best if I have them write on a specific topic rather than just ask them to keep a daily journal. For example, I recently asked a couple to keep separate journals for a week on the topic of work, what it meant to them, their earliest experiences, and so forth.

Using Intake Forms

One way to include gender issues from the beginning of therapy is in the intake forms. For example, on my intake form for adults I include the question, "What did your father think of your birth?" Another example is, "What were the different expectations for boys and girls in your family?"

During the intake process it is recommended that the woman therapist put gender issues out front early. After all, the male client chose to see a woman therapist. The therapist can ask him why and go beyond the usual answers of "to understand women better" or "to help in my relationship with women" or "my wife, partner, or fiancée said I needed to" or "I thought I could talk to a woman more easily." Any of these responses leaves the door wide open for "Why did you think a woman might help you with this better than a man?" And then, "What is important to you about being a man?" "What is important to you about women?"

As I noted in the beginning of this chapter, more men are coming to therapy today. And more men are coming to women therapists. Most men who specifically seek out a woman therapist for individual therapy expect her to be more knowledgeable about relationship issues than a man would be or they are ashamed of their emotional reactions and vulnerability and feel safer with a woman. Many women are turning more to their husbands, to the men in their lives, for the type of friendship women used to get from other women. Many men, particularly men under fifty, want a different type of relationship than they saw in their parents' generation, but they frequently do not have the skills to change and at the same time they are afraid of intimacy.

Also, times are changing in therapy. There are more female therapists and more male clients and a resultant surge in this male client–female therapist dyad. Male clients at all points on the adult development scale are finding their way to individual therapy, and frequently they are choosing to go to female therapists. Men continue in ever-increasing numbers to come to therapy for help with a variety of issues: relationships, anxiety, depression, sense of puzzlement, wounding. They also come to therapy with a mixture of skills to deal with their feelings and their inner life as it affects them day to day.

To be most effective with their male clients, women therapists must be knowledgeable about gender issues. One way to obtain this knowledge is to use paradigms from feminist therapy, gender-sensitive therapies, and gender-aware therapies. The new psychology of men presents the most helpful understanding of men's issues today. Also, the applications of feminist therapy principles and gender-aware therapy provide a powerful framework and constructive tools for women therapists helping men.

To turn Henry Higgins' question on its head, "Why can't a man be more like a woman?" In today's world he is—just as modern women are coping with issues once considered men's province. More men now are learning to open up and explore their feminine side. But like all of us, men need help in dealing with new and sometimes scary changes. They need to learn the new language and they need a knowledgeable and empathic professor to do it. Could it be that women therapists will play Henry Higgins without the arrogance and without the patriarchy?

References

Allen, J., & Gordon, S. (1990). Creating a framework for change. In R. Meth & R. Pasick (Eds.), *Men in therapy: The challenge of change* (pp. 131–151). New York: Guilford Press.

American Psychological Association. (1975). Report of the Task Force on Sex Role Bias and Sex Role Stereotyping in Psychotherapeutic Practice. *American Psychologist, 30,* 1169–1175.

Betcher, W., & Pollack, W. (1993). *In a time of fallen heroes: The re-creation of masculinity.* New York: Macmillan.

Brooks, G. (1991). Traditional men in marital and family therapy. In M. Bogard (Ed.), *Feminist approaches for men in family therapy* (pp. 51–74). New York: Haworth Press.

Brooks, G. (1998). *A new psychotherapy for traditional men.* San Francisco: Jossey-Bass.

Broverman, I. K., Broverman, D. M., Clarkson, F. E., Rosenkrantz, P. S., & Vogel, S. R. (1970). Sex-role stereotypes and clinical judgements of mental health *Journal of Consulting and Clinical Psychology, 34,* 1–7.

Carlson, N. (1987). Woman therapist: Male Client. In M. Scher, M. Stevens, G. Good, & G. Eichenfield (Eds.), *The handbook of counseling and psychotherapy with men* (pp. 39–50). Newbury Park, CA: Sage.

Crites, J., & Fitzgerald, L. (1980). The competent male. In T. M. Skovholt, P. G. Schauble, & R. Davis (Eds.), *Counseling men* (pp. 41–51). Monterey, CA: Brooks/Cole.

Eisler, R. M. (195). The relationship between masculine gender role stress and men's health risk: The validation of the construct. In R. F. Levant & W. S. Pollack (Eds.), *A new psychology of men* (pp. 207–225). New York: Basic Books.

Erickson, B. M. (1993). *Helping men change: The role of the female therapist.* Newbury Park, CA: Sage.

Fischer, A. R., & Good, G. E. (1997). Masculine gender roles, recognition of emotions, and interpersonal intimacy. *Psychotherapy, 34,* 160–170.

Good, G. E., Gilbert, L. A., & Scher, M. (1990). Gender aware therapy: A synthesis of feminist therapy and knowledge about gender. *Journal of Counseling and Development, 68,* 376–380.

Gray, J. (1992). *Men are from Mars, women are from Venus: A practical guide for improving communication and getting what you want in your relationships.* New York: HarperCollins.

Johnson, N. (1995, August). Feminist frames of women's strength: Visions for the future. Presidential address to the Division of the Psychology of Women presented at the annual meeting of the American Psychological Association, New York.

Levant, R. (1990). Psychological services designed for men: A psychoeducational approach. *Psychotherapy, 27*(3), 309–315.

Levant, R. (1992). Toward the reconstruction of masculinity. *Journal of Family Psychology, 5*(3–4), 379–402.

Levant, R., Hirsch, L., Celentano, E., Cozza, T., Hill, S., MacEachern, M., Marty, N., & Schnedeker, J. (1992). The male role: An investigation of norms and stereotypes. *Journal of Mental Health Counseling, 14,* 325–377.

Levant, R., & Kelly, J. (1989). *Between father and child.* New York: Viking.

Levinson, D. (1978). *The seasons of a man's life.* New York: Knopf.

Meth, R., & Pasick, R. (1990). *Men in therapy: The challenge of change.* New York: Guilford Press.

Napier, A. (1991). Heroism, men, and marriage. *Journal of Marital and Family Therapy, 9*(1), 19–35.

O'Neil, J. M., Good, G. E., & Holmes, S. (1995). Fifteen years of theory and research on men's gender role conflict: New paradigms for empirical research. In R. F. Levant & W. S. Pollack (Eds.), *A new psychology of men* (pp. 164–206). New York: Basic Books.

Osherson, S., & Krugman, S. (1990). Men, shame, and psychotherapy. *Psychotherapy, 27*(3), 327–339.

Philpot, C., Brooks, G., Lusterman, D., & Nutt, R. (Eds.). (1997). *Bridging separate gender worlds: Why men and women clash and how therapists can bring them together.* Washington, DC: American Psychological Association.

Pleck, J. (1980). Men's power with women, other men, and society: A men's movement analysis. In T. M. Skovholt, P. G. Schauble, & R. Davis (Eds.), *Counseling men* (pp. 30–40). Monterey, CA: Brooks/Cole.

Pollack, W. (1998). *Real boys: Rescuing our sons from the myths of boyhood.* New York: Random House.

Pollack, W. (2000). *Real boys' voices.* New York: Random House.

Pollack, W., & Levant, R. (1998). *New psychotherapy for men.* New York: Wiley.

Scher, M. (1990). Effect of gender role incongruities on men's experience as clients in psychotherapy. *Psychotherapy, 27*(3), 322–326.

Seligman, M., & Csikszentmihalyi, M. (2000). Positive psychology: An introduction. *American Psychologist, 55*(1), 5–14.

Shay, J., & Maltas, C. (1998). Reluctant men in couple therapy: Corralling the Marlboro man. In W. Pollack & R. Levant (Eds.), *New psychotherapy for men* (pp. 97–126). New York: Wiley.

Silverberg, R. (1986). *Psychotherapy for men: Transcending the masculine mystique.* Springfield, IL: Thomas.

Toomer, J. (1980). Males in psychotherapy. In T. M. Skovholt, P. G. Schauble, & R. Davis (Eds.), *Counseling men* (pp. 92–100). Monterey, CA: Brooks/Cole.

Worell, J., & Johnson, N. (Eds.). (1997). *Shaping the future of feminist psychology: Education, research, and practice.* Washington, DC: American Psychological Association.

Worell, J., & Remer, P. (1992). *Feminist perspectives in therapy: An empowerment model for women.* West Sussex, U.K.: Wiley.

Wyche, K., & Rice, J. (1997). Feminist therapy: From dialogue to tenets. In J. Worell & N. Johnson (Eds.), *Shaping the future of feminist psychology: Education, research, and practice* (pp. 57–71). Washington, DC: American Psychological Association.

CHAPTER TWENTY

Male Therapist, Male Client

Reflections on Critical Dynamics

Murray Scher

Two men in a room is a scary and unusual phenomenon. Just what are they doing there? Being intimate? Unlikely. Trusting each other? Less likely. Being competitive? Very likely. What makes this pairing scary? Nothing really, save that it frightens us, especially if we are women. What makes this scenario unusual? Men rarely seek each other out individually. A bunch of men in a room might not be less scary but it would be more usual. What contributes to the feelings evoked by two men together is the male gender role and how it molds both male behavior and our expectations of men.

In this chapter I examine a situation in which two men are together in a room, in which they are intimate, in which they trust each other, and in which they likely are competitive. Examining the therapeutic encounter between a male client and a male therapist is an exciting prospect. The excitement lies in uncovering that which should be most obvious but has not always been. Exploring the contribution of gender roles to the psychotherapy transaction is a relatively new occurrence (Gilbert & Scher, 1999) and is continually being expanded, as witnessed by this volume. I believe productive therapy is more likely to occur if the therapist is cognizant of gender roles. To practice any other way excludes a major component of individual behavior (Good, Gilbert, & Scher, 1990).

GENDER ROLES IN PSYCHOTHERAPY

Therapy is an intricate enterprise. Therapy with men necessitates patience and skill. Male therapists working with male clients are hard-pressed to stay cognizant of what is going on in the encounter, what is going on in themselves, what they can surmise about the client, and what elements of the male gender role are being tapped and to remain unafraid of the client and what he is being and presenting. All of this is no easy task and requires commitment and study on the part of therapists. This chapter is an attempt to help prepare, orient, and inform male therapists who work with male clients.

Why Look at This Pairing?

In the relatively short history of examining the male gender role as it relates psychologically to the behavior of men, the effect of that role on psychotherapy has been actively explored (Scher, 1979a, 1979b, 1981, 1984, 1990). It is important to keep examining men in therapy because increasing numbers of men are coming for therapy. Therapy does not appear to have quite the stigma for men that it once did because sports figures, political figures, and other men who have high status and are visible are more forthcoming about their own therapy experiences. Consequently, a greater variety of men will be entering consulting rooms, and we need to be sensitive to their needs and particular histories.

Although the psychotherapy profession includes a large proportion of women, many men will find themselves in a therapeutic encounter with another man, and that necessitates an understanding of the intersection of male roles and psychotherapy. That understanding is the focus of this chapter. Several of the major elements of the male gender role are examined, as are the construction of human relationships and the elements peculiar to the therapeutic encounter.

Male Gender Role

The male gender role has been thoroughly explored in other writings (Gilbert & Scher, 1999), and so it is unnecessary to repeat that exploration here. However, I want to focus on several elements of the male gender role that are significant in therapy. Those elements are competition, emotional constriction, rationality, fear of dependence, and homophobia.

Competition. Men are taught to be competitive, and virtually all men are either subtly or blatantly competitive. Competition in and of itself is not negative or positive, but how it is used and how it manifests itself in relationships determines its utility. In the male-male pairing it is potent and must not be ignored. Power differentials in therapy elicit competition. Therapists have more power than clients do, and clients struggle against that power differential (Scher, 1990). Male clients in my practice are much more likely to forget their checkbooks or to have run out of checks than female clients are when it is time to pay for a session. This "forgetfulness" is a reminder of the power that clients have, sometimes the only power the clients feel as they are experiencing dependence on therapists, and in the case of men that dependence is frightening. Therapists are also competitive with clients and must be mindful of this competition or the therapy can founder.

Emotional constriction. The image of a man in our culture is one that personifies coolness and restricted affect. Men are not easily moved and are very constrained in their expression of whatever they are feeling. It is a cliché that men do not cry. That is only part of what they do not do emotionally, because men are not expected to experience powerful feelings of any kind. Somehow if they do, they will be vulnerable. This vulnerability is in direct contradiction to the expectation that control and power will characterize a man's relation to the rest of the world. The constriction of emotion begins early in a man's life and is reinforced until his death, which just might be an untimely one if he tries to contain all of the feelings human beings normally experience.

Obviously therapy, which depends on some emotional abreaction in almost every case, is a challenge for men who have learned to be very removed from their feelings. I remember seeing a young man for therapy over a period of two years. He was most appealing and a joy to work with. The therapy was drawing to a close because he was graduating from college and I was working in the college counseling center. At our last session as we were saying good-bye I touched on my sadness at not seeing him again and tears began to run down my cheeks. Looking at me with a combination of fear and anger he said rather strongly, "Don't do that!"

Rationality. Of the many means men use to stay in control, rationality is a most significant one. It is a widespread belief that rationality makes men superior to women who, of course, are the embodiment of emotionality and therefore are irrational. Logic is the handmaiden or handboy of rationality. Therapy is usually necessitated when rational explanations and solutions fail. This failure of rationality causes the male client to feel disconcerted and disoriented. He comes into therapy seeking to reassert the rational underpinnings of his world and has a great deal of trouble embracing the irrational.

Male therapists, no strangers to rationality and logic themselves, have to fight the inclination to support the rational explanations sought. After all, if rationality would solve the problem, the client would not be in therapy. It is the effects of the destruction of that refuge that necessitate therapy. This is a situation in which the client feels especially frightened and in which the therapist must be careful to gently introduce the recognition and inspection of feelings so as to move the client to a sense of safety with emotions.

Fear of dependence. Males in our culture are raised to be independent and autonomous. Those qualities are the sine qua non of what makes a male into a man. Oddly enough, to reach independence one must develop through a stage of both physical and psychological dependence on the parents. At the same time one experiences dependence our culture prescribes independence as an important quality for men. These twin messages create ambivalence in the developing male and in the man he becomes. He both desires dependence and shuns it. The reactions to his ambivalence span the gamut from irritation with to physical violence against the object of his dependence, usually a partner or spouse.

Issues of dependence and independence enter the consulting room with the client. The client is dependent on the therapist by the nature of the therapy process. The process is usually unknown to the client, whereas the therapist is steeped in it. Therefore, clients rely on therapists to take care of them by introducing them to the therapeutic process and making sure that the process moves toward the particular goals set. The client often struggles against his feelings of dependence on the therapist. This struggle happens in general and is exacerbated in clients whose personal history involves unresolved dependency needs or a sense of failure to reach independence. The power and control issues of the therapist are also a factor here, and it is important to emphasize that therapists benefit mightily from their own therapy so as to be cognizant of what they are doing in the therapeutic encounter.

Paul was a young man I saw in therapy. His parents had treated him poorly insofar as they were quite neglectful of him. He had learned early that he could depend on no adults for anything more than furnishing his basic needs for survival. There was in him a yearning to be dependent, to be taken care of and loved. He struggled against that need because of his powerful fear of being disappointed and betrayed once again. He did well in therapy but would periodically disappear. I would write him and tell him I was there when he wanted to come back and I hoped it would be soon. He returned several times. We are still struggling with dependence issues, but they are not articulated. My sense is he is not ready to conceptualize them or talk about them yet, because they are far too primitive.

Homophobia. The worst thing you can call a young boy is a girl. Males are terrified of finding anything feminine in themselves (O'Neil, 1981). This terror is one of the roots of the noxious plant we call homophobia. Homophobia is central to the socialization of men in our culture, and it begins very early. The belief that the attraction to, love of, and consummation of that love with another man is anathema to being a man is deeply ingrained. Homosexuality is a very frightening concept for many people in our culture. Therefore, the vast majority of men shun any possibility of appearing homosexual, which necessitates truncating their relationships with other men. As boys the affection, love, and attraction they feel for their male playmates is stifled. When they reach adolescence men are taught to suppress the occasional and normal sexual feelings they experience for their chums. To not suppress them often leads to a homosexual panic, a frequent presenting problem in college counseling centers.

Therapists do well to be sensitive to the homophobic content of the male gender role. It is especially important for male therapists to be aware of this issue in their clients because it is liable to surface as clients experience appreciation of the therapists' care of them and as the emotional intimacy of the therapeutic encounter deepens. Confusing intimacy and affection with sex is not unusual, especially in young men. If necessary it is often helpful to make clients' fears explicit and to reassure clients about their fears.

Gene was a man who had long suppressed his yearnings for a good father. He found in his therapist a warm, wise, kindly, and charming man. Gene relaxed very slowly into feeling taken care of by someone he respected and liked. At a certain point in the therapy the therapist became aware of Gene's emotional absence. After this emotional absence had gone on for several weeks with no explanation, the therapist inquired about its origin. Gene acknowledged it and talked about a dream he had in which the therapist was naked. This dream terrified Gene because he began to worry about being sexual with the therapist. As they talked and Gene was assured that there might be other meanings to the dream and that his fear also related to homophobia he relaxed and exploring the dream became a most productive task for him.

It is essential for therapists to be aware of the male gender role and how it affects their clients and therapy. Not being aware severely hampers effective therapy (Gilbert & Scher, 1999). There are other elements to the male role than those mentioned; for a fuller explication, see Scher (1990). The subtle and not so subtle interweaving of male gender role elements will become clearer as this chapter progresses.

WHAT DO WE KNOW ABOUT MALE THERAPISTS AND MALE CLIENTS TOGETHER?

The male-male pairing in therapy is examined with all therapy, but it has not been specifically reviewed from a gender role perspective except in the work of Heppner and Gonzales (1987). The gender role perspective provides a sociological or sociopsychological underpinning to the psychological stew that is the therapeutic encounter.

The elements that men bring with them as a result of their cultural loading have already been considered earlier in this chapter. What is necessary, beyond understanding how complex is the interweaving of these elements both in the individuals and in their interactions, is how the therapist finds his way through this cobweb-filled, often very dark, sometimes rank, and always lush forest. I briefly explore here what I have said about men in therapy in the past and then go on to what I think now and how I find my way with the men who come to my consulting room.

Men are often frightening for other men, and therefore it is wise for male therapists to remember the importance of concern, good humor, and interest for and in the treatment of men. The initial contact, as in all therapeutic encounters, is important, and therapists who are successful in treating men will demonstrate honesty, consideration, and restrained affection (Scher, 1979b).

I have emphasized understanding the need to be careful with men. This care is essential because of an intriguing artifact in the treatment of men that requires that therapists be "prepared to contend with the frail, hurt, underloved, overprotected little boy who dwells within many men" (Scher, 1979a, p. 537). The issue of establishing intimacy is directly connected to this vulnerability. Developing intimate relationships is required for men to move beyond the limitations of the male gender role. Such achievement is possible in the therapeutic encounter, but therapists must remember the trepidation with which men approach each other and act accordingly (Scher, 1990).

Working with men often tests the limits of a therapist's patience because men are resistant to therapy and uncomfortable with help seeking. To aid in liberating men from the constraints of the male role counselors have to be supportive, be willing to model nonstereotyped male behavior, be understanding of the feminist viewpoint, and most important be "willing to give permission to be different, and willing to use whatever therapeutic modality is necessary to free their clients. The counselor who wants to help . . . will also have to be challenging and direct, possess a sense of humor, have a sense of the absurd, and be a loving and supportive person" (Scher, 1981, p. 201).

In an attempt to summarize some of what I have said in the past about therapy with men I want to quote from an article about working with a young man, whom I have called Bruce, who is HIV positive (Scher, 1994). I first started seeing him ten years ago; now I see him only occasionally. This quotation brings the issues of transference and countertransference, which will be explored later, to the fore. "I am impressed with the intricate dance of love and fear I did with this smitten young man. I had to confront so much of my own fears of death and aging and disability in an attempt to aid him in considering his own" (p. 91). Bruce tested and tried me, and we both grew from the experience. I tried to be caring and compassionate without being condescending or pitying. It was difficult but I feel fortunate that he, like so many other men, have shared their pain and terror with me.

What I learned early on in thinking about therapy with men and still believe is that the male gender role is a major factor in what brings men to therapy and how that therapy is to proceed, especially when the therapist is a man, because all men in our culture are socialized to the predominant male gender role. I am aware that there are variations based on racial, ethnic, geographic, and even religious factors. However, there is great similarity among men, no matter what their history. Essentially in my earlier writings I suggested the importance of restraint, humor, kindness, affection, and concern in working with male clients. I still hold those things to be important but I do not work with men in the ways I once did. I now turn to how I conceptualize therapy with men currently and then look at how I do therapy with men.

THERAPY WITH MEN IN THE TWENTY-FIRST CENTURY

Tony was so contained and tightly wound that I was not sure we would ever get close to his pain and trauma. He had come to therapy at the insistence of his physician, who had prescribed antidepressants only because he could not get Tony to go for therapy. Finally, as the medication began to help Tony, the physician could insist successfully that therapy was a necessity. Tony, an attorney, had been abandoned by his wife. She had literally run off with a high school boyfriend, leaving Tony with a sheaf of bills, a raided bank account, and two small children. She quickly filed for divorce, gave him custody of the children, and moved a thousand miles away. Tony was traumatized, overwhelmed, and terrified.

How did I work with Tony? Somewhat differently from the way I would have fifteen or twenty years ago. This different approach is a result of the changes in men and in me. Of course, both these sets of changes reflect differences in our culture and in the gender roles of men. Our culture is somewhat kinder to men in some ways and perhaps more harsh than it has always been. There is greater recognition and acceptance of the gentler side of men and greater tolerance for role behavior that is different from former expectations. However, the old role constraints are still quite alive and robust, so in some ways there are even greater stresses for men because disparities are more extreme. For example, men are now expected to be very involved with their children and at the same time even more occupationally successful than before; the struggle to meet both of these expectations is exceptionally stressful and induces shame and guilt of a very powerful variety. Male shame is a double whammy because it is shameful to feel ashamed.

Men are now expected to be more introspective and emotionally astute, and many are. When a major baseball star such as Mark McGwire can openly speak of being in therapy and the benefit of it for him the playing field changes. Nobody was shocked that he had gone for therapy, only that he admitted it directly, openly, and unapologetically. My practice is sometimes almost exclusively male, and I live in a conservative place and have a general practice. The times have changed, and it is sometimes difficult for men to deal with the openness to their feelings that is expected. They get two messages: be in touch with your emotions, and real men are in control of their emotions. Ultimately the first can lead to the second, but it takes some time, and also control may mean yielding to the emotions rather than determining them.

Perhaps it would be clearest to say that men are in a transitional period as the traditional gender roles become less rigid and we move toward a deeper acceptance of the continuum of qualities we all share as opposed to the assumption of difference between men and women (Gilbert & Scher, 1999). There is an old Chinese curse, "May you live in interesting times!" Transitional periods are interesting times and therefore are stressful and difficult. I see the results of this stress often with current clients. Men of all ages are experiencing these trials: young men because of their older role models and what the culture teaches them (although elements of the culture of the young are very different), middle-aged men because they came of age when the rules began to dissolve, and older men because they see that their lives could have been different and have regrets and guilt about what might have been and what they might have done.

So when I worked with Tony I had to be aware of his shame at being abandoned, at being financially raped, and at being very depressed and despondent. I also had to be aware of his guilt at having failed as a husband, at adoring but not wanting to be sole parent for his children (and being most willing to do it at the same time), and at disappointing his family, friends, and colleagues. It would have been very easy (and I once would have done it) to allow Tony to regress in the safety of the consulting room. This regression would not have been good for him. Therefore, I was careful to be sympathetic but not overly so and to maintain a certain rigidity in my reaction to his pain. I rarely shed a tear when he wept copiously, I did not encourage him to get deeper into the pain but rather to understand better the cultural and personal underpinnings of it, and I offered many suggestions of how to deal with his life and his trauma. Tony's depression dissipated, he got off medication, he maintained his practice (although he was not as wildly successfully as he had been), and he reported feeling little shame and guilt for what had happened. I would like you to believe that I helped him get to this point through planning and forethought; actually, I do not want you to believe that—the reality is better. The reality is that my unconscious, as a result of changes in my understanding of therapy with men, my own evolution, and the changes in male gender role expectations, conspired to focus on the adult in Tony rather than the wounded man-boy.

Do Male Therapists Need to Be Different?

I am not always pleased with the path our culture has taken. Many of the attempts to change gender roles have come to a difficult impasse because of the pressures of the economic times and of the cultural forces at work. There are also historical changes as a result of the passage of time. Many of the changes fought for by early thinkers and writers about gender roles have entered the communal consciousness, but the vigilance to maintain these changes has not and the forces of suppression and repression are always at work and should not be underestimated. Many young people have little doubt about the need for financial equity between the sexes, but they still believe that women should have primary responsibility for the rearing of children and so the workplace does not get structured to accommodate more enlightened attitudes. For example, a female attorney, a partner at a large law firm, could not get maternity leave but the female staff members could. All the other partners were male. Her choices were to use vacation, take leave without pay, or resign. Are secretaries seen as more valuable than professionals are, or are professionals to be men only?

In such a world male therapists must be different from what we once were. We must be even more aware of the inconsistencies and subterfuge that maintain gender role status quo or even undo some of the advances of recent times. Male therapists must continue to understand their beliefs and biases about male gender roles. There have been changes in men and changes in the world in which men dwell, and therapists must know how those changes affect both their clients and themselves.

Men are apparently more liberal and accommodating toward women. Men are apparently more interested in their children. Men are apparently less competitive and more cooperative. These are excellent changes, but they have not yet taken hold completely. Male therapists who know that this process is ongoing can continue to work toward the solidification of alterations in male gender role expectations in an attempt to further the positive development of men in our culture.

Lance, a thirty-year-old auto mechanic, came to see me when his physician referred him because of Lance's lack of interest in sex. Impotence was not the problem; he had no libido and no interest in his wife or other women. Lance was very involved in the rearing of his three sons, reported being in love with his wife, and was committed to his marriage. He had no idea why he was not interested in sex with his wife or other women. He had been faithful during their ten-year marriage. He reported that he continued to masturbate, but even that activity was less interesting, frequent, and compulsive for him. Lance remained in therapy for about a year. During therapy the focus was on his childhood and upbringing by a very strong mother. His father was absent and not very supportive of his mother. She was forced to fend for herself and her two children and suffered a good deal at the hands of the men for whom she worked. Lance developed rather strong attitudes and anger about the subservient position of women in our culture and resolved never to treat women in that manner. He did not; in fact, he hired women to work as mechanics in the large and successful auto repair business he managed. He was not interested in gender stereotypes or dictates.

What emerged in the course of his therapy was an idealization of women. He had gone to an extreme in protecting and defending women because of the way his mother had been treated when she was vulnerable. This idealization made him not want to sully women with sex. How exactly this idea took shape or gained power in his unconscious never became clear. What did happen, though, was through gentle persistence (Scher, 1980) on my part in terms of exploring his history with all the women in his life and continual reassurance about the importance of physical relationships and how they could be expressions of love and life he began to regain interest in sex. Very slowly and carefully, with my instruction and encouragement, Lance began to resurrect his sexual relationship with his wife. He terminated therapy when he felt secure in his retrieved sexual interest.

Differences from Traditional Therapy

How can we understand this case in a different way from the traditional views of men doing therapy with men? The way in which therapy with men by men has changed in the time that we have been examining this interaction through the lens of male gender roles is that such therapy is predicated on men being less fragile in their commitment to therapy, more aware of the oppression of women by our culture, and more open about their feelings. As a therapist I am more respectful of the emotional strength of men, the struggles they experience in a world that seduces and abandons them regularly, and how the dead hand of old men torments them.

As I have watched the evolution of my work with men I have become aware that men who come to therapy are more often self-referred than they once were. Consequently, their commitment to therapy is stronger and I am able to be more direct and less concerned about their fleeing when they get uncomfortable. I am still aware of discomfort on the part of the client but less inclined to reduce it for fear of an early termination of therapy. The increased determination to use therapy for their healing enables me to work on deeper levels with my male clients because I know they will hang in for the long haul if necessary.

The changes in our culture that make it more acceptable for men to experience and express their feelings in conjunction with a greater willingness to seek therapy together form a potent mix in the therapeutic encounter. I rarely feel the kind of concern that I have to do the right and careful thing or I am going to lose this client. My ability to be more relaxed also enables the client to trust me more and therefore relax more himself. The endeavor feels much more collaborative than it once did when I was concerned with making the client want and need therapy so he could get the assistance he was clear he desired but that frightened him because it necessitated his depending on me to some extent. As a result of self-referral the dependence is less frightening, although still present, because the client's presence is his choice.

An understanding of the oppression of women in our culture and a nascent understanding of the constraints inherent in male gender roles are helpful for men in comprehending some of their interactions with women as well as their thoughts and feelings about women. Interestingly enough, as men grasp more about what happens to women and how that affects men and the manner in which they behave they better understand themselves, their needs, and their behaviors. I am not sure what effect this understanding has on homosexual men, but I assume that a deeper understanding of oppression is a helpful experience for them, too.

Although the difficulties men experience are very far from over, there is a kind of strength and determination that seems more obvious. This determination is to lead lives that are fuller and more rewarding. Certainly there is variation here by age, class, race, ethnicity, and other defining characteristics. However, there has been a revolution in expectations for men, and the general attempt at self-care is an example of this transformation. Unfortunately, as usual many men carry things to an extreme and become obsessed with fitness of all kinds, but the vast majority of men seem to have adopted a more reasonable approach to caring for themselves. Unfortunately, our culture projects images of men who are wildly successful, totally buffed, and eerily in charge of all they survey as the ideal. This image causes stress because the means to that ideal are often at odds with living suitably (Faludi, 1999). This is an area in which continued work in proclaiming the danger in male gender roles and their personification in the media and entertainment industries is still a mandate for those of us concerned with men—and women, too, for that matter.

The dead hand of old men is the manner in which past generations have trained and molded men to strive to live in ways that are unhealthy at best and destructive at worst. Our fathers and forefathers have left us a legacy of self-hate and self-recrimination with a healthy dose of shame and guilt, which we all struggle to overcome. Men know least the men they love most, their fathers. This fact ensures the difficulty in knowing parts of themselves and the constant struggle to be known by those they love and themselves.

Old men continue to send young men to die. That callousness wounds all men and must be repaired. The recent air war in Kosovo was an intriguing departure from the norm; the U.S. president, a flawed but emotionally aware man, did not allow a single soldier to be placed in easy danger of dying. What a change in the ethos of war. And even better, the country supported him and expected that of him; men are no longer just cannon fodder.

THERE IS HOPE

Hope results from the many elements that have come together at the end of the twentieth century. Some of those elements are the grotesque history of mankind, especially in the twentieth century (which occasionally we learn something from), the rise and scholarship of feminism, the rule breaking of the 1960s, and the men's movement. The symbol I am most fond of in demonstrating the changes in how men behave and how they are treated in our culture is the advent of changing tables in men's rooms all over the country (Scher, 1996.) This occurrence is a demonstration that men are not only interested in their children but also are willing to care for them and that care and interest are culturally sanctioned. This is a major change and ensures that both fathers and children will be altered from what they might have been by their interaction.

There is a long way to go until we are safe from the destructive elements of the male gender role and of the history of men and the world, but I believe that there is a chance that we will move to a world in which we will all be safer. Male therapists working with male clients have a responsibility and an opportunity to advance that world. To do so these therapists will understand that changes in men are a result of pressures in our culture, what those pressures are and whence they come, and how to use those changes.

Changing the Therapist

As I mentioned earlier the parts of the male gender role most inimical to the optimal functioning of the male therapist are emotional constriction, homophobia, and competition. These qualities of men are guaranteed to keep therapists from most effectively connecting to their male clients. The emotional constriction makes empathy more difficult, the homophobia creates a further emotional constriction in the press toward avoiding intimacy, and the competition keeps men apart because they must treat each other as rivals, thus ensuring condescension and distance. Male therapists who are unaware of their internalization of these qualities of men and how they express them will be less effective than therapists who are continually tracking their place on these male behavioral continua. Therapists' insight into themselves in regard to these qualities is most helpful in aiding male clients to grasp their own stereotypical behaviors.

The pervasive nature of these behaviors is revealed to me again and again. I have learned that I can never surrender the lens of the male gender role in examining my own behavior and psyche. For example, while working with a man who had done a great deal of reading in the literature of the men's movement and believed that he had internalized much of what had been written and was living his life according to the model of a liberated man, I found myself feeling condescending toward him because I could find ways he was not doing as he preached and also that I was far more evolved than he. It was hard for me to accept how poorly I was responding to him because I was feeling so competitive with him, especially because he disagreed with my pronouncements about the men's movement. All men striving to be different from the traditional are pioneers and deserving of credit for that effort. When I relaxed, let go of my need for his recognition, and allowed myself to like him and to grasp how hard he struggled, the therapy went better and I liked myself more.

Countertransference

This confession raises the issue of countertransference, which underlies a good deal of what I have talked about when considering male therapists working with male clients. I think that countertransference issues are more significant with men working with men than women working with men. I suspect male therapists are more alert to countertransference issues with their female clients than with their male clients. This difference may have much to do with the subtle but pervasive manner in which competition and homophobia suffuse male-male relationships. I have written elsewhere about the power elements in therapy with men (Scher, 1990) and the direct and indirect manner in which they surface. When power elements surface the male therapist goes into competitive mode and does not easily give the competitiveness up; once he does, he begins to feel closer and therefore more vulnerable to the client, which raises homophobic issues and necessitates a pulling back. I once saw a very successful businessman whom I liked enormously. He said something one day about wanting to have a social relationship with me. I said that I thought in other contexts or perhaps in the future we could be friends. He replied, "I thought we were friends." Of course, he was right; we also had a professional relationship, which was a good one, because we were friends. His clarity helped me to understand my countertransference issues and how I was slowing the therapy because of them. In this case the client helped me to be different, but that is not the only way.

The way to improve ourselves as therapists for men is to be as kind, patient, and thoughtful with ourselves as we have learned to be with our male clients. The gist of most books about therapy with men is that therapists should be more understanding and less demanding. This approach has worked well, because men are becoming much more likely to seek therapy than in the past. Certainly the change in demeanor of therapists is not the only reason, but it has had an impact.

The male gender role, with its emphasis on success, prods men to work hard and to be unrelenting in their demands on themselves to do their job quickly and excellently. This artifact of the male role causes male therapists to work hard but not necessarily to work well. If we can offer ourselves the patience and consideration we have learned to offer our clients we can blossom and develop as they do. I am very likely to offer my interpretations and reactions to what my clients say rather than to force them on them or to utter them as if they came from Sinai. For example, I often say after a client has recounted a dream, "Would you be interested in my thoughts about your dream?" or after something in the psyche of the client has become very clear to me because of its repeated presentation in the session and sometimes across sessions, I might say, "I may be wrong, but I have a hunch that . . ." or "This may be a throw-away idea, but . . ." This sort of presentation protects both client and therapist. The need to be right creates condescension and conflict, neither of which are great helps in therapy. Treating myself more gingerly allows me to take more risks, and although I am not always right I discover that I am likely more often usefully correct than I have been at times when I was driven to be an expert and guru.

Seeking internal quiet and external patience is an excellent means for the therapist to be centered, attentive, and clear. Such pursuit also offers the client an opportunity to choose introspection and a quieter pace in dealing with his difficulties. This is a very new approach for most men, who are impressed with the need for speed and immediate success. The therapeutic encounter is a place apart, a sacred space and time for being different from the way men are in ordinary life. This place of difference offers strength and a value, which should be recognized and capitalized on. Even if a solution to the problem is not found, the ability to slow down, value oneself and one's thoughts, and consider the difficulty are precious qualities.

To work successfully with men, therapists ought not to be afraid either of clients or of their problems. Of course, depending on the population one works with the caveat of reasonable fear or wariness still pertains. Clients are usually frightened by what troubles them, and if the therapist is not frightened by it or them the clients are able to react and accept more fully whatever is going on in their lives and in themselves. An easy example is the anger most men have. It is an acceptable emotion, and many men have vast reserves of it. Anger can be frightening because it often leads to violence and destruction. The anger is usually a cover for a more profound feeling such as hurt. If the man is terrified of his anger he cannot get around it or below it or past it to contemplate his hurt very easily. A therapist who is frightened by the anger retards therapy. Conversely, a therapist who is unafraid helps the client to reduce the anger to more manageable proportions. Becoming a more capable therapist with men requires consideration, caring, and acceptance both for the client and for oneself.

Therapists do well to know themselves and know their clients. To know oneself one must be introspective and astute. Personal therapy is essential to delve into the dark and hidden places and to appreciate better the bright and open places. It is also helpful to understand the difficult and often shameful position of being a client. Therapists should study the population with whom they work so as to know the basic demographics and cultural pressures. Therapists ought also know the intricacies of gender roles and never lose sight of them in the consulting room (Good et al., 1990). Therapists must be unafraid of clients and their problems, although therapists may experience fear.

All of the dicta in the preceding paragraph are a result of my experience as a therapist, my own therapy, and conversations with colleagues, clients, and supervisees. These dicta pertain to all clients and so must be taken very seriously by male therapists working with male clients. Men are likely more afraid of other men than they are of women, and so they have to work to not be so afraid. Men are usually more competitive with other men than with women and this too must be known. Men in our culture, including gay men, are unlikely to escape all traces of homophobia, and therapists must be aware of it in the consulting room because clients will be.

There is no one way to be an excellent therapist for men, but a deep kindness, respect, and patience will go a long way toward helping clients trust and bond with the therapist. My experience is that men want to bond with other men; it may be the eternal search for a good father, or it may be something inherent in our species, but it is there nonetheless. Encouraging this bond while maintaining one's professional role and hewing to the limits and boundaries of the therapeutic interaction is a marvelous gift to the client and to the world.

References

Faludi, S. (1999, August 16). Rage of the American male. *Newsweek,* p. 31.

Gilbert, L. A., & Scher, M. (1999). *Gender and sex in counseling and psychotherapy.* Boston: Allyn & Bacon.

Good, G. E., Gilbert, L. A., & Scher, M. (1990). Gender aware therapy: A synthesis of feminist therapy and knowledge about gender. *Journal of Counseling and Development, 68,* 376–380.

Heppner, P. P., & Gonzales, D. S. (1987). Men counseling men. In M. Scher, M. Stevens, G. Good, & G. A. Eichenfield (Eds.), *Handbook of counseling and psychotherapy with men.* Beverly Hills, CA: Sage.

O'Neil, J. M. (1981). Patterns of gender role conflict and strain: Sexism and fear of femininity in men's lives. *Personnel and Guidance Journal, 60,* 203–210.

Scher, M. (1979a). The little boy in the adult male client. *Personnel and Guidance Journal, 57,* 537–539.

Scher, M. (1979b). On counseling men. *Personnel and Guidance Journal, 57,* 252–254.

Scher, M. (1980). The art of gentle persistence: A therapeutic necessity. *VOICES, 15*(4), 67–73.

Scher, M. (1981). Men in hiding: A challenge for the counselor. *Personnel and Guidance Journal, 60,* 199–202.

Scher, M. (1984). Men in therapy: Commonalities and politics. *VOICES, 20*(3), 41–45.

Scher, M. (1990). Effect of gender role incongruities on men's experience as clients in psychotherapy. *Psychotherapy, 27,* 322–326.

Scher, M. (1994). Drowning in a sea of letters. *VOICES, 30*(1), 88–92.

Scher, M. (1996, August). *Changing tables and changing men.* Address at the annual meeting of Division 51 of the American Psychological Association, Toronto, Canada.

SECTION SIX

MULTICULTURAL AND DIVERSITY-RELATED CONSIDERATIONS

CHAPTER TWENTY-ONE

African-Centered Therapeutic and Counseling Interventions for African American Males

Leon D. Caldwell
Joseph L. White

*From the end of the Civil War in 1865 to the 1960s, Euro-Americans appeared
to control Black Life in the United States. Operating through social custom,
law, economic and political power, and stereotypical images, White power
defined and maintained a subordinate status for Black males.*
—J. L. White and J. H. Cones, *Black Man Emerging:
Facing the Past and Seizing a Future in America*

In this chapter we offer culturally specific interventions for working with African
American males from an African-centered worldview. Cultural considerations are
viewed as prerequisites for new paradigms of mental health interventions for African
American males. We offer two conceptual precursors for working with African American males. First, the therapist needs to engage in the process of self-interrogation to
address race-based biases, stereotypes, attitudes, and behaviors. Second, the therapist
needs to understand the cultural impositions and limitations of traditional intervention
strategies and introduce culturally responsive interventions that evolve from the cultural
worldview of African Americans.

We are not advocating ethnic matching as the only viable solution to addressing
mental health needs. However, the counselor should acknowledge the limits of interpreting African American mental health from psychology's traditional Eurocentric worldview. Mental health interventions and strategies for African American males must be
culturally authentic to address the essence of distortions of black masculinity and resulting behaviors. The intervention paradigm must shift from the prevention of problem behaviors (symptom) to the restoration of a culturally consistent definition of
mental health.

PRECURSORS TO INTERVENTION

Given that most mental health professionals do not live in a vacuum, they must always
be aware of how implicit societal messages about African American males affect their
practice. The following precursors are basic to establishing a level of self-awareness

before providing services to African American men, specifically, and ethnically different clients in general.

Acknowledging Racism

The historical facts of the enslavement of Africans in America's chattel slave system continue to plague the contemporary life functioning of African American males. Despite the Emancipation Proclamation of 1863 and other subsequent government interventions intended to provide a veil of constitutional participation, African Americans continue to suffer from the subsequent three hundred plus years of oppressive social and economic conditions (Ani, 1994; Kambon, 1998a; White & Cones, 1999). Therapists working with African American males must first realize the historical circumstances that gave birth to the psychological dislocation of the African in America (White & Cones, 1999). The stripping of legal and civil rights and the violent (physical and psychological) imposition of an oppositional cultural worldview continue to plague the formation of a healthy black male identity (Akbar, 1984; Lee, 1999; Parham, White, & Ajamu, 1999).

The realities of racism and violent oppression, whether physical or psychological, take their toll on the social, psychological, cultural, and spiritual vitality of a people (Kambon, 1998a; Lee, 1999; Parham et al., 1999; White & Cones, 1999). The literature suggests that an important part of working with African American males is acknowledging the impact of racism and oppression, in all forms, on the lives of black males (Franklin, 1989; Grier & Cobbs, 1968; Lee, 1999; Thomas & Sillen, 1972; White & Cones, 1999). Lee (1999) suggests that as a result of coping and adapting to racism clients may manifest the following clinical issues: (1) problems of aggression and control, (2) cultural alienation or disconnection, (3) self-esteem issues, (4) dependency issues, (5) help-seeking attitudes and behaviors, and (6) racial identity issues. We encourage therapists working with African American males to include the impact of racism in conceptualizing their presenting issues.

Self-Interrogation and Self-Confrontation

What is less discussed and more important than the realization of racist social conditions is therapists' self-interrogation and self-confrontation of their own racist socialization. Moving beyond intellectualizing to personalizing racism and oppression will be helpful for therapists working with African American male clients. The process of self-interrogation and self-confrontation may reveal subliminal messages learned as a natural by-product of socialization.

We suggest that mental health providers proactively confront their stereotypes of black males by addressing the following issues:

1. What are your impressions of African American masculinity?

2. What were your first experiences with a black male?

3. What have you learned from your family, friends, and education about slavery, the civil rights movement, and the black power movement?

4. Do you hold images of black males as absent fathers, superstar athletes, entertainers, criminals, or comedians?

We suggest discussing these questions with colleagues, friends, and other interested parties to help in the self-interrogation and self-confrontation process. Clearly, we are not suggesting that only culturally different therapists benefit from these exercises. To be quite frank, African American therapists should also engage in the previously mentioned process to address their socialized class-based images and stereotypes.

Another consideration for mental health providers working with African American males is to dismiss notions of a monolithic black male experience and behavior pattern. The social construct of class and geography foster divergent views among African American males (Lee, 1999). For example, black males from the South may be more prone to comply with interventions that include spirituality than black males from the northeast corridor of the United States. This difference may be plausible because of the Bible Belt's influence on the Deep South. Geographically appropriate strategies are necessary if we are to consider the range of African American experiences in America, because society often conditions us to associate African American males only with the inner city.

Also, therapists should be mindful of the media's influence on perpetuating perceptions of African American cultural aesthetics and functioning. Media images may subliminally inform our expectations of African American male behaviors and attitudes. The following scenario illustrates this point:

> A psychologist at a college counseling center passed by her client three times in the waiting room before declaring him a no-show for the first session. Each time she glanced in at the waiting area she would politely smile at a young black male slouched in a chair wearing baggy jeans, an oversized denim FUBU jacket, a purple bandana, and a pair of unlaced construction boots before disappearing into the hallway of offices. Finally, as was policy, on the third walk-through she told the receptionist that her three o'clock appointment was a no-show. She admitted being surprised by this because his intake file indicated that his presenting problem was making a decision on which medical school to attend. Could this have been her client?

Finally, therapists may want to enhance the quality of their services by seeking cultural experiences that help to contextual African American male clients. Counselors are encouraged to personalize African American culture by reading books written by African Americans, attending Kwanzaa celebrations, attending Black History month programs, visiting a black church or mosque, or conversing with an African American male of a different background. Surface-level cultural connections are offered here as a starting point to obtaining more information and exposure to more complex aspects of African American culture.

The preceding considerations are intended to lead the therapist in a process of being honest with one's own race-based attitudes and behaviors that is crucial when working with African American males. Once mental health providers have interrogated and confronted themselves, they can find a safe, nonjudgmental outlet (for example, a supervisor, peer, or nonpsychologist friend) with whom they feel safe discussing this developmental process. We believe that this process is essential to providing culturally competent and ethical psychological services. In addition, although these issues are difficult to confront and discuss they are a necessary component of providing services to culturally different clients (Sue, Arrendondo, & McDavis, 1992).

Parham (1999) suggests the following five self-evaluation questions when considering working with African American clients:

1. Am I aware of my own biases and assumptions regarding African American people?

2. Do I have a thorough working knowledge of the history, experiences, and cultural dynamics of African Americans?

3. Do I have a keen awareness of my cultural heritage and how it relates to the realities and dynamics of the culture of African Americans?

4. Am I aware of the traditional and recently developed theoretical issues of counseling theory from an Afrocentric perspective?

5. Can I accurately label and demonstrate specific skills that may be more culturally sensitive to African American clients?

To confront our socialization toward race and gender in America we suggest the following additional questions when working with African American males:

6. What stereotypes of black males do I have?

7. What are my fears and attractions to black males?

UNDERSTANDING THE INFLUENCE OF CULTURAL WORLDVIEW IN INTERVENTION STRATEGIES

It is important to consider the concept of cultural worldview when designing counseling and therapeutic interventions for African American males. Cultural worldview is the process that gives people a general design for living and patterns for interpreting reality (Nobles, 1986). Traditional African culture norms, values, and behaviors serve as the foundation for African American culture (Akbar, 1994; Ani, 1994; Kambon, 1998b, 1999; Nobles, 1986). Therefore therapists may want to acknowledge the cultural limitations of psychological constructs, assessments, and interpretations that emerge from Eurocentric norms and standards (Parham et al., 1999; Sue & Sue, 1999).

It is likely that counselors or therapists who implement intervention strategies without considering worldview orientation are not maximizing their effectiveness. Traditional mental health intervention strategies have emerged from a Eurocentric worldview. Although these interventions may be successful for those from this worldview, their value is questionable when addressing the needs of those from a different worldview system.

Parham (1993) provides an example of an African American value system in Table 21.1. Understanding of this worldview has implications for the delivery of services and the expectations of the therapeutic relationship. Consideration must be given to the cultural appropriateness of an intervention strategy by examining its cultural worldview assumptions. It is important for counselors and therapists to understand how these assumptions influence African American males' conception and perception of mental health services.

Interventions for African American males that emerge from traditional mental health (Eurocentric worldview) are susceptible to misinterpretation, misdiagnosis, and low utilization rates. Likewise case conceptualizations of African American male clients' presenting problems ought to consider an African American worldview and reality. Traditional (Eurocentric) perceptual lenses are limited in providing a comprehensive conceptualization of African American male behaviors given the worldview differences illustrated. Therapists are encouraged to augment conceptualizations of presenting problems and assessment instruments with rival hypotheses based on an African American world-

Table 21.1. African American Value System.

European American Culture	Dimensions	African American Culture
Dualistic, fragmented	Self	Holistic, spiritness made evident
Suppressed in favor of rationality	Feelings	Legitimate, expressed, vitality, aliveness
Individual, competitive, autonomous	Survival	Collective or group: "I am because we are, and because we are, therefore I am."
Written, formal, detached	Language	Oral, expressive, call response
Metric units, an investment commodity, future oriented	Time	Events, cyclical
Control forces of nature	Universe	Harmony, ontological priniciple of consubstan-tiation, balance, self-determination
Final	Death	Extension of life
Material possessions, individual achievement	Worth	Contribution to one's community

view and experiences. The following case example demonstrates an alternate conceptualization using an African-centered worldview that takes into account the sociopolitical history of African American males.

DAVID'S STORY

David is a twenty-six-year-old African American male who was mandated by the municipal courts to seek psychological help for his aggressive behavior at work that led him to assault a white coworker. The counselor at the community mental health agency, as ordered by the court, administered to David the Minnesota Multiphasic Personality Inventory (MMPI-2; Butcher, Dahlstrom, Graham, Tellegen, & Kaemmer, 1990), the Beck Depression Inventory (BDI; Beck, Steen, & Brown, 1996), a life functioning assessment, and a clinical interview to rule out any psychotic personality traits and suicidal or homicidal ideation. In the interview it was revealed that David is the oldest of four children from an affluent Chicago suburb; he has been experiencing sleep agitation and a loss of appetite since returning from Ghana, West Africa, six months ago. He has only traffic violations on his record, which prompted the judge to decide on counseling and probation as a sentence. David's MMPI-2 revealed a valid report with elevated scores on scales

2 (Depression), 5 (Paranoia), and 7 (Schizophrenia). However, his BDI scores did not indicate any significant level of depression or suicidality. The counselor in the agency referred David to a psychiatrist for a medical evaluation for psychotropic drugs.

The counselor's conceptualizations were consistent with a traditional protocol. However, a number of cultural factors should have been considered before David was referred to the psychiatrist. One consideration is the impact of the visit to Ghana on David's attitudes toward whites and America. The counselor should have probed more into David's trip to see if he visited the slave dungeons in Ghana and explored the impact, spiritually and psychologically, of this visit. His behavior and his MMPI-2 scores may have been a result of living through the brutal experience of slavery through spiritual reconnection with ancestors. This experience could have affected his sleep, appetite, and general disposition toward European Americans, whom he may now identify as his oppressors. In addition, most black men reared in America live with a level of paranoia (Ridley, 1984). Appropriate interventions for David may in fact not have anything to do with psychotropic drugs. More appropriate intervention strategies would include offering the opportunity to process his experiences in Ghana (for example, use the movie *Sankofa* as a process stimulus), consulting a traditional African healer to discuss ancestral discovery, or conducting research about David's family history and African cultural heritage. An intervention strategy for David may be to simply offer him healthy ways to cope with the discovery of his African heritage, which includes the brutality of Europeans.

A therapeutic approach that allows David to deal with his racial identity and consciousness issues could provide a healthy outlet for coping with the possible pain, guilt, or anger prompted by his visit to Ghana. Appropriate intervention strategies would seek not to deny David's feelings but to assist him in developing a healthier range of options to deal with his feelings than assaulting his white coworkers.

Mental health service providers are challenged to step out of the traditional (Eurocentric) box to understand black male experiences and worldview when providing conceptualizations and intervention strategies. The case example demonstrates that there are culturally relevant alternative explanations for David's behaviors that may rule out pathology and alternative treatments to medication. Psychologists should seek to include conceptualizations and interventions that reflect knowledge about the African American male experience.

AFRICAN- AND AFRICAN AMERICAN–CENTERED INTERVENTION STRATEGIES

Strategies that emerge from an African-centered frame of reference conceptualize African American mental health using the standards and norms of behavior that reflect African and African American cultural experiences (Nobles, 1986; Parham et al., 1999). These intervention strategies are important because they allow for a richer contextualization of the client's presenting problem that may be neglected in using conceptualizations from traditional psychological theory orientations. David's case example illustrates this point.

An overwhelming majority of the theories and models that are taught in programs accredited by the American Psychological Association reflect a Eurocentric worldview. As a result, it is safe to assume that an overwhelming majority of the intervention strategies from these programs also reflect a Eurocentric worldview. Although this training is extremely beneficial when working with clients who share this worldview, it has left a void for approaches for those clients (African American males) who may not share this worldview. Our position is that therapists and counselors should carefully scrutinize the cultural worldview assumptions of intervention strategies before implementation.

African-centered psychologists (Akbar, 1991; Kambon, 1999; Myers, 1989; Nobles, 1986) have developed theories of psychological functioning that reflect an African American's authentic African identity. Using precolonial African principles and standards of living, African-centered psychologists have developed therapeutic interventions appropriate for African Americans. For example, NTU (pronounced "in-too") psychotherapy, developed by Phillips (1990), is primarily based on core principles of ancient African and African-centered worldviews. This therapeutic approach is spiritually based and uses the principles of the *Nguzo Saba*—seven principles of Kwanzaa (see Phillips, 1990, pp. 62–63) as guidelines for harmonious living.

The goals of NTU therapy for African American males are twofold. The first goal is to assist them to function harmoniously and authentically within themselves and relationships in respect to a natural order. The second goal is for clients to function within the seven principles of Kwanzaa as a standard of living and code of conduct. Phillips (1990) provides key concepts, therapeutic tasks, and techniques for employing this approach (pp. 62–63). For example, within the principle of *Umoja* (unity), a key concept is harmony; the resulting therapeutic tasks are experiences that foster closeness of being through group action, and the techniques are rituals (such as libations, prayer, and Afrodrama). This intervention strategy recognizes the importance of the relationship between the African American male and the therapist as consistent with the person-to-person African-centered worldview. And the therapist values the sacredness and spirituality of the therapeutic relationship.

Phillips (1990) outlines five phases of the NTU therapy process: (1) harmony, (2) awareness, (3) alignment, (4) actualize, and (5) synthesize. Each phase addresses the goals of therapy through the use of techniques of human psychology. This theoretical approach serves as an exemplar for a therapeutic intervention that is derived from an African American male cultural frame of reference (see Phillips, 1990, 1998 for greater detail).

A caveat for therapists interested in African-centered intervention strategies and approaches may want to consider the racial identity and consciousness of their African American male clients. Although these interventions seem culturally intuitive, therapists should acknowledge that many males of African descent have been socialized and miseducated to deny their own cultural history (Akbar, 1999; Hilliard, 1997).

MASCULINITY APPROACHES:
INTERVENTIONS AND STRATEGIES

White and Cones (1999) address the psychological issues confronting African American males from a comprehensive view of black masculinity development. Lee (1999) suggests that we consider the oppression of African American masculinity from slavery until today. As mentioned previously the contemporary media continues to distort black masculinity (for example, *The RuPaul Show* on television). These images then become not only the European model for black masculinity but more importantly and detrimentally they become the internalized self-image for many black males (Hopkins, 1977; Lee, 1999; White & Cones, 1999).

In lectures around the country at colleges and universities on the psychology of African American males, we open by asking participants to identify images of black men in the media, social science literature, and popular culture. Without much prompting, students quickly identify images such as "absent father," "pimp," "drug dealer," "player," "gangster," "academic underachiever," and so forth. These images are not only the popular media models for black masculinity, but they also become the internalized self-image of many black males (White & Cones, 1999). These images of masculinity offered by popular culture leave much to be desired. The obvious problem with media definitions of black masculinity is that they are admittedly distorted and are predicated on a model of cultural deprivation (Parham et al., 1999).

Black masculinity approaches offer numerous strategies that address the social realities and cultural disconnection of black boys and men. White and Cones (1999) detail interventions that seek to connect the African American male with positive culturally centered definitions, images, and practices of black masculinity. A major thrust of black masculinity interventions and strategies is to educate the black male about the tools of distortion (such as media, popular culture, and social science) and then to provide interventions that reformulate a healthy, vibrant, and liberating black masculine identity.

White and Cones (1999) highlight fatherhood training, rites of passage programs, and cultural history education as interventions to assist black males in the redefinition and formulation of an authentic black masculine identity. Images of the angry black man, gangster, absent father, and other negative overgeneralizations of black males are confronted. A resulting intervention is to explore the range of options available for the definition and model of black masculinity. These options should include but are not limited to the supportive father, the committed husband, the loyal friend, the culturally centered and successful businessman, and the compassionate brother. A reformulation of a distorted black male image would allow for the fullest expression of black functioning and identity regardless of social conditions.

In fatherhood training, young African American men learn what it is like to become an integral part of family life. Young fathers learn to look beyond parenting as a duty and see it as an opportunity for growth and fulfillment. Experiencing the development of children as they learn to walk, talk, skip, jump, and play games can be a very rewarding experience. Young fathers can rediscover the joy and spontaneity of life in the African American family (Stanoli, 1994).

Manhood training and rites of passage programs for African American boys are growing in popularity around the United States. An essential strategy of the masculinity intervention approach is intergenerational dialogue. African American boys should have the opportunity to engage in dialogue (meaning having a two-way conversation) with older African American men. There are many black manhood training formats, but most involve a common core of African American history, values, and principles of living. Guided by both individual and group mentors, most programs emphasize responsibility for self and others, wellness and bodily care, educational skills, respect for others, teamwork, problem solving, conflict resolution skills, household management, economic and life management skills, responsibility for family and community betterment, discipline, respect for women, responsible behavior, and drug use prevention. Boys and young men learn how to incorporate the African principles of spirituality, connectedness to others, harmony with nature, and collective work and responsibility into their daily lives as key factors of masculinity. They are taught that Africans were the original men of the earth and have a long history of respect for learning and education. Boys and young men are encouraged to identify with African pioneers in science, economics and trade, and mathematics. They are taught that men of African descent built engineering marvels such as the Pyramids. They could not have accomplished these significant human achievements with little education or while on drugs (Lee, 1992).

These interventions can be used in various modalities and settings. Because the formats are flexible, fatherhood training, Afrocentric education, and manhood training for African American boys and men can be readily adapted to wellness and prevention efforts in community mental health centers, churches, neighborhood agencies, civic groups, and college and university counseling centers. Community mobilization and activism to employ all available resources become important strategies.

One example of such an intervention was the Black Male Student Empowerment Summit that was originally convened by a black fraternity on a predominantly white university campus in the Northeast. This one-day summit allowed the students (graduate and undergraduate) to engage in an intergenerational dialogue about topics relevant to retention and graduation in college (for example, relationships, spirituality, and definitions of success) and success as a black male faculty, staff, and community member (for example, responsibility, accountability, and mentoring). The morning began with a welcoming address to set the tone and expectations, then an icebreaker, followed by a keynote address, then small-group discussions cofacilitated by teams of students, faculty, and staff, who were instructed to foster a comfortable environment in which students could express themselves freely. Students, faculty, and staff presented brief commentaries to introduce each group topic and provide small-group dialogue stimulus. The day concluded with an action-planning session in which participants were given self-monitored outcome expectations. In the following semester black male think tanks convened monthly to discuss a topic consistent with the theme of the summit. Noteworthy about this intervention was that students developed it and it was initially fully funded by faculty, staff, community contributions, and participants' registration fees (which were less than ten dollars). This type of intervention used community resources to provide an opportunity for the reformulation of models of black masculinity and functioning for a healthy existence and survival on a predominantly white campus.

Masculinity interventions must employ all available community resources and look to expand the limited range of options presented to black males that reflect images of self-liberation from distortions of an authentic black model of masculinity. To be effective, these interventions must rely on African worldview models for positive definitions and roles for African American masculinity. Again these models do not need to be created, they already exist (see Akbar, 1991; Gyeyke, 1996; Hilliard, 1997; Nobles, 1986); the challenge is translating ancient and traditional models for implementation in an American reality. In the absence of culturally and spiritually illuminating models of masculinity, intervention strategies are excellent vehicles to provide black males with a range of options for redefining and reformulating a masculine identity and lifestyle that is culturally sustaining and psychologically healthy.

BLACK AESTHETIC APPROACHES

Black aesthetic interventions and approaches use black cultural expressions (that is, music, art, dance, poetry, and the like) as a means to address black male issues (Pasteur & Toldson, 1982). Art in black culture has always been a medium of expression and communication. Pasteur and Toldson (1982) introduced black art forms (that is, poetry, music, dance, folklore, and graphic expression) as a means of promoting positive mental health. For example, during African drum and dance classes African American male participants are encouraged to connect the power and rhythm of the drum to their everyday life. The men participating in the drum class are assigned different parts of a rhythm and taught how playing each part in unity creates a sound that makes the dancers move. They are taught how together they create a powerful sound that causes movement through vibration, but alone they create noise. The drum teaches the need for concentration, listening, mental strength, and physical stamina. The drummers are challenged to listen to each part and see how their part fits into the collective sound. The lesson of the drum is that all African American men can play a part in moving the community if they are prepared to play their part. Another advantage of this strategy is the channeling of emotions. The Djembe (pronounced "jim-bay") is a drum played by hand. Brothers in the drum class can use their rage and frustration in the playing of the drum. We have witnessed, at the Annual Conference of the Association of Black Psychologists, the African drum's power of facilitating the release of mental anguish and creating a psychologically healthy outlet for the pains and joys of being a male of African descent in America.

Contemporary popular music also provides a means by which to spark dialogue and teaching. Lee (1989) explicates a group counseling model for adolescent boys that uses popular music to stimulate group discussion. Facilitating a positive self-identity is the emphasis of the group exercises and discussions. Popular music that promotes a racially conscious theme, encourages social and political activism, or speaks to the plight of black males is used to address relevant psychodevelopmental issues. Employing music or art that is relevant to the black male requires a culturally savvy and therapeutically astute facilitator to translate culturally specific expressions into therapeutically general constructs. There are similar requirements for individual therapy but greater opportunities to receive the clients' interpretations.

PRACTICAL CONSIDERATIONS FOR INTERVENTION STRATEGIES WITH AFRICAN AMERICAN MALES

Even the most well-intentioned intervention strategy must meet black cultural criteria before it can be deemed appropriate. The culturally responsive counselor must understand but not attempt to unnaturally duplicate black dialect, slang, and mannerisms (Franklin, 1989; Lee, 1999). It must be understood that different settings for service delivery render different attitudes toward mental health. Whenever necessary the therapist should provide services in nonthreatening settings (that is, community centers, churches, and recreational facilities). The therapist must be mindful of mental health's history as a sociopolitical tool used to justify slavery and the perpetuation of racial intellectual inferiority (Guthrie, 1998; Thomas & Sillen, 1972). The culturally responsive counselor must be aware of the need to promote an interpersonal orientation in service delivery.

Lee (1999) outlines five crucial stages in counseling African American males:

Stage 1: Initial contact or appraisal stage. During the appraisal stage African American men are seeking to find some trustworthiness in the counselor. It is important that mental health providers be authentic and genuine. African American male clients are assessing whether the counselor is "being real" (p. 45).

Stage 2: Investigative stage. Lee states that in the investigative stage the African American male seeks to minimize credentials and seek commonality with the counselor. This stage may require the counselor to step out of the professional role to interact with the client on a common ground (that is, sports, family, or current events).

Stage 3: Involvement stage. At the involvement stage the African American male client makes the decision of whether to trust the counselor based on the counselor's self-disclosure. The counselor's decision to engage in self-disclosure and share himself or herself will promote trust and the building of the counseling relationship.

Stage 4: Commitment stage. During the commitment stage the African American male client may make the decision to prematurely terminate counseling. This decision in based on his evaluation of the counselor's ability to relate to him on a personal level.

Stage 5: Engagement stage. In the engagement stage the decision is made that the counselor is real and trustworthy. According to Lee this is the stage in which authentic counseling begins.

These stages offer important insight into the need for mental health providers to address African American clients' perceptions of the counseling process and relationship. Astute counselors may want to recognize the conditions with which clients come to counseling and routinely address their expectations of the counseling process.

Culturally responsive counselors may want to use the strengths of the peer networks and extended families of black male clients. There are culturally loaded definitions of family, help seeking, psychologist, and other traditional mental health concepts. Mental health professionals must challenge their notion of the therapy hour and be willing to commit to nontraditional models of the therapeutic relationship. Franklin (1989) provides a guide to therapy that suggests that counselors consider the circumstances that black males bring to counseling, how the counseling process is conducted and who is included, the need to be knowledgeable of black slang and vernacular, and the need for attentiveness to dress and style. Counselors' ability to make themselves less culturally intrusive and more interpersonally genuine can assist in building the much-needed respect and trust of black male clients.

Culturally responsive counselors may also want to use various modalities of intervention strategies and techniques. Psychoeducational interventions that teach new skills or behaviors, social support networks that promote gatherings of men at various levels of functioning, and the use of metaphors, prayer, ritual, guided imagery visualizations, rap, and poetry (otherwise known as spoken word or ciphers) can prove to be culturally relevant mediums of expression for African American males. Therapists offering acceptance of various forms of expressions may be an intervention in itself.

The use of ritual mediation and ancestral worship must also be considered in the repertoire of interventions for African American males. The use of deep breathing exercises, meditation, and relaxation techniques may have both a physiological and emotional effect on black males. The initial use of these techniques may be somewhat awkward (as previously mentioned, because of racial identity and consciousness), but the challenge is to see the benefits for personal growth both spiritually and physically. With this intervention the use of bibliotherapy may be useful. Parham et al. (1999) provide an extensive bibliography with excellent sources of cultural empowerment and discussion stimulus about African American culture and mental health.

JAMAL'S STORY

Jamal is an eighteen-year-old African American high school senior. He lives in a working-class neighborhood on the edge of Philadelphia. His mother is a nurse, and his father works in the naval shipyards. Jamal's mother and father are separated, but they have a good working relationship as parents. He sees his father two or three times a month; they go out to dinner, attend ball games, and sometimes talk about Jamal's future. Jamal has a twelve-year-old brother who lives with him and his mom. Jamal dresses in a moderate hip-hop style: baggy pants, expensive sneakers, and athletic jackets. Jamal is part of a rap crew that competes in neighborhood and citywide contests. They write their own verses and hold impromptu competitions with other crews at parties and dances. Some of their raps were featured on a radio show. Jamal plays football and runs the two hundred– and four hundred–meter track events. He has been offered a four-year football scholarship to a Division I school contingent on his grades and SAT scores. He has two part-time jobs, one at a print shop and the other as a referee for elementary school and playground basketball leagues. His uncle, who is a recreation director, helped him get the referee jobs.

Until two years ago, Jamal was a mediocre student. His grades were mostly C's and D's, and his reading and math scores were two to three years below grade level. He and his friends thought that doing well in school was for girls and white folks. Through her church, Jamal's mother found out about a male mentorship program jointly sponsored by a black fraternity and a local university. She and his father pressured Jamal for several weeks until he agreed to give the program a try. In his two years in the program, Jamal has been exposed to career planning, study skills, problem solving, social skills development, and life planning, and he meets a number of black men in different occupations. As part of the mentorship program, he studied the *Nguzo Saba* (the seven principles of Kwanzaa). *Nguzo Saba* was developed by Maulana Karenga as the basic foundation for a black value system. The principles, adopted as a guiding philosophy by many African American organizations, are *Umoja* (unity), *Kujichagulia* (self-determination), *Ujima* (collective work and responsibility), *Ujamaa* (cooperative economics), *Nia* (purpose), *Kuumba* (creativity), and *Imani* (faith).

While Jamal was enrolled in the mentorship program, his parents sought out an African-centered family therapist to help the family improve its communication. Using a combination of psychoeducational and African-centered approaches, the therapist exposed the family to major Afrocentric concepts such as spirituality, harmony, connectedness to others, and syntheses of opposing views through mediation, conciliation, and dialogue. In between and at therapy sessions, the family practiced communication exercises using spirituality, harmony, connectedness to others, and synthesis as communication guidelines.

Toward the end of the family therapy sessions, Jamal's father joined an African American male consciousness-raising group in his church. In the consciousness-raising group, Jamal's father and fellow group members discuss excerpts from film versions of Richard Wright's *Native Son,* Lorraine Hansberry's *A Raisin in the Sun,* and Spike Lee's *Malcolm X, Get on the Bus,* and *Glory.* They analyze stereotypes of black men and reflect on how they see themselves as fathers and husbands. The men recall their own identity struggles as adolescents and how they resolved conflicting values and choices. They look back on their own childhood and discuss the roles of their fathers and other men who influenced them. Relationships with women are important components of these men's lives. They explore their feelings about women as companions, mothers, and lovers and how they manage conflict in heterosexual relationships. Finally, they examine the role of spirituality, purpose, meaning, and feelings in their lives.

The combination of mentorship for Jamal guided by the seven principles of *Nguzo Saba,* African-centered family therapy, and his father's participation in the African American consciousness-raising group was successful for both the family and Jamal. His grades and self-confidence improved, the family learned to communicate more effectively, and the overall conflict level between Jamal and his parents was reduced to a level at which new patterns of family interaction could emerge.

The psychological challenges confronting African American males are a response to a socialization process, education, and institutions that distort their authentic cultural core. Accordingly, interventions that seek to confront distorted and antiself behavior must employ strategies that address the ancient *Kemetic* (African) dictum of "Man Know Thyself" (Akbar, 1999). African American males must be introduced to thoughts, activities, and environments that illuminate their spirits. The maintenance and preservation of a "perfectible" self as defined in an African worldview must be the impetus for interventions for African American males (Nobles, 1986). Interventions lacking consideration of an African worldview may address only the manifestations of antisocial behavior and suboptimal functioning (Myers, 1989) and never address the greater need of instilling a culturally authentic definition of self, behavior, and mental health through spiritual illumination.

References

Ani, M. (1994). *Yurugu: An African-centered critique of European cultural thought and behavior.* Trenton, NJ: African World.

Akbar, N. (1984). *Chains and images of psychological slavery.* Jersey City, NJ: New Minds.

Akbar, N. (1991). *Visions for black men.* Nashville, TN: Winston-Derek.

Akbar, N. (1994). *Light from ancient Africa.* Tallahassee, FL: Mind Productions.

Akbar, N. (1999). *Breaking the chains of psychological slavery.* Tallahassee, FL: Mind Productions.

Beck, A. T., Steen, R. A., & Brown, G. K. (1996). *Beck Depression Inventory-II.* San Antonio, TX: The Psychological Corporation.

Butcher, J. N., Dahlstrom, W. G., Graham, J., Tellegen, A., & Kaemmer, B. (1990). *Minnesota Multiphasic Personality Inventory-2.* Minneapolis, MN: University of Minnesota Press.

Franklin, A. J. (1989). Therapeutic interventions with urban black adolescents. In R. L. Jones (Ed.), *Black adolescents* (pp. 309–337). Berkeley, CA: Cobb & Henry.

Grier, W., & Cobbs, P. (1968). *Black rage.* New York: Basic Books.

Guthrie, R. (1998). *Even the rat was white* (2nd ed.). Needham Heights, MA: Allyn & Bacon.

Gyeyke, K. (1996). *African cultural values: An introduction.* Accra, Ghana: Sankofa.

Hilliard. A. G. (1997). *SBA: The reawakening of the African American mind.* Gainesville, FL: Makare.

Hopkins, R. (1997). *Educating black males: Critical lessons in schooling, community, and power.* Albany, NY: State University of New York Press.

Kambon, K.K.K. (1998a). *African/black psychology in the American context: An African centered approach.* Tallahassee, FL: Nubian Nation.

Kambon, K.K.K. (1998b). An African-centered paradigm for understanding the mental health of Africans in America. In R. L. Jones (Ed.), *African American mental health: Theory, research, and intervention* (pp. 33–50). Hampton, VA: Cobb & Henry.

Kambon, K.K.K. (1999). *The African personality in America: An African-centered framework.* Tallahassee, FL: Nubian Nations.

Lee, C. C. (1989). Counseling the black adolescent: Critical roles and functions for counseling professionals. In R. L. Jones (Ed.), *Black adolescents* (pp. 293–308). Berkeley, CA: Cobb & Henry.

Lee, C. C. (1992). *Empowering young black males.* Ann Arbor, MI: Eric Clearinghouse.

Lee, C. C. (1999). Counseling African American men. In L. E. Davis (Ed.), *Working with African American males: A guide to practice* (pp. 39–53). Thousands Oaks, CA: Sage.

Myers, L. J. (1989). *Understanding an Afrocentric worldview: Introduction to an optimal psychology.* Dubuque, IA: Kendall/Hunt.

Nobles, W. W. (1986). *African psychology: Towards its reclamation, reascension, and revitalization.* Oakland, CA: Black Family Institute.

Parham, T. A. (1993). *Psychological storms: The African American struggle for identity.* Chicago: African American Images.

Parham, T. A. (1999, August). *Counseling African Americans.* Paper presented at the annual meeting of the American Psychological Association, Boston.

Parham, T. A., White, J. L., & Ajamu, A. (1999). *The psychology of blacks: An African centered perspective* (3rd ed.). Englewood Cliffs, NJ: Prentice Hall.

Pasteur, A. B., & Toldson, I. L. (1982). *Roots of soul: The psychology of black expressiveness.* Garden City, NY: Anchor Press/Doubleday.

Phillips, F. B. (1990). NYU psychotherapy: An Afrocentric approach. *Journal of Black Psychology, 17*(1), 55–74.

Phillips, F. B. (1998). Spirit-energy and NTU psychotherapy. In R. L. Jones (Ed.), *African American mental health: Theory, research, and intervention* (pp. 357–377). Hampton, VA: Cobb & Henry.

Ridley, C. R. (1984). Clinical treatment of the nondisclosing black client: A therapeutic paradox. *American Psychologist, 39,* 1234–1244.

Stanoli, A. (1994, May 29). They turn young men into fathers. *Parade Magazine,* pp. 16–17.

Sue, D. W., Arrendondo, P., & McDavis, R. J. (1992). Multicultural counseling competencies and standards: A call to the profession. *Journal of Counseling Development, 70,* 477–484.

Sue, D. W., & Sue, S. (1999). *Counseling the culturally different.* New York: Wiley.

Thomas, A., & Sillen, S. (1972). *Racism and psychiatry.* Secaucus, NJ: Citadel.

White, J. L., & Cones, J. H. (1999). *Black man emerging: Facing the past and seizing a future in America.* New York: Freeman.

CHAPTER TWENTY-TWO

Machismo Revisited in a Time of Crisis

Implications for Understanding and Counseling Hispanic Men

J. Manuel Casas
Joseph A. Turner
Christopher A. Ruiz de Esparza

As we proceed into the twenty-first century, it is apparent that the status of men and the role of masculinity (that is, the social construction) are in a continued state of flux. Indeed, these concerns are mirrored by contemporary writers who note, "[M]asculinity in Western society is in deep crisis . . . [and furthermore] masculinity *is a crisis* for men today—[in] that the masculine gender is a precarious and dangerous achievement and is highly damaging to men" (Horrocks, 1994, p. 1). Two important factors, that of economic changes since the 1980s and the empowerment of previously marginalized groups, have played a significant role in the way masculinity is played out in the United States.

CRISIS OF MASCULINITY

The 1980s concurrently saw a drastic decrease in male-typed industrial and white-collar jobs (3.8 million according to Petras & Morely, 1995) and greater growth in service or domestic (female-typed) jobs and the associated increase in percentage of women in the workforce (14.8 percent in the late 1800s and early 1900s versus 46.5 percent in 1992; Reskin & Padavic, 1994). This was a drastic change from the booming need for service and technical over manufacturing jobs that stemmed from the Industrial Revolution (in which the need for male physical strength was replaced by automation and its upkeep; Lederer & Botwin, 1982) in that it represented a heyday for white, middle-class, educated men (and a death toll for minorities and women shut out of these opportunities). As these employment trends and the workforce demographics have changed, women (and the corresponding feminist movement, which argues against the patriarchal system; Porter, 1992; Seidler, 1991) and affirmative action (along with the gay and lesbian civil rights movement, which has challenged traditional conceptions of masculinity and associated behaviors; Morgan, 1992; Shepherd & Wallis, 1989) have been earmarked as

Appreciation is given to the following clinicians who provided information regarding issues that need to be taken into account in working with Hispanic men: Chris Menkin, Alejandro Vasquez, Sylvia Worholic, and Fernando Cordero.

scapegoats in the "who is to blame" debate that arose from white, middle-class men's reaction to these power changes (Faludi, 1999).

This shift in power since the 1980s (Coyle & Morgan-Sykes, 1998) has caused a "masculinity crisis" in which men are socialized early in life toward "forceful[ness] and stoic[ism]" (Sleek, 1994, p. 6) and as adults are expected to embrace emotionality and be sensitive and available. Indeed, the existing crisis is more and more often targeted as having its roots in the early socialization of children in general. As one *New York Times* writer points out, males as children are not receiving enough direct parent contact and guidance and, subsequently, are more and more influenced by peer groups. Children and youth ultimately get less direction on how to control their emotions and behave like an adult man and yet are expected to act appropriately (Bradsher, 1999).

In short, what men have been raised to do and be is increasingly attacked and negated. Throughout this discussion, though, it is important to note that when using such terms as "emotions" and "men" (as in the preceding *New York Times* article), one must consider who is defining "emotions" and "men." Although this issue is discussed more fully later in this chapter, a reminder of cross-cultural implications in defining what these constructs represent must temper these debates.

Attempts to Cope

What does this crisis of masculinity look like and how is it evidenced? Movies such as *Fight Club* (Lindon, Bell, & Fincher, 1999) and *American Beauty* (Jinks, Cohen, & Mendes, 1999) depict men as having lost their sense of control, power, and meaning in the world. The nameless insomniac narrator in *Fight Club* feels empty and unhappy in his job and disconnected from a vapid and commercialized surrounding culture. Soon to be a victim of corporate downsizing and trapped in an unhappy marriage, Lester Burnham in *American Beauty* regresses into a more clearly defined adolescent masculine role to regain a sense of control in his life. Both of these themes are reflected in Susan Faludi's *Stiffed: The Betrayal of the American Man* (1999). Faludi draws on a sociohistorical perspective and interviews displaced shipyard workers, male domestic violence group members, zealous football fans, Citadel students, and religious group and support group members to describe the current state of affairs. From these interviews Faludi states, "It was already apparent to me that whatever the [masculinity] crisis was, it did not stem from a preening sense of entitlement and control" (p. 8). Instead, Faludi contends, the pre–World War II collectivist style geared toward helping society has been replaced with a self-serving, top-heavy, middle-management system that glamorizes the individual "star" and functions to discourage the previously existing mentor-style relationship among men at work. Another result of these changes has been men adopting the mindless consumerism mentality (that is, a promised fulfillment from superficial beauty and possessions) that has been shed by women. A survey of *Psychology Today* readers (Neimark, 1994) highlights how the shift in masculinity has coincided with a shift in men's perceptions of their bodies: men overestimate the importance of their appearance relative to women's actual desire. Indeed, the American Sports Data firm (as cited in Neimark, 1994) indicates that "8.5 million men now have health club memberships . . . [and] spend an average of 90.8 days a year in the club . . . nine days a year more than women" (p. 34). These facts are further borne out as the rates of exercise-induced anorexia and steroid abuse in men increase.

There is an impasse created, then, in which men, who have been socialized to view themselves as in control, separate from their community, and in charge, may not have adequate skills and organization with other men to band together to discuss the nature and effect of the current changes. Young (1994) writes that men may shy away from becoming associated with a men's movement because of the stigma attached to some of the men's groups. She writes, when "I mentioned that I was writing about the men's movement and added, 'but not the guys who go into the woods and beat drums,' the typical response from both women and men was, 'Is there any other kind?'" (p. 18). Such attitudes reflect the lack of awareness of the ideological diversity and representation of men's movements as well as the men who are currently participating in them. From Sheehy's (1998) perspective, men's movements fall into one of five categories: Resurgent Angry Macho Man (RAMM, those who return to the earlier male-dominant, female-subservient model), Sensitive New Age Guy (SNAG, those who grow out of their macho stance to discover their nurturing side), Dominant Male Model (DOM, those who call for men to reclaim happiness through achieving, being on top, and being in control), Messenger of God (MOG, those who believe love, affection, and spiritual leadership are the new roles and areas in which men should lead), and the Partner and Leader (PAL, those who instead of focusing on control or dominance look to other men for support in evaluating negative aspects of male-typical socialization). Young (1994) views efforts of men to overcome the current crisis via the men's movement as falling into two broad categories: mythopoetic (that is, a focus on spiritual healing and rediscovering masculine prototypes as typified by Robert Bly's retreats for men) and sociopolitical issues–related groups (that is, a focus on balancing male gender oppression in custody-related decisions and sentencing bias against men in the criminal justice system, for example).

Impact on Hispanic Culture

The popular discourse and media attention toward the issue at hand has mainly focused on non-Hispanic, middle-class, white men and their reactions to the masculinity crisis, yet strong adherence to masculine attitudes, values, and behaviors and the concomitant crisis are not tied solely to U.S. male culture. Gilmore's (1990) cross-cultural research on men and masculinity indicates that male-typed values and behaviors play out in most cultures. However, the importance given to such values and behaviors and the manner in which they are played out can vary significantly among those cultures and subcultures that find themselves at different points on the traditional-modern culture continuum (Brown & Landrum-Brown, 1995; Casas & Casas, 1994; Sue & Sue, 1990); the more traditional cultures or subcultures generally give more importance to those values and behaviors associated with masculinity. Over the years, varied researchers and authors (Gonzalez, 1982; Mirandé, 1988; Peñalosa, 1968) have taken the position that traditional Latino culture is one that gives great and often exaggerated importance and value as well as unique characteristics to masculine roles and behaviors. In support of this point, among many persons in the United States, the term *macho* or *machismo*, which is ascribed to men who strongly and adamantly adhere to traditional male values, attitudes, and behaviors, has become synonymous with Latino men. Given this fact, one could assume that compared with non-Hispanic U.S. males, traditional Latino males, who may find themselves marginalized in U.S. society for a variety of socioeconomic and political reasons, might experience a similar if not more severe crisis associated with the changing status of male gender identity.

In an effort to stimulate thought regarding how Hispanic males, and in particular those who adhere strongly to the "traditional" Hispanic culture, are coping with the changing faces of machismo and with the problems and issues associated with these changes, the purpose of this chapter is to (1) provide a historical and research-based perspective from which to understand what is known about machismo in the Hispanic population; (2) identify selective social, economic, and psychological factors that mediate the status of and the roles associated with machismo; (3) briefly review the literature that can be used to demonstrate a significant relationship between a strong adherence to male gender identity and social, mental, and physical well-being; and (4) offer clinical suggestions based on practitioners' experiences that can be considered when working with Hispanic men from a gender and culturally appropriate and sensitive perspective.

To ensure that the material provided in this chapter is accurately understood and used within appropriate sociocultural parameters, the following caveats are put forth: throughout this chapter the terms *Hispanic* and *Latino* and sometimes *Mexican American* are used interchangeably (because the authors have opted to employ the terms that are used by the researchers and authors cited or discussed in the text) and much of the information presented herein is couched in terms of hypotheses and potential themes within some Hispanic subcultures because such information cannot be generalized to all Hispanic men. One must keep in mind that because the Hispanic population differs across numerous variables (including race, ethnicity, nationality, level of acculturation, level of racial identity, socioeconomic level, level of education, and immigration and generational status), it is impossible to treat this population as a homogeneous entity (for more information relative to these variables, refer to Casas & Vasquez, 1996). Even from an internal psychological perspective, according to Mirandé (1997), "Latino men are internally diverse, so that intraethnic differences are perhaps as great or greater than interethnic differences" (p. 114).

HISTORICAL AND RESEARCH-BASED PERSPECTIVE OF MACHISMO

As noted previously, in an effort to explain the origins of machismo and describe, validate, or disprove its pervasiveness within the Hispanic culture, a select group of researchers, from varied disciplines, using differing research methodologies and approaches, have subjected Hispanic men and families to careful scrutiny and critique regarding the role of machismo and assumed power differential in family and societal structures (Baca-Zinn, 1982; Benavides, 1992; Cromwell & Ruiz, 1979; Gonzalez, 1982). Relative to its origins, varied authors contend that machismo as a construct can only be understood within an economic (de la Cancela, 1986) and historical context. For example, G. Bernal and Alvarez (1983), in discussing Hispanics, point out that the combination of traditional agrarian economics and culture, Catholicism, and a reliance on hierarchical power structures typically results in males presiding over females in family and economic decisions.

Early Studies

Origins aside, much of what is known about machismo is based on early descriptive studies that were mainly conducted by anthropologists and sociologists. With respect to the anthropologists (see Madsen, 1964), their findings, obtained from traditionally oriented rural communities, have tended to be little more than a reiteration of the often contradictory and stereotypic characteristics that are popularly believed to be an inherent part of machismo (for example, bravery, strength, bravado, responsibility, male dominance, honor, respect, virility, aggression, sexual promiscuity, excessive use of alcohol, stoicism, lack of emotion and aloofness, sexism, autonomy, good provider and protector; for more details and discussion of these characteristics, see Barker & Loewenstein, 1997; Bracero, 1998; Morales, 1996; Padilla & Ruiz, 1973; Pasick, Gordon, & Meth, 1990; Ramirez, 1999; Ruiz, 1981; Valdes, Baron, & Ponce, 1987). As for the sociologists (see de la Cancela, 1986), the majority of whose work is much more recent, the tendency has been to provide psychodynamic, historical, and environmental interpretations of the prevalence of machismo.

In all fairness, a few sociologists (see Baca-Zinn, 1982) and psychologists (see Cromwell & Ruiz, 1979) have conducted some research to more substantially validate and measure selective aspects of machismo within Hispanic subgroups. Unfortunately, their approach to studying machismo has tended to be atheoretical in nature and much too frequently simplistic in its conceptualization.

To address this concern, several researchers have proposed using specific theories to direct future research ventures that are seeking to better understand the construct of machismo from differing perspectives. From a psychological perspective, Casas, Wagenheim, Banchero, and Mendoza-Romero (1995) have proposed using gender schema theory as the base from which to examine this construct; in addition, they called for the need to also use a sociological approach to understand machismo within a contextual sphere. Addressing machismo from both a psychological and sociological frame of reference reflects current efforts to examine complex social issues from interdisciplinary perspectives (Baldwin & Hecht, 1995).

Prevalence of Machismo

From a research perspective, there are a variety of views on the prevalence of machismo within the Hispanic culture. Although some contend that the construct is very pervasive and as such plays an important and pivotal role in defining the traditional culture itself (Gonzalez, 1982; Mirandé, 1988; Peñalosa, 1968), others believe it is nothing more than a stereotypic myth inaccurately ascribed to the Hispanic culture as a whole (Baca-Zinn, 1982). Still others contend that machismo is much less ingrained and has played a less determining role in defining the culture than previously thought (Benavides, 1992). Benavides (1992) contends that the Mexican culture is actually matriarchal. He also takes the position that the whole culture is oriented toward the respect and love of the mother, who raises the children, cares for the household, and passes down the family history.

Still others would grant that, although the construct has played a defining role through the traditional culture, machismo is on the decline as a result of acculturation, modernity, and economic advancements (Cromwell & Ruiz, 1979; Gonzalez, 1982). The few studies that support this view have tended to limit their focus to assessing the prevalence of traditional family sex roles (Gonzalez, 1982), conjugal household decision making (Cromwell & Ruiz, 1979), and conjugal interaction (that is, the sharing of household duties; Baca-Zinn, 1982).

Despite diverse research findings regarding the degree of machismo that exists among Hispanics, given the growing body of literature that underscores both the crisis noted earlier and the potentially negative effect that strong and strict adherence to one's gender identity (that is, machismo) can have on one's mental and physical well-being in today's rapidly changing society, the construct of masculine gender identity among Hispanics begs to be systematically studied, understood, and taken into consideration within the counseling or therapeutic process.

SELECTIVE VARIABLES THAT MEDIATE
THE STATUS OF MACHISMO

As noted previously, for a variety of sociocultural reasons, there is an inherent difficulty in discussing Hispanic men as a homogeneous group. Nonetheless, certain social, economic, and psychological variables affect all Hispanic males and in turn differentially mediate the status and acceptance of the roles associated with machismo. In this section, we address three psychosocial contextual variables (that is, population growth, socioeconomic status, and stereotypes) in some detail to help the reader understand how different variables can influence machismo. We then present a list of other variables to stimulate thought regarding the contextual complexity of machismo, a complexity that must be understood when considering this construct in the counseling process.

Population Growth

For a variety of social and political reasons, the size and rate of growth of the Hispanic population in the United States has been well documented (Gomez & Fassinger, 1994; Webster, 1994). Since 1984, this group has seen at least a 53 percent population increase relative to a 10 percent increase for the total U.S. population (Cuellar, Arnold, & Gonzalez, 1995). According to the 1990 census, Hispanics number 25 million, or 9.8 percent of the U.S. population. This increase is due to a high fertility rate and a continuing rate of documented and undocumented immigration (Castex, 1998). From the perspective of intragroup diversity, although this group is growing as a whole some Hispanic ethnic and cultural subgroups are growing faster than others. For instance, whereas Mexican Americans and Puerto Ricans have a high fertility rate, Cuban Americans have a fertility rate that is lower than that of non-Hispanics (Casas & Vasquez, 1996). Immigration will not only contribute to the growth of this group but also continue to infuse into the United States Hispanics who are entrenched in traditional male and female gender traits, attitudes, and behaviors and who will very likely continue to model and nurture such characteristics in their families.

Socioeconomic Status

Another factor that affects a Hispanic male's gender identity is economic status. It is a well-known fact that a significant number of Hispanics find themselves in the lowest economic strata. Using 1993 U.S. Census data, Castex (1998) points out: "In 1992, 26.2 percent of [Latina/o] families had incomes below the poverty level, compared with 10.3 percent of [non-Latina/o] families. . . . [O]f all [Latina/o] children, 39.9 percent lived in poverty in 1992" (p. 256). Additionally, Latino families earn disproportionately lower incomes than their non-Latino counterparts. A major reason is that Latinos in general find themselves greatly underrepresented in middle-management and professional positions (Collins, 1997). Again, it should be noted that not all Hispanic individuals or ethnic or national subgroups find themselves in the lowest economic strata.

Those in Hispanic subgroups who find themselves plagued with financial disadvantages also have a higher probability of being marginalized in U.S. society (Ponterotto & Casas, 1991) and in turn are more prone to experience related social and psychological problems (Casas & Vasquez, 1996). For instance, with respect to male gender identity, one could expect that some men who find themselves at the lowest economic rung in society might feel that for a variety of reasons (both internal and external) they have fallen short of meeting the expectations that are relegated to men within their respective sociocultural context. Such feelings might easily be translated into depression, low self-esteem, and high-risk behaviors (for example, high rates of alcohol consumption). These feelings could also result in men overcompensating for their perceived lack of economic and social power by ascribing greater importance to prescribed macho attributes that focus on power and authority. One could expect that ascribing such importance to these attributes would influence how these men relate to women, their families, and other men who have equal or less status in society.

On a more positive side, it should be noted that the Latino middle class is growing in size and in turn gaining economic power. For instance, in California, 20 percent of the Latino middle class earns at least $50,000 per household per year. The significant increase in middle-class Hispanics is best underscored by the fact that academics and corporations are devoting more time and resources to tracking Hispanic buying habits, attitudes, and tastes (Acuña, 1999). Based on available information, one can expect that improved economic status concomitant with acculturation will result in changes in Hispanic males' adherence to traditional male gender roles. This change may be gradual, however. A recent study comparing Hispanic school and corporate professionals with non-Hispanic white professionals, students, and counseling outpatients found Hispanic professionals to have significantly higher masculinity and lower self-acceptance levels than all other groups (Long & Martinez, 1997).

Stereotypes

In sharp contrast to the recognition and appreciation for diversity within Latino cultures, the typical representation of this group within the U.S. culture in general has been largely based on stereotyped images (Carranza & Hidalgo de Trucios, 1993; Cross & Maldonado, 1971; Marin, 1984; Niemann, Jennings, Rozelle, & Baxter, 1994; Triandis et al., 1982). Such images have been overwhelmingly negative and pathological as rated by non-Hispanic white respondents. Specifically, Hispanic men have been characterized as ambitionless, lower class, poorly groomed, chauvinistic, and alcohol abusers (Niemann et al., 1994). Paradoxically, Hispanics in general have also been characterized as hardworking, competitive, ethical (Triandis et al., 1982), faithful, and passionate (Carranza & Hidalgo de Trucios, 1993). The immutability of these stereotypic characterizations of Hispanics was underscored in a study conducted by Wampold, Casas, and Atkinson (1981).

One of the effects of these powerfully pervasive and conflicting beliefs and messages has been their internalization by Hispanics themselves. Specifically, Mexican Americans endorsed adjectives such as ambitious, uneducated, competitive, cooperative, dependent, unfriendly, and unethical (Dworkin, 1965), as well as dirty, uneducated, dumb, lazy, irresponsible, and inferior (Casas, Ponterotto, & Sweeney, 1987). Relative to men, hard worker, proud, believe in God, family oriented, laborers, and alcohol abusers were common self-descriptions reported by Niemann et al. (1994). Needless to say, from a counseling perspective the internalization and acceptance of these pervasive stereotypes take a toll on the self-concept and gender identity of Hispanic males.

Other Variables

Other selective variables that interactively mediate the status and acceptance of the roles associated with machismo include the following: demographic (for example, age, family size and composition, and place of residency [Laramie, Wyoming, versus Santa Ana, California, or the barrio versus the suburbs]), sociohistorical (for example, generational status, length of time living in the United States, and experiences with racism), sociopolitical (for example, immigration versus citizen status), socioeconomic (for example, educational attainment, labor force participation, and individual and family income), sociopsychological (for example, level of acculturation, actual and perceived power, and self-entitlement), and sociocultural (for example, type of mass media accessed and involvement in popular culture). Finally, another factor of important concern is the actual level of identification with one's gender role. More specifically, a Hispanic man's identification with the culture's prescribed gender roles can vary significantly as a result of the interacting social, psychological, and contextual variables noted previously. In turn such variance can strongly affect how a Hispanic man defines and interacts with his environment and how the environment influences him.

RELATIONSHIP BETWEEN MACHISMO AND WELL-BEING

Beyond the drive to simply document and describe machismo in subgroups within the Hispanic culture, a need exists to consider the relationship between the adherence to a traditional male gender identity and physical, mental, and social well-being. The well-documented discrepancy between men's and women's life expectancy is even more disturbing given the overall lower death age for minority men (Kilmartin, 1994). Research has overwhelmingly borne out the relationship between holding traditional male gender role attitudes and values and health- and behavior-related problems, although the focus of these data has predominantly been non-Hispanic white men. We contend that when couched within a theoretical framework (namely, the gender role strain model), these data can be extrapolated to those groups and subgroups of Hispanic men who also hold traditional male gender roles and values.

Gender Role Strain

In brief, Pleck's (1981) gender role strain model proposes that men experience stress because of the contradiction between male-typed roles that society and culture demand (that is, masculine attitudes, beliefs, and behaviors) and the naturally occurring emotions, desires, and drives within a man. Because the internal experiences and drives (such as the urge to express one's emotions) run counter to what is expected of a man (such as stoicism), a conflict-related dissonance is experienced.

In using this model, Eisler and Skidmore (1987) demonstrated a relationship between high gender role stress in men and the inclination toward high-risk behaviors (for example, drug and alcohol abuse and unsafe and promiscuous sex practices) and episodes of violence directed toward both self and others. Even in researching the adherence to traditional male gender roles rather than role stress per se, researchers have found similarly negative outcomes across settings, populations, and age groups, thus establishing a disturbingly clear relationship. Because of the serious and even life-threatening nature of these outcomes, we present a select portion of the literature in this chapter.

In addressing the correlates of masculine ideology, researchers have found this variable to be related to type A dispositions, a lack of behaviors integral to close personal relationships, and attitudes toward and actual use of condoms (Bunting & Reeves, 1983; Pleck, Sonenstein, & Ku, 1993). Specific to adolescent males and their endorsements of masculine ideology, associations have been found for four problem areas: school difficulties, use of alcohol and other drugs, delinquency, and sexual behavior (Pleck, Sonenstein, & Ku, 1994).

Avoiding Mental Health Services

The restriction or deadening of one's emotions, said by some authors to be one of the hallmarks of traditional male gender identity, is considered to be an underlying factor in the development of psychosomatic symptoms (Flannery, 1978; Nemiah, 1977; Silverberg, 1986). There is mounting evidence on the chronic suppression of negative affect (Emmons, 1992; Pennebaker, 1992), indirect expression of negative emotions and hostility (Barefoot, 1992), and even unexpressed positive emotion as related to various diseases including heart disease, hypertension, insomnia, asthma, high cholesterol, ulcers, irritable bowel syndrome, and cancer. Sutkin and Good (1987) found that men unable to communicate their feelings may find it easier to seek medical than mental health services. Perhaps expressing distress through physical complaints is a primary way that men can understand their problems and thus find relief from their burdens.

Theoretical discussions on violence have suggested that cultures that encourage men to exhibit masculinity via control, dominance, and power could implicitly validate and perhaps explicitly encourage violence. Finn's (1986) research demonstrated that men, more so than women, held traditional sex role attitudes and that these beliefs predicted the endorsement of physical force in the context of marital relationships. More broadly Koval, Ponzetti, and Cate (1982) found important characteristics in profiling men who abuse their wives: patriarchal beliefs, emotional inexpressiveness, isolation resulting from difficulty in maintaining personal relationships, and dissatisfaction with or loss of current employment (Good, Borst, & Wallace, 1994).

Social drinking has been found to be a vehicle for facilitating communication between men (Burda & Vaux, 1987, 1988). As their inhibitions decrease with alcohol use, men may be able to overcome internally and externally proscribed rules that bar male-male emotional exchange. Pasick et al. (1990) view addictive behavior such as the abuse of alcohol and drugs, sex, and gambling, in part, as related to the male gender role in that these addictions temporarily meet the needs of men to feel omnipotent. The euphoria that accompanies the rush of a man addicted to alcohol, drugs, sex, or gambling is often associated with feelings of powerfulness.

In a similar vein to social support or help, some data support the contention that adherence to traditional gender roles or gender role stress is related to professional help-seeking attitudes (see Good & Wood, 1995; Komiya, Good, & Sherrod, 1999). The stigma attached to seeking help is mediated more readily for women than for men, and as such women are more willing to both recognize a need for help and share this need with others (Johnson, 1988). Moreover, stigma for men plays an especially important role relative to help seeking when the problem is of a sexual nature (Metz & Seifert, 1990, 1993) in that they are less willing than their female counterparts to initiate such discussions.

Sharpe and Heppner (1991) have observed that poor outcomes on almost all frequently used measures of psychological well-being are associated with high levels of gender role conflict. If men are successfully meeting society's standards of traditional "maleness," they may do so at the expense of their own health (Leafgren, 1990).

The data and conclusions presented here speak to the vital importance of further research with diverse groups and subgroups of men for whom traditional gender roles play a formative part in shaping their worldview. Because research has been concerned with non-Hispanic, white men's health relative to gender role adherence and stress, this concern should similarly be extended to Hispanic men. The variety of health and social implications here are such that both life duration and quality of life can be significantly compromised—especially as levels of gender role stress increase as a result of changing social rules and expectations. With this knowledge, it is appropriate to turn the current discussion toward mental health treatment issues with Hispanic men.

PROVIDING COUNSELING TO HISPANIC MALES FROM A CULTURALLY AND GENDER-SENSITIVE PERSPECTIVE

When taken together, the changing demographic nature of the Hispanic community along with the physical, psychological, and social outcomes associated with an adherence to a traditional masculine identity merit the need for clinicians, administrators, and mental health policy makers to consider the Hispanic male's level of masculine gender identity relative to the counseling experience (Casas et al., 1995). We believe that culturally sensitive mental health service delivery begins before the client walks through the door. Working from this perspective, in this section, we direct attention toward service delivery from a global, comprehensive perspective with respect to both personnel and services.

As stated earlier, one of the main reasons for this chapter is to stimulate thought in the mental health community on ways to most effectively meet the needs of the Hispanic male population. Thus, we put forth suggestions with the goal of providing culturally sensitive services. These suggestions range from outreach to the actual treatment process and are based on one author's (Casas's) experiences working as a consultant to mental health services as well as interviews with clinicians who work with a significant number of Hispanic clients.

Given the clinical and practical focus of this chapter and drawing from the suggestions that are put forth, the last part of this section contains an overview of a theoretical model proposed by Atkinson, Thompson, and Grant (1993) that counselors and clinicians can use to move beyond their traditional roles and by so doing more effectively use the information and address the suggestions provided herein.

To be effective and give credence to suggestions and recommendations, it is of utmost importance that counselors be aware of the stereotypically based values and attitudes that can influence their ability to effectively work with Hispanic men. For more information on this issue, we refer the reader to Wampold et al. (1981). Needless to say, lack of such awareness results in the provision of services that fall short of meeting the needs of Hispanic male clients.

Many of the suggestions in this section are based on the premises that Hispanics, as a whole, have consistently underutilized mental health services (Rodriguez, 1987) and that Hispanics in general continue to be inadequately served by the mental health systems (Myers, Echemendia, & Trimble, 1991). Working from these premises, the suggestions focus on ways to improve utilization of services and increase the probability that Hispanic males are adequately served by mental health systems.

With respect to utilization, some issues need to be carefully considered. It could be hypothesized that for traditional Hispanic men, self-esteem and a sense of control are tied to solving problems autonomously, and research has shown that men who align closely with male gender roles avoid situations in which they may view themselves as weak or helpless (as discussed earlier relative to help-seeking behaviors). As with other segments of society (U.S. Department of Health and Human Services, 1999), Hispanic males may view therapy or counseling as humiliating and stigmatizing (Johnson, 1988) because they view mental health services as reserved for *locos* (crazy people). Although these men may not self-refer to counseling, they may be required to access mental health services because of their interfacing with social services, the educational system, or the criminal justice system.

Outreach: Making Counseling a Viable Option for Hispanic Men

Every effort should be made to make counseling, like a visit to a medical doctor, an integral part of a boy's life. Such a perspective needs to be nurtured very early on in life. There should be enough counselors in schools (whenever possible) to enable them to meet regularly with students as friends and as mentors. Counseling should not be relegated solely to boys and their families who already have problems but should be used as a means to prevent problems.

Efforts should be taken to ensure that the Hispanic community is informed regarding what counseling is all about and that counseling is not solely for *los locos* (that is, the crazy ones). On the contrary, it is a resource that can help Hispanic men and their families reach their desired goals in a more efficient manner.

To bring mental health issues to the forefront, local television and radio stations should provide free public announcements in both English and Spanish that address mental health issues from a nonsensationalistic, helping, and learning perspective. That is to say, mental health services should be described as services that can teach individuals, and men in particular, to improve their ability to take care of themselves and more importantly their families. Whenever possible such information should be presented by individuals who are known and respected in the Hispanic community. Radio announcements should be made at a time when they can reach a maximum male audience. For example, if a community has a significant number of Hispanic men who work in the agricultural business, a good time to reach them would be when they are commuting to and from work.

Setting: Availability, Accessibility, and Cultural Appropriateness

Efforts should be made to ensure that mental health and social services are easily accessible to the clientele. Clients with low incomes may not have cars; consequently, service agencies should be within walking distance of public transportation. Nobody who is experiencing problems should have to take two to three buses or travel a long distance to obtain help. Thus to get men to use needed services, it might be necessary to make mental health and social services easily available in nontraditional settings: adult night schools, the employment office, or the work-benefits office. Consideration should be given to colocating services for those men who may need additional types of help (for example, mental health, social services, public health, probation, and employment). Other less-stigmatized services may be used as the entry points to mental health services. Such colocation would complement the desire expressed by many persons for one-stop shopping (such as at discount department stores).

Service hours need to be flexible. Many low-income Hispanic men work two jobs to make a living. If such men are in need of mental or social health services they must be provided with the opportunity of accessing needed services outside the professional's 8 A.M. to 5 P.M. mentality. To underscore this point, field workers who need to take an hour off for personal reasons are told by their supervisors that they might as well take the whole day off without pay (C. Menkin, personal communication, November 10, 1999).

To reach traditional Hispanic males who are highly represented in the lower levels of the agricultural business (that is, fieldworkers), mental health and social services might consider using a mobile approach. More specifically, these services could get approval from the growers to use a van to bring social and mental health information to their workers. Although there might be some resistance from the growers for such an effort, with appropriate coordination between county agencies and concerned individuals such resistance can be overcome. The bottom line that has to be put forth is what is in the best interest of the community.

Relative to the sites themselves, every effort should be made to make them user-friendly. For Hispanic men user-friendly sites would mean that men are represented at all staff levels, from receptionists to service providers. Going into a counseling center in which the majority of key players are women can be quite challenging for traditional Hispanic men. It can contribute to the belief that counseling is a "woman's business"— that is, it is run by women to meet women's needs. To counter such beliefs, it might be helpful if concerned therapists and community leaders worked with the county mental health association and the county mental health department to develop culturally and linguistically sensitive educational materials that put mental health problems and concerns into a realistic perspective, a perspective that shows that these problems occur across gender and among all kinds of families and, most important, that they are not insurmountable.

With respect to Hispanic males who are less acculturated, the counseling centers should do all that is necessary to ensure that the total ambience of the center is culturally friendly. The decorations should be reflective of the Hispanic culture. All reading materials should be in both English and Spanish; staff persons should not only be bilingual but also bicultural. It is not enough to say *"buenos dias"*; there needs to be follow-up. Given that many Hispanic men may be very self-conscious about seeking out mental health services, every effort should be made to reduce the amount of time that these men have to spend in a large waiting room. Small, comfortable rooms should be available to accommodate these men while they wait for their therapists. Nobody likes being exposed, least of all Hispanic men who are dealing with mental health issues.

Process: Taking Steps to Ensure the Effectiveness of Counseling

Throughout the counseling process, one must be aware of Latino value orientations; over the years a variety of researchers have documented these orientations to endure across generations (Altarriba & Bauer, 1998; G. Bernal & Alvarez, 1983; Bracero, 1998; Castex, 1998; Vasquez-Nuttall, Avila-Vivas, & Morales-Barreto, 1984; Zuniga, 1998). Such values include the importance of distinct male and female gender roles, family identity and cohesiveness, strong sense of community, concept of *respeto* and dignity, present time orientation, overt respect for elders and children, and strong religious beliefs and a respect for spirituality. The degree of adherence to these values varies as a result of the mediating variables noted earlier. Counselors should consider and use clients' high adherence to any of these values when appropriate to facilitate and expedite the counseling process. To this end, it may be necessary for counselors to turn to individuals who are strongly rooted in the Hispanic culture for guidance and direction.

From a preventative perspective, teachers should be trained to understand the gender identity developmental process that children undergo. In particular, they should understand the role that culture and socioeconomic factors play in such a process. Such understanding should in turn be translated into educational and socialization activities that help children develop healthy and realistic perspectives relative to their gender identity development. Teachers should use their knowledge and experience to help parents deal with the gender identity issues that their children face. Dealing with such issues is often a difficult task but one that cannot be ignored. To this end, counselors could provide classes and workshops for teachers through university extension programs and adult night school. In turn, teachers who avail themselves of such classes could be appropriately compensated for their willingness to more effectively meet the needs of their students.

According to some research (Atkinson, Wampold, Lowe, Matthews, & Ahn, 1998), when providing counseling to racial or ethnic minority persons, it is often more important to match client and counselor values than it is to match client and counselor race or ethnicity. Given the low number of racial and ethnic minority counselors, this finding is very important. With respect to the men addressed in this chapter, such matching could include the values given to the extended family, the importance of men taking a leadership role in looking out for the welfare of their families, and the importance of maintaining respect across generations. Because many counselors have not been directly trained to work with Hispanic populations (Myers et al., 1991) and as such may not be familiar with the values that are important to traditional Hispanic males, county mental health departments should be encouraged to provide cultural diversity training programs that focus on the local Hispanic populations and that are easily accessible to all service providers.

To expedite the counseling process with Hispanic men who have never been involved in counseling, it would be helpful if a mental health staff person were designated to take the time to educate the client regarding what the process seeks to attain as well as what the process entails (for example, goals, expectations, what is going to occur, what the therapist is going to do, and what the client can do to ensure successful outcomes). To streamline this effort, counseling centers could develop a video that not only explains the counseling process but also models the behaviors that are inherent in the process with respect to both counselor and client. Such a videotape could be extremely helpful if the types of questions that clients need to ask to maximize the benefits from their being involved in counseling were modeled and reinforced. To ensure that the most relevant information is attended to, the first time the tape is shown to the client, a mental health staff person might be present. Such a person might discuss with the client those aspects of the tape that they believe are most relevant to the client and the presenting problem or problems. The more specific the tape is to the client's presenting problem, the better. From a cost-effective perspective, the video could be used more than once to remind the clients what they can expect from being in counseling.

When working with traditionally socialized Hispanic males, consideration should be given to the use of nontraditional treatment formats such as classes, small groups or seminars, or workshops (Robertson & Fitzgerald, 1992). Such formats should maximize the positive aspect of the machismo role (that is, father, head of family, provider, and so forth; F. Cordero, personal communication, November 10, 1999). Again, to avoid the stigma associated with mental health issues, whenever possible, such treatment formats should be provided in non–mental health settings. For instance, Hispanic males may be less reluctant to go to an educational or religious setting for help. If so, social service and mental health agencies might work to provide help within such a setting. Needless to say, ensuring the success of such a venture will require quite a bit of planning and collaboration across agencies and settings.

Counseling agencies that want to help Hispanic males need to reexamine the business-as-usual approach that is used with all clients across the board. As noted previously, many Hispanic males do not access counseling until they are on the brink of having serious problems or until they are referred by other social service agencies. Consequently, mental health services should do everything possible to accommodate and help these men from the onset. Accommodation may entail having to postpone administering all the demographic and diagnostic instruments that are necessary for reimbursement from the federal or state government; the welfare of the client should take precedence over the financial well-being of the institution. The major objective of counselors working with such male clients should be to ensure their leaving the session with the feeling that they have been heard and respected and that initial efforts have been taken to help them get back on track.

When working with Hispanic males who are heads of families, counselors should couch early discussions in a framework in which the male is validated and considered an expert on his family and that he functions as a consultant in the meeting rather than as one who is being counseled; similarly, it would be inconsiderate to criticize the male partner in front of his family (C. Menkin, personal communication, November 10, 1999; S. Warholic, personal communication, November 2, 1999; Zuniga, 1998). With this perspective in mind, the counselor might take a systemic approach in which no one individual is seen as "the problem." The problem is the result of a variety of negative factors (such as poverty, underemployment, and substandard living conditions) that are affecting the family within a complex ecological system. The challenge for the counselor is to help the family members understand the effect of such factors on the family's well-being. Once the problem is put into perspective, the counselor, working with other social service professionals, should help the family and especially the male to identify and use all their socioculturally based strengths (including pride, family commitment, and extended family) to address the problem.

Given their small number, Hispanic Spanish-speaking psychologists who live in small to midsize cities may find themselves frequently confronting dual-relationship issues, issues for which there are no simple answers. More specifically, these psychologists may need to be an integral part of the Hispanic community and consequently have frequent social interaction with many of their clients. Without such interaction, their acceptance and credibility in the community may be greatly challenged. To ensure appropriate boundaries, though more lax than what the American Psychological Association might desire, it would be helpful for these psychologists to develop a support network that they might use to establish and maintain effective working relationships with their clients and with the community at large.

Three-Dimensional Model

The previously described guidelines and suggestions alone cannot provide absolute principles in mental health service provision given the heterogeneity of the Hispanic clientele. A model that would facilitate implementing the guidelines and suggestions provided herein is necessary. Such a model should help counselors to flexibly conceptualize, organize, and guide different types of interventions as needed by Hispanic clients. To this end, Atkinson et al. (1993) put forth a three-dimensional model that focuses on the diverse roles and strategies that a counselor may have to undertake when working with racial or ethnic minority clients in general. In this model, Atkinson et al. (1993) suggest that when selecting such roles and strategies three factors need to be considered, each of which exists on a continuum: (1) client level of acculturation to the dominant society (high or low), (2) locus of problem etiology (external to internal), and (3) goals of helping (prevention, including education or development, to remediation). On the basis of these factors, Atkinson et al. (1993) identified eight therapist roles that intersect with the extremes of each of the three continua:

1. *Adviser.* The therapist serves as an adviser when the client is low in acculturation, the problem is externally located, and prevention is the goal of treatment.

2. *Advocate.* The therapist serves as an advocate when the client is low in acculturation, the problem is external in nature, and the goal of treatment is remediation.

3. *Facilitator of indigenous support systems.* The therapist serves as a facilitator of indigenous support systems when the client is low in acculturation, the problem is internal in nature, and prevention is the goal of treatment.

4. *Facilitator of indigenous healing systems.* The therapist serves as a facilitator of indigenous healing systems when the client is low in acculturation, the problem is internal in nature, and remediation is the treatment goal.

5. *Consultant.* The therapist serves as a consultant when the client is high in acculturation, the problem is external in nature, and prevention is the treatment goal.

6. *Change agent.* The therapist serves as a change agent when the client is high in acculturation, the problem is external in nature, and remediation is the goal of treatment.

7. *Counselor.* The therapist serves as a counselor when the client is high in acculturation, the problem is internal in nature, and prevention is the primary goal of treatment.

8. *Psychotherapist.* The therapist serves as a psychotherapist when the client is high in acculturation, the problem is internal in nature, and remediation is the goal of therapy.

According to Casas et al. (1995), in addition to using the modified approaches contained in the Atkinson et al. (1993) model described earlier, counselors must use other frameworks and perspectives beyond those traditionally used that have been based on remediation models (that is, treating the client after a specific problem has surfaced). To this end, counselors can incorporate preventive and developmental interventions as alternative options for Hispanic men who may not want to access mental health services and wait until they are in crisis.

The overarching purpose of this chapter has been to stimulate thought and hypotheses within the mental health profession regarding the current masculinity crisis and to draw specific attention and concern to Hispanic men who may be at particular risk of distress relative to adherence to traditional male gender roles. Efforts to document the nature and function of machismo for Hispanic men thus far have largely relied on descriptive methods that at best shed a superficial light on this issue and at worst serve to perpetuate stereotypical representations of this group that affect both Hispanics and others.

It is our contention that Hispanic men will undoubtedly interface with the mental health system, but unaddressed questions regarding the quality of care these men will receive remain: What can applied psychology training programs do to ensure that students receive adequate preparation to work with this population? What can academicians and researchers do to approach the lack of theoretically relevant research of gender relative to Hispanic men's issues? How can our existing systems, organizations, and practitioners provide culturally appropriate and sensitive services to Hispanic men? We have addressed the latter question and now briefly turn attention to the former questions.

The current literature indicates that despite American Psychological Association requirements, psychology training programs are doing an inadequate job of preparing their students to work with racial or ethnic minorities (Mintz, Bartels, & Rideout, 1995; Quintana & Bernal, 1995). Mental health training programs must provide course work, research, and practicum opportunities for students to work with Hispanic male populations; one way of addressing this issue is through diversifying the faculty and student bodies (Atkinson, Brown, Casas, & Zane, 1996; M. E. Bernal, 1996) to provide visibility and support for these endeavors. To effect changes in the future, psychology research and practice efforts and investments must be made with current students (for example, by offering financial aid to minority students, holding multicultural research festivals and brown-bag forums to discuss male issues, and soliciting outside experts to speak in seminars).

Current academicians and researchers must put forth greater efforts to go beyond cursory, simplistic, and atheoretical examinations of cultural phenomena and instead delve into the complex and interactive identities of individuals (for example, a Puerto Rican man from a low socioeconomic background dealing with child-rearing issues or a Mexican American gay man navigating through coming-out issues and potential rejection from his culture of origin); when couched within theoretical frameworks, seemingly disparate data become contextualized, organized, and interpretable. Such data can help practitioners provide effective services to men who may find themselves in a gender identity–related crisis.

References

Acuña, A. (1999, October 20). Changes in state's ethnic balance are accelerating. *Los Angeles Times*, p. A3.

Altarriba, J., & Bauer, L. M. (1998). Counseling Cuban Americans. In D. R. Atkinson, G. Morton, & D. W. Sue (Eds.), *Counseling American minorities* (5th ed., pp. 280–296). Boston: McGraw-Hill.

Atkinson, D. R., Brown, M. T., Casas, J. M., & Zane, N.W.S. (1996). Achieving ethnic parity in counseling psychology. *Counseling Psychologist, 24*(2), 230–258.

Atkinson, D. R., Thompson, C. E., & Grant, S. K. (1993). A three-dimensional model for counseling racial/ethnic minorities. *Counseling Psychologist, 21*(2), 257–277.

Atkinson, D. R., Wampold, B. E., Lowe, S. M., Matthews, L., & Ahn, H.-N. (1998). Asian American preferences for counselor characteristics: Application of the Bradley-Terry-Luce model to paired data comparison data. *Counseling Psychologist, 26*(1), 101–123.

Baca-Zinn, M. (1982). Chicano men and masculinity. *Journal of Ethnic Studies, 10*, 20–44.

Baldwin, J. R., & Hecht, M. L. (1995). The layered perspective of cultural (in)tolerance(s): The roots of a multidisciplinary approach. In R. L. Wiseman (Ed.), *Intercultural communication theory* (pp. 55–91). Thousand Oaks, CA: Sage.

Barefoot, J. C. (1992). Developments in the measurement of hostility. In H. S. Friedman (Ed.), *Hostility, coping, and health* (pp. 13–31). Washington, DC: American Psychological Association.

Barker, G., & Loewenstein, I. (1997). Where the boys are: Attitudes related to masculinity, fatherhood, and violence toward women among low-income adolescent and young adult males in Rio de Janeiro, Brazil. *Youth and Society, 29*(2), 166–196.

Benavides, J. (1992, October 17). Mujeres rule the roosters. *Santa Barbara News Press*, p. B1.

Bernal, G., & Alvarez, A. I. (1983). Culture and class in the study of families. *Family Therapy Collections, 6*, 33–50.

Bernal, M. E. (1996). How did you do it? *Counseling Psychologist, 24*(2), 269–272.

Bracero, W. (1998). Intimidades: Confianza, gender, and hierarchy in the construction of Latino-Latina therapeutic relationships. *Cultural Diversity and Ethnic Minority Psychology, 4*(4), 264–277.

Bradsher, K. (1999, November 21). The Nation: Fear of crime trumps the fear of lost youth. *New York Times*, p. 3.

Brown, M. T., & Landrum-Brown, J. (1995). Counselor supervision: Cross-cultural perspectives. In J. G. Ponterotto, J. M. Casas, L. A. Suzuki, & C. M. Alexander (Eds.), *Handbook of multicultural counseling* (pp. 263–286). Thousand Oaks, CA: Sage.

Bunting, A. B., & Reeves, J. B. (1983). Perceived male sex orientation and beliefs about rape. *Deviant Behavior, 4*(3–4), 281–295.

Burda, P. C., & Vaux, A. C. (1987). The social support process in men: Overcoming sex-role obstacles. *Human Relations, 40*(1), 31–43.

Burda, P. C., & Vaux, A. C. (1988). Social drinking in supportive contexts among college males. *Journal of Youth and Adolescence, 17*(2), 165–171.

Carranza, J., & Hidalgo de Trucios, S. J. (1993). Condition-dependence and sex traits in the male great bustard. *Ethology, 94*(3), 187–200.

Casas, J. M., & Casas, A. (1994). *Acculturation: Theory, models, and implications.* Santa Cruz, CA: Network.

Casas, J. M., Ponterotto, J. G., & Sweeney, M. (1987). Stereotyping the stereotyper: A Mexican American perspective. *Journal of Cross-Cultural Psychology, 18*(1), 45–57.

Casas, J. M., & Vasquez, M.J.T. (1996). Counseling the Hispanic: A guiding framework for a diverse population. In P. B. Pedersen, J. G. Draguns, W. J. Lonner, & J. E. Trimble , (Eds.), *Counseling across cultures* (4th ed., pp. 146–176). Thousand Oaks, CA: Sage.

Casas, J. M., Wagenheim, B. R., Banchero, R., & Mendoza-Romero, J. (1995). Hispanic masculinity: Myth or psychological schema meriting clinical consideration? In A. M. Padilla, (Ed.), *Hispanic psychology: Critical issues in theory and research* (pp. 231–244). Thousand Oaks, CA: Sage.

Castex, G. M. (1998). Providing services to Hispanic/Latino populations: Profiles in diversity. In D. R. Atkinson, G. Morten, & D. W. Sue, (Eds.), *Counseling American minorities* (5th ed., pp. 255–267). Boston: McGraw-Hill.

Collins, L. V. (1997). *Memorandum for reporters, editors, news directors: Facts for Hispanic Heritage Month* [On-Line]. Available: http://www.census.gov/Press-Release/fs97-10.html

Coyle, A., & Morgan-Sykes, C. (1998). Troubled men and threatening women: The construction of "crisis" in male mental health. *Feminism and Psychology, 8*(3), 263–284.

Cromwell, R. E., & Ruiz, R. A. (1979). The myth of macho dominance in decision making within Mexican and Chicano families. *Hispanic Journal of Behavioral Sciences, 1,* 355–373.

Cross, W. C., & Maldonado, B. (1971). The counselor, the Mexican-American, and the stereotype. *Elementary School Guidance and Counseling, 6*(1), 27–31.

Cuellar, I., Arnold, B., & Gonzalez, G. (1995). Cognitive referents of acculturation: Assessment of cultural constructs in Mexican Americans. *Journal of Community Psychology, 23*(4), 339–356.

de la Cancela, V. (1986). A critical analysis of Puerto Rican machismo: Implications for clinical practice. *Psychotherapy, 23*(2), 291–296.

Dworkin, A. G. (1965). Stereotypes and self-images held by native-born and foreign-born Mexican Americans. *Sociology and Social Research, 49*(2), 214–224.

Eisler, R. M., & Skidmore, J. R. (1987). Masculine gender role stress: Scale development and component factors in the appraisal of stressful situations. *Behavior Modification, 11*(2), 123–136.

Emmons, R. A. (1992). The repressive personality and social support. In H. S. Friedman, (Ed.), *Hostility, coping, and health* (pp. 141–150). Washington, DC: American Psychological Association.

Faludi, S. (1999). *Stiffed: The betrayal of the American man.* New York: Morrow.

Flannery, J. G. (1978). Alexithymia, II: The association with unexplained physical distress. *Psychotherapy and Psychosomatics, 30,* 193–197.

Finn, J. (1986). The relationship between sex role attitudes and attitudes supporting marital violence. *Sex Roles, 14*(5–6), 235–244.

Gilmore, D. D. (1990). *Manhood in the making: Cultural concepts of masculinity.* New Haven, CT: Yale University Press.

Gomez, M. J., & Fassinger, R. E. (1994). An initial model of Latina achievement: Acculturation, biculturalism, and achieving styles. *Journal of Counseling Psychology, 41*(2), 205–215.

Gonzalez, A. (1982). Sex roles of the traditional Mexican American family: A comparison of Chicano and Anglo students' attitudes. *Journal of Cross-Cultural Psychology, 13,* 330–339.

Good, G. E., Borst, T. S., & Wallace, D. L. (1994). Masculinity research: A review and critique. *Applied and Preventive Psychology, 3*(1), 3–14.

Good, G. E., & Wood, P. K. (1995). Male gender role conflict, depression, and help seeking: Do college men face double jeopardy? *Journal of Counseling and Development, 74*(1), 70–75.

Horrocks, R. (1994). *Masculinity in crisis: Myths, fantasies, and realities.* New York: St. Martin's Press.

Jinks, D., Cohen, B. P., & Mendes, S. D. (1999). *American Beauty* [Film]. Dreamworks.

Johnson, M. E. (1988). Influences of gender and sex role orientation on help-seeking attitudes. *Journal of Psychology, 122*(3), 237–241.

Kilmartin, C. T. (1994). *The masculine self.* New York: Macmillan.

Komiya, N., Good, G. E., & Sherrod, N. B. (1999). Emotional openness as a predictor of college students' attitudes toward seeking psychological help. *Journal of Counseling Psychology, 46*(4), 520–524.

Koval, J. E., Ponzetti, J. J., & Cate, R. M. (1982). Programmatic intervention for men involved in conjugal violence. *Family Therapy, 9*(2), 147–154.

Leafgren, F. (1990). Men on a journey. In D. Moore & F. Leafgren (Eds.), *Problem solving strategies and interventions for men in conflict* (pp. 3–10). Alexandria, VA: American Association for Counseling and Development.

Lederer, W., & Botwin, A. (1982). Where have all the heroes gone? Another view of changing masculine roles. In E. Solomon & N. Levy (Eds.), *Men in transition: Theory and therapy* (pp. 241–246). New York: Plenum.

Lindon, A., Bell, R. (Producers), & Fincher, D. A. (Director). (1999). *Fight Club* [Film]. Twentieth Century Fox.

Long, V. O., & Martinez, E. A. (1997). Masculinity, femininity, and Hispanic professional men's self-esteem and self-acceptance. *Journal of Psychology, 131*(5), 481–488.

Madsen, W. (1964). *The Mexican Americans of South Texas.* New York: Holt, Rinehart & Winston.

Marin, G. (1984). Stereotyping Hispanics: The differential effect of research method, label, and degree of contact. *International Journal of Intercultural Relations, 8*(1), 17–27.

Metz, M. E., & Seifert, M. H. (1990). Men's expectations of physicians in sexual health concerns. *Journal of Sex and Marital Therapy, 16*(2), 79–88.

Metz, M. E., & Seifert, M. H. (1993). Differences in men's and women's sexual health needs and expectations of physicians. *Canadian Journal of Human Sexuality, 2*(2), 53–59.

Mintz, L. B., Bartels, K. M., & Rideout, C. A. (1995). Training in counseling ethnic minorities and race-based availability of graduate school resources. *Professional Psychology: Research and Practice, 26*(3), 316–321.

Mirandé, A. (1988). Que gacho es ser macho: It's a drag to be a macho man. *Aztlan, 17,* 63–69.

Mirandé, A. (1997). *Hombres y machos: Masculinity and Latino culture.* Boulder, CO: Westview Press.

Morales, E. (1996). Gender roles among Latino gay and bisexual men: Implications for family and couple relationships. In J. Laird & R. J. Green (Eds.), *Lesbians and gays in couples and families: A handbook for therapists* (pp. 272–297). San Francisco: Jossey-Bass.

Morgan, D.H.J. (1992). *Discovering men.* New York: Routledge.

Myers, H. F., Echemendia, R. J., & Trimble, J. E. (1991). The need for training ethnic minority psychologists. In H. Myers, P. Wohlford, L. P. Guzman, & R. Echemendia, (Eds.), *Ethnic minority perspectives on clinical training and services in psychology* (pp. 3–11). Washington, DC: American Psychological Association.

Neimark, J. (1994, November–December). The beefcaking of America. *Psychology Today, 27,* 32.

Nemiah, J. C. (1977). Alexithymia: Theoretical considerations. *Psychotherapy and Psychosomatics, 28,* 199–206.

Niemann, Y. F., Jennings, L., Rozelle, R. M., & Baxter, J. C. (1994). Use of free responses and cluster analysis to determine stereotypes of eight groups. *Personality and Social Psychology Bulletin, 20*(4), 379–390.

Padilla, A. M., & Ruiz, R. A. (1973). *Latino mental health: A review of literature.* Washington, DC: U.S. Government Printing Office.

Pasick, R. S., Gordon, S., & Meth, R. L. (1990). Helping men understand themselves. In L. Meth & R. S. Pasick (Eds.), *Men in therapy: The challenge of change* (pp. 152–180). New York: Guilford Press.

Peñalosa, F. (1968). Mexican family roles. *Journal of Marriage and the Family, 30,* 680–689.

Pennebaker, J. W. (1992). Inhibition as the linchpin of health. In H. S. Friedman (Ed.), *Hostility, coping, and health* (pp. 127–139). Washington, DC: American Psychological Association.

Petras, J. F., & Morely, M. (1995). *Empire or republic? American global power and domestic decay.* New York: Routledge.

Pleck, J. H. (1981). *The myth of masculinity.* Cambridge, MA: MIT Press.

Pleck, J. H., Sonenstein, F. L., & Ku, L. C. (1993). Masculinity ideology: Its impact on adolescent males' heterosexual relationships. *Journal of Social Issues, 49*(3), 11–29.

Pleck, J. H., Sonenstein, F. L., & Ku, L. C. (1994). Attitudes toward male roles among adolescent males: A discriminant validity analysis. *Sex Roles, 30*(7–8), 481–501.

Ponterotto, J. G., & Casas, J. M. (1991). *Handbook of racial/ethnic minority counseling research:* Springfield, IL: Charles C. Thomas.

Porter, D. (1992). *Between men and feminism.* New York: Routledge.

Quintana, S. M., & Bernal, M. E. (1995). Ethnic minority training in counseling psychology: Comparisons with clinical psychology and proposed standards. *Counseling Psychologist, 23*(1), 102–121.

Ramirez, M., III. (1999). *Multicultural psychotherapy: An approach to individual and cultural differences* (2nd ed.). Boston: Allyn & Bacon.

Reskin, B. F., & Padavic, I. (1994). *Women and men at work.* Thousand Oaks, CA: Pine Forge Press.

Robertson, J. M., & Fitzgerald, L. F. (1992). Overcoming the masculine mystique: Preferences for alternative forms of assistance among men who avoid counseling. *Journal of Counseling Psychology, 39,* 240–246.

Rodriguez, O. (1987). *Hispanics and human services: Help-seeking in the inner city* (Monograph No. 14). New York: Fordham University, Hispanic Research Center.

Ruiz, R. (1981). Cultural and historical perspective in counseling Hispanics. In D. W. Sue (Ed.), *Counseling the culturally different: Theory and practice* (pp. 186–214). New York: Wiley.

Seidler, V. J. (1991). *Recreating sexual politics: men, feminism, and politics.* New York: Routledge.

Sharpe, M. J., & Heppner, P. P. (1991). Gender role, gender-role conflict, and psychological well-being in men. *Journal of Counseling Psychology, 38,* 323–330.

Sheehy, G. (1998). *Understanding men's passages: Discovering the new map of men's lives.* New York: Random House.

Shepherd, S., & Wallis, M. (1989). *Coming on strong: Gay politics and culture.* Boston: Unwin Hyman.

Silverberg, R. A. (1986). *Psychotherapy for men: Transcending the masculine mystique.* Springfield, IL: Thomas.

Sleek, S. (1994, November). Psychology looks at a new masculinity. *APA Monitor, 26*(11), 6–7.

Sue, D. W., & Sue, D. (1990). *Counseling the culturally different: Theory and practice.* New York: Wiley.

Sutkin, L. F., & Good, G. (1987). Therapy with men in health-care settings. In M. Scher, M. Stevens, G. Good, & G. A. Eichenfield (Eds.), *Handbook of counseling and psychotherapy with men* (pp. 372–387). Newbury Park, CA: Sage.

Triandis, H. C., Lisansky, J., Setiadi, B., Chang, B., Marin, G., & Betancourt, H. (1982). Stereotyping among Hispanics and Anglos: The uniformity, intensity, direction, and quality of auto- and heterostereotypes. *Journal of Cross-Cultural Psychology, 13*(4), 409–426.

U.S. Department of Health and Human Services. (1999). *Mental health: A report of the surgeon general.* Rockville, MD: U.S. Department of Health and Human Services, Substance Abuse and Mental Health Services Administration, Center for Mental Health Services, National Institutes of Health, National Institute of Mental Health.

Valdes, L. F., Baron, A., Jr., & Ponce, F. Q. (1987). Counseling Hispanic men. In M. Scher, M. Stevens, G. Good, & G. A. Eichenfield, (Eds.), *Handbook of counseling and psychotherapy with men* (pp. 203–217). Newbury Park, CA: Sage.

Vasquez-Nuttall, E., Avila-Vivas, Z., & Morales-Barreto, G. (1984). Working with Latin American families. *Family Therapy Collections, 9,* 74–90.

Wampold, B. E., Casas, J. M., & Atkinson, D. R. (1981). Ethnic bias in counseling: An information processing approach. *Journal of Counseling Psychology, 28*(6), 498–503.

Webster, C. (1994). Effects of Hispanic ethnic identification on marital roles in the purchase decision process. *Journal of Consumer Research, 21*(2), 319–331.

Young, C. (1994, July). Man troubles: Making sense of the men's movement. *Reason,* pp. 18–25.

Zuniga, C. L. (1998). *Hispanic parent participation in school activities and the relationship to student success.* Unpublished doctoral dissertation, University of Wisconsin, Madison

CHAPTER TWENTY-THREE

Asian American Masculinity and Therapy

The Concept of Masculinity in Asian American Males

David Sue

In the portrayal of masculinity, Asian men have not been given a "fair shake." Stereotypes of being poor at sports, good in mathematics, and villains in mass media contribute to feelings of inferiority. It "becomes pretty easy to buy right into them and develop a poor self image" (Niiya, 1996, p. 7). During a brainstorming session, ethnically diverse college students identified "being in control," "decisive," "aggressive and assertive," "ambitious," "analytical," "competitive," "independent and self-reliant," "individualistic," and a "strong personality" as the ideal characteristics of a good manager. In the same study (Cheng, 1996), college students also played the role of assessor to evaluate the qualities of ethnically diverse volunteer candidates for the position of team manager using Bem's (1974) Sex Role Inventory. Euro-American men were the most likely to be selected as possessing managerial qualities, followed by Euro-American women and then minority women. None of the four African American men or the thirteen Asian American men were selected. On Bem's Sex Role Inventory, Asian American men were rated as "cheerful," "gentle," "naïve," "shy," "quiet," "too nice, not tough enough," "understanding," and "passive," which are "feminine" characteristics. The only "masculine" characteristic that they scored high on was "analytic." They were seen as not qualifying for the masculine-defined role of team manager. Interestingly, during a poststudy interview, most of the Asian American men described many of the characteristics (deferent, humble, polite, respectful, and team player) ascribed to them as assets and traits that mature adults or managers should possess.

Asian American men frequently are not seen to possess the traditional masculine characteristics (physical appearance and behavioral qualities) valued in U.S. society. The personal commentary by Brian Niiya at the beginning of this chapter indicates his belief that Asian American men need to adopt a new definition of masculinity. In fact, Niiya argues that "Asian American men can play a unique role in transforming masculinity" because they are not tall, white, and privileged. "I eventually learned that intelligence, wit, compassion, and emotional honesty were vital components in any new definition of masculinity for me" (Niiya, 1996, p. 7). Indeed, societal gender role expectations for American men are changing from being strong, self-reliant, competitive, in control, and emotionally restrained (Brooks, 1996) to greater sensitivity, appropriate emotionality, gentleness, and more egalitarian relationships (Andronico, 1996; Leafgren, 1990; Moore, 1990).

OBSTACLES TO GENDER REDEFINITION

Although many acculturated Asian American men such as Niiya can understand and personally apply the concept of gender role conflict and change for themselves, those with a traditional collectivistic orientation may have difficulty acknowledging this phenomenon. Both the definition of masculinity and the process by which it is considered may be problematic for Asian American males. For example, to deal with changes in gender role expectations, many in the men's movement stress the importance of introspection and self-reflection. Leafgren (1990) observed, "Most men are unable to listen to their internal self and use that as a standard by which to gauge their well-being, their worth, the value of their existence" (p. 5). In general, traditional Asian Americans do not engage in self-exploration activities or voice struggles through introspective processes. The Korean novelist Chang-Rae Lee describes his father as "unencumbered by those needling questions of existence and self-consciousness" (1995, p. 58). Even among acculturated Asian American college students the preference for dealing with problems with counselors is consultation and advice rather than self-exploration. As Atkinson, Kim, and Caldwell (1998) point out, there appears to be "a general rejection of the psychotherapy role by Asian American students" (p. 421). The introspective process by which gender role conflicts and changes are considered may be unacceptable to many Asian American males.

Consciousness-raising intrapsychic approaches fit in well with the individualistic nature of American society. However, in traditional Asian cultures, individual needs are subordinated to those of the family or community. Intense focus on individual needs is considered to be self-indulgent. In addition, masculine characteristics are defined not by individual qualities and characteristics but primarily in relationship with others such as providing and achieving success for the family. For traditionally oriented Asian American men, the goals of men's consciousness raising make no sense. Self-worth, masculinity, or other characteristics cannot be defined outside of a relationship. However, the Asian American population is heterogeneous and can differ on many other dimensions that may influence their reaction to gender role conflicts, making generalizations difficult.

DIVERSITY OF ASIAN AMERICANS AND PACIFIC ISLANDERS

There are up to forty distinct subgroups of Asian Americans who may differ in language, religious beliefs, and values (Sandhu, 1997). Most, to varying degrees, expect children to defer to parental authority without question, exhibit strong interdependence among family members, and raise children to believe that success in school will contribute directly to family honor (Blair & Qian, 1998). Differences among groups also exist. Japanese Americans are the most assimilated of all the Asian American populations. Their parenting style is similar to that of Euro-Americans (Meston, Heiman, Trapnell, & Carlin, 1999). Filipino American families tend to be the most egalitarian for females and in relationships among couples, whereas Korean Americans maintain a strong hierarchical family structure. Chinese Americans control their children through the use of shame and guilt. Southeast Asians (Vietnamese, Laotian, Cambodian, and Hmong) remain highly patriarchal and value sons over daughters (Blair & Qian, 1998). Sixty percent of Asian Americans live in the western United States, where they make up about 8 percent of the population. Educational attainment is high but varies according to the subgroup. In 1994, about 40 percent of Asian Americans and Pacific Islanders had at least a bachelor's degree, although there are large intergroup differences. About 58 percent of Asian Indians have at least a bachelor's degree versus 6 percent or less among the Tongans, Cambodians, Laotians, and Hmong (U.S. Bureau of the Census, 1995). Intragroup differences include the degree of acculturation; generational status; native born, immigrant, or refugee status; and socioeconomic levels. Each of these factors can influence the way gender role conflict is perceived, which makes any generalizations exceedingly difficult.

Although Asian American boys and men may be differentially affected by gender changes in American society according to their ethnic group or level of acculturation, they face additional challenges as a group. They are not only exposed to the values of the majority culture in the United States but influenced by traditional Asian cultural values and affected by racism and stereotyping. In this chapter, I focus on these factors as they relate to the development of Asian American boys and men.

TRADITIONAL ASIAN VALUES

Asian American males are influenced not only by Euro-American norms and values but also by the traditional values that they have been exposed to in their families and communities. These values are often in conflict with those advocated in the larger society. Asian men live in two different worlds, each with differing gender role expectations. These roles are often contradictory, leading to stress and conflict. As with other norms and values, gender roles can be subject to acculturation pressures (E. J. Kim, O'Neil, & Owen, 1996). In addition, Asian American males tend to acculturate at a slower rate than do Asian American females and therefore are more likely to be influenced by traditional cultural values (Mok, 1999; Sue & Morishima, 1982; Weiss, 1970). This slower assimilation likely results because Asian American males have the responsibility of continuing the family lineage (L. Nguyen & Peterson, 1992; N. A. Nguyen & Williams, 1989). Males, therefore, are defined by their acceptance of cultural values and the degree of success they have in imbuing their families and children with these standards. Many of the traditional values are in direct opposition to the exploration of conflicts over masculinity. The hierarchical nature of traditional Asian American families resists egalitarian considerations, and emotional restraint prevents emotional explorations and discussions of sensitivity. See Table 23.1 for contrasting values and norms between Asian Americans and Euro-Americans.

A married Korean American professor with two children who has lived in the United States since 1968 is facing a cultural conflict. He "must" return to Korea to take care of his aged mother, stating, "I am a man of Asian values (filial piety) . . ." (Choi, 1999, p. 7). In his absence, he was hoping that his children would stay with his wife (their mother). Instead, his two offspring were pursuing their own careers and content to remain in contact with their mother by e-mail or telephone.

The preceding situation reveals several aspects of traditional Asian culture. First, Yearn Hong Choi's self-evaluation depends on his display of filial piety and his desire for interdependence among the family members. Second, Choi decries American society, in which individualism prevails over family values. Among traditional Asian American men, masculinity is not determined by personality or physical appearance but by adhering to traditional values and successfully inculcating these values into their offspring. Many believe their masculinity is threatened if traditional values are not maintained in the family. If the stress is severe, violence and other unhealthy forms of behaviors such as alcohol abuse

Table 23.1. Areas of Potential Difference Between Asian American and Euroamerican Males.

Asian American Males	Euroamerican Males
Collectivism: individual needs are subordinated to those of the group	Individual focus, independence
Hierarchical relationships in which males are given higher status	Egalitarian relationships
Restraint of strong emotions indicates maturity	Expression of assertiveness and emotions is emotionally healthy
Respect for authority	Challenge areas of disagreement
Modesty is a virtue	Self-aggrandize to get ahead

Sources: E. C. Chang, 1996; House & Pinyuchon, 1998; Leong, 1998.

may develop. Exposure to conflicting values over gender roles has also led to increasing tension among Asian men and women.

GENDER ROLE CONFLICTS

On November 9, 1997, Cambodian immigrant, Sovanny Heng, killed his estranged wife and her mother. Some in the community believed that cultural conflict contributed to this event. (Wilson & Sisovann, 1997)

For many Asian American men, living in the United States has resulted in the reconfiguration of gender relationships. Men have suffered a loss of status in both their public and private lives. As Espiritu (1999) observed, "The patriarchal authority of Asian immigrant men, particularly those of the working class, has been challenged due to the social and economic losses that they suffered in their transition to the status of men of color in the United States" (p. 628). In their traditional culture, men had the most authority in the family and had the highest economic status. In the United States, both of these areas have been altered. In the case of the Heng tragedy, the wife wanted greater independence and was seeking a divorce, both of which are rare in Cambodian culture. Among Southeast Asian immigrants, Laotian and Cambodian women are described as being the most subservient to their husbands (Ho, 1990). Domestic violence committed by husbands for hierarchical or gender role violation was justified among older Chinese immigrants and recent immigrants but not among those who were more assimilated (Yick & Agbayani-Siewert, 1997).

Economic reversals also threaten male status. Many disadvantaged male immigrants can get employment only in ethnic businesses in which little English is required, whereas women have opportunities in the areas of child care, garment work, and electronic assembly (Espiritu, 1999). The unemployment rate for Cambodian men has been as high as 80 percent (Uli, 1991). In general, immigrant women often maintain their previous occupational status, whereas their husbands are either unemployed or underemployed

(Min, 1998). Men are often no longer considered to be the primary economic providers for their families and may turn to physical violence to express their control and frustration (Song-Kim, 1992). In a sample of 150 immigrant Korean women in Chicago, 60 percent reported being battered by their spouses. Of the Korean men who were abusive, 58 percent had lower-level jobs in the United States than they had held in Korea. To assert their masculinity, the men might have used physical powers in a destructive manner (Lum, 1988).

FATHERHOOD ROLE

Levant (1996) describes his Fatherhood Project at Boston University to help men develop appropriate communication skills with their children and to become aware of their own feelings. He believes the program helps men to overcome their socialization of being stoic and fearing intimacy. In the same vein, May (1990) stresses the importance of self-disclosure and self-acceptance. In traditional Asian cultures, the father role is being a provider and the head of the family. A man's success is determined by having well-behaved and high-achieving children. Sensitivity and democratic discussion with children are not part of the role description for the father.

Estrangement often occurs between Asian American fathers and their more acculturated children, who are exposed to democratic relationships in mass media and among their majority-culture friends. This conflict can produce attempts by the fathers to establish even more control and to use physical punishment (L. C. Lee & Zhan, 1998). Acculturated Vietnamese male college students were at high risk for having poor relationships with their fathers (Dinh, Sarason, & Sarason, 1994). In one sample of Asian and Caucasian adolescents, most Caucasian students identified parental figures as their role models. In contrast, only 18 percent of 99 Asian American adolescents identified parents as role models; of these, only three selected their fathers (Lorenzo, Pakiz, Reinherz, & Frost, 1995).

Traditionally oriented Asian American fathers feel that their masculinity is being threatened in that they are no longer regarded with respect and admiration by their acculturated children. Contact with the norms and values of the majority culture also influences the definition of fatherhood. Men who were less acculturated engaged in the least child care, and those who were more acculturated engaged more extensively and directly in fathering (Jain & Belsky, 1997).

ASIAN VALUES AND THE WORKPLACE

Norm and value differences often have implications in the workplace. In one study, Asian American male managers were found to make fewer self-disclosures and talked less frequently about their accomplishments to their supervisors than their Euro-American counterparts. Instead, the Asian American managers used tactics such as working harder or working more hours, which did not impress their supervisors. Their respect for authority (hierarchical relationships) and modesty (not drawing attention to the self for accomplishments) undermined their ability to penetrate the glass ceiling. The norms and traditions of Asian cultures are not valued in American society. However, behaviors accepted as normative by Euro-Americans can also be misinterpreted in other cultures. In Japanese corporations, Euro-American men have complained of a "bamboo ceiling." Part of this problem appears to be due to differences in acceptable nonverbal communications. In Japan, subordinates are supposed to avert their gaze to a superior. Euro-American men often continue eye contact, which the Japanese interpret as aggressiveness or defiance (Hamada, 1996).

IMPACT OF TRADITIONAL VALUES ON PERSONALITY MEASURES

In part because of their exposure to traditional values, Asian American students are described as conforming, inhibited, and socially introverted on personality measures (E. C. Chang, 1996; Leong, 1998). These characteristics have more negative implications for Asian males than for females because the male role in the United States is defined as aggressively getting ahead and being strong, self-reliant, competitive, and in control (Brooks, 1996). Although societal expectations for men have changed, characteristics such as sensitivity, emotional expressiveness, and egalitarian relationships are even more difficult for Asian American men than for Euro-American men because these expectations conflict with traditional Asian norms and values.

PORTRAYAL OF ASIAN AMERICAN MASCULINITY IN THE UNITED STATES

In general, the popular culture of the United States is male centered; male characters are the most visible and most prestigious. For Asian Americans, the situation is reversed. Asian men are "invisible" or have been stereotyped in American society and are not depicted as possessing ideal masculine characteristics. Asian males are underrepresented in mass media because of the stereotype that they are submissive (Wynter, 1993). The shortage of Asian American actors on television and in movies affects the way Asian American men are perceived. As one Asian American woman observed, "When you're growing up at 12 or 13 years old, the images of what you are attracted to are burned into your mind. . . . Most of the teen idols are young (white) men. . . . We don't have Asian male teen idols" (Ni, 1995, p. 1). There are also few Asian male role models on television. As one individual remarked, "Here in San Diego, we have about a dozen Asian American women on the air in one capacity or another and NO Asian American men" (McFadden, 1999, p. C4).

Little is done to address Asian American masculinity in films and television programs. In contrast, female Asian Americans have developed roles in movies (*Joy Luck Club, Picture Bride,* and *Double Happiness*) and are often shown as being unhappy with their stereotyped, one-dimensional, patriarchal male partners (Feng, 1996). Asian American men in mainstream media are presented in roles of waiters, cooks, servants, laundry workers, or martial arts experts (such as Bruce Lee and Jackie Chan). Even when they are shown in more prominent roles, the characters lack depth (Mok, 1998). Full character development of Asian American males can generally only be seen in plays and movies produced by Asian Americans such as the *American Sons,* by Okazaki. In this production, the Asian American males show a range of emotions and conflicts associated with their experiences with racism, identity conflicts, and the emasculated image of Asian American men.

The writer and poet David Mura (1996) talks about his apprehensions over fatherhood and his relief when his first child was a girl. "I felt I could help her deal with female

Asian stereotypes better than helping my son deal with the ways the culture would emasculate him" (p. 8). He was worried about the psychological development of a son in a society that portrayed Asian males as objects of ridicule or villains. Later, David Mura had two sons and resolved to help them face the issue of Asian American identity and masculinity.

The emphasis on the Eurocentric standards of male and female physical appearance has also affected the psychological state of Asian males and females. Many Asian Americans are dissatisfied with their appearance and that of their opposite sex counterparts (Arkoff & Weiner, 1966; Chen & Yang, 1986; Huang & Ying, 1991; Pang, Mizokawa, Morishima, & Oldstad, 1985). One Asian American boy responded, "I thought Asian girls were ugly and unexciting" (L. C. Lee & Zhan, 1998, p. 139). Some changes are occurring, as in these responses by two Asian American male actors (Ni, 1995, p. 1): "But I think Asian Americans need to begin to look at ourselves not just in terms of, 'Are we tall enough, strong enough, or big enough?' We don't necessarily have to measure ourselves the same way" and "I always thought I was not attractive. As I grew up I realized being sexy is not just how you look, but your personality and how you carry yourself." In many ways, these comments reflect much of the same reexamination that is occurring in many men regarding the shortcomings of the current definition of masculinity.

IDENTITY ISSUES

Erick Liu, a son of immigrants from Taiwan, has completely assimilated into the white mainstream and does not feel Asian American. Instead, he believes that the stress of ethnic identity in Asians is "unnecessary and contrived." (Y. Chang, 1998)

Theo Mizuhara, a top DJ in Los Angeles, obtained success but not in a manner his parents had stressed. Theo dropped out of school but got a GED. He finds it difficult to consider himself a role model for Asian males since they abandoned him when he left school (Chambers, 1996).

Many Asian American males face identity issues that are directly related to how they define and respond to masculinity. Consideration of identity is important because some evidence suggests that positive self-esteem is related to pride in ethnic identity (Nesdale, Rooney, & Smith, 1997). However, faced with a society that provides few Asian role models and that devalues or ignores Asian Americans, acculturation conflicts may occur and be manifested in conformity, traditional identity, or Asian American identity (Kitano & Maki, 1996; Sue & Sue, 1999). In addition, the definition of masculinity may differ according to the different group identity.

Conformity: Low Ethnic Identity, High Assimilation

In the conformity identity, Asian American males have completely accepted the majority cultural values and rarely accept their traditional cultural values. Some denigrate their own appearance and cultural background and totally accept masculinity as defined by American society. In one sample, Japanese American college men indicated dissatisfaction with their height and upper body development (Arkoff & Weaver, 1966). Similar attitudes were also found with Japanese American children (Pang, Mizokawa, Morishima, & Olstad, 1985). This dissatisfaction is probably due to the acceptance of the Euro-American standard of physical appearance.

At one high school, S. J. Lee (1994) observed a group of Asian American students she identified as "New Wavers." The students were described as those who "liked to party" and skip classes and were peer rather than family oriented. They believed that Asian stereotypes prevented them from gaining acceptance from white students. One student, Lee Chau, was proud of his physical prowess: "I'm not a wimp. I can defend myself. A lot of Asians can't fight" (S. J. Lee, 1994, p. 423). The goal of New Wavers seemed to be gaining acceptance by non-Asians. Others in this category may also be completely assimilated and not reject being Asian but believe that it is a relatively unimportant characteristic in American society.

For Asian American men in this category, individual-focused counseling approaches considering gender issues would be appropriate. Such men would be receptive to consciousness-raising groups that consider the impact and limiting elements of society's definitions of masculinity. However, it may be difficult for some men at this level to acknowledge the impact of their ethnicity or cultural background because the accepted standard is Euro-American. Raising issues of ethnicity might be uncomfortable for them because the topics would single them out, and they would rather not be reminded that racial differences exist. The topic of masculinity could be approached historically, culturally, and within family settings to encourage discussion and to educate all members.

Traditional: High Ethnic Identity, Low Assimilation

Asian American males in the traditional category maintain their traditional cultural orientation and often include recent immigrants or those living in ethnic enclaves. Masculinity is considered in a family or group context. For example, traditionally oriented Asian American male students stress the importance of doing well academically for the family and feelings of obligation to their parents for their sacrifices (S. J. Lee, 1994). There is little focus on the individual outside of a social context. For a married Asian American man, masculinity is defined in terms of being head of the family, providing for the economic and social well-being of the family, and having offspring who are successful and who demonstrate filial piety. Recent immigrants often feel that these aspects of their lives are being threatened:

> Mr. G. is a Korean American with a wife and two children. To provide for his family, he works more than 60 hours a week at a laundromat. He was visited by childhood protective services when his children reluctantly described his disciplinary methods. He feels that his children are growing away from him and arguments with his wife have increased.
> (Toarmino & Chun, 1997)

Mr. G. would have difficulty understanding the intrapsychic approaches to the consideration of gender role changes because the self is defined in relationship to others. Self-exploration in either a group or individual sessions would generally be ineffective. Instead, for individuals with the traditional orientation, problems would be discussed in the context of culture conflict and differing expectations from Asian and Euro-American perspectives. Dichotomous thinking would be pointed out and modified or reframed. For example, in the earlier example, Mr. Choi reconciled the fact that his adult children moved far away from him and his wife (in traditional Asian cultures, the adult children and parents are often in the same household or live nearby because they are supposed to take care of their aging parents) by stating, "My children still believe that they honor and love their parents, although they are apart from us" (Choi, 1999, p. 7). Mr. Choi can be praised for fulfilling his role as a son (adhering to traditional values toward his parents) and as a parent (his children succeeded academically, but because they live in a different culture they show filial piety in a different way). Similarly, in Mr. G.'s case, it is important to acknowledge that many problems are caused by culture conflict and adjustment to living in the United States. Positive adjustments that he has made in coming to the United

States could be pointed out, and different means of evaluating his success as a man, husband, and father could be developed.

Asian American Identity: High Ethnic Identity, High Assimilation

Individuals in the Asian American identity grouping may be thought of as bicultural in orientation. Some have rediscovered or actively sought and developed their Asian identity after being assimilated. They tend to be outspoken about racism and its effect on how Asian American masculinity is perceived in the United States. Individuals in this group often fight racism in public areas such as activism through changing and challenging discriminatory laws. They may be open to a discussion of the changing views of masculinity in society but need acknowledgment of the emasculation of Asian males and to address these issues through societal changes. Participation in consciousness-raising groups would necessitate the inclusion of material on Asian men and a willingness to address the issues of racism in American society. Individuals in this group might have difficulty accepting any difficulty as personal rather than external.

MODIFIED COGNITIVE THERAPY WITH ASIAN MEN

Mahalik, in Chapter Twenty-Five, recommends the use of cognitive therapy. This approach is congruent with men's socialization experiences because it focuses on cognitions rather than the expression of emotions and involves a problem-solving or action-oriented emphasis. For nearly the same reasons, cognitive therapy, with appropriate modifications, can be useful for Asian males whose cultural background supports emotional restraint and practical solutions. The approach can be useful for Asian males regardless of identity or generational status. For example, Atkinson et al. (1998) found that Asian American groups demonstrated a consistent preference for counseling that involved consultation for problems with an external etiology (racism in society). For problems with an internal cause (depression due to the death of a parent), they preferred the counselor to act primarily as a facilitator of family and community support. This would make sense because of the Asian value of self-sufficiency in solving one's own problems and allows avoiding a personal discussion of issues that might lead to shame. Regardless of acculturation level, Asian American students rated intrapsychic exploration low among preferred counselor roles.

The cognitive therapy approach with its identification and alterations of cognitions allows Asian men to develop the skills to deal with their own problems. However, instead of focusing primarily on shoulds and irrational statements, Asian males would identify conflicts of male roles and values between the different cultural standards and receive support for resolving them. The traditional Asian male role means maintaining a patriarchy, earning a living for the family, and raising a successful family. Conflicts in employment status among the spouses and acculturation of the children can threaten male status. The cognitive approach allows the Asian male to identify acculturation conflicts as the source of family problems and helps to prevent embarrassment. In addition, healthy ways of accommodating the cultural differences can be addressed. New ways of defining or reframing successful relationships among family members and peers can be acknowledged. Asian males can practice both the cognitive aspect (interpreting conflicts differently) and behavioral components associated with changed cognitions. Thus, cognitive therapy, modified to consider cultural conflicts and norms, may be useful in working with problems faced by Asian men.

SUMMARY AND CONCLUSION

Asian men may experience gender role changes and conflict in a very different manner than Euro-Americans. The worldview of traditional Asians is based on a collectivistic orientation. Intrapsychic conflicts over masculinity issues may be incomprehensible because maleness is not defined individually but as a function of how the individual relates to others. Asian men may have additional adjustment difficulties. In a male-oriented society, as exists in the United States, Asian males occupy an "invisible" status. They are rarely portrayed as models either in films or in the mass media. Indeed, the characterizations are generally negative or one-dimensional. Under these circumstances, highly acculturated Asian men may develop a sense that they do not meet the standard of masculinity in this society.

As indicated, the receptivity of Asian American males to a discussion of gender role conflicts depends to a large extent on their degree of acculturation and ethnic identity. Self-exploration approaches still appear to be uncomfortable for even acculturated Asian American males (Atkinson et al., 1998) and may be a reason why they continue to underutilize mental health services (Chin, 1998). For traditionally oriented Asian American males, reframing and discussing culture conflicts can help resolve issues of living up to cultural values. For more acculturated Asian American males, a more didactic presentation that includes a discussion of Asian males in American society might be a better first step than introspective techniques in the consciousness-raising process. In general, Asian Americans have been receptive to cognitive-behavioral methods. One promising approach is that by Mahalik (1999), who believes that gender role conflict should be dealt with as an example of cognitive distortion. He helps clients examine how experiences as men in American society have contributed to this problem and the difficulty of living up to internalized masculine standards. This approach may be useful for Asian American men, with the addition of the notion of culture conflict and aspects of racism in identifying cognitive distortions. The male consciousness-raising movement is still a relatively recent phenomenon. Because of cultural differences in the way masculinity is defined, it will be a challenge to develop strategies to include Asian American men.

References

Andronico, M. P. (1996). *Men in groups.* Washington, DC: American Psychological Association.

Arkoff, A., & Weaver, H. B. (1966). Body image and body dissatisfaction in Japanese-Americans. *Journal of Social Psychology, 68,* 323–330.

Atkinson, D. R., Kim, B.S.K., & Caldwell, R. (1998). Ratings of helper roles by multicultural psychologists and Asian American students. *Journal of Counseling Psychology, 45,* 414–423.

Bem, S. L. (1974). The measurement of psychological androgeny. *Journal of Consulting and Clinical Psychology, 42,* 155–162.

Blair, S. L., & Qian, Z. (1998). Family and Asian students' educational performance. *Journal of Family Issues, 19,* 355–374.

Brooks, G. R. (1996). Treatment for therapy-resistant men. In M. P. Andronico (Ed.), *Men in groups* (pp. 7–20). Washington, DC: American Psychological Association.

Chambers, V. (1996, October 11–13). Radio's most surprising voice. *USA Weekend,* p. 8.

Chang, E. C. (1996). Cultural differences in optimism, pessimism, and coping predictors of subsequent adjustment in Asian American and Caucasian American college students. *Journal of Counseling Psychology, 43,* 113–123.

Chang, Y. (1998, June 22). Asian identity crisis. *Newsweek,* p. 68

Chen, C. L., & Yang, D.C.Y. (1986). The self image of Chinese-American adolescents: A cross-cultural comparison. *International Journal of Social Psychiatry, 32,* 19–26.

Cheng, C. (1996). "We choose not to compete." The "merit" discourse in the selection process, and Asian and Asian American men and their masculinity. In C. Cheng (Ed.), *Masculinities in organizations* (pp. 177–200). Thousand Oaks, CA: Sage.

Chin, J. L. (1998). Mental health services and treatment. In L. C. Lee & N.W.S. Zane (Eds.), *Handbook of Asian American psychology* (pp. 485–504). Thousand Oaks, CA: Sage.

Choi, Y. H. (1999, September 7). Commentary: Asian values meet Western realities. *Los Angeles Times,* p. 7.

Dinh, K. T., Sarason, B. R., & Sarason, I. G. (1994). Parent-child relationships in Vietnamese immigrant families. *Journal of Family Psychology, 8,* 471–488.

Espiritu, Y. L. (1999). Gender and labor in Asian immigrant families. *American Behavioral Scientist, 42,* 628–634.

Feng, P. (1996). Redefining Asian American Masculinity: Steven Okazaki's "American sons." *Cineaste, 22,* 27–30.

Hamada, T. (1996). Unwrapping Euro-American masculinity in a Japanese multinational corporation. In C. Cheng (Ed.), *Masculinities in organizations* (pp. 160–176). Thousand Oaks, CA: Sage.

Ho, C. K. (1990). An analysis of domestic violence in Asian American communities: A multicultural approach to counseling. In L. Brown & M.P.P. Root (Eds.), *Diversity and complexity in feminist therapy* (pp. 129–150). New York: Hayworth.

House, R. M., & Pinyuchon, M. (1998). Counseling Thai Americans: An emerging need. *Journal of Multicultural Counseling and Development, 26,* 194–204.

Huang, L. N., & Ying, Y. W. (1991). Chinese children and adolescents. In J. T. Gibbs & L. N. Huang (Eds.), *Children of color: Psychological interventions with minority youth* (pp. 30–66). San Francisco: Jossey-Bass.

Jain, A., & Belsky, J. (1997). Fathering and acculturation: Immigrant Indian families with young children. *Journal of Marriage and the Family, 59,* 873–883.

Kim, E. J., O'Neil, J. M., & Owen, S. V. (1996). Asian-American men's acculturation and gender-role conflict. *Psychological Reports, 79,* 95–104.

Kitano, H.H.L., & Maki, M. T. (1996). *Continuity, change, and diversity: Counseling Asian Americans.* Thousand Oaks, CA: Sage.

Leafgren, F. (1990). Men on a journey. In D. Moore & F. Leafgren (Eds.), *Men in conflict* (pp. 3–10). Alexandria, VA: American Association for Counseling and Development.

Lee, C-R. (1995). *Native speaker.* New York: Berkeley Publishing.

Lee, L. C., & Zhan, G. (1998). Psychosocial status of children and youths. In L. C. Lee & N.W.S. Nolan (Eds.), *Handbook of Asian American psychology* (pp. 137–164). Thousand Oaks, CA: Sage.

Lee, S. J. (1994). Behind the model-minority stereotype: Voices of high- and low-achieving Asian American students. *Anthropology and Education Quarterly, 25,* 413–429.

Leong, F.T.L. (1998). Career development and vocational behaviors. In L. C. Lee & N.W.S. Zane (Eds.), *Handbook of Asian American psychology* (pp. 359–400). Thousand Oaks, CA: Sage.

Levant, R. F. (1996). The male code and parenting: A psychoeducational approach. In M. P. Andronico (Ed.), *Men in groups* (pp. 229–242). Washington, DC: American Psychological Association.

Lorenzo, M. K., Pakiz, B., Reinherz, H. Z., & Frost, A. (1995). Emotional and behavioral problems of Asian American adolescents: A comparative study. *Child and Adolescent Social Work Journal, 12,* 197–212.

Lum, J. (1988, March). Battered Asian women. *Rice,* pp. 50–52.

Mahalik, J. R. (1999). Interpersonal psychotherapy with men who experience gender role conflict. *Professional Psychology: Theory, Research, and Practice, 30,* 5–13.

May, R. (1990). Finding ourselves: Self-esteem, self-disclosure, and self-acceptance. In D. Moore & F. Leafgren (Eds.), *Problem-solving strategies and intervention for men in conflict* (pp. 180–200). Alexandria, VA: American Association for Counseling and Development.

McFadden, K. (1999, March 25). Readers weigh in on lack of Asian-American men on air. *Seattle Times,* p. C4.

Meston, C. M., Heiman, J. R., Trapnell, P. D., & Carlin, A. S. (1999). Ethnicity, desirable responding, and self-reports of abuse: A comparison of European- and Asian-ancestry undergraduates. *Journal of Consulting and Clinical Psychology, 67,* 139–144.

Min, P. G. (1998). *Changes and conflicts: Korean immigrant families in New York.* Needham Heights, MA: Allyn & Bacon.

Mok, T. A. (1998). Getting the message: Media images and stereotypes and their effect on Asian Americans. *Cultural Diversity and Mental Health, 4,* 185–202.

Mok, T. A. (1999). Asian American dating: Important factors in partner choice. *Cultural Diversity and Ethnic Minority Psychology, 5,* 103–117.

Moore, D. (1990). Helping men become more emotionally expressive: A ten-week program. In D. Moore & F. Leafgren (Eds.), *Men in conflict* (pp. 183–200). Alexandria, VA: American Association for Counseling and Development.

Mura, D. (1996, June 28–30). Of racism, sexism, and fatherhood. *USA Weekend,* pp. 8–9.

Nesdale, D., Rooney, R., & Smith, L. (1997). Migrant ethnic identity and psychological distress. *Journal of Cross-Cultural Psychology, 28,* 569–588.

Nguyen, L., & Peterson, C. (1992). Depressive symptoms among Vietnamese-American college students. *Journal of Social Psychology, 133,* 65–71.

Nguyen, N. A., & Williams, H. L. (1989). Transition from East to West: Vietnamese adolescents and their parents. *Journal of the American Academy of Child and Adolescent Psychiatry, 142,* 798–805.

Ni, C.-C. (1995, February 23). Shedding their shirts—and a stereotype entrepreneurship: Sexless computer nerds. *Los Angeles Times,* p. 1.

Niiya, B. (1996, June 8). The Rafu Shimpo: New definitions of masculinity. Asian men never had the John Wayne option. *Los Angeles Times,* p. 7.

Pang, V. O., Mizokawa, D., Morishima, J. K., & Olstad, R. G. (1985). Self-concepts of Japanese-American children. *Journal of Cross-Cultural Psychology,16,* 99–109.

Sandhu, D. S. (1997). Psychocultural profiles of Asian and Pacific Islander Americans: Implications for counseling and psychotherapy. *Journal of Multicultural Counseling and Development, 25,* 7–22.

Song-Kim, Y. I. (1992). Battered Korean women in urban United States. In S. Furuto, R. Biswas, D. K. Chung, K. Murase, & E. Ross-Sheriff (Eds.), *Social work practice with Asian-Americans* (pp. 213–226). Newbury Park, CA: Sage.

Sue, D. W., & Sue, D. (1999). *Counseling the culturally different* (3d ed.). New York: Wiley.

Sue, S., & Morishima, J. K. (1982). *The mental health of Asian Americans.* San Francisco: Jossey-Bass.

Toarmino, D., & Chun, C. A. (1997). Issues and strategies in counseling Korean Americans. In C. C. Lee (Ed.), *Multicultural issues in counseling* (2d ed., pp. 233–254). Alexandria, VA: American Counseling Association.

Uli, S. (1991). Unlikely heroes: The evolution of female leadership in a Cambodian ethnic enclave. In M. Burawoy (Ed.), *Ethnography unbound* (pp. 161–177). Berkeley and Los Angeles: University of California Press.

U.S. Bureau of the Census. (1995). *Population profile of the United States.* Washington, DC: U.S. Government Printing Office.

Weiss, M. S. (1970). Selective acculturation and the dating process: The patterning of Chinese-Caucasian interracial dating. *Journal of Marriage and the Family, 32,* 273–282.

Wilson, K.A.C., & Sisovann, P. (1997, November 11). Success story that turned to tragedy. *Seattle Post-Intelligencer,* pp. B1, B2.

Wynter, L. E. (1993, June 14). Asian-American men are left adrift in TV news. *Wall Street Journal,* p. B1.

Yick, A. G., & Agbayani-Siewert, P. (1997). Perceptions of domestic violence in a Chinese American community. *Journal of Interpersonal Violence, 12,* 832–846.

CHAPTER TWENTY-FOUR

Psychotherapy with Gay and Bisexual Men

Douglas C. Haldeman

The degree to which a clinician can work effectively with gay and bisexual clients depends in large measure on the degree to which he or she can understand the distinctive challenges faced by most gay and bisexual men. Nearly every gay or bisexual man reports, in his developmental years, some scarring experiences directly related to sexual orientation. The less severe end of the spectrum of such experiences includes verbal harassment and social rejection; the extreme end includes discrimination and violent crimes. For some, a rejecting home environment provides no refuge from a hostile society. Furthermore, religious and educational institutions may reinforce negative social messages about homosexuality and bisexuality. Finally, the presence of social stigma and danger of discrimination and violence are rarely balanced with visible images of happy, productive gay and bisexual men.

It is no surprise therefore that gay and bisexual men seek psychotherapy in proportionally greater numbers than heterosexual men. Although many adolescents experience taunting and rejection to some degree, for the gay or bisexual person it is often more pervasive, more severe in nature, and directly linked to an immutable characteristic—sexual orientation.

The recent inclusion of modules in training programs specifically designed to address clinical issues in working with gay and bisexual men is by no means a universal phenomenon. Pilkington and Cantor (1996) have noted that many psychologists in training do not receive adequate information about gay and bisexual clients. For that reason, in this chapter I offer a knowledge base and a conceptual framework for clinicians in their work with gay and bisexual men.

PREREQUISITES

Effective and ethical therapy with gay and bisexual men is more likely when therapists meet certain prerequisites.

Recognizing Diversity Among Gay and Bisexual Men

It should first be noted that gay and bisexual men comprise a very diverse group. Because of differences in background and social experience, race and culture, ability status, and generation, gay and bisexual men can appear very different from one another. It is therefore essential that the clinician refrain from assuming that the life experiences of gay and bisexual men are necessarily similar to one another.

Knowing Normative Development

Only some gay and bisexual clients focus on issues directly associated with sexual orientation. For example, clients coming out as gay or bisexual may indeed focus primarily on sexual orientation. The therapist needs to provide a supportive environment for exploration of issues associated with coming out but also needs to possess some knowledge of the normative developmental steps thereof to assist the client in solidifying a gay or bisexual identity.

For instance, clients in the early stages of coming out need support and reassurance and may engage in social behaviors mimetic of adolescence. Clients who have been victimized because of their sexual orientation, through either discrimination in the workplace or harassment or violence in their lives, need an atmosphere of healing to be created by the therapist's support and understanding.

For other gay and bisexual clients, sexual orientation is an important element of life experience but is not in and of itself a central focus of therapy. Regardless of whether sexual orientation is at the center or on the periphery of the gay or bisexual client's therapeutic agenda, a competent therapist needs a knowledge base in the normative life experiences of gay and bisexual men. This knowledge base includes some understanding of the multiple sources of oppression that may affect gay and bisexual men, a modicum of cultural literacy about the gay and bisexual communities, and a willingness to confront homophobia and heterocentrism.

CONFRONTING HOMOPHOBIA AND HETEROCENTRISM

Homophobia is a term that is used to describe a set of attitudes that devalue homosexual orientation. It is not a phobia in the clinical sense of the word but has achieved such common cultural currency that it is used here to describe attitudes generally prejudicial against homosexuality, bisexuality, and individuals who identify as such. Regardless of our sexual orientation, we all are socialized with messages and images that normalize heterosexuality and stigmatize homosexuality. It is to be expected that even the most self-aware will carry some vestiges of homophobia into adult life. Therefore, the psychotherapist must be particularly self-scrutinizing relative to his or her own homophobia and must be alert to the need for consultation when unsure or personally conflicted.

Homophobia in the Therapist

The most dangerous manifestation of homophobia on the part of the therapist is the belief that homosexuality and bisexuality are in and of themselves mental illnesses or barriers to productive, fulfilling lives. Although the mental health professions have discredited this belief, some persist in portraying homosexuality as a disorder. This erroneous practice runs counter to a substantial database comparing nonclinical samples of homosexual and heterosexual subjects. This research reveals that there are no significant differences between the groups on a variety of measures relative to psychological, social, familial, or vocational functioning. Further, a follow-up analysis of those studies purporting to show homosexuality per se as pathological has found them to be lacking in scientific rigor (Gonsiorek, 1991).

Homophobia in Clients

Therapists working with gay and bisexual clients should assess the level of homophobia manifested by clients. Homophobic attitudes may cause some gay and bisexual men to have distorted self-images, fear disclosure of their sexual orientation to others, and suffer from impairment in relationship or sexual functioning. Gay and bisexual individuals most likely to enjoy optimal mental health are those who have embraced their sexual orientation. Heterosexual men, on the other hand, may manifest covert or overt forms of antigay oppression if they are not asked to examine their homophobic attitudes.

Social Context

A therapist working with gay and bisexual men must understand the social context and life experiences of gay and bisexual men. This understanding requires an acknowledgment that gay and bisexual men enjoy fulfilling relationships in their families of choice, even if such families do not totally resemble the nuclear heterocentric family. The therapist recognizes the gay or bisexual man's capacity for a productive career, while understanding that particular stressors related to being "out" on the job may affect his comfort at work or even his general mental health.

Further, it is critical that the therapist refrain from framing a gay or bisexual client's problems as a product of his sexual orientation, unless this is the reason specifically given. It is both unscientific and offensive to infer that all problems are due to the individual's sexual orientation when they may actually be normative responses to social stressors.

Heterocentrism

Heterocentrism is the tendency to hold heterosexuality as the norm for behavior and assume that all people are heterosexual. Sometimes, even questions that seem innocuous such as "Are you married?" can appear insensitive to a gay or bisexual client. Counselors and therapists should never assume knowledge of a client's sexual orientation until it is directly stated or inferred. In the latter case, it is important to follow up with a question about the individual's identity, because both bisexual- and gay-identified individuals may discuss relationships with partners of both sexes.

Often, well-intentioned therapists make assumptions about the similarity of life experience between gay and heterosexual individuals. Such assumptions may be an overidentification with a client's experience and may unintentionally devalue a client's distress. For example, when a gay or bisexual client reports on harassment experiences in early life, it is usually not helpful for a therapist to reassure him that nearly everyone goes through rejection and taunting in youth. Although the statement may be true, it is invalidating to suggest that the concerns common to most people—social rejection, relationship difficulties, and career decisions—are experienced in the same way by gay and bisexual individuals.

SEXUAL IDENTITY VERSUS SEXUAL BEHAVIOR

Therapists should not assume that sexual orientation is necessarily congruent with sexual identity. An individual may have a primarily homosexual sexual orientation while maintaining a primarily heterosexual sexual identity. Such is the case of a heterosexually married homosexual man. Dave is a thirty-eight-year-old father of two children, ages five and eight. He and his wife have been married for ten years. He reports having struggled with homoerotic feelings all of his life but married in the hopes that they would diminish in a loving relationship with a woman. He has never disclosed his homoerotic feelings. He is a devoted father and loves his children very much, although his wife has complained for some time of Dave's emotional and sexual distance.

At her instigation, the two have been seeing a marital therapist for some time to work on intimacy enhancement. Dave reports that he has been having anonymous sexual contacts at road stops over the past year. Although he feels tremendous guilt after each such encounter, he is concerned that his life is passing him by and that he is living a lie. He cannot bring himself to tell his wife about his same-sex attractions and also fears that leaving the marriage would have a devastating effect on his children.

The therapist must guard against advising Dave—either that he face the truth about himself, come out, and leave his family or that he resign himself to the choices he has made and sublimate his sexual desires. This is an extremely complicated issue that Dave must solve for himself. The case highlights the folly of the "heterosexual experiments" favored by so-called reparative therapists. Such experiments do not eradicate homoerotic feelings, and they ensnare women and children in the client's often hidden agenda.

For some therapists, Dave's case may elicit a desire to make suggestions. In reality, the best observations are those that cause Dave to think more deeply about his situation and in so doing to be able to balance his own needs with the needs of his family. For instance, Dave might consider that perhaps his wife is blaming herself for his lack of enthusiasm in the relationship. Dave should also be reminded that anonymous sex in public places is both illegal and dangerous. Nevertheless, at this point the therapist's primary task is to provide a context in which Dave can weigh the cost associated with disrupting the family against the cost of continuing to live a life that is incongruent with who he is and come to his own conclusion.

EFFECTS OF SOCIAL STIGMA

The harm internalized from negative messages and experiences about sexual orientation affects nearly all gay and bisexual men. These experiences include harassment, discrimination, and even violence (Herek, 1991). They may have a profound effect on the way in which the individual perceives himself and his life and may be exacerbated by the fact that there may be little or no social or institutional support for the gay or bisexual individual coping with these stressors (DiPlacido, 1998).

Social Stigma and History of Harassment

The psychological sequelae of negative life experiences relative to sexual orientation may be exponentially more difficult for ethnic minority gay and bisexual men (Greene, 1994), older gay and bisexual men (Berger & Kelly, 1996), and gay and bisexual men living in rural environments (D'Augelli & Garnets, 1995). The internalization of untoward life experiences related to sexual orientation results in an array of problems ranging from poor self-image to overt self-hatred (Gonsiorek, 1993). It is thus important for therapists working with gay and bisexual clients to assess the individual's history of harassment, discrimination, and violence. Additionally, it is useful to remember that the attitudinal and behavioral manifestations of having survived these experiences are not always obvious or conscious (Shidlo, 1994).

Changing Sexual Orientation

Given the numerous potential psychological, social, and physical sources of abuse, it is not surprising that some men attempt to change their sexual orientation. Clients presenting with such a request should not be uncritically encouraged but should receive accurate information about sexual orientation and a thoughtful questioning about their motives. Even if it were desirable to do so, there is no evidence to suggest that sexual orientation can be changed. The majority of individuals seeking to change their homosexual or bisexual orientation do so in response to considerable internalized social pressure (Haldeman, 1994). Further, the American Psychological Association's policy on the issue, Appropriate Therapeutic Responses to Sexual Orientation, requires the therapist to refrain from using discriminatory practices (for example, basing treatment on pathology-based views of homosexuality or bisexuality) and from misrepresenting scientific or clinical data. This policy further requires a discussion of treatment alternatives and reasonable outcomes and clear informed consent (American Psychological Association, 1998).

ISSUES OF INTIMACY

The degree to which all men, regardless of sexual orientation, are able to bond with one another in intimate ways depends in part on confronting and resolving homophobia and heterophobia. Gay and bisexual men define themselves in part by homoerotic and homoemotional romantic attachment. However, some gay and bisexual men report having been tormented by male peers, rejected by fathers for not being "masculine" enough, berated by coaches for being unathletic, and railed at by preachers for being "sinners." This background can hardly establish a good foundation for social or romantic relationships with other men. If other men are perceived as dangerous and rejecting, the gay or bisexual individual may find it difficult to form bonds other than of a transitory or purely erotic nature. A sense of security with one's male self and with other males, whether gay, bisexual, or heterosexual, is a necessary element in the resolution of intimacy issues for gay and bisexual men (Haldeman, 1998).

Greg is a forty-two-year-old bank executive who has been "out" since he was in his early twenties. He is good-looking and outgoing and usually is seeing someone romantically. He reports chronic difficulties in long-term relationships, claiming that after six months to a year, he invariably distances himself from his partner. He seeks help in understanding this pattern and in changing his behavior.

Greg's story suggests two basic avenues for therapeutic inquiry—the historical and the habitual. From a historical perspective, it would be important to assess Greg's early life experiences with other men and determine the degree to which these experiences affect his intimacy-avoidant behavior. Greg was the youngest of three sons in a family that prized athletic achievement above all else. Therefore, his two older brothers, both of whom played football, received most of the attention from Greg's father. Although Greg does not describe his relationship with his father as contentious or unpleasant, he does recall feeling that his father had no idea what to do with his youngest, sensitive son. At the same time, Greg remembers having adored his father and that when he was little, the two of them would play endlessly. Greg recalls the subsequent distancing he experienced from his father as emotionally traumatic.

This case has some of the hallmarks of the stereotyped "sissy boy," and it is mentioned here for precisely that reason. Homophobic theorists incorrectly blame gay and bisexual individuals or their mothers for what is actually rejection by their fathers or male siblings and peers. Such rejection for young gay men, particularly when it is preceded by a strong bond between father and son, can result in male intimacy-avoidant behavior in adult life. Therefore, it is important to explore the background and retrieve unprocessed emotional material to assist the individual in establishing healthy primary relationships in adulthood.

Further, some homophobic therapies posit that the end point of this process should be heterosexual relationship orientation. This goal is wholly inappropriate for a person such as Greg, who is completely satisfied with his sexual orientation. By midlife, relationship patterns are well established. For many gay and bisexual men, the relative ease and availability of sex serve to offer a sense of emotional connection with other men, substituting for a long-term relationship. To replace this pattern with more stable attachments, some clients need to relinquish some of the autonomy they have come to take for granted. As we grow older, giving up autonomy becomes more difficult. Certain behavioral skills, such as communication and problem-solving techniques, need to be taught to the individual who has not struggled with a committed relationship.

GAY CULTURAL LITERACY

Gay cultural literacy is an ability to view the lives of gay and bisexual men through the appropriate lens—a gay-bisexual sensibility, as opposed to a heterocentric one. When considering the behavior of individuals, the therapist considers the norms appropriate to gay and bisexual men. For an individual, the norms may include a valuing of variety seeking in sexual behavior, a particular emphasis placed on the man's circle of friends and community, and different levels of self-disclosure in the various social contexts of the man's life.

New Rules for Gay Couples

For couples, this gay sensibility is partly characterized by a lack of institutional support for the relationship. Gay men become responsible for creating their own "rules" in committed relationships. In many instances, these guidelines may conform to heterocentric expectations, but not always. For instance, heterosexual marriage generally includes an expectation for sexual monogamy. This expectation may be applicable to some gay male relationships, but for some others it would be inappropriately heteromimetic. The resulting relationships, then, might be open, or nonmonogamous.

In a primary relationship between two men, there are no automatic role expectations, and it is up to the couple to decide how to organize their married life. Some couples may merge their finances, others may keep them separate, and still others may mix them. The same principle holds true for decisions about division of labor, the use of leisure time, and so on. The therapist's role is not to judge such choices or to borrow inappropriate inferences drawn from heterosexuals but to assess the degree to which the decisions about the relationship are adaptive for the individuals involved. Above all, any tendency to assume what is normal for gay and bisexual men based on a heterocentric model should be avoided.

The Newly Out

The therapist may need to recognize that the gay community can be a difficult place for people to navigate, especially the newly out. The therapeutic process is greatly facilitated by a therapist's understanding of the challenges gay men face in attempting to develop friendships and intimate relationships (for example, focus on looks and youth and difficulty interacting with others in bars).

IN OR OUT OF THE CLOSET

Decisions about if, when, and how to "come out" have major implications for gay and bisexual couple relationships. Paul and Tony have been together for five years; both are in their early thirties. They live in a large city on the West Coast. Both report that they are generally satisfied with their relationship; they enjoy sports and other leisure activities and have a wide circle of friends.

Paul comes from a conservative, religious family that he always sees on holidays and periodically sees on other occasions. He has not disclosed to them that he is gay and sees no reason to do so. Tony, on the other hand, comes from the East Coast, and his entire family has known for some time that he is gay.

At issue is how to deal with the disparity between the degree of openness the two consider appropriate at this point in their relationship. Tony would like them to start spending holidays together, whereas Paul does not wish to arouse suspicion on the part of his family. Tony wants to dismantle the second bedroom, which is set up as "Paul's room" in case someone who does not know the true nature of the couple's relationship comes over.

This couple presents with issues relative to both personal and relationship development. Sometimes, both partners in a gay male relationship differ with respect to how open they are willing to be about their personal sexual orientation and about the relationship itself. This difference speaks to an important underlying issue—is this relationship the primary family of choice for both Paul and Tony?

If so, the relationship needs to be considered first. Although Paul cannot be forced to come out to his family if that is not his wish, Tony should not be expected to subjugate his needs for honesty in the service of his partner's secretiveness. Ultimately, decisions must be made together, often borne of compromise.

FAMILY ISSUES

Until gay men are legally able to marry, the primary family structures of gay and some bisexual men will always include people who are not legally or biologically related. Therapists working with gay male couples must have some knowledge of and respect for gay relationships and be able to view the male couple as a family unit. Gay male couples are both similar to and different from heterosexual couples (Peplau, Veniegas, & Campbell, 1996).

Relationships Issues

Like heterosexual couples, gay male couples form relationships because of a desire for companionship (Klinger, 1996) and express satisfactions with their relationships similar to those of heterosexual couples (Kurdek, 1995). However, sometimes they react in disparate ways to common relationship issues. Communication difficulties, sexual problems, and dual-career issues are universal but may be viewed differently by gay male couples. Further, issues of disclosure as a couple to family or work colleagues, the additive effects of gender socialization, and HIV status are examples of concerns specific to gay male couples (Cabaj & Klinger, 1996).

External Issues

External issues, such as pressure from families of origin or previous partners, may arise. These issues are further complicated when children and decisions about parenting are involved. Aging and changes in physical health may present medical and legal issues for which gay couples enjoy no automatic solutions. There are numerous permutations of universal family issues that gay couples may face, as well as the aforementioned concerns specific to gay couples. A therapist working with gay couples is sensitive to the potential negative effects of social stigma, is knowledgeable about the diverse nature of these relationships, and respects the meaning and value of the relationships.

Parenting Competency

Research has clearly established that there are no significant differences between gay men and heterosexual men relative to parenting competency (Allen & Burrell, 1996; Bigner & Bozett, 1990; Patterson, 1996a). Nevertheless, this is an area in which the effect of social and institutional stigma can be particularly pernicious. In a number of instances, gay and bisexual parents have lost custody of their children, been prohibited from living with their domestic partners, or been prevented from adopting or being foster parents on the basis of their sexual orientation (Editors of the *Harvard Law Review*, 1990; Patterson, 1996a).

Gay and bisexual parents are often confronted with the commonly held but scientifically baseless misconceptions that gay parents influence a child's gender role identity, conformity, and sexual orientation. A number of reviews have clearly indicated that there is no basis for concern as to a child's gender role identity if his or her parent is gay (Patterson, 1996b). Furthermore, children of gay and bisexual parents do not differ from the children of heterosexual parents in their emotional development or the likelihood of their becoming homosexual (Bailey, Bobrow, Wolfe, & Mikach, 1995; Golombok & Tasker, 1996). Considering the misinformation that the gay or bisexual parent is battling in society at large, it is particularly important that he not need to convince his therapist as well.

Families of Gay and Bisexual Clients

Families of origin may be unprepared to accept a gay or bisexual family member because of negative stereotypes or familial, ethnic, or cultural norms or religious beliefs (Chan, 1995; Greene, 1994; Matteson, 1996). The acknowledgment of a family member's homosexuality or bisexuality can precipitate a family crisis resulting in the expulsion of the individual, counterrejection of parents or siblings by the gay or bisexual family member, parental guilt, or conflicts in the parents' relationship (Griffin, Wirth, & Wirth, 1996; Savin-Williams & Dube, 1998).

Even when family reactions are positive, adjustments are necessary to accommodate a new understanding of the gay or bisexual family member, because most families do not anticipate having gay members. Many families are faced with their own "coming out" process when a family member discloses the fact that he is gay or bisexual (Bass & Kaufman, 1996; Savin-Williams & Dube, 1998).

Even when the gay or bisexual man's relationship to his family of origin is close, the chosen or extended family can take on added importance. Because of the absence of social sanction for his marital relationship, the gay or bisexual man's relationships with his family of friends and community can assume added significance when there is stress with his family of origin (Kurdek, 1988; Weston, 1992). His relationship with his therapist may also assume greater significance, particularly in times of stress. Therefore, the therapist working with gay and bisexual men needs to have an above-average level of understanding about family dynamics.

GAY AND BISEXUAL MEN OF COLOR

One of the paradoxes of life for white gay and bisexual men is that they appear to be entitled to white, heterosexual privilege—that is, until they disclose their sexual orientation or until it is suspected by others. The same cannot be said for racial or ethnic minority gay and bisexual men, who are often doubly stigmatized and rejected in both ethnic and gay communities. Racial or ethnic minority gay and bisexual men must negotiate the norms, values, and beliefs regarding sexual orientation from both minority and mainstream cultures (Chan, 1995; Greene, 1994; Rust, 1996). The dissonance between such cultural norms and the individual's sense of being gay or bisexual can be a major source of stress, particularly if there is no one group or community to which a racial or ethnic minority man who is gay or bisexual can anchor his identity and feel at home.

This problem may be even more challenging for gay and bisexual ethnic minority youth and for those exploring their sexual orientation. A therapist working with gay and bisexual men of color should understand that clients may be affected by the ways in which their cultures view homosexuality and bisexuality and that they may also be affected by racism from within the gay community (Gock, 1992; Greene, 1994; Morales, 1996). The complex dynamics associated with factors such as cultural values about gender roles, religion and procreative beliefs, degree of individual and family acculturation, and the personal and cultural history of discrimination and oppression are all potential influences on identity integration and personal and social functioning (Chan, 1995; Greene, 1994).

John is an African American man in his midforties. He grew up in a large, very religious family on the East Coast. At the age of eighteen, he told his family that he believed he was gay. He was told to leave the family home and never return. He is angry with his family for having rejected him and angry with the gay community for its domination by well-off white men and its racism. He has had a number of short-term relationships. Once others get close to him and realize how angry he is, they withdraw.

John has been diagnosed with major depressive disorder and borderline personality disorder. Previous therapists have worked with him on anger management skills, which he says have been useless.

In John's case previous treatments may have actually exacerbated his problems, because they have not validated John's legitimate anger over having been rejected by both his family and the gay community. He is diagnosed as having borderline personality disorder instead of being seen as having a normal response to being thrown out of his home and then marginalized as an overweight person of color in a predominantly white male gay community. If the therapist working with John is white, it may evoke transference issues that should be explored. Additionally, in this situation the therapist may wish to research any local community resources that may be applicable to gay people of color.

BISEXUAL MEN

Bisexual men may face their own sense of cultural homelessness. Gay men may regard them with suspicion because of their access to heterosexual privilege. Yet heterosexual men may reject them as gay men who are still engaged in "hetero-pretense."

Bisexual men may face a variety of stressors in addition to those that derive from prejudice due to same-sex attractions. Bisexuality has historically been invalidated, both in the society at large and in the context of psychological theory and practice. This invalidation has largely occurred through the dichotomization of sexual orientation into heterosexual and homosexual categories, thereby negating any legitimacy to a bisexual orientation (Eliason, 1997; Fox, 1996). Consequently, bisexuality is often inaccurately characterized as a transitional state. Bisexual men who do not adopt either a heterosexual or homosexual identity may be viewed as developmentally arrested or otherwise psychologically impaired (Fox, 1996).

Negative attitudes, misinformation, and lack of social support in both heterosexual and homosexual communities can exacerbate the problems of bisexual men. Therefore, therapists working with them validate their experiences, refrain from encouraging them to select either a heterosexual or homosexual identity, and offer referrals to relevant community resources, when appropriate.

GENERATIONAL ISSUES

It is often said that the gay community is youth oriented, placing older gay and bisexual men at a social disadvantage and creating increased risk for marginalization. Nevertheless, young gay, bisexual, and questioning men face their own problems (D'Augelli, 1998) relative to harassment at school, among peers, and at home. These concerns are complicated by the normative developmental tasks of adolescence. Youth who identify as gay or bisexual at an early age are also at increased risk for violence (Hunter, 1990), substance abuse (Garofalo, Wolf, Kessel, Palfrey, & DuRant, 1998), and suicide attempts (Remafedi et al., 1998). Sometimes, the counseling relationship is the only area in the gay, bisexual, or questioning youth's life in which he feels truly safe.

Therapists should recognize that older gay and bisexual men have had many significant developmental experiences (such as coming out) during different historical periods than younger generations. Older gay and bisexual men grew into adulthood with peers who share characteristics that may make them distinct as a generation (Kimmel, 1995). These cohort effects may significantly influence gay identity development, as well as psychological and social functioning (Frost, 1997). Gay and bisexual older men face special transitions and life tasks such as normative changes in health, retirement, finances, and social support (Slater, 1995). End of life-span tasks for gay and bisexual older men can become complicated with heterosexism or the lack of legal protection that is afforded to heterosexual couples facing medical and financial concerns (Berger & Kelly, 1996). Because they have already addressed issues related to being an oppressed minority, older gay and bisexual men are in an advantaged position to address ageism and old-age transitions. Therapists should recognize that older gay and bisexual men are a diverse group, that normative changes in aging may be positive as well as negative, and that these changes are not necessarily rooted in the individual's sexual orientation.

DISABILITY ISSUES

Gay and bisexual men with physical or sensory disabilities may experience a wide range of challenges associated with the social stigmas of both disability and sexual orientation. The individual's self-concept may be affected to varying degrees by this stigma, which in turn would affect his sense of autonomy and personal agency, sexuality, and self-confidence (Shapiro, 1993). Gay and bisexual men with disabilities, just like their heterosexual counterparts, may be especially vulnerable to the effects of "looksism" (that is, basing social value on physical appearance and marginalizing those who do not conform) (Saad, 1997).

Another area of concern involves the way in which ability status affects the person's relationships with partners, family, caregivers, and health care professionals. Family support may be adversely influenced by awareness of the individual's sexual orientation (Rolland, 1994). Saad (1997) recommends that therapists not assume that a person with sensory or physical disabilities is asexual but inquire about the person's sexual history and current sexual functioning. Further, many disabled gay men have reported coercive sexual encounters (Swartz, 1995). Given the prejudice, discrimination, and lack of social support both within and beyond the gay community, it is important that therapists recognize that when physical or sensory disabilities are present, social barriers and negative attitudes may limit life choices (Shapiro, 1993).

GAY OR BISEXUAL AND HETEROSEXUAL MEN: THE BENEFITS OF CONNECTION

An especially troubling aspect of the pervasive gulf between gay and bisexual men and heterosexual men is the loss of the many possible benefits of close connection.

History of Distrust

During the adolescence of many gay and bisexual men and heterosexual men, the mutual dynamic of oppression, fear, and mistrust sets the tenor for mutual relating. Without personal corrective experiences and education, this way of relating may continue unabated into adulthood. Gay and bisexual men learn to fear and resent the unquestionable power of heterosexual privilege. Those who wield it will always be superior, and the best one can hope for is to protect oneself against its abuse, either by living in hiding or by ghettoizing. Gay and bisexual men also learn that the world of heterosexual men is a dangerous country, the inhabitants of which can threaten one's safety at any time. Ultimately, no matter how much they wish to belong, even though they may be fundamentally like the rest of them, they never will. As a result, most gay and bisexual men develop some degree of heterophobia—the belief that the dominant heterosexual culture is hostile.

Heterosexual males learn early that it is their right to torment those suspected of being gay or bisexual because they represent the antithesis of the socially constructed vision of masculinity. Such behavior sets them apart from their sissy-boy victims, so that nobody mistakes them for anything less than "real men." They learn that even if they have a gay family member, they must keep their mouths shut when a buddy or coworker tells a homophobic joke, lest they be suspected of sympathizing with those who are gay or, worse, being gay themselves.

Costs of Homophobia and Heterophobia

The costs associated with both homophobia and heterophobia are significant. Homophobia can lead some gay and bisexual men to believe that "gay masculinity" is an oxymoron. Nonetheless, the integration of a masculine identity into the ego structure is a sometimes daunting but necessary task. When gay and bisexual men understand that there are many and not just one hegemonic masculinity, they are free to define and experience their sense of maleness in a way that makes sense for them. Thus, one needs neither to reject traditional aspects of maleness nor to overcompensate for a failed sense of personal masculinity.

Benefits of Change

Heterophobia has a negative effect on the ways in which gay and bisexual men relate to one another. Heterophobia is, for most gay and bisexual men, a contaminant of all male-male relationships, whether platonic or romantic. The gay or bisexual man who has come to terms with his feelings of fear and anger at heterosexual men invariably has more successful intimate relationships than those who have not.

Equally, heterosexual men need to confront their homophobia. The hatred of gay and bisexual men and the fear of being perceived as such inhibit development of close relationships with other men and stifle emotional expression in relationships with women and men. Richard Mohr, in *A More Perfect Union* (1994), states:

> Straight men, while your dignity is not at stake in establishing justice for gays, your freedom is. As long as you define yourself in terms of some type and find your worth in putting down those of another type, then you will be trapped by the expectations and requirements of your type and you will always be subject to social blackmail for failure to live up to type. If you use anti-gay attitudes and behaviors to prop up your perception of your gender, and hold your gender, rather than your accomplishments, as what defines you as good, then you will never be able just to be yourself, you will never realize the distinctive human potential for freedom—the ability to develop your own capacities in your own way. (p. 137)

Mohr points out that freedom awaits the heterosexual male who is able to successfully challenge his homophobia. Clatterbaugh (1990) echoes this point: "Gay men do occupy a special place in the study of masculinity. . . . [T]he best way to get at the social construction of masculinity is to look at how gay men have been treated both historically and in contemporary society" (p. 155).

Gay and bisexual men have something to teach their heterosexual peers in the exercise of such freedom. One indirect advantage of social marginalization derives from having "broken the rules" so completely in acknowledging homosexual or bisexual orientation that all culturally assigned gender rules are now up for review. The tyranny of gender-based stereotypy that plagues many heterosexual men is not an issue for many gay and bisexual men, because they are already outside the mainstream and therefore have little to lose.

As a result, gay and bisexual men generally feel freer to express their emotions, if they wish, and to be more forgiving of themselves for failing to live up to socially reinforced gender expectations. Those males characterized by Wade (1998) as dependent on the reference group for their sense of identity stand to benefit the most from gay and bisexual men by challenging discriminatory attitudes, reducing anxiety and hypermasculinity, and increasing ego integration and autonomy.

Therapists who work effectively with gay and bisexual men recognize their diversity. Differences of generation, race and culture, social class, education, profession, relationship status, degree of "outness," health or physical ability status, and history of abuse or victimization all affect the issues a gay or bisexual man may bring to psychotherapy. Sexual orientation itself may be at issue, but more often than not the gay or bisexual man in therapy is dealing with issues similar to those brought by heterosexual men—relationship, career, health, and existential concerns. It may be tempting to forget altogether that his sexual orientation makes him different from the majority of men.

It is essential to remember, however, that he is indeed different, in that he invariably carries with him the experience of social disapproval at best and discrimination and violence at worst. Losing the perspective that these experiences are part of the core of his relationships with other men makes it difficult to see him clearly. An ability to understand him and to help him see where he is going is predicated in part on understanding where he has been.

Social stigma affects people powerfully, particularly when it is part of one's early life experience. From an individual, couple, and family perspective, as we have seen, the world is a different place for gay and bisexual men. Additionally, the therapist may encounter what has been referred to as the "gay spirit" in some gay and bisexual clients. Gay spirit is a dimension of the gay experience borne of struggle and pain but also, according to some cultural anthropologists, of the unique blend of male and female qualities present in some gay and bisexual men (Thompson, 1994).

Psychotherapy can be helpful in creating opportunities for corrective socioemotional experiences for gay men seeking to address their social aversion to heterosexual men and for heterosexual men willing to confront their antigay attitudes. The distance that many gay and bisexual men experience with their heterosexual counterparts is rooted in early social learning. Mutual communion opens the door to learning about each other in a different way—a learning that reduces the distance and promotes reconciliation. Thus, gay and bisexual men are able to reduce their defenses, and heterosexual men discontinue abusing their gay and bisexual brothers in a misguided sense of their own masculinity. In the end, both groups experience improved relationships with men of all sexual orientations. Therein lies the discovery that promotes a true personal masculinity and the recognition that we are in fact brothers after all.

References

Allen, M., & Burrell, N. (1996). Comparing the impact of homosexual and heterosexual parents on children: Meta-analysis of existing research. *Journal of Homosexuality, 32*(2), 19–35.

American Psychological Association. (1998). Appropriate therapeutic responses to sexual orientation in the proceedings of the American Psychological Association, Incorporated, for the legislative year 1997. *American Psychologist, 53*(8), 882–939.

Bailey, J., Bobrow, D., Wolfe, M., & Mikach, S. (1995). Sexual orientation of adult sons of gay fathers. Special issue: Sexual orientation and human development. *Developmental Psychology, 31*(1), 124–129.

Bass, E. & Kaufman, K. (1996). *Free your mind: The book for gay, lesbian, and bisexual youth and their allies.* New York: HarperCollins.

Berger, R., & Kelly, J. (1996). Gay men and lesbians growing older. In R. Cabaj & T. Stein (Eds.), *Textbook of homosexuality and mental health* (pp. 305–316). Washington, DC: American Psychiatric Press.

Bigner, J., & Bozett, F. (1990). Parenting by gay fathers. In F. Bozett & M. Sussman (Eds.), *Homosexuality and family relations* (pp. 155–176). New York: Harrington Park Press.

Cabaj, R., & Klinger, R. (1996). Psychotherapeutic interventions with lesbian and gay couples. In R. Cabaj & T. Stein (Eds.), *Textbook of homosexuality and mental health* (pp. 485–502). Washington, DC: American Psychiatric Press.

Chan, C. (1995). Issues of sexual identity in an ethnic minority: The case of Chinese American lesbians, gay men, and bisexual people. In A. D'Augelli & C. Patterson (Eds.), *Lesbian, gay, and bisexual identities over the lifespan: Psychological perspectives* (pp. 87–101). New York: Oxford University Press.

Clatterbaugh, K. (1990). *Contemporary perspectives on masculinity* Boulder, CO: Westview Press.

D'Augelli, A. (1998). Developmental implications of victimization of lesbian, gay, and bisexual youth. In G. Herek (Ed.), *Psychological perspectives on lesbian and gay issues: Vol. 4. Stigma and sexual orientation* (pp. 187–210). Thousand Oaks, CA: Sage.

D'Augelli, A., & Garnets, L. (1995). Lesbian, gay, and bisexual communities. In A. D'Augelli & C. Patterson (Eds.), *Lesbian, gay, and bisexual identities over the lifespan: Psychological perspectives.* New York: Oxford University Press.

DiPlacido, J. (1998). Minority stress among lesbians, gay men, and bisexuals: A consequence of heterosexism, homophobia, and stigmatization. In G. Herek (Ed.), *Psychological perspectives on lesbian and gay issues. Stigma and sexual orientation: Understanding prejudice against lesbians, gay men, and bisexuals* (pp. 138–159). Thousand Oaks, CA: Sage.

Editors of the *Harvard Law Review.* (1990). *Sexual orientation and the law.* Cambridge, MA: Harvard University Press.

Eliason, M. (1997). The prevalence and nature of biphobia in heterosexual undergraduate students. *Archives of Sexual Behavior, 26*(3), 317–325.

Fox, R. (1996). Bisexuality in perspective: A review of theory and research. In B. Firestein (Ed.), *Bisexuality: The psychology and politics of an invisible minority* (pp. 3–50). Newbury Park, CA: Sage.

Frost, J. (1997). Group psychotherapy with the gay male: Treatment of choice. *Group, 21*(3), 267–285.

Garofalo, R., Wolf, R., Kessel, S., Palfrey, S., & DuRant, L. (1998). The association between health risk behaviors and sexual orientation among a school-based sample of adolescents. *Pediatrics, 101*(5), 895–902.

Gock, T. (1992). The challenges of being gay, Asian, and proud. In B. Berzon (Ed.), *Positively gay* (pp. 247–252). Millbrae, CA: Celestial Arts.

Golombok, S., & Tasker, F. (1996). Do parents influence the sexual orientation of their children? Findings from a longitudinal study of lesbian families. *Developmental Psychology, 32*(1), 3–11.

Gonsiorek, J. (1991). The empirical basis for the demise of the mental illness model of homosexuality. In J. Gonsiorek & J. Weinrich (Eds.), *Homosexuality: Research implications for public policy* (pp. 115–136). Newbury Park, CA: Sage.

Gonsiorek, J. (1993). Mental health issues of gay and lesbian adolescents. In L. Garnets & D. Kimmel (Eds.), *Psychological perspectives on lesbian and gay male experiences* (pp. 469–485). New York: Columbia University Press.

Greene, B. (1994). Ethnic minority lesbians and gay men: Mental health and treatment issues. *Journal of Consulting and Clinical Psychology, 62*(2), 243–251.

Griffin, C., Wirth, M., & Wirth, A. (1996). *Beyond acceptance: Parents of lesbians and gays talk about their experiences.* New York: St. Martin's Press.

Haldeman, D. (1994). The practice and ethics of sexual orientation conversion therapy. *Journal of Consulting and Clinical Psychology, 62*(2), 221–227.

Haldeman, D. (1998). Ceremonies and religion in same-sex marriage. In R. Cabaj & D. Purcell (Eds.), *On the road to same-sex marriage* (pp. 141–164). San Francisco: Jossey-Bass.

Herek, G. (1991). Stigma, prejudice, and violence against lesbians and gay men. In J. Gonsiorek & J. Weinrich (Eds.), *Homosexuality: Research implications for public policy* (pp. 60–80). Newbury Park, CA: Sage.

Hunter, J. (1990). Violence against lesbian and gay male youths. *Journal of Interpersonal Violence, 5,* 295–300.

Kimmel, D. (1995). Lesbians and gay men also grow old. In L. Bond, S. Cutler, & A. Grams (Eds.), *Promoting successful and productive aging* (pp. 289–303). Thousand Oaks, CA: Sage.

Klinger, R. (1996). Lesbian couples. In R. Cabaj & T. Stein (Eds.), *Textbook of homosexuality and mental health* (pp. 339–352). Washington, DC: American Psychiatric Press.

Kurdek, L. (1988). Perceived social support in gays and lesbians in cohabiting relationships. *Journal of Personality and Social Psychology, 54,* 504–509.

Kurdek, L. (1995). Lesbian and gay couples. In A. D'Augelli & C. Patterson (Eds.), *Lesbian, gay, and bisexual lives over the lifespan* (pp. 243–261). New York: Oxford University Press.

Matteson, D. (1996). Counseling and psychotherapy with bisexual and exploring clients. In B. Fierstein (Ed.), *Bisexuality: The psychology and politics of an invisible minority* (pp. 185–213). Newbury Park, CA: Sage.

Mohr, R. (1994). *A more perfect union: Why straight Americans must stand up for gay rights.* Boston: Beacon Press.

Morales, E. (1996). Gender roles among Latino gay and bisexual men: Implications for family and couple relationships. In J. Laird & R. Green (Eds.), *Lesbians and gays in couples and families: A handbook for therapists* (pp. 272–297). San Francisco: Jossey-Bass.

Patterson, C. (1996a). Lesbian and gay parenthood. In M. Bornstein (Ed.), *Handbook of parenting* (pp. 255–274). Hillsdale, NJ: Erlbaum.

Patterson, C. (1996b). Lesbian and gay parents and their children. In R. Savin-Williams & K. Cohen (Eds.), *The lives of lesbians, gays, and bisexuals: Children to adults* (pp. 274–304). Fort Worth, TX: Harcourt Brace.

Peplau, L., Veniegas, R., & Campbell, S. (1996). Gay and lesbian relationships. In R. Savin-Williams & K. Cohen (Eds.), *The lives of lesbians, gays, and bisexuals: Children to adults* (pp. 250–273). Fort Worth, TX: Harcourt Brace.

Pilkington, N., & Cantor, J. (1996). Perceptions of heterosexual bias in professional psychology programs: A survey of graduate students. *Professional Psychology: Research and Practice, 27*(6), 604–612.

Remafedi, G., French, S., Story, M., Resnick, M., Michael, D., & Blum, R. (1998). The relationship between suicide risk and sexual orientation: Results of a population-based study. *American Journal of Public Health, 88*(1), 57–60.

Rolland, J. (1994). In sickness and health: The impact of illness on couples' relationships. *Journal of Marital and Family Therapy, 20*(4), 327–347.

Rust, P. (1996). Managing multiple identities: Diversity among bisexual women and men. In B. Fierstein (Ed.), *Bisexuality: The psychology and politics of an invisible minority* (pp. 53–83). Thousand Oaks, CA: Sage.

Saad, C. (1997). Disability and the lesbian, gay man, or bisexual individual. In M. Sipski & C. Alexander (Eds.), *Sexual function in people with disability and chronic illness: A health professional's guide*. Gaithersburg, MD: Aspen.

Savin-Williams, R., & Dube, E. (1998). Parental reactions to their child's disclosure of gay/lesbian identity. *Family Relations, 47*, 1–7.

Shapiro, J. (1993). *No pity*. New York: Times Books.

Shidlo, A. (1994). Internalized homophobia: Conceptual and empirical issues in measurement. In B. Greene & G. Herek (Eds.), *Psychological perspectives on lesbian and gay issues. Lesbian and gay psychology: Theory, research, and clinical applications* (pp. 176–205). Thousand Oaks, CA: Sage.

Slater, S. (1995). *The lesbian family life cycle*. New York: Free Press.

Swartz, D. (1995). Cultural implications of audiological deficits on the homosexual male. *Sexuality and Disability, 13*(2), 159–181.

Thompson, M. (1994). *Gay soul: Finding the heart of gay spirit and nature*. San Francisco: HarperCollins.

Wade, J. (1998). Male reference group identity dependence: A theory of male identity. *Counseling Psychologist, 26*(3), 349–383.

Weston, K. (1992). *Families we choose*. New York: Columbia University Press.

CHAPTER TWENTY-FIVE

Counseling Men
with Religious Affiliations

Michael R. Maples
John M. Robertson

N orth Americans tend to be highly religious. Using religious affiliation as a measure, less than 10 *percent* of North Americans are atheist, agnostic, or nonreligious
(Barrett & Johnson, 1998). In a 1999 Gallup poll, 87 percent of North Americans
indicated that religion was "very important" or "fairly important" in their lives, a percentage that remained fairly consistent throughout the 1990s. Fully 86 percent of Americans believe in God, and an additional 8 percent believe in some form of a universal spirit
or higher power (Gallup Organization, 1999).

Most religious individuals in North America are Christians. As a group, Christians
form 85 percent of the total population in North America. The largest Christian groups
include Protestants (30 percent of the total population) and Roman Catholics (24 percent). Another 31 percent of the population belongs to other Christian denominations
such as Orthodox, Anglican, and many other smaller groups (Barrett & Johnson, 1998).
The remaining 15 percent of the population is divided among nonreligious preferences
(9 percent of the total population), Jewish (2 percent), Muslim (2 percent), Buddhist (1
percent), Hindu (0.04 percent), and other groups (0.06 percent).

It may be useful to note that many people in North America draw a distinction
between religiosity and spirituality (Richards & Bergin, 1997). Religiosity generally refers
to an active affiliation with an organized religious community and typically includes
participation in various rituals and public activities sponsored by that group. Spirituality tends to be a more inclusive term and describes a sense of "closeness, harmony, or
connection" with a transcendent being or power (Richards & Bergin, 1997, p. 13). Spiritual activities tend to be more personal, more private, and less dogmatic than religious
activities.

The North American religious landscape has been changing since the 1950s. Two
trends are especially worth noting. The first is the growth of non-Christian religious
groups. Although Christians remain the largest collection of religious congregations, the
representation of non-Christian religions in the United States has grown significantly.
From 1949 to 1998, the percentage of non-Christian religious affiliation doubled from
3 percent to 6 percent of the total population (Barrett & Johnson, 1998; Braden, 1950).
This increase in religious heterogeneity is the result of many cultural and political
changes that have taken place, including the effects of higher education, a growing
awareness of other worldviews, and immigration patterns (Demerath, 1998; Hoge, 1996).

Non-Christian houses of worship are no longer restricted to a handful of major cities in the United States.

One result of this increase in religious diversity for counselors is that they are encountering men from a wider array of religious affiliations. These encounters may be distinctly cross-cultural, as when the client belongs to one faith and the counselor is inclined toward another. In fact, cross-cultural differences between counselor and client are highly likely. Although the population at large remains religiously affiliated at a very high rate (approximately 91 percent), counselors generally are not. Only 37 percent of clinical and counseling psychologists, for example, have a moderate or high level of religious affiliation and participation (Barrett & Johnson, 1998; Shafranske, 1995, as cited in Shafranske, 1996).

All counselors—not simply the pastoral counselors who work in the context of a particular denomination or religious setting—will confront issues related to religious diversity. Pastoral or spiritual counselors typically undergo significant theological training sponsored by their denominations and are able to understand and use the language of their groups. Although most psychologists and counselors lack the formal training in theological knowledge that comes from an academic study of various religions (Shafranske, 2000), they find themselves working with men who have a wide variety of religious attitudes and values. In these situations, counselors need to be cognizant and respectful of a client's religious beliefs and culture. Such respect falls under the ethical guidelines for psychologists and other counselors regarding awareness of client differences (American Counseling Association, 1995; American Psychological Association, 1992; Richards & Bergin, 1997).

A second trend is the growth in the number of conservative Christian evangelicals and fundamentalists in North America. These groups take a literal interpretation of the Bible, stress spiritual rebirth followed by the development of a personalized relationship with God, and espouse conservative attitudes on social and political issues (Hoge, 1996).

In 1949, 27 percent of all Christian church members belonged to fundamentalist and evangelical churches (Braden, 1950). Fifty years later, these same groups comprised 36 percent of all church members in North America (Barrett & Johnson, 1998; Bedell, 1997).

Large numbers of men have become active in the evangelical tradition, a movement that crosses Christian denominational lines. One illustration of this trend is the organization called Promise Keepers (Promise Keepers, 2000). This group attracts tens of thousands of men to football stadiums to hear lectures and music about conservative Christian teachings and values. Attendees are told that men in traditional masculine roles must be godly and purposeful in their lives. Speakers promote the belief that to be fully masculine, men must submit to God and obey Christian teachings. Specifically, men are encouraged to promote the values of "fidelity, leadership, and compassion." They are asked to become benevolent authorities in their own homes, to take their responsibilities of parenting seriously, to become active leaders in their communities, and to submit to God while doing so.

Although Promise Keepers has a wide following, the movement also has its critics. Many women and men have expressed concern with what appears to be an attempt to restore male-dominated home and work environments; these critics fear that the influence of Promise Keepers may be to disenfranchise women. Others call the movement cultist, exclusive, or inattentive to the heterogeneity of men's personal problems and characteristics (see, for example, Gilkeson, 1997; Leichman, 1995; Stodghill, 1997). Even so, the Promise Keepers movement is popular, boasting that 453,000 men attended nineteen conferences held in the United States in 1998. The group's 1999 annual revenue was $41 million (Promise Keepers, 2000).

IS RELIGION UNMASCULINE?

At first glance, it would appear that men are much less religious than women. Evidence indicates that men are not as active as women in religious activities. Specifically, men do not attend religious services and ceremonies as frequently as do women, and they do not engage in prayer as often (Field, 1993; Francis & Wilcox, 1996; Poloma & Gallup, 1991).

But less involvement in religious activities does not mean that men are less interested than women in religious or spiritual ideas. When religious behavior and religious belief are considered separately, gender differences are not found at any significant level (Sloane & Potvin, 1983; Thompson, 1991). Even though men do not engage in religious behavior as often as women do, they have religious beliefs and attitudes at rates very similar to those for women.

Nevertheless, men often perceive religion as a "feminine" endeavor (Rohr, 1988). With this perception can come the idea that religious activity and religious beliefs must be of little value or that they are inherently incomplete or flawed in some way and require the infusion of "masculine" characteristics (Podles, 1999; Rohr, 1988). The larger social struggle for gender equity influences attitudes toward religion. Men who regard traditionally feminine values as inferior may transfer that view toward religion because so many more women than men attend religious services.

Thompson (1991) suggests two gender-based explanations for the perception that religion is unmasculine. The first possibility follows in the tradition of Durkheim (1915) and acknowledges the reality that for a long time women were disenfranchised from the competitive North American workplace. The dominant values were achievement oriented and masculine driven. As a result, women were left out of the picture and became oriented toward the communal aspects of life. Religious activities and groups were a natural setting in which women could live these values and make important social connections and contributions.

A second argument comes from the tradition of gender socialization theorists (see Gilligan, 1982). According to this view, men are much less socialized toward qualities found in many Christian groups, such as passivity (accepting God's will for one's life and submitting oneself to the church), communality (the importance of attendance at meetings and cooperative social action activities), and expressiveness (public prayer, confession of sins, group singing, and proselytizing). As a result, some men may have assumed that they must become more "feminine" in order to become more spiritual.

But others have conceptualized spiritual well-being differently for men than for women. V. O. Long and Heggen (1988) looked at how members of the Christian clergy perceived spirituality for men versus women. They found that clergy had different expectations for men and women. Christian leaders described a spiritually healthy man as "dominant in the home, self-reliant, independent, comfortable leading in church, and enjoys teaching adults in church" (p. 218). A spiritually healthy woman was described as being "obedient, seeks advice from others, submissive in the home, and enjoys teaching children in church" (p. 218).

Still other authors speak of spiritual health in terms of androgyny. For instance, Rohr and Martos (1992) discuss human spirituality as having both masculine and feminine aspects. The masculine manifestation of the spiritual self was more related to the left side of the brain and included logic, order, persuasion, and clarity. The feminine manifestation included creativity, affect, connection, and union. The problem according to these authors is that women are much more willing to move into their masculine selves in the formation of spiritual androgyny than are men. According to this view, men are left spiritually incomplete and unhealthy. Given the traditional masculine emphasis on separation and independence, men feel alienated from other men, from their families, from their cultural context, and ultimately from their God (Rohr & Martos, 1992).

Gender expectations concerning religious participation are found in many world religions. Muslim men have traditionally participated actively in mosque worship, whereas Muslim women have assumed more supportive roles in the life of the mosque. Women typically have not been present in mosque worship, with the exception of Friday prayer (Haddad & Lummis, 1987; Hedayat-Diba, 2000). Historically, Jewish men have been the teachers and rabbis, and women have taken a more dominant role in raising the children, at least until the children enter adolescence (Cohen, 1983). Jewish men traditionally have led the religious rituals held at home as well.

Thus, in many religious traditions the traits that defined a man as spiritually healthy have been very similar to those that have defined him as masculine. One further clarification needs to be made. Several investigators have examined the question of whether there is a distinction between "feminine" orientation and female participation in religious activities. Several theorists have suggested that religiosity is more highly related to a "feminine" outlook on life than it is to anything biologically female. This view may explain why men who possess traits such as nurturance, submissiveness, and communality are more likely to have a religious affiliation than those who do not (Francis & Wilcox, 1996; Gaston & Brown 1991; Thompson 1991).

WHY ARE MEN DRAWN TO RELIGION?

What role does religion play in the lives of men and what factors account for the religious revival among men in groups such as the Promise Keepers? Three possible explanations might be offered. The first is that some men may turn to religious groups to find relief from the demands and costs of traditional masculine expectations. Some men feel dissatisfaction with cultural male norms. They may be troubled by their inability to live up to culturally imposed expectations of success and achievement. The rewards of achievement may be unfulfilling and not worth further effort, or the anxiety that naturally accompanies competition may become problematic. The pursuit of economic success and social respect may create for them a sense of strain, isolation, and alienation from friends and family (Rohr & Martos, 1992). These aspects of the masculine role have been detailed in various measures and have been referred to as "gender-role conflict" (O'Neil, Helms, Gable, David, & Wrightsman, 1986), "sex-role strain" (Pleck, 1981), and "gender-role stress" (Eisler & Skidmore, 1987).

This underlying dissatisfaction with the consequences of the traditional male role may nudge some men to explore more fully what Rohr and Martos (1992) describe as the "feminine" aspects of spirituality: union, relatedness, and generativity. In effect, a religious setting can become a place in which men suffering from significant gender role strain might find some relief, as well as a broader way of thinking about gender-related values. Men looking for solace for these reasons will look for religious settings that tend to de-emphasize the importance of traditional gender role behavior in their theology and practice.

A second factor that may influence some men to explore spiritual or religious perspectives is the father-son relationship. Much has been written in the literature on masculinity about men and their search for their fathers (see Osherson, 1986). Some men may be drawn to the notion of God, Allah, or Yahweh because of the language often used by religious groups. Across many religions, the Supreme Being is presented in mostly masculine terms or is said to be male in some way. For example, the God of the religions based on the Torah, the New Testament, and the Koran (Judaism, Christianity, and Islam, respectively) is understood mostly in male terms. At times, he is portrayed in strong and highly assertive terms—judging, jealous, instrumental, even militant.

Yet this same God is also represented in more feminine ways. He is said to care for what he has created, much as a caring parent provides for his children. This God can be approached via prayer, and his sensitive side can be swayed by petition. As increasing numbers of today's men seek ways to operationalize a greater emotional awareness than they experienced with their own fathers, they may seek someone to replace an emotionally and perhaps physically absent father (Abramovitch, 1997; Osherson, 1986). The God of monotheistic religion can become this father figure—a loving authority. The language found in many current religious ideologies encourages adherents to relate to God in very human terms. They are invited to take a "walk with God," to pray to him as a "heavenly father," or to develop a "loving relationship" with him. For men with poor histories with their fathers, this language can have a distinct appeal.

A third factor that may account for the appeal religion has for some men is the sense of forgiveness and pardon that many religions offer. Counselors can benefit from knowing how their male clients think along these lines. The belief in a God who expresses virtues such as love and forgiveness can be a model to a man who operates within a theistic framework. The implications are many. For example, men who experience a sense of forgiveness from God can also experience liberation from the excessive guilt and low self-esteem that results from maladaptive self-perceptions. Or a man might be more willing to let go of various hurts and emotional pains he has experienced if he believes that his God has done the same for him.

Roy was a forty-year-old African American man whose problems with depression and low self-worth worsened after he returned to the conservative religion of his upbringing. Much earlier in life, he had been physically abusive toward his wife, but after working with a counselor he had developed new anger management skills and had displayed no abusive actions toward his wife for almost sixteen years; he had never abused his two daughters. Nevertheless, his return to religion at midlife had filled him with a severe sense of self-loathing and shame for his past behaviors.

He turned to a counselor to address these issues. His wife attended his sessions for several weeks and openly expressed her love and forgiveness. On the whole, this couple seemed relatively healthy to the counselor. Finally, Roy spoke of his religious past. As a youth, his father had caught him in a variety of "sinful" behaviors, such as drinking alcohol, engaging in impermissible sexual behavior, and fighting. Roy's father would force him to sit and listen while he read from the Bible to Roy. At one point, he told Roy that there was no way to ensure his eternal salvation after all that he had done. Roy eventually left his father's religion behind. But as an adult, Roy had returned to religion after the death of his father. The familiar sense of self-loathing and a fear of eternal punishment returned.

Roy's counselor was familiar with Roy's religious system, which stressed grace, forgiveness, and rebirth for a penitent sinner. Consultation and a cotherapy with a spiritual counselor of his denomination were vital in helping Roy broaden his views of his own religion. He learned that he could focus on his own personal spirituality, not the punitive religious teachings of his father. He learned that some of what he learned as a boy was actually at odds with what his denominational doctrine taught. Once Roy believed that forgiveness was obtainable from his God, his depressive symptoms lessened.

CAN RELIGION BENEFIT MEN?

Recent research has shown that religious affiliation is associated with lower levels of alcohol abuse, less depression, lower rates of suicide, better physical health, lower levels of aggression, higher levels of marital satisfaction, and lower levels of psychological distress than is nonaffiliation. Although some of these findings are mixed, are based on correlational data, or do not exclude third variable explanations, they are worth noting in more detail.

Alcohol Use

Men are more likely than women to consume alcohol and to develop some form of substance dependency in their lives (Kessler, et al., 1994; Robins & Regier, 1991). Men who attend religious services or who otherwise indicate some form of religious commitment tend to evidence higher rates of abstinence from alcohol or report lower rates of abuse for alcohol and other drugs than do men without a religious commitment (Gartner, 1996).

This finding may not be surprising given the spiritual nature of programs such as Alcoholics Anonymous (AA). This group teaches that to recover from addiction, a man must turn to a Higher Power. He must admit that he himself is helpless in finding a complete recovery (Buxton, Smith, & Seymour, 1987). The actual cause of AA's success remains unclear, but several of AA's techniques have been proposed as active ingredients—prayer, humbleness, inner peace, the admission of personal inadequacies, and the appeal for aid from other sources (Thoresen et al., 1998).

Depression

Although depression has significantly higher rates of formal diagnosis among women than among men in the United States (Prior, 1999), this gender difference masks an important distinction. Men who experience higher levels of masculine role conflict have higher levels of depression than other men (Good & Mintz, 1990) and lower levels of self-esteem (Sharpe & Heppner, 1991). As Cochran and Rabinowitz (2000) note, men tend to underreport their depression. Warren (1983) has described this tendency as the "male intolerance of depression," and Real (1997) has referred to it as "male covert depression" in his mass-market book entitled *I Don't Want to Talk About It: Overcoming the Legacy of Male Depression.*

Research has shown that women and men report some distinctly different patterns of symptoms of depression. Women tend to become tearful and report feelings of self-dislike, whereas men tend to avoid crying, withdraw from others, and experience pessimism and self-criticism (Shepherd & Robertson, 1999). Men also tend to somaticize their feelings of depression (Funabiki, Bologna, Pepping, & Fitzgerald, 1980; Oliver & Toner, 1990; Padesky & Hammen, 1981). In any case, when depression occurs in men, it is no less debilitating than it is for women.

Religious commitment has been shown to have a significant negative correlation with depressive symptoms (Gartner, 1996). That is, the higher the level of religious commitment, the lower the likelihood of depression.

Counselors have used various approaches in treating religious men with depression. Cognitive-behavioral techniques have incorporated a spiritual element such as religious imagery or scriptural teaching in an overall behavior modification or cognitive reframing program (Propst, 1988); these techniques have been found to reduce depressive symptomatology in religious clients. Some reports suggest that for religious men these approaches are even more effective than the use of cognitive-behavioral techniques that are nonreligious (Propst, 1996; Thoresen et al., 1998).

Suicide

In the United States, men commit suicide 4.5 times more frequently than women, even though women actually have higher rates of suicidal ideation and suicidal attempts (Canetto & Sakinofsky, 1998; National Institute of Mental Health, 1999). Men who are members of minority groups—particularly Native Americans and gay men—face an especially high risk (Westefeld et al., 2000).

Religious individuals report less suicidal ideation and more negative attitudes about suicide than do nonreligious persons (see Bascue, Inman, & Kahn, 1982; Minear & Bruch, 1980–1981; Reynolds & Nelson, 1981). There are several possible explanations for this difference: many religions strictly condemn suicide; certain religious beliefs may provide the believer with a sense of purpose and meaning in life and strength in times of difficulty; and when a suicidal man belongs to a supportive religious community, he has a built-in support system with people ready to offer assistance. Given the prominent role that organized religion plays in the lives of some ethnic minorities (Weatherford & Weatherford, 1999; Westefeld et al., 2000), mental health collaboration with clergy may help further reduce the incidence of suicide among minority men.

Physical Health

Men die sooner than women for all ten of the leading causes of death in the United States ("Cardiovascular Disease at the Millennium," 2000). Given this fact, research investigating the relation between religion and physical health merits some attention. Several studies (see Thoresen et al., 1998) have shown that men who are actively religious have higher levels of physical health than men who are not.

Cardiovascular health has been improved by various forms of meditation. Various meditation protocols have been developed, based on Christian, Buddhist, and Hindu teachings (Ornish, 1990; Propst, 1988). Although these techniques have been found effective in decreasing angina and reducing arterial blockage, it is not entirely clear what role meditation plays. Typically, meditation is used in conjunction with other forms of treatment such as diet and moderate exercise. The extent to which these other activities are influenced by meditation remains unclear (Ornish, 1990; Thoresen et al., 1998). Benson (1996) found that the critical component of meditation, relaxation, was associated with lowered heart rates, lowered blood pressure, lessened activity in the sympathetic branch of the nervous system, and lowered levels of oxygen consumption.

Religious affiliation may have other health benefits. Some religious groups promote the avoidance of such unhealthy behaviors as smoking and the excessive use of alcohol (Gartner, 1996). Religious individuals appear to cope better than nonreligious individuals when they are physically ill (Bergin & Richards, 2000). Religious participation may increase longevity, particularly among men (see Larson, 1985). Still, the exact nature of the relationship between religion and physical health remains somewhat unclear because most studies do not adequately control for possible confounds (Gartner, 1996; McCullough, Larson, & Worthington, 1998; Thoresen et al., 1998).

Aggression

The male tendency toward various forms of aggression is well documented (D. Long, 1987). Gartner (1996) reviewed seven studies of delinquency and recidivism rates. The studies of delinquency are somewhat dated, but they showed lower rates of delinquency among subjects who participated in religious activities than among nonparticipants

(Albrecht, Chadwick, & Alcorn, 1977; Burkett & White, 1974; Higgins & Albrecht, 1977; Nye, 1958; Robins, 1974; Rohrbaugh & Jessor, 1975; Stark, Kent, & Doyle, 1982). Two additional studies found lower rates of recidivism among prison inmates who participated in church-sponsored ministries (Ames, Larson, Gartner, & O'Connor, 1990; Young et al., 1990).

Marital Satisfaction

Three reviews of the literature (Gartner, 1996; Larson, 1985; McCullough et al., 1998) have shown that regular attendance at religious services is related to self-reported marital satisfaction and to low incidence of divorce. The explanation for this correlation is unclear. Perhaps men who attend religious services frequently have internalized prohibitions of marital discord or divorce (Gartner, 1996). Maybe men who are happy in their domestic relationships are more likely to seek out additional relationships and support systems. It is also possible that single people may feel that religious meetings are designed mostly for couples and families but not adult single persons.

Although much literature reports a positive relationship between religiosity and various health concerns germane to men, other literature shows an association between religion and poor psychological well-being (see Gartner, 1996). Religious orthodoxy appears to have a positive correlation with authoritarianism (Argyle & Beit-Hallahmi, 1975), and several researchers indicate that there may be a positive correlation between authoritarianism and religiosity (see Beit-Hallahmi & Nevo, 1987; Dubey, 1986; Hassan & Khalique, 1981). Others have shown an association between religious orthodoxy and dogmatic thinking, an inability to tolerate ambiguity, and rigidity (Hassan & Khalique, 1981; McNeel & Thorsen, 1985).

It would seem therefore that men who are oriented to more orthodox or fundamentalist perspectives (such as Christian fundamentalists, Orthodox Jews, and Muslim fundamentalists) may demonstrate some of these traits. These tendencies toward dogmatism and rigidity can result in poor relationships at home and in the workplace. Further, these men may resist seeking therapy, particularly with a counselor who does not share their views.

Many religious and spiritually based interventions have been developed and promoted to counselors. A comprehensive discussion of these interventions is found in Richards and Bergin (1997). Here we list only some of the most popular ones presented by Ball and Goodyear (1991), Lovinger (1996), Pargament (1997), Propst (1980, 1988), Richards and Bergin (1997, 2000), and Richards and Potts (1995). Silent prayer, ritual prayer, participation in sacred rituals, involvement in social welfare activities, and various religious writings all have been used, either in session or as homework. Counselors also have used cognitive-behavioral and relaxation techniques with religious imagery and concepts (Propst, 1980, 1996).

COMMON PRESENTING ISSUES
AMONG ACTIVELY RELIGIOUS MEN

In this section, we discuss issues that counselors may frequently encounter when working with men who are actively religious. Although some of these concerns may be specific to men of a particular religion, most cross religious boundaries. Issues that have strong masculinity overtones include resistance to seeking help, sexuality issues (sexual behavior, birth control, abortion, homosexuality, and acquired immunodeficiency syndrome [AIDS]), cultural issues (values conflicts and intercultural relationships), marriage and family problems, and issues of concern to professional clergy.

Resistance

Generally, men are reluctant to seek personal counseling. But men from some religious groups may be even more cautious, not wanting their religious beliefs to be undermined by a counselor. In most cases, male clients want to receive services from a counselor who is not antagonistic to their religious beliefs. Many actively religious men ask directly about counselors' beliefs, looking for hints of bias.

In some cases, this caution is well placed. Religious teachings and psychological theory have often been at odds. Many psychologists have suggested that religious faith and behavior are irrational, detrimental to self-actualization, or out-of-date in the face of modern science (Ellis, 1971; Richards & Bergin, 1997). Opponents of religion include such luminaries as Sigmund Freud (1927/1961), B. F. Skinner (1953), and Albert Ellis (1971). On the other hand, influential figures such as Erik Erikson (1950/1963) and Carl Jung (1932/1969) have been more supportive of religion, and even Ellis has toned down his vehemence somewhat (Wulff, 1996).

Given this uneasy history between psychology and religion, many religious men view the mental health professions with suspicion. These men ask counselors very pointed questions about their religious tolerance or even about their own religious beliefs. These questions are best confronted directly and openly rather than seen exclusively as another example of male reluctance to seek help.

Sexuality Issues

One nearly universal religious teaching dictates that sexual intercourse is reserved for men and women who are married to each other. Although many unmarried religious men are sexually active, they engage in sexual activity with some level of recognition that they are acting in opposition to religious teaching. Men who are sexually active—and this includes masturbation in several religions—may experience troubling feelings of guilt and a fear of punishment if their behaviors are discovered. Sexuality can become a matter of embarrassment that may generalize to all sexual behaviors, even within marriage.

Ulrich, Richards, and Bergin (2000) suggest that for some Christians, sexual inhibitions after marriage may be due to misunderstanding their churches' teachings about sexuality. In such cases, the counselor may need to work with a client to clarify his church's teaching and to explore other possible explanations for sexual inhibition.

Although birth control has been accepted by many over the past century, it still remains forbidden in several faiths, including Roman Catholicism, Orthodox Judaism, and Mormonism. This prohibition is rooted in the commandment of God to populate the earth, a commandment that is still taken seriously in some church teachings. To use contraceptives is therefore tantamount to directly disobeying God in the teachings of some religions.

However, many religions, even some conservative Christian religions, permit contraception for the purpose of limiting a married couple's number of children. But they do not permit birth control for unmarried couples (Dobbins, 2000). Roman Catholic men are especially likely to confront the issue of birth control. Although the Roman Catholic church officially retains its prohibition on both abortion and birth control, many North American Catholics approve of and use contraception of some form (Shafranske, 2000).

This distinction between what is taught by religious authority and what is practiced in the group may present male clients with a difficult dilemma. They are in the position of having to reconcile their own responsibility to prevent unwanted pregnancies while retaining a sense of belonging to their religion.

A similar conflict can be experienced over the question of abortion. Again, men of many faiths in North America may experience some dissonance between what their religion teaches and what they feel is an acceptable personal choice. Many religious groups including Roman Catholics, Eastern Orthodox Christians, conservative Christian Protestants, Latter-day Saints, Orthodox Jews, Buddhists, and Muslims forbid abortion (Richards & Bergin, 2000). A man who belongs to one of these groups and has unintentionally impregnated his partner is likely to face directly the issue of abortion. This confrontation may be further complicated when the man's partner is more accepting of abortion than he is.

Any man seeking counseling about the issue of abortion will certainly need to address his religious beliefs in therapy, in addition to exploring the psychological sequelae of the decision. Experiences of guilt, fear of punishment, shame, and self-loathing are not uncommon in such cases. The man may also be concerned with how to protect his partner emotionally during this time and may not sufficiently tend to his own emotional well-being.

Homosexuality is another human reality that most religions consider immoral and sinful (Richards & Bergin, 2000). Though some religions are careful to condemn homosexual behavior and not the homosexual individual, a homosexual man is likely to experience rejection of his sexuality by family and peers who believe that it is morally wrong and contrary to God's intentions for sexual behavior. Such rejection by others on religious grounds may become internalized and experienced as a condemnation by God. The result can be loneliness, depression, abandonment of religion, and sometime suicide.

Religious institutions vary in how they respond to a man who desires to be public about his sexual orientation. Many openly gay men find themselves feeling at odds with their faith community, and some certainly face overt hostility and rejection. Openly gay men also find themselves barred from religious ordination and positions of leadership within their organization. For example, a gay man in the Latter-day Saints church who is in open conflict with the church teachings on homosexuality may find himself facing a church council with the power of censure or even excommunication (Ulrich et al., 2000). If he feels a sense of responsibility for the emotional welfare of his family, the possibility of bringing shame on his family may be sufficient to keep a man "in the closet."

At the same time, it is useful for counselors to know about the many gay-friendly movements that exist within the larger religious communities. Among Christians, for example, groups have formed for Roman Catholics (Dignity), Eastern Orthodox members (AXIOS), Southern Baptists (Honesty), Presbyterians (More Light Presbyterians), United Methodists (Affirmation), Lutherans (Lutherans Concerned), United Church of Christ members (Coalition), Christian Scientists (Emergence International), Pentecostals (Alliance), Latter-day Saints (Affirmation), Seventh-day Adventists (Kinship), and Quakers (Friends for Lesbian and Gay Concerns). One denomination has been organized specifically for gay, bisexual, and lesbian Christians—the Universal Fellowship of Metropolitan Community Churches.

Jewish gay men find various forms of assistance from the World Congress of Gay, Lesbian, and Bisexual Jewish Organizations, headquartered in Washington, D.C. Muslim gay men find support from the organization Al-Fatiha, located in New York City.

Men with AIDS may find themselves isolated from their religious communities. Even groups that have been ideologically open to homosexuality have been slow to develop outreach to members with AIDS. Although some religions are gradually coming to an awareness of the need to minister to men (and women) with AIDS, this form of support remains controversial to many people in religious communities (Weatherford & Weatherford, 1999).

Cultural Issues

Noteworthy differences exist among religions with regard to the relationship of religion and culture. Simply put, religion is less central to the cultural identity of some groups in North America than it is to others. For example, many groups compartmentalize religion so that it becomes one aspect of the larger culture. Overtly religious activities may be something that a man does for an hour or two on weekends, but during the rest of the week he pursues these activities only intermittently. Very few men in North American cities attend religious services or rituals on a daily basis. At most, they may look to religion to provide general guidelines for how to act in business, how to relate to others, and how to distinguish right from wrong. Ethnicity, region, and socioeconomic status certainly influence these patterns, but the general expectation for these groups is that men attend weekend rituals and behave in moral ways during the rest of the week.

Other groups see a closer interaction between religion and culture. For men of Eastern or Middle Eastern religions, faith permeates all areas of their lives. Islam, Hinduism, and Judaism (particularly Orthodox Judaism) illustrate this perspective. Religious practices direct devout men to pray every day, often on a schedule with the use of organized prayers. In addition, these groups influence countless daily decisions—what the diet will contain, how men will behave with women, and especially whom men will marry. Men in these groups do not simply choose a religion to live by; rather, religious behavior forms the center of their cultural identity as well.

As many men from non-Christian cultures come to North America through migration, cross-cultural issues are likely to manifest themselves. These issues are both cultural and religious. These two domains are not easily separated. To illustrate, Muslim men may look with disapproval on certain aspects of the North American culture. They are likely to believe that practices such as premarital sexual intercourse and divorce undermine the stability of their families (Haddad & Lummis, 1987). Although women traditionally do not attend mosque worship in most parts of the world, both Muslim men and women in the United States are presented with a culture that allows women to participate more fully in the religious community. Islamic beliefs of masculine authority and power are likely to be challenged by the dissonance of seeing women participate more fully in the mosques in the United States.

These men may become concerned about women who are too "liberated" and are likely to interpret this liberation as running counter to their religious culture. Men may see a woman's assuming of some domestic or religious leadership as a challenge to their traditional way of relating, thus requiring a redefinition of their role as leaders in these domains. Men may encounter this difficulty with their female children as well. As these families enter their second and third generations in North America, acculturation is likely to pull children further from traditional religious and cultural customs. This situation creates much consternation in both father and mother, who are concerned with the preservation of their religious culture (Haddad & Lummis, 1987).

Interreligious marriages and romantic relationships can create considerable difficulties, especially for men who have emigrated from countries with strongly religious cultures. In Islam and Hinduism, dating as practiced in the West is literally a foreign concept. Most marriages are arranged by families. As a Hindu assimilates into the North American culture, he is likely to encounter this American way of dating. Given the Western acceptance of premarital sexual intercourse (even by many Christians), the Hindu or Muslim who is surrounded by others who are dating non-Muslims will have to face issues arising from interreligious dating. Counselors seeing Muslim men may be called on to help explain the cultural practices of North American dating, a process that does not necessarily lead to marriage in the United States or Canada.

Rasheev came to a university counseling center from an orthodox Hindu culture. He was a twenty-five-year-old graduate student at the time of the intake and was brought to the counseling center by a professor, who was also Hindu. Rasheev presented symptoms of a depression that was seriously impairing his performance as both a student and a classroom instructor. After several sessions, he gained the courage to report that he had been in a six-month relationship with a woman from the United States. This was Rasheev's first romantic relationship because his family expected that he would enter into an arranged marriage within his caste. After dating this woman for several weeks, Rasheev had learned that she was not a virgin. He shared this information with his father, who was already distressed that his son was dating. Rasheev's father then ordered him to terminate the romantic relationship; Rasheev had complied with this directive.

In counseling, Rasheev reported that he had felt enormous conflict between his affection for the woman and his cultural religious expectations. His girlfriend had become highly distressed over the breakup and soon began developing signs of depression herself. Rasheev felt great shame for causing this problem and felt that he had failed to protect someone he cared for and had hoped to marry. He could not escape the feeling that he had wronged her and he believed that this behavior was going to have karmic consequences. In part, counseling was directed toward helping him understand North American dating norms for men so that he could compare them with his own cultural beliefs. This discussion led to an exploration of various issues related to his acculturation as a man. After exploring his feelings of responsibility to his family and what he had come to identify as their religious culture, he chose to enter into a prearranged marriage. Even so, North American expectations for men had come to influence his thinking. He demanded the right to approve or reject any woman presented to him, a request his family reluctantly accepted.

Family and Relationship Issues

In many religions, males are granted rights and responsibilities not given to women. For example, men can be ordained in some traditions but not in others. In other religions, restrictions prevent women from entering a place of worship for certain ceremonies. Similarly, men are sometimes afforded a higher status in their families because of their role in religion.

Frank complained that from an early age his parents had expected him to become a Catholic priest. He had been enrolled in high school and college seminaries by his mother, who spoke openly about her dream of seeing her son become "Father Frank." Frank, however, had other plans. He wanted to be married. Even when he started dating women in his early twenties, he carried with him some sense of the male prestige that his parents had given him from an early age. In relationships, this sense of male privilege had prevented him from establishing healthy relationships with women. Relationships ended prematurely, because women complained about his attempts to control too many aspects of their lives.

Religious cultures often have significant expectations for men. Men may be asked to provide for their families or to spread the message of their religion. Men in the Latter-day Saints tradition are expected to serve as missionaries for two years beginning at age nineteen. Missionaries typically have little if any contact with family and others from home (including girlfriends). Although the missionary effort can afford men the chance to acquire a significant feeling of accomplishment (if successful as missionaries), it can also place significant strain on them emotionally. The strain is particularly evident if they have a romantic attachment and are asked to serve in missions overseas.

Men in Judaism also have enjoyed a special place within the family and religious community. Traditionally, the passage of the Jewish male youth into adulthood was marked with ceremony and communal celebration in the bar mitzvah. For more liberal Jewish groups, female youth now participate in a female ceremony of passage called bat mitzvah. Historically, the bar mitzvah marked a ritualistic identification of a youth as a man. But masculinity to a Jew involves more than changing his identity from boy to man. According to Miller and Lovinger (2000, p. 280), "masculinity is intertwined with learnedness" as he learns the Jewish Talmud and Torah. The emphasis on learning is even more pronounced among men in Orthodox Judaism, who must learn and observe the halakah tradition of Jewish law. A man's inability to observe the rituals of Judaism, again particularly among Orthodox Jews, can lead to feelings of guilt, anxiety, and failure to live up to the expectations of others in his religious culture (Rabinowitz, 2000).

Because God is often conceptualized as male, a man's authority within the household is seen by some religions as an extension of God's authority. This view has a basis in the scriptures of Islam, Judaism, and Christianity. The notions of masculine authority in the family and in opposite sex relationships is often explained on a religious basis.

In many religions, men have a specific feeling that they are responsible for the welfare of the family. The idea that men are to be in charge appears to cross cultural and religious boundaries, and in many cases this idea carries the weight of religious doctrine. This perspective is clearly seen in current evangelical Christianity. One of the major tenets of the Promise Keepers movement is the idea that men must have domestic authority. The justification is that a relationship with God allows a man to be an effective leader, particularly in the home (Stodghill, 1997). The document "Seven Promises of a Promise Keeper" (Promise Keepers) outlines the core tenets or statements of faith. Of the seven promises, three describe the relationships that a man is to have with his wife and family, with other men, and with his church pastor. The other promises involve relationships with God, other denominations, other races, and other persons whom the man may meet in business, social, or romantic interactions. Central to keeping these promises is the expectation that he must be an effective leader over others.

The concept of the responsible religious man is found in other religions as well. Religiously minded men, imbued with a feeling of authority as a religious right, may be at risk for abuse of that power. It is not unusual for counselors to encounter clients who were victims of abuse at the hands of others claiming religious authority. Some children can be abused by religious authority figures. Other children can be abused by fathers intent on providing punishment in order bring their children closer to God. At times, this punishment becomes cruel, with devastating and lasting emotional consequences.

In some religions, the inability to provide materially for the family carries with it a shameful cultural stigma. For example, Muslim men are expected to be the providers for their families, and when they cannot do so they experience cultural shame (Hedayat-Diba, 2000).

The very definition of family varies according to religious and cultural factors. Men from some non-Western religions such as Islam and Hinduism are expected to maintain close ties with their extended family, and they retain a feeling of obligation toward these members. This value contrasts with the Western concept of individuating from one's family of origin (Hedayat-Diba, 2000; Keller, 2000). The Muslim male, who accepts responsibility for the care of ill and aged family members, cannot accept the North American practice of placing the elderly in nursing homes (Haddad & Lummis, 1987). When the family is defined as the basic cultural unit (for example, in Islam, Judaism, Hinduism, and some branches of Christianity), a man may look on nonfamily or cross-cultural care-givers with suspicion and disapproval. This belief must be addressed when counseling men from these cultures. These men are likely to be quite resistant to discussing their problems with a stranger who may be ignorant or even disrespectful of their religion (Hedayat-Diba, 2000). Many of these men may not seek counseling on their own but may be referred by a family member or by another member of the religious community. Because of the value that these men, particularly Muslims, place on privacy, problems are likely to be addressed within the family before seeking outside help (Meleis & LaFever, 1984). This pattern often results in the development of severe symptoms before a counselor becomes involved. Further, a therapist may not receive ready support and consultation from the man's family members or other religious community leaders. These interested observers might be protectively critical, especially during assessment of the client (Hedayat-Diba, 2000; Sharma, 2000).

Another family issue that troubles men is attachment or even enmeshment. This problem may occur for immigrant men who come to the United States for education and then meet resistance from their families when they decide to remain in the United States. Men who are enmeshed in their families can become severely depressed. Family enmeshment appears to be more common in some religions (such as Judaism) than in others (Miller & Lovinger, 2000; Yeung & Greenwald, 1992). In such cases, families may attempt to resolve problems within the family system instead of seeking assistance from professional sources outside the family. Dysfunctional family dynamics will likely lead to an exacerbation of psychological concerns. Some suggest that this pattern may help account for the slightly higher rates of depression in Jewish men (Yeung & Greenwald, 1992).

Issues in the Lives of Male Professional Clergy

Men dominate the power structures of most religious organizations. Given the ratio of ministers to congregants in most Christian churches, many of today's ministers are greatly overworked (Fox, 1995). Although the ordained ministry brings status and meaning to male clergy, it also brings enormous responsibility, stress, and public scrutiny.

Clergy live under great emotional pressure. They feel called to minister to the needs of others but have few ways of providing for their own psychological well-being. As a result, these men are at risk for depression, anxiety, substance abuse, family problems, and even suicide (McAllister, 1993). Clergy and their family members often find themselves living under the strain of being in the proverbial fishbowl. Scrutiny is high. Expectations and demands from others are constant.

The pressures are especially strong in the Roman Catholic church, in which priests must be chaste and celibate. This lifestyle forces on men a personal isolation from women and prevents them from developing any family of their own. Many of these men struggle with loneliness and a lack of approved outlets for their sexual needs. For some Catholic clergy, the results are severe and include alcoholism and (for a small minority) sexual abuse of others, including children. This latter tragedy has received considerable attention from the popular press in recent decades as victims have initiated lawsuits against the offending clerics. Many of the litigants are men who were abused in their youth and are bringing lawsuits in adulthood. Although the vast majority of Roman Catholic priests are not child molesters, the publicized cases cast a distinct shadow of suspicion over their adult heterosexual orientation. Further, their heterosexuality may be questioned because they have decided not to marry and start families of their own. Stories of priests leaving the church to marry are not uncommon.

Any of these issues may lead male clergy to seek counseling from mental health professionals. Counselors need to recognize the role given these men by members of their respective faiths. Shafranske (2000) provides some useful guidelines to counselors who treat Catholic clergy, monks, or nuns. Of great importance is the need to provide clergy with an environment of confidentiality, which can be particularly difficult if the treatment is mandated by the Church or if the counseling will be covered by an individual church's insurance plan.

GUIDELINES IN COUNSELING RELIGIOUSLY AFFILIATED MEN

Religion has always had the power to inspire and comfort people, but it has also had the ability to create conflict and stress. This tension is often in the background when men seek help from counselors. Therefore, counselors would do well to acknowledge a man's religious convictions as a significant part of his personal history. Although religious counseling per se is best left to pastoral counselors or other professionals trained in the theology of a client's belief system, other personal counseling offered by professionals must be mindful of the role of religion in the man's life.

Counselors must also acknowledge their own limitations when providing therapy to a religious man, such as ignorance about significant teachings from his religion, a lack of awareness about stereotypes that the man may encounter, or prejudice against religion in general.

There appears to be a need for clear ethical guidelines when providing psychotherapy to actively religious men. Ethical guidelines have been presented for working with religious clients in general (Richards & Bergin, 1997, pp. 143–169) and for working with women (Fitzgerald & Nutt, 1986). However, we are aware of no ethical guidelines for working with religious men as therapy clients. Following are some suggestions for providing personal counseling to men who have strong religious convictions:

Principle One. Counselors recognize that although men do not engage in religious behavior as frequently as women do, men are just as likely as women to have strong religious beliefs (Sloane & Potvin, 1983; Thompson, 1991). These beliefs will influence their core values, their relationships, their behavior, and their views of the world. The absence of an overt religious affiliation does not mean that men are not influenced by religious or spiritual teachings. It is useful for therapists to ask male clients about their religious values and behavior and to use this information when developing diagnostic impressions and treatment plans.

Principle Two. Counselors are aware that many values about gender may be rooted in religious teachings. These religiously based values may define for men their relationship roles and their codes of personal conduct. These values may place strains and expectations on men relative to their friendship, family, and work roles that are different from those placed on women.

Principle Three. Counselors are cautious about making unwarranted generalizations about a man's views of masculinity based solely on his stated religious affiliation. Although doctrines and practices of a man's religious system influence the concerns he presents to a counselor, it is important to recognize that within each larger tradition (for example, Judaism, Christianity, Islam, and Buddhism), there are many varieties and expressions of faith.

Principle Four. Counselors are aware that the general reluctance of men in North America to seek help (Cheatham, Shelton, & Ray, 1987; Vessey & Howard, 1993) can be exacerbated for men with active religious affiliations. These men may feel hesitant to seek help because they know that others hold negative stereotypes about their religion or because their religious tradition counsels against seeking outside help. To increase the sense of safety for male clients who are taking a risk by seeking help, counselors can identify and reduce their own religious prejudices and stereotypes and avoid any promotion of their own religious views to their male clients.

Principle Five. Most religious systems present teachings that have implications for gender role attitudes and behavior. Counselors familiarize themselves with these themes from a man's religious culture before working directly with him on gender issues. In treating presenting issues that are influenced by these gender role teachings, counselors are cautious about recommending any changes in religious behavior as treatment techniques (for example, attending religious rituals and events, using religious imagery, or praying). Addressing masculinity issues from a religious perspective requires that counselors become familiar with applicable teachings and that they regard this information with appropriate levels of sensitivity and respect.

Principle Six. Given that many men in North America are socialized to accept such traditional masculine values as self-reliance, leadership, and competition, counselors are sensitive to the risks of usurping religious authority. Counselors are willing to refer men to religious officials when the issues involve interpreting spiritual teachings or clarifying behavior based on religious rules. Counselors clarify their roles in working with male clients, emphasizing areas of competence as well as limitations of professional jurisdiction. Referral to a religious leader or coordination of therapy with such a leader may be necessary.

Principle Seven. Counselors acknowledge that simply talking about masculinity may open up difficult questions for men who are religiously active. Because they know that this exploration may lead to a sense of uncertainty for men about parts of their faith, counselors inform clients at the outset about the risks involved in carefully examining the social and personal implications of various religious teachings.

Principle Eight. Counselors recognize that when they minimize or disregard male clients' religious beliefs about masculinity, they may actually be doing them harm. As a result, clients may experience less respect for their counselors' expertise or trustworthiness. When counselors suspect that clients may be misunderstanding their own religion's teachings on topics with implications for masculinity (for example, homosexuality, women's roles in the family, masturbation, or discipline of children), counselors collaborate with experts from the clients' religion to help clarify these questions.

Principle Nine. Counselors are aware of possible dual-role issues when male clients come from the same religious affiliation or congregation as their own, and they address such issues with their clients. This issue is especially problematic when the therapist and client both live in a small community with only one local congregation. When this religious faith stresses the importance of active involvement in congregational activities, issues of personal-professional boundaries are complicated. Dual-role issues may also be present when both are in leadership positions within the same congregation.

Principle Ten. Counselors recognize that values about gender relations are deeply rooted in religious traditions and that some of these teachings perpetuate gender inequity (Brinkerhoff & MacKie, 1988; Wilson, 1978). To illustrate, women in some faiths are not permitted to be members of the clergy, to be leaders over men, or to participate in certain ceremonies. According to their Code of Conduct (American Psychological Association, 1992), psychologists must respect the rights and dignity of others, become aware of differences regarding religion and other variables, and "not knowingly participate in or condone unfair discriminatory practices." Although counselors respect the rights of their clients to hold their own views about gender equality, they also support male clients who strive for gender equity in their families, their social roles, or their religious communities.

References

Abramovitch, H. (1997). Images of the "father" in psychology and religion. In M. E. Lamb (Ed.), *The role of the father on child development* (3rd ed., pp.19–32). New York: Wiley.

Albrecht, S. L., Chadwick, B. A., & Alcorn, D. S. (1977). Religiosity and deviance: Application of an attitude behavior contingent consistency model. *Journal for the Scientific Study of Religion, 16,* 263–274.

American Counseling Association. (1995). *Code of ethics and standards of practice.* Alexandria, VA: Author.

American Psychological Association. (1992). Ethical principles of psychologists and code of conduct. *American Psychologist, 47*(12), 1597–1611.

Ames, D., Larson, D., Gartner, J., & O'Connor, T. (1990, August). *Participation in a volunteer prison ministry program and recidivism.* Paper presented at the annual meeting of the American Psychological Association, Boston.

Argyle, M., & Beit-Hallahmi, B. (1975). *The social psychology of religion.* London: Routledge & Kegan Paul.

Ball, R. A., & Goodyear, R. K. (1991). Self-reported professional practices of Christian psychologists. *Journal of Psychology and Christianity, 10,* 144–153.

Barrett, D. B., & Johnson, T. M. (1998). Religion: World religious statistics. In D. Calhoun (Ed.), *1998 Britannica book of the year* (p. 314). Chicago: Encyclopedia Britannica.

Bascue, L. O., Inman, D. J., & Kahn, W. J. (1982). Recognition of suicidal lethality factors by psychiatric nursing assistants. *Psychological Reports, 51,* 197–198.

Bedell, K. B. (1997). *Yearbook of American and Canadian churches.* Nashville, TN: Abingdon Press.

Beit-Hallahmi, B., & Nevo, B. (1987). Jews in Israel: The dynamics of an identity change. *International Journal of Psychology, 22,* 75–81.

Benson, H. (1996). *Timeless healing.* New York: Scribner.

Bergin, A. E., & Richards, P. S. (2000). Religious values and mental health. In A. E. Kazdin (Ed.), *Encyclopedia of psychology* (Vol. 7, pp. 59–62). Washington, DC: American Psychological Association.

Braden, C. S. (1950). Church membership: Principal religions of the world. In W. Yust (Ed.), *1950 Britannica book of the year* (p. 183). Chicago: Encyclopedia Britannica.

Brinkerhoff, M. B., & MacKie, M. (1988). Religious sources of gender traditionalism. In D. L. Thomas (Ed.), *The religion and family connection: Social science perspective* (Religious Studies Center Specialized Monograph No. 3, pp. 232–257). Provo, UT: Religious Studies Center.

Burkett, S. R., & White, M. (1974). Hellfire and delinquency: Another look. *Journal for the Scientific Study of Religion, 13,* 455–462.

Buxton, M. E., Smith, D. E., & Seymour, R. B. (1987). Spirituality and other points of resistance to the 12-step recovery process. *Journal of Psychoactive Drugs, 19,* 275–286.

Canetto, S. S., & Sakinofsky, I. (1998). The gender paradox in suicide. *Suicide and Life-Threatening Behavior, 28,* 1–23.

Cardiovascular disease at the millennium: A progress report. (2000, January). *Harvard Men's Health Watch, 4,* 1–2.

Cheatham, H. E., Shelton, T. O., & Ray, W. J. (1987). Race, sex, causal attribution and help-seeking behavior. *Journal of College Student Personnel, 28,* 559–568.

Cochran, S. V., & Rabinowitz, F. E. (2000). *Men and depression: Clinical and empirical perspectives.* San Diego, CA: Academic Press.

Cohen, S. M. (1983). *American modernity and Jewish identity.* New York: Tavistock.

Demerath, N. J., III. (1998). Excepting exceptionalism: American religion in comparative belief. *Annals of the American Academy of Political and Social Sciences, 558,* 28–39.

Dobbins, R. D. (2000). Psychotherapy with Pentecostal Protestants. In P. S. Richards & A. E. Bergin (Eds.), *Handbook of psychotherapy and religious diversity* (pp. 155–184). Washington, DC: American Psychological Association.

Dubey, R. S. (1986). Authoritarianism in Indian leaders. *Psychological Research Journal, 10,* 16–23.

Durkheim, E. (1915). *The elementary forms of the religious life*. New York: Free Press.

Eisler, R. M., & Skidmore, J. R. (1987). Masculine gender role stress: Scale development and components factors in appraisal of stressful situations. *Behavior Modification, 11*, 123–136.

Ellis, A. (1971). *The case against religion: A psychotherapist's view*. New York: Institute for Rational Living.

Erikson, E. H. (1963). *Childhood and society* (2nd ed.). New York: Norton. (Original work published 1950)

Field, C. D. (1993). Adam and Eve: Gender in English Free Church constituency. *Journal of Ecclesiastical History, 44*, 63–79.

Fitzgerald, L. F., & Nutt, R. (1986). The Division 17 principles concerning the counseling/psychotherapy of women: Rationale and implementation. *Counseling Psychologist, 14*, 180–216.

Fox, T. (1995). *Sexuality and Catholicism*. New York: Braziller.

Francis, L. J., & Wilcox, C. (1996). Religion and gender orientation. *Personality and Individual Difference, 20*, 119–121.

Freud, S. (1961). *The future of an illusion* (J. Strachey, Ed. and Trans.). New York: Norton. (Original work published 1927)

Funabiki, D., Bologna, N., Pepping, M., & Fitzgerald, K. (1980). Revisiting sex differences in the expression of depression. *Journal of Abnormal Psychology, 89*, 1980–2002.

Gallup Organization. (1999). Religion. In *Gallup Poll Topics* [On-line]. Available: www.gallup.com/poll/indicators/indreligion3.asp.

Gartner, J. (1996). Religious commitment, mental health, and prosocial behavior: A review of the empirical literature. In E. P. Shafranske (Ed.), *Religion and the clinical practice of psychology* (pp. 187–214). Washington, DC: American Psychological Association.

Gaston, J. E., & Brown, L. B. (1991). Religious and gender prototypes. *International Journal for the Psychology of Religion, 1*, 232–241.

Gilkeson, D. (1997). Keeping an eye on Promise Keepers. In *MenWeb* [On-line]. Available: www.vix.com/menmag/pkgikes.htm

Gilligan, C. (1982). *In a different voice*. Cambridge, MA: Harvard University Press.

Good, G. E., & Mintz L. B. (1990). Depression and the male gender role: Evidence for compounded risk. *Journal of Counseling and Development, 69*, 17–21.

Haddad, Y. Y., & Lummis, A. T. (1987). *Islamic values in the United States*. New York: Oxford University Press.

Hassan, M. K., & Khalique, A. (1981). Religiosity and its correlates in college students. *Journal of Psychological Researches, 25*, 129–136.

Hedayat-Diba, Z. (2000). Psychotherapy with Muslims. In P. S. Richards & A. E. Bergin (Eds.), *Handbook of psychotherapy and religious diversity* (pp. 289–314). Washington, DC: American Psychological Association.

Higgins, P. C., & Albrecht, G. L. (1977). Hellfire and delinquency revisited. *Social Forces, 55*, 952–958.

Hoge, D. R. (1996). Religion in America: The demographics of belief and affiliation. In E. P. Shafranske (Ed.), *Religion and the clinical practice of psychology* (pp. 21–41). Washington, DC: American Psychological Association.

Jung, C. G. (1969). Psychotherapists or the clergy. In H. Read, M. Fordham, & G. Adler (Eds.), *The collected works of C. G. Jung* (2nd ed., Vol. 11, pp. 327–347). Princeton, NJ: Princeton University Press. (Original work published 1932)

Keller, R. R. (2000). Religious diversity in North America. In P. S. Richards & A. E. Bergin (Eds.), *Handbook of psychotherapy and religious diversity* (pp. 27–55). Washington, DC: American Psychological Association.

Kessler, R. C., McGonagle, K. A., Zhao, S., Nelson, C. B., Hughes, M., Eshleman, S., Wittchen, H-U, & Kendler, K. S. (1994). Lifetime and 12 month prevalence of DSM-III-R psychiatric disorders in the United States: Results from the National Comorbidity Survey. *Archives of General Psychiatry, 51*, 8–19.

Larson, D. B. (1985). Religious involvement. In G. Rekers (Ed.), *Family building* (pp. 121–147). Ventura, CA: Regal Books.

Leichman, G. (1995). A promise worth keeping. In *MenWeb* [On-line]. Available: www.vix.com/menmag.promiswo.htm

Long, D. (1987). Working with men who batter. In M. Scher, M. Stevens, G. Good, & G. A. Eichenfield (Eds.), *Handbook of counseling and psychotherapy with men* (pp. 305–320). Newbury Park, CA: Sage.

Long, V. O., & Heggen, C. H. (1988). Clergy perceptions of spiritual health for adults, men, and women. *Counseling and Values, 32,* 213–220.

Lovinger, R. J. (1996). Considering the religious dimension in assessment and treatment. In E. P. Shafranske (Ed.), *Religion and the clinical practice of psychology* (pp. 327–364). Washington, DC: American Psychological Association.

McAllister, R. J. (1993). Mental health treatment of religion professionals. In R. D. Parsons (Series Ed.) & R. J. Wicks & R. D. Parsons (Vol. Eds.), *Clinical handbook of pastoral counseling:: Vol. 2. Series in pastoral psychology, theology, and spirituality.* New York: Paulist Press.

McCullough, M. E., Larson, D. B., & Worthington, E. L., Jr. (1998). Mental health. In D. B. Larson, J. P. Swyers, & M. E. McCullough (Eds.), *Scientific research on spirituality and health: A consensus report* (pp. 129–152). Rockville, MD: National Institute for Healthcare Research.

McNeel, S. P., & Thorsen, P. L. (1985). A developmental perspective on Christian faith and dogmatism. *High School Journal, 68,* 211–220.

Meleis, A., & LaFever, C. (1984). The Arab American and psychiatric care. *Perspectives in Psychiatric Care, 12,* 72–86.

Miller, L., & Lovinger, R. J. (2000). Psychotherapy with Conservative and Orthodox Jews. In P. S. Richards & A. E. Bergin (Eds.), *Handbook of psychotherapy and religious diversity* (pp. 259–286). Washington, DC: American Psychological Association.

Minear, J. D., & Bruch, L. R. (1980–1981). The correlations of attitudes toward suicide with death anxiety, religiosity, and personal closeness to suicide. *Omega Journal of Death and Dying, 11,* 317–324.

National Institute of Mental Health. (1999). *Suicide fact sheet* [On-line]. Available: http://www.nimh.nih.gov/research/suicide.htm

Nye, F.I. (1958). *Family relationships and delinquent behavior.* New York: Wiley.

Oliver, S. J., & Toner, B. B. (1990). The influence of gender role typing on the expression of depressive symptoms. *Sex Roles, 22,* 775–790.

O'Neil, J. M., Helms, B. J., Gable, R. K., David, L., & Wrightsman, L. S. (1986). Gender-Role Conflict Scale: College men's fear of femininity. *Sex Roles, 14,* 335–350.

Ornish, D. (1990). *Dr. Dean Ornish's program for reversing heart disease.* New York: Random House.

Osherson, S. (1986). *Finding our fathers: How a man's life is shaped by his relationship with his father.* New York: Fawcet Columbine.

Padesky, C. A., & Hammen, C. L. (1981). Sex differences in depressive symptoms expression and help-seeking among college students. *Sex Roles, 7,* 309–320.

Pargament, K. I. (1997). *The psychology of religion and coping: Theory, research, and practice.* New York: Guilford Press.

Pleck, J. (1981). *The myth of masculinity.* Cambridge, MA: MIT Press.

Podles, L. J. (1999). *The church impotent: The feminization of Christianity.* Dallas, TX: Spence.

Poloma, M. M., & Gallup, G. H., Jr. (1991). *Varieties of prayer: A survey report.* Philadelphia, PA: Trinity Press International.

Prior, P. M. (1999). *Gender and mental health.* New York: New York University Press.

Promise Keepers. (2000). *Official Web-site of Promise Keepers.* [On-line]. Available: www.promisekeepers.org.

Propst, L. R. (1980). The comparative efficacy of religious and nonreligious imagery for the treatment of mild depression in religious individuals. *Cognitive Therapy and Research, 4,* 167–178.

Propst, L. R. (1988). *Psychotherapy in a religious framework: Spirituality in the emotional healing process.* New York: Human Sciences Press.

Propst, L. R. (1996). Cognitive-behavioral therapy in the religious person. In E. P. Shafranske (Ed.), *Religion and the clinical practice of psychology* (pp. 391–407). Washington, DC: American Psychological Association.

Rabinowitz, A. (2000). Psychotherapy with Orthodox Jews. In P. S. Richards & A. E. Bergin (Eds.), *Handbook of psychotherapy and religious diversity* (pp. 237–258). Washington, DC: American Psychological Association.

Real, T. (1997). *I don't want to talk about it: Overcoming the legacy of male depression.* New York: Scribner.

Reynolds, D. K., & Nelson, F. L. (1981). Personality, life situation, and life expectancy. *Suicide and Life-Threatening Behavior, 11,* 99–110.

Richards, P. S., & Bergin, A. E. (1997). *A spiritual strategy for counseling and psychotherapy.* Washington, DC: American Psychological Association.

Richards, P. S., & Bergin, A. E. (2000). Religious diversity and psychotherapy: Conclusions, recommendations, and future directions. In P. S. Richards & A. E. Bergin (Eds.), *Handbook of psychotherapy and religious diversity* (pp. 469–489). Washington, DC: American Psychological Association.

Richards, P. S., & Potts, R. W. (1995). Using spiritual interventions in psychotherapy: Practices, successes, failures, and ethical concerns of Mormon psychotherapists. *Professional Psychology: Research and Practice, 26,* 163–170.

Robins, L. N. (1974). *Deviant children grow up.* Huntington, NY: Krieger.

Robins, L., & Regier, D. (Eds.). (1991). *Psychiatric disorders in America: The Epidemiologic Catchment Area Study.* New York: Free Press.

Rohr, R. (1988). Masculine spirituality. *Praying, 26,* 5–9, 22.

Rohr, R., & Martos, J. (1992). *The wild man's journey: Reflections on male spirituality* (Rev. ed.). Cincinnati, OH: St. Anthony Messenger Press.

Rohrbaugh, J., & Jessor, R. (1975). Religiosity in youth: A control against deviant behavior. *Journal of Personality, 43,* 136–155.

Shafranske, E. P. (1996). Religious beliefs, affiliations, and practices of clinical psychologists. In E. P. Shafranske (Ed.), *Religion and the clinical practice of psychology* (pp. 149–163). Washington, DC: American Psychological Association.

Shafranske, E. P. (2000). Psychotherapy with Roman Catholics. In P. S. Richards & A. E. Bergin (Eds.), *Handbook of psychotherapy and religious diversity* (pp. 59–88). Washington, DC: American Psychological Association.

Sharma, A. R. (2000). Psychotherapy with Hindus. In P. S. Richards & A. E. Bergin (Eds.), *Handbook of psychotherapy and religious diversity* (pp. 341–365). Washington, DC: American Psychological Association.

Sharpe, M. J., & Heppner, P. P. (1991). Gender role, gender-role conflict, and psychological well-being in men. *Journal of Counseling Psychology, 38,* 323–330.

Shepherd, D. S., & Robertson, J. M. (1999). *Male hidden depression and gender role conflict: An empirical study.* Manuscript submitted for publication.

Skinner, B. F. (1953). *Science and human behavior.* New York: Macmillan.

Sloane, D. A., & Potvin, R. H. (1983). Age differences in adolescent religiousness. *Review of Religious Research, 25,* 142–154.

Stark, R., Kent, L., & Doyle, D. P. (1982). Religion and delinquency: The ecology of a lost relationship. *Journal of Research in Crime and Delinquency, 19,* 4–24.

Stodghill, R., III. (1997, October 6). God of our fathers. *Time, 150,* 34–40.

Thompson, E. H., Jr. (1991). Beneath the status characteristic: Gender variations in religiousness. *Journal for the Scientific Study of Religion, 30,* 381–394.

Thoresen, C., Worthington, E. L., Jr., Swyers, J. P., Larson, D. B., McCullough, M. E., & Miller, W. R. (1998). Religious/spiritual interventions. In D. B. Larson, J. P. Swyers, & M. E. McCullough (Eds.), *Scientific research on spirituality and health: A consensus report* (pp. 104–128). Rockville, MD: National Institute for Healthcare Research.

Ulrich, W. L., Richards, P. S., & Bergin, A. E. (2000). Psychotherapy with Latter-Day Saints. In P. S. Richards & A. E. Bergin (Eds.), *Handbook of psychotherapy and religious diversity* (pp. 185–210). Washington, DC: American Psychological Association.

Vessey, J. T., & Howard, K. I. (1993). Who seeks psychotherapy? *Psychotherapy, 30*(4), 546–553.

Warren, L. W. (1983). Male intolerance of depression: A review with implications for psychotherapy. *Clinical Psychology Review, 3,* 147–156.

Weatherford, R. J., & Weatherford, C. B. (1999). *Somebody's knocking at your door: AIDS and the African-American Church.* New York: Haworth Pastoral Press.

Westefeld, J. S., Range, L. M., Rogers, J. R., Maples, M. R., Bromley, J. L., & Alcorn, J. (2000). Suicide: An overview. *The Counseling Psychologist, 28,* 445–510.

Wilson, J. (1978). *Religion in American society.* Englewood Cliffs, NJ: Prentice Hall.

Wulff, D. M. (1996). The psychology of religion: An overview. In E. P. Shafranske (Ed.), *Religion and the clinical practice of psychology* (pp. 43–70). Washington, DC: American Psychological Association.

Yeung, P. P., & Greenwald, S. S. (1992). Jewish Americans and mental health: Results of the NIMH Epidemiologic Catchment Area Study. *Social Psychiatry and Psychiatric Epidemiology, 27,* 292–297.

Young, M., Gartner, J., O'Connor, T., Larson, D., Wright, K., & Rosen, B. (1990, August). *Participation in a volunteer ministry program and recidivism: A ten year follow-up.* Paper presented at the annual meeting of the American Psychological Association, Boston.

A Final Word

Gary R. Brooks
Glenn E. Good

From our vantage point, major changes have been taking place in terms of manhood and masculinity *subito presto* (literally, "suddenly fast"). Further, these ongoing changes in masculinity will provide substantial challenges to contemporary men. Fortunately, it also appears that the prognosis for efficacious counseling of men and boys is far brighter than it has been at any time in the past. Public and professional interest is burgeoning. Boys' and men's needs are being articulated more clearly, obstacles are being recognized, and creative new interventions are being offered. Indeed, the parallel processes of elucidating men's problems and developing effective interventions are accelerating with the expansion of the scientific bases for our work and the improved communication among practitioners, researchers, and therapy consumers. Given the growth of organizations dedicated to these efforts, there is every reason to believe that the future augurs well for improved understanding of the complexities of masculinity and for the discovery of the most compassionate avenues for the well-being of men.

RESOURCES FOR ADDITIONAL INFORMATION AND PROFESSIONAL INVOLVEMENT

We commend those who wish to promote the mental and physical health of men and who seek greater involvement in the effort to enhance the lives of men and their loved ones. The following are a few organizations dedicated to this mission.

Society for the Psychological Study of Men and Masculinity (SPSMM: Division 51 of the American Psychological Association)

SPSMM seeks to advance the knowledge of the psychology of men through research, education, training, public policy, and improved clinical practice.

Contact:
Division 51 Administrative Office
c/o American Psychological Association
750 First St.
Washington, DC 20002–4242
(202) 336–6013
division@apa.org (email)

Special Interest Group on Men, Masculinity, and Men's Studies

This is a special interest group (SIG) of the Division of Counseling Psychology (Division 17) of the American Psychological Association. This SIG seeks to serve primarily as a liaison between APA Divisions 17 and 51 for members who are interested in advancing the psychology of men, masculinity, and men's studies.

Contact:
Division 17 Administrative Office
c/o American Psychological Association
750 First St.
Washington, DC 20002–4242
(202) 336–6013
division@apa.org (email)

American Men's Studies Association

AMSA is an organization of men and women dedicated to teaching, research, and clinical practice in the field of men's studies.

Contact:
Membership Office
329 Afton Ave.
Youngstown, OH 44512–2311
(216) 782–2736

Men's Health Network

MHN is an informational and educational organization recognizing men's health as a specific social concern.

Contact:
Men's Health Network
P.O. Box 75972
Washington, DC 20013
202–543–6461
info@menshealthnetwork.org (email)
http://www.menshealthnetwork.org

ABOUT THE EDITORS

Glenn E. Good, Ph.D., is an associate professor in the Department of Educational, School, and Counseling Psychology at the University of Missouri-Columbia. Dr. Good has provided more than 120 presentations at national and international conferences and authored more than sixty scholarly articles, chapters, and books. He is coeditor (with Murray Scher, Mark Stevens, and Gregg Eichenfield) of the *Handbook of Counseling and Psychotherapy with Men* (Sage, 1987). Dr. Good is a fellow of the Society of Counseling Psychology and of the Society for the Psychological Study of Men and Masculinity (SPSMM) of the APA. He has served as president of the SPSMM, representative to the APA Council of Representatives, and chair of the Missouri psychology licensing board. He is the two-time recipient of the SPSMM Researcher of the Year Award, the Kathryn Hopwood Award for meritorious contributions to counseling psychology, the Annuit Coeptis Award given by the American College Personnel Association, and numerous university teaching and mentorship awards. He also maintains a private practice in Columbia, Missouri. His life is enriched by his wonderful wife, Laurie, and their two delightful daughters, Jennifer and Allison.

Gary R. Brooks, Ph.D., received his doctorate from the University of Texas at Austin in 1976. He currently is a professor at Baylor University, after completing twenty-eight years in the Veterans Affairs system. He is a fellow of the APA and has been president of the APA's Division of Family Psychology and the SPSMM. He has written more than thirty articles and book chapters. He has authored or coauthored four previous books: *The Centerfold Syndrome* (Jossey-Bass, 1995), *Men and Sex: New Psychological Perspectives* (Wiley, 1997), *Bridging Separate Gender Worlds* (APA Press, 1997), and *A New Psychotherapy for Traditional Men* (Jossey-Bass, 1998). He received the 1996 Distinguished Practitioner Award and the 2002 Researcher of the Year Award of the SPSMM and the 1997 Texas Distinguished Psychologist Award.

ABOUT THE CONTRIBUTORS

Leon D. Caldwell, Ph.D., is an assistant professor of educational psychology at the University of Nebraska, Lincoln. He received his doctorate in counseling psychology from Pennsylvania State University (1998). His research and publication interests are in the areas of black psychology, career development, mental health service delivery to underserved populations, and school counseling. He also coordinates a student course in Ghana, West Africa.

Aaron Carlstrom is currently a Ph.D. candidate in urban education (counseling psychology specialization) at the University of Wisconsin-Milwaukee. He holds a bachelor's degree in psychology from Marquette University and a master's degree in educational psychology (community counseling specialization) from the University of Wisconsin-Milwaukee. In addition to organizational consulting and men's issues, his clinical and research interests are in the areas of vocational psychology, multiculturalism, temporal perspective, spirituality, decision making, and student success and retention interventions.

J. Manuel Casas, Ph.D., received his doctorate from Stanford University with a specialization in counseling psychology. Currently, he is a professor in the Counseling, Clinical, and School Psychology Program at the University of California, Santa Barbara. He has published widely and serves on numerous editorial boards. He is the coauthor of the *Handbook of Racial/Ethnic Minority Counseling Research* and is one of the editors of the *Handbook of Multicultural Counseling.* His most recent research and publication endeavors have focused on Hispanic families and children who are at risk for experiencing educational and psychosocial problems, including drug and alcohol abuse. His research in this area gives special attention to the resiliency factors that can help Hispanic families avoid and overcome such problems. His expertise and that of his colleagues in this area have made it possible to bring numerous research grants to the campus. He serves as a consultant to various private and governmental agencies and organizations.

Sam V. Cochran, Ph.D., is director of the University Counseling Service and a clinical professor in the Counseling Psychology Program at the University of Iowa in Iowa City. He received his doctorate in counseling psychology from the University of Missouri in 1983. Since that time he has worked with men in therapy, written about men's issues, and researched depression in men. He is the coauthor of three books: *Deepening Psychotherapy with Men, Men and Depression: Clinical and Empirical Perspectives,* and *Man Alive: A Primer of Men's Issues.* He has also written several articles and book chapters on assessing and treating depression in men as well as on psychotherapy with men.

Will H. Courtenay, Ph.D., L.C.S.W., received his doctorate from the University of California at Berkeley and is a licensed clinical social worker. He is a member of the clinical faculty in the Department of Psychiatry at Harvard Medical School and at the University of California, San Francisco School of Medicine. His research focuses on how psychological, behavioral, and social factors—including beliefs about masculinity—influence the health of men and boys, and on evidence-based gender-specific health interventions with men. He is a regular contributor to professional journals and is currently completing a book on men's health (Vanderbilt University Press). Dr. Courtenay serves as editor of the *International Journal of Men's Health* and is on the editorial board of the *Journal of Men's Health and Gender.* He provides consultation, program development assistance, continuing education, and training to colleges, public health departments, medical centers, and health professionals nationwide. He is also a psychotherapist in Berkeley and San Francisco, California.

Margaret Evanow is a Ph.D. candidate (counseling psychology) in the Department of Urban Education at the University of Wisconsin-Milwaukee. She holds an M.S. degree in educational psychology (community counseling specialization) from the University of Wisconsin-Milwaukee. In addition to gender-based issues, her clinical and research interests are in the area of interpersonal violence and familial abuse. Currently, she coordinates a school-based intervention to reduce and prevent adolescent violence in an urban setting. She also coordinates an aftercare treatment program for women recovering from alcohol and drug addictions.

Douglas C. Haldeman, Ph.D., is a counseling psychologist in independent practice in Seattle. He serves on the clinical faculty in the Department of Psychology at the University of Washington and is the author of numerous publications about the competent and ethical treatment of lesbian, gay, and bisexual clients in psychotherapy. Dr. Haldeman has lectured internationally and in the media on the topic of sexual orientation conversion therapy and is coauthor of the APA's 1997 "Resolution on Appropriate Therapeutic Responses to Sexual Orientation" and the 2000 "Guidelines for Psychotherapy with Lesbian, Gay, and Bisexual Clients." He was awarded the 1996 Distinguished Psychologist Award from the Washington State Psychological Association and the 1999 Outstanding Professional Contribution Award from the Society for the Psychological Study of Lesbian, Gay, and Bisexual Issues (APA Division 44). He has served as president of APA's Division 44 and chair of APA's Committee on Lesbian, Gay, and Bisexual Concerns, and currently serves on the executive board of the Society for the Psychological Study of Men and Masculinity (APA Division 51) and the APA Ethics Committee.

Mary J. Heppner, Ph.D., is an associate professor in the Department of Educational and Counseling Psychology and an associate director of the Career Center at the University of Missouri-Columbia. She has written two books and numerous articles and book chapters, primarily in the areas of career development of adults and rape prevention interventions. Her most recent book is *Career Counseling: Process, Issues and Techniques* (Allyn & Bacon, 1997). She won the 1999 Kemper Award for Outstanding Teaching and the 1999 Early Scientist Practitioner Award from Division 17 (Counseling Psychology) of the APA.

P. Paul Heppner, Ph.D., received his doctorate in 1979 from the University of Nebraska-Lincoln and was a Fulbright Research Scholar at the University of Goteborg (Sweden), the University College Cork (Ireland), and National Taiwan Normal University (Taiwan); he was also a visiting fellow at the University of London and a visiting faculty member at the University of the Western Cape (South Africa). He has been an active researcher, having published over one hundred articles and chapters; his primary areas of interest are the relationship between coping or problem solving and psychological adjustment, health psychology, supervision, and men and masculinity. He is a frequent presenter at conferences and symposiums across the United States and Canada and has been an invited speaker in Sweden, Norway, England, Taiwan, Korea, Hong Kong, and South Africa. He has served on several national and international editorial boards and as the editor of *The Counseling Psychologist.* He has contributed to professional psychology in numerous ways, such as by serving counseling psychology in various roles, including most recently as the president of the Society of Counseling Psychology (APA Division 17), as a frequent site visitor, and as a frequent external reviewer of tenure and promotion. On the University of Missouri campus, he has been awarded the prestigious Kemper Fellowship for Excellence in Teaching and has been very active in developing the doctoral training program, including serving as training director and most recently as one of the founders and codirectors of the Center for Multicultural Research, Training, and Consultation.

Hope I. Hills, Ph.D. (Virginia Commonwealth University, 1986), currently consults with businesses and is president of the Circle Consulting Group, Inc., in Milwaukee, Wisconsin. She teaches at both the Department of Urban Education (Counseling Psychology Program) at the University of Wisconsin-Milwaukee and the College of Business at Marquette University and maintains a small private practice. Her publications and presentations have focused on paradoxical interventions, interpersonal theory, multicultural training, and women in academia and organizational consulting. Since leaving the faculty of the University of Missouri's Counseling Psychology Program in 1991, she has consulted with many organizations, helping leaders recognize that ongoing leadership problems can be effectively approached through awareness of their early decisions about self and others. Because management and executive ranks remain largely male, she has developed interventions designed to break through men's reluctance to look at this more personal perspective on performance. She loves Milwaukee, where she lives with her husband, Dave, a retired Milwaukee Symphony musician whom she originally met on the Internet.

Carl Isenhart, Psy.D., L.P., is a psychologist and coordinator of the Addictive Disorders Section at the Minneapolis Veterans Affairs Medical Center. He is an assistant professor in the Department of Psychiatry and clinical assistant professor in the Department of Psychology at the University of Minnesota. He holds a Certificate of Proficiency in the Treatment of Alcohol and Other Psychoactive Substance Use Disorders from the APA's College of Professional Psychology, and he is a trainer in motivational interviewing. He has published journal articles, reviews, and book chapters. He is conducting research in the areas of assessment of substance use disorders, motivation and stages of change, and masculinity and male gender roles.

Norine G. Johnson, Ph.D., is former president of the APA and past president of the Division of the Psychology of Women. As president of the APA in 2001, one of her major initiatives was Psychology: Building a Healthy World. She served as cochair of the APA

Presidential Task Force on Adolescent Girls and senior volume editor of *Beyond Appearances: A New Look at Adolescent Girls,* a professional book published by the APA in 1999. She is coeditor with Judith Worell of *Shaping the Future of Feminist Psychology: Research, Education, and Practice* (1997). She is president of Affect, Behavior, Cognition Systems and an owner of Access for Change, a full-time independent behavioral health practice in Quincy, Massachusetts. She is a clinical assistant professor in the Boston University Medical School, Department of Neurology. She has over ninety-five publications and presentations in the areas of health care, women's issues, adolescent girls' issues, psychotherapy, neuropsychological applications, and child and adolescent psychology. She received her doctorate in clinical psychology from Wayne State University and did her postdoctoral work in a two-year program for mental health planners and administrators sponsored by Harvard Medical School.

Mark S. Kiselica, Ph.D., N.C.C., L.P.C., is associate professor and chairperson of the Department of Counselor Education at the College of New Jersey. He has conducted fifty juried convention presentations and is the author or editor of forty juried publications, including *Multicultural Counseling with Teenage Fathers: A Practical Guide* (Sage, 1995), *Confronting Prejudice and Racism During Multicultural Training* (American Counseling Association, 1999), and *Handbook of Counseling Boys and Adolescent Males: A Practitioner's Guide* (Sage, 1999). He is a former consulting scholar to the Clinton administration's Fatherhood Initiative and the immediate past president of the Society for the Psychological Study of Men and Masculinity (APA Division 51). Dr. Kiselica was named Counselor Educator of the Year (1996–1997) by the American Mental Health Counselors Association and was the recipient of the Publication in Counselor Education and Supervision Award for 1999.

Ronald F. Levant, Ed.D., A.B.P.P., earned his doctorate in clinical psychology and public practice from Harvard University in 1973. Since then he has been a clinician in solo independent practice, clinical supervisor in hospital settings, clinical and academic administrator, and academic faculty member. He has served on the faculties of Boston, Rutgers, and Harvard Universities. He is currently dean and professor at the Center for Psychological Studies, Nova Southeastern University. Dr. Levant has authored, coauthored, edited, or coedited more than 200 publications, including 13 books and 130 refereed journal articles and book chapters in family and gender psychology and in advancing professional psychology. Dr. Levant has also served as president of the Massachusetts Psychological Association, president of APA Division 43 (Family Psychology), cofounder and the first president of APA Division 51 (the Society for the Psychological Study of Men and Masculinity), two-term member and two-term chair of the APA Committee for the Advancement of Professional Practice, two-term member of the APA Council of Representatives, member at large of the APA Board of Directors, and two terms as recording secretary of the APA. As a member of the board of directors, he chaired the task force that resolved the long-standing issue of representation of small state psychological associations and divisions on the APA Council of Representatives through the creation of the "Wildcard Plan," which brought an expanded council into being in January 1999. He is currently serving as president-elect of the APA.

David Lisak, Ph.D., is an associate professor of psychology at the University of Massachusetts-Boston, where he conducts and supervises research on the causes and consequences of interpersonal violence. In particular, he has studied the motives and characteristics of "undetected" rapists—men who rape but are never prosecuted. He also studies the long-term effects of childhood abuse in adult men, and the relationship between early abuse and the later perpetration of interpersonal violence. His research has been published in leading journals of psychology, trauma, and violence, and he is the founding editor of the journal *Psychology of Men and Masculinity.* In addition to his research and teaching, Dr. Lisak serves as faculty for the National Judicial Education Program and the American Prosecutors Research Institute, and has served as a consultant to judicial, prosecutor, and law enforcement education programs across the country. He has conducted workshops in more than thirty states across the United States, and consults widely with universities and other institutions regarding sexual assault prevention and policies. He also serves as an expert witness and consultant in sexual violence and homicide cases across the country. Dr. Lisak received his doctorate from Duke University.

James R. Mahalik, Ph.D., completed his doctorate in counseling psychology at the University of Maryland in 1990. He is currently an associate professor in the Department of Counseling, Developmental, and Educational Psychology at Boston College. His research interests focus on how gender role conformity influences men's and women's psychological and physical well-being, including health-risk behaviors and help seeking.

Michael R. Maples is a Ph.D. candidate (counseling psychology) in the Division of Psychological and Quantitative Foundations at the University of Iowa. He is currently a predoctoral intern with University Counseling Services at Kansas State University. He holds bachelor degrees in psychology and English from the University of Tennessee, Knoxville. In addition to men's issues, his clinical and research interests are in the areas of college student development, vocational psychology, and religion.

Irmo D. Marini, Ph.D., C.R.C., is an associate professor and graduate coordinator of the master of science program in rehabilitation counseling at the University of Texas-Pan American. He obtained his Ph.D. in rehabilitation from Auburn University in 1992. Dr. Marini has made more than fifty international, national, and state presentations as well as having over thirty publications on disability-related studies. He serves on four journal editorial boards and is a commissioner for the Commission on Rehabilitation Counselor Certification. Dr. Marini was the recipient of two research awards while at Arkansas State University and currently maintains a private practice in forensic rehabilitation consulting.

Laurie B. Mintz, Ph.D., is an associate professor in the APA-accredited Counseling Psychology Program in the Department of Educational, School, and Counseling Psychology at the University of Missouri-Columbia. In addition, she maintains a part-time private practice in Columbia, Missouri. Her doctorate in counseling psychology was granted by Ohio State University in 1987. Dr. Mintz has provided more than fifty presentations at national and international conferences and has authored more than thirty scholarly articles and book chapters. In addition, she has been quoted in over one hundred magazines, newspapers, and radio stations. She has also won three teaching awards and served on the editorial board of three journals. She is married and the mother of two daughters.

Carol L. Philpot, Psy.D., is dean and professor of psychology at the School of Psychology, Florida Institute of Technology, where she directs the marriage and family track and teaches the psychology of gender. She is a fellow of the APA and a past president of APA's Division of Family Psychology. She is on the editorial boards of the *Journal of Family Psychology* and the *Family Psychology and Counseling Series.* She has authored numerous articles and book chapters in the areas of gender-sensitive psychotherapy, clinical training, family assessment, and family therapy. She is coauthor of *Bridging Separate Gender Worlds,* published by the APA in 1997.

William S. Pollack, Ph.D., is assistant clinical professor of psychology in the Department of Psychiatry at Harvard Medical School, the director of the Center for Men and Young Men and of continuing education (psychology) at McLean Hospital, a founding member and fellow of the Society for the Psychological Study of Men and Masculinity (APA Division 51), and a member of the Boston Psychoanalytic Society. He is the author of the best-seller *Real Boys: Rescuing Our Sons from the Myths of Boyhood,* based on his research project *Listening to Boys' Voices* (Random House [1998]; paperback, Holt/Owl [1999]), on the inner emotional lives of boys; coauthor (with Dr. Bill Betcher) of *In a Time of Fallen Heroes: The Re-Creation of Masculinity* (Guilford Press, 1995); and coeditor (with Dr. Ron Levant) of *A New Psychology of Men* (Basic Books, 1995) and a book redefining psychological treatment for males: *A New Psychotherapy for Men* (Wiley, 1998). His newest book is *Real Boys' Voices* (Random House, 2000). Dr. Pollack lives in Newton, Massachusetts, with his wife and daughter, where he maintains a private practice in psychotherapy, psychoanalysis, and organizational consultation.

Fredric E. Rabinowitz, Ph.D., received his doctorate in counseling psychology from the University of Missouri-Columbia. He is a full professor of psychology at the University of Redlands in California. He has presented nationally on men and psychotherapy and has written and cowritten journal articles and book chapters on the topic. Dr. Rabinowitz has coauthored three books with Dr. Sam Cochran: *Man Alive: A Primer of Men's Issues* (Brooks/Cole, 1994), *Men and Depression: Clinical and Empirical Perspectives* (Academic Press, 2000), and *Deepening Psychotherapy with Men* (American Psychological Association, 2002). He has received the Outstanding Teaching Award and Professor of the Year Award at the University of Redlands. Dr. Rabinowitz has served as the director of the university's Salzburg, Austria, Overseas Program, for several years as chair of the Psychology Department and has also been the mental health director of the local community mental health center in Redlands. His private psychotherapy practice focuses on the issues of men. He founded and has been a coleader of an ongoing men's therapy group in Redlands since 1987. He is the incoming president of APA Division 51, the Society for the Psychological Study of Men and Masculinity (2005).

John M. Robertson, Ph.D., is a licensed psychologist in independent practice in the northeast Kansas area, in Lawrence, and Manhattan. He has retired from University Counseling Services, Kansas State University, where he also taught for the Department of Psychology and was a member of the graduate faculty in the Department of Counseling and Educational Psychology. His doctorate in counseling psychology was granted by the University of California at Santa Barbara. In addition to providing individual counseling to men, he has conducted groups for men on recovering from sexual and physical abuse, managing aggression and violence, developing emotional expressiveness, and improving relationship skills. His published research has addressed a variety of issues related to masculinity: the gender biases therapists have toward male clients, emotional expressiveness in men, predictors of aggression in boys, male depression symptoms, the help-seeking preferences of college men, the experiences of voluntary male homemakers, and the measurement of psychological distress in men.

Christopher A. Ruiz de Esparza is a first-year doctoral student in the Counseling, Clinical, School Psychology Program at the University of California, Santa Barbara. He received his B.A. in psychology from Stanford University with an emphasis in health and development. There he participated as a program assistant for the Stanford Community Partnership, a project funded by the U.S. Department of Education to assess alcohol and other drug use and prevention throughout diverse higher education communities. Currently, Ruiz de Esparza's research interests are in developing effective counseling treatments and community interventions for diverse populations.

Murray Scher, Ph.D., received his doctorate in counseling psychology from the University of Texas at Austin in 1971. A former professor of psychology at Tusculum College in Greeneville, Tennessee, he has been in the full-time independent practice of psychology since 1975. Widely published in the area of gender roles in psychotherapy, primarily male gender roles, Dr. Scher has presented frequently and been honored with the 1998 Practitioner of the Year Award from APA Division 51, the Society for the Psychological Study of Men and Masculinity. He was also honored by that division in being invited to present with a group of pioneers in the study of men at a symposium on the beginnings of the men's movement. Dr. Scher was the first editor of the classic *Handbook of Counseling and Psychotherapy with Men.* He has also been editor or coeditor for a number of special issues of journals on gender roles in psychotherapy. His most recent book, coauthored with Lucia Gilbert, is *Gender and Sex in Counseling and Psychotherapy.* He is past president of the American Academy of Psychotherapists. Married for forty years, Scher has a thirty-three-year-old daughter; his wife and child continue to remind him of the importance of staying cognizant of the power and impact of gender roles.

David Sue, Ph.D., is a professor of psychology and an associate at the Center for Cross-Cultural Research at Western Washington University, where he served as the chairman of the Mental Health Counseling Program for thirteen years. He received his doctorate in clinical psychology at Washington State University. He has coauthored the books *Counseling the Culturally Different* (3rd ed.) and *Understanding Abnormal Behavior* (6th ed.). He has published numerous articles in the field of multicultural counseling and training.

Joseph A. Turner received his master's degree in psychology from Salisbury State University, Salisbury, Maryland, in 1996. At present, he is a doctoral student in the Counseling, Clinical, and School Psychology Program at the University of California, Santa Barbara. Complementing his doctoral work, he currently works as a research associate for the Multiagency Integrated System of Care evaluation team at University of California, Santa Barbara. His research interests include lesbian, gay, bisexual, transgender, gender, and racial-ethnic minority issues and identity development; mental health service utilization; and program development and evaluation.

Joseph L. White, Ph.D., has for the past thirty-eight years enjoyed a distinguished career in the field of psychology and mental health as a teacher, mentor, administrator, clinical supervisor, writer, consultant, and practicing psychologist. He is currently professor emeritus of psychology and psychiatry at the University of California, Irvine, where he spent most of his career as a teacher, supervising psychologist, mentor, and director of ethnic studies and cross-cultural programs. Dr. White received his Ph.D. in clinical psychology from Michigan State University in 1961. Dr. White is the author of several papers and three books: *The Psychology of Blacks: An African-American Perspective* (1984, 1990, 1999); *The Troubled Adolescent* (1989); and *Black Man Emerging: Facing the Past and Seizing a Future in America* (1998). He was a pioneer in the field of black psychology and is affectionately referred to as one of the "fathers of black psychology" by his students, mentees, and younger colleagues. His seminal article in *Ebony* magazine in 1970, "Toward a Black Psychology," was instrumental in beginning the modern era of African American and ethnic psychology. In addition to his teaching and research, Dr. White has been a practicing psychologist and consultant. He has served as a supervising psychologist and staff affiliate psychologist to five hospitals and three clinical practices in Southern California. He has worked as a consultant with school districts, universities, private organizations, drug prevention programs, and government agencies. Dr. White was appointed to the California State Psychology Licensing Board by Governor Edmund G. Brown Jr., and served as chairman for three years. He is currently a member of the board of trustees of the Menninger Foundation in Topeka, Kansas.

NAME INDEX

SUBJECT INDEX

A

African Americans: acknowledging racism, 324; African American value system, 327; African and African American-centered intervention strategies, 328–329; black aesthetic approaches, 331–332; case study (David's story), 327–328; case study (Jamal's story), 333–335; influence of cultural worldview, 326–327; masculinity approaches, 329–331; NTU psychotherapy, 329; practical considerations, 332–333; precursors to intervention, 323–326; self-interrogation and self-confrontation, 324–326

AIDS epidemic, 265, 393

Alcoholics Anonymous (AA), 138, 139, 143, 389

Alexithymia, 207, 209, 217; myths and realities regarding, 26–27

Al-Fatiha, 393

American Beauty (cinema), 338

American Civil War, 150

American Counseling Association, 385

American Medical Association, 31, 32, 34, 35, 38

American Psychiatric Association, 125

American Psychological Association, 147, 238, 292, 328, 373, 385; Code of Conduct, 399; Division of the Psychology of Women, 295

American Sons (Okazaki), 362

American Sports Data, 338

Americans with Disabilities Act, 100, 174

Annual Conference of the Association of Black Psychologist, 332

Appropriate Therapeutic Responses to Sexual Orientation (American Psychological Association), 373

Asian American men: areas of potential difference between Asian American and Euroamerican men, 360; Asian values and workplace, 361–362; concept of masculinity, 357–366; diversity of Asian Americans and Pacific Islanders, 358–359; fatherhood role, 361; gender role conflicts, 360–361; identity issues, 363–365; impact of traditional values on personality measures, 362; modified cognitive therapy with, 365; obstacles to gender redefinition, 358; portrayal of Asian American masculinity in United States, 362–363; and traditional Asian values, 359–360

B

Beck Depression Inventory (BDI), 327, 328

Black Male Student Empowerment Summit, 331